arihant
SUCCESS AND NOTHING LESS



# Ignite

## Topicwise MCQs

*"Give Fire to **Your Prelims Prep**"*

# Economic & Social Development

For **Civil Services** & **State PCS**
Preliminary Examination

MentorsHut

arihant
SUCCESS AND NOTHING LESS

**ARIHANT PUBLICATION (INDIA) LIMITED**



卐 **Administrative & Production Offices**

**Regd. Office**

'Ramchhaya' 4577/15, Agarwal Road, Darya Ganj, New Delhi -110002
Tele: 011- 47630600, 43518550

卐 **Head Office**

Kalindi, TP Nagar, Meerut (UP) - 250002 Tel: 0121-7156203, 7156204

卐 **Sales & Support Offices**

Agra, Ahmedabad, Bengaluru, Bareilly, Chennai, Delhi, Guwahati, Hyderabad, Jaipur, Jhansi, Kolkata, Lucknow, Nagpur & Pune.

卐 **PRICE:** ₹ 395.00

卐 **PO No:** TXT-XX-XXXXXXX-X-XX

Published by Arihant Publications (India) Ltd.

For further information about the books published by Arihant, log on to www.arihantbooks.com or e-mail at info@arihantbooks.com

Follow us on

# Preface

The *Ignite Series* is more than just a resource - it's your ultimate guide to conquering one of the toughest examinations in India. With nearly **10 lakh aspirants** filling the forms for the UPSC Civil Services Preliminary Examination each year and **only around 15,000 qualifying for Mains**, the success rate stands at a staggering 1.5%. Designed by the authors of the bestselling *Pulse Handwritten Notes for Prelims*, this series is meticulously crafted to transform your preparation and significantly enhance your chances of success.

What truly sets the *Ignite Series* apart is its ability to **bridge the gap between rote learning and deep conceptual understanding**. Packed with over **6,000+ carefully designed MCQs**, the series offers comprehensive coverage of the Prelims syllabus, ensuring no topic is left unexplored. Each question is strategically designed to challenge your knowledge and sharpen your problem-solving skills.

In an exam where every mark counts, **standing out isn't optional - it's essential.** To equip you for this challenge, the *Ignite Series* introduces a **three-tiered evaluation system**, testing your knowledge at Factual, Conceptual and Analytical levels. This innovative approach mirrors the demands of the UPSC, ensuring you are thoroughly prepared to tackle its dynamic and unpredictable nature. Additionally, topic-**wise Previous Years' Questions (PYQs)** included at the end of each chapter provide valuable insights into trends and patterns, helping you craft a data-driven strategy.

Understanding concepts is important, but **retaining and applying them under pressure** is the key to success. To make this process seamless, every question in this series is accompanied by **detailed explanations**, enriched with **infographics, tables and maps** that simplify complex topics.

Recognizing the importance of self-assessment, the series offers **free access to 3 All India Mock Tests.** These simulated tests replicate real exam conditions, allowing you to benchmark your performance, identify areas of improvement, and refine your preparation strategy. By offering a clear picture of where you stand, these tests ensure that you are not just prepared but **exam-ready**.

With the *Ignite Series*, you're not merely preparing for an exam - you're gearing up to outshine the competition and achieve your dreams. Let this book be the tool that empowers you to break into the top **1.5%** and take a giant step toward becoming a civil servant.

This masterpiece wouldn't have been possible without the **tireless efforts of the entire MentorsHut family**, who dedicated countless hours to creating a resource that truly serves aspirants.

To our daughter, **Prisha Mangtani**, your unwavering patience and love have been our greatest source of strength throughout this journey. Thank you for your sacrifices and for inspiring us to give our best.

We at MentorsHut remain committed to excellence and continuous improvement. Your feedback is invaluable to us. If you have suggestions or ideas to make this series even better, please don't hesitate to reach out to us at **info@mentorshut.com.**

Here's wishing you the very best for your preparation - may this series **ignite the spark of excellence within you** and guide you toward achieving your goals.

**Amit Mangtani,**
**CA Shalini Wadhwani**
Founders, MentorsHut

# Contents

## Topical PYQ Trend Last 8 Years'

| Section | 2024 | 2023 | 2022 | 2021 | 2020 | 2019 | 2018 | 2017 |
|---|---|---|---|---|---|---|---|---|
| Introduction to Economics | 2 | 1 | 1 | 1 | - | - | 1 | - |
| National Income Accounting | - | - | 1 | - | - | - | 2 | - |
| Human Development and Unemployment | 1 | 1 | 1 | 1 | 1 | 2 | 1 | 1 |
| Public Finance | - | 2 | 2 | 3 | 1 | - | 3 | 3 |
| Monetary Policy | 1 | 2 | 3 | 3 | 2 | 2 | 1 | 2 |
| Inflation and Business Cycle | - | 1 | - | 1 | 1 | - | - | - |
| Banking in India | 1 | - | 1 | 1 | 1 | 4 | 4 | 3 |
| External Sector | - | 1 | 2 | 2 | 4 | 5 | 2 | 2 |
| Money and Capital Market | 6 | 2 | 3 | 2 | 2 | 1 | 1 | - |
| Agriculture | 1 | 3 | 1 | 1 | 5 | 2 | 4 | 3 |
| Industry and Infrastructure | 2 | 3 | 1 | 1 | 1 | 3 | - | 2 |
| Bretton Woods & Other Institutions | - | 2 | 2 | 0 | 2 | 1 | 1 | - |
| WTO | - | - | - | 0 | 1 | 0 | 1 | 3 |
| Social Sector Initiatives | 2 | 2 | - | 0 | 2 | 1 | 4 | 7 |
| Miscellaneous | 0 | 1 | 2 | 0 | - | 3 | 1 | 2 |
| **Total** | **16** | **21** | **20** | **16** | **23** | **24** | **24** | **28** |

## Overall PYQ Trend Last 8 Years'

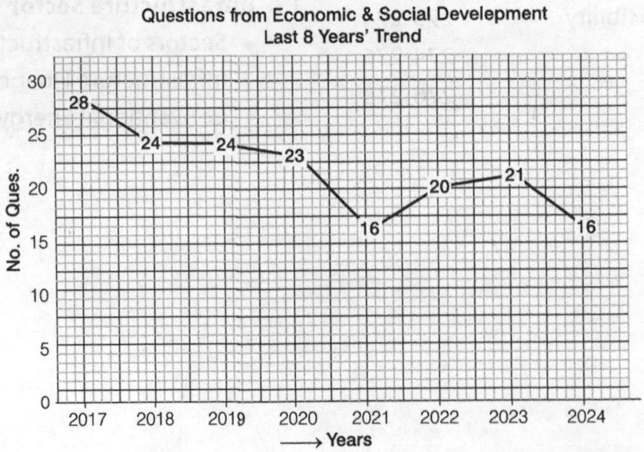

CHAPTER 01

# Basic Concepts of Economics

## Assessment Round

### Topic 1 : Economics

**1.** With reference to the concept of 'Opportunity Cost', consider the following statements:

1. It refers to the value of the next best alternative that is forgone when a choice is made.
2. It is zero when there are no alternative uses of resources.
3. It is applicable to both individual and societal decisions.

How many of the statements given above is/ are correct?

(a) Only one
(b) Only two
(c) All three
(d) None

**2.** Which of the following correctly distinguishes 'Opportunity Cost' from 'Sunk Cost'?

(a) Opportunity cost is incurred after a decision is made, while Sunk cost is incurred before the decision.
(b) Opportunity cost reflects potential future benefits, whereas Sunk cost represents past expenditures that cannot be recovered.
(c) Sunk cost is always higher than Opportunity cost because it involves irreversible spending.
(d) Opportunity cost applies only to financial decisions, while Sunk cost applies to all types of decisions.

**3.** Consider the following hypothetical scenarios:

1. A factory has idle machines that are used to produce goods without displacing any other production.
2. A person volunteers their time for a charity event on a day when they had no other commitments.
3. A student decides to study in the library during a time when they had no other planned activities.
4. A company uses leftover raw materials from a previous production process to create a new product.

In which of the given above scenarios can opportunity cost be considered zero?

(a) 1 and 3 only
(b) 1, 2, and 4 only
(c) 2 and 4 only
(d) 1, 2, 3 and 4

**4.** With reference to the 'Factors of Production', consider the following statements:

1. Land refers to all natural resources available for production, including forests, minerals, and water.
2. Labour includes both physical and mental efforts contributed by workers to produce goods and services.
3. Capital is only the money invested in a business and does not include physical assets like machinery or buildings.

How many of the statements given above is/ are correct?

(a) Only one
(b) Only two
(c) All three
(d) None

**5.** Which of the following are true about the differences between Physical Capital and Human Capital?

1. Physical capital is tangible and can be bought and sold whereas human capital is intangible and inherent to individuals.
2. Unlike physical capital, human capital can be transferred from one person to another.
3. Investment in human capital includes education, training, and healthcare while investment in physical capital involves purchasing machinery, equipment and infrastructure.

Select the correct answer from the codes given below:

(a) 1 and 3 only
(b) 1, 2 and 3
(c) 3 only
(d) 1 and 2 only

**6.** Consider the following factors with the correct type of capital:

| | Factors | Type of Capital |
|---|---|---|
| 1. | Computer software used in a business | Human Capital |
| 2. | Technical training received by employees | Physical Capital |
| 3. | Office furniture and equipment | Human Capital |
| 4. | A worker's experience and expertise | Physical Capital |

How many of the above pairs are correctly matched?

(a) Only two pairs (b) Only three pairs
(c) All four pairs (d) None

**7.** Which of the following are considered key factors in the formation of human capital?

1. Investment in education and training.
2. Access to quality healthcare.
3. Availability of physical capital like machinery and equipment.
4. Social and cultural environment that promotes skill development.

Select the correct answer from the codes given below:

(a) 1 and 2 only
(b) 1, 2 and 4 only
(c) 2 and 3 only
(d) 1, 2, 3 and 4

**8.** Consider the following types of capital with their appropriate examples:

| Type of Capital | Examples |
|---|---|
| 1. Fixed Capital | Raw materials used in production |
| 2. Working Capital | Inventory of finished goods |
| 3. Fixed Capital | Office equipment like computers |
| 4. Working Capital | Cash available for day-to-day operations |

How many of the above pairs is/are correctly matched?

(a) Only one pair
(b) Only two pairs
(c) Only three pairs
(d) All four pairs

**9.** With reference to the differences between fixed capital and working capital, consider the following statements:

1. Fixed capital is invested in long-term assets that are used in the production process over several years.
2. Working capital is primarily used to finance the daily operations of a business, such as purchasing raw materials and paying wages.
3. Depreciation affects fixed capital over time, reducing its value.
4. Working capital does not involve any tangible assets.

Which of the statements given above are correct?

(a) 1 and 2 only
(b) 1, 2 and 3 only
(c) 2 and 4 only
(d) 3 and 4 only

**10.** With reference to the relationship between ICOR and economic growth, consider the following statements:
1. A country with a high ICOR may experience slower economic growth due to the inefficiency in converting capital into output.
2. Developing countries often have a lower ICOR compared to developed countries due to higher marginal returns on investment.
3. ICOR is directly related to the rate of savings in an economy i.e. higher savings typically lead to a lower ICOR.

Which of the statements given above are correct?
(a) 1 and 2 only (b) 1 and 3 only
(c) 2 and 3 only (d) 1, 2 and 3

**11.** Which of the following scenarios would likely lead to a lower Incremental Capital Output Ratio (ICOR) in an economy?
(a) Increased investment in advanced technology that boosts productivity.
(b) A significant rise in the cost of capital goods.
(c) Poor management of capital resources leading to waste and inefficiency.
(d) A shift towards more capital-intensive industries.

## Topic 2 : Economy

**12.** Consider the following activities:
1. A mother cooking meal for her family.
2. A teacher offering free tutoring services to underprivileged students.
3. A person donating blood to a charity.
4. A farmer selling produce at a local market.

Which of the given above activities can be classified as 'Non-Economic Activities'?
(a) 1 and 2 onlys
(b) 2, 3 and 4 only
(c) 1, 2 and 3 only
(d) 1, 2, 3 and 4

**13.** Consider the following activities:
1. Fishing
2. Manufacturing of textiles
3. Mining
4. Information technology services

Which of the given activities are considered 'Primary Sector' activities in the economy?
(a) 1 and 3 only (b) 1, 2 and 4 only
(c) 2 and 4 only (d) 1, 2, 3 and 4

**14.** Consider the following economic activities with the correct sector of the economy:

| Economic Activity | Sector of Economy |
|---|---|
| 1. Agriculture | Primary Sector |
| 2. Intellectual Property | Secondary Sector |
| 3. Construction of buildings | Tertiary Sector |
| 4. Manufacturing of steel | Secondary Sector |

How many of the above pairs is/are correctly matched?
(a) Only one pair (b) Only two pairs
(c) Only three pairs (d) All four pairs

**15.** Consider the following statements about 'India's structural transformation':
1. Structural transformation typically involves a shift of labour from agriculture to manufacturing and then to services.
2. It is often associated with an increase in productivity and income levels.
3. All economies experience structural transformation at the same pace and in the same manner.

How many of the statements given above is/are correct?
(a) Only one (b) Only two
(c) All three (d) None

**16.** With reference to India's structural transformation, consider the following statements:
1. India bypassed the manufacturing stage during the process of structural transformation.
2. The services sector has emerged as the largest contributor to India's GDP.
3. Despite the structural transformation, a large portion of India's workforce is still employed in agriculture.

Which of the statements given above are correct?
(a) 1 and 2 only (b) 2 and 3 only
(c) 1 and 3 only (d) 1, 2 and 3

**17.** With reference to the Real Sector of the economy, consider the following statements:

1. The real sector includes the production of goods and services such as manufacturing, agriculture, and services.
2. Activities in the real sector directly contribute to the Gross Domestic Product (GDP).
3. The Real Sector also encompasses financial activities like banking and insurance.

How many of the statements given above is/are correct?

(a) Only one (b) Only two
(c) All three (d) None

**18.** Consider the following economic activities:

1. Manufacturing automobiles
2. Providing financial advice through investment banks
3. Growing and harvesting crops
4. Offering retail services in a supermarket

Which of the given above activities are part of the Real Sector in an economy?

(a) 1 and 2 only (b) 1, 3 and 4 only
(c) 2, 3 and 4 only (d) 1, 2, 3 and 4

## Topic 3 : Economic System

**19.** Consider the following statements about the 'Capitalist Economic System':

1. In a capitalist economy, private individuals or businesses own the means of production.
2. Private property rights are a fundamental feature of capitalism.
3. The government plays a significant role in regulating prices and controlling production in a capitalist economy.

How many of the statements given above is/are correct?

(a) Only one (b) Only two
(c) All three (d) None

**20.** Which of the following is a key characteristic of a command economy?

(a) Market forces determine the allocation of resources.
(b) The government makes all significant decisions about the production and distribution of goods.
(c) Prices of goods and services are determined by supply and demand.
(d) Private ownership of property and businesses is promoted.

**21.** Consider the following statements:

1. Capitalist economies rely on free markets to allocate resources, while socialist economies rely on central planning.
2. Capitalist economies may experience market failures, leading to negative externalities like pollution and income inequality.

Which of the statements given above is/are correct?

(a) 1 only
(b) 2 only
(c) Both 1 and 2
(d) Neither 1 nor 2

**22.** The concept of the 'Invisible Hand' in economics refers to which of the following?

(a) Government intervention that guides economic activities toward the public good.
(b) The unseen forces of supply and demand that guide individuals to unintentionally promote society's welfare through their self-interested actions.
(c) The role of central banks in managing the money supply to stabilise the economy.
(d) The invisible power of monopolies to control markets and prices.

**23.** In a laissez-faire economy, which of the following is primarily the role of the government?

(a) Regulate and control all aspects of economic activity.
(b) Intervene only in cases of market failures and provide public goods.
(c) Allow markets to operate with minimal government intervention, letting supply and demand determine prices.
(d) Set prices for essential goods and services to ensure fairness and equity.

## Topic 4 : Types of Goods

**24.** Which of the following characteristics are true for 'public goods'?

1. Non-excludability
2. Non-rivalry
3. Provided by private markets
4. Subject to the free-rider problem

Select the correct answer from the codes given below:

(a) 1 and 3 only (b) 1, 2 and 4 only
(c) 2 and 3 only (d) 1, 2, 3 and 4

**25.** Consider the following goods and services:

1. National defence
2. Street lighting
3. Public parks
4. Private healthcare services

Which of the given above are the examples of 'Public Goods'?

(a) 1 and 3 only
(b) 1, 2 and 3 only
(c) 2 and 4 only
(d) 1, 3 and 4 only

**26.** Why does the private sector typically not provide public goods?

(a) Because the production costs of public goods are too high for private firms to bear profitably.
(b) Because public goods are non-excludable and non-rivalrous, leading to the free-rider problem where individuals can benefit without paying.
(c) Because public goods are associated with low consumer demand, making them unprofitable for private enterprises.
(d) Because government regulations restrict the private sector from entering markets for public goods to ensure equity and fairness.

**27.** Which of the following are examples of merit goods?

1. Public transportation
2. Vaccinations
3. Cigarettes
4. Primary education

Select the correct answer from the codes given below:

(a) 1, 2 and 4 only (b) 2 and 3 only
(c) 1, 2, 3 and 4 (d) 1 and 4 only

**28.** With reference to consumer and capital goods, consider the following statements:

1. Consumer goods are those that are used directly by consumers to satisfy their wants.
2. Capital goods are used in the production of other goods and services and are not directly consumed.
3. A car used by a family for personal transportation is an example of a capital good.

How many of the statements given above is/ are correct?

(a) Only one (b) Only two
(c) All three (d) None

**29.** Consider the following examples with their appropriate classification:

| Examples | Classification |
|---|---|
| 1. A restaurant's kitchen equipment | Capital Good |
| 2. Television set for home use | Consumer Good |
| 3. Construction cranes | Capital Good |
| 4. Personal car used for commuting | Consumer Good |

How many of the given above pairs is/are correctly matched?

(a) Only one pair (b) Only two pairs
(c) Only three pairs (d) All four pairs

## Topic 5 : Microeconomics–Concept of Demand and Supply

**30.** With reference to the 'Law of Demand', consider the following statements:

1. It states that as the price of a good decreases, the quantity demanded increases.
2. It is applicable to all goods, including Giffen goods.

Which of the statements given above is/are correct?

(a) 1 only (b) 2 only
(c) Both 1 and 2 (d) Neither 1 nor 2

**31.** Which of the following can increase the demand for a good?

1. An increase in the population size
2. A decrease in the price of complementary goods
3. An increase in the price of substitute goods
4. An expectation of higher future prices

Select the correct answer from the codes given below:

(a) 1 and 3 only
(b) 2 and 4 only
(c) 1, 2, 3 and 4
(d) 1 and 2 only

**32.** With reference to the 'Price Elasticity of Demand', consider the following statements:

1. It measures the responsiveness of quantity demanded to a change in the price of the good.
2. A product with a price elasticity of demand greater than 1 is considered inelastic.
3. Necessities tend to have a lower price elasticity of demand than luxuries.

How many of the statements given above is/are correct?

(a) Only one (b) Only two
(c) All three (d) None

**33.** If a good has a price elasticity of demand (PED) greater than 1, which of the following scenarios is likely to occur?

1. A 10% increase in the price of the good will result in a more than 10% decrease in the quantity demanded.
2. The good is likely to have close substitutes available in the market.
3. The good is likely a necessity rather than a luxury.
4. Total revenue will decrease if the price of the good is increased.

Select the correct answer from the codes given below:

(a) 1 and 4 only (b) 1, 2 and 4 only
(c) 2 and 3 only (d) 1, 2, 3 and 4

**34.** Consider the following goods with their correct elasticity characteristic:

| Goods | Elasticity Characteristic |
|---|---|
| 1. Branded luxury handbags | Elastic demand |
| 2. Essential medicines | Inelastic demand |
| 3. High-end electronics with substitutes | Elastic demand |
| 4. Basic utilities (water, electricity) | Inelastic demand |

How many of the above pairs is/are correctly matched?

(a) Only one pair (b) Only two pairs
(c) Only three pairs (d) All four pairs

**35.** With reference to the complementary and substitute goods, consider the following statements:

1. If the price of tea increases, the demand for its substitute good i.e. coffee is likely to increase.
2. The demand for cars and gasoline, which are complementary goods, will both decrease if the price of gasoline rises significantly.
3. If two goods are substitutes, an increase in the price of one will lead to a decrease in the demand for the other.

Which of the statements given above are correct?

(a) 1 and 2 only (b) 2 and 3 only
(c) 1 and 3 only (d) 1, 2 and 3

**36.** Consider the following statements:

1. Cross-Price Elasticity of Demand is positive for substitute goods and negative for complementary goods.
2. If the Cross-Price elasticity of Demand between two goods is zero, the goods are likely to be unrelated.

Which of the statements given above is/are correct?

(a) 1 only (b) 2 only
(c) Both 1 and 2 (d) Neither 1 nor 2

**37.** Which of the following bring out the difference between 'Giffen goods' and 'Veblen goods'?

(a) Giffen goods are inferior goods for which demand increases as the price increases, while Veblen goods are luxury goods for which demand increases due to their status symbol associated with higher prices.

(b) Giffen goods are luxury items with a positive income elasticity of demand, while Veblen goods are essential goods with a negative income elasticity of demand.

(c) Giffen goods are characterised by a backward-bending supply curve, while Veblen goods are characterised by a downward-sloping demand curve.

(d) Giffen goods are consumed by the wealthy, while Veblen goods are consumed by the poor.

**38.** Consider the following statements:

1. A good is considered a normal good if its Income Elasticity of Demand is positive.
2. If the Income Elasticity of Demand for a good is greater than 1, the good is considered a luxury.
3. Inferior goods have a negative Income Elasticity of Demand, meaning that demand decreases as income increases.

Which of the given above statements is/are true about the 'Income Elasticity of Demand'?

(a) 1 and 2 only (b) 1, 2 and 3
(c) 2 only (d) 1 and 3 only

**39.** Which of the following goods are likely to have a high positive Income Elasticity of Demand?

1. High-end electronics 2. Basic food staples
3. Designer clothing
4. Public transportation

Select the correct answer from the codes given below:

(a) 1 and 3 only (b) 2 and 4 only
(c) 1, 3 and 4 only (d) 1, 2 and 3 only

**40.** Consider the following concepts with their correct descriptions:

| Concepts | Descriptions |
|---|---|
| 1. Law of Supply | As price decreases, quantity supplied decreases. |
| 2. Law of Demand | As price decreases, quantity demanded increases. |
| 3. Price Elasticity of Demand | Measures how much quantity demanded responds to price changes. |
| 4. Marginal Utility | Additional satisfaction from consuming one more unit of a good. |

How many of the above pairs is/are correctly matched?

(a) Only one pair (b) Only two pairs
(c) Only three pairs (d) All four pairs

**41.** Engel's Law suggests that as a household's income increases, the proportion of income spent on food:

(a) Increases because food is a necessity and higher income allows for more food consumption.

(b) Remains constant as food expenditure is not related to income changes.

(c) Decreases because the income elasticity of demand for food is less than one, leading to a smaller proportion of income being spent on food.

(d) Increases at the same rate as income because food consumption rises with income.

## Topic 6 : Market Structure

**42.** Consider the following statements about 'Perfect Competition':

**Statement I**: In a perfectly competitive market, all firms are price takers.

**Statement II**: There are significant barriers to entry in a perfectly competitive market, allowing existing firms to maintain economic profits.

Which one of the following is correct in respect of the above statements?

(a) Both Statement I and Statement II are correct, and Statement II is the correct explanation for Statement I.

(b) Both Statement I and Statement II are correct, but Statement II is not the correct explanation for Statement I.

(c) Statement I is correct, but Statement II is incorrect.

(d) Statement I is incorrect, but Statement II is correct.

**43.** Which of the following are true characteristics of an oligopolistic market?
1. Few firms dominate the market.
2. Firms are interdependent in their pricing and output decisions.
3. There are no barriers to entry for new firms.
4. Non-price competition, such as advertising, plays a significant role.

Select the correct answer from the codes given below:
(a) 1 and 2 only (b) 1, 2 and 4 only
(c) 2 and 3 only (d) 1, 2, 3 and 4

**44.** Consider the following market structures with their correct characteristics:

| Market Structures | Characteristics |
|---|---|
| 1. Perfect Competition | Firms are price takers with no control over prices. |
| 2. Monopoly | A single firm dominates the market with significant barriers to entry. |
| 3. Monopolistic Competition | Many firms offer differentiated products. |
| 4. Oligopoly | A few firms dominate the market with significant interdependence. |

How many of the above pairs is/are correctly matched?
(a) Only one pair (b) Only two pairs
(c) Only three pairs (d) All four pairs

**45.** Which of the following are examples of market failures?
1. Pollution from a factory
2. Under-provision of public goods
3. Perfect competition
4. Information asymmetry in financial markets

Select the correct answer from the codes given below:
(a) 1 and 2 only
(b) 1, 2 and 4 only
(c) 3 and 4 only
(d) 1, 2, 3 and 4

**46.** Which of the following correctly bring out the difference between monopolistic competition and perfect competition?
(a) Firms in monopolistic competition produce identical products, while firms in perfect competition produce differentiated products.
(b) Firms in monopolistic competition face no barriers to entry, while firms in perfect competition face significant barriers to entry.
(c) Firms in monopolistic competition have some market power due to product differentiation, while firms in perfect competition have no market power and produce identical products.
(d) Firms in monopolistic competition earn long-run economic profits, while firms in perfect competition only earn normal profits in the long run.

# OMR SHEET

**Assessment Round**

| | | | | | | | | | | | | | | | | | | | |
|---|---|---|---|---|---|---|---|---|---|---|---|---|---|---|---|---|---|---|---|
| 1 | a | b | c | d | 31 | a | b | c | d | 61 | a | b | c | d | 91 | a | b | c | d |
| 2 | a | b | c | d | 32 | a | b | c | d | 62 | a | b | c | d | 92 | a | b | c | d |
| 3 | a | b | c | d | 33 | a | b | c | d | 63 | a | b | c | d | 93 | a | b | c | d |
| 4 | a | b | c | d | 34 | a | b | c | d | 64 | a | b | c | d | 94 | a | b | c | d |
| 5 | a | b | c | d | 35 | a | b | c | d | 65 | a | b | c | d | 95 | a | b | c | d |
| 6 | a | b | c | d | 36 | a | b | c | d | 66 | a | b | c | d | 96 | a | b | c | d |
| 7 | a | b | c | d | 37 | a | b | c | d | 67 | a | b | c | d | 97 | a | b | c | d |
| 8 | a | b | c | d | 38 | a | b | c | d | 68 | a | b | c | d | 98 | a | b | c | d |
| 9 | a | b | c | d | 39 | a | b | c | d | 69 | a | b | c | d | 99 | a | b | c | d |
| 10 | a | b | c | d | 40 | a | b | c | d | 70 | a | b | c | d | 100 | a | b | c | d |
| 11 | a | b | c | d | 41 | a | b | c | d | 71 | a | b | c | d | 101 | a | b | c | d |
| 12 | a | b | c | d | 42 | a | b | c | d | 72 | a | b | c | d | 102 | a | b | c | d |
| 13 | a | b | c | d | 43 | a | b | c | d | 73 | a | b | c | d | 103 | a | b | c | d |
| 14 | a | b | c | d | 44 | a | b | c | d | 74 | a | b | c | d | 104 | a | b | c | d |
| 15 | a | b | c | d | 45 | a | b | c | d | 75 | a | b | c | d | 105 | a | b | c | d |
| 16 | a | b | c | d | 46 | a | b | c | d | 76 | a | b | c | d | 106 | a | b | c | d |
| 17 | a | b | c | d | 47 | a | b | c | d | 77 | a | b | c | d | 107 | a | b | c | d |
| 18 | a | b | c | d | 48 | a | b | c | d | 78 | a | b | c | d | 108 | a | b | c | d |
| 19 | a | b | c | d | 49 | a | b | c | d | 79 | a | b | c | d | 109 | a | b | c | d |
| 20 | a | b | c | d | 50 | a | b | c | d | 80 | a | b | c | d | 110 | a | b | c | d |
| 21 | a | b | c | d | 51 | a | b | c | d | 81 | a | b | c | d | 111 | a | b | c | d |
| 22 | a | b | c | d | 52 | a | b | c | d | 82 | a | b | c | d | 112 | a | b | c | d |
| 23 | a | b | c | d | 53 | a | b | c | d | 83 | a | b | c | d | 113 | a | b | c | d |
| 24 | a | b | c | d | 54 | a | b | c | d | 84 | a | b | c | d | 114 | a | b | c | d |
| 25 | a | b | c | d | 55 | a | b | c | d | 85 | a | b | c | d | 115 | a | b | c | d |
| 26 | a | b | c | d | 56 | a | b | c | d | 86 | a | b | c | d | 116 | a | b | c | d |
| 27 | a | b | c | d | 57 | a | b | c | d | 87 | a | b | c | d | 117 | a | b | c | d |
| 28 | a | b | c | d | 58 | a | b | c | d | 88 | a | b | c | d | 118 | a | b | c | d |
| 29 | a | b | c | d | 59 | a | b | c | d | 89 | a | b | c | d | 119 | a | b | c | d |
| 30 | a | b | c | d | 60 | a | b | c | d | 90 | a | b | c | d | 120 | a | b | c | d |

## Calculate Your Score

| | |
|---|---|
| **Correct (✓)** | |
| **Incorrect (✓)** | |
| **Unattempted** | |
| **Total Score** | |
| **Accuracy (%)** | |

## Reasons for Incorrect Answers?

| | |
|---|---|
| 1. Lack of Knowledge/Existing Source Insufficient | |
| 2. Lack of Multiple Revision | |
| 3. Common Sense Mistakes | |

**Note :**

1. Calculate total score as correct answers carry 2 marks each 1/3rd marks will deducted for **Incorrect** Answers.
2. Calculate Accuracy (%) by dividing the number of correct answers to the total number of attempted questions.

## Past Learning

**1.** With reference to the sectors of the Indian economy, consider the following pairs: **(2024)**

| | Economic activity | Sector |
|---|---|---|
| 1. | Storage of agricultural produce | Secondary |
| 2. | Dairy farm | Primary |
| 3. | Mineral exploration | Tertiary |
| 4. | Weaving cloth | Secondary |

How many of the pairs given above is/are correctly matched?

(a) Only one (b) Only two
(c) Only three (d) All four

**2.** With reference to physical capital in Indian economy, consider the following pairs: **(2024)**

| | Item | Category |
|---|---|---|
| 1. | Farmer's plough | Working capital |
| 2. | Computer | Fixed capital |
| 3. | Yarn used by the weaver | Fixed capital |
| 4. | Petrol | Working capital |

How many of the pairs given above is/are correctly matched?

(a) Only one (b) Only two
(c) Only three (d) All four

**3.** Consider the investments in the following assets : **(2023)**

1. Brand recognition 2. Inventory
3. Intellectual property 4. Mailing list of clients

How many of the above is/are considered intangible investments?

(a) Only one (b) Only two
(c) Only three (d) All four

**4.** Which of the following activities constitute real sector in the economy? **(2022)**

1. Farmers harvesting their crops
2. Textile mills converting raw cotton into fabrics
3. A commercial bank lending money to a trading company
4. A corporate body issuing Rupee Denominated Bonds overseas

Select the correct answer from the codes given below:

(a) 1 and 2 only (b) 2, 3 and 4 only
(c) 1, 3 and 4 only (d) 1, 2, 3 and 4

**5.** Other things remaining unchanged, market demand for a good might increase if: **(2021)**

1. Price of its substitute increase
2. Price of its complement increase
3. The good is an inferior good and income of the consumers increases
4. Its price falls

Which of the above statements are correct?

(a) 1 and 4 only (b) 2, 3 and 4 only
(c) 1, 3 and 4 only (d) 1, 2 and 3 only

**6.** If a commodity is provided free to the public 1, by the Government, then: **(2018)**

(a) the opportunity cost is zero.
(b) the opportunity cost is ignored.
(c) the opportunity cost is transferred from the consumers of the product to the tax- paying public.
(d) the opportunity cost is transferred from the consumers of the product to the Government.

**7.** Consider the following statements : **(2018)**

Human capital formation as a concept is better explained in terms of a process which enables:

1. individuals of a country to accumulate more capital.
2. increasing the knowledge, skill levels and capacities the people of the country.
3. accumulation of tangible wealth.
4. accumulation of intangible wealth.

Which of the statements given above is/are correct?

(a) 1 and 2 only (b) 2 only
(c) 2 and 4 only (d) 1, 3 and 4 only

**8.** Despite being a high saving economy, capital formation may not result in significant increase in output due to: **(2018)**

(a) weak administrative machinery
(b) illiteracy
(c) high population density
(d) high capital-outputs ratio

# Detailed Solutions

## Assessment Round

**1.** (*c*) All three

- **Statement 1 is correct:** Opportunity cost is a fundamental concept in economics that represents the benefits an individual, investor or business misses out on when choosing one alternative over another.
- **Statement 2 is correct:** Opportunity cost can indeed be zero in situations where a resource has no alternative uses. For instance, if a specific skill or resource can only be used in one way and there is no other opportunity or alternative for its use, then the opportunity cost of using that resource in that particular way is zero because there is no forgone alternative.
- **Statement 3 is correct:** Individuals face opportunity costs when making personal choices (e.g., choosing between studying or going out with friends), while societies face opportunity costs when allocating resources (e.g., deciding between spending on healthcare or education).

**Thus, option (c) is the correct answer.**

**2.** (*b*) Opportunity cost reflects potential future benefits, whereas Sunk cost represents past expenditures that cannot be recovered.

- **Opportunity Cost** refers to the value of the next best alternative that is foregone when a decision is made. It reflects the potential future benefits. E.g. investing in a stock or putting the money in a savings account. If you choose to invest in the stock, the opportunity cost is interest rate that you have earned from the savings account.
- **Sunk Cost** refers to resources that have already been spent and cannot be recovered. They are past expenditures that should not influence current or future economic decisions because they remain the same regardless of the outcome of any decision.

**Thus, option (b) is the correct answer.**

**3.** (*d*) 1, 2, 3 and 4

Zero Opportunity Cost occurs when a decision or action does not involve any sacrifice of other alternatives.

- **Statement 1 is correct:** Since the machines were idle and not being used for any other production, there is no forgone alternative. Using the idle machines does not displace any other production activity. Therefore, the opportunity cost is zero.
- **Statement 2 is correct:** Volunteering does not displace any other valuable use of time, as volunteering time when there are no other commitments incurs no opportunity cost.
- **Statement 3 is correct:** Studying when there are no other planned activities means there is no Opportunity cost, as nothing else is being sacrificed.
- **Statement 4 is correct:** Using leftover raw materials that would otherwise go to waste involves no opportunity cost, as they are not being diverted from any other productive use.

**Therefore, the correct answer is (d) 1, 2, 3 and 4.**

**4.** (*b*) Only two

- **Statement 1 is correct:** Land as a factor of production includes all natural resources available for production, such as forests, minerals, water, and other natural resources. These resources are considered part of 'Land' because they are naturally occurring and are used in the production of goods and services.
- **Statement 2 is correct:** Labour includes both physical and mental efforts contributed by workers to produce goods and services. This factor of production encompasses all human efforts, whether manual or intellectual, that are used in the production process.
- **Statement 3 is incorrect:** Capital as a factor of production is not limited to just the money invested in a business. It also includes physical assets like machinery, buildings, equipment, and tools that are used in the production process.

**Therefore, option (b) is the correct answer.**

**5.** (*a*) 1 and 3 only

Physical capital is tangible and includes assets like machinery, buildings, and equipment that can be bought and sold. Human capital is intangible and represents the skills, knowledge, and abilities inherent to individuals, which cannot be bought or sold in the same way.

- **Statement 1 is correct**: Physical capital is tangible and tradable while human capital is intangible and tied to individuals.
- **Statement 3 is correct**: As investment in human capital includes education and training, while investment in physical capital involves acquiring machinery and nfrastructure.
- **Statement 2 is incorrect**: Human capital is inherently tied to the individual to the individual who possesses the skills and knowledge and cannot be transferred like physical capital.

**Therefore, the correct answer is (a) 1 and 3 only.**

**6.** (*d*) None

Types of capital refer to the various resources that are used in the production of goods and services. Different types of capital play distinct roles in the economic process like

**Physical Capital:** Tangible assets that are used in the production process to produce goods and services.

**Human Capital:** The skills, knowledge, experience, and abilities of individuals that contribute to economic production.

**Pair 1 is incorrect**: Computer software is considered physical capital because it is a man-made asset used in the production process to enhance efficiency and productivity.

**Pair 2 is incorrect**: Technical training improves the skills and knowledge of employees, which is considered human capital.

**Pair 3 is incorrect**: Office furniture and equipment are tangible assets that are used in the production process, making them physical capital.

**Pair 4 is incorrect**: A worker's experience and expertise are examples of human capital because they reflect the accumulated knowledge and skills that improve a worker's productivity.

**Thus, option (d) is the correct answer.**

**7.** (*b*) 1, 2 and 4 only

Human capital is intangible and is developed through investment in education, training and healthcare. It increases productivity and efficiency in the workforce.

- **Statement 1 is correct**: Education and training are fundamental in developing skills, knowledge, and capabilities, which are critical components of human capital.
- **Statement 2 is correct**: As access to quality healthcare ensures a healthy workforce, which contributes to human capital formation.
- **Statement 4 is correct**: Social and cultural environment that encourages learning and skill development plays a significant role in the formation of human capital.
- **Statement 3 is incorrect**: Physical capital like machinery and equipment contributes to production capacity but is not directly involved in human capital formation.

**Thus, option (b) is the correct answer.**

**8.** (*c*) Only three pairs

- **Pair 1 is incorrect**: Fixed capital refers to long-term assets used in the production process, such as machinery and raw materials are not fixed capital, they are part of working capital.
- **Pair 2 is correct**: Working capital includes assets that are used in the day-to-day operations of a business, such as inventory of finished goods.
- **Pair 3 is correct**: Office equipment like computers are examples of fixed capital because they are long-term.
- **Pair 4 is correct**: Cash available for day-to-day operations is a classic example of working capital, as it is essential for the daily functioning.

**Thus, option (c) is the correct answer.**

**9.** (*b*) 1, 2 and 3 only

- **Statement 1 is correct**: Fixed capital is invested in long-term assets like machinery, buildings, and equipment, which are used in the production process over several years.
- **Statement 2 is correct**: Working capital is primarily used to finance the day-to-day operations of a business, including purchasing raw materials, paying wages, and covering other short-term expenses.

- **Statement 3 is correct**: Depreciation affects fixed capital over time, reducing its value as assets like machinery and equipment wear out or become obsolete.
- **Statement 4 is incorrect**: Working capital can involve tangible assets, such as inventory and raw materials, which are part of the short-term assets used in daily business operations.

**Therefore, option (b) is the correct answer.**

***10.*** (*a*) 1 and 2 only

The Incremental Capital-Output Ratio (ICOR) measures the amount of additional capital required to produce an additional unit of output. It reflects the efficiency of capital investment.

A higher ICOR suggests that more capital is required to achieve a certain level of output, indicating inefficiency in the use of capital. A lower ICOR indicates that the economy is using its capital more efficiently.

- **Statement 1 is correct**: A higher ICOR suggests that more capital is required to achieve a certain level of output, indicating inefficiency in the use of capital. This inefficiency can slow down economic growth because it implies that the country is not using its investments as effectively as it could be.
- **Statement 2 is correct**: Developing countries often exhibit lower ICORs compared to developed countries because they typically have higher marginal returns on investment. In developing economies, there are often significant unmet needs and opportunities for investment in infrastructure, education, and technology.
- **Statement 3 is incorrect**: ICOR is primarily a measure of the efficiency of capital in producing output, rather than a direct reflection of the savings rate. While savings can influence the amount of capital available for investment, ICOR is concerned with how effectively that capital is used.

**Thus, option (a) is the correct answer.**

***11.*** (*a*) Increased investment in advanced technology that boosts productivity.

A lower ICOR indicates that the economy is using its capital more efficiently, generating more output per unit of capital invested. Investment in advanced technology improves productivity, which would lower the ICOR.

**Thus, option (a) is the correct answer.**

***12.*** (*c*) 1, 2 and 3 only

Non-economic activities are activities that do not involve any monetary gain or economic benefit like activities performed out of love, affection, social or religious obligation.

- **Statement 1 is correct**: As mother cooking meals for her family is a non-economic activity as it is done for personal satisfaction without monetary compensation.
- **Statement 2 is correct**: Offering free tutoring services is a non-economic activity since there is no exchange of money.
- **Statement 3 is correct**: Donating blood is a non-economic activity performed for social welfare.
- **Statement 4 is incorrect**: Selling produce at a market is an economic activity involving the exchange of goods for money as they are economic activity aiming for economic gain.

**Thus, option (c) is the correct answer.**

***13.*** (*a*) 1 and 3 only

Primary Sector activities involve the extraction and harvesting of natural resources. They include activities that directly use natural resources, such as farming, fishing, forestry and mining.

- **Option 1 is correct**: Fishing is an activity directly related to the extraction of natural resources, which belongs to the primary sector.
- **Option 2 is incorrect**: Manufacturing is a secondary sector activity as it involves processing raw materials into finished goods, which is a **secondary sector** activity.
- **Option 3 is correct**: Mining involves the extraction of minerals and other natural resources, also part of the primary sector.
- **Option 4 is incorrect**: IT services belong to the tertiary sector in which information technology services involve providing technological solutions and support, which is a **tertiary sector** activity.

**Therefore, the correct answer is (a) 1 and 3 only.**

**14.** (*b*) Only two pairs

- **Pair 1 is correct**: Agriculture is a part of the primary sector as it involves the extraction and production of natural resources, such as crops and livestock.
- **Pair 2 is incorrect**: Intellectual property activities, such as creating patents or copyrights, are part of the tertiary sector, not the secondary sector, as they involve services related to intellectual and creative work.
- **Pair 3 is incorrect**: The construction of buildings falls under the **secondary sector** because it involves transforming raw materials into finished goods, such as buildings and infrastructure.
- **Pair 4 is correct**: Manufacturing of steel is part of the secondary sector, which includes industries involved in the processing and manufacturing of goods.

**Therefore, option (b) is the correct answer.**

**15.** (*b*) Only two

India's structural Transformation refers to the shift in the economic structure of the country from being predominantly agrarian to becoming more diversified, with increasing contributions from the industrial and services sectors.

- **Statement 1 is correct**: Structural transformation often involves a reallocation of labour from the agriculture sector to the manufacturing and services sectors as the economy develops.
- **Statement 2 is correct**: Structural transformation is generally associated with rising productivity and income levels as resources shift to more productive sectors like manufacturing and services.
- **Statement 3 is incorrect**: The pace and nature of structural transformation can vary significantly across different economies, depending on various factors like policy, resources, and historical context. For example, India experienced a significant shift from agriculture directly to the services sector, largely bypassing the manufacturing-led stage of industrialisation.

**Therefore, the correct answer is (b) Only two.**

**16.** (*d*) 1, 2 and 3

- **Statement 1 is correct**: India has largely bypassed the manufacturing stage during its structural transformation. Unlike many other developing countries that experienced a manufacturing-led growth phase.
- **Statement 2 is correct**: Services (tertiary sector) has been the fastest growing in India and is now the largest contributor to GDP:50-55%. As the services sector is now the largest contributor to India's GDP, reflecting the structural shift in the economy. Agriculture and Allied Sectors (Primary Sector) Contribution to GDP: 15-18% in recent years, but it employs a significant portion of the workforce (around 40-50%). Industry (Secondary Sector): Manufacturing, a key component of this sector, has not grown as fast as services but remains crucial for economic development and employment. Contribution to GDP: 25-30%.
- **Statement 3 is correct**: The decline in agriculture's contribution to GDP, a significant portion of India's workforce is still employed in the agricultural sector.

**Therefore, option (d) is the correct answer.**

**17.** (*b*) Only two

The real sector of the economy deals with the production side, while the nominal economy deals with the financial side.

- **Statement 1 is correct**: The real sector involves all production activities, including manufacturing, agriculture and services. It refers to all activities involving the creation of goods and provision of services that constitute the real, or tangible, economy.
- **Statement 2 is correct**: The real sector's activities directly contribute to GDP as it includes all economic activities within the real sector.
- **Statement 3 is incorrect**: Financial activities like banking and insurance belong to the financial sector, not the real sector, which deals with the management of money, investments, and financial services.

**Therefore, the correct answer is (b) Only two.**

**18.** *(b)* 1, 3 and 4 only

Real sector involves all production activities, including manufacturing, agriculture, and services. These activities directly contribute to GDP. It includes activities related to manufacturing, agriculture, and services that meet consumer needs.

- **Statement 1 is correct**: Manufacturing is a key activity in the real sector.
- **Statement 3 is correct**: Agricultural production is a primary component of the real sector.
- **Statement 4 is correct**: Retail services are part of the service industry, which is included in the real sector.
- **Statement 2 is incorrect**: Financial services belong to the financial sector, not the real sector. This is not a part of the real sector, it is a part of the financial sector, which involves managing money, investments, and financial services.

**Thus, option (b) is the correct answer.**

**19.** *(b)* Only two

Capitalism is often thought of as an economic system in which private actors own and control property in accord with their interests, and demand and supply freely set prices in markets in a way that can serve the best interests of society.

- **Statement 1 is correct**: In a capitalist economy, the means of production (such as factories, land and machinery) are owned by private individuals or businesses.
- **Statement 2 is correct**: Private property rights are essential in a capitalist economy, allowing individuals and businesses to own and control resources.
- **Statement 3 is incorrect**: In a pure capitalist system, the government has a limited role in regulating prices and controlling production, with market forces determining these aspects instead.

**Therefore, the correct answer is (b) Only two.**

**20.** *(b)* The government makes all significant decisions about the production and distribution of goods.

In a **command economy**, the **government** exercises complete control over economic activity. This means that the allocation of resources, the **production of goods and services,** and their **distribution** are all centrally planned and managed by the state.

A command economy typically has the following features:

- **State ownership** of the means of production (land, labour, capital and entrepreneurship). Private ownership of businesses and property is either restricted or non-existent.
- **Government control** of labour, determining where people work and what wages they receive.
- **Limited role for market forces,** meaning that supply and demand do not influence economic decisions.
- **Centralised economic planning,** where the government creates long-term plans (often for five years or more) to achieve specific economic outcomes, such as industrialisation, infrastructure development, or employment generation.

**Thus, option (b) is the correct answer.**

**21.** *(c)* Both 1 and 2

Socialist economic systems in which the means of production (such as factories, resources, and capital) are owned and controlled by the state or the public rather than by private individuals. The main goal of a socialist economy is to ensure equal distribution of wealth and resources.

- **Statement 1 is correct**: Capitalist economies allocate resources through the market mechanism, while socialist economies use central planning to distribute resources.
- **Statement 2 is correct**: Capitalist economies can experience market failures, such as environmental degradation and income inequality, when the market does not allocate resources efficiently.

**Therefore, the correct answer is (c) Both 1 and 2.**

**22.** (*b*) The unseen forces of supply and demand that guide individuals to unintentionally promote society's welfare through their self-interested actions.

The 'Invisible Hand' represents the self-regulating nature of the marketplace. It suggests that when individuals seek to maximise their own gains, they inadvertently contribute to the economic well-being of society as a whole. The 'Invisible Hand' is a metaphor introduced by Adam Smith work, **The Wealth of Nations.**

**Thus, Option (b) is the correct answer.**

**23.** (*c*) A laissez-faire economy is characterised by minimal government intervention, where the forces of supply and demand are allowed to operate freely to determine prices and allocate resources.

**Thus, Option (c) is the correct answer.**

**24.** (*b*) 1, 2 and 4

Public goods are **non-excludable** and non-rivalrous, meaning that they can be consumed by anyone, and one person's consumption does not reduce the availability of the good to others. These characteristics make public goods unique and often require government intervention for their provision because private markets may fail to supply them adequately.

- **Option 1 is correct**: Non-excludability is a characteristic of public goods, meaning that once the good is provided, it is not possible to exclude anyone from using it. For example, once a lighthouse is built, all ships benefit from it, whether they contributed to its construction or not.
- **Option 2 is correct**: Non-rivalry is another characteristic of public goods, meaning that one person's use of the good does not diminish the ability of others to use it. For instance, one person's enjoyment of national defence does not reduce the level of protection available to others.
- **Option 3 is incorrect**: Public goods are typically not provided by private markets because they are non-excludable and non-rivalrous. Private markets find it difficult to charge individuals directly for their use, making it unprofitable. As a result, public goods are usually provided by the government or funded through taxation.
- **Option 4 is correct**: Public goods are subject to the free-rider problem, where individuals can benefit from the good without paying for it, leading to under-provision of the good if left to private markets.

**Therefore, the correct answer is (b) 1, 2 and 4 only.**

**25.** (*b*) 1, 2 and 3 only

- **Option 1 is correct**: National defence is a classic example of a public good that is non-excludable and non-rivalrous.
- **Option 2 is correct**: Street lighting is non-excludable and non-rivalrous, making it a public good.
- **Option 3 is correct**: Public parks are non-excludable and non-rivalrous, fitting the definition of a public good.
- **Option 4 is incorrect**: Private healthcare Services are not public goods. Private healthcare is excludable (only those who pay for the service can receive it) and rivalrous (resources used for one person's healthcare are not available for another).

**Thus, option (b) is the correct answer.**

**26.** (*b*) **The free-rider problem** is the main reason private firms are reluctant to provide public goods. Since these goods are non-excludable (anyone can benefit regardless of payment) and non-rivalrous (one person's use does not reduce availability for others), it becomes challenging for firms to charge all beneficiaries, thus **undermining potential profits** and discouraging private provision.

**Thus, option (b) is the correct answer.**

**27.** (*a*) 1, 2 and 4 only

- **Option 1 is correct**: Public transportation is often subsidised due to its positive externalities as it provides benefits like reduced traffic congestion, lower pollution levels, and increased accessibility for individuals who cannot afford private transport.
- **Option 2 is correct**: Vaccinations are typically considered a merit good due to their public health benefits by preventing the spread of infectious diseases.

- **Option 4 is correct:** Primary education a merit good with significant positive externalities such as better job prospects and personal development, as well as societal benefits like improved literacy rates.
- **Option 3 incorrect:** Cigarettes are a demerit good because their consumption has negative externalities, such as health issues and second-hand smoke, which can harm society.

**Therefore, the correct answer is (a) 1, 2 and 4 only.**

***28.*** (*b*) Only two

- **Statement 1 is correct:** Consumer goods are goods that are used directly by consumers to satisfy their personal needs and wants. Examples include food, clothing, electronics and household items.
- **Statement 2 is correct:** Capital goods are goods that are used in the production of other goods and services. They are not directly consumed by consumers but are used by businesses to produce consumer goods or provide services. Examples include machinery, tools and equipment used in factories.
- **Statement 3 is incorrect:** A car used by a family for personal transportation is an example of a consumer good because it is used directly by consumers to satisfy their need for personal transportation. A car would be considered a capital good if it were used by a business for production purposes, such as for deliveries or transporting employees.

**Therefore, the correct answer is (b) Only two.**

***29.*** (*d*) All four pairs

- **Pair 1 is correctly matched:** A restaurant's kitchen equipment is a capital good, used in the production of food services.
- **Pair 2 is correctly matched:** Television set for home use is a consumer good because it is purchased for personal enjoyment.
- **Pair 3 is correctly matched:** Construction cranes is a capital good as they are used in construction projects.
- **Pair 4 is correctly matched:** Personal car used for commuting is a consumer good as it is used by individuals for personal trans portation.

**Thus, all four pairs are correctly matched. Therefore, the correct answer is (d).**

***30.*** (*a*) 1 only

- **Statement 1 is correct:** The Law of Demand states that, all else being equal, as the price of a good decreases, the quantity demanded increases. This reflects an inverse relationship between price and quantity demanded.
- **Statement 2 is incorrect:** The Law of Demand is not applicable to all goods, specifically Giffen goods. Giffen goods are an exception to the law of demand; for these goods, an increase in price leads to an increase in quantity demanded due to the unique relationship between the price and the consumer's perceived necessity or income effect. Example: rice, wheat, public transportation.

**Therefore, the correct answer is (a) 1 only.**

***31.*** (*c*) 1, 2, 3 and 4

- **Statement 1 is correct:** An increase in the population size can lead to an increase in the demand for a good because more people may want to buy the product, thereby raising overall demand.
- **Statement 2 is correct:** A decrease in the price of complementary goods can increase the demand for a good. When the price of a complementary good falls, consumers are more likely to buy both goods together, increasing the demand for the related good.
- **Statement 3 is correct:** An increase in the price of substitute goods can increase the demand for a good. If the price of a substitute rises, consumers may switch their preference to the relatively cheaper good, thereby increasing its demand.
- **Statement 4 is correct:** An expectation of higher future prices can lead to an increase in current demand. Consumers may choose to purchase more now to avoid paying higher prices in the future, thereby increasing the current demand.

**Therefore, the correct answer is (c) 1, 2, 3 and 4.**

***32.*** (*b*) Only two

Price Elasticity of Demand (PED) measures how much the quantity demanded of a good change in response to a change in its price. It is calculated as the percentage change in quantity demanded divided by the percentage change in price.

- **Statement 1 is correct**: In mathematical terms, it is calculated as the percentage change in quantity demanded divided by the percentage change in price.
- **Statement 3 is correct:** Necessities typically have a lower price elasticity of demand compared to luxuries because consumers continue to purchase them even when prices rise. This is because necessities are essential for daily life, such as food, water, and basic healthcare
- **Statement 2 is incorrect**: A high elasticity of greater than 1 indicates that consumers are very responsive to price changes, meaning that a small change in price results in a large change in the quantity demanded. Types of Price Elasticity:
  - **Elastic Demand (PED > 1)**: Quantity demanded changes more than the price change; consumers are highly responsive to price changes.
  - **Inelastic Demand (PED < 1)**: Quantity demanded changes less than the price change; consumers are less responsive to price changes.
  - **Unitary Elastic Demand (PED = 1)**: Quantity demanded changes exactly in proportion to the price change.

**Thus, option (b) is the correct answer.**

**33.** (*b*) 1, 2 and 4 only

- **Statement 1 is correct**: If a good has a Price Elasticity of Demand (PED) greater than 1, it means the demand is elastic. A 10% increase in the price will lead to a more than 10% decrease in the quantity demanded, reflecting high sensitivity to price changes.
- **Statement 2 is correct**: Goods with elastic demand often have close substitutes available. Consumers can easily switch to alternatives if the price of the good increases, making demand more responsive to price changes.
- **Statement 3 is incorrect**: Goods with a PED greater than 1, it is more likely to be a luxury good rather than a necessity. Necessities typically have inelastic demand (PED less than 1).
- **Statement 4 is correct**: If the price of a good with elastic demand (PED > 1) increases, total revenue will decrease because the percentage decrease in quantity demanded will be greater than the percentage increase in price.

**Therefore, the correct answer is (b) 1, 2 and 4 only.**

**34.** (*d*) All four pairs

- **Pair 1 is correct**: Branded luxury handbags have **elastic demand** because they are non-essential luxury items with many substitutes. Consumers are likely to reduce their purchases if prices increase.
- **Pair 2 is correct**: Essential medicines have **inelastic demand** as they are necessary for health and survival, and consumers will purchase them regardless of price changes.
- **Pair 3 is correct**: High-end electronics with substitutes also have **elastic demand** because consumers can easily switch to alternative products if prices rise.
- **Pair 4 is correct**: Basic utilities like water and electricity have **inelastic demand** because they are essential for daily living, and consumption does not significantly decrease with price increases.

**All four pairs are correctly matched.**

**Therefore, the correct answer is (d) All four pairs.**

**35.** (*a*) 1 and 2 only

Complementary and substitute goods are concepts in economics that describe the relationship between two or more products based on how they are consumed or used.

**Complementary goods** are goods that are typically consumed together, where the use or consumption of one good enhances the use or consumption of the other (**Joint Demand**). It has **Negative Cross-Price Elasticity**: When the price of one good decreases, the demand for its complementary good often increases, and vice versa.

**Substitute goods** are goods that can be used in place of one another (Alternative). It has **positive Cross-Price Elasticity**: When the price of one good increases, the demand for its substitute also increases, showing a positive cross-price elasticity of demand.

- **Statement 1 is correct:** When the price of tea increases, consumers might switch to coffee, a substitute, leading to an increase in its demand.
- **Statement 2 is correct:** As cars and gasoline are complementary goods; a significant increase in the price of gasoline will reduce the demand for both gasoline and cars.
- **Statement 3 is incorrect:** If two goods are substitutes, an increase in the price of one would lead to an increase, not a decrease, in the demand for the other.

**Thus, option (a) is the correct answer.**

**36.** (*c*) Both 1 and 2

Cross-Price Elasticity of Demand (CPED) measures how the quantity demanded of one good responds to a change in the price of another good. It helps determine the relationship between two goods and whether they are substitutes, complements, or unrelated.

- **Statement 1 is correct** because substitute goods have a positive cross-price elasticity; when the price of one good increases, consumers switch to its substitute, increasing demand for the substitute.
- Complementary goods have a negative cross-price elasticity; an increase in the price of one good reduces the demand for its complement because the goods are typically used together.
- **Statement 2 is correct** because if the cross-price elasticity between two goods is zero, it suggests that the goods are unrelated and a change in the price of one does not affect the demand for the other.

**Therefore, the correct answer is (c) Both 1 and 2.**

**37.** (*a*) **Giffen Goods:** These are a type of **inferior good** where an **increase in the price leads to an increase in quantity demanded,** which is **contrary to the law of demand.** This occurs because the **income effect of a price increase outweighs the substitution effect.**

Giffen goods are typically **essential items for which cheaper alternatives are not available.** When the price of a Giffen good rises, low-income consumers may end up buying more of it because they can no longer afford to switch to more expensive substitutes.

**Veblen Goods:** These are luxury goods for which demand increases as the price increases because they serve as a status symbol. The higher price makes the good more desirable to some consumers, who associate higher prices with greater prestige or quality. This behaviour is contrary to typical demand patterns and reflects consumer preferences for conspicuous consumption.

**Thus, option (a) is the correct answer.**

**38.** (*b*) 1, 2 and 3

Income Elasticity of Demand (YED) measures how **the quantity demanded of a good change in response to a change in consumer income.** It helps determine whether a good is a normal good or an inferior good based on how demand responds to income changes.

- **Statement 1 is correct: A good is considered a normal good if its income elasticity of demand is positive** because normal goods see an increase in demand as income rises.
- **Statement 2 is correct: If the Income Elasticity of demand for a good is greater than 1, the good is considered a luxury** because luxuries have an income elasticity greater than 1, indicating that demand increases more than proportionately with income.
- **Statement 3 is correct: Inferior goods have a negative Income Elasticity of Demand** because inferior goods see a decrease in demand as income increases.

**Thus, option (b) is the correct answer.**

**39.** (*a*) 1 and 3 only

High Positive Income Elasticity of Demand refers to a situation where the demand for a good increase significantly in response to an increase in consumer income.

**Goods with high positive Income Elasticity of Demand** are typically luxury goods or non-essential items. For these goods, as consumers' income increases, the demand for these goods rises more than proportionally.

- **Option 1 is correct:** Luxury items like high-end electronics often have a high positive Income Elasticity of Demand, meaning demand increases significantly with rising income.

- **Option 2 is incorrect:** Basic food staples are typically having a low or even negative income elasticity, as they are necessities and not luxuries.
- **Option 3 is correct:** Designer clothing is also considered a luxury good, with demand rising more than proportionately as income increases.
- **Option 4 is incorrect:** Public transportation generally has a low-income elasticity, as it is more of a necessity than a luxury. As incomes increase, people may prefer personal modes of transportation (like cars) over public transportation.

**Thus, option (a) is the correct answer.**

**40.** (*d*) All four pairs

- **Pair 1 is correct:** The **Law of Supply** states that as the price of a good decreases, the quantity supplied also decreases, assuming all other factors remain constant. This reflects a **direct relationship** between price and quantity supplied.
- **Pair 2 is correct:** The Law of Demand states that as the price of a good decreases, the quantity demanded increases, assuming all other factors remain constant. This reflects an **inverse relationship** between price and quantity demanded.
- **Pair 3 is correct: Price Elasticity of Demand** measures the responsiveness of the quantity demanded of a good to changes in its price. It indicates how sensitive consumers are to price changes.
- **Pair 4 is correct: Marginal Utility** refers to the additional satisfaction or utility that a consumer gains from consuming one more unit of a good or service.

**All four pairs are correctly matched.**
**Therefore, the correct answer is (d) All four pairs.**

**41.** (*c*) **Statement (c) is correct:** According to Engel's Law, as income increases, the proportion of income spent on food decreases because food has a lower income elasticity of demand compared to other goods and services. Even though absolute spending on food might increase, it takes up a smaller percentage of total income.

- **Statement (a) is incorrect :** because although higher income may allow for more food consumption, the proportion of income spent on food does not increase.
- **Statement (b) is incorrect :** because the proportion of income spent on food does change with income changes, specifically decreasing as income increases.
- **Statement (d) is incorrect :** because food consumption does not increase at the same rate as income; instead, the proportion of income spent on food decreases.

**Thus, option (c) is the correct answer.**

**42.** (*c*) Statement I is correct, but Statement II is incorrect.

- **Statement I is correct:** Because in a perfectly competitive market, all firms are **price takers.** This means that individual firms have **no control over the market price** and must accept the market price determined by the forces of supply and demand. This is because there are many sellers offering identical products, and consumers can switch between sellers without any cost.
- **Statement II is incorrect:** In a perfectly competitive market, there are **no significant barriers** to entry. This characteristic ensures that new firms can **freely enter or exit the market.** As a result, existing firms cannot maintain economic profits in the long run because any economic profits would attract new entrants, driving profits down to a normal level due to increased competition.

**Thus, option (c) is the correct answer.**

**43.** (*b*) 1, 2 and 4 only

- **Statement 1 is correct:** In an oligopolistic market, few firms dominate the market. This small number of large firms controls most of the market share.
- **Statement 2 is correct:** Firms in an oligopoly are interdependent in their pricing and output decisions. The actions of one firm directly affect the others, leading to strategic decision-making and mutual dependence.
- **Statement 3 is incorrect:** There are barriers to entry in an oligopolistic market, which

prevents new firms from easily entering the market. These barriers can include high startup costs, economies of scale, and strong brand loyalty among existing firms.

- **Statement 4 is correct:** Non-price competition, such as advertising, product differentiation, and customer service, plays a significant role in oligopolistic markets. Firms use these strategies to compete without altering prices significantly.

**Thus, option (b) is the correct answer.**

**44.** (*d*) All four pairs

- **Pair 1 is correct:** In a perfect competition market structure, there are many firms selling identical products, and each firm is a price taker with no control over the market price.
- **Pair 2 is correct:** A monopoly is characterised by a single firm that dominates the market, and there are significant barriers to entry that prevent other firms from entering the market.
- **Pair 3 is correct:** In monopolistic competition, there are many firms that offer differentiated products, allowing them to have some control over their prices.
- **Pair 4 is correct:** An oligopoly consists of a few firms that dominate the market. These firms are interdependent, meaning each firm's decisions affect the others.

**Therefore, the correct answer is (d) All four pairs.**

**45.** (*b*) 1, 2 and 4 only

Market failures occur when free markets fail to allocate resources efficiently, leading to a loss of economic and social welfare. In such cases, the market does not achieve a socially optimal outcome, resulting in overproduction, underproduction or misallocation of resources.

- **Option 1 is correct: Pollution from a factory** represents a negative externality, a common market failure.
- **Option 2 is correct: Under-provision of public goods** (like national defence or public parks) are non-excludable and non-rivalrous, leading to free-rider problems.
- **Option 3 is incorrect: Perfect competition** represents an ideal market structure, not a market failure. In fact, perfect competition is considered a benchmark for a well-functioning market where resources are allocated efficiently, and prices reflect the true cost of production and consumer preferences.
- **Option 4 is correct: Information asymmetry** in which one party has more or better information than another, it can lead to market failures because one party has better information than the other, leading to suboptimal decision-making and potential market inefficiencies (e.g., adverse selection and moral hazard)

**Therefore, the correct answer is (b) 1, 2 and 4 only.**

**46.** (*c*) **Monopolistic Competition:** Firms produce differentiated products, meaning each firm offers a product that is slightly different from its competitors, which gives them some market power to set prices above marginal cost.

- **Examples** include restaurants, clothing brands, and consumer goods, where companies differentiate their products through quality, branding or features.

**Perfect Competition:** Firms produce **identical or homogeneous products**, meaning there is no differentiation between products offered by different firms. Firms in perfect competition are price takers, meaning they have **no market power** to set prices. Prices are determined by the market, and firms must accept the market price.

- **Examples** include agricultural markets like wheat or corn, where products are largely undifferentiated.

**Key difference** is that firms in monopolistic competition differentiate their products, giving them some market power. In contrast, firms in perfect competition sell identical products and are price takers with no market power.

**Thus, option (c) is the correct answer.**

## Past Learning (Answers)

| | | | | | | | |
|---|---|---|---|---|---|---|---|
| 1 (b) | 2 (b) | 3 (c) | 4 (a) | 5 (a) | 6 (c) | 7 (c) | 8 (d) |

CHAPTER 02

# National Income Accounting

## Assessment Round

### Topic 1 : Gross Domestic Product (GDP)

**1.** With reference to the 'Gross Domestic Product (GDP)', consider the following statements:

1. It includes the market value of both final goods and intermediate goods.
2. It includes the value of intermediate goods to avoid double counting.
3. It includes all goods and services produced by the citizens of a country regardless of their location.

How many of the statements given above is/are correct?

(a) Only one (b) Only two
(c) All three (d) None

**2.** Consider the following activities:

1. A factory producing cars for domestic consumption
2. A family providing unpaid household services
3. A company exporting software services abroad
4. The resale of second-hand goods in the domestic market

How many of the above activities is/are included in the calculation of a country's GDP?

(a) Only one (b) Only two
(c) Only three (d) All four

**3.** In the context of GDP calculation, which of the following are considered part of the domestic territory of a country?

1. A factory located within the country but owned by a foreign corporation
2. Indian embassies in foreign countries
3. Indian companies operating in foreign Special Economic Zones (SEZs)
4. A ship registered in India but operating between foreign countries

Select the correct answer using the codes given below:

(a) 1 and 2 only
(b) 1, 2 and 4 only
(c) 2 and 4 only
(d) 1, 2, 3 and 4

**4.** What is a defining characteristic of a final good in national income accounting?

(a) It refers to a product that is used as a raw material in the production of other goods.
(b) It refers to goods that are only used in industrial processes.
(c) It is a good that cannot be resold after consumption.
(d) It is a good that contributes to the Gross Domestic Product (GDP) by being consumed or invested without further transformation.

**5.** Consider the following goods:

1. A car sold to a consumer
2. Raw materials used by a manufacturer
3. A computer purchased by a company for office use
4. Flour purchased by a bakery

How many of the above goods can be classified as Final Goods?

(a) Only one (b) Only two
(c) Only three (d) All four

**6.** Arrange the following types of national income estimates in the correct chronological order of their release:

1. Advance Estimates
2. First Revised Estimates
3. Provisional Estimates
4. Final Estimates

Select the correct answer using the codes given below:

(a) 1, 3, 2, 4 (b) 3, 1, 2, 4
(c) 1, 2, 3, 4 (d) 3, 2, 1, 4

**7.** With reference to the Nominal and Real GDP, consider the following statements:

1. Real GDP is the value of GDP at the current prevailing prices.
2. Nominal GDP is calculated in such a way that the goods and services are evaluated at some constant prices.
3. The ratio of Real GDP to Nominal GDP is known as GDP Deflator.

Which of the given above statements are correct?

(a) 1 and 2 only (b) 2 and 3 only
(c) 1, 2 and 3 (d) None of these

**8.** Consider the following statements:

1. Nominal GDP can rise even if the total production of goods and services falls.
2. Real GDP accounts for inflation while Nominal GDP does not.
3. Nominal GDP will always be higher than Real GDP in an economy experiencing deflation.

How many of the statements given above is/are correct?

(a) Only one (b) Only two
(c) All three (d) None

**9.** Why is it important to periodically update the base year used in GDP calculations?

(a) To reflect changes in inflation rates more accurately.
(b) To ensure GDP measures are based on current consumption patterns and technological advancements.
(c) To avoid changes in international trade impacting domestic GDP estimates.
(d) To reduce the impact of global exchange rates on Real GDP.

**10.** When choosing a base year for GDP calculation in India, several factors are considered. Which of the following are general criteria for selecting a base year?

1. The base year should reflect a normal economic scenario without major distortions like natural disasters or economic crises.
2. The base year should represent a period of significant economic reforms.
3. The base year should have reliable and comprehensive data on economic activity.
4. The base year should always be a year of low inflation to avoid overstating economic growth.

Select the correct answer using the codes given below:

(a) 1, 2 and 3 only
(b) 1 and 3 only
(c) 2 and 4 only
(d) 1, 3 and 4 only

**11.** Consider the following activities:

1. Unpaid household work
2. Transfer payments like pensions and scholarships
3. Sale of second-hand goods
4. Income from lotteries and gambling

How many of the above activities is/are excluded from the calculation of national income?

(a) Only one
(b) Only two
(c) Only three
(d) All four

**12.** Consider the following activities:

1. Salaries paid to government employees
2. Construction of new residential buildings
3. Illegal drug trade
4. An individual purchasing shares of a company

How many of the given above activities is/are included in the calculation of a country's GDP?

(a) Only one
(b) Only two
(c) Only three
(d) All four

**13.** With reference to the concept of Externalities, consider the following statements:

1. It refers to the unintended side effects of economic activities that affect third parties.
2. A positive externality benefits third parties while a negative externality imposes a cost on them.
3. Externalities are always internalised in a perfectly competitive market.

Which of the given statements are correct?

(a) 1 and 2 only (b) 1 and 3 only
(c) 2 and 3 only (d) 1, 2 and 3

**14.** It is argued that GDP does not cover up externalities in the production of goods and services. If there are positive externalities then:

(a) The socially desirable GDP will be lower than the commercially desirable GDP.
(b) The socially desirable GDP will be higher than the commercially desirable GDP.
(c) The socially desirable GDP cannot be produced with the intervention of the state.
(d) The commercially desirable GDP will not be able to utilise all economic resources efficiently.

**15.** Consider the following examples:

1. Unemployment benefits
2. Pension payments
3. Wages paid to government employees
4. Scholarships granted by the government

How many of the given above examples is/are considered 'Transfer Payments'?

(a) Only one (b) Only two
(c) Only three (d) All four

**16.** Which of the following best describes the concept of 'Green GDP'?

(a) A measure of economic growth that focuses solely on industrial output.
(b) A metric that adjusts Gross Domestic Product (GDP) by accounting for environmental degradation and resource depletion.
(c) An indicator used to measure the total amount of green energy produced in a country.
(d) A measure of economic development that excludes public services.

## Topic 2 : Other Indicators of National Income (NI)

**17.** With reference to the difference between Gross Domestic Product (GDP) and Gross National Product (GNP), consider the following statements:

1. GDP measures the total value of goods and services produced within a country's borders, while GNP measures the total income earned by the residents of a country.
2. GNP includes income earned by a country's citizens abroad, while GDP does not.
3. GDP includes the value of production by foreign residents within a country, whereas GNP excludes it.

How many of the statements given above is/are correct?

(a) Only one
(b) Only two
(c) All three
(d) None

**18.** Consider the following cases:

1. An Indian company earns profits from its subsidiary operating in the United States.
2. A foreign company operating in India generates revenue from selling products domestically.
3. An Indian professional working in Dubai sends remittances back to India.
4. A factory owned by a foreign investor in India produces goods for export.

How many of the above activities contribute to India's GNP but not to India's GDP?

(a) Only one
(b) Only two
(c) Only three
(d) All four

**19.** Which of the following are included in Net Factor Income from Abroad (NFIA)?

1. Income earned by Indian workers employed abroad.
2. Dividends received by Indian residents from their investments in foreign companies.
3. Income earned by foreign nationals working within India.
4. Profits repatriated by foreign companies operating in India.

Select the correct answer from the codes given below:

(a) 1 and 2 only (b) 1, 2 and 3 only
(c) 1, 3 and 4 only (d) 1, 2, 3 and 4

**20.** Consider the following pairs:

| Hypothetical Scenario | Possible Relationship Between GDP and GNP |
|---|---|
| 1. Citizens earning income only from domestic sources, with no significant foreign income or outflows | GNP equals GDP |
| 2. High profits from foreign companies operating within the domestic economy | GDP is higher than GNP |
| 3. Large income earned by domestic residents from their foreign investments | GNP is higher than GDP |
| 4. Foreign workers repatriating income back to their home countries | GDP is higher than GNP |

How many of the pairs given above is/are correctly matched?

(a) Only one (b) Only two
(c) Only three (d) All four

**21.** Consider the following statements:

1. Factor Cost includes subsidies granted by the government to reduce the cost of production.
2. Market Price is always higher than Factor Cost, as it includes both taxes and subsidies.
3. Market Price is equal to Factor Cost plus indirect taxes minus subsidies.

Which of the statements given above are correct?

(a) 1 and 3 only (b) 2 and 3 only
(c) 1 and 2 only (d) 1, 2 and 3

**22.** Consider the following statements about 'Depreciation':

1. It refers to that portion of the capital goods which goes in the maintenance and replacement of existing goods due to wear and tear.
2. It takes into account unexpected and sudden destruction caused due to natural calamities.
3. To obtain gross investment in an economy, depreciation is subtracted from the net investment.

Which of the statement(s) given above is/are correct?

(a) 1 and 2 only (b) 2 and 3 only
(c) 1 only (d) 1 and 3 only

**23.** Which of the following are not included in the 'Personal Disposable Income (PDI)' earned by the households?

1. Undistributed profits
2. Corporate tax
3. Transfer payments made by the governments
4. Income tax

Select the correct answer from the codes given below:

(a) 1, 2 and 4 only
(b) 1 and 2 only
(c) 2, 3 and 4 only
(d) 1, 2, 3 and 4

**24.** With reference to 'Per Capita Income (PCI)', consider the following statements:

1. It is calculated by dividing the GDP of a country with its total population.
2. A higher PCI always indicates a better standard of living for the population.
3. PCI can rise even if income inequality increases within the country.

Which of the given above statements are correct?

(a) 1 and 2 only (b) 1 and 3 only
(c) 2 and 3 only (d) 1, 2 and 3

**25.** Which of the following best describes the relationship between Per Capita Income and population growth rate in a country?
(a) In a country with a high population growth rate, Per Capita Income will likely increase faster than national income.
(b) In a country with a high population growth rate, Per Capita Income will likely increase slower than national income.
(c) Per Capita Income is not affected by population growth rates in any country.
(d) Per Capita Income and national income grow at the same rate, regardless of population growth.

**26.** Which of the following economic indicators is commonly referred to as national income?
(a) Gross Domestic Product (GDP)
(b) Net National Product (NNP) at Market Prices
(c) Net National Product (NNP) at Factor Cost
(d) Gross National Product (GNP)

## Topic 3 : Methods of Estimating National Income (NI)

**27.** Which of the following are included in the 'Expenditure Method' of calculating national income?
1. Household consumption of durable goods
2. Imports of capital goods
3. Government spending on infrastructure projects
4. Investment in machinery by private companies

Select the correct answer from the codes given below:
(a) 1 and 3 only
(b) 1, 3 and 4 only
(c) 2 and 3 only
(d) 1, 2 and 4 only

**28.** Arrange the following components of the Expenditure Method for calculating GDP in decreasing order of their contribution to India's GDP in the latest year based on Economic Survey 2024:
1. Private Consumption Expenditure (PCE)
2. Government Expenditure
3. Net Exports (Exports-Imports)
4. Gross Fixed Capital Formation (Investment)

Select the correct answer from the options below:
(a) 1, 4, 2, 3
(b) 1, 2, 4, 3
(c) 4, 1, 3, 2
(d) 3, 1, 2, 4

**29.** What is the significance of 'Gross Fixed Capital Formation (GFCF)' for economic growth?
(a) It directly measures the standard of living in an economy.
(b) It indicates the level of consumption in an economy.
(c) It reflects the investment in physical assets that contribute to long-term economic productivity.
(d) It measures the total exports of a country.

**30.** Consider the following items:
1. Construction of buildings and infrastructure
2. Purchase of machinery and equipment
3. Acquisition of intellectual property (e.g., patents)
4. Spending on repair and maintenance of existing buildings.

How many of the above is/are included under 'Gross Fixed Capital Formation (GFCF)'?
(a) Only one (b) Only two
(c) Only three (d) All four

**31.** Which of the following factors can increase the 'Aggregate Demand' of an economy?
1. Protectionist tendencies by the various countries
2. Direct income transfers to farmers
3. Increasing the FDI limit for various sectors
4. Credit availability in an economy

Select the correct answer from the codes given below:
(a) 2, 3 and 4 only
(b) 2 and 3 only
(c) 1 and 4 only
(d) 1, 2, 3 and 4

**32.** Which of the following are considered components of the Income Method when calculating national income?

1. Interest earned on capital
2. Depreciation on capital goods
3. Mixed income from self-employed individuals
4. Dividends received from corporate stocks

Select the correct answer using the codes given below:

(a) 1, 3 and 4 only
(b) 2 and 3 only
(c) 1, 2 and 4 only
(d) 1, 3 and 4 only

**33.** Consider the following:

1. Wages and salaries in cash or kind
2. Bonuses paid to employees
3. Employer's contribution to social security schemes
4. Dividends paid to shareholders

How many of the given above is/are included under 'Compensation to Employees (CE)'?

(a) Only one (b) Only two
(c) Only three (d) All four

## Topic 4 : New GDP Series

**34.** Which of the following indicators is referred to as the 'Official GDP' of India?

(a) Gross Domestic Product (GDP) at Market Prices
(b) Gross National Product (GNP) at Factor Cost
(c) Net National Product (NNP) at Market Prices
(d) Gross Domestic Product (GDP) at Factor Cost

**35.** With reference to the changes introduced in the new GDP series in India (2015), consider the following statements:

1. The base year for GDP calculation was changed from 2004-05 to 2011-12.
2. The new series incorporates data from the corporate sector, particularly MCA-21 database.
3. The calculation of GDP shifted from the factor cost method to market prices.

How many of the given above statements is/are correct?

(a) Only one (b) Only two
(c) All three (d) None

**36.** Which of the following best describes the concept of Basic Price in economic terms?

(a) The price of goods and services including taxes but excluding subsidies.
(b) The price of goods and services after accounting for indirect taxes and subsidies.
(c) The price received by producers for their goods and services before taxes are added and excluding subsidies.
(d) The market price paid by consumers for goods and services, including indirect taxes.

**37.** Consider the following statements:

1. Higher inflation in a particular year may lead to higher differences between the Real and Nominal GDP.
2. An increase in the share of net indirect taxes may lead to the increase in differences between GVA and GDP.

Which of the statement(s) given above is/are correct?

(a) 1 only
(b) 2 only
(c) Both 1 and 2
(d) Neither 1 nor 2

**38.** Which of the following statements best explains why Gross Value Added (GVA) is used to measure sectoral performance in the economy?

(a) GVA excludes the impact of indirect taxes and subsidies, giving a clearer picture of the production output of each sector.
(b) GVA is adjusted for inflation, making it a better indicator of sectoral performance than GDP.
(c) GVA includes international income flows, whereas GDP does not.
(d) GVA is based on market prices, making it a better measure of sectoral output.

## Topic 5 : Business Cycle

**39.** Identify the phase of the economic cycle based on the following statements:

1. This phase is characterised by rising employment, increasing GDP and higher consumer confidence.
2. Businesses experience increased demand, and there is a general sense of optimism in the economy.
3. The phase leads up to the peak, after which growth begins to slow down.

Which phase of the economic cycle is described by the above statements?

(a) Recession (b) Expansion
(c) Trough (d) Peak

**40.** Consider the following features:

1. Decline in Gross Domestic Product (GDP)
2. Rising unemployment
3. Increased consumer spending
4. Decline in business investments

How many of the given above is/are typical features of a 'Recession'?

(a) Only one (b) Only two
(c) Only three (d) All four

**41.** With reference to the concept of 'Technical Recession', consider the following statements:

1. It occurs when a country experiences two consecutive quarters of negative GDP growth.
2. India experienced a technical recession for the first time in 2020 during the COVID-19 pandemic.
3. It is characterised by job losses, high inflation and a long-term economic slump.

How many of the statements given above is/are correct?

(a) Only one (b) Only two
(c) All three (d) None

**42.** Which of the following measures are typically considered economic stimulus measures during a recession?

1. Lowering interest rates by the central bank
2. Government spending on infrastructure projects
3. Raising taxes on households
4. Providing direct cash transfers to individuals

Select the correct answer from the codes given below:

(a) 1 and 2 only (b) 1, 2 and 4 only
(c) 1, 3 and 4 only (d) 2, 3 and 4 only

**43.** Consider the following types of economic recovery with their appropriate characteristics:

| Type of Economic Recovery | Characteristics |
|---|---|
| 1. V-shaped recovery | Characterised by a sharp decline followed by a rapid and sustained economic rebound. |
| 2. K-shaped recovery | The recovery is uneven, where some sectors or populations recover faster than others. |
| 3. U-shaped recovery | The recovery is slow and steady, after a long period of economic contraction. |
| 4. W-shaped recovery | The economy faces alternating periods of recovery and recession, creating a double-dip effect |

How many of the given above pairs is/are correctly matched?

(a) Only one (b) Only two
(c) Only three (d) All four

**44.** Arrange the following types of economic recovery from best (quickest and strongest recovery) to worst (slowest recovery):

1. Z-shaped recovery 2. V-shaped recovery
3. L-shaped recovery 4. U-shaped recovery

Select the correct answer from the options below:

(a) 1, 2, 4, 3 (b) 2, 1, 3, 4
(c) 1, 4, 2, 3 (d) 2, 4, 3, 1

## Topic 6 : Measure of Development and Welfare

**45.** Which of the following can be the limitation(s) of GDP as an index for the welfare of a country?

1. It does not account for economic inequalities.
2. Several non-monetary exchanges are not accounted in its calculation.
3. Environmental costs are neglected.

Select the correct answer using the codes given below.

(a) 1 and 2 only (b) 2 and 3 only
(c) 1 and 3 only (d) 1, 2 and 3

**46.** With reference to the 'Economic Growth' and 'Economic Development', consider the following statements:

1. Growth is a narrower concept that focuses on the increase in a country's output while development is broader, addressing overall improvements in well-being.
2. Development requires growth, but growth does not necessarily lead to development.
3. Both growth and development can be measured by increases in GDP.

How many of the statements given above is/are correct?

(a) Only one (b) Only two
(c) All three (d) None

**47.** Which of the following may generally indicate the development levels of a country?

1. Per capita income
2. Average literacy level
3. Status of health indicators

Select the correct answer from the codes given below:

(a) 1 only
(b) 1 and 3 only
(c) 2 only
(d) 1, 2 and 3

**48.** Consider the following:

1. Higher tax revenues for the government
2. Improvement in human development indicators
3. Reduced income inequality
4. Increase in per capita income (population is assumed constant)

How many of the given above outcomes is/are necessarily true in the context of increasing GDP?

(a) Only one
(b) Only two
(c) Only three
(d) All fou

**49.** Consider the following dimensions:

1. Life expectancy at birth
2. Mean years of schooling
3. Gross National Income (GNI) per capita
4. Environmental sustainability

How many of the given above is/are components of the Human Development Index (HDI)?

(a) Only one (b) Only two
(c) Only three (d) All four

**50.** With reference to the concept of 'Sustainable Development', consider the following statements:

1. The concept of sustainable development was popularised by the Brundtland Commission in 1987.
2. Sustainable development focuses only on environmental protection and does not consider economic or social dimensions.
3. SDGs are legally binding for all United Nations member countries.

Which of the statements given above is/are correct?

(a) 1 and 3 only (b) 2 and 3 only
(c) 1 only (d) 1, 2 and 3

**51.** Consider the following goals:

1. No Poverty
2. Climate Action
3. Zero Hunger
4. Peace, Justice and Strong Institutions

How many of the given above are official SDGs as outlined by the United Nations?

(a) Only one (b) Only two
(c) Only three (d) All four

## Topic 7 : Other Concepts

**52.** With reference to Potential Output in an economy, consider the following statements:

1. Potential output represents the maximum level of output an economy can achieve without causing inflationary pressures.
2. The actual output of an economy can exceeds its potential output during periods of high inflation.
3. The difference between actual output and potential output is known as the output gap.

Which of the statements given above are correct?

(a) 1 and 2 only (b) 1 and 3 only
(c) 2 and 3 only (d) 1, 2 and 3

**53.** Which of the following statements are correct about the concept of 'GDP Deflator'?
1. It includes the prices of all goods and services produced domestically.
2. It is affected by changes in import prices.
3. It is a more comprehensive measure of inflation than the CPI.
4. It reflects price changes in the basket of goods consumed by households.

Select the correct answer from the codes given below:
(a) 1 and 3 only (b) 2 and 4 only
(c) 1, 3 and 4 only (d) 1, 2 and 3 only

**54.** Consider the following statements about 'Inventories':
1. These include the stock of unsold finished goods and semi-finished goods but not raw materials.
2. Inventory is a stock variable but change in inventory is a flow variable.
3. Change in the inventory of a firm is treated as an investment.

Which of the given above statement(s) is/are correct?
(a) 1 only (b) 1 and 2 only
(c) 2 and 3 only (d) 3 only

**55.** Consider the following activities:
1. Unpaid care work by family members
2. Paid childcare services
3. Nursing care for the elderly
4. Teaching services in public schools

How many of the above is/are part of the Care Economy?
(a) Only one
(b) Only two
(c) Only three
(d) All four

**56.** Which of the following best describes the concept of a Circular Economy?
(a) An economic system focused on continuous extraction of natural resources for production.
(b) An economic system driven primarily by increased consumption and disposal of goods.
(c) An economic system that aims to minimise waste by reusing, repairing, recycling, and regenerating products and materials.
(d) An economic model that emphasises rapid industrialisation and mass production.

**57.** Which of the following best describes the term 'Hindu Rate of Growth'?
(a) It refers to the rapid industrialisation phase of the Indian economy during the post-liberalisation period.
(b) It describes the sluggish economic growth experienced by India before economic reforms in 1991.
(c) It refers to the high growth rate of India's economy due to the influence of Hindu culture on economic practices.
(d) It describes the growth in India's agricultural sector during the Green Revolution.

## Past Learning

**1.** With reference to the Indian economy, consider the following statements: **(2015)**
1. The rate of growth of Real Gross Domestic Product has steadily increased in the last decade.
2. The Gross Domestic Product at market prices (in rupees) has steadily increased in the last decade.

Which of the statements given above is/are correct?
(a) 1 only (b) 2 only
(c) Both 1 and 2 (d) Neither 1 nor 2

**2.** The national income of a country for a given period is equal to the: **(2013)**
(a) total value of goods and services produced by the nationals
(b) sum of total consumption and investment expenditure
(c) sum of personal income of all individuals
(d) money value of final goods and services produced

# OMR SHEET

**Assessment Round**

| Q | Options | Q | Options | Q | Options | Q | Options |
|---|---|---|---|---|---|---|---|
| 1 | a b c d | 31 | a b c d | 61 | a b c d | 91 | a b c d |
| 2 | a b c d | 32 | a b c d | 62 | a b c d | 92 | a b c d |
| 3 | a b c d | 33 | a b c d | 63 | a b c d | 93 | a b c d |
| 4 | a b c d | 34 | a b c d | 64 | a b c d | 94 | a b c d |
| 5 | a b c d | 35 | a b c d | 65 | a b c d | 95 | a b c d |
| 6 | a b c d | 36 | a b c d | 66 | a b c d | 96 | a b c d |
| 7 | a b c d | 37 | a b c d | 67 | a b c d | 97 | a b c d |
| 8 | a b c d | 38 | a b c d | 68 | a b c d | 98 | a b c d |
| 9 | a b c d | 39 | a b c d | 69 | a b c d | 99 | a b c d |
| 10 | a b c d | 40 | a b c d | 70 | a b c d | 100 | a b c d |
| 11 | a b c d | 41 | a b c d | 71 | a b c d | 101 | a b c d |
| 12 | a b c d | 42 | a b c d | 72 | a b c d | 102 | a b c d |
| 13 | a b c d | 43 | a b c d | 73 | a b c d | 103 | a b c d |
| 14 | a b c d | 44 | a b c d | 74 | a b c d | 104 | a b c d |
| 15 | a b c d | 45 | a b c d | 75 | a b c d | 105 | a b c d |
| 16 | a b c d | 46 | a b c d | 76 | a b c d | 106 | a b c d |
| 17 | a b c d | 47 | a b c d | 77 | a b c d | 107 | a b c d |
| 18 | a b c d | 48 | a b c d | 78 | a b c d | 108 | a b c d |
| 19 | a b c d | 49 | a b c d | 79 | a b c d | 109 | a b c d |
| 20 | a b c d | 50 | a b c d | 80 | a b c d | 110 | a b c d |
| 21 | a b c d | 51 | a b c d | 81 | a b c d | 111 | a b c d |
| 22 | a b c d | 52 | a b c d | 82 | a b c d | 112 | a b c d |
| 23 | a b c d | 53 | a b c d | 83 | a b c d | 113 | a b c d |
| 24 | a b c d | 54 | a b c d | 84 | a b c d | 114 | a b c d |
| 25 | a b c d | 55 | a b c d | 85 | a b c d | 115 | a b c d |
| 26 | a b c d | 56 | a b c d | 86 | a b c d | 116 | a b c d |
| 27 | a b c d | 57 | a b c d | 87 | a b c d | 117 | a b c d |
| 28 | a b c d | 58 | a b c d | 88 | a b c d | 118 | a b c d |
| 29 | a b c d | 59 | a b c d | 89 | a b c d | 119 | a b c d |
| 30 | a b c d | 60 | a b c d | 90 | a b c d | 120 | a b c d |

## Calculate Your Score

**Correct (✓)**

**Incorrect (✓)**

**Unattempted**

**Total Score**

**Accuracy (%)**

## Reasons for Incorrect Answers?

1. Lack of Knowledge/Existing Source Insufficient
2. Lack of Multiple Revision
3. Common Sense Mistakes

**Note :**

1. Calculate total score as correct answers carry 2 marks each 1/3rd marks will deducted for **Incorrect** Answers.
2. Calculate Accuracy (%) by dividing the number of correct answers to the total number of attempted questions.

# Detailed Solutions

## Assessment Round

**1.** (*d*) None

Gross Domestic Product (GDP) is the total monetary value of all final goods and services produced within a country's borders in a specific period, typically a year or a quarter. It is a comprehensive measure of a nation's overall economic activity and serves as an indicator of the health of the economy.

- **Statement 1 is incorrect:** GDP only includes the market value of **final goods and services,** not intermediate goods, to avoid double counting.
- **Statement 2 is incorrect:** GDP **does not include intermediate goods** specifically to avoid double counting. Only the value of final goods and services is included.
- **Statement 3 is incorrect:** GDP includes all goods and services **produced within the country,** regardless of who produces them (domestic or foreign entities). It does not include the production of citizens abroad; that would be measured under **Gross National Product (GNP).**

**None of the statements are correct and thus, the correct answer is (d) None.**

**2.** (*b*) Only two

- **Statement 1 is correct:** A factory producing cars for domestic consumption is included in GDP as it represents the production of final goods.
- **Statement 2 is incorrect:** Unpaid household services are not included in GDP, as they do not involve market transactions.
- **Statement 3 is correct:** Exporting software services is included in GDP under exports.

  GDP=C+I+G+(X-M) Where:

  C = Consumption (spending by households)

  I = Investment (spending by businesses)

  G = Government spending

  X - M = Net exports (exports minus imports)
- **Statement 4 is incorrect:** The resale of second-hand goods is not included, as the value of these goods was already counted when they were first sold.

**Two activities are included in GDP and thus, the correct answer is (b) Only two.**

**3.** (*b*) 1, 2 and 4 only

- **Statement 1 is correct:** A factory located within the country but owned by a foreign corporation is part of the country's domestic territory because it is producing within the country's borders.
- **Statement 2 is correct:** Indian embassies in foreign countries are considered part of India's domestic territory for GDP purposes.
- **Statement 3 is incorrect:** Indian companies operating in foreign special economic zones (SEZs) are part of the foreign country's GDP, not India's, as they are located outside India's domestic territory.
- **Statement 4 is correct:** A ship registered in India but operating between foreign countries is part of India's domestic territory for GDP calculation.

  **Other areas considered as part of domestic territory**

  - **Offshore oil rigs and installations:** Offshore oil rigs, gas extraction facilities, and similar installations that are **owned or operated** by residents of the country in **international waters** are considered part of the domestic territory.
  - **Territorial enclaves:** These include military bases, embassies, and consulates located in other countries that belong to the home country.

**Thus, the correct answer is (b) 1, 2 and 4 only.**

**4.** (*d*) It is a good that contributes to the Gross Domestic Product (GDP) by being consumed or invested without further transformation.

A **final good** is directly included in the calculation of **Gross Domestic Product (GDP)** because it represents the end product of the production process. It is either consumed or used for investment and does not undergo further transformation.

**Intermediate goods,** in contrast, are not counted in GDP as they are used to produce final goods. Examples of final goods include personal computers, cars, and clothing.

**Thus, option (d) is the correct answer.**

**5.** (*b*) Only two

- **A car sold to a consumer** is classified as a Final Good because it is purchased for end-use and not for further production.
- **Raw materials used by a manufacturer** are **not** classified as Final Goods, as they are used for further production. Thus, it is an intermediate good, as it will be used in the production process to create other goods.
- **A computer purchased by a company for office use is a Final Good,** as it is used for the company's consumption and not for resale or further production.
- **Flour purchased by a bakery** is not a Final Good, as it is used in further production like to make bread or other baked goods.

**Two goods are classified as Final Goods and therefore, the correct answer is (b) Only two.**

**6.** (*a*) 1, 3, 2, 4

- **Advance Estimates:** These are released first to provide an early indication of national income for the fiscal year. It is released **before the end of the financial year,** typically in January or February with the purpose of providing an **early projection** of the national income (like GDP) for the entire financial year, based on **partial data** available for key sectors up to that point.
- **Provisional Estimates:** After the fiscal year ends usually in May month, with the **purpose** of to provides a **more accurate** reflection of national income for the fiscal year that has just ended based on full-year data from key sectors, but some data points might still be preliminary.
- **First Revised Estimates:** These estimates revise the earlier figures based on more complete data and are typically released a year after the provisional estimates around **January of the following year** after the financial year has ended.
- **Final Estimates:** These are the last and most accurate estimates, incorporating all available data and revisions, and are released after all sources of data are confirmed and usually released **two to three years after** the financial year.

**Therefore, the correct chronological order is (a) 1, 3, 2, 4.**

**7.** (*d*) None of these

- **Statement 1 is incorrect: Real GDP** is calculated using **constant prices,** which means it adjusts for inflation and reflects the true value of goods and services in terms of purchasing power. It is **not** the value at **current prevailing prices** that's Nominal GDP.
- **Statement 2 is incorrect: Nominal GDP** is calculated at **current prices,** while Real GDP is calculated at **constant prices** (adjusted for inflation).
- **Statement 3 is incorrect:** The **GDP Deflator** is the ratio of **Nominal GDP** to Real GDP, and it is used to measure the **price level changes** in the economy.

**Therefore, the correct answer is (d) None of these.**

**8.** (*b*) Only two

- **Statement 1 is correct: Nominal GDP** can rise if prices increase, even if the actual production of goods and services falls, because it is based on current prices, which can rise due to inflation.
- **Statement 2 is correct: Real GDP** adjusts for **inflation,** providing a clearer picture of the actual growth of an economy by isolating changes in the quantity of goods and services produced, whereas **Nominal GDP** does not account for inflation and can be distorted by price changes.
- **Statement 3 is incorrect:** In an economy experiencing deflation (falling prices), **Real GDP** may actually be **higher** than **Nominal**

GDP. This is because Real GDP uses constant prices, which may be higher than the current, deflated prices used in Nominal GDP.

**Therefore, the correct answer is (b) Only two.**

**9.** (*b*) To ensure GDP measures are based on current consumption patterns and technological advancements.

- **A base year** is a specific year chosen as a reference point for comparing economic data, such as GDP. It is used to measure the value of goods and services in other years by adjusting for inflation.
- It is important to periodically update the base year because **economic structures, consumption patterns,** and **technological advancements** evolve over time. Using an outdated base year might not accurately reflect the current economy. By updating the base year, GDP calculations stay relevant and provide more accurate estimates of a country's economic performance.

**Thus, option (b) is the correct answer.**

**10.** (*b*) 1 and 3 only

- **Statement 1 is correct:** The base year should reflect a **normal economic scenario** without major disruptions, ensuring the data used is representative of typical economic activity.
- **Statement 2 is incorrect:** While economic reforms are important, the base year does not necessarily need to coincide with major reforms.
- **Statement 3 is correct:** The base year should have **reliable and comprehensive** data to accurately measure economic activity.
- **Statement 4 is incorrect:** The base year is not necessarily chosen based on **low inflation** but rather to represent normal economic conditions.

**Therefore, the correct answer is (b) 1 and 3 only.**

**11.** (*d*) All four

**The calculation of national income** focuses on activities that involve legal, market-based production of goods and services, contribute to economic output, and generate income for individuals or entities within the economy. This ensures that national income reflects the real economic value generated in a country.

1. **Unpaid household work** is excluded because it does not involve a market transaction.
2. **Transfer payments** (like pensions and scholarships) are not counted as they do not involve the production of goods or services.
3. **Sale of second-hand goods** is excluded because these goods were already counted when they were initially produced and sold.
4. **Income from lotteries and gambling is excluded**, as it is considered a windfall gain and does not reflect productive economic activity.

**Therefore, the correct answer is (d) All four.**

**12.** (*b*) Only two

**National Income** (**GDP** = C+I+G+(X-M)

- C : Consumption (spending by households)
- I : Investment (spending by businesses on capital goods)
- G : Government spending
- X : Exports
- M : Imports (subtracted as they are not part of domestic production)

1. **Salaries paid to government employees are included in GDP under government spending.**
2. **Construction of new residential buildings** is included in GDP as part of **investment.**
3. **Illegal drug trade is not** included in GDP because it represents illegal activity.
4. **Purchasing shares of a company** is **not** included in GDP, as it is a financial transaction, not a production of goods or services.

**Therefore, the correct answer is (b) Only two.**

**13.** (*a*) 1 and 2 only

- **Statement 1 is correct: Externalities** are unintended side effects of economic activities that impact individuals or groups who are not directly involved in the transaction.
- **Statement 2 is correct:** Positive externalities confer benefits (e.g., education, vaccination), while **negative externalities** impose costs (e.g., pollution, traffic congestion) on third parties.

- **Statement 3 is incorrect:** Externalities are **not always internalised** in a perfectly competitive market. Markets often fail to account for externalities unless government intervention or specific policies are implemented to address them. For externalities to be **internalised**, there typically needs to be:
  - **Government intervention** (e.g., taxes, subsidies, or regulation).
  - **Private negotiations** between affected parties (e.g., coase theorem).
  - **Market-based mechanisms** (e.g., cap-and-trade systems for pollution).

**Therefore, the correct answer is (a) 1 and 2 only.**

***14.*** (*b*) The socially desirable GDP will be higher than the commercially desirable GDP.

- **Positive externalities** occur when the production or consumption of a **good benefits third parties**, but these benefits are **not reflected in the market price.** This leads to underproduction of such goods in a free market.
- As a result, the socially desirable GDP, which takes into account the broader societal benefits, will be higher than the commercially desirable GDP produced by the market. The market tends to underproduce goods with positive externalities because it does not capture their full value to society.

**Thus, option (b) is the correct answer.**

***15.*** (*c*) Only three

- **Option 1 is correct: Unemployment benefits** are **Transfer Payments** because they are payments made without any direct exchange of goods or services.
- **Option 2 is correct: Pension payments are** also **Transfer Payments,** as they are provided to individuals without any exchange for current work or services.
- **Option 3 is incorrect: Wages paid to government employees are not Transfer Payments;** they are payment for services rendered.
- **Option 4 is correct: Scholarships granted by the government** are **Transfer Payments,** as they are payments given without any work or service provided in return.

**Therefore, the correct answer is (c) Only three.**

***16.*** (*b*) A metric that adjusts Gross Domestic Product (GDP) by accounting for environmental degradation and resource depletion.

**Green GDP** is an economic measure that adjusts traditional GDP to account for the **environmental costs** of economic activity, including **pollution, resource depletion,** and the degradation of ecosystems. It provides a more holistic view of economic growth by considering the environmental impact of production.

**Thus, option (b) is the correct answer.**

***17.*** (*c*) All three

**GNP=GDP+Net Factor Income from Abroad (NFIA)**

**Net Factor Income from Abroad (NFIA):** This is the difference between income earned by residents from abroad (such as salaries, interest, dividends) and income earned by foreign residents within the country.

- **Statement 1 is correct:** GDP measures the total output produced within a country's **borders,** while GNP focuses on the **income earned** by the country's residents, regardless of where they are located.
- **Statement 2 is correct:** GNP includes income earned by a country's citizens **abroad,** such as foreign investments or remittances, while GDP only considers domestic production.
- **Statement 3 is correct:** GDP counts the value of production by foreign residents and businesses within a country, while GNP excludes this, focusing solely on the income generated by the country's citizens.

**Therefore, the correct answer is (c) All three.**

***18.*** (*b*) Only two

- **Statement 1 is correct: An Indian company earning profits from its subsidiary in the** U.S. contributes to **India's GNP** because the income is earned by an Indian entity abroad, but it does **not** contribute to **India's GDP** as the production occurred outside India.

- **Statement 2 is incorrect: A foreign company operating in India** contributes to **India's** GDP, but not to India's GNP, as the income generated belongs to a foreign entity.
- **Statement 3 is correct: An Indian professional working in Dubai sending remittances** contributes to **India's GNP**, as it is income earned by an Indian citizen abroad. It does not contribute to **India's GDP** because the production or service generating the income occurred outside India.
- **Statement 4 is incorrect: A foreign-owned factory producing goods in India** contributes to India's GDP but not to India's GNP, as the income is earned by foreign investors.

**Therefore, the correct answer is (b) Only two.**

***19.*** (*a*) 1 and 2 only

- **Statement 1 is correct: Income earned by Indian workers abroad** is included in **NFIA,** as it represents income earned by residents from foreign sources.
- **Statement 2 is correct: Dividends from foreign investments** by Indian residents are also included in **NFIA,** as they represent income earned from foreign sources.
- **Statement 3 is incorrect: Income earned by foreign nationals** working in India is **not** included in NFIA; it is considered part of the income earned within India as it represents income that stays within the domestic economy and would count as part of GDP.
- **Statement 4 is incorrect: Profits repatriated by foreign companies** are excluded from NFIA, as they represent income earned by foreign entities within India and it is the outflows from the domestic economy to other countries.

**Therefore, the correct answer is (a) 1 and 2 only.**

***20.*** (*d*) All four

- **Pair 1 is correctly matched:** When **citizens earn income only from domestic sources** and there are no significant foreign income or outflows, **GDP** equals **GNP** as there is no factor income from abroad or outflows affecting the relationship.
- **Pair 2 is correctly matched: High profits from foreign companies** operating domestically increase **GDP**, but not **GNP**, since the income belongs to foreign entities, making **GDP higher than GNP.**
- **Pair 3 is correctly matched: Income earned by domestic residents from foreign investments** raises GNP, as it represents income from abroad, making **GNP higher than GDP.**
- **Pair 4 is correctly matched: Foreign workers repatriating income** to their home countries means that income earned domestically flows abroad, making **GDP higher than GNP.**

**Therefore, the correct answer is (d) All four.**

***21.*** (*a*) 1 and 3 only

- **Statement 1 is correct: Factor Cost** refers to the cost of production incurred by producers, and it includes subsidies because they reduce the cost of production for the producer.
- **Statement 2 is incorrect: Market Price** is not necessarily always higher than **Factor Cost.** It depends on the balance between **taxes** and **subsidies.** If subsidies are large, Market Price could be lower than Factor Cost.
- **Statement 3 is correct: Market Price** is calculated as **Factor Cost + Indirect Taxes - Subsidies.**

**Therefore, the correct answer is (a) 1 and 3 only.**

***22.*** (*c*) 1 only

- **Statement 1 is correct: Depreciation** refers to the loss of value of capital goods due to **wear and tear** over time, and the need for maintenance or replacement of these goods.
- **Statement 2 is incorrect:** Depreciation does not account for unexpected and sudden destruction (such as natural calamities). These are classified under capital losses or extraordinary losses, not regular depreciation.
- **Statement 3 is incorrect:** To obtain **net investment,** you subtract depreciation from **gross investment,** not the other way around. **Gross investment** is the total investment, including depreciation.

**Thus, option (c) is the correct answer.**

**23.** (*a*) 1, 2 and 4 only

| |
|---|
| **Personal income= National income - undistributed profit** - Net interest payment made by household - **Corporate tax + Transfer payment** to the household from government and firms. |
| **Personal Disposable Income (PDI)= Personal Income** - Personal tax payment - Non-tax payment. |

- **Option 1 is correct: Undistributed profits** refer to profits retained by corporations and not distributed to shareholders or households. It is **not included** in Personal Disposable Income (PDI).
- **Option 2 is correct: Corporate tax** is a tax paid by businesses and does not affect **household income,** so it is **not included** in PDI.
- **Option 3 is incorrect: Transfer payments** are payments made by the government (such as pensions or unemployment benefits) to individuals, which **are included** in the PDI as they represent disposable income available to households.
- **Option 4 is correct: Income tax** is deducted from personal income to calculate Personal Disposable Income, so it is **not included** in PDI.

**Hence, the correct answer is (a) 1, 2 and 4 only.**

**24.** (*b*) 1 and 3 only

- **Statement 1 is correct: Per Capita Income** is calculated by dividing a country's total **income** (such as GDP) by its **total population,** providing an average income per person.
- **Statement 2 is incorrect:** A higher **Per Capita Income** does not always indicate a better standard of living, as it does not account for income inequality, cost of living, or the distribution of wealth.
- **Statement 3 is correct: Per Capita Income** can increase even if **income inequality** worsens, as a rise in total income does not necessarily mean income is distributed evenly among the population. For instance, if the rich are getting richer while the poor stay the same or get poorer, the average income (PCI) may rise, but it doesn't reflect the income distribution or well-being of the population.

**Therefore, the correct answer is (b) 1 and 3 only.**

**25.** (*b*) In a country with a high population growth rate, Per Capita Income will likely increase slower than national income.

- **Per Capita Income (PCI)** is calculated by dividing the national income (GDP) by the total population. Therefore, population growth directly affects PCI.
- In countries with a **high population growth rate, Per Capita Income** (which is national income, divided by population) tends to **grow slower** than **national income.** This is because the increased income must be spread across a larger population, diluting the income per person. If the population grows faster than national income, Per Capita Income may even decline.

**Thus, option (b) is the correct answer.**

**26.** (*c*) Net National Product (NNP) at Factor Cost

**Net National Product (NNP) at Factor Cost** is commonly referred to as **national income.** It represents the total income earned by the residents of a country, after accounting for depreciation, and is adjusted for subsidies and indirect taxes, providing a more accurate reflection of the economic income generated by the nation.

**Thus, option (c) is the correct answer.**

**27.** (*b*) 1, 3 and 4 only

**Expenditure method** calculates national income by summing up all expenditures on final goods and services in the economy. This method focuses on **demand-side** measurement by adding consumption, investment,
government expenditure, and net exports and it represents the spending habits of consumers, businesses, and the government.

- **Option 1 is correct: Household consumption of durable goods** (e.g., cars, electronics) is part of consumer spending and included in the **Expenditure Method.**
- **Option 2 is incorrect: Imports of capital goods** are **subtracted** from the calculation, as

imports represent goods produced abroad and not domestically, so this is **not included.**

- **Option 3 is correct: Government spending** on infrastructure and other projects is included as part of government expenditure in the **Expenditure Method.**
- **Option 4 is correct: Investment in machinery** by private companies is included as part of **investment expenditure,** which is a key element in the Expenditure Method.

**Therefore, the correct answer is (b) 1, 3 and 4 only.**

**28.** (*a*) 1, 4, 2, 3

In the **Expenditure Method, Private Consumption** typically remains the largest contributor to GDP, followed by **Gross Fixed Capital Formation (Investment). Government Expenditure** also plays a substantial role, while **Net Exports** often contribute the least or negatively due to a trade deficit. This order aligns with trends from India's **Economic Survey 2024**, which highlighted strong consumption and investments as major growth drivers.

**Chart I. Private consumption Steady as Investment Drivers Growth**

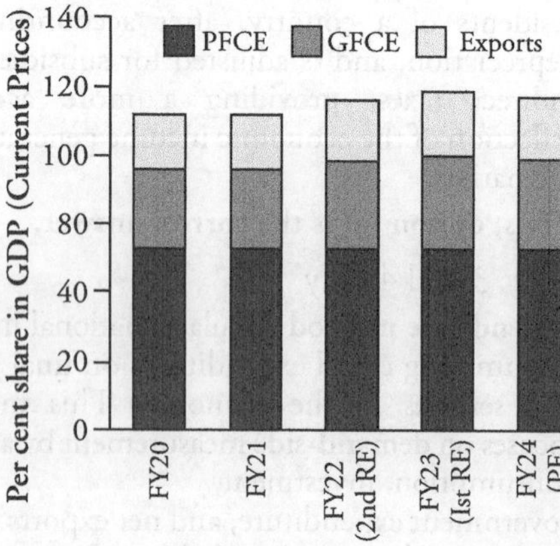


**Therefore, the correct answer is (a) 1, 4, 2, 3.**

**29.** (*c*) It reflects the investment in physical assets that contribute to long-term economic productivity.

**GFCF or Gross Investment** is significant because it measures investment in **physical assets** such as machinery, infrastructure, and buildings, which contribute to the **long-term productive capacity** of an economy. Higher GFCF indicates a stronger foundation for sustained economic growth as it leads to increased production capabilities in the future.

**Thus, option (c) is the correct answer.**

**30.** (*c*) Only three

- **Gross Fixed Capital Formation (GFCF)** represents the investment in physical assets such as machinery, infrastructure, buildings, and equipment that are used to produce goods and services over a long period.
- It is an important indicator because it reflects the level of **capital investment** in an economy, which in turn determines the **capacity for future production and economic growth.**
- **Option 1 is correct: Construction of buildings and infrastructure** is included in GFCF because it involves investment in fixed assets.
- **Option 2 is correct: Purchase of machinery and equipment** is part of **GFCF,** as it contributes to long-term production capacity.
- **Option 3 is correct: Acquisition of intellectual property** (e.g., patents) is included in GFCF, as it represents investments in non-physical, long-term assets.
- **Option 4 is incorrect: Spending on repair and maintenance** of existing buildings is **not** included in **GFCF** since it does not involve new investments in fixed assets but rather maintaining existing ones.

**Therefore, the correct answer is (c) Only three.**

**31.** (*a*) 2, 3 and 4 only

**Aggregate Demand (AD)** refers to the total quantity of goods and services demanded across all sectors of an economy at a given overall price level and during a specific period. **It represents the total spending on an economy's goods and services that is similar to Expenditure method. Thus;**

**Aggregate Demand** (AD) = Consumption (C) + Investment (I) + Government Purchase (G) + Net Exports (NX)

- **Statement 1 is incorrect: Protectionism** usually involves imposing tariffs or trade barriers to restrict imports. This can reduce international trade, potentially lowering demand for exports, which may decrease aggregate demand rather than increase it.
- **Statement 2 is correct**: Direct Income Transfers increase the **disposable income** of farmers, which can boost **consumption spending** (C), thus increasing Aggregate Demand.
- **Statement 3 is correct**: Increasing the FDI limit for various sectors will facilitate more investment in Indian economy and thus having a positive effect on Aggregate Demand.
- **Statement 4 is correct**: Increased credit availability in an economy will decrease the lending rates. This would encourage more borrowing by the firms for more investment in the economy. Thus, having a positive effect on Aggregate Demand.

**Thus, option (a) is the correct answer.**

***32.*** (*d*) 1, 3 and 4 only

**Income method** calculates national income by summing all incomes earned by factors of production (land, labour, capital and entrepreneurship). It focuses on income distribution among the population and captures the earnings of individuals and businesses from wages, rent, interest, and profits.

**National Income=Wages+Rent+Interest + Profits + Mixed Income**

- **Interest earned on capital** is a part of the **Income Method,** representing the returns to capital.
- **Depreciation is not included** in the Income Method, as it is a non-cash charge related to capital consumption.
- **Mixed income** from the self-employed is included as it represents a combination of wages and profits.
- **Dividends** received from stocks are included as they represent a return on investments.

**Thus, the correct answer is (d) 1, 3 and 4 only.**

***33.*** (*c*) Only three

**Compensation to Employees** is the total remuneration, both monetary and non-monetary, provided by employers to employees in exchange for their labour or services. It includes various components such as wages, salaries, and benefits. In national income accounting, Compensation to Employees is a key part of the Income Method.

- **Option 1 is correct: Wages and salaries in cash** are included as they represent direct payment to employees for their labour. **Wages and salaries in kind** are included as non-monetary compensation, such as benefits or goods provided to employees.
- **Option 2 is correct: Bonuses paid to employees** are included as they are part of **monetary compensation** for work performed.
- **Option 3 is correct: Employer's contributions to social security schemes** are included as they are part of the total compensation provided by employers.
- **Option 4 is incorrect: Dividends paid to shareholders** are **not** included as they are returns to shareholders and not considered employee compensation.

**Therefore, the correct answer is (c) Only three.**

***34.*** (*a*) Gross Domestic Product (GDP) at Market Prices

**India's Official GDP is calculated as Gross Domestic Product (GDP) at Market Prices,** which represents the total value of all goods and services produced within the country, including taxes and excluding subsidies on products. This measure reflects the current market prices and is widely used in official government reports to assess the economic performance of the country.

**Thus, option (a) is the correct answer.**

***35.*** (*c*) All three

- **Statement 1 is correct**: The base year for calculating GDP was changed from **2004-05 to 2011-12** in the new series, which reflects a more updated structure of the economy.
- **Statement 2 is correct**: The new GDP series of 2015 incorporates data from the **MCA-21 database**, which includes detailed information from the corporate sector.
- **Statement 3 is correct**: The calculation of GDP shifted from being measured at factor cost to being measured at market prices, aligning with international standards.

**Therefore, the correct answer is (c) All three.**

**36.** (*c*) The price received by producers for their goods and services before taxes are added and excluding subsidies.

- **Basic Price** refers to the amount received by producers from the sale of their goods and services **before indirect taxes** (like VAT or GST) are added and **excluding subsidies.** It represents the income retained by producers for their output without any government-imposed charges or benefits affecting the price.
- **Market Price,** on the other hand, includes taxes and is the price paid by consumers.

**Basic price = Factor cost + Production taxes – Production subsidy**

**Market price = Basic price + Product taxes – Product subsidy**

**Thus, option (c) is the correct answer.**

**37.** (*c*) Both 1 and 2

- **Statement 1 is correct:** Nominal GDP differs from Real GDP as the later doesn't include inflation, while the former does. As a result, Nominal GDP will most often be higher than real GDP in an expanding economy. So, only higher inflation indicated higher differences between the Real and Nominal GDP.
- **Statement 2 is correct:** Gross Value Added (GVA) measures the value of goods and services produced in an economy, excluding net indirect taxes (taxes minus subsidies). When the share of net indirect taxes increases, the difference between GDP (which includes net indirect taxes) and GVA (which excludes net indirect taxes) will also increase.

**Thus, option (c) is the correct answer.**

**38.** (*a*) GVA excludes the impact of indirect taxes and subsidies, giving a clearer picture of the production output of each sector.

- GVA is a measure of the value added by each sector in the production process, excluding the impact of indirect taxes and subsidies. This provides a more accurate reflection of the productive performance of individual sectors, as it focuses on the actual output rather than market distortions caused by taxation or subsidies.
- While, **GDP** includes taxes and subsidies, which can inflate or reduce the apparent size of different sectors. GVA, by focusing purely on the value of production, provides a **clearer picture of sectoral performance.**
- **GVA is not adjusted for inflation,** and it does not include **international income flows,** which are aspects related to other economic measures.

**Thus, option (a) is the correct answer.**

**39.** (*b*) The **Expansion** phase of the economic cycle is characterised by increased economic activity, with rising **employment, GDP growth,** and **consumer confidence.** Businesses see greater demand, and the overall sentiment in the economy is optimistic. This phase continues until the economy reaches its peak, after which growth begins to slow down.

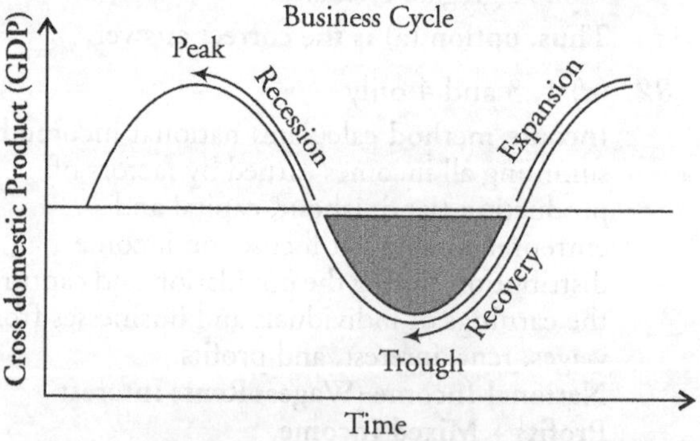


**Thus, option (b) is the correct answer.**

**40.** (*c*) Only three

A **recession** is an indication of declining economic activity that lasts for an extended period, typically across multiple sectors of the economy. It is officially recognised when there is a decline in a country's Gross Domestic Product (GDP) for two consecutive quarters. However, other indicators, such as rising unemployment and falling production, are also used to identify a recession.

- **Option 1 is correct: Decline in GDP** is a typical feature of a recession, as the economy contracts and overall output decreases.

- **Option 2 is correct: Rising unemployment** is another characteristic of a recession, as businesses cut jobs to reduce costs.
- **Option 3 is incorrect: Increased consumer spending** is not a feature of a recession; instead, consumers tend to reduce spending during economic downturns.
- **Option 4 is correct: Decline in business** investments is also common in recessions, as businesses hold off on expanding or investing due to uncertainty.

**Therefore, the correct answer is (c) Only three.**

***41.*** (*b*) Only two

- **Statement 1 is correct:** A Technical Recession is defined as a situation where a country's GDP contracts for two consecutive quarters.
- **Statement 2 is correct:** India entered a **Technical Recession** in 2020 when it saw two consecutive quarters of negative GDP growth during the COVID-19 pandemic.
- **Statement 3 is incorrect:** A **Technical Recession** refers to short-term economic contraction and does not imply a prolonged economic depression, which is a more severe and extended downturn. While a **Technical Recession** may involve economic challenges, it does not always lead to high inflation or long-term slumps.

**Therefore, the correct answer is (b) Only two.**

***42.*** (*b*) 1, 2 and 4 only

- **Lowering interest rates** by the central bank is a common stimulus measure to make borrowing cheaper, encouraging businesses and consumers to spend and invest more.
- **Government spending on infrastructure projects** is used to create jobs and stimulate demand in the economy.
- **Raising taxes** is generally not considered a stimulus measure during a recession as it could reduce disposable income and economic activity.
- **Direct cash transfers** to individuals, such as stimulus checks, are used to boost consumer spending during times of economic downturn.

**Therefore, the correct answer is (b) 1, 2 and 4 only.**

***43.*** (*d*) All four

- **V-shaped recovery** is matched with **A**, where the economy undergoes a sharp and brief decline followed by a quick and robust recovery.
- **K-shaped recovery** is matched with **B**, indicating an uneven recovery where some industries or segments of the population recover quickly, while others struggle.
- **U-shaped recovery** is matched with **C**, where the recovery is slow and gradual after a longer recessionary period.
- **W-shaped recovery** is matched with **D**, representing a double-dip scenario, where the economy experiences recovery followed by another recession.

**All pairs are correctly matched, so the correct answer is (d) All four.**

***44.*** (*a*) 1, 2, 4, 3

- **Z-shaped** recovery is considered as the **best** and fastest type, where the economy recovers quickly and surpasses the pre-crisis growth trajectory before stabilizing.
- **V-shaped** recovery is next, where the economy experiences a sharp contraction followed by a rapid and strong rebound.
- **U-shaped** recovery involves a more prolonged downturn before recovery, where the economy takes time to bounce back after staying in recession for a while.
- **L-shaped** recovery is the worst case, where the economy faces a sharp downturn followed by prolonged stagnation with no clear recovery.

**Thus, option (a) is the correct answer.**

***45.*** (*d*) 1, 2 and 3

- **Statement 1 is correct:** The rise in GDP may be concentrated in the hands of a very few individuals or firms. For the rest, the income may, in fact, have fallen.
- **Statement 2 is correct:** Non-monetary transactions are not taken into consideration, such as domestic services women perform at home are not paid for, even though they contribute to welfare and economic value.
- **Statement 3 is correct:** Externalities such as environmental degradation, which is a negative externality are not accounted for in GDP. In

this case, GDP shall be overestimating the actual welfare. As a result, activities that harm the environment can still increase GDP, but this does not reflect sustainable welfare.

**Therefore, option (d) is correct answer.**

**46.** (*b*) Only two

- **Statement 1 is correct: Growth** refers to an increase in the country's economic output whereas development includes broader social progress, such as education and health.
- **Statement 2 is correct: Economic growth** does not always lead to **economic development** because growth may benefit only specific sectors or regions, creating disparities in wealth distribution. Development involves broader improvements in well-being, such as healthcare, education, and income equality, which may not occur if growth is unevenly distributed.

  Hence, growth alone is insufficient for ensuring overall social progress.
- **Statement 3 is incorrect: GDP** measures **growth,** but it does not fully capture **development,** which also involves social and human progress indicators like life expectancy and literacy rates.

**Thus, option (b) is the correct answer.**

**47.** (*d*) 1, 2 and 3

- **Option 1 is correct**: Per capita income shows living standard and economic status. This is a widely used measure of economic development, indicating the average income of individuals in a country.
- **Option 2 is correct**: Literacy levels are important for social and economic development, as they reflect access to education and skills needed for improving the quality of life. Literacy rate shows educational achievement and is used in some form in the HDI.
- **Option 3 is correct**: Health indicators like life expectancy, infant mortality rates, and access to healthcare are crucial for assessing the overall well-being and development of a country's population.

**Thus, option (d) is the correct answer.**

**48.** (*b*) Only two

- **Outcome 1 is correct: Higher tax revenues for the government** are typically a direct outcome of increasing GDP. As the economy grows, the government collects more revenue through **taxes** (both direct and indirect) because of higher **economic activity,** including increased production, sales, and higher individual incomes.
- **Outcome 2 is incorrect**: Improvement in human development indicators (such as health, education, and life expectancy) is not necessarily guaranteed by GDP growth alone. While higher GDP provides the government with more resources to invest in public services, whether or not these resources are effectively allocated toward improving human development depends on government priorities and policies. Thus, GDP growth does not automatically result in better social outcomes.
- **Outcome 3 is incorrect**: Reduced income inequality is not necessarily an outcome of increasing GDP. In fact, GDP growth can sometimes widen inequality if the benefits of growth are concentrated in the hands of a few, particularly in sectors that benefit more from industrialisation or capital accumulation. Inequality may remain or even increase if the gains from growth are not distributed equitably.
- **Outcome 4 is correct**: Increase in per capita income (assuming a constant population) is necessarily true because per capita income is derived by dividing GDP by the total population. When GDP increases and the population remains unchanged, the average income per person rises, resulting in an increase in per capita Income.

**Thus, the correct answer is (b) Only two.**

**49.** (*c*) Only three

The Human Development Index (HDI) is calculated using three main dimensions:

- **Life expectancy at birth,** which measures the health dimension.
- **Mean years of schooling and expected years of schooling,** representing the education dimension.

- **Gross National Income (GNI) per capita,** which measures the standard of living.
- **Environmental sustainability** is not a part of the HDI calculation but is considered in other indices or reports. Thus, three of the above are HDI components.

**Thus, option (c) is the correct answer.**

***50.*** (*c*) 1 only

- **Statement 1 is correct:** The term was popularised in the 1987 report by the **Brundtland Commission,** officially titled 'Our Common Future,' which emphasized this integrated approach. **Sustainable development** seeks to balance the needs of the present with the capacity of future generations to meet their own needs, ensuring long-term environmental, social, and economic health.
- **Statement 2 is incorrect:** Sustainable development focuses on three key pillars: environmental, **economic,** and **social** dimensions, promoting a holistic approach to progress.
- **Statement 3 is incorrect:** The SDGs are **not legally binding.** Countries are encouraged to take ownership and establish national frameworks to achieve the goals, but compliance is voluntary.

**Therefore, the correct answer is (c) 1 only.**

***51.*** (*d*) All four

All four mentioned goals–**No Poverty (SDG 1), Climate Action (SDG 13),** Zero Hunger (SDG 2), and **Peace, Justice, and Strong Institutions** (SDG 16)—are part of the 17 **United Nations Sustainable Development Goals.** These goals are designed to address global challenges like poverty, inequality, climate change, and peace by 2030.

**Thus, option (d) is the correct answer.**

***52.*** (*d*) 1, 2 and 3

- **Statement 1 is correct: Potential Output** is the maximum sustainable level of output an economy can achieve without increasing inflation, assuming full employment and optimal use of resources.
- **Statement 2 is correct:** During periods of **high inflation,** the actual output may temporarily exceed the **Potential Output,** but this situation is not sustainable in the long term.
- **Statement 3 is correct:** The **output gap** is the difference between the actual output of an economy and its **Potential Output.** A positive output gap indicates an economy is operating above its potential, while a negative gap indicates underperformance.
  - **For example,** imagine a factory that can produce **100 cars per day** if all its machines and workers are used at full capacity. This is the **potential output** of the factory — the most it can produce **without overworking the machines or workers.**
  - If demand increases and the factory pushes to produce **110 cars per day,** the workers may have to work overtime, and machines may wear out faster, leading to **higher costs and inflationary pressures.** This would mean the actual output exceeds the potential output, but it's not sustainable in the long term.
  - In an **economy,** potential output works in a similar way, it represents the maximum sustainable production level without causing inflation.

**Therefore, the correct answer is (d) 1, 2 and 3.**

***53.*** (*a*) **1 and 3 only**

- **Statement 1 is correct:** The GDP Deflator includes the prices of all goods and services produced domestically, making it a comprehensive measure of price level changes.
- **Statement 2 is incorrect:** The GDP Deflator **does not directly include import prices,** as it focuses on domestically produced goods and services.
- **Statement 3 is correct:** The GDP Deflator is considered a more comprehensive measure of inflation compared to the **CPI,** as it includes all goods and services produced in an economy, whereas CPI focuses only on a **basket of goods** consumed by households.

- **Statement 4 is incorrect**: The GDP Deflator reflects price changes in all goods and services produced in the economy, not just the basket of goods consumed by households (which is measured by CPI).

**Therefore, the correct answer is (a) 1 and 3 only.**

***54.*** (*c*) 2 and 3 only

- **Statement 1 is incorrect**: In economics, the stock of unsold finished goods, or semi-finished goods, or raw materials which a firm carries from one year to the next is called Inventory.
- **Statement 2 is correct**: Inventory is a stock variable. It may have a lower value at the beginning of the year; it may have a higher value at the end of the year. In such a case inventories have increased (or accumulated). However, change in inventory is flow variable as its takes place over a period of time.
- **Statement 3 is correct**: Inventories are treated as capital. Addition to the stock of capital of a firm is known as investment. Therefore, change in the inventory of a firm is treated as investment.

**Thus, option (c) is the correct answer.**

***55.*** (*c*) Only three

The Care Economy refers to the sector of the economy that encompasses paid and unpaid work related to caregiving and nurturing, which is essential for maintaining households and communities.

- **Option 1 is correct: Unpaid care work** by family members is a core component of the **Care Economy**, which includes activities like caring for children, the elderly, and the sick, often performed without monetary compensation.
- **Option 2 is correct: Paid childcare services** are also part of the Care Economy, as these services are provided to meet the care needs of others.
- **Option 3 is correct: Nursing care for the elderly** is included because it directly contributes to the well-being and support of individuals who require assistance.
- **Option 4 is incorrect: Teaching services in public schools** are **not** typically classified under the Care Economy, as they fall under the formal education sector, even though they contribute to social well-being.

**Therefore, the correct answer is (c) Only three.**

***56.*** (*c*) An economic system that aims to minimise waste by reusing, repairing, recycling, and regenerating products and materials.

A Circular Economy is an economic model designed to minimise waste and make the most of resources. It involves extending the lifecycle of products through recycling, reusing, and regenerating materials to create a closed-loop system, reducing the need for new resources and decreasing environmental impacts. For example, National Circular Economy Roadmap for reduction of plastic waste in India.

**Thus, option (c) is the correct answer.**

***57.*** (*b*) It describes the sluggish economic growth experienced by India before economic reforms in 1991.

The term '**Hindu Rate of Growth**' was coined by economist **Raj Krishna** to describe the **slow and stagnant economic growth** that India experienced from the 1950s to the 1980s, before the economic reforms of 1991. During this period, India's GDP growth was around **3.5% per year**, which was seen as insufficient for the country's developmental needs. This term has no religious connotation but rather reflects the economic policies and structural inefficiencies that limited India's growth.

**Thus, option (b) is the correct answer.**

## Past Learning (Answers)

1 (b) 2 (d)

CHAPTER 03

# Poverty, Inequality and Unemployment

## Assessment Round

### Topic 1 : Meaning of Poverty

*1.* With reference to the 'International Poverty Line' set by the World Bank, consider the following statements:

1. It is currently set at $2.15 per day.
2. It is uniform across all countries, regardless of differences in the cost of living.
3. It considers access to clean water and sanitation.

How many of the statements given above is/are correct?

(a) Only one
(b) Only two
(c) All three
(d) None

*2.* Which of the following indicators are included in the 'Multi-dimensional Poverty Index (MPI)'?

1. Access to clean drinking water
2. Child mortality
3. Years of schooling
4. Income level above the international poverty line

Select the correct answer from the codes given below:

(a) 1 and 4 only
(b) 2 and 3 only
(c) 1, 2 and 3 only
(d) 1, 2, 3 and 4

*3.* Which of the following is the primary purpose of the International Poverty Line set by the World Bank?

(a) To measure the wealth distribution in developed countries.
(b) To assess the minimum income required to meet basic needs globally, adjusted for price differences across countries.
(c) To determine the level of taxation required in each country.
(d) To evaluate the availability of public services like clean water and sanitation in developing countries.

*4.* Match the following poverty estimation methods with their key characteristics:

| Poverty Estimation Method | Key Characteristic |
|---|---|
| 1. Headcount Ratio | A. Measures the intensity of poverty |
| 2. Poverty Gap Index | B. Reflects the proportion of poor |
| 3. Multi-dimensional Poverty Index (MPI) | C. Includes education and health indicators |
| 4. Sen Index | D. Combines incidence and intensity |

Select the correct answer using the codes given below:

(a) 1-B, 2-A, 3-C, 4-D (b) 1-A, 2-B, 3-D, 4-C
(c) 1-B, 2-C, 3-A, 4-D (d) 1-C, 2-D, 3-B, 4-A

**5.** Consider the following pairs of poverty-related terms and their descriptions:

| Term | Description |
|---|---|
| 1. Poverty Gap | A. Measures the share of children who cannot read and understand simple text by age 10. |
| 2. Poverty Intensity | B. Reflects the depth of poverty by indicating how far, on average, the poor are from the poverty line. |
| 3. Learning Poverty | C. Captures the degree of deprivation among the poor, factoring in both the number of poor and the severity of their poverty. |

How many of the above pairs is/are correctly matched?

(a) Only one pair (b) Only two pairs
(c) All three pairs (d) None

## Topic 2 : Types of Poverty

**6.** With reference to the 'Absolute Poverty', consider the following statements:

1. It is defined by the inability to meet basic needs such as food, clothing and shelter.
2. It is measured by comparing individual's income to a fixed threshold that is consistent across all countries.
3. The World Bank's international poverty line is an example of an absolute poverty measure.

How many of the statements given above is/are correct?

(a) Only one (b) Only two
(c) All three (d) None

**7.** With reference to the types of poverty, consider the following statements:

1. Chronic poverty is long-term and persistent, often passed down through generations.
2. Situational poverty is a temporary state caused by an external event, such as a natural disaster.
3. Seasonal poverty occurs at particular times of the year, often in relation to agricultural cycles.

How many of the statements given above is/are correct?

(a) Only one (b) Only two
(c) All three (d) None

**8.** What is the primary difference between Absolute Poverty and Relative Poverty?

(a) Absolute poverty is a measure of poverty based on a fixed income threshold necessary to meet basic needs, while relative poverty compares an individual's income with the average income in society.
(b) Absolute poverty focuses on poverty in developed countries, while relative poverty is used to measure poverty in developing countries.
(c) Absolute poverty is concerned with access to luxury goods, while relative poverty is concerned with basic survival needs.
(d) Absolute poverty measures poverty in rural areas, while relative poverty measures poverty in urban areas.

**9.** Which of the following best describes the concept of the 'Churning Poor'?

(a) People who remain consistently below the poverty line without any opportunity for improvement.
(b) People who are temporarily poor, frequently moving in and out of poverty due to unstable income or employment.
(c) People who have escaped poverty and have stable incomes but remain vulnerable to falling back into poverty.
(d) People who are poor due to seasonal unemployment, such as agricultural workers during the off-season.

**10.** With reference to the 'Gini Coefficient', consider the following statements:

1. The Gini Coefficient measures income inequality within a population.
2. A Gini Coefficient of 0 indicates perfect equality, while a Gini Coefficient of 1 indicates maximum inequality.
3. The Gini Coefficient is derived from the Lorenz Curve and published by the World Bank.

How many of the statements given above is/are correct?

(a) Only one (b) Only two
(c) All three (d) None

***11.*** Consider the following statements about the 'Lorenz Curve':

1. It represents the cumulative distribution of income or wealth among a population.
2. The greater the distance between the Lorenz Curve and the line of perfect equality, the higher the income inequality.

Which of the statements given above is/are correct?

(a) 1 only
(b) 2 only
(c) Both 1 and 2
(d) Neither 1 nor 2

***12.*** What are the likely implications of a high Gini Coefficient and a Lorenz Curve that is significantly bowed away from the line of perfect equality?

1. Increased income inequality could lead to social unrest and political instability.
2. High levels of income inequality may hinder economic growth by reducing overall demand in the economy.
3. A high Gini Coefficient typically indicates that a small proportion of the population controls a large share of the total income or wealth.

Select the correct answer using the codes given below:

(a) 1 and 2 only
(b) 2 and 3 only
(c) 1 and 3 only
(d) 1, 2 and 3

***13.*** What does the Kuznets Curve hypothesize about the relationship between income inequality and economic development?

(a) Income inequality decreases as economic development progresses, following a linear path.
(b) Income inequality first increases and then decreases as a country develops economically.
(c) Income inequality remains constant regardless of economic development.
(d) Income inequality is unrelated to economic development and follows no specific pattern.

## Topic 3 : Poverty Line Estimation (PLE)

***14.*** With reference to the measurement of absolute poverty in India, consider the following statements:

1. Absolute poverty in India is measured using a fixed poverty line that is adjusted for inflation over time.
2. The poverty line in India is based solely on the consumption expenditure required to meet minimum calorie intake.
3. The Tendulkar Committee recommended a shift from calorie-based poverty measurement to a broader approach that includes health and education.

How many of the statements given above is/are correct?

(a) Only one (b) Only two
(c) All three (d) None

***15.*** How many of the given below reasons justifies why income levels are not used as a direct indicator for estimating the poverty line?

1. Income levels can fluctuate frequently, making them an unreliable measure of long-term poverty.
2. People may underreport their income due to informal or unaccounted sources.
3. Income does not capture the actual living conditions or access to basic necessities.
4. Income-based data is more readily available and accurate than consumption data.

Select the correct answer from the codes given below:

(a) Only one (b) Only two
(c) Only three (d) All four

***16.*** Consider the following committees:

1. Lakdawala Committee
2. Tendulkar Committee
3. Rangarajan Committee
4. Hashim Committee

Which of the given above committees were constituted to measure the poverty line in India?

(a) 1 and 3 only (b) 2 and 4 only
(c) 1, 2 and 3 only (d) 1, 2, 3 and 4

**17.** Which of the following are key features of the 'Poverty Line Basket (PLB)' used to estimate poverty in India?

1. The PLB includes a basket of goods and services necessary to meet basic human needs.
2. The price levels for consumption in the PLB are uniform across all states in India.
3. The PLB was first introduced by the Alagh Committee.

Select the correct answer from the codes given below:

(a) 1 and 2 only
(b) 1 and 3 only
(c) 2 and 3 only
(d) 1, 2 and 3

**18.** Arrange the following committees constituted for poverty line estimation in the correct chronological order of their establishment:

1. Tendulkar Committee
2. Alagh Committee
3. Lakdawala Committee
4. Rangarajan Committee

Choose the right answer from the codes given below:

(a) 2-3-1-4
(b) 3-2-4-1
(c) 1-2-3-4
(d) 2-1-3-4

**19.** With reference to the recommendations of the 'Tendulkar Committee on Poverty Estimation', consider the following statements:

1. The Tendulkar Committee recommended shifting from a calorie-based poverty line to a poverty line based on consumption expenditure.
2. The committee proposed a uniform poverty line across rural and urban areas in India.
3. The Tendulkar Committee introduced the concept of multi-dimensional poverty in India.

How many of the statements given above is/are correct?

(a) Only one (b) Only two
(c) All three (d) None

**20.** With reference to the recommendations of the Tendulkar and Rangarajan Committees on poverty estimation, consider the following statements:

1. Both committees recommended a shift from the calorie-based poverty line to a broader measure of consumption expenditure.
2. The Tendulkar Committee proposed a uniform poverty line for both rural and urban areas while the Rangarajan Committee suggested separate poverty lines for rural and urban areas.

Which of the statements given above is/are correct?

(a) 1 only (b) 2 only
(c) Both 1 and 2 (d) Neither 1 nor 2

**21.** Which of the following reasons explain higher calorie requirements in rural areas as compared to urban areas?

(a) Rural populations have limited access to medical facilities, necessitating higher calorie intake for better health.
(b) The rural environment requires higher energy expenditure due to higher prevalence of physical labour-intensive activities such as agricultural work and manual labour.
(c) The cost of food is lower in rural areas, leading to increased consumption of calories.
(d) Rural diets are richer in fats and proteins, leading to a naturally higher calorie intake.

**22.** Which of the following components were included in the poverty estimation methodology recommended by the Tendulkar Committee?

1. Health expenditure
2. Education expenditure
3. Nutritional requirements based on calorie intake
4. Clothing and footwear

Select the correct answer from the codes given below:

(a) 1 and 3 only
(b) 2 and 4 only
(c) 1, 2 and 4 only
(d) 1, 2, 3 and 4

**23.** Which of the following statements accurately describe about the 'Uniform Reference Period (URP)' method used in NSSO expenditure surveys?

1. URP collects consumption data based on a 30-day recall period for all items.
2. URP is effective in capturing seasonal variations in consumption.
3. URP tends to under report the consumption of infrequently purchased items.

Select the correct answer from the codes given below:

(a) 1 and 2 only (b) 1 and 3 only
(c) 2 and 3 only (d) 1, 2 and 3

**24.** Which of the following statements accurately describe the Mixed Reference Period (MRP) method used by NSSO for estimating poverty?

1. MRP uses a 30-day recall period for non-durable goods and a 365-day recall period for durable goods.
2. MRP provides a more accurate reflection of both short-term and long-term consumption patterns compared to the URP method.
3. MRP applies a uniform recall period across all categories of goods and services.

Select the correct answer from the codes given below:

(a) 1 and 2 only (b) 2 and 3 only
(c) 1 and 3 only (d) 1, 2 and 3

## Topic 4 : Key Terminologies of Unemployment

**25.** Consider the following statements about the concept of 'Labour Force':

1. It includes all individuals aged 15-64 years who are either employed or actively seeking employment.
2. Labour Force Participation Rate (LFPR) is calculated as the percentage of the labour force in the working-age population.
3. It excludes those who are not actively seeking work, such as students, homemakers and retirees.

Which of the given above statements are correct ?

(a) 1 and 2 only (b) 2 and 3 only
(c) 1 and 3 only (d) 1, 2 and 3

**26.** Which of the following groups are typically not included in the labour force?

1. Full-time students who are not working or seeking work.
2. Retired individuals who are not seeking employment.
3. Individuals engaged in unpaid domestic work.

Select the correct answer from the codes given below:

(a) 1 and 2 only
(b) 2 and 3 only
(c) 1 and 3 only
(d) 1, 2 and 3

**27.** Consider the following statements:

1. Code on Wages, 2019 applies to all employees in organised sectors but excludes those in unorganised sectors.
2. Under the Code on Wages, 2019, the Central Government is responsible for setting the minimum wages across all sectors in India.
3. The Code on Wages, 2019, introduces the concept of a National Floor Wage, which acts as a baseline for setting minimum wages across different states.

How many of the statements given above is/are correct?

(a) Only one (b) Only two
(c) All three (d) None

**28.** With reference to the National Floor Wage under the Code on Wages, 2019, consider the following statements:

1. The National Floor Wage sets the baseline wage that must be paid to all workers across India, irrespective of the state.
2. States are permitted to set their minimum wages above the National Floor Wage, but not below it.
3. The National Floor Wage is mandated to be revised annually by the Central Government.

How many of the statements given above is/are correct?

(a) Only one (b) Only two
(c) All three (d) None

**29.** Match the following wage concepts with their correct descriptions:

| Wage Concept | Description |
|---|---|
| 1. Minimum Wage | The baseline wage set by the government below which no state can fix its minimum wage. |
| 2. Floor Wage | The lowest legal wage that employers are required to pay to workers as per government regulations. |
| 3. Living Wage | A wage that is sufficient to cover the basic needs of workers, ensuring a decent standard of living. |

How many of the pairs given above is/are correctly matched?

(a) Only one pair (b) Only two pairs
(c) All three pairs (d) None

**30.** With reference to the concepts of Minimum Wage and Living Wage in India, consider the following statements:

1. A Minimum Wage is the legally mandated lowest wage that must be paid to workers, ensuring they can meet their basic needs.
2. A Living Wage is higher than a Minimum Wage and is designed to provide a decent standard of living, including the ability to save for the future.
3. The concept of Minimum Wage is explicitly recognised and mandated by the Indian Constitution.

How many of the statements given above is/are correct?

(a) Only one (b) Only two
(c) All three (d) None

## Topic 5 : Categorisation of Workforce

**31.** Which of the following types of employment typically come under the formal workforce?

1. Government employees working in public sector undertakings.
2. Full-time employees in registered private companies.
3. Daily wage labourers working on construction sites without formal contracts.

Select the correct answer from the codes given below:

(a) 1 and 2 only (b) 2 and 3 only
(c) 1 and 3 only (d) 1, 2 and 3

**32.** Which of the following characteristics define employment that falls under the formal workforce?

1. The employment is governed by labour laws and regulations.
2. Employees receive regular salaries and benefits such as health insurance and pensions.
3. The employment is primarily in the agriculture sector.

Select the correct answer from the codes given below:

(a) 1 and 2 only (b) 2 and 3 only
(c) 1 and 3 only (d) 1, 2 and 3

**33.** With reference to the 'E-Shram portal' in India, consider the following statements:

1. The E-Shram portal is a government initiative to create a national database of unorganised workers.
2. The registration on the E-Shram portal provides workers with an accident insurance cover under the Pradhan Mantri Suraksha Bima Yojana (PMSBY).

Which of the statements given above is/are correct?

(a) 1 only (b) 2 only
(c) Both 1 and 2 (d) Neither 1 nor 2

**34.** Which of the following benefits are associated with registration on the E-Shram portal?

1. Access to accident insurance under the Pradhan Mantri Suraksha Bima Yojana (PMSBY).
2. Priority access to government welfare schemes for unorganised workers.
3. Guaranteed minimum wage as per the government's wage policy.

Select the correct answer from the codes given below:

(a) 1 and 2 only (b) 2 and 3 only
(c) 1 and 3 only (d) 1, 2 and 3

**35.** Which of the following workers are considered part of the gig economy?

1. Food delivery personnel working for platforms like Swiggy or Zomato.
2. A consultant providing specialised services on a contract basis for multiple clients.
3. A factory worker employed under a permanent contract with full benefits.

Select the correct answer from the codes given below:

(a) 1 and 2 only
(b) 1 and 3 only
(c) 2 and 3 only
(d) 1, 2 and 3

**36.** Consider the following statements:

1. Gig workers are recognised as employees under the Indian labour laws and are entitled to the same benefits as full-time workers.
2. The Code on Social Security, 2020, includes provisions for the social security of gig and platform workers.
3. Gig workers are entitled to health insurance and pension benefits under the Employees' Provident Fund Act, 1952.

Which of the statements given above is/are correct?

(a) 1 and 2 only (b) 2 only
(c) 1 and 3 only (d) 1, 2 and 3

**37.** With reference to the protection of gig workers in India, consider the following statements:

1. The Code on Wages, 2019, mandates a minimum wage for all gig workers in India.
2. The Gig and Platform Workers Welfare Board is responsible for addressing grievances and ensuring the welfare of gig workers.
3. The Code on Social Security, 2020, mandates the creation of a social security fund for gig and platform workers.

Which of the statements given above is/are correct?

(a) 1 and 2 only
(b) 2 and 3 only
(c) 3 only
(d) 1, 2 and 3

## Topic 6 : Types of Unemployment

**38.** Consider the following statements about 'Structural Unemployment':

1. This type of unemployment arises due to a mismatch between workers' skills and the demands of the job market.
2. It is often caused by technological changes or shifts in the economy.

Which of the statements given above is/are correct?

(a) 1 only (b) 2 only
(c) Both 1 and 2 (d) Neither 1 nor 2

**39.** Consider the following types of unemployment with specific examples:

| Type of Unemployment | Example |
|---|---|
| 1. Structural Unemployment | A. Workers in coal mining losing jobs due to the shift to renewable energy. |
| 2. Frictional Unemployment | B. A software engineer taking time off to find a better job. |
| 3. Seasonal Unemployment | C. Farm workers becoming unemployed after the harvest season. |
| 4. Cyclical Unemployment | D. Factory workers laid off during an economic recession. |

How many of the pairs given above is/are correctly matched?

(a) Only one pair (b) Only two pairs
(c) Only three pairs (d) All four pairs

**40.** With reference to the 'Frictional Unemployment', consider the following statements:

1. It occurs when workers are temporarily between jobs while searching for new employment.
2. It is typically a long-term form of unemployment.
3. It is generally higher during periods of economic recession.

How many of the statements given above is/are correct?

(a) Only one (b) Only two
(c) All three (d) None

**41.** Which of the following statements are correct?

1. Seasonal unemployment occurs when workers are employed only during certain times of the year.
2. Disguised unemployment occurs when more workers are employed than are actually needed, leading to lower productivity.
3. Both types of unemployment can be found in the agriculture sector.

Select the correct answer from the codes given below:

(a) 1 and 2 only (b) 2 and 3 only
(c) 1 and 3 only (d) 1, 2 and 3

**42.** Consider the following scenario:

'A manufacturing worker loses their job because the company has automated the production process using new technologies, replacing the need for manual labour. The worker finds it difficult to get another job as most companies in the sector are adopting similar technologies.'

What type of unemployment is the worker experiencing?

(a) Cyclical Unemployment
(b) Structural Unemployment
(c) Frictional Unemployment
(d) Seasonal Unemployment

## Topic 7 : Measurement of Unemployment

**43.** Which of the following statements best describes the 'Usual Principal Status (UPS)' approach to measuring unemployment?

(a) It measures the number of people who were unemployed at any time during a specific day.
(b) It assesses the employment status of an individual based on their activity over a short reference period, typically a week.
(c) It identifies the primary activity status of an individual over a longer reference period, usually a year, to determine whether they are employed or unemployed.
(d) It tracks fluctuations in employment status on an hourly basis to capture short-term unemployment.

**44.** Match the following approaches of measuring unemployment with their respective descriptions:

| Approach | Description |
|---|---|
| 1. Current Weekly Status (CWS) | A. Estimates the proportion of labour force unemployed in a week, identifying short-term unemployment. |
| 2. Usual Principal Status (UPS) | B. Captures the primary activity status over a long period, usually identifying chronic unemployment. |
| 3. Current Daily Status (CDS) | C. Tracks daily fluctuations in employment, providing a comprehensive picture of labour force utilisation. |

Select the correct answer from the codes given below:

(a) 1-A, 2-B, 3-C (b) 1-B, 2-C, 3-A
(c) 1-C, 2-A, 3-B (d) 1-B, 2-A, 3-C

**45.** Which of the following surveys or censuses are primary sources for measuring unemployment in India?

1. Periodic Labour Force Survey (PLFS)
2. Economic Census
3. Census of India
4. National Family Health Survey (NFHS)

Select the correct answer from the codes given below:

(a) 1 and 2 only (b) 1, 2 and 3 only
(c) 2 and 4 only (d) 1, 2, 3 and 4

**46.** With reference to the 'Economic Census' in India, consider the following statements:

1. It is conducted and published by the Ministry of Statistics and Programme Implementation (MoSPI).
2. It provides comprehensive data on all establishments in India, covering both formal and informal sectors.
3. It covers both agriculture and non-agricultural establishments.

How many of the statements given above is/are correct?

(a) Only one (b) Only two
(c) All three (d) None

**47.** Which of the following statements correctly describe about 'Periodic Labour Force Survey (PLFS)' in India?

1. PLFS is designed to provide quarterly estimates of labour force indicators for urban areas.
2. It replaced the Employment-Unemployment Survey (EUS) as the primary source of labour market data in India.
3. PLFS provides both quarterly estimates for urban areas and annual estimates for both urban and rural areas.

Select the correct answer from the codes given below:

(a) 1 and 2 only (b) 2 and 3 only
(c) 1 and 3 only (d) 1, 2 and 3

**48.** Consider the following statements:

1. The unemployment rate in urban areas is higher than in rural areas.
2. The unemployment rate for females is lower than that for males in both urban and rural areas.
3. The overall unemployment rate in India has shown a declining trend over the past few years.

How many of the above statements is/are correct?

(a) Only one (b) Only two
(c) All three (d) None

## Topic 8 : Government Initiatives

**49.** Consider the following government initiatives:

1. National Rural Livelihoods Mission (NRLM)
2. Stand Up India Scheme
3. Swachh Bharat Abhiyan
4. Deen Dayal Upadhyaya Grameen Kaushalya Yojana (DDU-GKY)

Which of the given above government initiatives are specifically aimed at improving the livelihoods of women and marginalised communities?

(a) 1 and 3 only
(b) 1, 2 and 4 only
(c) 2, 3 and 4 only
(d) 1, 3 and 4 only

**50.** With reference to the implementation of MGNREGA, consider the following statements:

1. MGNREGA mandates that at least one-third of the beneficiaries should be women.
2. MGNREGA funds are provided directly by the Central Government, and State Governments do not contribute.
3. Social audits are a mandatory part of the MGNREGA implementation process to ensure transparency and accountability.

How many of the statements given above is/are correct?

(a) Only one (b) Only two
(c) All three (d) None

**51.** With reference to the Mahatma Gandhi National Rural Employment Guarantee Act (MGNREGA), consider the following statements:

1. MGNREGA guarantees 100 days of wage employment per year to every adult member of a rural household.
2. The wages under MGNREGA are equal across all states in India.
3. MGNREGA includes provisions for the creation of durable assets in rural areas.

How many of the statements given above is/are correct?

(a) Only one (b) Only two
(c) All three (d) None

**52.** With reference to the 'Atal Pension Yojana (APY)', consider the following statements:

1. It is a government-backed pension scheme primarily aimed at workers in the unorganised sector.
2. The scheme guarantees a minimum monthly pension of ₹ 5,000 for all subscribers after the age of 60.
3. Contributions to the APY are eligible for tax benefits under Section 80C of the Income Tax Act.
4. APY is available to all Indian citizens between the ages of 18 and 40.

How many of the statements given above is/are correct?

(a) Only one (b) Only two
(c) Only three (d) All four

**53.** Consider the following individuals and their circumstances.

1. Ravi-A 25-year-old self-employed individual who runs a small grocery store in a rural area.
2. Meena - A 42-year-old government school teacher who is already a member of the Employees' Provident Fund (EPF).
3. Anil - A 35-year-old factory worker in the unorganised sector who has no other pension or social security benefits.
4. Sunita - A 30-year-old software engineer working in a private IT firm and contributing to the National Pension System (NPS).

Which of the given above would be eligible to enroll in the Atal Pension Yojana (APY)?

(a) 1 and 3 only
(b) 1, 2 and 4 only
(c) 2 and 3 only
(d) 1, 3 and 4 only

**54.** With reference to the 'Pradhan Mantri Shram Yogi Maandhan (PMSYM)', consider the following statements:

1. PMSYM is a voluntary and contributory pension scheme for workers in the unorganised sector.
2. The scheme provides a minimum assured pension of ₹ 3,000 per month after the age of 60.
3. To be eligible for PMSYM, the monthly income of the beneficiary should not exceed ₹ 10,000.

How many of the statements given above is/are correct?

(a) Only one (b) Only two
(c) All three (d) None

## Topic 9 : Labour Codes

**55.** With reference to the new labour codes adopted in India, consider the following statements:

1. The Code on Wages, 2019, consolidates laws related to minimum wages, payment of wages, and equal remuneration.
2. The Industrial Relations Code, 2020, governs the rules regarding trade unions, industrial disputes, and standing orders.
3. The Code on Social Security, 2020, mandates a universal social security scheme covering all workers, including those in the unorganised sector.

How many of the statements given above is/are correct?

(a) Only one (b) Only two
(c) All three (d) None

**56.** With reference to the implementation of the Code on Wages, 2019, consider the following statements:

1. The Code on Wages, 2019, ensures equal remuneration for men and women for work of similar nature.
2. The minimum wages under the Code apply only to the employees in the public sector and do not cover private sector workers.
3. The Code on Wages provides for the Constitution of advisory boards at the central and state levels to recommend minimum wages.

How many of the statements given above is/are correct?

(a) Only one
(b) Only two
(c) All three
(d) None

**57.** Consider the following statements:

1. The Occupational Safety, Health, and Working Conditions Code, 2020, mandates that employers provide safe working conditions and welfare measures for workers.
2. The Code on Social Security, 2020, includes provisions for maternity benefits and employee provident funds.

Which of the statements given above is/are correct?

(a) 1 only
(b) 2 only
(c) Both 1 and 2
(d) Neither 1 nor 2

# OMR SHEET

**Assessment Round**

| | | | | | | | |
|---|---|---|---|---|---|---|---|
| 1 | ⓐ ⓑ ⓒ ⓓ | 31 | ⓐ ⓑ ⓒ ⓓ | 61 | ⓐ ⓑ ⓒ ⓓ | 91 | ⓐ ⓑ ⓒ ⓓ |
| 2 | ⓐ ⓑ ⓒ ⓓ | 32 | ⓐ ⓑ ⓒ ⓓ | 62 | ⓐ ⓑ ⓒ ⓓ | 92 | ⓐ ⓑ ⓒ ⓓ |
| 3 | ⓐ ⓑ ⓒ ⓓ | 33 | ⓐ ⓑ ⓒ ⓓ | 63 | ⓐ ⓑ ⓒ ⓓ | 93 | ⓐ ⓑ ⓒ ⓓ |
| 4 | ⓐ ⓑ ⓒ ⓓ | 34 | ⓐ ⓑ ⓒ ⓓ | 64 | ⓐ ⓑ ⓒ ⓓ | 94 | ⓐ ⓑ ⓒ ⓓ |
| 5 | ⓐ ⓑ ⓒ ⓓ | 35 | ⓐ ⓑ ⓒ ⓓ | 65 | ⓐ ⓑ ⓒ ⓓ | 95 | ⓐ ⓑ ⓒ ⓓ |
| 6 | ⓐ ⓑ ⓒ ⓓ | 36 | ⓐ ⓑ ⓒ ⓓ | 66 | ⓐ ⓑ ⓒ ⓓ | 96 | ⓐ ⓑ ⓒ ⓓ |
| 7 | ⓐ ⓑ ⓒ ⓓ | 37 | ⓐ ⓑ ⓒ ⓓ | 67 | ⓐ ⓑ ⓒ ⓓ | 97 | ⓐ ⓑ ⓒ ⓓ |
| 8 | ⓐ ⓑ ⓒ ⓓ | 38 | ⓐ ⓑ ⓒ ⓓ | 68 | ⓐ ⓑ ⓒ ⓓ | 98 | ⓐ ⓑ ⓒ ⓓ |
| 9 | ⓐ ⓑ ⓒ ⓓ | 39 | ⓐ ⓑ ⓒ ⓓ | 69 | ⓐ ⓑ ⓒ ⓓ | 99 | ⓐ ⓑ ⓒ ⓓ |
| 10 | ⓐ ⓑ ⓒ ⓓ | 40 | ⓐ ⓑ ⓒ ⓓ | 70 | ⓐ ⓑ ⓒ ⓓ | 100 | ⓐ ⓑ ⓒ ⓓ |
| 11 | ⓐ ⓑ ⓒ ⓓ | 41 | ⓐ ⓑ ⓒ ⓓ | 71 | ⓐ ⓑ ⓒ ⓓ | 101 | ⓐ ⓑ ⓒ ⓓ |
| 12 | ⓐ ⓑ ⓒ ⓓ | 42 | ⓐ ⓑ ⓒ ⓓ | 72 | ⓐ ⓑ ⓒ ⓓ | 102 | ⓐ ⓑ ⓒ ⓓ |
| 13 | ⓐ ⓑ ⓒ ⓓ | 43 | ⓐ ⓑ ⓒ ⓓ | 73 | ⓐ ⓑ ⓒ ⓓ | 103 | ⓐ ⓑ ⓒ ⓓ |
| 14 | ⓐ ⓑ ⓒ ⓓ | 44 | ⓐ ⓑ ⓒ ⓓ | 74 | ⓐ ⓑ ⓒ ⓓ | 104 | ⓐ ⓑ ⓒ ⓓ |
| 15 | ⓐ ⓑ ⓒ ⓓ | 45 | ⓐ ⓑ ⓒ ⓓ | 75 | ⓐ ⓑ ⓒ ⓓ | 105 | ⓐ ⓑ ⓒ ⓓ |
| 16 | ⓐ ⓑ ⓒ ⓓ | 46 | ⓐ ⓑ ⓒ ⓓ | 76 | ⓐ ⓑ ⓒ ⓓ | 106 | ⓐ ⓑ ⓒ ⓓ |
| 17 | ⓐ ⓑ ⓒ ⓓ | 47 | ⓐ ⓑ ⓒ ⓓ | 77 | ⓐ ⓑ ⓒ ⓓ | 107 | ⓐ ⓑ ⓒ ⓓ |
| 18 | ⓐ ⓑ ⓒ ⓓ | 48 | ⓐ ⓑ ⓒ ⓓ | 78 | ⓐ ⓑ ⓒ ⓓ | 108 | ⓐ ⓑ ⓒ ⓓ |
| 19 | ⓐ ⓑ ⓒ ⓓ | 49 | ⓐ ⓑ ⓒ ⓓ | 79 | ⓐ ⓑ ⓒ ⓓ | 109 | ⓐ ⓑ ⓒ ⓓ |
| 20 | ⓐ ⓑ ⓒ ⓓ | 50 | ⓐ ⓑ ⓒ ⓓ | 80 | ⓐ ⓑ ⓒ ⓓ | 110 | ⓐ ⓑ ⓒ ⓓ |
| 21 | ⓐ ⓑ ⓒ ⓓ | 51 | ⓐ ⓑ ⓒ ⓓ | 81 | ⓐ ⓑ ⓒ ⓓ | 111 | ⓐ ⓑ ⓒ ⓓ |
| 22 | ⓐ ⓑ ⓒ ⓓ | 52 | ⓐ ⓑ ⓒ ⓓ | 82 | ⓐ ⓑ ⓒ ⓓ | 112 | ⓐ ⓑ ⓒ ⓓ |
| 23 | ⓐ ⓑ ⓒ ⓓ | 53 | ⓐ ⓑ ⓒ ⓓ | 83 | ⓐ ⓑ ⓒ ⓓ | 113 | ⓐ ⓑ ⓒ ⓓ |
| 24 | ⓐ ⓑ ⓒ ⓓ | 54 | ⓐ ⓑ ⓒ ⓓ | 84 | ⓐ ⓑ ⓒ ⓓ | 114 | ⓐ ⓑ ⓒ ⓓ |
| 25 | ⓐ ⓑ ⓒ ⓓ | 55 | ⓐ ⓑ ⓒ ⓓ | 85 | ⓐ ⓑ ⓒ ⓓ | 115 | ⓐ ⓑ ⓒ ⓓ |
| 26 | ⓐ ⓑ ⓒ ⓓ | 56 | ⓐ ⓑ ⓒ ⓓ | 86 | ⓐ ⓑ ⓒ ⓓ | 116 | ⓐ ⓑ ⓒ ⓓ |
| 27 | ⓐ ⓑ ⓒ ⓓ | 57 | ⓐ ⓑ ⓒ ⓓ | 87 | ⓐ ⓑ ⓒ ⓓ | 117 | ⓐ ⓑ ⓒ ⓓ |
| 28 | ⓐ ⓑ ⓒ ⓓ | 58 | ⓐ ⓑ ⓒ ⓓ | 88 | ⓐ ⓑ ⓒ ⓓ | 118 | ⓐ ⓑ ⓒ ⓓ |
| 29 | ⓐ ⓑ ⓒ ⓓ | 59 | ⓐ ⓑ ⓒ ⓓ | 89 | ⓐ ⓑ ⓒ ⓓ | 119 | ⓐ ⓑ ⓒ ⓓ |
| 30 | ⓐ ⓑ ⓒ ⓓ | 60 | ⓐ ⓑ ⓒ ⓓ | 90 | ⓐ ⓑ ⓒ ⓓ | 120 | ⓐ ⓑ ⓒ ⓓ |

## Calculate Your Score

| | |
|---|---|
| **Correct (✓)** | |
| **Incorrect (✓)** | |
| **Unattempted** | |
| **Total Score** | |
| **Accuracy (%)** | |

## Reasons for Incorrect Answers?

| | |
|---|---|
| 1. Lack of Knowledge/Existing Source Insufficient | |
| 2. Lack of Multiple Revision | |
| 3. Common Sense Mistakes | |

**Note :**

1. Calculate total score as correct answers carry 2 marks each 1/3rd marks will deducted for **Incorrect** Answers.
2. Calculate Accuracy (%) by dividing the number of correct answers to the total number of attempted questions.

## Past Learning

**1.** Consider the following statements : **(2023)**

1. The Self-Help Group (SHG) programme was originally initiated by the State Bank of India by providing microcredit to the financially deprived.
2. In an SHG, all members of a group take responsibility for a loan that an individual member takes.
3. Regional Rural Banks and Scheduled Commercial Banks support SHGs.

How many of the above statements is/are correct?

(a) Only one (b) Only two
(c) All three (d) None

**2.** In India, which one of the following compiles information on industrial disputes, closures, retrenchments and lay-offs in factories employing workers? **(2022)**

(a) Central Statistics Office
(b) Department for Promotion of Industry and Internal Trade
(c) Labour Bureau
(d) National Technical Manpower Information System

**3.** With reference to casual workers employed in India, consider the following statements: **(2021)**

1. All casual workers are entitled for Employees Provident Fund Coverage.
2. All casual workers are entitled for regular working hours and overtime payment.
3. The government can by a notification specify that an establishment or industry shall pay wages only through its bank account.

Which of the given above statements are correct?

(a) 1 and 2 only
(b) 2 and 3 only
(c) 1 and 3 only
(d) 1, 2 and 3

**4.** With reference to the Indian economy after the 1991 economy liberalization, consider the following statements: **(2020)**

1. Worker productivity (? per worker at 2004-05 price) increase in urban areas while it decreased in rural areas.
2. The percentage share of rural areas in workforce steadily increased.
3. In rural areas, the growth in non-farm economy increased.
4. The growth rate in rural employment decreased.

Which of the given above statements is/are correct?

(a) 1 and 2 only (b) 3 and 4 only
(c) 3 only (d) 1, 2 and 4 only

**5.** In a given year in India, official poverty lines are higher in some states than in others because: **(2019)**

(a) poverty rates vary from State to State
(b) price levels vary from State to State
(c) Gross State Product varies from State to State
(d) quality of public distribution varies from State to State

**6.** Increase in absolute and per capita real GNP do not connote a higher level of economic development, if: **(2018)**

(a) industrial output fails to keep pace with agricultural output.
(b) agricultural output fails to keep pace with industrial output.
(c) poverty and unemployment increase.
(d) imports grow faster than exports.

**7.** Disguised unemployment generally means: **(2013)**

(a) large number of people remain unemployed
(b) alternative employment is not available
(c) marginal productivity of labour is zero
(d) productivity of workers is low

**8.** To obtain full benefits of demographic dividend, what should India do: **(2013)**

(a) Promoting skill development
(b) Introducing more social security schemes
(c) Reducing infant mortality rate
(d) Privatisation of higher education

# Detailed Solutions

## Assessment Round

**1.** (*a*) Only one

The International Poverty Line set by the World Bank is a global benchmark used to measure and compare poverty levels across different countries. It is the minimum daily income required to meet basic needs, adjusted for differences in cost of living across countries.

- **Statement 1 is correct:** The World Bank currently sets the International Poverty Line at **$2.15 per day, measured in 2017** purchasing power parity (PPP) terms. This line is used to estimate global poverty by assessing the minimum income required to meet basic needs, adjusted for price differences between countries.
- **Statement 2 is incorrect:** While the International Poverty Line is set at a specific dollar amount ($2.15 per day), it is **adjusted using Purchasing Power Parity (PPP)** to account for differences in the cost of living between countries.
- **Statement 3 is incorrect:** It is based on income levels and does **not directly consider access to specific services such as clean water and sanitation.**

**Thus, option (a) is the correct answer.**

**2.** (*c*) 1, 2 and 3 only

**The Multi-dimensional Poverty Index** (MPI) is a measure developed by the United Nations Development Programme (UNDP) and the Oxford Poverty and Human Development Initiative (OPHI) that captures the multiple deprivations that people face in areas such as education, health, and standard of living.

**Indicators included in the MPI:**

- **Access to clean drinking water:** This is an indicator under the **standard of living** dimension in the MPI. Lack of access to clean drinking water is considered a deprivation.
- **Child mortality:** This is an indicator under the **health** dimension in the MPI. It reflects whether any child in the household has died, indicating poor health outcomes and healthcare access.
- **Years of schooling:** This is an indicator under the **education** dimension in the MPI. It measures the number of years of education completed by household members, reflecting educational attainment.
- **Income level above the international poverty line:** This is **not** an indicator in the MPI. The MPI does not consider income directly but instead focuses on deprivations in specific basic needs and services.

**Thus, option (c) is the correct answer.**

**3.** (*b*) To assess the minimum income required to meet basic needs globally, adjusted for price differences across countries.

The International Poverty Line set by the World Bank is designed to estimate global poverty by establishing the minimum income needed to meet basic living needs, adjusted for purchasing power parity (PPP) to reflect price differences across countries. It serves as a benchmark to identify individuals living in extreme poverty worldwide.

**Thus, option (b) is the correct answer.**

**4.** (*a*) 1-B, 2-A, 3-C,4-D

- **Headcount Ratio:** It reflects the **proportion of poor** in a population. It is the percentage of people whose income or consumption is below the poverty line.
- **Poverty Gap Index:** It measures the **intensity of poverty.** It takes into account not only the number of poor individuals but also the extent to which their incomes fall below the poverty line, providing an indication of the depth of poverty.
- **Multi-dimensional Poverty Index (MPI):** The MPI includes various indicators beyond income, such as **education and health indicators.** It captures multiple deprivations that people face across different aspects of life, providing a more comprehensive measure of poverty.

- **Sen Index**: This index combines both the **incidence** (how widespread poverty is) and intensity (how severe poverty is) of poverty. It provides a more nuanced measure by taking into account the distribution of income among the poor.

**Therefore, the correct answer is (a) 1-B, 2-A, 3-C, 4-D.**

**5.** (*d*) None

- **Pair 1 is incorrect**: The **Poverty Gap** does not measure literacy or education. Instead, it reflects the **depth of poverty**, indicating how far, on average, the poor are from the poverty line. It highlights the shortfall between the income of the poor and the poverty threshold, providing a more nuanced understanding of poverty. Thus, it is correctly matched with (B).
- **Pair 2 is incorrect: Poverty Intensity** captures the **degree of deprivation** experienced by the poor. It factors in both the number of poor people and the **severity** of their poverty, combining these two aspects to measure how intensely poverty affects a population. This is correctly matched with (C).
- **Pair 3 is incorrect: Learning Poverty** measures the share of children who cannot read and understand a **simple text** by age 10, indicating significant **educational deprivation**. This concept highlights the gap in early childhood education and literacy, which is crucial for long-term development. It is correctly matched with (A).

**Thus, option (d) is the correct answer.**

**6.** (*b*) Only two

- **Statement 1 is correct**: Absolute poverty is defined by the inability to meet basic needs such as food, clothing, and shelter. It reflects a level of poverty where individuals do not have enough resources to secure these basic life necessities.
- **Statement 2 is incorrect**: While absolute poverty uses a fixed threshold, the threshold can be adjusted for different countries based on Purchasing Power Parity (PPP) to account for differences in the cost of living.
- **Statement 3 is correct**: The World Bank's international poverty line (currently set at \$2.15 per day in 2017 PPP) is an example of an absolute poverty measure.

**Therefore, the correct answer is (b) Only two.**

**7.** (*c*) All three

- **Statement 1 is correct**: Chronic poverty is a **long-term and persistent** form of poverty that often lasts for several years or even across generations. It is characterised by a lack of access to essential resources and opportunities, making it difficult for individuals and families to escape poverty.
- **Statement 2 is correct**: Situational poverty is a **temporary state** of poverty that occurs due to an external event or crisis, such as a natural disaster, economic recession, job loss, or severe illness.
- **Statement 3 is correct**: Seasonal poverty **occurs at specific times** of the year, typically in relation to agricultural cycles or seasonal employment. For example, agricultural workers may experience poverty during off-harvest seasons when there is less work available.

**Thus, option (c) is the correct answer.**

**8.** (*a*) Absolute poverty defines poverty based on a **universal threshold**, which determines if individuals can afford basic necessities like food, shelter and clothing.

Relative poverty, on the other hand, is a **comparative measure**, assessing how an individual's income relates to the broader societal income levels, focusing on income inequality rather than subsistence.

**Thus, option (a) is the correct answer.**

**9.** (*b*) People who are temporarily poor, frequently moving in and out of poverty due to unstable income or employment.

The **churning poor** refers to individuals or households that **move in and out of poverty** over time. Their income or employment status is often unstable, meaning they may temporarily rise above the poverty line but can fall back below it during economic downturns, loss of employment, or personal financial crises. This group experiences frequent transitions between being poor and not poor, making their poverty status fluid.

**Thus, option (b) is the correct answer.**

***10.*** (*b*) Only two

- **Statement 1 is correct:** The **Gini Coefficient** is a measure of income inequality within a population. It quantifies the degree of inequality in income distribution among a population, ranging from perfect equality to maximum inequality.
- **Statement 2 is correct:** A Gini Coefficient of **0 indicates perfect equality**, where everyone has the same income. A Gini Coefficient of 1 (or 100 if expressed as a percentage) **indicates maximum inequality**, where all the income is concentrated in the hands of a single person or household.
- **Statement 3 is incorrect:** The Gini Coefficient is derived from the **Lorenz Curve**, which graphically represents the distribution of income or wealth within a population. While the World Bank does publish Gini Coefficients as part of its data on global inequality, it is **not the only organisation** that does so. Gini coefficients can be calculated and published by various organizations, including national statistical agencies and other international bodies.

**Therefore, the correct answer is (b) Only two.**

***11.*** (*c*) Both 1 and 2

- **Statement 1 is correct:** The **Lorenz Curve** represents the cumulative distribution of income or wealth among a population. It plots the cumulative percentage of total income received against the cumulative percentage of recipients, starting with the poorest and ending with the richest.

  It is a graphical representation that shows the proportion of total income earned by the bottom x% of the population.
- **Statement 2 is correct:** The **greater the distance between the Lorenz Curve and the line of perfect equality,** the higher the income inequality. The line of perfect equality is a 45-degree line representing a scenario where income or wealth is distributed equally among all members of the population. The more the Lorenz Curve deviates from this line, the more unequal the distribution of income or wealth.

**Therefore, the correct answer is (c) Both 1 and 2.**

***12.*** (*d*) 1, 2 and 3

- **Statement 1 is correct:** High income inequality as indicated by a High Gini Coefficient and a significantly bowed Lorenz Curve can lead to social unrest and political instability as large segments of the population may feel marginalised.
- **Statement 2 is correct:** High levels of income inequality can reduce overall demand in the economy because lower-income households have less purchasing power, potentially hindering economic growth.
- **Statement 3 is correct:** A high Gini Coefficient often indicates that a small portion of the population holds a disproportionately large share of the total income or wealth, exacerbating economic disparities.

**Thus, option (d) is the correct answer.**

***13.*** (*b*) Income inequality first increases and then decreases as a country develops economically.

- The **Kuznets Curve** is a U-shaped graph that shows the relationship between economic growth and **various factors**, such as income inequality, environmental quality, or forest cover.
- The Kuznets Curve hypothesizes that as an economy develops, income inequality initially rises because of the shift from agriculture to industry. Over time, as more of the population gains access to education, higher wages, and social services, income inequality begins to decline, creating an inverted 'U' shape on the graph of inequality versus economic development.

**Thus, option (b) is the correct answer.**

***14.*** (*b*) Only two

- **Statement 1 is correct:** Absolute poverty in India is measured using a **fixed poverty line that is adjusted for inflation over time.** This poverty line is based on consumption expenditure and is periodically updated to reflect changes in the cost of living due to inflation.

- **Statement 2 is incorrect**: The poverty line in India was initially based on the consumption expenditure required to meet a minimum calorie intake. However, the poverty line is not based solely on calorie intake anymore; it **now includes a broader range** of basic consumption needs beyond just food, such as clothing, shelter, and other essential items.
- **Statement 3 is correct**: The **Tendulkar Committee** recommended a shift from a strictly calorie-based measurement of poverty to a broader approach that also includes expenses related to health, education, and other basic needs. This recommendation led to a more comprehensive understanding of poverty, incorporating factors beyond just food consumption.

**Therefore, the correct answer is (b) Only two.**

***15.*** (*c*) Only three

- **Statement 1 is correct: Income levels can fluctuate frequently**, particularly in economies with large informal sectors or seasonal employment. This makes income an unreliable measure for assessing long-term poverty, as temporary income changes do not reflect persistent poverty conditions.
- **Statement 2 is correct**: In many cases, people working in the **informal sector** or relying on unaccounted sources of income may **underreport their earnings**. This results in inaccurate data, making it difficult to assess true poverty levels based solely on income.
- **Statement 3 is correct: Income** does not provide a full picture of poverty because it does not necessarily reflect **living conditions** or access to **basic necessities** like healthcare, housing, education, or food security. These factors are often better captured through **consumption patterns**, which measure what people are actually spending on essentials.
- **Statement 4 is incorrect: Income-based data** is often less reliable than consumption data, especially in economies with significant informal sectors. Consumption data tends to be more stable over time and gives a better picture of people's actual living standards, as it reflects what individuals are spending on to meet their daily needs.

**Thus, three reasons are correct, making the correct answer (c) Only three.**

***16.*** (*d*) 1, 2, 3 and 4

The following committees were constituted to measure the poverty line in India:

- **Lakdawala Committee**: Constituted in **1993**, the Lakdawala Committee recommended that the poverty line should be based on consumption expenditure needed to obtain minimum calorie requirements and other basic needs, using state-specific price indices.
- **Tendulkar Committee**: The Tendulkar Committee was established in **2005** to review the methodology for poverty estimation. It recommended moving away from a purely calorie-based definition of poverty to a broader definition that includes expenditure on health, education, and other essentials.
- **Rangarajan Committee**: Constituted in 2012, the Rangarajan Committee was tasked with reviewing the poverty estimation methodology. It proposed a new poverty line based on a broader set of consumption requirements, including food, education, health, clothing, and shelter.
- **Hashim Committee**: The Hashim Committee was an expert group established by the Planning Commission of India in 2010 to develop a methodology for identifying Below Poverty Line (BPL) households in urban areas.

**Therefore, the correct answer is (d) 1, 2, 3 and 4**

***17.*** (*b*) 1 and 3 only

The Poverty Line Basket (PLB) is crucial in determining the poverty line in India and includes a selection of goods and services essential for basic needs. However, **the price levels in the PLB vary from state to state due to differences in cost of living.**

- **Statement 1 is correct**: The Poverty Line Basket (PLB) includes a basket of goods and services necessary to meet basic human needs, such as food, clothing, shelter, health, and education.

- **Statement 2 is incorrect:** The price levels for consumption in the PLB are not uniform across all states in India.
- **Statement 3 is correct:** The Poverty Line Basket (PLB) concept was first introduced by the Alagh Committee in the 1970s which constructed separate poverty lines for rural and urban areas based on nutritional requirements and consumption expenditure.

**Therefore, the correct answer is (b) 1 and 3 only.**

***18.*** (*a*) 2-3-1-4

- **Alagh Committee (1979):** The first committee to estimate the poverty line in India.
- **Lakdawala Committee (1993):** Revised the methodology for poverty estimation.
- **Tendulkar Committee (2005):** Recommended a broader approach to poverty measurement.
- **Rangarajan Committee (2012):** Further revised the poverty line estimation.

**Thus, option (a) is the correct answer.**

***19.*** (*b*) Only two

- **Statement 1 is correct:** The **Tendulkar Committee** recommended shifting from a strictly calorie-based poverty line to a poverty line based on **consumption expenditure.** This approach considers a broader range of needs, including food, education, and health, rather than just calorie intake.
- **Statement 2 is correct:** The committee proposed a **uniform poverty** line across rural and urban areas in India, based on a common consumption basket, adjusted for price differences between rural and urban areas. This was a departure from previous methods that used separate poverty lines for rural and urban areas.
- **Statement 3 is incorrect:** The Tendulkar Committee did not introduce the concept of **multi-dimensional poverty** in India. It was developed later by the UNDP and OPHI.

**Thus, option (b) is the correct answer.**

***20.*** (*c*) Both 1 and 2

- **Statement 1 is correct:** Both the **Tendulkar Committee** (2009) and the **Rangarajan Committee** (2014) recommended a shift from the earlier calorie-based approach of estimating poverty, which focused on food intake, to a broader measure of **consumption expenditure.** This broader measure includes essential items such as **health, education, and clothing,** in addition to food, reflecting a more holistic view of the cost of living and poverty.
- **Statement 2 is correct:** The **Tendulkar Committee** proposed a **uniform poverty line** across rural and urban areas, reflecting differences in living standards but using the same threshold for both. On the other hand, the **Rangarajan Committee** recommended separate poverty lines for rural and urban areas to better capture the distinct cost of living and consumption patterns in these regions.

**Thus, option (c) is the correct answer.**

***21.*** (*b*) The physical activities commonly performed in rural areas, such as farming and other forms of manual labour, require more energy which increases the calorie needs of rural populations compared to their urban counterparts.

**Thus, option (b) is the correct answer.**

***22.*** (*d*) 1, 2, 3 and 4

The **Tendulkar Committee** recommended a comprehensive approach to poverty estimation that included several components beyond just calorie intake. It aimed to create a more realistic measure of poverty by considering multiple aspects of consumption expenditure.

**All four components** (health expenditure, education expenditure, nutritional requirements based on calorie intake, and clothing and footwear) were included in the poverty estimation methodology recommended by the Tendulkar Committee.

**Therefore, the correct answer is (d) 1, 2, 3 and 4.**

**23.** (*b*) 1 and 3 only

The National Sample Survey Office (NSSO), now part of the **National Statistical Office (NSO)** in India, uses various reference periods to collect consumption expenditure data during its surveys.

1. **URP**: A uniform 30-day recall period for all items; simpler but less accurate for infrequently purchased items.
2. **MRP**: Combines 30-day recall for frequent purchases and 365-day recall for infrequent purchases; more accurate and comprehensive.
3. **MMRP**: Further refines MRP by using a 7-day recall for perishables; enhances precision in food consumption data.

Currently, the **Modified Mixed Reference Period (MMRP)** method is use by the National Statistical Office (NSO) in India.

- **Statement 1 is correct**: URP collects consumption data using a 30-day recall period for all items, which can lead to consistent reporting across households.
- **Statement 2 is incorrect**: URP is less effective in capturing seasonal variations since it relies on a single recall period.
- **Statement 3 is correct**: URP tends to underreport the consumption of infrequently purchased items because it only considers a 30-day recall period, which may not accurately reflect purchases made less frequently.

**Thus, option (b) is the correct answer.**

**24.** (*a*) 1 and 2 only

- **Statement 1 is correct**: The MRP method uses a 30-day recall period for non-durable goods and a 365-day recall period for durable goods, helping to capture both frequent and infrequent purchases.
- **Statement 2 is correct**: MRP offers a more comprehensive view of consumption patterns by varying the recall periods for different types of goods, improving accuracy over the URP method.
- **Statement 3 is incorrect**: MRP does not use a uniform recall period. **Instead, it uses different recall periods** (30 days for non-durables and 365 days for durables) to more accurately capture consumption data.

**Thus, option (a) is the correct answer.**

**25.** (*d*) 1, 2 and 3

- **Statement 1 is correct**: The **labour force** includes all individuals within the working-age population (typically aged 15-64 years) who are either **employed** or **actively seeking employment.** This definition encompasses both those currently working and those who are unemployed but looking for work.
- **Statement 2 is correct**: The **Labor Force Participation Rate (LFPR)** is calculated as the percentage of the labour force within the working-age population. It represents the proportion of people who are actively engaged in the labour market, either by working or seeking work.
- **Statement 3 is correct**: The labour force **excludes** those who are not actively seeking work, such as students, homemakers, retirees, and individuals who are unable or unwilling to work.

**Therefore, the correct answer is (d) 1, 2 and 3.**

**26.** (*d*) 1, 2 and 3

- **Statement 1 is correct**: Full-time students who are not seeking employment are not included in the labour force.
- **Statement 2 is correct**: Retired individuals who are not seeking employment are also excluded from the labour force.
- **Statement 3 is correct**: Individuals engaged in unpaid domestic work, such as homemakers, are not considered part of the labour force unless they are actively seeking paid employment.

**Therefore, the correct answer is (d) 1, 2 and 3.**

**27.** (*a*) Only one

- **Statement 1 is incorrect**: The Code on Wages, 2019 applies to **all employees** in both the organised and unorganised sectors. It aims to ensure that all workers receive a **minimum wage**, irrespective of the sector they work in.
- **Statement 2 is incorrect**: While the **Central Government sets the national floor wage, the minimum wages are primarily set by the State Governments**, taking into account the local conditions.

- **Statement 3 is correct**: The Code on Wages, 2019, introduces the concept of a **National floor wage**, which serves as a baseline wage below which no state can set its minimum wage.

**Therefore, the correct answer is** (a) **Only one.**

***28.*** (*b*) Only two

- **Statement 1 is correct**: The **national floor wage** under the **Code on Wages, 2019** provides a **reference point** for states to set their minimum wages but does not mandate a uniform **minimum wage** across all states. Instead, it acts as a baseline below which no state can set its minimum wage, but states have the freedom to determine wages based on their local conditions.
- **Statement 2 is correct**: States are **permitted** to set their **minimum wages above** the national floor wage, but they **cannot set wages below** the floor wage. The national floor wage serves as a **minimum threshold,** ensuring that workers across the country receive a certain baseline wage, while states may adjust their rates higher depending on the cost of living and other factors.
- **Statement 3 is incorrect**: The **national floor wage** is not necessarily **revised annually** by the Central Government. While the wage is subject to periodic revision to account for changes in inflation and cost of living, there is no strict mandate for annual revisions. The frequency of revision is determined based on economic conditions and policy decisions.

**Therefore, the correct answer is (b) Only two.**

***29.*** (*a*) Only one pair

- **Pair 1 is incorrect**: The minimum wage is the **lowest legal wage** that employers are required to pay to workers as per government regulations. It is set to ensure that workers receive a fair wage for their labour.
- **Pair 2 is incorrect**: The floor wage is the **baseline wage set by the government below which no state can fix its minimum wage.** This ensures a uniform standard below which workers cannot be paid, serving as a national benchmark.
- **Pair 3 is correct**: The living wage is a wage that is **sufficient to cover the basic needs** of workers, ensuring a decent standard of living. It considers not just basic survival needs but also education, healthcare, and other essentials for a reasonable quality of life.

**Therefore, the correct answer is** (a) **Only one pair.**

***30.*** (*b*) Only two

- **Statement 1 is correct**: A Minimum Wage is the **legally mandated** lowest wage that employers must pay to workers to meet their basic needs.
- **Statement 2 is correct**: A Living Wage is intended to provide a **higher standard of living than a Minimum Wage,** covering not just basic needs but also allowing for savings and other essentials.
- **Statement 3 is incorrect**: The Indian Constitution does not explicitly recognise or mandate the concept of a Minimum Wage; however, **Article 43** of the Directive Principles of State Policy suggests that the State shall **endeavour to secure a living wage for all.** However, it is enforced under the **Minimum Wages Act, 1948,** and other labour laws.

**Therefore, the correct answer is (b) Only two.**

***31.*** (*a*) 1 and 2 only

- **Statement 1 is correct**: Government employees and those working in public sector undertakings (PSUs) are part of the formal workforce. They have official employment contracts, access to social security benefits, and regulated working conditions.
- **Statement 2 is correct**: Full-time employees in registered private companies also come under the formal workforce. These employees have formal employment contracts and are entitled to social security benefits, regulated wages, and working conditions as per labour laws.
- **Statement 3 is incorrect**: Daily wage labourers working without formal contracts are typically part of the informal workforce.

**Therefore, the correct answer is** (a) **1 and 2 only.**

**32.** (*a*) 1 and 2 only

- **Statement 1 is correct:** Employment governed by labour laws and regulations is characteristic of the formal workforce.
- **Statement 2 is correct:** Employees in the formal workforce receive regular salaries and benefits like health insurance and pensions.
- **Statement 3 incorrect:** The agriculture sector is primarily associated with informal employment, not formal.

**Therefore, the correct answer is (a) 1 and 2 only.**

**33.** (*c*) Both 1 and 2

The E-Shram portal is a government initiative in India aimed at creating a national database of unorganised workers, launched in August 2021 by the Ministry of Labour and Employment.

- **Statement 1 is correct:** The E-Shram portal is a government initiative designed to create a **comprehensive national database of unorganised workers**, which includes various categories of informal labour across the country.
- **Statement 2 is correct:** Registration on the E-Shram portal provides workers with an **accident insurance cover under the Pradhan Mantri Suraksha Bima Yojana (PMSBY).** The PMSBY provides accidental death and disability cover for registered unorganised workers, enhancing their social security.

According to PIB as of July 2024, more than **29.79 crore** unorganised workers have been registered under the **e-Shram portal** in India. The total number of people working in the unorganised sector was approximately **43.99 crore** during 2019-20 according to the Economic Survey 2021-22.

**Therefore, the correct answer is (c) Both 1 and 2.**

**34.** (*a*) 1 and 2 only

- **Statement 1 is correct:** Registration on the E-Shram portal provides unorganised workers with access to accident insurance under the Pradhan Mantri Suraksha Bima Yojana (PMSBY).
- **Statement 2 is correct:** Registered workers on the E-Shram portal **may receive priority access** to various government welfare schemes tailored for the unorganised sector.
- **Statement 3 is incorrect:** While the E-Shram portal provides various benefits, it **does not guarantee** a minimum wage as it is governed separately under labour laws and do not depend on E-Shram registration.

**Therefore, the correct answer is (a) 1 and 2 only.**

**35.** (*a*) 1 and 2 only

- **Statement 1 correct:** Food delivery personnel working for platforms like Swiggy or Zomato are part of the gig economy, as they work on a flexible and on-demand basis.
- **Statement 2 correct:** Consultants often work on a freelance or contractual basis for various clients, rather than being employed full-time by a single employer. Therefore, it also considered part of the gig workforce.
- **Statement 3 incorrect:** A factory worker employed under a permanent contract with full benefits does not fall under the gig economy, as this type of employment is traditional and structured.

**Therefore, the correct answer is (a) 1 and 2 only.**

**36.** (*b*) 2 only

- **Statement 1 is incorrect:** Gig workers are **not recognised as employees** under traditional Indian labour laws. They do not receive the same benefits as full-time employees, such as job security, health benefits, or paid leave.
- **Statement 2 is correct:** The **Code on Social Security, 2020 includes provisions for the social security of gig and platform workers.** It aims to provide them with access to social security benefits like health and maternity benefits, old age protection, and other welfare measures.
- **Statement 3 is incorrect:** Gig workers are **not entitled to benefits under the Employees' Provident Fund Act, 1952,** which covers traditional employees in formal employment. The EPF Act mandates retirement and pension benefits for workers classified as employees, which does not include gig workers.

**Therefore, the correct answer is (b) 2 only.**

**37.** (*c*) 3 only

- **Statement 1 is incorrect:** The **Code on Wages, 2019** does not mandate a minimum wage specifically for gig workers. It primarily covers employees in formal employment settings.
- **Statement 2 is incorrect:** There is no specific **Gig and Platform Workers Welfare Board** currently established under Indian law to address grievances and ensure the welfare of gig workers.
- **Statement 3 is correct:** The **Code on Social Security, 2020 includes provisions for the creation of a social security fund for gig and platform workers.** This fund aims to provide social security benefits such as health and maternity benefits, life and disability cover, and old age protection to gig workers.

**Therefore, the correct answer is (c) 3 only.**

**38.** (*c*) Both 1 and 2

- **Statement 1 is correct: Structural unemployment** arises when there is a mismatch between the skills of workers and the demands of the job market. This mismatch can occur due to changes in the economy, such as when certain industries decline while others grow, requiring different skills.
- **Statement 2 is correct:** Structural unemployment is often caused by **technological changes or shifts in the economy.** For example, technological advancements can render certain skills obsolete, while shifts in consumer demand or global trade can change the types of jobs available.

**Therefore, the correct answer is (c) Both 1 and 2.**

**39.** (*d*) All four pairs

- **Structural Unemployment - Example A: Correct.** Structural unemployment occurs when there is a long-term change in the economy that alters the demand for certain skills. Workers in coal mining losing jobs due to the shift to renewable energy.
- **Frictional Unemployment - Example B: Correct. Frictional unemployment** happens when workers are temporarily unemployed while transitioning from one job to another. A software engineer taking time off to find a better job is an example that involves a short-term break in employment.
- **Seasonal Unemployment - Example C: Correct.** Farm workers becoming unemployed after the harvest season is an example of seasonal unemployment because their jobs depend on specific seasons.
- **Cyclical Unemployment - Example D: Correct.** Cyclical unemployment is related to the business cycle and occurs during periods of economic downturn. Factory workers laid off during an economic recession exemplify cyclical unemployment.

**Therefore, the correct answer is (d) All four pairs.**

**40.** (*a*) Only one

- **Statement 1 is correct: Frictional unemployment** occurs when workers are temporarily between jobs while they search for new employment. This type of unemployment is often short-term and results from the normal job search process, career transitions, or moving to new locations.
- **Statement 2 is incorrect:** Frictional unemployment is **not typically a long-term form of unemployment.** It is generally short-term, as it arises from people transitioning between jobs.
- **Statement 3 is incorrect:** Frictional unemployment is **not generally higher during periods of economic recession.** In fact, during recessions, overall unemployment tends to rise due to cyclical factors, but **frictional unemployment may decrease as fewer people voluntarily leave their jobs to look for** new ones due to uncertainty in the job market.

**Therefore, the correct answer is (a) Only one.**

**41.** (*d*) 1, 2 and 3

- **Statement 1 is correct:** Seasonal unemployment occurs when workers are only employed during specific seasons or times of the year, such as during harvest season in agriculture.
- **Statement 2 is correct: Disguised unemployment** occurs when more people are employed than required, resulting in reduced productivity, as the additional workers do not

significantly contribute to output. Here MP is zero or very low.

- Marginal productivity is **zero** or **very low**. This means that adding more workers does not increase total output because the existing workforce is already sufficient to produce the maximum output possible with the given resources. This commonly found in the agricultural sector.

- **Statement 3 is correct:** Seasonal unemployment is common in industries like agriculture, tourism, and construction, where demand for labour fluctuates throughout the year.

**Therefore, the correct answer is (d) 1, 2 and 3.**

**42.** (*b*) Structural Unemployment

**Structural Unemployment** happens when there is a mismatch between the skills workers possess and the skills required by employers. In this case, the worker's job was made redundant due to **automation** and new **technological advancements.** As other companies in the industry are also adopting similar technologies, the worker is unable to find employment with their current skill set. This reflects a structural shift in the labour market, where certain types of jobs become obsolete due to innovation and technological changes.

**Thus, option (b) is the correct answer.**

**43.** (*c*) Unemployment in India is measured using various approaches and methods by National Statistical Office (NSO) under the **Ministry of Statistics and Programme Implementation (MoSPI).** The measurement is primarily done through periodic labour force surveys, which assess employment and unemployment status using different reference periods.

- Usual Principal Status (UPS)
- Current Weekly Status (CWS)
- Current Daily Status (CDS)
- **CWS** and **CDS** offer short-term perspectives, capturing weekly and daily employment status, respectively. The **Usual Principal Status (UPS)** approach is used to identify an individual's employment status over a long reference period, typically a year. This method helps to determine whether a person is employed or unemployed based on their primary activity status during that period.

**Thus, option (c) is the correct answer.**

**44.** (*a*) 1-A, 2-B, 3-C

- **Current Weekly Status (CWS):** The CWS approach estimates the proportion of the labour force that is unemployed over a short reference period of one week. It helps identify short-term unemployment by capturing whether individuals were without work and seeking employment during the week.
- **Usual Principal Status (UPS):** This approach captures the primary activity status of an individual over a longer reference period, usually a year. It identifies chronic or long-term unemployment.
- **Current Daily Status (CDS):** It tracks daily fluctuations in employment status, providing a detailed and comprehensive picture of labour force utilisation.

**Thus, the correct answer is (a) 1-A, 2-B, 3-C.**

**45.** (*b*) 1, 2 and 3 only

- **Periodic Labour Force Survey (PLFS) : Correct.** The PLFS is a **primary source** for measuring unemployment in India. It **provides quarterly estimates for urban areas** and annual estimates that cover both urban and rural areas of employment and unemployment along with labour force participation and worker population ratios.
- **Economic Census: Correct.** The Economic Census provides comprehensive data on all economic establishments in India, including those in the informal sector, which indirectly helps in assessing employment and unemployment levels.
- **Census of India: Correct.** The Census of India collects data on various socio-economic indicators, including employment and economic activity status. This data can be used to analyse employment trends, though it is not as focused on unemployment as the PLFS.
- **National Family Health Survey (NFHS): Incorrect.** The NFHS primarily collects data on health, nutrition, and population, and does not focus on measuring employment or unemployment.

**Therefore, the correct answer is (b) 1, 2 and 3 only.**

**46.** (*b*) Only two

- **Statement 1 is correct:** The **Economic Census** is conducted and published by the Ministry of Statistics and Programme Implementation (MoSPI).
- **Statement 2 is correct:** The Economic Census provides comprehensive data on all establishments in India, including those in both the formal and informal sectors.
- **Statement 3 is incorrect:** The Economic Census in India primarily covers **non-agricultural establishments** such as manufacturing, trade, services, and other non-agricultural sectors. It typically excludes agricultural activities and related operations, **except for activities related to agricultural services or processing units** that may be counted as part of the non-agricultural sector.
- The Economic Census provides **comprehensive data** on all economic establishments engaged in various economic activities **whereas Other Surveys (like PLFS, NSS Surveys, etc.) have specific focuses,** like employment status, consumer expenditure, health, education, and other socio-economic indicators.

**Therefore, the correct answer is (b) Only two.**

**47.** (*d*) 1, 2 and 3

- **Statement 1 is correct:** PLFS provides quarterly estimates of labour force indicators, including employment and unemployment, specifically for urban areas.
- **Statement 2 is correct: The PLFS replaced the Employment-Unemployment Survey (EUS)** conducted by the National Sample Survey Office (NSSO)**in 2017** as the primary source of labour market data in India. The PLFS offers more frequent and updated data compared to the EUS.
- **Statement 3 is correct:** PLFS provides **quarterly estimates for urban areas** and annual estimates that cover both urban and rural areas.

**Therefore, the correct answer is (d) 1, 2 and 3.**

**48.** (*b*) Only two

- **Statement 1 is correct:** According to the latest **PLFS data,** the **unemployment rate in urban areas** is consistently higher than in rural areas due to limited job opportunities in the formal sector and a higher percentage of educated individuals seeking jobs in urban areas.
- **Statement 2 is incorrect:** The unemployment rate for **females** is generally **higher** than that for males, particularly in urban areas, due to socio-economic factors, fewer job opportunities for women, and workforce participation gaps.
- **Statement 3 is correct:** The overall unemployment rate in India has shown a **declining trend** in recent years as the economy recovers from the disruptions caused by the pandemic.

**Therefore, the correct answer is (b) Only two.**

**49.** (*b*) 1, 2 and 4 only

- **National Rural Livelihoods Mission (NRLM): Correct.** The NRLM aims to reduce poverty by promoting diversified and gainful self-employment and skilled wage employment opportunities for rural poor households, particularly targeting women and marginalised communities.
- **Stand Up India Scheme: Correct.** The Stand-Up India scheme specifically focuses on empowering marginalised communities. It aimed at promoting entrepreneurship among women, Scheduled Castes (SC), and Scheduled Tribes (ST) by providing loans for setting up greenfield enterprises in the non-farm sector.
- **Swachh Bharat Abhiyan: Incorrect.** The Swachh Bharat Abhiyan is a nationwide campaign initiated to clean up the streets, roads, and infrastructure of India's cities and rural areas. It is not specifically targeted at improving livelihoods but rather aims at sanitation and hygiene.
- **Deen Dayal Upadhyaya Grameen Kaushalya Yojana (DDU-GKY): Correct.** The DDU-GKY focuses on providing skill training to rural youth from poor families, with a special emphasis on socially disadvantaged groups such as SC/ST and women, thereby improving their livelihood opportunities.

**Therefore, the correct answer is (b) 1, 2 and 4 only.**

**50.** (*b*) Only two

- **Statement 1 is correct:** The Mahatma Gandhi National Rural Employment Guarantee Act (MGNREGA) **guarantees 100 days of wage employment** per year to every rural household whose adult members volunteer to do unskilled manual work.
- **Statement 2 is incorrect:** The wages under MGNREGA are **not equal across all states in India.** The wage rates under MGNREGA are notified by the Central Government and can vary from state to state depending on various factors such as the cost of living and prevailing minimum wages in the state.
- **Statement 3 is correct:** MGNREGA does include provisions for the **creation of durable assets** in rural areas. The types of works permissible under MGNREGA are aimed at enhancing the livelihood resource base of rural areas, such as water conservation, drought-proofing, irrigation, and land development.

**Therefore, the correct answer is (b) Only two.**

**51.** (*b*) Only two

- **Statement 1 is correct:** MGNREGA mandates that at **least one-third of the beneficiaries should be women,** promoting gender equality in rural employment.
- **Statement 2 is incorrect:** MGNREGA is funded by both the **Central and State Governments,** with the **Central Government bearing the majority** of the cost.
- **Statement 3 is correct:** Social audits are a **mandatory** part of MGNREGA to ensure transparency, accountability, and public participation in monitoring the implementation of the scheme.

**Therefore, the correct answer is (b) Only two.**

**52.** (*c*) Only three

- **Statement 1 is correct: The Atal Pension Yojana** is indeed aimed primarily at workers in the **unorganised sector** to provide them with a guaranteed pension after retirement.
- **Statement 2 is incorrect:** The APY guarantees a pension ranging from ₹ 1,000 to ₹ 5,000 per month, depending on the contributions made by the subscriber and the age at which they join the scheme.
- **Statement 3 is correct:** Contributions to the APY are **eligible for tax benefits under Section 80C** of the Income Tax Act, providing additional financial incentives for saving for retirement.
- **Statement 4 is correct:** The **APY** is available to **all Indian citizens** between the ages of 18 and 40. Subscribers need to contribute for a minimum of 20 years or more to avail of the pension benefits after the age of 60 and who are **not part of any other formal pension scheme.**

**Therefore, the correct answer is (c) Only three.**

**53.** (*d*) 1, 3 and 4 only

- **Ravi:** Eligible. As a 25-year-old self-employed individual without any formal pension, within the eligible age **range of 18 to 40 years.**
- **Meena:** Not eligible. As is **already a member of the Employees' Provident Fund (EPF)** and is also above the maximum age limit of 40 years for enrolling in APY.
- **Anil:** Eligible. As a 35-year-old worker in the unorganised sector with no other pension benefits, Anil can enrol in APY.
- **Sunita:** Eligible. She is also eligible if she meets the eligibility criteria for both schemes because a person can invest in NPS and APY together, if they fulfil the eligibility criteria.

**Therefore, the correct answer is (d) 1, 3 and 4 only.**

**54.** (*b*) Only two

- **Statement 1 is correct: Pradhan Mantri Shram Yogi Maandhan (PMSYM)** is indeed a voluntary and contributory pension scheme aimed at providing social security to workers in the unorganised sector.
- **Statement 2 is correct:** The scheme provides a minimum assured pension of ₹ 3,000 per month after the beneficiary attains the age of 60.
- **Statement 3 is incorrect:** To be eligible for PMSYM, the monthly income of the beneficiary should **not exceed ₹ 15,000,** not ₹ 10,000.

**PMSYM:** Specifically targets workers in the **unorganised sector.** This includes street vendors, mid-day meal workers, head loaders, brick kiln workers, cobblers, rag picker etc.

Contributions are **fixed** based on the age of entry. Both the subscriber and the government contribute an **equal amount** to the pension fund.

**Eligibility Criteria**

- Available to **unorganised sector** workers aged **18 to 40 years.**
- The worker's **monthly income should not exceed ₹ 15,000.**
- The subscriber should not be covered under any other statutory social security schemes like **EPF, ESIC,** or **NPS**, and should not be an income tax payer.

- Administered by the **Life Insurance Corporation of India (LIC)** and overseen by the Ministry of Labour and Employment whereas **APY** administered by the **Pension Fund Regulatory and Development Authority** (PFRDA) and overseen by the Ministry of Finance.

**Therefore, the correct answer is (b) Only two.**

**55.** (*c*) All three

- **Statement 1 is correct: The Code on Wages, 2019**, consolidates and simplifies four previous labour laws related to wages: the Payment of Wages Act, 1936; the Minimum Wages Act, 1948; the Payment of Bonus Act, 1965; and the Equal Remuneration Act, 1976.
  - It covers regulations related to minimum wages, payment of wages, and **equal remuneration for all workers** in India.
- **Statement 2 is correct: The Industrial Relations Code, 2020**, consolidates three previous laws: the Trade Unions Act, 1926; the Industrial Employment (Standing Orders) Act, 1946; and the Industrial Disputes Act, 1947.
  - This code governs the rules and regulations regarding trade unions, industrial disputes, standing orders, and conditions of employment in industrial establishments.
- **Statement 3 is correct: The Code on Social Security, 2020**, aims to extend social security benefits to all employees and workers, including those in the unorganised sector, **gig workers, and platform workers.**
  - It consolidates nine laws related to social security, including the Employees' Provident Funds Act, 1952, the Employees' State Insurance Act, 1948, and the Unorganised Workers' Social Security Act, 2008.

**Therefore, the correct answer is (c) All three.**

**56.** (*b*) Only two

- **Statement 1 is correct**: The Code on Wages, 2019, includes provisions for ensuring **equal** remuneration for men and women performing work of a similar nature.
- **Statement 2 is incorrect**: The minimum wages under the Code **apply to both public and private sector** workers, covering a broad range of employment types.
- **Statement 3 is correct**: The Code on Wages provides for the **Constitution of advisory boards at both the central and state levels** to recommend minimum wages and ensure fair wage practices.

**Therefore, the correct answer is (b) Only two.**

**57.** (c) Both 1 and 2

- **Statement 1 is correct**: The Occupational Safety, Health, and Working Conditions Code, 2020 mandates that employers provide **safe working conditions and welfare measures for workers**

  The code consolidates various laws relating to occupational safety, health, and working conditions, ensuring that workplaces adhere to standards that protect the health and safety of workers.
- **Statement 2 is correct**: The Code on Social Security, 2020 includes provisions for **maternity benefits and employee provident funds among other social security benefits.**

**Therefore, the correct answer is (c) Both 1 and 2.**

## Past Learning (Answers)

1 (b) 2 (c) 3 (d) 4 (b) 5 (b) 6 (c) 7 (c) 8 (a)

CHAPTER 04

# Public Finance-Fiscal Policy

## Assessment Round

### Topic 1 : Types of Fiscal Policy

**1.** Consider the following actions:

1. Increasing income taxes for high-income earners
2. Adjusting the central bank's interest rate to influence lending
3. Providing subsidies for renewable energy projects
4. Reducing the corporate tax rate to attract business investment

How many of the given above actions fall under fiscal policy?

(a) Only one
(b) Only two
(c) Only three
(d) All four

**2.** In the context of Indian economy, which of the following measures would be considered an 'Expansionary Fiscal Policy'?

1. Increasing government spending on infrastructure projects.
2. Reducing corporate tax rates to stimulate business investment.
3. Introducing new subsidies for agricultural inputs.

Select the correct answer from the codes given below:

(a) 1, 2 and 3
(b) 1 and 3 only
(c) 2 and 3 only
(d) 1 and 2 only

**3.** Consider the following pairs:

| List I (Fiscal Measures) | List II (Type of Fiscal Policy) |
|---|---|
| 1. Increased defence spending | Expansionary |
| 2. Cutting back on social welfare programmes | Contractionary |
| 3. Increasing excise duties on luxury goods | Contractionary |
| 4. Higher exemption in the income tax rates | Expansionary |

How many of the given above pairs is/are correctly matched?

(a) Only one pair
(b) Only two pairs
(c) Only three pairs
(d) All four pairs

**4.** With reference to the 'Pro-cyclical Fiscal Policy', consider the following statements:

1. This policy refers to the government's action of increasing spending during economic booms and cutting spending during the recession period.
2. This type of policy tends to reinforce the current economic trend, potentially exacerbating economic volatility.

Which of the statements given above is/are correct?

(a) 1 only
(b) 2 only
(c) Both 1 and 2
(d) Neither 1 nor 2

**5.** Consider the following fiscal measures:

1. Increasing government spending on infrastructure during a recession.
2. Reducing income tax rates during a period of economic expansion.
3. Implementing austerity measures during an economic boom.

How many of the given above is/are the examples of 'Counter-cyclical Fiscal Policies'?

(a) Only one (b) Only two
(c) All three (d) None

## Topic 2 : Budget

**6.** With reference to the 'Budgetary Process in India', consider the following statements:

1. The Union Budget is presented by the Finance Minister on the last week of February every year.
2. The Finance Bill is introduced and passed by the Rajya Sabha before being sent to the Lok Sabha for voting.
3. The Appropriation Bill legally authorises the government to withdraw funds from the Consolidated Fund of India (CFI).

Which of the given above statements is/are correct?

(a) 1 and 2 only (b) 2 and 3 only
(c) 3 only (d) 1, 2 and 3

**7.** Consider the following statements:

1. Indian Constitution confers responsibility upon the Minister of Finance to ensure that Budget is laid before both House of Parliament.
2. Public Accounts of India and the Contingency Fund of India are not subject to the vote of Parliament.

Which of the statements given above is/are correct?

(a) 1 only (b) 2 only
(c) Both 1 and 2 (d) Neither 1 nor 2

**8.** Consider the following statements about 'Demand for Grants':

1. Demand for Grants is presented to the Lok Sabha and includes both charged and non-charged expenditures.
2. Rajya Sabha has the power to vote on the Demand for Grants presented in the budget.
3. Guillotine process ensures that all demands are discussed in detail before being put to vote.

Which of the statements given above is/are correct?

(a) 1 and 2 only (b) 2 and 3 only
(c) 1 only (d) 1 and 3 only

**9.** Consider the following statements:

1. The National Informatics Centre (NIC) helps the budget division in the process of consolidation of the budget data.
2. Department of Revenue under the Ministry of Finance is responsible for the formulation of Budget.

Which of the given above statements is/are Incorrect?

(a) 1 only (b) 2 only
(c) Both 1 and 2 (d) Neither 1 nor 2

**10.** Which of the following estimates are presented in the Budget Document?

1. Budget Estimates of the next financial year
2. Revised Estimates of the ongoing financial year
3. Actual Estimates of the previous financial year

Select the correct answer from the codes given below :

(a) 1 only (b) 1 and 2 only
(c) 1 and 3 only (d) 1, 2 and 3

**11.** Which of the following statements are correct about the 'Consolidated Fund of India' under the Indian Constitution?

1. It includes all revenues received by the Government of India.
2. It is the source of all government expenditures, including charged expenditures that do not require parliamentary approval.
3. It includes all borrowings and loans received by the government.
4. It cannot be used for making payments without the prior approval of Parliament.

Select the correct answer using the codes given below:

(a) 1, 2 and 3 (b) 1, 3 and 4
(c) 2 and 4 only (d) 1, 2, 3 and 4

**12.** Which of the following receipts goes to the 'Public Account of India'?
1. Post Office Savings Account
2. Kisan Vikas Patra
3. Sukanya Samriddhi Account
4. Public Provident Fund

Select the correct answer from the codes given below:
(a) 1 and 4 only (b) 2 and 3 only
(c) 2, 3 and 4 only (d) 1, 2, 3 and 4

**13.** With reference to Gender Budgeting in India, consider the following statements:
1. Ministry of Women and Child Development is the nodal agency for Gender Budgeting in India.
2. It provides a separate budget for women.
3. Gender Budgeting in India was first introduced in the Union Budget of 2007-08.

Which of the statements given above are correct?
(a) 1 only (b) 2 and 3 only
(c) 1 and 3 only (d) 1, 2 and 3

**14.** Which of the following best describes a key distinction between Zero-Based Budgeting (ZBB) and Outcome Budgeting?
(a) ZBB involves justifying all expenses each budget cycle, while Outcome Budgeting focuses on aligning spending with desired results or objectives.
(b) ZBB requires only incremental adjustments to previous budgets, while Outcome Budgeting involves analyzing every expense from scratch.
(c) ZBB emphasises long-term projects exclusively, whereas Outcome Budgeting is based on short-term goals.
(d) ZBB is more suitable for corporate settings, while Outcome Budgeting is exclusively for government use.

## Topic 3 : Components of Budget

**15.** Consider the following budget components:
1. Grants-in-aid to state governments.
2. Expenditure on defence equipment.
3. Repayment of public debt.
4. Salaries of government employees.

How many of the given above is/are included in the Revenue Budget?
(a) Only one (b) Only two
(c) Only three (d) All four

**16.** Which of the following does not fall under the category of 'Capital Receipts'?
1. Borrowing by the government from Reserve Bank.
2. Loans received from foreign governments and international organisation.
3. Interest and dividend on investments made by the government.
4. Deposits in Post-Office Savings Accounts.

Select the correct answer from the codes given below:
(a) 3 only (b) 3 and 4 only
(c) 1, 2 and 3 (d) 2 and 3 only

**17.** With reference to the 'Revenue Expenditure' of the government, consider the following statements:
1. It is provided in every annual budget of the government.
2. Some part of revenue expenditure can be used for creation of physical assets.
3. Interest payments on debt incurred by the government do not form part of revenue expenditure.

Which of the statements given above is/are correct?
(a) 1 and 2 only (b) 3 only
(c) 2 and 3 only (d) 1, 2 and 3

**18.** Consider the following items:
1. Interest payment on Debt
2. Grants given to the State Government
3. Salaries of Employees
4. Subsidies
5. Pensions

Which of the given above are the main items of 'Revenue Expenditure'?
(a) 3, 4 and 5 only (b) 1, 3 and 5 only
(c) 1, 2, 3, 4 and 5 (d) 1 and 4 only

**19.** Which of the following are the components of 'Capital Expenditure'?

1. Expenditure on the acquisition of land.
2. Loans given by the central government to state governments.
3. Repayment of loans to international financial institutions.
4. Grants-in-aid for the creation of capital assets.

Select the correct answer from the codes given below:

(a) 1 and 2 only (b) 1, 2 and 3 only
(c) 2 and 4 only (d) 1, 2, 3 and 4

**20.** Which of the following is/are part of 'Non-Tax Revenue Receipts'?

1. Dividends paid by PSUs and RBI to government
2. License fee received by the government
3. Disinvestment of shares of PSUs

Select the correct answer from the codes given below:

(a) 2 only (b) 1 and 3 only
(c) 1 and 2 only (d) 1, 2 and 3

**21.** Consider the following pairs:

| Budget Component | Example |
|---|---|
| 1. Revenue Receipts | Interest income from loans given by the government |
| 2. Capital Receipts | Proceeds from the disinvestment of public sector units |
| 3. Revenue Expenditure | Salaries paid to government employees |
| 4. Capital Expenditure | Construction of highways and bridges |

How many pairs given above is/are correctly matched?

(a) Only one pair
(b) Only two pairs
(c) Only three pairs
(d) All four pairs

**22.** In the context of the Union Budget, which of the following are included in 'Effective Capital Expenditure'?

1. Grants-in-aid given to state governments for the creation of capital assets.
2. Expenditure on defence equipment and infrastructure.
3. Interest payments on government borrowings.
4. Expenditure on social sector schemes like health and education.

Select the correct answer from the codes given below:

(a) 1 and 2 only (b) 3 and 4 only
(c) 1, 2 and 4 only (d) 1, 2, 3 and 4

## Topic 4 : Types of Deficits and Deficit Financing

**23.** Consider the following statements:

1. Revenue deficit refers to the excess of government's revenue expenditure over revenue receipts.
2. Fiscal deficit is the difference between the government's total expenditure and its total receipts excluding borrowing.
3. Primary deficit is the fiscal deficit of current year excluding interest liabilities on previous borrowings.

How many of the given above statements is/are correct?

(a) Only one (b) Only two
(c) All three (d) None

**24.** Which of the following could be the possible implications of government incurring a 'Revenue Deficit'?

1. Government is dissaving and using savings of the other sectors of economy.
2. Higher fiscal deficit of the government.
3. Government borrowings will also be used for consumption requirements.

Select the correct answer from the codes given below:

(a) 3 only (b) 1 and 2 only
(c) 1, 2 and 3 (d) 2 and 3 only

**25.** Government of India wants to reduce Revenue deficit without creating liabilities. For this it asked general public to provide viable solutions. As a concerned citizen, which of the following will be your advice?

1. Printing more money by RBI
2. Borrowing from foreign countries
3. Increasing direct taxes
4. Rationalisation of Subsidies

Select the correct answer using the codes given below:

(a) 1, 2 and 4 only (b) 2 and 4 only
(c) 3 and 4 only (d) 1 and 2 only

**26.** Which of the following components are included in the calculation of the Fiscal Deficit?

1. Capital Expenditure 2. Interest Payments
3. Revenue Receipts 4. Borrowings

Select the correct answer using the codes given below:

(a) 1, 2 and 3 only (b) 1, 3 and 4 only
(c) 1, 2, 3 and 4 (d) 1, 2 and 4 only

**27.** With reference to the 'Effective Revenue Deficit (ERD)', consider the following statements:

1. The deficit excludes grants for capital asset creation, providing a clearer measure of the government's revenue shortfall.
2. A high Effective Revenue Deficit over multiple years indicates that a significant portion of the government's expenditure is non-productive.

Which of the statements given above is/are correct?

(a) 1 only (b) 2 only
(c) Both 1 and 2 (d) Neither 1 nor 2

**28.** With reference to the 'Monetised Deficit', consider the following statements:

1. Monetised Deficit is an indicator of the extent to which the government is relying on the central bank to finance its deficit by printing money.
2. It directly increases the money supply in the economy.
3. A high Monetised Deficit can lead to deflationary pressures in the economy.

How many of the statements given above is/are correct?

(a) Only one (b) Only two
(c) All three (d) None

**29.** Consider the following methods:

1. Printing currency (monetisation of the deficit)
2. Borrowing from the public through the sale of bonds
3. Borrowing from international markets
4. Reducing public expenditure

Which of the given above can be the sources of 'Deficit Financing'?

(a) 1, 2 and 3 only (b) 1 and 3 only
(c) 2 and 4 only (d) 1, 2, 3 and 4

**30.** Which of the following are potential outcomes of extensive Deficit Financing?

1. Increase in inflation
2. Higher public debt
3. Crowding out of private investment
4. Increase in foreign exchange reserves

Select the correct answer using the codes given below:

(a) 1 and 2 only (b) 1, 2 and 3 only
(c) 3 and 4 only (d) 1, 2, 3 and 4

**31.** Consider the following pairs of the types of deficit and their purposes:

| Deficit Type | Purpose |
|---|---|
| 1. Fiscal Deficit | Indicates total borrowing needs of the government. |
| 2. Primary Deficit | Shows the deficit without interest liabilities, highlighting fresh borrowing. |
| 3. Revenue Deficit | Reflects shortfall in government's operational receipts versus expenses. |
| 4. Effective Revenue Deficit | Adjusts revenue deficit by excluding capital-creating grants to states. |

How many of the given above pairs is/are correctly matched?

(a) Only one pair (b) Only two pairs
(c) Only three pairs (d) All four pairs

## Topic 5 : Fiscal Consolidation

**32.** Consider the following fiscal measures:

1. Increasing excise duties on luxury goods.
2. Introducing austerity measures in public spending.
3. Implementing a universal basic income scheme.
4. Privatising non-strategic public sector enterprises.

How many of the given above measures is/are typically associated with 'Fiscal Consolidation'?

(a) Only one (b) Only two
(c) Only three (d) All four

**33.** Consider the following factors:

1. Slower-than-expected economic growth
2. Increase in tax rates on corporate income
3. Higher-than-budgeted spending on welfare programmes
4. Inadequate monitoring of government projects

How many of the given above factors is/are likely causes of fiscal slippage?

(a) Only one (b) Only two
(c) Only three (d) All four

**34.** Which of the following measures can lead to the reduction of fiscal deficit?

1. Rationalisation of subsidies
2. Higher exemption limits in the income tax regime
3. Enhancing tax compliance through digitisation and better enforcement
4. Introduction of tax on virtual digital assets

Select the correct answer from the codes given below:

(a) 2 and 3 only (b) 1, 2 and 4 only
(c) 1, 3 and 4 only (d) 1, 2, 3 and 4

**35.** Which of the following documents are tabled in the Parliament along with 'Annual Financial Statement (AFS)'?

1. Medium-term Fiscal Policy Statement
2. Fiscal Policy Strategy Statement
3. Macroeconomic Framework Statement
4. Economic Survey of India

Select the correct answer from the codes given below:

(a) 1 only (b) 1 and 2 only
(c) 1, 2 and 3 only (d) 1, 2, 3 and 4

**36.** Which of the following committee was constituted to review the implementation of 'Fiscal Responsibility and Budget Management Act, 2003'?

(a) NK Singh Committee
(b) Arvind Subramanian Committee
(c) Urjit Patel Committee
(d) Rathin Roy Committee

**37.** Consider the following statements with reference to the 'Fiscal Responsibility and Management Act (FRBM)':

1. FRBM Act applies to both the central government and state governments.
2. FRBM Act provide for Fiscal Council that is responsible for the administration of the fiscal rules.
3. NK Singh Committee recommended fiscal deficit target range rather than absolute target.

Which of the given above statements is/are correct?

(a) 1 only (b) 1 and 3 only
(c) 2 and 3 only (d) None of these

**38.** Which of the following are provisions under the 'Fiscal Responsibility and Budget Management (FRBM) Act, 2003'?

1. Setting targets for the reduction of the fiscal deficit and revenue deficit.
2. Introduction of a Medium-Term Fiscal Policy Statement to be presented annually in Parliament.
3. Banning the Reserve Bank of India (RBI) from purchasing primary issuance of central government securities.
4. Establishing 'escape clauses' that allow deviations from fiscal targets under specific conditions.

Select the correct answer from the codes given below:

(a) 1 and 2 only (b) 2 and 4 only
(c) 1, 3 and 4 only (d) 1, 2, 3 and 4

**39.** With reference to the 'FRBM Amendment Act, 2012', consider the following statements:
1. The amendment introduced the concept of Effective Revenue Deficit.
2. The amendment mandated presenting a Medium-Term Expenditure Framework Statement annually.
3. The amendment set a fixed target of reducing the fiscal deficit to 3% of GDP by 2015.

Which of the statements given above are correct?
(a) 1 and 2 only
(b) 1 and 3 only
(c) 2 and 3 only
(d) 1, 2 and 3

## Topic 6 : Total Liabilities of the Government

**40.** With reference to public debt, consider the following statements:
1. Public debt includes all borrowings by the government from both internal and external sources.
2. The central government's public debt is managed by the Reserve Bank of India (RBI).
3. Public debt is classified into two categories: marketable debt and non-marketable debt.

How many of the statements given above is/are correct?
(a) Only one (b) Only two
(c) All three (d) None

**41.** Which of the following are considered components of public debt in India?
1. Treasury Bills
2. External loans from foreign governments
3. Special securities issued to financial institutions
4. Tax Revenues

Select the correct answer using the codes given below:
(a) 1 and 2 only
(b) 1, 2 and 3 only
(c) 2 and 4 only
(d) 1, 2, 3 and 4

**42.** With reference to public debt management, consider the following statements:
1. Marketable debt can be traded in the secondary market, providing liquidity to investors.
2. Non-marketable debt includes borrowings like National Savings Certificates (NSCs) and Provident Funds.
3. The government can only borrow externally from multilateral institutions like the IMF and World Bank.

Which of the statements given above are correct?
(a) 1 and 2 only
(b) 2 and 3 only
(c) 1 and 3 only
(d) 1, 2 and 3

**43.** Consider the following types of government borrowings:
1. Sovereign Bonds issued in international markets
2. Loans from the Reserve Bank of India (RBI)
3. Government Savings Bonds
4. Receipts from disinvestment of public sector enterprises

How many of the above is/are considered part of public debt?
(a) Only one (b) Only two
(c) Only three (d) All four

**44.** With reference to the 'Public Debt in India', consider the following statements:
1. India's public debt is primarily composed of internal debt, which is raised through government securities.
2. External debt constitutes a small percentage of India's total public debt.
3. The interest payments on India's public debt form a significant part of the government's revenue expenditure.

Which of the statements given above are correct?
(a) 1 and 2 only
(b) 2 and 3 only
(c) 1 and 3 only
(d) 1, 2 and 3

**45.** With reference to public debt trends in India, consider the following statements:

1. India has a higher proportion of marketable debt compared to non-marketable debt.
2. India's public debt is predominantly long-term, reducing the risk of refinancing in the short term.

Which of the statements given above is/are correct?

(a) 1 only (b) 2 only
(c) Both 1 and 2 (d) Neither 1 nor 2

**46.** Which of the following entities are typically allowed to subscribe to India's government securities (public debt)?

1. Commercial banks
2. Insurance companies
3. Foreign Institutional Investors (FIIs)
4. Non-resident Indians (NRIs)

Select the correct answer from the codes given below:

(a) 1 and 2 only (b) 2 and 3 only
(c) 1, 2 and 4 only (d) 1, 2, 3 and 4

**47.** Consider the following statements about the 'India's Public Debt':

1. India's public debt has consistently been below 50% of GDP in the last decade.
2. India's external public debt is largely denominated in Indian rupees to minimize exchange rate risks.

Which of the statements given above is/are correct?

(a) 1 only
(b) 2 only
(c) Both 1 and 2
(d) Neither 1 nor 2

**48.** What is a significant implication of a negative Interest Rate - Growth Differential (IRGD) for a country's debt management?

(a) It can help reduce the debt-to-GDP ratio
(b) It implies a higher GDP growth rate than borrowing costs
(c) It indicates that debt accumulation could increase due to higher interest burdens
(d) It results in lower fiscal deficit requirements

**49.** Which of the following are considered non-marketable debt instruments in India?

1. Provident Fund Deposits
2. National Savings Certificates (NSCs)
3. Treasury Bills issued through auctions
4. Special Securities issued to the RBI

Select the correct answer from the codes given below:

(a) 1 and 2 only
(b) 1, 2 and 4 only
(c) 3 and 4 only
(d) 1, 2, 3 and 4

**50.** Which of the following are classified as public account liabilities under the Government of India's financial system?

1. National Small Savings Fund (NSSF)
2. Central Government Loans
3. Deposits under the Public Provident Fund (PPF)
4. Securities issued against Small Savings

Select the correct answer from the codes given below:

(a) 1 and 3 only
(b) 1, 3 and 4 only
(c) 2 and 4 only
(d) 1, 2, 3 and 4

**51.** With reference to the 'Extra-Budgetary Resources (EBRs)' in India, consider the following statements:

1. EBRs are funds raised by the government through public sector enterprises or special purpose vehicles without reflecting in the Union Budget.
2. These are used to finance public sector projects without increasing the fiscal deficit.
3. EBRs are fully accounted for in the government's fiscal deficit calculation.

How many of the statements given above is/are correct?

(a) Only one
(b) Only two
(c) All three
(d) None

**52.** With reference to the Ways and Means Advances (WMA) provided by the Reserve Bank of India (RBI), consider the following statements:

1. WMAs are provided to both the central and state governments by the Reserve Bank of India.
2. The interest rate on WMA is always higher than the market borrowing rate for government securities.
3. The government must repay the WMA within a specified period, after which it is treated as an overdraft.

How many of the statements given above is/are correct?

(a) Only one (b) Only two
(c) All three (d) None

**53.** With reference to the 'Small Saving Schemes' in India, consider the following statements:

1. The interest rates on small saving schemes are revised quarterly by the government.
2. The principal and interest earned from investments in small saving schemes are exempt from taxation under the Income Tax Act.

Which of the statements given above is/are correct?

(a) 1 only (b) 2 only
(c) Both 1 and 2 (d) Neither 1 nor 2

**54.** Which of the following statements correctly describe about the 'National Small Savings Fund (NSSF)'?

1. NSSF acts as a depository for the funds collected through small saving schemes like Public Provident Fund (PPF), Kisan Vikas Patra, etc.
2. The fund is used to provide loans to the central and state governments.
3. The returns generated by the NSSF are distributed to the contributors of small saving schemes annually.
4. NSSF is managed by the Reserve Bank of India (RBI).

Select the correct answer from the codes given below:

(a) 1 and 2 only (b) 1, 2, and 3 only
(c) 2 and 4 only (d) 1, 2, 3 and 4

**55.** With reference to the borrowing powers of the central and state governments in India, consider the following statements:

1. The central government has the exclusive power to borrow funds on the security of the Consolidated Fund of India.
2. States require the approval of the central government to borrow if they are indebted to it.
3. Both central and state governments can borrow from external sources without restrictions.

Which of the statements given above are correct?

(a) 1 and 2 only (b) 1 and 3 only
(c) 2 and 3 only (d) 1, 2 and 3

**56.** Which of the following were key recommendations made by the '15th Finance Commission'?

1. Devolution of 41% of the divisible pool of taxes to the states.
2. Introduction of performance-based incentives for states in areas such as power sector reforms and solid waste management.
3. Establishment of a non-lapsable fund for defence and internal security.

Select the correct answer from the codes given below:

(a) 1 and 2 only
(b) 2 and 3 only
(c) 1 and 3 only
(d) 1, 2 and 3

**57.** Which of the following criteria were used by the 15th Finance Commission for the distribution of tax revenues among the states?

1. Population
2. Forest and Ecology
3. Demographic Performance
4. Income Distance

Select the correct answer from the codes given below:

(a) 1 and 3 only
(b) 1, 2 and 4 only
(c) 2, 3 and 4 only
(d) 1, 2, 3 and 4

**58.** Which of the following factor distinguishes the 16th Finance Commission from previous Finance Commissions?
(a) It will solely focus on improving states' revenue collection mechanisms.
(b) It will incorporate climate change impacts into its fiscal recommendations for the first time.
(c) It will completely revise the tax-sharing formula between the central and state governments.
(d) It will exclude considerations of demographic changes when making recommendations for resource allocation.

**59.** With reference to the differences between statutory and discretionary grants in India, consider the following statements:
1. Statutory grants are constitutionally required and are generally formula-based.
2. Discretionary grants are allocated by the central government at its discretion and may vary each year.
3. Statutory grants must be approved by Parliament annually, while discretionary grants do not require parliamentary approval.

Which of the statements given above are correct?
(a) 1 and 2 only
(b) 2 and 3 only
(c) 1 and 3 only
(d) 1, 2 and 3

## Topic 7 : Disinvestment

**60.** With reference to the disinvestment policy of the Government of India, consider the following statements:
1. Disinvestment refers to the government's sale or liquidation of its equity in public sector enterprises (PSEs).
2. The proceeds from disinvestment are used exclusively for reducing the fiscal deficit.
3. Strategic disinvestment involves the sale of a substantial portion of the government's shareholding in a PSE along with the transfer of management control.

Which of the statements given above are correct?
(a) 1 and 2 only (b) 1 and 3 only
(c) 2 and 3 only (d) 1, 2 and 3

**61.** With reference to the 'Disinvestment in India', consider the following statements:
1. Minority disinvestment occurs when the government retains a majority stake in the public sector enterprise after selling a portion of its equity.
2. The Department of Investment and Public Asset Management (DIPAM) is responsible for managing disinvestment in India.
3. Disinvestment always leads to the privatization of public sector enterprises.

Which of the statements given above are correct?
(a) 1 and 2 only (b) 1 and 3 only
(c) 2 and 3 only (d) 1, 2 and 3

**62.** Which of the following are considered strategic sectors under the Government of India's Disinvestment policy?
1. Atomic energy
2. Railways
3. Banking and Insurance
4. Defence

Select the correct answer from the codes given below:
(a) 1 and 2 only (b) 3 and 4 only
(c) 1, 3 and 4 only (d) 1, 2, 3 and 4

**63.** Consider the following statements about the Government of India's disinvestment policy:
1. In strategic sectors, the government will maintain a bare minimum presence with the remaining stake being disinvested.
2. In non-strategic sectors, the government aims to completely exit by selling its entire stake.
3. Strategic disinvestment in non-strategic sectors is aimed at boosting efficiency and encouraging private sector participation.

Which of the following statements are correct?
(a) 1 and 2 only (b) 2 and 3 only
(c) 1 and 3 only (d) 1, 2 and 3

# OMR SHEET

**Assessment Round**

| | | | | | | | |
|---|---|---|---|---|---|---|---|
| 1 | ⓐ ⓑ ⓒ ⓓ | 31 | ⓐ ⓑ ⓒ ⓓ | 61 | ⓐ ⓑ ⓒ ⓓ | 91 | ⓐ ⓑ ⓒ ⓓ |
| 2 | ⓐ ⓑ ⓒ ⓓ | 32 | ⓐ ⓑ ⓒ ⓓ | 62 | ⓐ ⓑ ⓒ ⓓ | 92 | ⓐ ⓑ ⓒ ⓓ |
| 3 | ⓐ ⓑ ⓒ ⓓ | 33 | ⓐ ⓑ ⓒ ⓓ | 63 | ⓐ ⓑ ⓒ ⓓ | 93 | ⓐ ⓑ ⓒ ⓓ |
| 4 | ⓐ ⓑ ⓒ ⓓ | 34 | ⓐ ⓑ ⓒ ⓓ | 64 | ⓐ ⓑ ⓒ ⓓ | 94 | ⓐ ⓑ ⓒ ⓓ |
| 5 | ⓐ ⓑ ⓒ ⓓ | 35 | ⓐ ⓑ ⓒ ⓓ | 65 | ⓐ ⓑ ⓒ ⓓ | 95 | ⓐ ⓑ ⓒ ⓓ |
| 6 | ⓐ ⓑ ⓒ ⓓ | 36 | ⓐ ⓑ ⓒ ⓓ | 66 | ⓐ ⓑ ⓒ ⓓ | 96 | ⓐ ⓑ ⓒ ⓓ |
| 7 | ⓐ ⓑ ⓒ ⓓ | 37 | ⓐ ⓑ ⓒ ⓓ | 67 | ⓐ ⓑ ⓒ ⓓ | 97 | ⓐ ⓑ ⓒ ⓓ |
| 8 | ⓐ ⓑ ⓒ ⓓ | 38 | ⓐ ⓑ ⓒ ⓓ | 68 | ⓐ ⓑ ⓒ ⓓ | 98 | ⓐ ⓑ ⓒ ⓓ |
| 9 | ⓐ ⓑ ⓒ ⓓ | 39 | ⓐ ⓑ ⓒ ⓓ | 69 | ⓐ ⓑ ⓒ ⓓ | 99 | ⓐ ⓑ ⓒ ⓓ |
| 10 | ⓐ ⓑ ⓒ ⓓ | 40 | ⓐ ⓑ ⓒ ⓓ | 70 | ⓐ ⓑ ⓒ ⓓ | 100 | ⓐ ⓑ ⓒ ⓓ |
| 11 | ⓐ ⓑ ⓒ ⓓ | 41 | ⓐ ⓑ ⓒ ⓓ | 71 | ⓐ ⓑ ⓒ ⓓ | 101 | ⓐ ⓑ ⓒ ⓓ |
| 12 | ⓐ ⓑ ⓒ ⓓ | 42 | ⓐ ⓑ ⓒ ⓓ | 72 | ⓐ ⓑ ⓒ ⓓ | 102 | ⓐ ⓑ ⓒ ⓓ |
| 13 | ⓐ ⓑ ⓒ ⓓ | 43 | ⓐ ⓑ ⓒ ⓓ | 73 | ⓐ ⓑ ⓒ ⓓ | 103 | ⓐ ⓑ ⓒ ⓓ |
| 14 | ⓐ ⓑ ⓒ ⓓ | 44 | ⓐ ⓑ ⓒ ⓓ | 74 | ⓐ ⓑ ⓒ ⓓ | 104 | ⓐ ⓑ ⓒ ⓓ |
| 15 | ⓐ ⓑ ⓒ ⓓ | 45 | ⓐ ⓑ ⓒ ⓓ | 75 | ⓐ ⓑ ⓒ ⓓ | 105 | ⓐ ⓑ ⓒ ⓓ |
| 16 | ⓐ ⓑ ⓒ ⓓ | 46 | ⓐ ⓑ ⓒ ⓓ | 76 | ⓐ ⓑ ⓒ ⓓ | 106 | ⓐ ⓑ ⓒ ⓓ |
| 17 | ⓐ ⓑ ⓒ ⓓ | 47 | ⓐ ⓑ ⓒ ⓓ | 77 | ⓐ ⓑ ⓒ ⓓ | 107 | ⓐ ⓑ ⓒ ⓓ |
| 18 | ⓐ ⓑ ⓒ ⓓ | 48 | ⓐ ⓑ ⓒ ⓓ | 78 | ⓐ ⓑ ⓒ ⓓ | 108 | ⓐ ⓑ ⓒ ⓓ |
| 19 | ⓐ ⓑ ⓒ ⓓ | 49 | ⓐ ⓑ ⓒ ⓓ | 79 | ⓐ ⓑ ⓒ ⓓ | 109 | ⓐ ⓑ ⓒ ⓓ |
| 20 | ⓐ ⓑ ⓒ ⓓ | 50 | ⓐ ⓑ ⓒ ⓓ | 80 | ⓐ ⓑ ⓒ ⓓ | 110 | ⓐ ⓑ ⓒ ⓓ |
| 21 | ⓐ ⓑ ⓒ ⓓ | 51 | ⓐ ⓑ ⓒ ⓓ | 81 | ⓐ ⓑ ⓒ ⓓ | 111 | ⓐ ⓑ ⓒ ⓓ |
| 22 | ⓐ ⓑ ⓒ ⓓ | 52 | ⓐ ⓑ ⓒ ⓓ | 82 | ⓐ ⓑ ⓒ ⓓ | 112 | ⓐ ⓑ ⓒ ⓓ |
| 23 | ⓐ ⓑ ⓒ ⓓ | 53 | ⓐ ⓑ ⓒ ⓓ | 83 | ⓐ ⓑ ⓒ ⓓ | 113 | ⓐ ⓑ ⓒ ⓓ |
| 24 | ⓐ ⓑ ⓒ ⓓ | 54 | ⓐ ⓑ ⓒ ⓓ | 84 | ⓐ ⓑ ⓒ ⓓ | 114 | ⓐ ⓑ ⓒ ⓓ |
| 25 | ⓐ ⓑ ⓒ ⓓ | 55 | ⓐ ⓑ ⓒ ⓓ | 85 | ⓐ ⓑ ⓒ ⓓ | 115 | ⓐ ⓑ ⓒ ⓓ |
| 26 | ⓐ ⓑ ⓒ ⓓ | 56 | ⓐ ⓑ ⓒ ⓓ | 86 | ⓐ ⓑ ⓒ ⓓ | 116 | ⓐ ⓑ ⓒ ⓓ |
| 27 | ⓐ ⓑ ⓒ ⓓ | 57 | ⓐ ⓑ ⓒ ⓓ | 87 | ⓐ ⓑ ⓒ ⓓ | 117 | ⓐ ⓑ ⓒ ⓓ |
| 28 | ⓐ ⓑ ⓒ ⓓ | 58 | ⓐ ⓑ ⓒ ⓓ | 88 | ⓐ ⓑ ⓒ ⓓ | 118 | ⓐ ⓑ ⓒ ⓓ |
| 29 | ⓐ ⓑ ⓒ ⓓ | 59 | ⓐ ⓑ ⓒ ⓓ | 89 | ⓐ ⓑ ⓒ ⓓ | 119 | ⓐ ⓑ ⓒ ⓓ |
| 30 | ⓐ ⓑ ⓒ ⓓ | 60 | ⓐ ⓑ ⓒ ⓓ | 90 | ⓐ ⓑ ⓒ ⓓ | 120 | ⓐ ⓑ ⓒ ⓓ |

## Calculate Your Score

| | |
|---|---|
| **Correct (✓)** | |
| **Incorrect (✓)** | |
| **Unattempted** | |
| **Total Score** | |
| **Accuracy (%)** | |

## Reasons for Incorrect Answers?

| | |
|---|---|
| 1. Lack of Knowledge/Existing Source Insufficient | |
| 2. Lack of Multiple Revision | |
| 3. Common Sense Mistakes | |

**Note :**

1. Calculate total score as correct answers carry 2 marks each 1/3rd marks will deducted for **Incorrect** Answers.
2. Calculate Accuracy (%) by dividing the number of correct answers to the total number of attempted questions.

## Past Learning

**1.** Consider the following statements: **(2024)**

**Statement I:** If the United States of America (USA) were to default on its debt, holders of US Treasury Bonds will not be able to exercise their claims to receive payment.

**Statement II:** The USA Government debt is not backed by any hard assets, but only by the faith of the Government.

Which one of the following is correct in respect of the above statements?

(a) Both Statement I and Statement II are correct and Statement II explains Statement I.
(b) Both Statement I and Statement II are correct, but Statement II does not explain Statement I.
(c) Statement I is correct, but Statement II is incorrect.
(d) Statement I is incorrect, but Statement II is correct.

**2.** Consider the following : **(2023)**

1. Demographic performance
2. Forest and ecology
3. Governance reforms
4. Stable government
5. Tax and fiscal efforts

For the horizontal tax devolution, the Fifteenth Finance Commission used how many of the above as criteria other than population area and income distance?

(a) Only two
(b) Only three
(c) Only four
(d) All five

**3.** With reference to the Indian economy, consider the following statements: **(2022)**

1. A share of the household financial savings goes towards government borrowings.
2. Dated securities issued at market-related rates in auctions form a large component of internal debt.

Which of the statements given above is/are correct?

(a) 1 only
(b) 2 only
(c) Both 1 and 2
(d) Neither 1 nor 2

**4.** Which among the following steps is most likely to be taken at the time of an economic recession? **(2021)**

(a) Cut in tax rates accompanied by increase in interest rate
(b) Increase in expenditure on public projects
(c) Increase in tax rates accompanied by reduction of interest rate
(d) Reduction of expenditure on public projects

**5.** Which one of the following is likely to be one of the most inflationary in its effects?

(a) Repayment of public debt **(2021)**
(b) Borrowing from the public to finance a budget deficit
(c) Borrowing from the banks to finance a budget deficit
(d) Creation of new money to finance a budget deficit

**6.** Along with the Budget, the Finance Minister also places other documents before the parliament which include 'The Macro Economic Framework Statement'. The aforesaid document is presented because this is mandated by: **(2020)**

(a) Long-standing parliamentary convention
(b) Article 112 and Article 110(1) of the Constitution of India
(c) Article 113 of the Constitution of India
(d) Provisions of the Fiscal Responsibility and Budget Management Act, 2003

**7.** Consider the following statements: **(2018)**

1. The Fiscal Responsibility and Budget Management (FRBM) Review Committee Report has recommended a debt to GDP ratio of 60% for the general (combined) government by 2023, comprising 40% for the Central Government and 20% for the State Governments.
2. The Central Government has domestic liabilities of 21% of GDP as compared to that of 49% of GDP of the State Governments.
3. As per the Constitution of India, it is mandatory for a State to take the Central Government's consent for raising any loan if the former owes any outstanding liabilities to the latter.

Which of the statements given above are correct?

(a) 1 only
(b) 2 and 3 only
(c) 1 and 3 only
(d) 1, 2 and 3

**8.** There has been a persistent deficit budget year after year. Which action/actions of the following can be taken by the Government to reduce the deficit? **(2016)**

1. Reducing revenue expenditure
2. Introducing new welfare schemes
3. Rationalizing subsidies
4. Reducing import duty

Select the correct answer from the codes given below:

(a) 1 only
(b) 2 and 3 only
(c) 1 and 3 only
(d) 1, 2, 3 and 4

**9.** Which of the following is/are included in the capital budget of the Government of India? **(2016)**

1. Expenditure on acquisition of assets like roads, buildings, machinery, etc.
2. Loans received from foreign governments
3. Loans and advances granted to the States and Union Territories

Select the correct answer from the codes given below:

(a) 1 only (b) 2 and 3 only
(c) 1 and 3 only (d) 1, 2 and 3

**10.** There has been a persistent deficit budget year after year. Which action/actions of the following can be taken by the Government to reduce the deficit? **(2015)**

1. Reducing revenue expenditure
2. Introducing new welfare schemes
3. Rationalizing subsidies
4. Expanding Industries

Select the correct answer from the codes given below:

(a) 1 and 3 only (b) 2 and 3 only
(c) 1 only (d) 1, 2, 3 and 4

**11.** With reference to the Fourteenth Finance Commission, which of the following statements is/are correct? **(2015)**

1. It has increased the share of States in the central divisible pool from 32 percent to 42 percent.
2. It has made recommendations concerning sector-specific grants.

Select the correct answer from the codes given below:

(a) 1 only (b) 2 only
(c) Both 1 and 2 (d) Neither 1 nor 2

**12.** In India, deficit financing is used for raising resources for **(2013)**

(a) economic development
(b) redemption of public debt
(c) adjusting the balance of payments
(d) reducing the foreign debt

# Detailed Solutions

## Assessment Round

**1.** (*c*) Only three

- **Statement 1 is correct: Increasing income taxes** for high-income earners is a fiscal policy measure because it involves government decisions on taxation, directly impacting revenue and income distribution.
- **Statement 2 is incorrect: Adjusting the central bank's interest rate** is part of monetary policy managed by the central bank, not fiscal policy. Fiscal policy is concerned with government spending and tax decisions, while monetary policy involves the regulation of interest rates and money supply.
- **Statement 3 is correct: Providing subsidies** for renewable energy projects is a fiscal policy action, as it involves government spending aimed at promoting a specific economic activity.
- **Statement 4 is correct: Reducing corporate tax rates** to stimulate investment is also a fiscal policy measure. Lowering taxes increases businesses' after-tax earnings, encouraging further investment and economic activity.

**Thus, the correct answer is (c) Only three.**

**2.** (*a*) 1, 2 and 3

**Fiscal policy** refers to the use of **government spending and taxation** by a country's government to influence the economy. Fiscal policy can be **either expansionary or contractionary**, depending on whether the government seeks to stimulate or cool down economic activity.

**Expansionary fiscal policy** is a macroeconomic policy that's used to stimulate the economy by increasing government spending, decreasing taxes, or both. It's also known as "loose" fiscal policy.

- **Statement 1 is correct:** By increasing government spending on infrastructure, the government injects more money into the economy, stimulating demand and promoting economic growth.
- **Statement 2 is correct:** Reducing corporate tax rates is also considered expansionary fiscal policy. Lower taxes increase the after-tax profits of businesses, encouraging them to invest more, which boosts economic activity.
- **Statement 3 is correct:** Introducing subsidies for agricultural inputs reduces costs for farmers, encouraging them to produce more, which increases economic activity. This is also a form of **expansionary fiscal policy** aimed at stimulating growth in the agricultural sector.

**Thus, the correct answer is (a) 1, 2 and 3.**

**3.** (*d*) All four pairs

- **Pair 1 is correctly matched: Increasing defence spending** is a form of **expansionary fiscal policy** because it involves higher government expenditure, which injects more money into the economy and boosts demand.
- **Pair 2 is correctly matched: Reducing social welfare programmes** is a form of **contractionary fiscal policy** as it decreases government spending, which can reduce demand in the economy.
- **Pair 3 is correctly matched: Increasing taxes,** including excise duties on luxury goods, is a **contractionary fiscal policy** because it reduces disposable income and consumption, especially of luxury items.
- **Pair 4 is correctly matched: Raising income tax exemptions** is an **expansionary fiscal policy** as it leaves people with more disposable income, encouraging consumption and investment.

**Therefore, the correct answer is (d) All four pairs.**

**4.** (*c*) Both 1 and 2

- **Statement 1 is correct: Pro-cyclical fiscal policy** refers to government actions that amplify the current phase of the economic cycle. During economic booms, the government may increase spending or cut taxes, and during recessions, it may reduce spending or increase taxes.

This is the **opposite of a counter-cyclical policy**, which aims to stabilize the economy.

- **Statement 2 is correct:** A pro-cyclical fiscal policy can **exacerbate economic volatility** by reinforcing existing trends—spending more during booms can lead to overheating, while cutting spending during recessions can deepen the downturn.

**Thus, the correct answer is (c) Both 1 and 2.**

**5.** (*a*) Only one

- **Statement 1 is correct: Increasing government spending on infrastructure during a recession** is a classic example of counter-cyclical fiscal policy. In a recession, the government aims to stimulate economic activity by injecting money into the economy through increased spending. This helps create jobs and boost demand.
- **Statement 2 is incorrect: Reducing income tax rates during a period of economic expansion** is **not** a counter-cyclical measure because reducing taxes will increase disposable income, which will increase demand, resulting in the economy overheating rather than stabilizing it. **And** during an economic expansion, a counter- cyclical policy would involve reducing demand, either by cutting government spending or raising taxes, to prevent the economy from overheating.
- **Statement 3 is incorrect: Implementing austerity measures during an economic boom is not a counter-cyclical measure.** Austerity measures involve reducing government spending and increasing taxes to reduce budget deficits. These measures are typically implemented during economic downturns to stabilise the economy, not during booms.

**Thus, the correct answer is (a) Only one.**

**6.** (*c*) 3 only

- **Statement 1 is incorrect:** The Union Budget is presented by the Finance Minister on 1st February each year, to allow the budgetary process to be completed before the start of the new financial year on 1st April.
- **Statement 2 is incorrect:** The **Finance Bill** is a Money Bill and can only be introduced in the Lok Sabha. After being passed by the Lok Sabha, it is sent to the Rajya Sabha, which can suggest amendments but cannot reject or amend it without the Lok Sabha's consent.
- **Statement 3 is correct:** The **Appropriation Bill** legally authorises the government to withdraw the necessary funds from the Consolidated Fund of India to meet its expenditures as approved by the Parliament.

**Thus, the correct answer is (c) 3 only.**

**7.** (*b*) 2 only

- **Statement 1 is incorrect:** The responsibility to ensure that the Budget is laid before Parliament is **conferred upon the President of India**, as per **Article 112** of the Indian Constitution. The **Finance Minister presents the Budget on behalf of the President** but the Constitution mandates the President to cause the **Annual Financial Statement** (Budget) to be laid before both Houses of Parliament.
- **Statement 2 is correct:** Expenditures from the **Public Accounts of India** and the **Contingency Fund of India are not subject to a vote in Parliament**, but they can be discussed.

  The **Contingency Fund** is used for emergency or unforeseen expenditures, and the money used is replenished through parliamentary approval later.

**Thus, the correct answer is (b) 2 only.**

**8.** (*c*) 1 only

- **Statement 1 is correct: Demand for Grants** is presented to the **Lok Sabha** as part of the budget and includes both **charged expenditures** (which are not subject to vote, such as salaries of judges and the President) and **non-charged expenditures** (which are subject to vote).
- **Statement 2 is incorrect:** The **Rajya Sabha does not have the power to vote** on the Demand for Grants. This power lies exclusively with the **Lok Sabha.**
- **Statement 3 is incorrect:** The **Guillotine process** is a parliamentary mechanism used to ensure that **all demands** for grants are **not discussed in detail** before being put to vote.

When time runs out for detailed discussions, the remaining demands are voted on without further discussion.

**Thus, the correct answer is (c) 1 only.**

***9.*** (*b*) 2 only

- **Statement 1 is correct:** The **National Informatics Centre** (**NIC**) assists by providing the technological infrastructure needed for the **consolidation of budget data.** NIC helps with automating and securing the data management process during budget formulation.
- **Statement 2 is incorrect:** The **Department of Economic Affairs** under the **Ministry of Finance** is primarily responsible for the **formulation of the Union Budget,** not the Department of Revenue.

**Thus, the correct answer is (b) 2 only.**

***10.*** (*d*) 1, 2 and 3

The ministries are required to provide **three different kinds** of figures relating to their expenditures and receipts during this process of budget preparation. These are: Budget Estimates, Revised Estimates and Actual Estimates.

- **Statement 1 is correct: Budget Estimates** (BE) are estimates for the **upcoming fiscal year.** It projects the government's expected revenue and expenditure for the next year.
- **Statement 2 is correct: Revised Estimates** (RE) provide **updated figures for the current fiscal year.** These are adjustments made based on actual receipts and expenditures during the ongoing year.
- **Statement 3 is correct: Actual Estimates** (AE) represent the actual revenue and expenditure figures for the last completed fiscal year (referred to as Actuals).

**Thus, the correct answer is (d) 1, 2 and 3.**

***11.*** (*d*) 1, 2, 3 and 4

- **Statement 1 is correct:** The **Consolidated Fund of India** includes **all revenues received** by the Government of India, including taxes, non-tax revenues, and other income.
- **Statement 2 is correct:** While the Consolidated Fund is the source of all government expenditures, **charged expenditures** (such as the salaries of the President, judges, and interest payments on loans) are **automatically charged** to the fund and **do not require parliamentary approval** for withdrawal. However, they are still accounted for and reported to Parliament.
- **Statement 3 is correct:** The **Consolidated Fund** includes **all borrowings** and loans received by the Government of India. This includes internal and external borrowing.
- **Statement 4 is correct:** Money from the Consolidated Fund **cannot be used** for making payments without the **prior approval of Parliament.** Expenditures from this fund must be authorised through the Appropriation Bill.

**Thus, the correct answer is (d) 1, 2, 3 and 4.**

***12.*** (*d*) 1, 2, 3 and 4

The **Public Account of India** is a separate account where certain receipts are credited, and the government acts as a trustee for the funds, using them without requiring parliamentary approval for expenditure. Each of the following falls under this category:

- **Statement 1 is correct: Post Office Savings Account** deposits go to the Public Account. Funds here are deposited by citizens and managed by the government, with interest paid to the depositors.
- **Statement 2 is correct: Kisan Vikas Patra** (KVP), a government savings instrument, is also credited to the Public Account. The funds collected under KVP are managed by the government and used as needed.
- **Statement 3 is correct: Sukanya Samriddhi Account** deposits, aimed at supporting the education and future of girl children, are part of the Public Account. This instrument collects funds from the public, held in trust.
- **Statement 4 is correct:** The **Public Provident Fund** (**PPF**) is included in the Public Account, as it represents citizen contributions held by the government in trust, with interest returned on maturity.

**All four receipts go to the Public Account of India and therefore, the correct answer is (d) 1, 2, 3 and 4.**

**13.** (*a*) 1 only

- **Statement 1 is correct**: The **Ministry of Women and Child Development (MWCD) acts as the central nodal agency** for gender budgeting and the Ministry of Finance has mandated the establishment of **Gender Budget Cells** in all central ministries and departments to support this process.
- **Statement 2 is incorrect**: Gender budgeting **does not involve creating a separate budget exclusively for women** but focuses on addressing **women's specific** needs through existing budgetary frameworks. The Gender Budget Statement is structured into three parts:
  - **Part-A** exclusively comprises schemes and programmes with a 100% gender-specific focus. Ex – SAMARTHYA. It now account for nearly **40% of GBS allocations**, partly due to the full inclusion of the **Pradhan Mantri Awas Yojana (PMAY).**
  - **Part-B** highlights gender-sensitive initiatives with allocations exceeding 30% but falling below 100% for women and girls within each scheme's budget. **Ex: PM AJAY-Adarsh Gram Yojana.**
  - **Part-C** encompasses schemes with a budget allocation of less than 30% for women. **Inclusion of a new section Part C** which now includes pro-women schemes with **up to 30% allocation** for women, such as the **PM Kisan Scheme.**
- **Statement 3 is incorrect**: India ratified the Convention on the Elimination of All Forms of Discrimination Against Women (CEDAW) (1979) in 1993, signalling its commitment to gender equality.
  - This commitment led to the **introduction of the first Gender Budget Statement in the Indian Budget of 2005-2006.** Since then, the government has consistently released the Gender Budget Statement alongside the Union Budget.

**Thus, the correct answer is (a) 1 only.**

**14.** (*a*) ZBB involves justifying all expenses each budget cycle, while Outcome Budgeting focuses on aligning spending with desired results or objectives.

- **Option (a) is correct: Zero-Based Budgeting (ZBB)** requires every budget cycle to begin from a 'zero base,' meaning that each expense must be **justified from scratch.** It does not rely on past expenditures, thus promoting detailed scrutiny of all costs. On the other hand, **Outcome Budgeting** does not start from zero but instead **focuses on aligning spending with specific objectives and measuring results.** This method ties funds to desired outcomes, ensuring resources contribute to the intended impact.
- **Option (b) is incorrect**: ZBB does not involve incremental adjustments; it eliminates any assumptions based on previous budgets by starting each new cycle from zero. Outcome Budgeting, meanwhile, analyzes expenses based on results rather than scrutinizing every line item.
- **Option (c) is incorrect**: Neither ZBB nor Outcome Budgeting strictly emphasises long-term or short-term projects. Both methods can be applied to various time frames, though Outcome Budgeting typically connects to achieving measurable results within a defined period.
- **Option (d) is incorrect**: Although ZBB is popular in corporate environments due to its granular control, it is also applicable in public finance. Similarly, Outcome Budgeting is widely used in government to ensure public funds achieve desired results but is not exclusive to government settings.

**Thus, option (a) is the correct answer.**

**15.** (*b*) Only two

- **Statement 1 is correct: Grants-in-aid to state governments** is part of **revenue expenditure** because it does not create any assets or reduce liabilities. It is a regular expenditure to assist states in financing their operations.
- **Statement 2 is incorrect**: **Expenditure on defence equipment** is **capital expenditure,** as it results in the creation of assets (defence equipment). Hence, it is **not part of the revenue budget.**
- **Statement 3 is incorrect**: **Repayment of public debt** is a **capital expenditure,** as it reduces the government's liabilities. Therefore, **it is not included in the revenue budget.**

- **Statement 4 is correct: Salaries of government employees** is part of **revenue expenditure** because it is a regular operational cost and does not create assets.

**Therefore, the correct answer is (b) Only two.**

***16.*** (*a*) 3 only

Capital Receipts are receipts that **either create liabilities or result in the reduction of assets.** These include loans and borrowings.

- **Statement 1 is incorrect: Borrowing by the government from the Reserve Bank falls under capital receipts.** Capital receipts refer to funds raised that increase the government's liability or reduce its assets. Borrowing increases the government's liability, so it is classified as a capital receipt.
- **Statement 2 is incorrect: Loans received from foreign governments and international organisations** are also categorized as **capital receipts** since they increase the government's liability, fitting within capital receipt parameters.
- **Statement 3 is correct: Interest and dividend on investments made by the government are revenue receipts**, not capital receipts, because they represent earnings from government investments and do not create any liabilities or reduce assets.
- **Statement 4 is incorrect:** Deposits in Post-Office Savings Accounts are part of the **Public Account and are considered capital receipts** because they create a liability for the government, as it has to repay these deposits.

**Therefore, the correct answer is (a) 3 only.**

***17.*** (*a*) 1 and 2 only

- **Statement 1 is correct: Revenue expenditure** is a regular feature of the government's annual budget. It includes **day-to-day expenses** required to run the government, such as salaries, subsidies and interest payments.
- **Statement 2 is correct:** Revenue expenditure does **not typically result in the creation of physical assets.** It is used for operational expenses like salaries, pensions, and subsidies. However, in certain cases, **revenue expenditures may support asset creation indirectly**, such as maintenance of existing infrastructure.

1. One such component is the 'Grants to states for the creation of capital assets'.

- **Statement 3 is incorrect: Interest payments on debt** are a significant component of revenue expenditure. The government pays interest on the borrowings it has taken, and this forms part of its recurring expenses.

**Thus, the correct answer is (a) 1 and 2 only.**

***18.*** (*c*) 1, 2, 3, 4 and 5

**Revenue expenditure** refers to the government's **regular expenses** that do not lead to the creation of assets or reduction of liabilities. It includes operational expenses such as interest payments, grants, salaries, subsidies, and pensions.

- **Option 1 is correct: Interest payment on debt** is a revenue expenditure as it involves regular payments to meet the interest liabilities on government borrowings. It does not create any assets or reduce liabilities.
- **Option 2 is correct: Grants given to the State Government** are part of revenue expenditure when they are not tied to specific capital projects and are provided for operational needs.
- **Option 3 is correct: Salaries of employees** are considered revenue expenditure as they are recurring costs required to maintain government operations and do not result in asset creation or liability reduction.
- **Option 4 is correct: Subsidies** are revenue expenditures because they are regular payments aimed at supporting various sectors and citizens, with no asset creation or liability reduction for the government.
- **Option 5 is correct: Pensions** are also part of revenue expenditure. They represent payments to retired government employees, providing financial support without contributing to new assets or reducing liabilities.

**Thus, option (c) is the correct answer.**

***19.*** (*d*) 1, 2, 3 and 4

**Capital Expenditure** are expenditures of the government which **result in creation of physical or financial assets or reduction in financial liabilities.**

- **Statement 1 is correct: Expenditure on the acquisition of land:** This is part of capital expenditure as it results in the creation of an asset.
- **Statement 2 is correct: Loans given by the central government to state governments:** This is also capital expenditure because it represents a transfer that creates an obligation (liability) for repayment or helps in creating assets for the state governments.
- **Statement 3 is correct: Repayment of loans to international financial institutions:** This is capital expenditure because it reduces the government's liabilities by paying off outstanding debts.
- **Statement 4 is correct: Grants-in-aid for creation of capital assets:** These grants are treated as capital expenditure because they are specifically used for creating long-term assets.

**Therefore, the correct answer is (d) 1, 2, 3 and 4.**

***20.*** (*c*) 1 and 2 only

**Non-Tax Revenue Receipts** refer to income earned by the government from sources other than taxes. This includes earnings from public sector units (PSUs), fees, fines, interest, and other miscellaneous sources.

- **Statement 1 is correct: Dividends paid by PSUs and RBI to the government is part of non-tax revenue receipts** because the government earns dividends as a shareholder in public sector enterprises and through profits from the Reserve Bank of India (RBI).
- **Statement 2 is correct: License fee received by the government** is also part of **non-tax revenue receipts.** License fees, such as telecom spectrum fees or mining licenses, are regular sources of income for the government.
- **Statement 3 is incorrect: Disinvestment of shares of PSUs is not part of non-tax revenue receipts,** but rather a **capital receipt (Non-Debt Capital Receipt)** as it involves the sale of government assets (equity in PSUs), leading to a reduction in government holdings.

**The correct answer is (c) 1 and 2 only.**

***21.*** (*d*) All four pairs

- **Pair 1 is correct:** Interest income is part of **non-tax revenue receipts.**
- **Pair 2 is correct: Disinvestment** refers to the sale or liquidation of government-owned assets or public sector undertakings (PSUs) to private players, or the reduction of the government's stake in these enterprises. These proceeds are considered as **capital receipts** as they involve selling government assets.
- **Pair 3 is correct: Salaries** are part of operational, recurring expenses, classified as **revenue expenditure.**
- **Pair 4 is correct:** Capital expenditure involves spending on long-term assets, such as infrastructure projects like highways and bridges.

**Therefore, the correct answer is (d) All four pairs.**

***22.*** (*a*) 1 and 2 only

- **Statement 1 is correct: Grants-in-aid given to state governments for the creation of capital assets** is part of Effective Capital Expenditure as it leads to the creation of assets, even though the expenditure is a grant to state governments.
- **Statement 2 is correct: Expenditure on defence equipment and infrastructure** is also part of Effective Capital Expenditure as it involves spending on long-term assets like defence equipment and infrastructure.
- **Statement 3 is incorrect: Interest payments on government borrowings is not part of capital expenditure.** Interest payments are classified under revenue expenditure, as they are recurring operational costs and do not create assets.
- **Statement 4 is incorrect:** Some expenditure on social sector schemes may include capital expenditures (e.g., building hospitals or schools), but **general expenditure** on health and education services is typically revenue expenditure, as **it does not directly result in asset creation.**

**Therefore, the correct answer is (a) 1 and 2 only.**

**23.** (*c*) All three

- **Statement 1 is correct:** Revenue deficit is The revenue deficit refers to the excess of government's revenue expenditure over revenue receipts.

**Revenue Deficit = Revenue Expenditure – Revenue Receipts**

- **Statement 2 is correct:** Fiscal deficit is the difference between the government's total expenditure and its total receipts (excluding borrowings). It shows the total borrowing requirement of the government.

**Fiscal Deficit = Total Expenditure (Revenue Expenditure + Capital Expenditure) - Total Receipts (Revenue Receipts + Non-Debt Capital Receipts)**

Non debt creating capital receipts are those which do not give rise to debt, as the name itself suggests. For instance, loan recovery and PSU proceeds from disinvestment in the Public Sector Undertakings.

It should be **noted** that, **revenue deficit is a part of fiscal deficit.**

**Fiscal Deficit = Revenue Deficit + Capital Expenditure – Non-Debt creating Capital Rreceipts**

- **Statement 3 is correct: Primary deficit** is the fiscal deficit of the current year excluding interest liabilities on previous borrowings. It indicates the extent to which the government is borrowing to cover its current expenses, excluding interest payments.

  **Gross Primary Deficit = Gross Fiscal Deficit – Net Interest Liabilities**

  Net interest liabilities consist of interest payments minus interest receipts by the government on net domestic lending.

**Thus, option (c) is the correct answer.**

**24.** (*c*) 1, 2 and 3

- **Statement 1 is correct: Government is dissaving and using savings of the other sectors of economy:** A revenue deficit indicates that the government is not generating enough revenue to meet its operational expenses, so it has **to rely on borrowing or using savings** from other sectors of the economy.
- **Statement 2 is correct: Higher fiscal deficit of the government:** A revenue deficit contributes to the overall fiscal deficit, as the government has to borrow to meet both its revenue and capital expenditure.
- **Statement 3 is correct: Government borrowings will also be used for consumption requirements:** If the government is incurring a revenue deficit, it means borrowings are being used not just for asset creation (capital expenditure), but also for meeting consumption-related expenses (revenue expenditure), which is not sustainable in the long run.

**Thus, option (c) is the correct answer.**

**25.** (*c*) 3 and 4 only

To reduce the revenue deficit without creating liabilities, the focus should be on **increasing revenue receipts** (through better taxation, compliance, and asset monetisation) and **reducing revenue expenditure** (through rationalisation of subsidies, efficient spending, and better public sector management).

- **Statement 1 is incorrect: Printing more money by RBI is not a viable solution** as printing more money can lead to inflation and does not solve the structural problem of the revenue deficit. It creates more liabilities in the form of inflationary pressures.
- **Statement 2 is incorrect: Borrowing increases liabilities**, so it **does not help** in reducing the revenue deficit without creating liabilities.
- **Statement 3 is correct: Increasing direct taxes** is a **viable solution** as it can increase government revenue without adding to liabilities.
- **Statement 4 is correct: Rationalising subsidies** can reduce the government's revenue expenditure, thus reducing the revenue deficit without creating liabilities.

**Therefore, the correct answer is (c) 3 and 4 only.**

**26.** (*a*) 1, 2 and 3 only

**Fiscal Deficit = Total Expenditure (Revenue + Capital Expenditure) - Total Receipts (Revenue Receipts + Non-Debt Capital Receipts)**

- **Option 1 is correct: Capital Expenditure** is included in the calculation of fiscal deficit, as it represents the government's spending on infrastructure and asset creation.
- **Option 2 is correct: Interest Payments** is also included in the fiscal deficit because it is a part of the government's total expenditure, which needs to be financed.
- **Option 3 is correct: Revenue Receipts** are **subtracted** from total expenditure when calculating the fiscal deficit, as they represent the government's earnings from taxes and other revenue sources.
- **Option 4 is incorrect: Borrowings are not included** directly in the calculation of the fiscal deficit, as the fiscal deficit represents the shortfall that needs to be covered by borrowing.

**Therefore, the correct answer is (a) 1, 2 and 3 only.**

**27.** (*c*) Both 1 and 2

- **Statement 1 is correct: Effective Revenue Deficit (ERD)** was introduced in the Union Budget of India in 2011-12 to give an accurate picture of the revenue deficit. ERD is calculated by **subtracting** the **grants given for the creation of capital assets from the revenue deficit.**

  Effective Revenue Deficit (ERD) = Revenue Deficit – Grants to states for creation of Capital Assets
- **Statement 2 is correct: A high ERD** over multiple years does **indicate that a significant portion of the government's expenditure is non-productive.** This is because ERD measures the excess of revenue expenditure over revenue receipts, excluding grants for capital asset creation. If ERD remains high for a prolonged period, it suggests that the government is spending more on non-productive activities than it is earning, which can be unsustainable.

**Therefore, the correct answer is (c) Both 1 and 2.**

**28.** (*b*) Only two

- **Statement 1 is correct:** Monetised Deficit refers to the portion of the fiscal deficit that is financed by the central bank, typically through the printing of money, indicating the government's reliance on this method.
- **Statement 2 is correct:** When the central bank prints new money to finance the government's deficit, it directly increases the money supply in the economy, which can lead to inflationary pressures.
- **Statement 3 is incorrect:** A high monetised deficit **does not lead to deflationary pressures;** rather, it can lead to **inflationary pressures** due to the increase in the money supply.

**Thus, the correct answer is (b) Only two.**

**29.** (*a*) 1, 2 and 3 only

**Deficit financing** refers to the government's practice of spending more than it earns, often to stimulate economic growth. The following methods can be used to finance this deficit:

- **Printing currency (monetisation of the deficit):** This involves the government creating new money to cover its expenses. It can be inflationary, as it increases the money supply.
- **Borrowing from the public through the sale of bonds:** The government can issue bonds to raise funds from the public. This creates a debt that must be repaid with interest in the future.
- **Borrowing from international markets:** The government can borrow funds from international financial institutions or other countries. This can increase the country's foreign debt.
- **Reducing public expenditure : It is not a method of deficit financing.** It is a measure to reduce the government's spending and bring it in line with its revenue, thereby reducing the deficit.

**Thus, the correct answer is (a) 1, 2 and 3 only.**

**30.** (*b*) 1, 2 and 3 only

- **Statement 1 is correct: Deficit Financing** involves the government borrowing to meet expenditure that exceeds its revenue. This can lead to an **increase in inflation** as excessive money supply drives demand up, potentially outpacing supply and causing price levels to rise.

- **Statement 2 is correct:** Extensive deficit financing results in **higher public debt**, as the government borrows funds domestically or internationally to cover its deficit.
  This accumulated debt becomes a liability, impacting the country's fiscal health.
- **Statement 3 is correct: Crowding out of private investment** can occur with high levels of deficit financing, as the government's borrowing from the financial system can reduce the available capital for private sector loans, raising interest rates and discouraging private investment.
- **Statement 4 is incorrect: Increase in foreign exchange reserves** is not a typical outcome of deficit financing. Foreign exchange reserves usually increase with trade surpluses or capital inflows, rather than through government borrowing.

**Therefore, the correct answer is (b) 1, 2 and 3 only.**

***31.*** (*d*) All four pairs

- **Pair 1 is correct: Fiscal Deficit** represents the total borrowing needs of the government. It indicates the difference between the government's total expenditure and total receipts (excluding borrowings), showing the extent of the shortfall covered through borrowing.
- **Pair 2 is correct: Primary** Deficit is calculated as the fiscal deficit minus interest payments. It reflects fresh borrowing requirements, highlighting the deficit without the burden of past debt interest.
- **Pair 3 is correct: Revenue Deficit** shows the shortfall between the government's operational income (revenue receipts) and its day-to-day operational expenditure. It signifies that revenue is insufficient to cover operational expenses, requiring other funding sources.
- **Pair 4 is correct: Effective Revenue Deficit** refines the revenue deficit by excluding grants given to states for capital creation. This adjustment provides a more accurate picture by considering funds that contribute to capital formation.

**Therefore, the correct answer is (d) All four pairs.**

***32.*** (*c*) Only three

**Fiscal Consolidation** refers to the policies and strategies implemented by the government to reduce fiscal deficits and stabilise the level of public debt in relation to national income. It involves efforts to balance government revenues and expenditures, ensuring long-term economic sustainability.

- **Statement 1 is correct: Increasing excise duties on luxury goods** is a measure increases government revenue and is associated with fiscal consolidation.
- **Statement 2 is correct: Austerity involves cutting government spending** to reduce deficits, which is directly related to fiscal consolidation.
- **Statement 3 is incorrect: Implementing a universal basic income scheme** will increases social welfare, it typically involves higher government spending, which is **not** associated with fiscal consolidation.
- **Statement 4 is correct: Privatising non-strategic public sector enterprises:** Privatisation generates revenue for the government and reduces the burden of maintaining loss-making enterprises, which is associated with fiscal consolidation.

**Thus, the correct answer is (c) Only three.**

***33.*** (*c*) Only three

**Fiscal slippage refers to a situation where a government's actual fiscal deficit exceeds its budgeted target.** This deviation usually arises from unexpected increases in expenditures (like subsidies, welfare spending, or project overruns) or shortfalls in revenue (due to slower economic growth or lower-than-anticipated tax collections).

- **Statement 1 is correct: Slower-than expected economic growth** can lead to fiscal slippage because it often results in lower than anticipated revenue from taxes. When economic growth lags, tax collections drop, which can increase the fiscal deficit.
- **Statement 2 is incorrect: Increase in tax rates on corporate income** generally raises government revenue rather than causing fiscal slippage. Higher tax rates on corporations contribute positively to

government receipts unless they discourage investment significantly, which is not directly implied here.

- **Statement 3 is correct: Higher-than-budgeted spending on welfare programmes** can cause fiscal slippage as it increases unplanned government expenditure, which can strain fiscal targets and result in a larger fiscal deficit.
- **Statement 4 is correct: Inadequate monitoring of government projects** often leads to inefficiencies, cost overruns, and wastage of resources. These unplanned expenses contribute to fiscal slippage by diverting funds from other critical areas.

**Thus, the correct answer is (c) Only three.**

***34.*** (*c*) 1, 3 and 4 only

**Measures to Reduce Fiscal Deficit:**

- Increase revenue: Raise taxes, close loopholes, reduce exemptions.
- Decrease spending: Cut unnecessary spending, rationalise subsidies.
- Borrow less: Reduce reliance on debt.
- Promote economic growth: Stimulate economic activity.
- Manage debt effectively: Refine debt management strategies.

**By implementing these measures, governments can work towards reducing their fiscal deficits and achieving sustainable economic growth.**

- **Option 1 is correct: Rationalisation of subsidies:** Reducing or better targeting subsidies can reduce government expenditure and help lower the fiscal deficit.
- **Option 2 is incorrect: Higher exemption limits in the income tax regime:** Increasing exemption limits would reduce tax revenue, which increases the fiscal deficit. Hence, this is not a measure to reduce the deficit.
- **Option 3 is correct: Enhancing tax compliance through digitization and better enforcement:** This can increase tax revenues by reducing evasion, thereby contributing to a reduction in the fiscal deficit.
- **Option 4 is correct: Introduction of tax on virtual digital assets:** Taxing digital assets can create a new revenue stream for the government, helping to reduce the fiscal deficit.

**Thus, the correct answer is (c) 1, 3 and 4 only.**

***35.*** (*c*) 1, 2 and 3 only

Along with the **Annual Financial Statement (AFS)**, the following documents are tabled in Parliament as per the provisions of the **Fiscal Responsibility and Budget Management (FRBM) Act:**

- **Medium-term Fiscal Policy Statement**: This outlines the fiscal targets for the next three financial years.
- **Fiscal Policy Strategy Statement**: This document outlines the government's fiscal policies and strategic priorities.
- **Macroeconomic Framework Statement**: This provides an assessment of the overall economic situation and projections for key economic indicators.
- **Economic Survey of India**, although presented before the budget, is not tabled with the Annual Financial Statement. It is a separate document prepared by the Ministry of Finance.

**Thus, the correct answer is (c) 1, 2 and 3 only.**

***36.*** (*a*) The **NK Singh Committee** was established in 2016 to review the **FRBM Act, 2003**. Its mandate was to assess the effectiveness of fiscal targets under the Act and recommend improvements.

The committee suggested adopting a flexible fiscal deficit target based on economic conditions and implementing a debt-to-GDP target.

**Thus, option (a) is the correct answer.**

***37.*** (*b*) 1 and 3 only

- **Statement 1 is correct**: The **FRBM** Act applies to both the central and state governments, though states have their own version of fiscal responsibility legislation based on the principles of the central FRBM Act.
- **Statement 2 is incorrect**: The FRBM Act does **not currently provide for a Fiscal Council**. The **NK Singh Committee** recommended the establishment of such a council, but it has not yet been implemented.

- **Statement 3 is correct**: The **NK Singh Committee** recommended a **fiscal deficit target range** rather than an absolute target, allowing for flexibility with a deviation of up to **0.5% of GDP** under certain conditions.

**Therefore, the correct answer is (b) 1 and 3 only.**

***38.*** (*d*) 1, 2, 3 and 4

- **Provision 1 is correct**: The **FRBM Act, 2003 sets targets for reducing fiscal deficit** and **revenue deficit** to ensure fiscal discipline.
- **Provision 2 is correct**: The Act mandates the presentation of a **Medium-Term Fiscal Policy Statement** annually in Parliament to provide a framework for fiscal policy over the next three years.
- **Provision 3 is correct**: The **FRBM Act** prohibits the **Reserve Bank of India (RBI)** from participating in the **primary issuance of government securities**, which prevents direct monetisation of the government's deficit.
- **Provision 4 is correct**: The Act includes **'escape clauses'** that allow for deviations from fiscal targets under exceptional circumstances, such as **economic crises or natural disasters.**

**Thus, the correct answer is (d) 1, 2, 3 and 4.**

***39.*** (*a*) 1 and 2 only

The Fiscal Responsibility and Budget Management (FRBM) Act has been amended several times, including in 2012, 2015, and 2018.

- 2012 and 2015 amendments: These amendments relaxed the target realisation year, introduced the **Effective Revenue Deficit (E.R.D) concept**, and added the **Medium-Term Expenditure Framework Statement.**
- 2018 amendment: This amendment incorporated the concept of "General Government debt" and **fixed a target of containing General Government debt at a level of 60 per cent of the GDP by the end of financial year 2024-25.**

- **Statement 1 is correct**: The 2012 amendment introduced the concept of Effective Revenue Deficit, which excludes grants for the creation of capital assets from the revenue deficit.
- **Statement 2 is correct**: As the amendment required the government to present a Medium-Term Expenditure Framework Statement annually, providing a rolling target for expenditure over the next three years.
- **Statement 3 is incorrect**: This amendment **did not set a fixed target** of reducing the fiscal deficit to 3% of GDP by 2015; it allowed for more flexibility in setting targets based on economic conditions.

**Thus, the correct answer is (a) 1 and 2 only.**

***40.*** (*c*) All three

- **Statement 1 is correct**: Public debt encompasses all liabilities incurred by the government through borrowing, regardless of whether the funds are sourced domestically or internationally.
- **Statement 2 is correct**: The RBI plays a crucial role in managing the central government's public debt. It acts as the government's debt manager, issuing securities, conducting auctions, and overseeing debt repayments.
- **Statement 3 is correct**: Public debt is typically classified into **marketable debt** and **non-marketable debt.**
  - **Marketable government securities** include G-secs and T-Bills issued through auction. Non-marketable securities include intermediate treasury bills issued to state governments and special securities issued to national Small Savings Fund among others.

**Thus, the correct answer is (c) All three.**

***41.*** (*b*) 1, 2 and 3 only

- **Option 1 is correct: Treasury Bills** are short-term, zero-coupon bonds issued by the government to meet short-term liquidity needs. They are considered a part of public debt.
- **Option 2 is correct: External loans from foreign governments:** These loans are taken from foreign governments and are also included in public debt.
- **Option 3 is correct: Special securities issued to financial institutions:** These securities are specifically issued to financial institutions and are part of public debt.

- **Option 4 is incorrect: Tax revenues** are not considered public debt. They are a source of government income, not a liability.

**Thus, the correct answer is (b) 1, 2 and 3 only.**

***42.*** (*a*) 1 and 2 only

- **Statement 1 is correct:** Marketable debt, such as government bonds and treasury bills, can be traded in the secondary market, offering liquidity to investors.
- **Statement 2 is correct:** Non-marketable debt includes borrowings like National Savings Certificates (NSCs) and Provident Funds, which are not traded in secondary markets.
- **Statement 3 is incorrect:** The government can borrow externally not just from multilateral institutions like the IMF and World Bank but also from other sources, including bilateral loans from foreign governments and commercial borrowings.

**Therefore, the correct answer is (a) 1 and 2 only.**

***43.*** (*c*) Only three

- **Statement 1 is correct: Sovereign Bonds issued in international markets:** These are a part of external debt. Governments issue these bonds in foreign currencies in international markets, and they are a component of public debt.
- **Statement 2 is correct: Loans from the Reserve Bank of India (RBI):** These loans are part of internal borrowing and are included in public debt. RBI lends money to the government through various instruments, such as Ways and Means Advances (WMA).
- **Statement 3 is correct: Government Savings Bonds:** These are part of **non-marketable public debt.** They are issued to the public as a secure investment instrument, and the government uses these to raise funds.
- **Statement 4 is incorrect: Disinvestment receipts** are not considered part of public debt, as they represent the sale of government equity in public sector enterprises rather than borrowing.

**Thus, correct answer is (c) Only three.**

***44.*** (*d*) 1, 2 and 3

- **Statement 1 is correct: India's public debt is primarily composed of internal debt,** which is raised through the issuance of government securities, bonds, and treasury bills. This internal borrowing forms the bulk of the government's debt obligations.
- **Statement 2 is correct:** External debt forms a relatively small proportion of India's total public debt compared to internal debt. The Indian government relies more on domestic borrowing than external sources to fund its deficit.
- **Statement 3 is correct:** Interest payments on public debt, especially internal debt, form a significant portion of the government's revenue expenditure. A considerable amount of the government's budget is allocated to service these debt obligations.

**Key Figures (as of recent estimates):**

- **Total Public Debt-to-GDP Ratio:** Approximately 88.5% in FY 2022-23.
- **Internal Debt:** Accounts for **about 95%** of the total public debt.
- **External Debt:** Constitutes around 5% of the total public debt.

**Thus, the correct answer is (d) 1, 2 and 3.**

***45.*** (*c*) Both 1 and 2

- **Statement 1 is correct: India has a higher proportion of marketable debt compared to non-marketable debt.** India's public debt is largely composed of marketable debt, such as government securities (G-secs) and treasury bills, which are traded in the financial markets. Non-marketable debt, such as special securities issued to the Reserve Bank of India (RBI) and liabilities from small savings schemes, constitutes a smaller portion of the total debt.
- **Statement 2 is correct: India's public debt is predominantly long-term, reducing the risk of refinancing in the short term.** A significant portion of India's public debt is long-term, which helps mitigate short-term refinancing risks. Long-term debt provides the government with more time to manage its

debt obligations and reduces immediate repayment pressures.

**Therefore, the correct answer is (c) Both 1 and 2.**

***46.*** (*d*) 1, 2, 3 and 4

- **Option 1 is correct: Commercial banks** in India are allowed to subscribe to government securities as part of their statutory liquidity ratio (SLR) requirements.
- **Option 2 is correct: Insurance companies** are key institutional investors in government securities, using them as safe investment avenues to match long-term liabilities.
- **Option 3 is correct: Foreign Institutional Investors (FIIs)** can invest in government securities, subject to limits set by the Reserve Bank of India (RBI) under specific frameworks.
- **Option 4 is correct: Non-Resident Indians (NRIs)** can also subscribe to certain categories of government securities under specific schemes allowed by the government.

**Thus, the correct answer is (d) 1, 2, 3 and 4.**

***47.*** (*d*) Neither 1 not 2

- **Statement 1 is incorrect:** India's public debt has actually increased significantly in recent years, often exceeding 50% of GDP. This increase is primarily due to government spending on various sectors, including infrastructure, healthcare, and education.
- **Statement 2 is incorrect:** While India has made efforts to reduce its external debt denominated in foreign currencies, a significant portion of its **external debt is still denominated in foreign currencies, primarily US dollars.** This exposes India to exchange rate risks, as fluctuations in exchange rates can affect the cost of servicing and repaying this debt.

**Thus, the correct answer is (d) Neither 1 nor 2.**

***48.*** (*c*) It indicates that debt amumulation could inearase due to higher interest burdens.

A **negative IRGD** (where the interest rate on government debt is higher than GDP growth) places additional stress on debt management. In this case, debt grows faster than the economy's ability to service it, leading to potential debt accumulation. This is particularly concerning for debt sustainability as it may require additional borrowing or revenue generation to meet obligations.

**Thus, option (c) is the correct answer.**

***49.*** (*b*) 1, 2 and 4 only

- **Option 1 is correct: Provident Fund Deposits** are not readily transferable or tradable in the market and are considered non-marketable debt instruments.
- **Option 2 is correct: National Savings Certificates (NSCs)** are also non-marketable, as they cannot be freely bought and sold in the open market.
- **Option 3 is incorrect: Treasury Bills** are short-term, zero-coupon bonds that are issued through auctions and are considered **marketable debt instruments.** They can be traded in the secondary market.
- **Option 4 is correct: Special Securities issued to the RBI**: These securities are issued specifically to the RBI and are not available for trading in the open market, making them non-marketable.

**Thus, option (b) is the correct answer.**

***50.*** (*b*) 1, 3 and 4

**Public account liabilities** represent funds that the government holds in trust, like small savings schemes and provident funds, which are not part of direct borrowings but are obligations the government must repay.

- **Option 1 is correct: National Small Savings Fund (NSSF)** is indeed a public account liability. It includes deposits from various small savings schemes like the National Savings Certificates, Post Office Savings Accounts, and Public Provident Fund.
- **Option 2 is incorrect: Central Government Loans** are considered **part of public debt** rather than public account liabilities.
- **Option 3 is correct**: PPF deposits are part of the National Small Savings Fund and hence are classified as public account liabilities.
- **Option 4 is correct**: Securities issued against small savings are also considered public

account liabilities as they represent the government's obligation to repay these deposits.

**Thus, option (b) is the correct answer.**

***51.*** (*b*) Only two

**Extra-Budgetary Resources (EBRs)** are funds that are **managed outside the regular government budget**. These funds are generated through various sources such as public sector undertakings, autonomous bodies, and special purpose vehicles.

EBRs are used to finance specific projects or programmes that are not included in the regular budget, often due to their self-financing nature or to avoid budgetary constraints.

- **Statement 1 is correct**: Extra-Budgetary Resources are funds raised outside the formal budget process, often through public sector enterprises or special purpose vehicles.
- **Statement 2 is correct**: EBRs are often used to finance projects without directly impacting the reported fiscal deficit.
- **Statement 3 is incorrect**: Not all EBRs are fully accounted for in the government's fiscal deficit calculation, which can lead to an underestimation of the true fiscal burden.

An example of **Extra-Budgetary Resources (EBRs)** in India is the **issuance of bonds by public sector enterprises like the Food Corporation of India (FCI)** to finance its food subsidy obligations. While the government backs these bonds, the funds raised through them are not directly reflected in the Union Budget but are used to meet expenditure needs, such as paying for food procurement.

**Therefore, the correct answer is (b) Only two.**

***52.*** (*b*) Only two

**Ways and Means Advances** (WMA) are temporary loans provided by the Reserve Bank of India (RBI) to the central and state governments to help them manage temporary mismatches in their receipts and expenditures. The WMA scheme was introduced on 1st April, 1997.

- **Statement 1 is correct**: WMAs are **short-term loan facilities provided by the RBI** to the central and state governments to manage temporary cash flow mismatches.
- **Statement 2 is incorrect**: The interest rate on a Ways and Means Advance (WMA) is typically **lower than the market borrowing rate for government securities**, meaning it is a cheaper option for the government to access short-term funds from the RBI compared to borrowing directly from the market.
- **Statement 3 is correct**: As the government is required to repay the WMA within a specified period (generally 90 days), and failure to do so results in the advance being treated as an overdraft.

**Thus, the correct answer is (b) Only two.**

***53.*** (*a*) 1 only

- **Statement 1 is correct**: The government regularly reviews and updates the interest rates on small saving schemes, typically on a **quarterly basis**. These changes are announced and implemented to keep the interest rates competitive and aligned with prevailing market conditions.
- **Statement 2 is incorrect**: While some small savings schemes like the **Public Provident Fund (PPF)** and **Sukanya Samriddhi Yojana (SSY)** provide **tax exemptions** on both principal and interest, not all schemes offer this benefit. The **National Savings Certificate** (NSC), for example, has taxable interest.

Hence, the principal and interest earned from all small saving schemes are not universally exempt from taxation.

**Therefore, the correct answer is (a) 1 only.**

***54.*** (*a*) 1 and 2 only

**The National Small Savings Fund (NSSF)** is a government-managed fund that serves as a depository for funds collected through various small savings schemes in India. These schemes include:

Public Provident Fund (PPF)

National Savings Certificates (NSCs)

Kisan Vikas Patra (KVP)

Post Office Monthly Income Scheme (POMIS)

Senior Citizens Savings Scheme (SCSS)

- **Statement 1 is correct**: The National Small Savings Fund (NSSF) acts as a depository for the funds collected through small saving schemes such as the Public Provident Fund (PPF), Kisan Vikas Patra (KVP), and others.

- **Statement 2 is correct:** The NSSF provides loans to both the central and state governments, using the funds deposited into the small saving schemes.
- **Statement 3 is incorrect:** The returns generated by the NSSF are not directly distributed to contributors. Instead, the returns are used to meet the liabilities of small savings schemes and to provide loans to governments.
- **Statement 4 is incorrect:** The NSSF is not managed by the Reserve Bank of India (RBI); rather, it is managed by the **Ministry of Finance.**

**Thus, the correct answer is (a) 1 and 2 only.**

**55.** (*a*) 1 and 2 only

- **Statement 1 is correct:** The **central government** has the exclusive authority to borrow funds on the security of the **Consolidated Fund of India**. This is part of its fiscal autonomy and aligns with its responsibility to manage national debt and large-scale financing needs for central initiatives.
- **Statement 2 is correct: State governments** in India have some autonomy to borrow funds independently. However, if a state has an outstanding loan or financial obligation to the central government, it requires **consent from the central government** before borrowing additional funds. This ensures states remain fiscally responsible and do not overextend liabilities that could impact federal finances.
- **Statement 3 is incorrect:** States cannot borrow from **external sources** independently, as the central government holds the sole authority for borrowing from foreign sources. External borrowings are managed by the Centre to ensure national fiscal stability and alignment with foreign relations and economic policies.

**Thus, the correct answer is (a) 1 and 2 only.**

**56.** (*d*) 1, 2 and 3

The **15th Finance Commission of India** was constituted in November 2017 under the chairmanship of **NK Singh**. It submitted its final report to the President of India in December 2020, covering the period from **2020-21** to **2024-25.**

- **Statement 1 is correct:** The 15th Finance Commission recommended the **devolution of 41% of the divisible pool of taxes to the states,** down from 42% recommended by the 14th Finance Commission.
- **Statement 2 is correct:** The 15th Finance Commission introduced **performance-based incentives** for states. Focused on four main themes: Social sector (health and education), Rural economy (agriculture and rural roads), Performance in power sector, Enhancing trade and exports.
- **Statement 3 is correct:** The 15th Finance Commission recommended the establishment of a **non-lapsable fund for defence and internal security** to address the needs of the defence sector.

Other important recommendation:

1. **Vertical Devolution:** The share of tax revenues that the Centre shares with the states has been maintained at 41%, slightly reduced from the previous 42%.
2. **Horizontal Devolution:** The allocation between states is based on multiple criteria:
   - 45% weightage to income
   - 15% each to population and area
   - 12.5% to demographic performance
   - 10% to forest and ecology
   - 2.5% to tax and fiscal efforts.
3. **Revenue Deficit Grants:** Recommended post-devolution revenue deficit grants amounting to **about ₹ 3 trillion** over five years. The number of states qualifying for these grants decreases from 17 in FY22 to 6 in FY26.
4. **Local Bodies:** Increased grants to local bodies to strengthen their financial position and improve governance.
5. **Disaster Risk Management:** Recommended setting up a National Disaster Risk Management Fund and State Disaster Risk Management Funds.
6. **Defence and Internal Security:** Suggested creating a non-lapsable fund for defence and internal security.

These recommendations aim to promote fiscal stability, equitable distribution of resources, and incentivise states to improve their performance in various sectors.

**Thus, all statements are correct (d) 1, 2 and 3.**

***57.*** (*d*) 1, 2, 3 and 4

**All four criteria** were used by the 15th Finance Commission in determining the distribution of tax revenues among the states with following weightage:

**Revenue-sharing formulas in the 14th and 15th Finance Commissions**

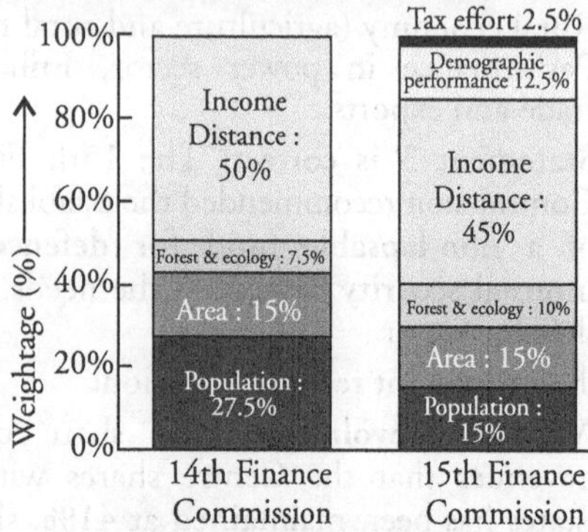


- **Population** and **Income Distance** are traditional criteria used in previous Finance Commissions.
- **Forest and Ecology** was included to incentivise states to maintain their forest cover.
- **Demographic Performance** was introduced to reward states that have successfully controlled their population growth.

**Thus, the correct answer is (d) 1, 2, 3 and 4.**

***58.*** (*c*) It will in carporate climate change impacts into its fiscal recommendations for the first time.

- The **16th Finance Commission** is notable for its expected inclusion of **climate change** impacts in fiscal transfers and resource allocation, addressing the vulnerability of states to environmental challenges.
- The other options, such as focusing solely on revenue collection, revising the tax-sharing formula entirely, or excluding demographic changes, do not reflect the specific distinctions of the 16th Fiance Commission.

**Thus, option (c) is the correct answer.**

***59.*** (*a*) 1 and 2 only

In India, grants-in-aid to states are categorised into two main types: **statutory grants** and **discretionary grants.**

- **Statement 1 is correct: Statutory grants** are constitutionally required and are often allocated based on a formula, such as the grants-in-aid under **Article 275.**
  - Charged on the Consolidated Fund of India.
  - These grants are given to states that need financial assistance. They are not available to every state but are targeted towards those with specific needs.
  - The Finance Commission recommends the amount and distribution of these grants
- **Statement 2 is correct: Discretionary grants** are provided at the **discretion of the central government** and can vary each year depending on budgetary allocations and specific needs.
  - Provided under **Article 282** of the Indian Constitution.
  - These grants can be given by both the Centre and the states for any public purpose, even if it is not within their legislative competence.
  - Often used for various developmental and welfare projects.
  - Not charged on the Consolidated Fund of India and are given at the discretion of the Centre or the states.
- **Statement 3 is incorrect: Both statutory and discretionary grants typically require parliamentary approval** as part of the budgetary process, though statutory grants are more formula-based and expected, while discretionary grants are more flexible.

**Thus, the correct answer is (a) 1 and 2 only.**

***60.*** (*b*) 1 and 3 only

- **Statement 1 is correct: Disinvestment** refers to the **sale or liquidation** of the government's equity in **public sector enterprises (PSEs)**. It is a way for the government to reduce its ownership in PSEs.
- **Statement 2 is incorrect:** The **proceeds from disinvestment** are **not exclusively** used for reducing the **fiscal deficit**. They can also be

used for other purposes, such as **capital expenditure**, infrastructure projects, or even as part of the National Investment Fund.

- **Statement 3 is correct: Strategic disinvestment** involves the sale of a substantial portion of the government's shareholding in a PSE along with the transfer of management control to a private entity.

**Therefore, the correct answer is (b) 1 and 3 only.**

***61.*** (*a*) 1 and 2 only

- **Statement 1 is correct**: In **Minority disinvestment** the government retains a majority stake, typically above 51%, ensuring management control remains with the government.

  Other types of Disinvestments
  - **Majority Disinvestment:** The government retains a minority stake, typically below 50%, transferring management control to private entities.
  - **Strategic Disinvestment:** Involves the sale of a substantial portion of the government's shareholding in a PSE along with the transfer of management control.
- **Statement 2 is correct: The Department of Investment and Public Asset Management (DIPAM)** is the government department responsible for managing the process of disinvestment.
- **Statement 3 is incorrect: Disinvestment does not always lead to privatisation.** Privatisation occurs when the government's stake falls below 50% or it relinquishes control over management, whereas disinvestment can occur even if the government retains a controlling stake.

**Therefore, option (a) 1 and 2 is the correct answer.**

***62.*** (*d*) 1, 2, 3 and 4

The Government of India's disinvestment policy classifies public sector enterprises (PSEs) into strategic and non-strategic sectors. Here are the strategic sectors where the government aims to maintain a bare minimum presence:

- **Atomic Energy, Space, and Defence:** These sectors are critical for national security and strategic interests.
- **Transport and Telecommunications:** like **Railways** essential for infrastructure development and connectivity.
- **Power, Petroleum, Coal, and Other Minerals:** Vital for energy security and resource management.
- **Banking, Insurance, and Financial Services:** Important for financial stability and economic growth.

In these strategic sectors, the government plans to retain a minimal presence, while the remaining enterprises will be privatized, merged, or closed. In non-strategic sectors, the government will exit all businesses except for a minimal presence.

**All four sectors listed are considered strategic sectors** under India's Disinvestment policy.

**Thus, the correct answer is option (d) 1, 2, 3 and 4.**

***63.*** (*d*) 1, 2 and 3

- **Statement 1 is correct:** In strategic sectors, the Government of India's disinvestment policy aims to maintain a bare minimum presence, allowing for disinvestment of the remaining stake.
- **Statement 2 is correct:** In non-strategic sectors, the government intends to completely exit by selling its entire stake, shifting control to private entities.
- **Statement 3 is correct:** Strategic disinvestment in non-strategic sectors is aimed at improving efficiency and encouraging private sector participation to foster competitiveness and growth.

**Hence, all the statements are correct, and the answer is (d) 1, 2 and 3.**

## Past Learning (Answers)

| | | | | | | | | | |
|---|---|---|---|---|---|---|---|---|---|
| 1 (a) | 2 (b) | 3 (c) | 4 (b) | 5 (d) | 6 (d) | 7 (c) | 8 (c) | 9 (d) | 10 (a) |
| 11 (a) | 12 (a) | | | | | | | | |

CHAPTER 05

# Public Finance-Taxation System

## Assessment Round

### Topic 1 : Concept of Taxation

**1.** With reference to the provisions of taxation in the Indian Constitution, consider the following statements:

1. Article 265 of the Indian Constitution states that no tax shall be levied or collected except by the authority of law.
2. Seventh Schedule of the Indian Constitution specifies the subjects on which the Union and State Governments can levy taxes.
3. The President has the authority to impose new taxes without the approval of the Parliament.

How many of the statements given above is/are correct?

(a) Only one (b) Only two
(c) All three (d) None

**2.** Under the Indian Constitution, different authorities have the power to levy various types of taxes. In this context, which of the following taxes can be levied by the State Governments?

1. Land Revenue
2. Corporation Tax
3. Stamp Duty
4. Customs Duty

Select the correct answer from the codes given below:

(a) 1 and 3 only (b) 2 and 4 only
(c) 1, 2 and 3 only (d) 2, 3 and 4 only

**3.** Consider the following pairs regarding types of taxes and the authority responsible for levying them:

| Type of Tax | Responsible Authority |
|---|---|
| 1. Income Tax | Central Government |
| 2. Property Tax | State Government |
| 3. Excise Duty on Alcohol | State Government |
| 4. Goods and Services Tax (GST) | Jointly by Central and State Governments |

How many pairs given above is/are correctly matched?

(a) Only one pair
(b) Only two pairs
(c) Only three pairs
(d) All four pairs

### Topic 2 : Important Terms

**4.** Consider the following statements:

1. Tax incidence refers to the entity on which the tax is legally imposed.
2. Tax burden refers to the entity that ultimately bears the economic cost of the tax.
3. Tax incidence and tax burden are always the same in any given tax situation.

Which of the statements given above are correct?

(a) 1 and 2 only
(b) 2 and 3 only
(c) 1 and 3 only
(d) 1, 2 and 3

**5.** With reference to the concept of 'Tax Base,' consider the following statements:

1. Tax base refers to the total amount of assets or income that can be taxed by a government.
2. A broader tax base allows the government to lower tax rates while still maintaining revenue.
3. The tax base can only include income from salaries and wages.

How many of the statements given above is/are correct?

(a) Only one (b) Only two
(c) All three (d) None

**6.** Which of the following measures have been taken by the Indian government to ensure a wider tax base and better compliance?

1. Implementation of Goods and Services Tax (GST)
2. Introduction of the PAN-Aadhaar linkage for taxpayers
3. the personal income tax exemption limit
4. Launching the Faceless Assessment Scheme

Select the correct answer from the codes given below:

(a) 1, 2 and 4 only (b) 2 and 3 only
(c) 1 and 4 only (d) 1, 2, 3 and 4

**7.** Which of the following best describes the concept of 'Tax Expenditure'?

(a) Government revenue collected from indirect taxes
(b) Financial assistance provided to businesses through grants
(c) Revenue forgone by the government due to tax exemptions, deductions, or credits to encourage specific activities or sectors
(d) Public spending on infrastructure and social services

**8.** Consider the following statements about 'Tax Elasticity':

1. It measures the percentage change in tax revenue to the percentage change in the tax rate.
2. It is high when the tax revenue changes significantly with small changes in the tax rate.
3. It is always greater than 1.

How many of the statements given above is/are correct?

(a) Only one
(b) Only two
(c) All three
(d) None

**9.** With reference to the concept of 'Tax Buoyancy' in India, consider the following statements:

1. High tax buoyancy indicates that tax revenues increase at a faster rate than the growth in GDP.
2. A tax system with high buoyancy is less effective in stabilising the economy during periods of economic fluctuation.

Which of the statements given above is/are correct?

(a) 1 only
(b) 2 only
(c) Both 1 and 2
(d) Neither 1 nor 2

**10.** According to the Laffer Curve, what happens to tax revenue when tax rates exceed an optimal level?

(a) Tax revenue continues to increase as tax rates increase
(b) Tax revenue remains constant regardless of changes in tax rates
(c) Tax revenue decreases as tax rates increase beyond a certain point
(d) Tax revenue becomes negative

**11.** Consider the following statements:

1. Tax avoidance is a strategy used by individuals and corporations to exploit loopholes in tax laws to minimise their tax burden.
2. Tax evasion involves deliberate misrepresentation or non-disclosure of income to reduce tax liabilities.
3. Both tax avoidance and tax evasion are legally punishable under the Indian Income Tax Act.

How many of the statements given above is/are correct?

(a) Only one (b) Only two
(c) All three (d) None

**12.** Which of the following correctly describes 'Tax Haven'?

(a) A country or jurisdiction that offers minimal or no tax liability to foreign individuals and businesses

(b) A country that imposes high taxes on both domestic and foreign income

(c) A financial institution that provides tax benefits to its customers

(d) A type of government policy designed to increase tax revenue

**13.** With reference to the concept of 'Inverted Duty Structure,' consider the following statements:

1. An inverted duty structure occurs when import duties on finished goods are lower than the import duties on raw materials.
2. An inverted duty structure can lead to higher production costs for domestic manufacturers.
3. The inverted duty structure always benefits domestic manufacturers by reducing their tax burden.

Which of the statements given above are correct?

(a) 1 and 2 only (b) 2 and 3 only
(c) 1 and 3 only (d) 1, 2 and 3

**14.** Pigouvian taxes are designed to correct the negative externalities of certain activities. In this context, which of the following can be considered examples of Pigouvian taxes?

1. Carbon tax on emissions from factories
2. Tax on sugary drinks to reduce consumption and promote public health
3. Fuel tax imposed to fund public transportation infrastructure
4. Congestion tax on vehicles entering a crowded urban area

Select the correct answer from the codes given below:

(a) 1 and 3 only (b) 1, 2 and 4 only
(c) 2 and 3 only (d) 1, 2, 3 and 4

**15.** Which of the following best describes the purpose of 'Withholding Tax'?

(a) To allow individuals to pay taxes at their discretion

(b) To collect tax at the source of income, ensuring compliance

(c) To provide tax rebates on income earned abroad

(d) To facilitate tax refunds for foreign investments

## Topic 3 : Methods of Taxation

**16.** Principles of taxation guide the formulation of a fair and efficient tax system. Which of the following principles can be considered fundamental to designing a robust tax policy?

1. Convenience 2. Economy
3. Universality 4. Efficiency

Select the correct answer from the codes given below:

(a) 1 and 2 only
(b) 1, 2 and 4 only
(c) 3 and 4 only
(d) 1, 2, 3 and 4

**17.** With reference to the methods of taxation, consider the following statements:

1. Progressive taxation imposes a higher tax rate on individuals with higher incomes.
2. Regressive taxation can lead to a greater financial burden on lower-income individuals compared to higher-income individuals.
3. Proportional taxation imposes a flat tax rate, regardless of the income level of individuals.

How many of the statements given above is/are correct?

(a) Only one
(b) Only two
(c) All three
(d) None

**18.** Which of the following best describes an 'Ad Valorem Tax'?

(a) A fixed amount of tax applied to each unit of a product

(b) A tax based on the assessed value of an item or property

(c) A tax only applicable to imported goods

(d) A tax levied at the point of sale of a product

**19.** Which of the following taxes are examples of ad valorem taxes in India?

1. Property Tax
2. Excise Duty on Petrol/Diesel
3. Goods and Services Tax (GST)
4. Custom Duty on imported goods

Select the correct answer from the codes given below:

(a) 1 and 2 only
(b) 1, 3 and 4 only
(c) 2 and 3 only
(d) 1, 2, 3 and 4

**20.** Consider the following statements:

1. Direct taxes are levied directly on individuals or entities, and the burden of these taxes cannot be shifted to others.
2. Indirect taxes are often considered regressive because they take a larger percentage of income from lower-income groups.
3. Corporate tax is an example of an indirect tax, as it is passed on to consumers through higher prices.

How many of the statements given above is/are correct?

(a) Only one
(b) Only two
(c) All three
(d) None

## Topic 4 : Direct Taxes

**21.** Direct taxes are taxes paid directly by individuals or organisations to the government. In this context, which of the following are considered examples of direct taxes in India?

1. Income Tax
2. Corporate Tax
3. Goods and Services Tax (GST)
4. Capital Gains Tax

Select the correct answer from the codes given below:

(a) 1, 2 and 4 only
(b) 1 and 3 only
(c) 2 and 4 only
(d) 1, 2, 3 and 4

**22.** Consider the following pairs regarding types of direct taxes and their descriptions in India:

| | Type of Direct Tax | Description |
|---|---|---|
| 1. | Capital Gains Tax | Tax on profits from the sale of capital assets |
| 2. | Securities Transaction Tax (STT) | Tax on the value of transactions of securities |
| 3. | Corporate Tax | Tax on profits made by domestic and foreign companies |
| 4. | Professional Tax | Tax levied on professionals such as doctors and lawyers |

How many pairs given above is/are correctly matched?

(a) Only one pair (b) Only two pairs
(c) Only three pairs (d) All four pairs

**23.** With reference to the income tax system in India, consider the following statements:

1. Income earned by a non-resident from a property located in India is taxable in India.
2. Income earned by agricultural activities is exempt from income tax under the Indian Income Tax Act.
3. The Government of India levies a uniform income tax rate for all individuals, irrespective of their income levels.

How many of the statements given above is/are correct?

(a) Only one (b) Only two
(c) All three (d) None

**24.** In India, which of the following types of income are subject to income tax?

1. Income from business or profession
2. Income received as gifts exceeding a certain limit
3. Income from sale of personal jewellery
4. Income from a lottery win

Select the correct answer from the codes given below:

(a) 1, 2 and 3 only (b) 1 and 3 only
(c) 2 and 4 only (d) 1, 2, 3 and 4

**25.** With reference to 'Corporate Tax' in India, consider the following statements:

1. It is a direct tax levied on the net income of companies.
2. Different tax rates apply to Indian and foreign corporations.
3. Corporate entities earning revenue from India but incorporated outside India are not liable to pay corporate tax in India.

Which of the statements given above are correct?

(a) 1 and 2 only
(b) 2 and 3 only
(c) 1 and 3 only
(d) 1, 2 and 3

**26.** With reference to the 'Minimum Alternate Tax (MAT)', consider the following statements:

1. MAT provisions were introduced to curb tax avoidance by companies using various exemptions and deductions.
2. MAT is payable only by domestic companies and does not apply to foreign companies operating in India.
3. MAT is calculated at a standard rate of 18.5% of the book profits for all companies.

Which of the statements given above is/are correct?

(a) 1 and 2 only
(b) 1 only
(c) 2 and 3 only
(d) 1, 2 and 3

**27.** Which of the following best describes the difference between 'Minimum Alternate Tax (MAT)' and 'Alternate Minimum Tax (AMT)' in India?

(a) MAT applies to all companies, while AMT applies only to certain individuals
(b) MAT is applicable to companies whereas AMT targets non-corporate taxpayers availing tax incentives.
(c) MAT provides tax rebates for corporate taxpayers, while AMT exempts all income of non-corporate entities
(d) MAT is levied on small businesses only, while AMT applies to large corporations

**28.** Which of the following types of income are classified as 'Capital Gains' under the Income Tax Act in India?

1. Profit from the sale of an investment property
2. Income earned from dividends
3. Gains from the sale of unlisted shares
4. Interest earned on fixed deposits

Select the correct answer from the codes given below:

(a) 1 and 3 only (b) 2 and 4 only
(c) 1, 2 and 3 only (d) 1, 3 and 4 only

**29.** With reference to the 'Digital Service Tax (DST)' in India, consider the following statements:

1. It is applicable to foreign e-commerce companies earning revenue from Indian users.
2. It is levied at a flat rate of 6% on the total revenue earned by foreign companies from digital services provided to Indian residents.
3. It is applicable to both business-to-business (B2B) and business-to-consumer (B2C) transactions.

How many of the statements given above is/are correct?

(a) Only one
(b) Only two
(c) All three
(d) None

**30.** Consider the following digital services:

1. Online advertising services provided by a foreign company to Indian businesses
2. Digital content streaming services provided by a non-resident company to Indian subscribers
3. Cloud computing services offered by an Indian company to global customers
4. E-commerce platforms facilitating the sale of goods by foreign companies to Indian consumers

How many of the given above services is/are subject to the Digital Service Tax (DST) in India?

(a) Only one (b) Only two
(c) Only three (d) All four

**31.** Which of the following is a primary reason for the introduction of the GAFA tax?
(a) To promote local technology startups
(b) To ensure fair taxation of digital services provided by large technology firms
(c) To fund digital infrastructure projects
(d) To regulate internet usage by tech giants

**32.** With reference to the 'Securities Transaction Tax (STT)', consider the following statements:
1. STT is applicable on all transactions involving the sale of securities on recognised stock exchanges in India.
2. STT encourages long-term investments by making frequent trading more expensive.
3. STT is applicable to both buyer and seller in all transactions involving securities.

Which of the statements given above is/are correct?
(a) 1 only (b) 2 only
(c) Both 1 and 2 (d) Neither 1 nor 2

**33.** Consider the following types of securities:
1. Equity shares traded on a recognised stock exchange
2. Debt securities issued by the government
3. Derivatives traded on recognised stock exchanges
4. Buying or selling of mutual fund units of an equity fund.

How many of the given above securities is/are subject to 'Securities Transaction Tax (STT)' in India?
(a) Only one (b) Only two
(c) Only three (d) All four

**34.** Which of the following best describes about the 'Tobin Tax'?
(a) A tax on luxury goods to promote equality
(b) A tax on short-term currency transactions aimed at reducing volatility
(c) A tax on corporate profits to increase government revenue
(d) A tax on income earned from foreign investments

**35.** Consider the following statements about 'Commodities Transaction Tax (CTT)':
1. It is applicable to agricultural commodities traded on recognised commodity exchanges.
2. It is a direct tax levied by the government on the sale of commodities.
3. The rate of CTT is the same for all types of commodities traded in India.

Which of the statements given above are incorrect?
(a) 1 and 2 only (b) 2 and 3 only
(c) 1 and 3 only (d) 1, 2 and 3

**36.** Which of the following transactions on a recognised exchange are subject to the 'Commodities Transaction Tax (CTT)' in India?
1. Trading of gold futures
2. Trading of wheat futures
3. Trading of crude oil futures
4. Trading of equity shares

Select the correct answer from the codes given below:
(a) 1 and 3 only (b) 1, 2 and 3 only
(c) 2 and 4 only (d) 1, 3 and 4 only

**37.** Consider the following statements:
1. Both cess and surcharge are levied as additional charges over and above the existing taxes.
2. Surcharge can be used for any purpose, while cess is earmarked for a specific purpose.
3. Both cess and surcharge are included in the Consolidated Fund of India.

How many of the statements given above is/are correct?
(a) Only one (b) Only two
(c) All three (d) None

**38.** With reference to cess and surcharge in India, consider the following statements:
1. The revenue generated from both cess and surcharge is not shared with State Governments.
2. Surcharge is applicable only to individuals with high incomes while cess can be applied to a broader range of taxpayers.

Which of the statements given above is/are correct?
(a) 1 only (b) 2 only
(c) Both 1 and 2 (d) Neither 1 nor 2

## Topic 5 : Indirect Taxes

**39.** With reference to the 'Goods and Services Tax (GST)' in India, consider the following statements:

1. GST is a single indirect tax levied on the supply of goods and services across India.
2. GST replaced multiple indirect taxes previously levied by the Central and State Governments.
3. GST is collected at the point of consumption, not at the point of origin.

Which of the statements given above are correct?

(a) 1 and 2 only (b) 1 and 3 only
(c) 2 and 3 only (d) 1, 2 and 3

**40.** With reference to the 'Goods and Services Tax (GST)' in the context of the Indian Constitution, consider the following statements:

1. GST Council is a constitutional body that makes recommendations on GST-related issues.
2. The President can unilaterally impose GST in any state without the approval of the GST Council.

Which of the statements given above is/are correct?

(a) 1 only (b) 2 only
(c) Both 1 and 2 (d) Neither 1 nor 2

**41.** Consider the following goods and services:

1. Electricity
2. Hotel services
3. Petroleum
4. Basic educational services upto secondary level

How many of the above is/are exempt from GST in India?

(a) Only one (b) Only two
(c) Only three (d) All four

**42.** Which of the following are zero-rated supplies under GST in India?

1. Export of goods
2. Inter-state supply of goods
3. Supply to Special Economic Zones (SEZs)
4. Intra-state supply of goods

Select the correct answer from the codes given below:

(a) 1 and 2 only (b) 1 and 3 only
(c) 2 and 4 only (d) 3 and 4 only

**43.** With reference to the 'Goods and Services Tax (GST)' system in India, consider the following statements:

1. It is a destination-based tax levied at the point of consumption.
2. Under the GST regime, input tax credit is available across the supply chain from the manufacturer to the retailer.
3. GST rates are uniform across all goods and services.

How many of the statements given above is/are correct?

(a) Only one (b) Only two
(c) All three (d) None

**44.** Consider the following features:

1. Multi-stage taxation levied on every value addition.
2. Dual GST model involving both Central and State Governments.
3. Uniform tax rates for all goods and services.
4. Digital compliance and filling system.

How many of the above features is/are applicable to the GST system in India?

(a) Only one
(b) Only two
(c) Only three
(d) All four

**45.** Consider the following taxes:

1. Central Excise Duty
2. Service Tax
3. Customs Duty
4. Value Added Tax (VAT)

How many of the given above taxes was/were subsumed under the Goods and Services Tax (GST) in India?

(a) Only one
(b) Only two
(c) Only three
(d) All four

**46.** With reference to the 'GST Composition Scheme' in India, consider the following statements:

1. It is available to small taxpayers with an annual turnover of up to INR 1.5 crore.
2. Under the composition scheme, taxpayers can file quarterly returns instead of monthly returns.
3. Taxpayers under the composition scheme are eligible to claim input tax credit.

Which of the statements given above are correct?

(a) 1 and 2 only
(b) 2 and 3 only
(c) 1 and 3 only
(d) 1, 2 and 3

**47.** Which of the following are eligible to opt for the GST Composition Scheme in India?

1. A wholesale trader with an annual turnover of INR 1 crore.
2. An e-commerce operator supplying goods through an online platform.
3. A small manufacturer with an annual turnover of INR 80 lakh.
4. A service provider with an annual turnover of INR 70 lakh providing consultancy services.

Select the correct answer from the codes given below:

(a) 1 and 3 only (b) 2 and 4 only
(c) 1, 2 and 3 only (d) 1, 3 and 4 only

**48.** With reference to the 'GST Council', consider the following statements:

1. It is a constitutional body formed under Article 279A of the Indian Constitution.
2. Union Finance Minister is the Chairperson of the GST Council.
3. All decisions in the GST Council require a three-fourths majority vote of the members present and voting.

Which of the statements given above are correct?

(a) 1 and 2 only (b) 2 and 3 only
(c) 1 and 3 only (d) 1, 2 and 3

**49.** Which of the following correctly describes about the 'Reverse Charge Mechanism (RCM)' under GST?

(a) A mechanism where the buyer is liable to pay tax instead of the seller.
(b) A mechanism where the seller is liable to pay tax on behalf of the buyer.
(c) A mechanism where the government directly collects tax from the end consumer.
(d) A mechanism where both buyer and seller share the tax liability equally.

**50.** With reference to the GST Compensation Cess in India, consider the following statements:

1. It is levied to compensate states for any revenue loss due to the implementation of GST.
2. It is applicable to all goods and services under GST.
3. The revenue from the GST Compensation Cess is credited to the Consolidated Fund of India.

How many of the statements given above is/are correct?

(a) Only one
(b) Only two
(c) All three
(d) None

**51.** With reference to Double Taxation Avoidance Agreement (DTAA), consider the following statements:

1. It aims to prevent taxpayers from being taxed twice on the same income in both countries involved in the agreement.
2. Under DTAA, taxpayers are allowed to choose which country's tax rate to apply to their income.
3. DTAA applies only to corporate entities and not to individual taxpayers.

Which of the statements given above is/are correct?

(a) 1 only
(b) 1 and 3 only
(c) 2 and 3 only
(d) 1, 2, and 3

**52.** Which of the following best describes the concept of Round Tripping in the context of international finance?
(a) Moving money abroad for investment in foreign markets
(b) Routing funds through foreign jurisdictions to reinvest in the original country
(c) Using international loans to expand operations abroad
(d) Transferring profits to tax havens for long-term foreign investments

**53.** Consider the following methods:
1. Routing investments through tax havens.
2. Using shell companies in foreign jurisdictions.
3. Buying undervalued assets abroad to sell back in the home country.

How many of the given above methods is/are typically associated with 'Round Tripping'?
(a) Only one
(b) Only two
(c) All three
(d) None

**54.** Which of the following best describes the primary purpose of a Shell Company?
(a) To conduct significant commercial activities within a specific sector
(b) To serve as the main business entity in a multinational corporation
(c) To represent government interests in foreign markets
(d) To hold assets and manage financial transactions without any substantial business operations

**55.** Which of the following best describes the 'Arm's Length Principle' in the context of transfer pricing?
(a) Ensuring that all international transactions are exempt from taxation
(b) Setting prices between related entities as if they were unrelated, to avoid tax manipulation
(c) Allowing companies to decide their prices without regulatory oversight
(d) Providing government subsidies for intra-company transactions

**56.** What is the primary objective of Base Erosion and Profit Shifting (BEPS) initiatives led by the OECD?
(a) To ensure tax incentives are given to multinational corporations
(b) To prevent multinational corporations from exploiting tax loopholes to shift profits
(c) To encourage countries to reduce corporate tax rates
(d) To mandate uniform tax rates across all participating countries

**57.** With reference to the 'Global Minimum Corporate Tax' initiative, consider the following statements:
1. It aims to prevent multinational companies from shifting profits to low-tax jurisdictions.
2. The minimum tax rate under this initiative is proposed to be 21%.
3. This initiative is led by the Organisation for Economic Co-operation and Development (OECD).

Which of the statements given above are correct?
(a) 1 and 2 only
(b) 1 and 3 only
(c) 2 and 3 only
(d) 1, 2 and 3

**58.** In the context of Advance Pricing Agreement (APA), which of the following is a key benefit?
(a) Exempting companies from filing tax returns in multiple countries
(b) Providing certainty on tax treatment of related-party transactions
(c) Reducing a company's overall tax burden by providing tax rebates
(d) Increasing tax rates for multinational entities

**59.** With reference to the 'Central Board of Direct Taxes (CBDT)', consider the following statements:

1. CBDT is responsible for formulating policies related to direct taxes in India.
2. It functions under the Ministry of Finance, Government of India.
3. It has the authority to issue guidelines for all state taxes.

Which of the statements given above are correct?

(a) 1 and 2 only
(b) 2 and 3 only
(c) 1 and 3 only
(d) 1, 2 and 3

**60.** With reference to the Central Board of Indirect Taxes and Customs (CBIC), consider the following statements:

1. It is responsible for the administration of GST, Customs, Central Excise and Service Tax in India.
2. It functions under the Department of Economic Affairs, Ministry of Finance.
3. It formulates policies and issues guidelines to ensure compliance with indirect tax laws.

How many of the statements given above is/are correct?

(a) Only one
(b) Only two
(c) All three
(d) None

**61.** With reference to the E-Way Bill System, consider the following statements:

1. It is mandatory for goods valued over ₹ 50,000 for inter-state transport.
2. It is not required for goods transported by non-motorised vehicles.
3. It can be generated only by registered businesses.

Which of the statements given above are correct?

(a) 1 and 2 only
(b) 2 and 3 only
(c) 1 and 3 only
(d) 1, 2 and 3

**62.** With reference to General Anti-Avoidance Rules (GAAR), consider the following statements:

1. GAAR provisions allow tax authorities to disregard transactions that lack commercial substance.
2. GAAR applies only to transactions exceeding a specific threshold.
3. It applies to both domestic and international transactions.

Which of the statements given above are correct?

(a) 1 and 2 only
(b) 1 and 3 only
(c) 2 and 3 only
(d) 1, 2 and 3

**63.** The Direct Tax Code (DTC) aims to reform India's tax structure. Which of the following potential benefits are associated with the implementation of the DTC?

1. Simplification of tax laws to improve compliance
2. Increased foreign direct investment due to a more predictable tax regime
3. Reduction in tax litigation through clearer definitions and rules
4. Enhanced ability for states to set direct tax rates independently

Select the correct answer from the codes given below:

(a) 1, 2 and 3 only
(b) 2 and 4 only
(c) 1, 3 and 4 only
(d) 1, 2, 3 and 4

# OMR SHEET

**Assessment Round**

| | | | | | | | | | | | | | | | | | | | |
|---|---|---|---|---|---|---|---|---|---|---|---|---|---|---|---|---|---|---|---|
| 1 | a | b | c | d | 31 | a | b | c | d | 61 | a | b | c | d | 91 | a | b | c | d |
| 2 | a | b | c | d | 32 | a | b | c | d | 62 | a | b | c | d | 92 | a | b | c | d |
| 3 | a | b | c | d | 33 | a | b | c | d | 63 | a | b | c | d | 93 | a | b | c | d |
| 4 | a | b | c | d | 34 | a | b | c | d | 64 | a | b | c | d | 94 | a | b | c | d |
| 5 | a | b | c | d | 35 | a | b | c | d | 65 | a | b | c | d | 95 | a | b | c | d |
| 6 | a | b | c | d | 36 | a | b | c | d | 66 | a | b | c | d | 96 | a | b | c | d |
| 7 | a | b | c | d | 37 | a | b | c | d | 67 | a | b | c | d | 97 | a | b | c | d |
| 8 | a | b | c | d | 38 | a | b | c | d | 68 | a | b | c | d | 98 | a | b | c | d |
| 9 | a | b | c | d | 39 | a | b | c | d | 69 | a | b | c | d | 99 | a | b | c | d |
| 10 | a | b | c | d | 40 | a | b | c | d | 70 | a | b | c | d | 100 | a | b | c | d |
| 11 | a | b | c | d | 41 | a | b | c | d | 71 | a | b | c | d | 101 | a | b | c | d |
| 12 | a | b | c | d | 42 | a | b | c | d | 72 | a | b | c | d | 102 | a | b | c | d |
| 13 | a | b | c | d | 43 | a | b | c | d | 73 | a | b | c | d | 103 | a | b | c | d |
| 14 | a | b | c | d | 44 | a | b | c | d | 74 | a | b | c | d | 104 | a | b | c | d |
| 15 | a | b | c | d | 45 | a | b | c | d | 75 | a | b | c | d | 105 | a | b | c | d |
| 16 | a | b | c | d | 46 | a | b | c | d | 76 | a | b | c | d | 106 | a | b | c | d |
| 17 | a | b | c | d | 47 | a | b | c | d | 77 | a | b | c | d | 107 | a | b | c | d |
| 18 | a | b | c | d | 48 | a | b | c | d | 78 | a | b | c | d | 108 | a | b | c | d |
| 19 | a | b | c | d | 49 | a | b | c | d | 79 | a | b | c | d | 109 | a | b | c | d |
| 20 | a | b | c | d | 50 | a | b | c | d | 80 | a | b | c | d | 110 | a | b | c | d |
| 21 | a | b | c | d | 51 | a | b | c | d | 81 | a | b | c | d | 111 | a | b | c | d |
| 22 | a | b | c | d | 52 | a | b | c | d | 82 | a | b | c | d | 112 | a | b | c | d |
| 23 | a | b | c | d | 53 | a | b | c | d | 83 | a | b | c | d | 113 | a | b | c | d |
| 24 | a | b | c | d | 54 | a | b | c | d | 84 | a | b | c | d | 114 | a | b | c | d |
| 25 | a | b | c | d | 55 | a | b | c | d | 85 | a | b | c | d | 115 | a | b | c | d |
| 26 | a | b | c | d | 56 | a | b | c | d | 86 | a | b | c | d | 116 | a | b | c | d |
| 27 | a | b | c | d | 57 | a | b | c | d | 87 | a | b | c | d | 117 | a | b | c | d |
| 28 | a | b | c | d | 58 | a | b | c | d | 88 | a | b | c | d | 118 | a | b | c | d |
| 29 | a | b | c | d | 59 | a | b | c | d | 89 | a | b | c | d | 119 | a | b | c | d |
| 30 | a | b | c | d | 60 | a | b | c | d | 90 | a | b | c | d | 120 | a | b | c | d |

## Calculate Your Score

| | |
|---|---|
| **Correct (✓)** | |
| **Incorrect (✓)** | |
| **Unattempted** | |
| **Total Score** | |
| **Accuracy (%)** | |

## Reasons for Incorrect Answers?

| | |
|---|---|
| 1. Lack of Knowledge/Existing Source Insufficient | |
| 2. Lack of Multiple Revision | |
| 3. Common Sense Mistakes | |

**Note :**

1. Calculate total score as correct answers carry 2 marks each 1/3rd marks will deducted for **Incorrect** Answers.
2. Calculate Accuracy (%) by dividing the number of correct answers to the total number of attempted questions.

## Past Learning

**1.** Which one of the following situations best reflects 'Indirect Transfers' often talked about in media recently with reference to India? **(2022)**

(a) An Indian company investing in a foreign enterprise and paying taxes to the foreign country on the profits arising out of its investment.

(b) A foreign company investing in India and paying taxes to the country of its base on the profits arising out of its investment.

(c) An Indian company purchases tangible assets in a foreign country and sells such assets after their value increases and transfers the proceeds to India.

(d) A foreign company transfers shares and such shares derive their substantial value from assets located in India.

**2.** Which one of the following effects of creation of black money in India has been main cause of worry to the Government of India? **(2021)**

(a) Diversion of resources to the purchase of real estate and investment in luxury housing.

(b) Investment in unproductive activities and purchase of precious stones, jewellery, gold, etc.

(c) Large donations to political parties and growth of regionalism.

(d) Loss of revenue to the State Exchequer due to tax evasion.

**3.** With reference to India's decision to levy an equalisation tax of 6% on online advertisement services offered by non-resident entities, which of the following statements is/are correct? **(2018)**

1. It is introduced as a part of the Income Tax Act that offers advertisement services in India.
2. Non-resident entities that offer advertisement services in Indian can claim a tax credit in their home country under the 'Double Taxation Avoidance Agreements'.

Select the correct answer using the codes given below:

(a) 1 only (b) 2 only
(c) Both 1 and 2 (d) Neither 1 nor 2

**4.** Consider the following items: **(2018)**

1. Cereal grains hulled 2. Chicken eggs cooked
3. Fish processed and canned
4. Newspapers containing advertising material

Which of the above items is/are exempted under GST (Goods and Services Tax)?

(a) 1 only (b) 2 and 3 only
(c) 1, 2 and 4 only (d) 1, 2, 3 and 4

**5.** What is/are the most likely advantages of implementing 'Goods and Services Tax (GST)'? **(2017)**

1. It will replace multiple taxes collected by multiple authorities and will thus create a single market in India.
2. It will drastically reduce the 'Current Account Deficit' of India and will enable it to increase its foreign exchange reserves.
3. It will enormously increase the growth and size of economy of India and will enable it to overtake China in the near future.

Select the correct answer using the codes given below:

(a) 1 only (b) 2 and 3 only
(c) 1 and 3 only (d) 1, 2 and 3

**6.** Consider the following statements: **(2017)**

1. Tax revenue as a percent of GDP of India has steadily increased in the last decade.
2. Fiscal deficit as a percent of GDP of India has steadily increased in the last decade.

Which of the statements given above is/are correct?

(a) 1 only (b) 2 only
(c) Both 1 and 2 (d) Neither 1 nor 2

**7.** The term 'Base Erosion and Profit Shifting' is sometimes seen in the news in the context of: **(2016)**

(a) mining operation by multinational companies in resource-rich but backward areas
(b) curbing of the tax evasion by multinational companies
(c) exploitation of genetic resources of a country by multinational companies
(d) lack of consideration of environmental planning and developmental costs in the implementation of projects

# Detailed Solutions

## Assessment Round

**1.** *(b)* Only two

- **Statement 1 is correct: Article 265 of the Indian Constitution states that no tax shall be levied or collected except by the authority of law.** This provision ensures that taxation in India is carried out according to the rule of law, meaning that taxes can only be imposed if there is a valid law passed by the Parliament or State Legislature authorising the tax. This protects citizens from arbitrary taxation.
- **Statement 2 is correct: The Seventh Schedule of the Indian Constitution contains three lists: the Union List, State List and Concurrent List, which specify the subjects on which the Union and State Governments can levy taxes.**
- The Union List includes subjects on which only the Central Government can levy taxes (e.g., income tax), while the State List includes subjects for state taxation (e.g., property tax).
- **Statement 3 is incorrect: The President does not have the authority to impose new taxes without the approval of the Parliament.** All taxes must be authorised by law, meaning that any new tax or modification of existing taxes must be passed by the Parliament (for central taxes) or the State Legislature (for state taxes).
- **The President cannot unilaterally impose taxes; the process of taxation requires legislative approval.**

**Therefore, the correct answer is (b) Only two.**

**2.** *(a)* 1 and 3 only

- **Option 1 is correct: Land Revenue is a tax that can be levied by the State Governments.** It is a direct tax imposed on landowners and its collection is the responsibility of the State Governments.
- **Option 2 is incorrect: Corporation Tax is levied by the Central Government**, not the State Governments. This tax is imposed on the income of companies and corporations operating in India.
- **Option 3 is correct: Stamp Duty is levied by the State Governments.** Stamp duty is a tax on legal documents, such as property transactions, agreements, and contracts. The rates of stamp duty may vary from state to state.
- **Option 4 is incorrect: Customs Duty is levied by the Central Government.** Customs duty is a tax imposed on goods imported into or exported from the country. The Central Government collects customs duty as part of its regulatory measures to control international trade and generate revenue from cross-border commerce.

**Therefore, the correct answer is (a) 1 and 3 only.**

**3.** *(d)* All four pairs

- **Pair 1 is correct: Income Tax is levied by the Central Government.** The Central Government is responsible for collecting income tax on individuals and businesses under the Income Tax Act, 1961. It applies to both salaried individuals and businesses based on their income.
- **Pair 2 is correct: Property Tax is levied by the State Governments** (and in many cases, it is collected by local municipal bodies). Property tax is imposed on real estate, including land and buildings. The rates and regulations for property tax may vary from state to state.
- **Pair 3 is correct: Excise Duty on Alcohol is levied by the State Governments.** While the Central Government collects excise duty on goods like petroleum and tobacco, excise duty on alcoholic beverages is a state subject. This makes it a significant revenue stream for State Governments, which control the taxation and sale of alcohol within their respective states.
- **Pair 4 is correct: GST (Goods and Services Tax) is levied jointly by the Central and**

**State Governments.** GST is a comprehensive indirect tax on goods and services and it is implemented under a dual structure. The **Central GST (CGST)** is collected by the Central Government, and the **State GST (SGST)** is collected by State Governments. For inter-state transactions, **Integrated GST (IGST)** is collected by the Central Government and shared with the states.

**Therefore, the correct answer is (d) All four pairs.**

**4.** *(a)* 1 and 2 only

- **Statement 1 is correct: Tax incidence refers to the legal responsibility of paying the tax,** meaning it is the entity on which the tax is officially levied. For example, in the case of a sales tax, the seller is responsible for collecting and remitting the tax to the government. The tax incidence specifies the party that is legally obligated to comply with tax laws and make the payment to the government.
- **Statement 2 is correct: Tax burden, or economic incidence, refers to the entity that ultimately bears the economic cost of the tax.** This burden is determined after the tax has been shifted through price changes or other mechanisms. For instance, while a business may have the legal obligation to pay a tax, the actual economic cost may be passed on to consumers in the form of higher prices. The tax burden identifies who feels the impact of the tax financially.
- **Statement 3 is incorrect: Tax incidence and tax burden are not always the same.** While the tax incidence refers to the party legally responsible for paying the tax, the tax burden shows who ultimately bears the economic impact of the tax. These two can differ when taxes are passed on to others. For example, with sales tax, the legal incidence is on the seller, but the economic burden may be passed on to consumers through price increases. Thus, **the entity paying the tax legally is not always the one bearing the financial cost.**

**Therefore, the correct answer is (a) 1 and 2 only.**

**5.** *(b)* Only two

- **Statement 1 is correct: The tax base is the total amount of assets, income, or value that is subject to taxation by a government.** The tax base represents the range of economic activities or assets, such as income, property and goods, that are subject to taxation. Larger the tax base, the more revenue the government can generate without necessarily increasing tax rates.
- **Statement 2 is correct: A broader tax base allows for lower tax rates** as more sources of income or assets are taxed, helping maintain or increase revenue. By expanding the tax base to include a wide variety of income sources or assets, governments can spread the tax burden across more entities, enabling them to keep tax rates relatively low while still generating sufficient revenue. This helps create a more balanced and fair taxation system.
- **Statement 3 is incorrect: The tax base can include various sources such as property, goods, services and investments, not just income from salaries and wages.** While salaries and wages are an important part of the tax base, other sources of income, such as business profits, capital gains, rental income, and taxes on goods and services, are also included. The tax base is therefore much broader than just income from employment, encompassing all taxable economic activity.

**Therefore, the correct answer is (b) Only two.**

**6.** *(a)* 1, 2 and 4 only

- **Option 1 is correct: The implementation of GST has helped formalise the economy and increase the tax base.** The Goods and Services Tax (GST) streamlined the indirect tax system by replacing a complex web of state and central taxes. It encouraged businesses to register and comply with tax laws, especially small and informal businesses that were previously outside the tax net. By formalising these businesses, GST has contributed to a broader tax base.
- **Option 2 is correct: Linking PAN with Aadhaar helps in tracking taxpayers and**

reduces tax evasion, thereby expanding the tax base. The Permanent Account Number (PAN) is used to track financial transactions, and linking it with Aadhaar ensures that individuals cannot use multiple PANs to evade taxes. This linkage enhances transparency in the tax system, making it easier for tax authorities to identify and monitor taxpayers, thereby widening the tax base.

- **Option 3 is incorrect: Increasing the personal income tax exemption limit reduces the number of taxpayers,** which does not help in widening the tax base. When the exemption limit is raised, fewer people fall under the taxable income bracket, which can shrink the tax base. While this may provide relief to lower-income groups, it does not contribute to expanding the number of taxpayers or the overall tax revenue.
- **Option 4 is correct: The Faceless Assessment Scheme promotes transparency and reduces corruption**, encouraging more people to comply with tax laws. The scheme eliminates the need for physical interaction between taxpayers and tax officers, reducing opportunities for corruption and favouritism. This increased transparency and impartiality boost confidence in the tax system, encouraging better compliance and helping to expand the tax base.

**Therefore, the correct answer is (a) 1, 2 and 4 only.**

**7.** *(c)* Revenue forgone by the government due to tax exemptions, deductions, or credits to encourage specific activities or sectors

Tax expenditure refers to the revenue that the government foregoes by providing tax exemptions, deductions, or credits to incentivise certain activities (like investment, research, or housing). This indirect spending supports policy goals without direct cash outflows.

**Thus, option (c) is the correct answer.**

**8.** *(b)* Only two

- **Statements 1 is correct: Tax elasticity is defined as the percentage change in tax revenue relative to the percentage change in the tax rate.** It measures how responsive tax revenue is to changes in the tax rate. It reflects the relationship between the tax rate set by the government and the total revenue collected.
- **Statement 2 is correct: A higher tax elasticity indicates that even a small change in the tax rate can lead to a significant change in tax revenue.**
- This is often seen in situations where the taxable base is highly responsive to changes in tax rates, such as consumption taxes on goods with high demand elasticity.
- **Statement 3 is incorrect: Tax elasticity can be less than, equal to, or greater than 1.** When tax elasticity is equal to 1, it means that a 1% change in the tax rate results in a 1% change in tax revenue. If tax elasticity is greater than 1, tax revenue is highly responsive to changes in the tax rate. Conversely, if tax elasticity is less than 1, changes in the tax rate have a smaller impact on tax revenue.

**Therefore, the correct answer is (b) Only two.**

**9.** *(a)* 1 only

- **Statement 1 is correct: High tax buoyancy indicates that tax revenues increase at a faster rate than the growth in GDP**, showing a robust response of tax collections to economic growth.
- In a tax system with high buoyancy, as the economy grows, tax revenues increase more than proportionally, providing the government with greater fiscal space to fund public services and reduce deficits.
- This reflects an efficient tax system where economic growth translates effectively into higher tax revenue without the need for increasing tax rates.
- **Statement 2 is incorrect: A tax system with high buoyancy typically acts as an automatic stabiliser**, meaning it collects more revenue during periods of economic growth and less during economic downturns.
- This helps to stabilise the economy because during periods of expansion, higher tax revenues prevent overheating by reducing disposable income, while in downturns, lower tax revenues leave more money in the

hands of individuals and businesses, helping to boost demand.

- **Thus, high buoyancy tax system aids in economic stabilisation, rather than destabilisation.**

**Therefore, the correct answer is (a) 1 only.**

***10.*** *(c)* Tax revenue decreases as tax rates increase beyond a certain point.

- **The Laffer Curve suggests that when tax rates exceed an optimal level, tax revenue starts to decrease.** This happens because higher tax rates can discourage work, saving and investment, which reduces the overall taxable income in the economy.
- The optimal tax rate is the point at which tax revenue is maximised. Beyond this point, increasing tax rates further results in declining tax revenue as individuals and businesses alter their behaviour to avoid high taxes.

**Thus, option (c) is the correct answer.**

***11.*** *(b)* Only two

- **Statement 1 is correct: Tax avoidance involves using legal methods and loopholes to minimise tax liabilities.** Tax avoidance is the practice of structuring financial affairs in a way that reduces the amount of tax owed, using provisions in the tax code. It involves taking advantage of deductions, exemptions, and other legal strategies to lower taxable income. While tax avoidance is legal, it often exploits loopholes in tax laws, which may be subject to scrutiny if the government changes its policies or laws.
- **Statement 2 is correct: Tax evasion involves illegal acts like misrepresenting or not disclosing income to reduce tax liabilities.** Tax evasion is a criminal offense that includes activities such as underreporting income, inflating deductions, or hiding money in offshore accounts. It is an illegal attempt to avoid paying taxes and is punishable by law. Tax evasion undermines the integrity of the tax system and can lead to severe penalties, including fines and imprisonment.
- **Statement 3 is incorrect: While tax evasion is legally punishable under the Indian Income Tax Act,** tax avoidance is not punishable as long as it remains within the boundaries of the law. Tax avoidance is considered a legal practice, even though it may involve exploiting loopholes in tax regulations. However, if tax avoidance crosses into illegal territory, such as deliberately misrepresenting information, it becomes tax evasion and is punishable under the law.

**Therefore, the correct answer is (b) Only two.**

***12.*** *(a)* A country or jurisdiction that offers minimal or no tax liability to foreign individuals and businesses.

**A tax haven is a country or jurisdiction that offers minimal or no tax liability to foreign individuals and businesses.** These countries or jurisdictions typically have very low tax rates, or in some cases, no tax at all on income or capital gains. Additionally, tax havens often provide strict confidentiality and limited transparency, making them attractive to businesses and individuals looking to minimize their tax liabilities while keeping financial details private.

**Thus, option (a) is the correct answer.**

***13.*** *(a)* 1 and 2 only

- **Statement 1 is correct: An inverted duty structure refers to a situation where the import duties on finished goods are lower than those on raw materials or intermediate goods.** This creates a disadvantage for domestic manufacturers who rely on imported raw materials or components. When they face higher import duties on these essential inputs compared to the lower duties on finished imported products, it becomes more expensive for them to produce goods domestically.
- **Statement 2 is correct: When raw materials attract higher duties than finished goods, domestic manufacturers face higher production costs,** which can reduce their competitiveness. The increased cost of raw materials makes it difficult for domestic manufacturers to compete with cheaper imported finished goods, potentially leading to lower demand for locally produced products and reduced market share for domestic industries.
- **Statement 3 is incorrect: An inverted duty structure typically disadvantages domestic**

manufacturers by increasing their costs, rather than benefiting them. Higher import duties on raw materials raise production costs, making domestically produced goods more expensive and less competitive compared to imported finished goods.

- This negatively impacts domestic industries, particularly those that rely on imported raw materials for their production processes.

**Therefore, the correct answer is (a) 1 and 2 only.**

***14.*** *(b)* 1, 2 and 4 only

A Pigouvian tax is designed to internalise the external costs of negative externalities.

- **Option 1 is correct: A carbon tax on emissions from factories is a classic example of a Pigouvian tax.** By imposing a tax on carbon emissions, the government aims to make polluters bear the social cost of their actions, thereby reducing environmental harm and encouraging cleaner production methods.
- **Option 2 is correct: A tax on sugary drinks is considered a Pigouvian tax** because it addresses the negative externalities associated with excessive sugar consumption, such as increased public health costs. By taxing sugary drinks, the government aims to discourage consumption, reduce health issues like obesity and diabetes, and lower the overall healthcare burden on society.
- **Option 3 is incorrect: A fuel tax imposed to fund public transportation infrastructure is not a Pigouvian tax.** While fuel taxes can have the effect of reducing fuel consumption and pollution, the primary purpose of this tax is to generate revenue for infrastructure projects, not to correct a negative externality. A Pigouvian tax specifically targets activities that create social costs, whereas a fuel tax for public transportation is primarily for funding purposes.
- **Option 4 is correct: A congestion tax on vehicles entering crowded urban areas is a Pigouvian tax.** It is intended to reduce traffic congestion, which is a negative externality caused by excessive vehicle use. By imposing a congestion tax, the government discourages driving in heavily congested areas, thus reducing traffic, lowering pollution, and improving the efficiency of transportation systems.

**Therefore, the correct answer is (b) 1, 2 and 4 only.**

***15.*** *(b)* To collect tax at the source of income, ensuring compliance

**Withholding tax** is designed to collect taxes directly from the source of income, typically by requiring the payer (such as an employer or institution) to deduct tax before disbursing income to the recipient. This ensures tax compliance and reduces the chance of tax evasion.

**Thus, option (b) is the correct answer.**

***16.*** *(b)* 1, 2 and 4 only

- **Option 1 is correct: The principle of convenience suggests that taxes should be collected in a manner that is convenient for the taxpayer.** This principle ensures that the process of paying taxes is as straightforward and hassle-free as possible, reducing the burden on taxpayers.
- **Option 2 is correct: The principle of economy emphasises that the cost of collecting taxes should be low relative to the revenue generated.** A tax system should be designed to minimise administrative costs, ensuring that a significant portion of the revenue collected goes to the government, rather than being consumed by the cost of collection.
- **Option 3 is incorrect: The principle of universality is not a fundamental principle of taxation.** While universality may refer to the idea that all taxpayers should contribute to the tax system, the more commonly recognised principles of taxation include equity, certainty, convenience, economy and efficiency.
- **Option 4 is correct: The principle of efficiency aims to ensure that the tax system does not create excessive economic distortions.** An efficient tax system should allocate resources optimally and avoid

negatively impacting economic decisions such as work, investment or consumption.

**Therefore, the correct answer is (b) 1, 2 and 4 only.**

**17.** *(c)* All three

- **Statement 1 is correct: Progressive taxation is a method where the tax rate increases as the taxpayer's income increases.** In a progressive tax system, individuals with higher incomes are subject to higher tax rates, placing a larger financial burden on wealthier individuals.
- This system is designed to promote equity by ensuring that those who earn more contribute a larger proportion of their income to taxes, helping to reduce income inequality.
- **Statement 2 is correct: Regressive taxation can place a disproportionate financial burden on lower-income individuals.** In a regressive tax system, lower-income earners pay a higher percentage of their income in taxes than higher-income earners.
- This occurs because regressive taxes, such as sales taxes or excise duties, take a larger share of income from those with lower earnings, making the tax system less equitable for poorer individuals.
- **Statement 3 is correct: Proportional taxation, also known as a flat tax, imposes the same tax rate on all income levels.** Under a proportional tax system, all taxpayers pay the same percentage of their income, regardless of their earnings.
- For example, if the tax rate is 10%, both low-income and high-income individuals would pay 10% of their income in taxes. This system is simpler to administer but may be seen as less fair than progressive taxation, as it does not account for differences in income levels.

**Therefore, the correct answer is (c) All three.**

**18.** *(b)* A tax based on the assessed value of an item or property

**Ad Valorem Tax** is a tax based on the assessed value of an item or property. For example, property taxes are typically ad valorem, as they are levied based on the current market value of the property.

**Thus, option (b) is the correct answer.**

**19.** *(b)* 1, 3 and 4 only

- **Option 1 is correct:** Property tax is an ad valorem tax since it is based on the assessed value of the property. Higher property values result in higher tax amounts, making it proportional to the asset's value.
- **Option 2 is incorrect:** Excise duty on petrol and diesel in India is not always ad valorem; it is often a specific tax, charged at a fixed amount per unit (e.g., per liter) rather than on the value.
- **Option 3 is correct:** GST is an ad valorem tax as it is calculated based on the sale price of goods and services. Higher-priced items lead to higher GST amounts.
- **Option 4 is correct:** Customs duty on imports is often calculated based on the value of goods, making it an ad valorem tax since it varies according to the item's price.

**Thus, the correct answer is (b) 1, 3 and 4 only.**

**20.** *(b)* Only two

- **Statement 1 is correct: Direct taxes are levied directly on individuals or entities,** such as income tax or property tax. These taxes are paid directly to the government by the person or entity on whom the tax is imposed, and the burden cannot be shifted to another party.
- **Statement 2 is correct: Indirect taxes are often considered regressive** because they tend to take a larger percentage of income from lower-income individuals. Since indirect taxes, such as Value Added Tax (VAT) or Goods and Services Tax (GST), are applied uniformly to goods and services, lower-income individuals, who spend a greater portion of their income on consumption, **end up paying a higher percentage of their income in taxes compared to wealthier individuals.**
- **Statement 3 is incorrect: Corporate tax is a direct tax imposed on a company's profit.** It is not classified as an indirect tax. Companies are required to pay corporate tax based on their profits, making it a direct obligation.

**Therefore, the correct answer is (b) Only two.**

**21.** *(a)* 1, 2 and 4 only

- **Option 1 is correct: Income Tax is a direct tax imposed on an individual's income.** It is levied directly on the income earned by individuals, whether from salaries, business profits, or other sources. The taxpayer pays this tax directly to the government, and the burden of the tax cannot be shifted to another entity or individual.
- **Option 2 is correct: Corporate Tax is a direct tax imposed on the net income or profit of companies.** This tax is levied on the profits made by corporations or businesses. Similar to income tax for individuals, corporate tax is a direct obligation of the company, and the tax burden falls on the corporation.
- **Option 3 is incorrect: Goods and Services Tax (GST) is an indirect tax levied on the supply of goods and services.** GST is included in the price of goods and services, and while the seller collects the tax, the ultimate burden of the tax is passed on to the consumer. This makes it an indirect tax, as the taxpayer (the consumer) pays the tax through their consumption, but it is collected by the intermediary (the business).
- **Option 4 is correct: Capital Gains Tax is a direct tax on the profit made from the sale of assets or investments.** This tax is levied on the gains made from selling assets like real estate, stocks, or bonds. Since the tax is imposed directly on the individual or entity making the profit, it qualifies as a direct tax.

**Therefore, the correct answer is (a) 1, 2 and 4 only.**

**22.** *(d)* All four pairs

- **Pair 1 is correct: Capital Gains Tax is a direct tax on the profits earned from the sale of capital assets like property or stocks.** This tax is imposed on the gain or profit made from selling assets such as real estate, stocks, or bonds. Since the tax is levied on the individual or entity making the profit, it qualifies as a direct tax.
- **Pair 2 is correct: Securities Transaction Tax (STT) is a tax levied on the transaction value of securities traded on stock exchanges.** STT is an indirect tax applied to the purchase or sale of securities, such as stocks, on recognized stock exchanges. Although it is a transaction-based tax, it is generally treated as a tax on financial transactions rather than on income.
- **Pair 3 is correct. Corporate Tax is a direct tax imposed on the profits of domestic and foreign companies operating in India.** This tax is levied on the net income or profits generated by companies, making it a direct tax obligation of the corporations themselves. Companies are required to file tax returns based on their income, and the tax is imposed on their profits after deductions and expenses.
- **Pair 4 is correct: Professional Tax is a direct tax levied by some state governments on professionals** such as doctors, lawyers, and others, based on their profession. It is a tax collected by certain state governments in India from individuals engaged in specific professions, trades, or employment. The tax is generally deducted by the employer, but it is a direct tax imposed on the individual professional.

**Therefore, the correct answer is (d) All four pairs.**

**23.** *(b)* Only two

- **Statement 1 is correct: Income earned by a non-resident from a property located in India is considered Indian-sourced income and is taxable in India.**
- According to Indian tax laws, any income generated from property situated in India, regardless of the residency status of the owner, is subject to taxation in India.
- Non-residents earning rental income or profits from property in India are taxed on such income under the provisions of the Indian Income Tax Act.
- **Statement 2 is correct: Income earned from agricultural activities is exempt from income tax under Section 10(1) of the Indian Income Tax Act.** This exemption acknowledges agriculture as a state subject under the Indian Constitution.
- Consequently, income derived from agricultural activities is not taxed by the central government, allowing states to regulate agricultural income. This provision is in place

to promote and support the agricultural sector in India.

- **Statement 3 is incorrect: The Government of India does not levy a uniform income tax rate for all individuals.** India uses a **progressive tax structure,** where the tax rates increase with higher income levels.
- The rates are divided into income slabs, with lower-income individuals paying lower tax rates and higher-income individuals paying higher rates. This progressive system ensures that wealthier individuals contribute more to the government's revenue while providing relief to lower-income earners.

**Therefore, the correct answer is (b) Only two.**

**24.** (d) 1, 2, 3 and 4

- **Statement 1 is correct: Income earned from business or profession is taxable under the head 'Income from Business or Profession' as per the Income Tax Act.** Taxpayers are required to report their business or professional income separately, and deductions related to business expenses are allowed under this head to calculate the taxable income.
- **Statement 2 is correct: Income received as gifts exceeding ₹ 50,000 in a financial year is taxable as 'Income from Other Sources',** subject to certain exemptions.
- Gifts received from specified relatives, or on special occasions like marriage, are exempt from taxation. However, if the total value of gifts from non-relatives exceeds ₹ 50,000 in a financial year, the amount is treated as income and taxed under the head 'Income from Other Sources.'
- **Statement 3 is correct: Income from the sale of personal jewellery is taxable as capital gains under the Income Tax Act.** When an individual sells personal jewellery, any profit made from the sale is treated as capital gains.
- Depending on the period for which the jewellery was held, the gain is classified as either short-term or long-term capital gains, or the applicable tax rates are levied accordingly.
- **Statement 4 is correct: Lottery winnings in India are taxed under a flat tax rate under Section 194B of the Income Tax Act, specifying 30% tax rate plus applicable cess and surcharge.**

**Therefore, the correct answer is (d) 1, 2, 3 and 4.**

**25.** *(a)* 1 and 2 only

- **Statement 1 is correct: Corporate tax is indeed a direct tax levied on the net income of companies.** It is imposed directly on the profits earned by businesses after accounting for expenses, deductions and allowances. This tax is paid directly by the company to the government and cannot be passed on to customers or employees, making it a direct tax.
- **Statement 2 is correct: Different tax rates apply for Indian and foreign corporations.** In India, domestic companies (those incorporated in India) and foreign companies (those earning revenue from India but incorporated elsewhere) are subject to different corporate tax rates.
- Domestic companies generally pay a lower tax rate, while foreign companies may face higher tax rates depending on the nature of their income and the specific provisions under the Income Tax Act.
- **Statement 3 is incorrect: Foreign corporations earning revenue from India are liable to pay corporate tax in India.**
- Foreign companies that earn income from business operations in India, such as from royalties, technical services, or sales, are required to pay corporate tax on the income they generate within India.
- This applies to revenue earned through a permanent establishment or other qualifying business activities within the country.

**Therefore, the correct answer is (a) 1 and 2 only.**

**26.** *(b)* 1 only

- **Statement 1 is correct: The MAT provisions were introduced to prevent tax avoidance by companies using various exemptions and deductions to reduce their tax liability.**
  - Minimum Alternate Tax (MAT) ensures that companies that benefit from various deductions and exemptions still pay a minimum amount of tax based on their book profits.

- The MAT mechanism was introduced to bring companies that effectively avoided paying taxes by reporting very low or zero taxable income, despite showing substantial book profits.

- **Statement 2 is incorrect: MAT is applicable to both domestic and foreign companies if they have a place of business in India and income that is taxable under the Indian Income Tax Act.**
  - Foreign companies with a place of business in India and earning taxable income are subject to MAT, just like domestic companies.
  - The intention is to bring all qualifying businesses under the MAT framework to ensure a minimum level of tax payment.
- **Statement 3 is incorrect: While MAT is generally calculated at a rate of 15% of the book profits (plus applicable surcharge and cess), it is not a standard rate of 18.5%.** The MAT rate was earlier set at 18.5%, but it has since been reduced to 15% of the book profits, along with applicable surcharge and cess.

**Therefore, the correct answer is (b) 1 only.**

***27.*** *(b)* MAT is applicable to companies, whereas AMT targets non-corporate taxpayers availing tax incentives.

MAT is specifically designed for companies to ensure they pay a minimum amount of tax even if their taxable income is reduced due to exemptions or deductions.

AMT, on the other hand, applies to non-corporate taxpayers (such as individuals, partnerships, or LLPs) who claim certain deductions to ensure they contribute a minimum tax.

**Thus, option (b) is the correct answer.**

***28.*** *(a)* 1 and 3 only

- **Statement 1 is correct: Profit from the sale of an investment property is classified as a capital gain under the Income Tax Act.** When an individual or entity sells an investment property and makes a profit, this profit is considered a capital gain. Depending on the holding period, it is classified as either short-term or long-term capital gain, with different tax rates applicable based on the duration of ownership.
- **Statement 2 is incorrect: Income earned from dividends is not classified as a capital gain.** Dividends are considered **income from other sources** under the Income Tax Act. They are taxed separately and are not treated as capital gains, as they do not arise from the sale of a capital asset but from holding shares in a company.
- **Statement 3 is correct: Gains from the sale of unlisted shares are classified as capital gains.** When unlisted shares are sold, the resulting profit is classified as a capital gain. The tax treatment depends on whether the shares were held for a short-term period (less than 24 months) or a long-term period (more than 24 months), with different tax rates applied to short-term and long-term capital gains.
- **Statement 4 is incorrect: Interest earned on fixed deposits is classified as income from other sources, not as capital gains.** Interest income from fixed deposits does not arise from the sale of a capital asset, and it is taxed as **income from other sources**, not as a capital gain.

**Therefore, the correct answer is (a) 1 and 3 only.**

***29.*** *(b)* Only two

- **Statement 1 is correct: The Digital Service Tax (DST) is indeed applicable to foreign e-commerce companies earning revenue from Indian users.** It was introduced to tax digital services provided by non-resident companies to Indian customers, particularly in the context of the growing digital economy. The aim is to ensure that foreign companies generating revenue from Indian users contribute to the Indian tax system, even if they do not have a physical presence in the country.
- **Statement 2 is incorrect: The DST is levied at a rate of 2%, not 6%, on the revenue earned by foreign companies from digital services provided to Indian residents.** The DST is specifically targeted at non-resident e-commerce operators and applies a 2% tax on their revenues from digital transactions involving Indian users.

- **Statement 3 is correct: DST is applicable to both business-to-business (B2B) and business-to-consumer (B2C) transactions,** ensuring comprehensive coverage of digital services. This broad application ensures that all forms of digital transactions, whether they involve businesses or consumers, are subject to the tax, thereby capturing a wide range of digital activities in the Indian market.

**Therefore, the correct answer is (b) Only two.**

***30.*** *(c)* Only three

**Statement 1 is correct: Online advertising services provided by a foreign company to Indian businesses are subject to the DST.** Digital Service Tax (DST) applies to revenue generated by non-resident companies from digital services offered to Indian users, including online advertising. This ensures that foreign companies profiting from the Indian market contribute to the country's tax revenue.

**Statement 2 is correct: Digital content streaming services provided by a non-resident company to Indian subscribers are subject to the DST.** Streaming platforms like Netflix or Spotify, if operated by non-resident entities, are subject to DST on the revenue earned from Indian subscribers. This tax ensures that such companies contribute to the Indian tax system despite their lack of physical presence in the country.

**Statement 3 is incorrect: Cloud computing services offered by an Indian company to global customers are not subject to the DST.** The DST is applicable only to non-resident companies earning revenue from Indian users. Since, the cloud computing services are provided by an Indian company, this revenue is not subject to DST but rather to regular Indian corporate tax laws.

**Statement 4 is correct: E-commerce platforms facilitating the sale of goods by foreign companies to Indian consumers are subject to the DST.** If a foreign e-commerce platform is facilitating sales to Indian consumers, the revenue earned from these transactions is taxable under the DST, ensuring that these platforms pay tax on their operations in the Indian market.

**Therefore, the correct answer is (c) Only three.**

***31.*** *(b)* **The primary reason for the introduction of the GAFA tax is to ensure fair taxation of digital services provided by large technology firms.** These companies often have complex tax structures that allow them to minimise their tax liabilities, despite earning significant revenue from digital services in multiple countries. The GAFA tax seeks to address this by taxing the revenue generated from digital activities within a specific country, ensuring that these companies pay their fair share of taxes.

**Therefore, option (b) is the correct answer.**

***32.*** *(c)* Both 1 and 2

- **Statement 1 is correct: STT is applicable on all transactions involving the sale of securities, such as equity shares, derivatives, and mutual fund units, that are conducted on recognised stock exchanges in India.**
  - It is a tax levied on the purchase and sale of securities that are listed on the stock exchanges.
  - It applies to various types of transactions including equities, derivatives and mutual funds, ensuring that the government collects tax revenue from financial market activity.
- **Statement 2 is correct: STT can discourage frequent trading because it adds a cost to each transaction.**
  - Every time a trade is executed, STT is imposed, which increases the overall transaction cost.
  - This additional cost may disincentivise frequent traders from engaging in high-frequency trades, encouraging them to adopt longer-term investment strategies to reduce the cumulative impact of transaction costs.

**Therefore, the correct answer is (c) Both 1 and 2.**

***33.*** *(c)* Only three

**Statement 1 is correct: Equity shares traded on a recognised stock exchange are subject to STT.** When investors buy or sell equity shares on recognised stock exchanges like the NSE or BSE, Securities Transaction Tax (STT) is levied on these transactions. STT is a tax on the value of the trade, ensuring that each transaction generates revenue for the government.

**Statement 2 is incorrect: Debt securities issued by the government are not subject to STT.** Government bonds and other debt securities are exempt from STT. STT is focused primarily on equity-related transactions and derivatives, and it does not apply to government-issued debt instruments.

**Statement 3 is correct: Derivatives traded on recognised stock exchanges are subject to STT.** STT applies to transactions involving derivatives like futures and options that are traded on recognised stock exchanges. The tax is levied on the value of the contract traded, with the applicable rates varying depending on the type of derivative.

**Statement 4 is correct:** An STT of 0.001% is levied by the government (Ministry of Finance) when you decide to buy or sell mutual fund units of an equity fund or a hybrid equity-oriented fund. There is **no STT on the sale of debt fund units.**

**Therefore, the correct answer is (c) Only three.**

***34.*** *(b)* **The Tobin tax is a tax on short-term currency transactions.** Economist James Tobin proposed this tax as a way to stabilise exchange rates by discouraging speculative trading in the foreign exchange markets. The Tobin tax is intended to reduce currency fluctuations by imposing a small tax on currency trades, making speculative trading less attractive.

**Therefore, option (b) the correct answer.**

***35.*** *(c)* 1 and 3 only

- **Statement 1 is incorrect: CTT is not applicable to agricultural commodities.** The Commodity Transaction Tax (CTT) is **only levied on non-agricultural commodities** traded on recognised commodity exchanges in India.
  - Agricultural commodities are exempt from CTT, meaning that the tax is not applicable to transactions involving agricultural products like wheat, rice, or pulses.
- **Statement 2 is correct: CTT is a direct tax levied by the government on the sale of commodities on recognised commodity exchanges.**
  - The CTT is imposed on the sale of non-agricultural commodities, such as metals and energy products, traded on recognised exchanges like MCX (Multi Commodity Exchange). It is a tax applied directly to the value of the transaction and is paid by the traders participating in these exchanges.
- **Statement 3 is incorrect: The rate of CTT varies depending on the type of commodity and the nature of the transaction.**
  - CTT rates are not uniform across all commodities and transactions. Different non-agricultural commodities may have different rates of CTT, depending on the type of commodity and whether the transaction involves futures, options, or other forms of trading.

**Therefore, the correct answer is (c) 1 and 3 only.**

***36.*** *(a)* 1 and 3 only

- **Option 1 is correct:** Trading of gold futures on a recognised commodity exchange is subject to CTT as it is a non-agricultural commodity.
- **Option 2 is incorrect: Trading of wheat futures on a recognised commodity exchange is not subject to CTT,** as wheat is an agricultural commodity. CTT is only applicable to non-agricultural commodities and agricultural commodities, such as wheat, are exempt from this tax.
- **Option 3 is correct:** Trading of crude oil futures on a recognised commodity exchange is subject to CTT as it is a non-agricultural commodity.
- **Option 4 is incorrect: Trading of equity shares on a recognised stock exchange is not subject to CTT; it is subject to Securities Transaction Tax (STT).** Equity shares are traded on stock exchanges and are subject to STT.

**Therefore, the correct answer is (a) 1 and 3 only.**

**37.** *(b)* Only two

- **Statement 1 is correct: Both cess and surcharge are additional charges levied over and above the base tax.** Cess is imposed for a specific purpose, such as education or health, and the funds collected are used exclusively for that purpose.
  - **Surcharge,** on the other hand, is an additional tax levied on individuals or entities that fall within higher income brackets. Unlike cess, **surcharge is not earmarked for any specific use** and is a tool used to generate additional revenue from high-income earners.
- **Statement 2 is correct: Surcharge can be used for any general government expenditure as it goes into the Consolidated Fund of India.** The revenue collected through surcharge becomes part of the government's general pool of funds and can be used for any purpose as needed.
  - Cess, however, is earmarked for specific purposes, such as the Swachh Bharat Cess or the Education Cess, and must be used only for the designated cause.
- **Statement 3 is incorrect: While surcharge is included in the Consolidated Fund of India, cess is credited to a separate fund and used exclusively for the purpose for which it was collected.**
  - Cess is specifically set aside for the purpose it is imposed for and is not part of the general revenue pool. This distinction ensures that funds collected via cess are only used for the designated purposes, unlike surcharge, which is available for general expenditure.

**Therefore, the correct answer is (b) Only two.**

**38.** *(c)* Both 1 and 2

- **Statement 1 is correct: The revenue generated from both cess and surcharge is not shared with state governments. Both cess and surcharge are retained by the Central Government**, and are not part of the divisible pool of taxes that are shared with the states under the provisions of the Indian Constitution.
- While taxes like income tax and GST are part of the divisible pool, cess and surcharge remain with the Central Government for specific purposes or additional revenue.
- **Statement 2 is correct: While surcharges are often applied to individuals with high incomes, cess can also be levied on a wide range of taxpayers or goods and services.**
- **A surcharge is generally imposed on high-income individuals or corporations** as an additional tax on their income tax liability. It is levied on the individuals having a minimum income of ₹ 50 lakh. Surcharge rates increases with the increase in income with the highest surcharge rate to be 25% for an income above 2 crore.
- **Cess, on the other hand, can be levied on a** broader base, including all taxpayers or specific goods and services, depending on the government's purpose. For instance, Health and Education Cess is applied to all taxpayers.

**Therefore, the correct answer is (c) Both 1 and 2.**

**39.** *(d)* 1, 2 and 3

- **Statement 1 is correct:** The Goods and Services Tax (GST) is a unified tax system that replaced multiple indirect taxes. It applies uniformly across the country, ensuring that goods and services are taxed at the same rate, making the tax structure simpler and more efficient.
- **Statement 2 is correct:** Before the implementation of GST, there were various indirect taxes levied by both Central and State Governments, including Value Added Tax (VAT), service tax, central excise duty, and entry tax. GST simplified the tax structure by merging these taxes into a single system, reducing tax complications and eliminating the cascading effect of taxes.
- **Statement 3 is correct:** GST is a destination-based tax collected at the point of consumption, not at the point of origin. Unlike previous indirect taxes, GST is levied where the goods or services are consumed, rather than where they are produced. This ensures that the revenue from GST goes to the state where the goods or services are

finally consumed, rather than the state where they were manufactured or provided.

**Therefore, the correct answer is (d) 1, 2 and 3.**

**40.** *(a)* 1 only

- **Statement 1 is correct: GST Council is a constitutional body established under Article 279A of the Indian Constitution.** The GST Council is responsible for making recommendations to the Union and State governments regarding issues related to the Goods and Services Tax (GST). These recommendations include tax rates, exemptions, thresholds, and special provisions for states. The Council consists of the Union Finance Minister, the Union Minister of State for Finance, and finance ministers from all states. It plays a crucial role in ensuring uniformity and coordination in the implementation of GST across India.
- **Statement 2 is incorrect: The President cannot unilaterally impose GST in any state without the approval of the GST Council.** GST decisions are made based on recommendations from the GST Council, which requires a consensus or a majority vote among its members. The Central Government or the President cannot impose GST on any state without following the due process of consultation and approval within the GST Council. This ensures that both the Central and State Governments have a say in GST matters.

**Therefore, the correct answer is (a) 1 only.**

**41.** *(c)* Only three

- **Option 1 is correct: Electricity is exempt from GST and continues to be taxed separately by the State Governments.** Electricity is **currently not included under the GST regime.** Instead, it is taxed by the State Governments through state-specific electricity duties. This means that consumers do not pay GST on their electricity consumption and it remains outside the GST framework.
- **Option 2 is incorrect: Hotel services are subject to GST based on the tariff of the rooms.** Hotels are subject to GST, and the applicable rate depends on the room tariff. For instance, rooms with tariffs below a certain threshold are taxed at a lower rate, while higher-priced rooms are subject to a higher GST rate. Therefore, hotel services are not exempt from GST.
- **Option 3 is correct: Petroleum products are currently outside the GST framework and are taxed separately by the Central and State Governments.** Key petroleum products such as crude oil, petrol, diesel and natural gas are not subject to GST. Instead, these products continue to be taxed through excise duties and value-added tax (VAT) imposed by the Central and State Governments, respectively.
- **Option 4 is correct:** Basic educational services provided by recognised educational institutions are exempt from GST, aimed at reducing the tax burden on essential services like education.

**Therefore, the correct answer is (c) Only three.**

**42.** *(b)* 1 and 3 only

- **Option 1 is correct: Export of goods is considered a zero-rated supply under GST, meaning it attracts no GST, but input tax credit can be claimed.** Under GST, the export of goods is zero-rated, which means that while no GST is charged on the export sale itself, the exporter can claim a refund of the input tax credit (ITC) on inputs used to produce the exported goods. This policy is designed to make Indian exports competitive in the global market.
- **Option 2 is incorrect: Inter-state supply of goods is not zero-rated; it is subject to IGST.** When goods are supplied across state borders within India, they are subject to Integrated Goods and Services Tax (IGST). This tax is levied to ensure that the revenue from interstate transactions is appropriately shared between the central and state governments (destination state).
- **Option 3 is correct: Supply to Special Economic Zones (SEZs) is also zero-rated, attracting no GST but allowing input tax credit.** Supplies made to Special Economic Zones (SEZs) are treated as zero-rated supplies under GST. This means that suppliers do not charge GST on these supplies, but they can claim a refund on the input tax credit for the

goods or services used in making these supplies.

- **Option 4 is incorrect: Intra-state supply of goods is subject to CGST and SGST, not zero-rated.** For goods supplied within the same state, Central Goods and Services Tax (CGST) and State Goods and Services Tax (SGST) are applicable. This is not a zero-rated supply but a standard supply subject to dual tax.

**Therefore, the correct answer is (b) 1 and 3 only.**

***43.*** *(b)* Only two

**Statement 1 is correct: GST is a destination-based tax, meaning it is levied at the point of consumption, not at the point of origin.** This means that GST is applied where the goods or services are consumed, not where they are produced or supplied. The destination-based approach ensures that the tax revenue accrues to the state where the final consumption takes place, which helps balance the revenue distribution among states.

**Statement 2 is correct: One of the key features of GST is the availability of input tax credit across the supply chain, which allows businesses to offset the tax paid on inputs against the tax payable on the output.** This feature is fundamental to GST as it eliminates the cascading effect of taxes by allowing businesses to claim credit for the taxes paid on their purchases, thus reducing the overall tax burden on the final consumer.

**Statement 3 is incorrect: GST rates are not uniform across all goods and services; there are multiple tax slabs (0%, 5%, 12%, 18% and 28%) depending on the type of goods and services.** GST is structured with various tax rates applicable to different categories of goods and services to address diverse economic needs and to align with the government's policy objectives.

**Therefore, the correct answer is (b) Only two.**

***44.*** *(c)* Only three

- **Statement 1 is correct: GST is a comprehensive indirect tax system.** GST integrates various indirect taxes into a single tax system, covering all stages of the supply chain from production to consumption. This helps in simplifying the tax structure and improve compliance by reducing the multiplicity of taxes.
- **Statement 2 is correct: The GST system in India follows a dual GST model involving both central (CGST) and State Governments (SGST).** Under this model, GST is levied and collected by both the Central and State Governments, with CGST collected by the Central Government and SGST collected by the State Government on intra-state supplies. For interstate supplies, the Integrated GST (IGST) is levied.
- **Statement 3 is incorrect: GST does not have uniform tax rates for all goods and services; there are multiple tax slabs.** GST rates are categorised into different slabs (0%, 5%, 12%, 18% and 28%) based on the type of goods or services, reflecting the diverse nature of goods and services and the government's policy objectives.
- **Statement 4 is correct: GST in India includes a digital compliance and filling system to streamline tax collection and filing processes.** The GST system incorporates a digital platform for compliance, including online registration, filing of returns, and payment of taxes, which enhances efficiency and transparency in tax administration.

**Therefore, the correct answer is (c) Only three.**

***45.*** *(c)* Only three

- **Option 1 is correct: Central Excise Duty, except for certain petroleum products, was subsumed under GST.** GST replaced most of the Central Excise Duty levied on goods, with the exception of petroleum products and a few other items.
- **Option 2 is correct: Service Tax was subsumed under GST**, as GST covers the taxation of services. Prior to GST, Service Tax was levied by the Central Government on various services, but under GST, it has been replaced by the tax on services included in the GST framework.
- **Option 3 is incorrect: Customs Duty was not subsumed under GST.** Customs Duty is still applicable on the import of goods and is not covered under the GST system. It remains

a separate levy administered by the Central Government.

- **Option 4 is correct: Value Added Tax (VAT) was subsumed under GST for most goods and services,** but some items like alcohol for human consumption and certain petroleum products were excluded from the GST regime. These items continue to be taxed separately by the State Governments or Central Government as applicable.

**Therefore, the correct answer is (c) Only three.**

**46.** *(a)* 1 and 2 only

- **Statement 1 is correct: The composition scheme is available to small taxpayers with an annual turnover of up to INR 1.5 crore, providing a simplified tax compliance regime.** This scheme is designed to ease the tax burden for small businesses by allowing them to pay tax at a reduced rate and adhere to simplified compliance procedures.
- **Statement 2 is correct: Under the composition scheme, taxpayers are required to file quarterly returns instead of monthly returns** which reduces the frequency of filling and simplifies compliance for small businesses. This is in contrast to regular GST taxpayers who must file returns on a monthly basis.
- **Statement 3 is incorrect: Taxpayers under the composition scheme are not eligible to claim input tax credit on their purchases.** One of the main features of the Composition Scheme is that it simplifies compliance but at the cost of losing the ability to claim input tax credit, which is available to regular taxpayers.

**Therefore, the correct answer is (a) 1 and 2 only.**

**47.** *(a)* 1 and 3 only

- **Statement 1 is correct: A wholesale trader with an annual turnover of INR 1 crore is eligible for the GST Composition Scheme as it is below the threshold limit of INR 1.5 crore for most states.** The Composition Scheme is available to taxpayers with turnover up to INR 1.5 crore, making this wholesale trader eligible.
- **Statement 2 is incorrect: An e-commerce operator supplying goods through an online platform is not eligible for the GST Composition Scheme.** Businesses that supply goods through e-commerce platforms are excluded from the Composition Scheme. This is because the scheme is not applicable to e-commerce operators and businesses that use e-commerce platforms for supply.
- **Statement 3 is correct: A small manufacturer with an annual turnover of INR 80 lakh is eligible for the Composition Scheme as it is below the threshold limit.** The threshold limit for the Composition Scheme is INR 1.5 crore, so this manufacturer qualifies for the scheme.
- **Statement 4 is incorrect: A service provider with an annual turnover of INR 70 lakh providing consultancy services is not eligible for the Composition Scheme.** While the Composition Scheme is available for certain types of service providers, consultancy services are generally excluded, and the scheme may apply to specific service providers only under special provisions if their turnover is below INR 50 lakh.

**Therefore, the correct answer is (a) 1 and 3 only.**

**48.** *(d)* 1, 2 and 3

- **Statement 1 is correct: The GST Council is indeed a constitutional body formed under Article 279A of the Indian Constitution to make recommendations to the Union and State on GST rates, exemptions, etc.** This council plays a crucial role in the administration of GST by making decisions on tax rates and other related matters.
- **Statement 2 is correct: The Union Finance Minister is the Chairperson of the GST Council.** The Council is chaired by the Union Finance Minister, and its meetings involve discussions and decisions on GST related issues.
- **Statement 3 is correct: All decisions in the GST Council require a three-fourths majority vote, and the voting weight is distributed with the Central Government having one-third and the State Governments**

having two-thirds. The voting power is weighted differently, with the Central Government having 33.33% of the vote and state governments collectively having 66.67%.

**Therefore, the correct answer is (d) 1, 2 and 3.**

***49.*** *(a)* **Under the Reverse Charge Mechanism (RCM), the liability to pay tax shifts from the supplier to the recipient of goods or services.** This means that in situations where RCM applies, it is the responsibility of the recipient (buyer) to pay the tax directly to the government rather than the supplier (seller). This mechanism is designed to ensure that tax is collected from the recipient, often to simplify compliance or address specific issues with suppliers.

**Therefore, option (a) is the correct answer.**

***50.*** *(a)* Only one

**Statement 1 is correct: It is levied to compensate states for any revenue loss they might face due to the transition to the GST system.** The GST Compensation Cess was introduced as a measure to ensure that states do not suffer revenue losses due to the implementation of GST, as it might affect their existing revenue streams from previous taxes.

**Statement 2 is incorrect: The GST Compensation Cess is not applicable to all goods and services.** It is specifically levied on certain luxury and sin goods such as tobacco, aerated drinks and high-end automobiles. This selective application targets goods that are considered non-essential or harmful rather than being a general tax applicable to all goods and services.

**Statement 3 is incorrect: The revenue from the GST Compensation Cess is not credited to the Consolidated Fund of India.** Instead, it is credited to a non-lapsable fund known as the GST Compensation Fund. This fund is specifically created to compensate states for any loss of revenue due to the GST implementation, ensuring that the compensation mechanism is dedicated and separate from the general revenue.

**Therefore, the correct answer is (a) Only one.**

***51.*** *(a)* 1 only

**Statement 1 is correct:** The main purpose of a Double Taxation Avoidance Agreement (DTAA) is to **prevent the same income from being taxed in both countries,** reducing the tax burden on individuals and corporations earning income in multiple jurisdictions.

By clarifying taxing rights between countries, DTAA mitigates tax overlap.

**Statement 2 is incorrect:** DTAA does not give taxpayers the flexibility to choose the tax rate of either country arbitrarily. Instead, it provides for either a **tax exemption** or **tax credit** method, where the taxpayer pays tax in one country and receives a tax credit in the other, subject to DTAA terms.

**Statement 3 is incorrect:** DTAA applies to **both corporate entities and individual taxpayers** who are residents of the signatory countries. This ensures that individuals and corporations alike avoid being doubly taxed on the same income.

**Therefore, the correct answer is (a) 1 only.**

***52.*** *(b)* Routing funds through foreign jurisdictions to reinvest in the original country

Round tripping refers to the practice of moving funds out of a country and routing them through foreign jurisdictions to reinvest in the original country, often to benefit from tax incentives or investment advantages.

**Thus, option (b) is the correct answer.**

***53.*** *(c)* All three

**Method 1 is correct:** Investors often route money through tax havens to benefit from lower tax rates and reintroduce it as foreign investment, making this a common round-tripping strategy.

**Method 2 is correct:** Shell companies are frequently used in round-tripping schemes to obscure ownership and facilitate reinvestment in the home country without tax implications.

**Method 3 is correct:** This strategy may be used in round-tripping to create capital gains which are then shifted back, simulating foreign investment.

**Therefore, the correct answer is (c) All three.**

**54.** *(d)* To hold assets and manage financial transactions without any substantial business operations

A shell company typically exists solely on paper, often used to hold assets or conduct financial transactions without engaging in substantial business operations. While they can serve legitimate purposes like asset protection, shell companies are sometimes misused for tax evasion, money laundering, or hiding ownership.

**Thus, option (d) is the correct answer.**

**55.** *(b)* Setting prices between related entities as if they were unrelated, to avoid tax manipulation

The **Arm's Length Principle** requires that prices set in transactions between related entities be comparable to those set between unrelated parties. This principle aims to prevent tax evasion by ensuring that profits are reported fairly in each country involved.

**Thus, option (b) is the correct answer.**

**56.** *(b)* To prevent multinational corporations from exploiting tax loopholes to shift profits

**BEPS initiatives**, led by the OECD, focus on addressing tax avoidance strategies that exploit gaps and mismatches in tax rules to shift profits and erode the tax base.

This ensures fair taxation by preventing profit shifting to low-tax jurisdictions.

**Thus, option (b) is the correct answer.**

**57.** *(b)* 1 and 3 only

**Statement 1 is correct:** The Global Minimum Corporate Tax initiative aims to prevent multinational corporations from shifting their profits to low-tax jurisdictions, ensuring they pay a fair share of tax in each country where they operate. This initiative is part of a broader effort to curb tax avoidance and maintain fair competition across borders.

**Statement 2 is incorrect:** The minimum tax rate agreed upon under this initiative is 15%, not 21%. This rate was established to balance competitiveness while ensuring sufficient tax collection in each jurisdiction.

**Statement 3 is correct:** The Organisation for Economic Co-operation and Development (OECD), in partnership with the G20, spearheaded this initiative as part of its Base Erosion and Profit Shifting (BEPS) Project, aiming for global tax fairness.

**Therefore, the correct answer is (b) 1 and 3 only.**

**58.** *(b)* Providing certainty on tax treatment of related-party transactions

- An Advance Pricing Agreement (APA) is an **arrangement between a taxpayer and a tax authority** that pre-determines the transfer pricing method for transactions between related parties.
- This helps avoid disputes by ensuring that the pricing is acceptable to both the taxpayer and the tax authority, reducing the risk of tax adjustments.
- The primary benefit of an APA is that it provides **clarity and certainty on the tax treatment of related-party transactions**. This minimizes the risk of transfer pricing disputes and ensures that multinational corporations are aware of their tax liabilities in advance, facilitating better tax compliance.

**Thus, option (b) is the correct answer.**

**59.** *(a)* 1 and 2 only

- **Statement 1 is correct:** CBDT formulates policies and administers laws related to direct taxes in India, such as income tax and corporate tax, ensuring the effective functioning of the direct tax system.
- **Statement 2 is correct:** CBDT is a **statutory authority that operates under the Department of Revenue in the Ministry of Finance**, overseeing direct tax administration in India.
- **Statement 3 is incorrect: CBDT does not regulate state taxes**; it is focused on central direct taxes. State taxes are administered independently by the respective state governments.

**Therefore, the correct answer is (a) 1 and 2 only.**

**60.** *(b)* Only two

- **Statement 1 is correct:** CBIC is indeed responsible for the administration of various indirect taxes in India, including GST, Customs, Central Excise and Service Tax.

- It plays a significant role in ensuring compliance and efficient collection of indirect taxes.
- **Statement 2 is incorrect:** CBIC functions under the **Department of Revenue, Ministry of Finance and not the Department of Economic Affairs.** The Department of Revenue oversees tax policies and administration for indirect taxes.
- **Statement 3 is correct:** CBIC formulates policies and issues procedural guidelines to ensure smooth compliance with indirect tax laws, addressing issues in tax enforcement and administration.

**Thus, the correct answer is (b) Only two.**

***61.*** *(a)* 1 and 2 only

The E-Way Bill System was introduced under GST to facilitate the tracking and movement of goods, reduce logistical bottlenecks, and curb tax evasion. This electronic bill is required for the transportation of goods over a certain value across state borders and for specific goods within states.

**Statement 1 is correct:** The E-Way Bill is mandatory for goods transported inter-state when the consignment value exceeds ₹ 50,000. This rule helps in monitoring high-value goods and minimising tax evasion in cross-border trade within India.

**Statement 2 is correct:** An E-Way Bill is not required for goods transported using non-motorised vehicles. This exemption aims to ease transportation for small traders and individuals using manual or animal-driven vehicles, thereby supporting traditional and low-scale transportation modes.

**Statement 3 is incorrect:** The E-Way Bill can be generated by **both registered and unregistered persons involved in the transport of goods,** with transporters able to generate the bill if needed. This feature ensures wider accessibility and convenience for various stakeholders in the supply chain.

**Thus, the correct answer is (a) 1 and 2 only.**

***62.*** *(d)* 1, 2 and 3

- **Statement 1 is correct:** GAAR enables tax authorities to **disregard or recharacterise transactions that lack commercial substance,** particularly those structured solely to achieve tax benefits without any substantial business purpose. This provision is **intended to prevent aggressive tax planning and ensure tax compliance.**
- **Statement 2 is correct:** GAAR applies **only to transactions that meet or exceed a specific financial threshold.** This ensures that GAAR provisions do not impact minor transactions or low-value transactions, thereby reducing the compliance burden for smaller taxpayers.
- **Statement 3 is correct:** GAAR provisions **apply to both domestic and international transactions** that meet the defined criteria for impermissible tax avoidance. This ensures a comprehensive approach to curbing tax avoidance practices, regardless of the origin of the transactions.

**Therefore, the correct answer is (d) 1, 2 and 3.**

***63.*** *(a)* 1, 2 and 3 only

**Statement 1 is correct:** One of the primary objectives of the DTC is to simplify the tax structure, making it easier for taxpayers to understand, thereby encouraging higher compliance and reducing confusion.

**Statement 2 is correct:** By introducing a predictable and transparent tax regime, the DTC aims to attract more foreign direct investment, fostering a stable environment for international investors.

**Statement 3 is correct:** The DTC's emphasis on clear rules and definitions is expected to reduce tax litigation by addressing ambiguities and providing clarity in tax matters.

**Statement 4 is incorrect:** The DTC does not grant states the authority to set their own direct tax rates; this remains under central jurisdiction to ensure uniformity in direct taxation.

**Thus, the correct answer is (a) 1, 2 and 3 only.**

## Past Learning (Answers)

| | | | | | | |
|---|---|---|---|---|---|---|
| 1 (d) | 2 (d) | 3 (d) | 4 (c) | 5 (a) | 6 (d) | 7 (b) |

# CHAPTER 06 Money and Monetary Policy

## Assessment Round

### Topic 1 : Concept of Money

*1.* Which of the following limitations of the barter system led to the introduction of money?

1. Lack of divisibility
2. Lack of portability
3. Difficulty in deferred payments
4. Lack of a standardised unit of account

Select the correct answer from the codes given below:

(a) 1 and 4 only (b) 2, 3 and 4 only
(c) 1, 2 and 3 only (d) 1, 2, 3 and 4

*2.* With reference to the concept of money, consider the following statements:

1. Money serves as a medium of exchange, facilitating trade and transactions.
2. Money has intrinsic value regardless of its form or use.
3. Money acts as a store of value, allowing individuals to save for future needs.

How many of the statements given above is/are correct?

(a) Only one (b) Only two
(c) All three (d) None

*3.* Consider the following types of money:

1. Commodity money 2. Fiat money
3. Digital currency 4. Barter system

How many of the given above is/are recognised as forms of money in economic systems?

(a) Only one (b) Only two
(c) Only three (d) All four

*4.* With reference to the Commodity Money, consider the following statements:

1. It has intrinsic value derived from the material it is made of and therefore also known as full-bodied money.
2. It includes items like gold, silver and precious stones.
3. It is easier to transport and store compared to fiat money.

Which of the statements given above are correct?

(a) 1 and 2 only (b) 1 and 3 only
(c) 2 and 3 only (d) 1, 2 and 3

*5.* Consider the following characteristics:

1. Issued by a central authority or government
2. Has intrinsic value based on physical commodity
3. Accepted as a medium of exchange because of government regulation
4. Not affected by inflation or deflation

How many of the above characteristics is/are correct for fiat money?

(a) Only one (b) Only two
(c) Only three (d) All four

*6.* Which of the following correctly describes about the 'legal tender' in an economy?

(a) Money that must be accepted if offered in payment of a debt.
(b) A type of currency that can be exchanged for gold or silver.
(c) Any form of commodity money used in trade.
(d) A non-monetary item used in bartering transactions.

**7.** Consider the following pairs:

| | Forms of Money | Examples in India |
|---|---|---|
| 1. | Legal Tender | Central Bank Digital Currency (CBDC) |
| 2. | Digital Currency | UPI Transactions |
| 3. | Full-bodied Money | Silver Coins |
| 4. | Near Money | Fixed Deposit Receipts |

How many of the above pairs is/are correctly matched?
(a) Only one pair (b) Only two pairs
(c) Only three pairs (d) All four pairs

**8.** Which of the following best describes the concept of Helicopter Money?
(a) A form of economic aid given to developing countries by international organisations to stimulate growth.
(b) A situation where a central bank prints large amounts of money and distributes it directly to the public to boost demand.
(c) A financial strategy where the government borrows from foreign institutions to inject liquidity into the economy.
(d) A program where commercial banks lower interest rates to stimulate borrowing and economic activity.

## Topic 2 : Electronic Money

**9.** With reference to 'Electronic Money', consider the following statements:
1. Electronic money includes both stored value cards and online wallets.
2. All forms of electronic money require internet access for transactions.
3. Its use is limited to domestic transactions and cannot be used for cross-border payments.

How many of the statements given above is/are correct?
(a) Only one (b) Only two
(c) All three (d) None

**10.** With reference to the concept of cryptocurrency, consider the following statements:
1. These are decentralised digital assets that operate on a blockchain technology.
2. These are backed by physical assets like gold or silver.
3. Transactions made with cryptocurrencies are generally irreversible.

How many of the statements given above is/are correct?
(a) Only one (b) Only two
(c) All three (d) None

**11.** Consider the following statements about 'Cryptocurrency':
1. They have intrinsic value because they are backed by a physical asset.
2. Most cryptocurrencies are not regulated by any central authority or government.
3. El Salvador was the first country to declare Bitcoin as legal tender.

Which of the statements given above are correct?
(a) 1 and 2 only (b) 1 and 3 only
(c) 2 and 3 only (d) 1, 2 and 3

**12.** Which of the following best describes a stablecoin in the context of cryptocurrencies?
(a) A cryptocurrency that is backed by a physical commodity like gold or silver.
(b) A digital currency designed to maintain a stable value by being pegged to a reserve of assets such as fiat currencies or commodities.
(c) A digital currency whose value fluctuates based on market demand and supply without any asset backing.
(d) A cryptocurrency that is not affected by inflation or deflation in the real economy.

**13.** Consider the following statements with reference to the regulation of cryptocurrency in India:
1. These are recognised as legal tender by the Reserve Bank of India (RBI).
2. The trading of cryptocurrencies is subject to taxation under the Income Tax Act.
3. Securities and Exchange Board of India (SEBI) currently regulates cryptocurrency trading in India.

How many of the statements given above is/are correct?
(a) Only one (b) Only two
(c) All three (d) None

**14.** With reference to India's Central Bank Digital Currency (CBDC), also known as the Digital Rupee, consider the following statements:

1. It is a form of digital currency which is issued and regulated by the RBI.
2. This will require users to mandatorily have a bank account with a commercial bank.
3. It is a liability on the balance sheet of the Reserve Bank of India (RBI).

How many of the statements given above is/are correct?

(a) Only one (b) Only two
(c) All three (d) None

**15.** Consider the following statements about 'Digital Rupee':

1. It is not recognised as legal tender and is only a digital asset used for specific transactions.
2. RBI has the authority to regulate the supply of the digital rupee in managing inflation and economic stability.
3. Users can convert their physical cash into digital rupee tokens through authorised banks and digital platforms.

Which of the statements given above are correct?

(a) 1 and 2 only (b) 2 and 3 only
(c) 1 and 3 only (d) 1, 2 and 3

**16.** With respect to the 'Digital Rupee', consider the following statements:

1. Digital Rupee can be transferred directly between users without the need for a bank intermediary.
2. It can be used to earn interest when held in digital wallets.
3. Digital Rupee mandatorily requires a smartphone with internet access for all transactions.

Which of the statements given above is/are correct?

(a) 1 and 2 only (b) 2 and 3 only
(c) 1 only (d) 1, 2 and 3

## Topic 3 : Money Supply

**17.** With reference to the components of the money supply in India, consider the following statements:

1. Reserve money (M0) includes both currency held by the public and reserves held by commercial banks.
2. Narrow money (M1) consists of currency with the public, demand deposits and other deposits with the RBI.
3. Broad money (M3) encompasses all components of M1 as well as time deposits with banks.

Which of the statements given above are correct?

(a) 1 and 2 only (b) 2 and 3 only
(c) 1 and 3 only (d) 1, 2 and 3

**18.** Which of the following best describes the role of high-powered money in the monetary system?

(a) It directly determines the interest rates set by commercial banks.
(b) It acts as the foundation for the creation of broad money in the economy.
(c) It is used exclusively for international trade and foreign exchange transactions.
(d) It represents the total wealth of a country including all assets and liabilities.

**19.** What does the money multiplier represent in the banking system?

(a) The total amount of loans a bank can issue based on its assets.
(b) The ratio of the central bank's reserves to the commercial banks' deposits.
(c) The maximum amount of commercial bank money that can be created from a unit of central bank money.
(d) The ratio of physical currency to digital currency in circulation.

**20.** Consider the following statements:

1. Increasing financial inclusion can potentially raise the money multiplier in an economy.
2. The digitalisation of the economy reduces the money multiplier by encouraging cash transactions.
3. A higher reserve requirement leads to a higher money multiplier.

Which of the statements given above is/are correct?

(a) 1 only (b) 2 and 3 only
(c) 1 and 3 only (d) 1, 2 and 3

## Topic 4 : Monetary Policy

**21.** Consider the following actions:
1. Increasing the Cash Reserve Ratio (CRR)
2. Regulating trade tariffs
3. Conducting Open Market Operations (OMOs)
4. Implementing a debt-to-GDP ratio policy

How many of the above actions is/are part of a central bank's monetary policy?
(a) Only one (b) Only two
(c) Only three (d) All four

**22.** Which of the following actions are consistent with a central bank's use of contractionary monetary policy?
1. Raising the repo rate
2. Selling government securities in the open market
3. Lowering the cash reserve ratio (CRR)

Select the correct answer from the codes given below:
(a) 1 and 2 only (b) 2 and 3 only
(c) 1 and 3 only (d) 1, 2 and 3

**23.** Consider the different stances of monetary policy with their appropriate examples:

| Stances of Monetary Policy | Examples |
|---|---|
| 1. Expansionary | Lowering of the reverse repo rate |
| 2. Hawkish | Signalling a willingness to fight inflation aggressively |
| 3. Accommodative | Providing cheap long-term loans to banks |
| 4. Dovish | Reducing interest rates to encourage borrowing and spending |

How many pairs given above is/are correctly matched?
(a) Only one pair (b) Only two pairs
(c) Only three pairs (d) All four pairs

**24.** What is the primary goal of the monetary policy framework adopted by the Reserve Bank of India (RBI)?
(a) To maintain exchange rate stability
(b) To control inflation and maintain price stability
(c) To reduce the fiscal deficit
(d) To increase foreign exchange reserves

**25.** With reference to the India's monetary policy framework, consider the following statements:
1. It uses WPI as the primary measure of inflation.
2. The inflation target in India is set by the Government of India in consultation with the RBI.
3. The RBI is required to explain its actions to the government if inflation deviates from the target range for three consecutive quarters.

How many of the statements given above is/are correct?
(a) Only one (b) Only two
(c) All three (d) None

**26.** Consider the following statements about 'Monetary Policy Committee (MPC)' in India:
1. It is a statutory body responsible for setting the benchmark interest rates in India.
2. MPC consists of six members with no member from the Government of India.
3. MPC's decision-making process is based on majority voting and all members have equal voting rights.

Which of the statements given above are correct?
(a) 1 and 2 only (b) 2 and 3 only
(c) 1 and 3 only (d) 1, 2 and 3

**27.** Which of the following statements about the 'Monetary Policy Committee (MPC)' is/are correct?
1. It is chaired by the RBI Governor.
2. All members of the MPC are appointed by the Government of India.
3. The MPC meets once every month to discuss monetary policy decisions.

Select the correct answer from the codes given below:
(a) 1 and 2 only (b) 1 only
(c) 2 and 3 only (d) 1, 2 and 3

## Topic 5 : Tools of Monetary Policy

**28.** Consider the following tools of monetary policy:

1. Open Market Operations (OMO)
2. Cash Reserve Ratio (CRR)
3. Moral Suasion
4. Repo Rate

How many of the above is/are quantitative tools of monetary policy?

(a) Only one (b) Only two
(c) Only three (d) All four

**29.** With reference to the Repo Rate, consider the following statements:

1. It is the rate at which the RBI lends money to commercial banks against government securities.
2. A decrease in the repo rate can result into higher liquidity into the economic system.
3. Repo rate is always higher than reverse repo rate.

Which of the statements given above are correct?

(a) 1 and 2 only (b) 1 and 3 only
(c) 2 and 3 only (d) 1, 2 and 3

**30.** Which of the following institutions are eligible to borrow under the Liquidity Adjustment Facility (LAF) operations conducted by the Reserve Bank of India (RBI)?

1. Commercial banks
2. Non-Banking Financial Companies (NBFCs)
3. Primary Dealers
4. Scheduled Co-operative Banks

Select the correct answer from the codes given below:

(a) 1 and 3 only (b) 1, 2 and 4 only
(c) 1, 3 and 4 only (d) 1, 2, 3 and 4

**31.** Which of the following best describes the 'Bank Rate'?

(a) The interest rate at which the central bank lends short-term loans to commercial banks.
(b) The interest rate at which commercial banks lend to customers for home loans and personal loans.
(c) The interest rate charged by the central bank on long-term loans extended to commercial banks and financial institutions.
(d) The rate at which the government borrows funds from international financial institutions.

**32.** With reference to the 'Standing Deposit Facility (SDF)', consider the following statements:

1. It is a tool used by the RBI to absorb surplus liquidity from the banking system without the need for collateral.
2. SDF allows banks to deposit their excess funds with the RBI, earning interest on these deposits.

Which of the statements given above is/are correct?

(a) 1 only (b) 2 only
(c) Both 1 and 2 (d) Neither 1 nor 2

**33.** With reference to the 'Marginal Standing Facility (MSF)' in India, consider the following statements:

1. It allows banks to borrow overnight funds from the Reserve Bank of India (RBI) against approved government securities.
2. The MSF rate serves as the upper bound of the Liquidity Adjustment Facility (LAF) corridor.
3. Banks can borrow up to 2% of their Net Demand and Time Liabilities (NDTL) under the MSF.

How many of the statements given above is/are correct?

(a) Only one (b) Only two
(c) All three (d) None

**34.** Consider the following statements:

1. Banks can borrow funds under the repo rate against securities that are above the SLR requirement.
2. MSF Rate is set higher than Repo rate.
3. MSF Rate provides a ceiling for the Liquidity Adjustment Facility (LAF) corridor while the repo rate provides a floor.

Which of the statements given above are correct?

(a) 1 and 2 only (b) 2 and 3 only
(c) 1 and 3 only (d) 1, 2 and 3

**35.** With reference to Open Market Operations (OMO) in India, consider the following statements:

1. RBI conducts OMO primarily through auctions, where government securities are bought or sold in the open market.
2. Purchase of government securities under OMO can injects liquidity into the banking system.

Which of the statement(s) given above is/are correct?

(a) 1 only (b) 2 only
(c) Both 1 and 2 (d) Neither 1 nor 2

**36.** With reference to the 'Market Stabilisation Scheme (MSS)' in India, consider the following statements:

1. It is used by the RBI to manage excess liquidity in the economy.
2. Under the MSS, the government issues treasury bills and bonds to absorb surplus liquidity from the banking system.
3. The funds raised through MSS can be used by the government for public spending and investment.

How many of the statements given above is/are correct?

(a) Only one (b) Only two
(c) All three (d) None

**37.** Which of the following are the objectives of reserve requirements set by the RBI?

1. Ensures banks have enough liquidity for withdrawals.
2. Allows the RBI to control lending and economic activity.
3. To provide a steady source of funds for the RBI's operational expenses.

Select the correct answer from the codes given below:

(a) 1 and 2 only (b) 2 and 3 only
(c) 1 and 3 only (d) 1, 2 and 3

**38.** What is the main characteristic of a 'Fractional Reserve Banking System'?

(a) Banks are required to hold 100% of their deposits as reserves.
(b) Banks can lend out a portion of their deposits while keeping a fraction as reserves.
(c) Banks do not need to hold any reserves against their deposits.
(d) Banks are only allowed to invest in government securities.

**39.** Consider the following statements:

1. CRR is maintained in cash with the RBI, whereas SLR can be maintained in cash, gold or government securities.
2. Banks earn interest on the funds kept as CRR with the RBI.
3. CRR helps in controlling inflation by regulating the money supply.

Which of the statements given above are correct?

(a) 1 and 2 only (b) 1 and 3 only
(c) 2 and 3 only (d) 1, 2 and 3

**40.** Consider the following statements:

1. Increasing the CRR reduces the money supply in the economy.
2. Reducing the SLR allows banks to have more funds available for lending.
3. Both CRR and SLR are used exclusively to control inflation.

Which of the statements given above are correct?

(a) 1 and 2 only (b) 2 and 3 only
(c) 1 and 3 only (d) 1, 2 and 3

**41.** Consider the following qualitative tools of monetary policy with their descriptions:

| Qualitative Tool | Description |
|---|---|
| A. Moral Suasion | Imposing lending restrictions on certain sectors |
| B. Credit Rationing | Persuading banks to adhere to policy guidelines |
| C. Selective Credit Controls | Allocating credit limits to specific banks |

How many pairs given above is/are correctly matched?

(a) Only one pair (b) Only two pairs
(c) All three pairs (d) None

**42.** Consider the following actions by a central bank:

1. Advising banks to increase lending to the agriculture sector.
2. Imposing credit ceilings on loans to speculative real estate projects.
3. Changing the repo rate to influence market interest rates.

How many of the above actions is/are examples of qualitative tools of monetary policy?

(a) Only one (b) Only two
(c) All three (d) None

**43.** Consider the following scenario:

In response to a sharp economic contraction caused by Covid-19 pandemic, the RBI is considering various measures to stimulate the economy. Consumer confidence is low, unemployment is rising, and businesses are struggling to stay afloat.

Which expansionary policy actions would the RBI likely to implement in addressing this economic downturn?

1. Lowering the repo rate
2. Increasing the SLR
3. Announcing a moratorium on loan repayments
4. Selling of government securities

Select the correct answer from the codes given below:

(a) 1 and 3 only (b) 2 and 4 only
(c) 1, 2 and 3 only (d) 1, 3 and 4 only

**44.** The economy is experiencing high inflation, with consumer prices rising rapidly over the past six months. The central bank wants to reduce inflation and stabilise the economy.

Which of the following monetary policy tools should the central bank use to combat inflation in this scenario?

1. Lowering the Cash Reserve Ratio (CRR)
2. Increasing the Repo Rate
3. Conducting Open Market Operations (OMO) by selling government securities
4. Implementing Selective Credit Controls to limit loans for non-essential consumer goods

Select the correct answer using the codes given below:

(a) 1 and 2 only (b) 2, 3 and 4 only
(c) 1, 3 and 4 only (d) 1, 2, 3 and 4

## Topic 6 : Other Terms

**45.** Which of the following best describes 'Monetary Policy Transmission'?

(a) The process through which the central bank directly controls inflation by setting fixed prices for essential goods and services.
(b) The process of transferring government funds from one sector of the economy to another for public expenditure.
(c) The direct intervention by the central bank to regulate stock market prices and real estate values.
(d) The mechanism through which changes in the central bank's monetary policy (such as interest rates) affect the broader economy, particularly inflation and output.

**46.** Consider the following factors:

1. Reduction in non-performing assets (NPAs) in the banking sector.
2. Greater use of external benchmarks for lending rates.
3. Increased competition among banks.
4. Government interventions in fixing lending rates for specific sectors.

How many of the given above factors can smoothen monetary policy transmission?

(a) Only one (b) Only two
(c) Only three (d) All four

**47.** What is the primary objective of Operation Twist as implemented by central banks?

(a) To increase the supply of money in the economy by printing additional currency.
(b) To lower long-term interest rates by selling short-term government securities and buying long-term government securities.
(c) To stabilise foreign exchange rates by intervening in the currency markets.
(d) To reduce inflation by raising short-term interest rates.

# OMR SHEET

**Assessment Round**

| | | | | | | | | | | | | | | | | | | | |
|---|---|---|---|---|---|---|---|---|---|---|---|---|---|---|---|---|---|---|---|
| 1 | a | b | c | d | 31 | a | b | c | d | 61 | a | b | c | d | 91 | a | b | c | d |
| 2 | a | b | c | d | 32 | a | b | c | d | 62 | a | b | c | d | 92 | a | b | c | d |
| 3 | a | b | c | d | 33 | a | b | c | d | 63 | a | b | c | d | 93 | a | b | c | d |
| 4 | a | b | c | d | 34 | a | b | c | d | 64 | a | b | c | d | 94 | a | b | c | d |
| 5 | a | b | c | d | 35 | a | b | c | d | 65 | a | b | c | d | 95 | a | b | c | d |
| 6 | a | b | c | d | 36 | a | b | c | d | 66 | a | b | c | d | 96 | a | b | c | d |
| 7 | a | b | c | d | 37 | a | b | c | d | 67 | a | b | c | d | 97 | a | b | c | d |
| 8 | a | b | c | d | 38 | a | b | c | d | 68 | a | b | c | d | 98 | a | b | c | d |
| 9 | a | b | c | d | 39 | a | b | c | d | 69 | a | b | c | d | 99 | a | b | c | d |
| 10 | a | b | c | d | 40 | a | b | c | d | 70 | a | b | c | d | 100 | a | b | c | d |
| 11 | a | b | c | d | 41 | a | b | c | d | 71 | a | b | c | d | 101 | a | b | c | d |
| 12 | a | b | c | d | 42 | a | b | c | d | 72 | a | b | c | d | 102 | a | b | c | d |
| 13 | a | b | c | d | 43 | a | b | c | d | 73 | a | b | c | d | 103 | a | b | c | d |
| 14 | a | b | c | d | 44 | a | b | c | d | 74 | a | b | c | d | 104 | a | b | c | d |
| 15 | a | b | c | d | 45 | a | b | c | d | 75 | a | b | c | d | 105 | a | b | c | d |
| 16 | a | b | c | d | 46 | a | b | c | d | 76 | a | b | c | d | 106 | a | b | c | d |
| 17 | a | b | c | d | 47 | a | b | c | d | 77 | a | b | c | d | 107 | a | b | c | d |
| 18 | a | b | c | d | 48 | a | b | c | d | 78 | a | b | c | d | 108 | a | b | c | d |
| 19 | a | b | c | d | 49 | a | b | c | d | 79 | a | b | c | d | 109 | a | b | c | d |
| 20 | a | b | c | d | 50 | a | b | c | d | 80 | a | b | c | d | 110 | a | b | c | d |
| 21 | a | b | c | d | 51 | a | b | c | d | 81 | a | b | c | d | 111 | a | b | c | d |
| 22 | a | b | c | d | 52 | a | b | c | d | 82 | a | b | c | d | 112 | a | b | c | d |
| 23 | a | b | c | d | 53 | a | b | c | d | 83 | a | b | c | d | 113 | a | b | c | d |
| 24 | a | b | c | d | 54 | a | b | c | d | 84 | a | b | c | d | 114 | a | b | c | d |
| 25 | a | b | c | d | 55 | a | b | c | d | 85 | a | b | c | d | 115 | a | b | c | d |
| 26 | a | b | c | d | 56 | a | b | c | d | 86 | a | b | c | d | 116 | a | b | c | d |
| 27 | a | b | c | d | 57 | a | b | c | d | 87 | a | b | c | d | 117 | a | b | c | d |
| 28 | a | b | c | d | 58 | a | b | c | d | 88 | a | b | c | d | 118 | a | b | c | d |
| 29 | a | b | c | d | 59 | a | b | c | d | 89 | a | b | c | d | 119 | a | b | c | d |
| 30 | a | b | c | d | 60 | a | b | c | d | 90 | a | b | c | d | 120 | a | b | c | d |

## Calculate Your Score

**Correct (✓)**

**Incorrect (✓)**

**Unattempted**

**Total Score**

**Accuracy (%)**

## Reasons for Incorrect Answers?

1. Lack of Knowledge/Existing Source Insufficient
2. Lack of Multiple Revision
3. Common Sense Mistakes

**Note :**

1. Calculate total score as correct answers carry 2 marks each 1/3rd marks will deducted for **Incorrect** Answers.
2. Calculate Accuracy (%) by dividing the number of correct answers to the total number of attempted questions.

## Past Learning

**1.** Consider the following statements in respect of the digital rupee:

1. It is a sovereign currency issued by the Reserve Bank of India RBI alignment with its monetary policy.
2. It appears as a liability on the RBI's balance sheet. It is insured against inflation by its very design.
3. It is freely convertible against commercial bank money and cash.

Which of the statements given above are correct?

(a) 1 and 2 only (b) 1 and 3 only
(c) 2 and 4 only (d) 1, 2 and 4 only

**2.** With reference to Central Bank digital currencies, consider the following statements : **(2023)**

1. It is possible to make payments in a digital currency without using US dollar or SWIFT system.
2. A digital currency can be distributed with a condition programmed into it such as a time-frame for spending it.

Which of the statements given above is/are correct?

(a) 1 only (b) 2 only
(c) Both 1 and 2 (d) Neither 1 nor 2

**3.** Consider the following statements : **(2023)**

**Statement I:** In the post-pandemic recent past, many Central Banks worldwide had carried out interest rate hikes.

**Statement II:** Central Banks generally assume that they have the ability to counteract the rising consumer prices via monetary policy means.

Which one of the following is correct in respect of the above statements?

(a) Both Statement I and Statement II are correct and Statement II is the correct explanation for Statement I.
(b) Both Statement I and Statement II are correct and Statement II is not the correct explanation for Statement I.
(c) Statement I is correct, but Statement II is incorrect.
(d) Statement I is incorrect, but Statement II is correct.

**4.** Which one of the following activities of the Reserve Bank of India is considered to be part of sterilisation? **(2023)**

(a) Conducting 'Open Market Operations'
(b) Oversight of settlement and payment systems
(c) Debt and cash management for the Central and State Governments
(d) Regulating the functions of Non-banking Financial Institutions

**5.** In India, which one of the following is responsible for maintaining price stability by controlling inflation? **(2022)**

(a) Department of Consumer Affairs
(b) Expenditure Management Commission
(c) Financial Stability and Development Council
(d) Reserve Bank of India

**6.** With reference to Non-Fungible Tokens (NFTs), consider the following statements: **(2022)**

1. They enable the digital representation of physical assets.
2. They are unique cryptographic tokens that exist on a blockchain.
3. They can be traded or exchanged at equivalency and therefore can be used as a medium of commercial transactions.

Which of the statements given above are correct?

(a) 1 and 2 only
(b) 2 and 3 only
(c) 1 and 3 only
(d) 1, 2 and 3

**7.** The money multiplier in an economy increases with which one of the following? **(2021)**

(a) Increase in the cash reserve ratio
(b) Increase in the banking habit of the population
(c) Increase in the statutory liquidity ratio
(d) Increase in the population of the country

**8.** If the RBI decides to adopt an expansionist monetary policy, which of the following would it not do? **(2020)**

1. Cut and optimise the Statutory Liquidity Ratio.
2. Increase the Marginal Standing Facility Rate.
3. Cut the Bank Rate and Repo Rate.

Select the correct answer using the codes given below:

(a) 1 and 2 only (b) 2 only
(c) 1 and 3 only (d) 1, 2 and 3

**9.** If you withdraw ₹ 1,00,000 in cash from your Demand Deposit Account at your bank, the immediate effect on aggregate money supply in the economy will be: **(2020)**

(a) to reduce it by ₹ 1,00,000
(b) to increase it by ₹ 1,00,000
(c) to increase to by more than ₹ 1,00,000
(d) to leave it unchanged

**10.** The money multiplier in an economy increases with which one of the following? **(2019)**

(a) Increase in the cash reserve ratio
(b) Increase in the banking habit of the population
(c) Increase in the statutory liquidity ratio
(d) Increase in the population of the country

**11.** Which one of the following statements correctly describes the meaning of legal tender money ? **(2018)**

(a) The money which is tendered in courts of law to defray the fee of legal cases
(b) The money which a creditor is under compulsion to accept in settlement of his claims
(c) The bank money in the form of cheques drafts, bills of exchange, etc.
(d) The metallic money in circulation in a country

**12.** Which of the following statements is/are correct regarding the Monetary Policy Committee (MPC)? **(2017)**

1. It decides the RBI's benchmark interest rates.
2. It is a 12-member body including the Governor of RBI and is reconstituted every year.
3. It functions under the chairmanship of the Union Finance Minister.

Select the correct answer using the codes given below:

(a) 1 only (b) 1 and 2 only
(c) 3 only (d) 2 and 3 only

**13.** With reference to Bitcoins, sometimes seen in the news, which of the following statements is/are correct? **(2016)**

1. Bitcoins are tracked by the Central Banks of the countries.
2. Anyone with a Bitcoin address can send and receive Bitcoins from anyone else with a Bitcoin address.
3. Online payments can be sent without either side knowing the identity of the other.

Select the correct answer using the codes given below:

(a) 1 and 2 only (b) 2 and 3 only
(c) 3 only (d) 1, 2 and 3

**14.** With reference to Indian economy, consider the following: **(2015)**

1. Bank rate
2. Open market operations
3. Public debt
4. Public revenue

Which of the above is/are component/ components of Monetary Policy?

(a) 1 only (b) 2, 3 and 4 only
(c) 1 and 2 only (d) 1, 3 and 4

**15.** When the Reserve Bank of India reduces the Statutory Liquidity Ratio by 50 basis points, which of the following is likely to happen? **(2015)**

(a) India's GDP growth rate increases drastically
(b) Foreign Institutional Investors may bring more capital into our country
(c) Scheduled Commercial Banks may cut their lending rates
(d) It may drastically reduce the liquidity to the banking system

# Detailed Solutions

## Assessment Round

**1.** *(d)* 1, 2, 3 and 4

- **Option 1 is correct:** Many goods cannot be divided into smaller portions without losing their value. For example, dividing a cow or a Plow might result in a loss of utility, whereas money can be divided into smaller units (such as coins or notes) without losing its value. **This divisibility of money makes it more convenient for trade and exchange.**
- **Option 2 is correct:** Barter goods can often be **bulky or perishable,** making them difficult to transport over long distances. For instance, transporting livestock or sacks of grain involves considerable effort and is impractical. **Money, on the other hand,** is portable and easy to carry, **allowing individuals to conduct transactions with ease.**
- **Option 3 is correct:** In barter systems, **deferred payments** are challenging because there is no standard unit of account to agree upon for future transactions. For instance, agreeing on how much grain should be delivered in exchange for livestock at a future date is complex without a common measure of value. **Money solves this issue by allowing for easy deferral of payments, providing a standardised unit of account that both parties can rely on for future transactions.**
- **Option 4 is correct:** The **lack of a standardised unit of account** in barter systems creates challenges in valuing goods and services consistently. For example, without a common measure of value, it is difficult to determine how many sacks of grain should be exchanged for a Plow. **Money provides** a common unit of account, **simplifying the valuation of goods and services, making trade more efficient, and standardised.**

**Therefore, the correct answer is (d) 1, 2, 3 and 4.**

**2.** *(b)* Only two

- **Statement 1 is correct:** Money serves as a **medium of exchange,** facilitating trade and transactions by providing a common platform for exchanging goods, and services. It eliminates the inefficiencies of a barter system, where individuals would need to find someone who wants their goods in exchange for something they need. Money simplifies this process, allowing individuals to trade goods and services more efficiently.
- **Statement 2 is incorrect: Money does not always have intrinsic value.** For example, modern fiat money (like currency notes) has no intrinsic value of its own. Its value is derived from the trust and acceptance of the people using it, and it is backed by government guarantees. While historically, some forms of money, such as gold and silver, had intrinsic value due to their material content, most modern forms of money, such as paper currency or digital money, do not.
- **Statement 3 is correct:** Money serves as a **store of value,** meaning individuals can save it and use it for future purchases. This characteristic allows people to preserve their wealth over time, plan for future expenses and delay consumption. The value stored in money is relatively stable over short periods, which helps in saving for future needs.

**Therefore, the correct answer is (b) Only two.**

**3.** *(c)* Only three

- **Option 1 is correct: Commodity money** is recognised as a form of money. It has intrinsic value because it is made of valuable materials such as gold, silver, or other commodities.
- **Option 2 is correct: Fiat money** is widely accepted in modern economies. It is issued by the government and does not have intrinsic value or backing by a physical commodity like gold or silver. Its value is derived from the trust that people place in the issuing authority (usually the government) and its acceptance for the payment of goods, and services.
- **Option 3 is correct: Digital currency,** including cryptocurrencies, is increasingly recognised as a form of money. With the rise

of digital payment systems and blockchain technology, cryptocurrencies like Bitcoin are used as a medium of exchange, a store of value, and a unit of account in certain contexts, though they are not yet universally accepted.

- **Option 4 is incorrect: Barter** is not a recognised form of money. It is an exchange system where goods and services are traded directly without the use of money. Since there is no universally accepted medium of exchange in barter, it does not meet the criteria for being classified as a form of money.

**Therefore, the correct answer is (c) Only three.**

**4.** *(a)* 1 and 2 only

- **Statement 1 is correct: Commodity money has intrinsic value** because it's worth is derived from the material it is made of, such as gold, silver, or other precious metals. These commodities are valuable in themselves due to their rarity, durability and other inherent properties, making them suitable as a medium of exchange and store of value.
- **Statement 2 is correct: Commodity money includes items like gold, silver and precious stones,** which are valuable not only as money but also as goods with intrinsic worth. Historically, these items were used in trade because people universally recognised their value beyond their function as money.
- **Statement 3 is incorrect: Commodity money is harder to transport and store compared to fiat money.** Precious metals like gold and silver are heavy, and require special arrangements for secure storage. On the other hand, fiat money, such as paper currency, is lightweight and easy to transport in large quantities. This makes fiat money more practical for everyday transactions.

**Therefore, the correct answer is (a) 1 and 2 only.**

**5.** *(b)* Only two

- **Option 1 is correct: Fiat money is issued by a central authority or government,** such as the Reserve Bank of India (RBI) in India or the Federal Reserve in the United States. These institutions are responsible for controlling the supply of money and regulating its use as the official currency within their respective countries.
- **Option 2 is incorrect: Fiat money does not have intrinsic value.** Unlike commodity money, which has value based on the material it is made from (such as gold or silver), fiat money derives its value from public trust and the backing of the government. Its value is not based on physical properties but rather on the confidence that people have in its use as a medium of exchange.
- **Option 3 is correct: Fiat money is accepted as a medium of exchange** primarily because of government regulation and legal tender laws. Governments declare fiat money to be legal tender, meaning it must be accepted for payment of debts and goods within the economy. This legal framework ensures its widespread acceptance in everyday transactions.
- **Option 4 is incorrect: Fiat money is subject to inflation and deflation.** Its value can fluctuate based on economic conditions, such as changes in monetary policy, supply and demand, or overall economic performance. Inflation can reduce the purchasing power of fiat money, while deflation can increase it. The value of fiat money is not stable and can be affected by various factors.

**Therefore, the correct answer is (b) Only two.**

**6.** *(a)* Money that must be accepted if offered in payment of a debt.

- **Option (a) is correct: Legal tender refers to money that must be accepted if offered in payment of a debt.** It is recognised by law as a valid form of payment for settling financial obligations. In most countries, legal tender includes coins and banknotes issued by the government or central bank, which must be accepted for transactions.
- **Option (b) is incorrect: Legal tender does not refer to currency that can be exchanged for gold or silver.** This would describe commodity-backed money, where the currency can be redeemed for a physical commodity like gold or silver. Legal tender, especially fiat money, is not backed by such

commodities and derives its value from legal and regulatory frameworks.

- **Option (c) is incorrect: Legal tender is not the same as commodity money.** Commodity money has intrinsic value because it is made of materials like gold or silver. Legal tender, especially fiat money, has no intrinsic value but is accepted in transactions because it is recognised by law as an official currency.
- **Option (d) is incorrect: Legal tender is not a non-monetary item used in bartering.** It specifically refers to recognised currency in an economy, such as coins and banknotes. Barter systems, on the other hand, involve the direct exchange of goods and services without using money.

**Thus, option (a) is the correct answer.**

**7.** *(c)* Only three pairs

- **Pair 1 is correct: Legal Tender in India includes Indian coins, banknotes and recently, central bank digital currency issued by the Reserve Bank of India.** Legal tender is recognised by law and must be accepted when offered for the payment of a debt. The inclusion of digital currency as legal tender is a recent development, aligning with global trends towards digital payments.
- **Pair 2 is incorrect: Digital Currency is a form of currency that exists only in digital form, but UPI transactions are not digital currency,** they are a form of digital payment using fiat money. UPI (Unified Payments Interface) enables transactions using existing bank balances, but it does not represent a new form of currency. Digital currency, as defined in economic terms, refers to currency that exists only in digital form and is yet to be officially issued by the Reserve Bank of India.
- **Pair 3 is correct: Full-bodied Money is money that has intrinsic value equal to its face value.** Historically, coins made of precious metals, like silver coins, were examples of full-bodied money. These coins had value because the material (silver or gold) was worth an amount equal to the face value stamped on the coin.
- **Pair 4 is correct: Near Money refers to financial assets that are not cash but can easily be converted into cash, such as Fixed** Deposit Receipts, Treasury Bills, or other short-term financial instruments. These assets are highly liquid and can be quickly converted into cash when needed, though they do not function as money directly

**Therefore, the correct answer is (c) Only three pairs.**

**8.** *(b)* A situation where a central bank prints large amounts of money and distributes it directly to the public to boost demand.

**Helicopter Money** refers to an unconventional monetary policy tool where a central bank prints new money and distributes it directly to the public or government to **stimulate demand,** and combat deflation. This approach is used to boost **consumer spending** in situations of economic stagnation, but it also carries the risk of causing inflation if not carefully managed.

**Thus, option (b) is the correct answer.**

**9.** *(a)* Only one

- **Statement 1 is correct: Electronic money includes stored value cards (like prepaid cards) and online wallets (like Paytm Wallet).** These are digital forms of money that allow users to store cash electronically. Stored value cards and online wallets can be used for a variety of transactions, and they offer a convenient way to carry, and spend money without the need for physical currency.
- **Statement 2 is incorrect: Not all forms of electronic money require internet access.** Stored value cards, for example, can function offline because the value is stored directly on the card rather than requiring access to an online account or network. Many transit systems, for example, use stored value cards that can be used without internet connectivity.
- **Statement 3 is incorrect: Electronic money can be used for both domestic and cross-border transactions.** Depending on the platform and regulatory compliance, electronic money can facilitate international payments. Platforms such as PayPal, for example, allow users to send and receive money across borders, while other forms of electronic money can also be used for domestic transactions.

**Therefore, the correct answer is (a) Only one.**

***10.*** *(b)* Only two

- **Statement 1 is correct: Cryptocurrencies are decentralised digital assets** that use blockchain technology to ensure secure, transparent and tamper-proof transactions. Blockchain operates as a distributed ledger that records all transactions in a secure and immutable manner, without the need for a central authority. This decentralisation is one of the key features of cryptocurrencies like Bitcoin and Ethereum.
- **Statement 2 is incorrect: Cryptocurrencies are not backed by physical assets like gold or silver.** Unlike commodity-backed currencies, cryptocurrencies derive their value from **supply and demand dynamics**, the security provided by blockchain technology, and the confidence of users. Their value fluctuates based on market sentiment, investor interest and usage, rather than being tied to any tangible asset.
- **Statement 3 is correct: Transactions made with cryptocurrencies are generally irreversible.** Due to the nature of blockchain technology, once a transaction is verified and added to the blockchain, it cannot be altered or reversed. This immutability ensures the integrity of the ledger but also means that errors or fraud cannot easily be undone, unlike in traditional banking systems where chargebacks may be possible.

**Therefore, the correct answer is (b) Only two.**

***11.*** *(c)* 2 and 3 only

- **Statement 1 is incorrect: Cryptocurrencies do not have intrinsic value** because they are not backed by physical assets like gold or silver. Their value is based on **supply and demand dynamics**, market perception, and the technology underlying them, such as blockchain. Cryptocurrencies derive their worth from the trust users place in them and their utility within decentralised networks, rather than any tangible asset.
- **Statement 2 is correct: Most cryptocurrencies operate on a decentralised model** and are not regulated by any central authority or government. This decentralisation is a key characteristic of cryptocurrencies like Bitcoin and Ethereum, where transactions, and issuance of new coins are managed by networks of computers, known as nodes, rather than a centralised entity. This system enhances transparency and security but also means less government control over the currency.
- **Statement 3 is correct: El Salvador was the first country to declare Bitcoin as legal tender in June 2021.** This decision allows Bitcoin to be used for all forms of transactions within the country, alongside the U.S. dollar, which is the other official currency. The move was significant in the global adoption of cryptocurrencies, marking a milestone where a digital currency could be used as legal tender in a national economy.

**Therefore, the correct answer is (c) 2 and 3 only.**

***12.*** *(b)* A digital currency designed to maintain a stable value by being pegged to a reserve of assets such as fiat currencies or commodities.

**Stablecoins** are cryptocurrencies designed to have a **stable value** by being **pegged** to assets like **fiat currencies** (e.g., the US dollar) or **commodities** (e.g., gold). This stability makes them less volatile than other cryptocurrencies, making them useful for transactions, savings and a store of value in the digital economy.

**Thus, option (b) is the correct answer.**

***13.*** *(a)* Only one

- **Statement 1 is incorrect: Cryptocurrencies are not recognised as legal tender by the Reserve Bank of India (RBI).** The RBI has made it clear that the only recognised legal tender in India is the Indian Rupee (INR). Cryptocurrencies such as Bitcoin, Ethereum, and others are not accepted as official currency for transactions, and do not have the status of legal tender in India.
- **Statement 2 is correct: The trading of cryptocurrencies is subject to taxation under the Income Tax Act in India.** Profits made from cryptocurrency transactions are considered capital gains and individuals are required to report them under the applicable tax regime. Depending on the holding period, they may be classified as short-term or long-term capital gains and taxed accordingly. This

taxation ensures that cryptocurrency earnings are treated similarly to other investment gains.

- **Statement 3 is incorrect: The Securities and Exchange Board of India (SEBI) does not currently regulate cryptocurrency trading.** While SEBI oversees securities and the stock market in India, cryptocurrencies do not fall under its jurisdiction as they are not officially classified as securities. As of now, India does not have a specific regulatory framework for cryptocurrencies, although discussions around potential regulations are ongoing.

**Therefore, the correct answer is (a) Only one.**

**14.** *(b)* Only two

- **Statement 1 is correct: The Digital Rupee is issued and regulated by the Reserve Bank of India (RBI)** as India's official Central Bank Digital Currency (CBDC). The RBI oversees the issuance and management of the Digital Rupee, which is designed to function as a digital version of the Indian Rupee (INR). It is backed by the central bank and operates under a similar framework to physical currency, ensuring its legitimacy, and widespread acceptance.
- **Statement 2 is incorrect: The Digital Rupee will not necessarily require users to have a bank account with a commercial bank.** The objective of the Digital Rupee is to be inclusive, providing access to digital currency for both banked and unbanked individuals. This allows even those without traditional banking infrastructure to use and hold the digital currency, promoting financial inclusion, and expanding the reach of digital payments in India.
- **Statement 3 is correct: The Digital Rupee is a liability on the balance sheet of the Reserve Bank of India (RBI),** just like physical currency notes. When the RBI issues Digital Rupees, they become a liability on its balance sheet, representing a claim by the holder on the central bank. This is similar to how paper money functions as a claim on the central bank, ensuring the value of the Digital Rupee.

**Therefore, the correct answer is (b) Only two.**

**15.** *(b)* 2 and 3 only

- **Statement 1 is incorrect: The Digital Rupee is recognised as legal tender in India,** meaning it must be accepted for all transactions where the Indian Rupee is accepted. The Digital Rupee, issued by the Reserve Bank of India (RBI), is treated as equivalent to physical currency in terms of its legal status. **Cryptocurrencies,** on the other hand, are not recognised as legal tender in India and businesses are not legally required to accept them as payment.
- **Statement 2 is correct: The Reserve Bank of India (RBI) has the authority to regulate the supply of the Digital Rupee,** which allows the central bank to control its issuance and manage the overall money supply in the economy. By regulating the Digital Rupee, the RBI can implement monetary policies aimed at controlling inflation, managing interest rates and stabilising the economy, similar to how it manages physical currency, and bank reserves.
- **Statement 3 is correct: Users can convert their physical cash into Digital Rupee tokens** through authorised banks and digital platforms. This process allows individuals to easily transition between physical currency and digital currency, making the adoption of the Digital Rupee more seamless. The ability to switch between cash and digital currency enhances the flexibility, and convenience of using the Digital Rupee for various transactions.

**Therefore, the correct answer is (b) 2 and 3 only.**

**16.** *(c)* 1 only

- **Statement 1 is correct: The Digital Rupee can be transferred directly between users without the need for a bank intermediary,** similar to peer-to-peer (P2P) transactions in digital payment systems. This allows for seamless transfers between individuals using digital wallets, making it faster and more convenient for users to send, and receive funds. This decentralised mechanism enhances accessibility and simplifies transactions, much like popular P2P payment platforms.

- **Statement 2 is incorrect: The Digital Rupee itself does not earn interest when held in digital wallets.** It functions similarly to physical cash, meaning it can be used for transactions but does not accrue interest over time. Interest is typically earned on savings or investments in bank accounts or other financial instruments, but the Digital Rupee, like cash, does not generate interest when simply stored.
- **Statement 3 is incorrect: The Digital Rupee may not necessarily require a smartphone with internet access for all transactions.** Depending on the implementation by the Reserve Bank of India (RBI), it may also support offline transactions or transactions through basic mobile phones. This could allow broader access to digital currency, particularly in areas with limited internet connectivity or among individuals who do not own smartphones.

**Therefore, the correct answer is (c) 1 only.**

***17.*** *(d)* 1, 2 and 3

- **Statement 1 is correct: Reserve money (M0) includes currency held by the public, currency with the banks and reserves held by commercial banks with the Reserve Bank of India (RBI).** It is the most liquid form of money in the economy and is also referred to as the monetary base or high-powered money. M0 forms the foundation of the money supply, as it represents the currency in circulation and the reserves that banks hold with the central bank.
- **Statement 2 is correct: Narrow money (M1) consists of currency with the public, demand deposits with banks and other deposits with the RBI.** M1 is a highly liquid component of the money supply, representing cash and readily accessible bank deposits. This form of money is immediately available for transactions, making it a key indicator of the liquidity in the economy.
- **Statement 3 is correct: Broad money (M3) includes all components of M1 plus savings deposits and time deposits with banks.** M3 is a broader measure of the money supply, as it encompasses not only the currency and demand deposits but also savings, and time deposits, which are less liquid but still part of the overall money supply in the economy.

**Therefore, the correct answer is (d) 1, 2 and 3.**

***18.*** *(b)* It acts as the foundation for the creation of broad money in the economy.

- **High-powered money,** also known as the **monetary base or reserve money (M0),** serves as the foundation of the monetary system. It includes currency in circulation (held by the public) and reserves held by commercial banks with the central bank (such as the Reserve Bank of India in India).
- **High-powered money is critical for the banking system** because it is the primary reserve that banks use to support the creation of loans and deposits. Through the process of **fractional-reserve banking,** banks hold only a fraction of their deposits in reserve and lend out the remaining portion. This lending process leads to the **multiplication of money** in the economy.
- **Broader forms of money,** such as **M1, M2, and M3,** are created from the base of high-powered money. When banks issue loans, new deposits are created in the banking system, expanding the money supply beyond the initial reserve base. The extent of money creation depends on the reserve ratio set by the central bank and the lending activities of commercial banks.
- The central bank controls the supply of high-powered money, which influences the overall money supply and **monetary policy** in the economy. By adjusting the reserve requirements or the monetary base, the central bank can influence inflation, interest rates, and economic growth.

**Thus, option (b) is the correct answer.**

***19.*** *(c)* The maximum amount of commercial bank money that can be created from a unit of central bank money.

- **The money multiplier** refers to the **maximum amount of commercial bank money** (such as deposits) that can be created from a unit of central bank money (like reserves). The concept is rooted in the **fractional-reserve banking system,** where commercial banks are required to hold only a fraction of their deposits as reserves with the central bank.

- **The process begins when central bank money, or high-powered money,** is deposited in a commercial bank. The bank keeps a portion of this as reserves (as required by the reserve ratio) and lends out the rest. The amount lent out is then deposited in another bank, and the process repeats, leading to the creation of additional money through deposits, and loans.
- **The larger the reserve ratio,** the smaller the money multiplier, as banks must hold a larger portion of their deposits as reserves and have less to lend. Conversely, a lower reserve ratio increases the money multiplier, allowing banks to create more money from the same amount of central bank reserves.
- **Through this mechanism,** the banking system multiplies the initial deposits, expanding the money supply. This multiplier effect amplifies the central bank's ability to influence the overall money supply and liquidity in the economy.

**Thus, option (c) is the correct answer.**

**20.** *(a)* 1 only

- **Statement 1 is correct: Increasing financial inclusion, such as by providing more people access to banking services, can raise the money multiplier.** When more individuals and businesses are included in the formal banking system, it results in a greater number of deposits within the banks. These deposits can then be used by banks to issue loans, which increases the overall money supply through the multiplier effect. More participants in the banking system lead to more transactions and a higher potential for money creation.
- **Statement 2 is incorrect: The digitalisation of the economy typically increases the money multiplier,** as it reduces the reliance on cash transactions. When more transactions occur digitally, money remains within the banking system rather than being withdrawn as cash. This ensures that more deposits are available for banks to lend, thus enhancing the money multiplier. Digital payments systems keep money circulating within financial institutions, increasing their lending capacity.
- **Statement 3 is incorrect: A higher reserve requirement reduces the money multiplier,** as banks must hold more reserves against deposits. This restricts their ability to lend out money, which directly lowers the potential for money creation through loans. The money multiplier is inversely related to the reserve ratio: the higher the reserve requirement, the smaller the money multiplier and the lesser the banks' ability to expand the money supply.

**Therefore, the correct answer is (a) 1 only.**

**21.** *(b)* Only two

- **Option 1 is correct: Increasing the Cash Reserve Ratio (CRR) is a monetary policy action** that requires banks to hold a higher proportion of their deposits as reserves with the central bank. When the CRR is increased, banks have less money available to lend, which reduces the overall money supply in the economy. This action is used by central banks to control inflation and manage liquidity in the banking system.
- **Option 2 is incorrect: Regulating trade tariffs is related to trade policy, not monetary policy.** Trade tariffs are taxes imposed on imports or exports and are part of a country's trade policy. They are designed to protect domestic industries or generate revenue, but do not directly influence the money supply or interest rates, which are the primary focus of monetary policy.
- **Option 3 is correct: Conducting Open Market Operations (OMOs) involves the buying or selling of government securities** by the central bank in the open market. When the central bank buys securities, it injects money into the banking system, increasing the money supply. Conversely, selling securities withdraws money from the system, reducing liquidity. OMOs are a key tool used by central banks to influence interest rates and control inflation.
- **Option 4 is incorrect: Implementing a debt-to-GDP ratio policy is typically a fiscal policy action,** not a monetary policy action.

The debt-to-GDP ratio reflects a country's level of debt relative to its economic output and is primarily a concern of fiscal policy, which deals with government spending, taxation, and debt management. Monetary policy, on the other hand, focuses on controlling the money supply and interest rates.

**Therefore, the correct answer is (b) Only two.**

**22.** *(a)* 1 and 2 only

- **Option 1 is correct: Raising the repo rate is a contractionary monetary policy action.** When the central bank raises the repo rate, it makes borrowing more expensive for banks, which in turn makes loans more costly for businesses and consumers. This leads to reduced borrowing, decreased spending and a slowdown in economic activity. By raising the repo rate, the central bank aims to control inflation by reducing the money supply.
- **Option 2 is correct: Selling government securities in the open market is a contractionary action.** When the central bank sells government securities, it withdraws money from the banking system, as buyers pay for the securities using their reserves. This reduces the amount of money available for banks to lend, thereby decreasing the money supply. Open market sales are used to reduce liquidity in the economy and control inflation.
- **Option 3 is incorrect: Lowering the cash reserve ratio (CRR) is an expansionary action.** When the CRR is lowered, banks are required to hold less money in reserve, allowing them to lend more. This increases the money supply in the economy and stimulates economic activity.

**Therefore, the correct answer is (a) 1 and 2 only.**

**23.** *(d)* All four pairs

- **Pair 1 is correct: Lowering of the reverse repo rate is an Expansionary monetary policy.** Reducing reverse repo rate will discourages the Commercial Banks to lend to the Central Bank for a lower return and encourage banks to lend more to businesses, and people.
- **Pair 2 is correct: Hawkish monetary policy signals a willingness to aggressively fight inflation.** A hawkish stance typically involves raising interest rates or implementing other restrictive measures aimed at curbing inflation. This type of policy seeks to tighten monetary conditions to slow down an overheating economy and keep inflation under control, even at the risk of slowing economic growth.
- **Pair 3 is correct: Accommodative monetary policy provides cheap long-term loans to banks** to encourage lending and stimulate economic growth. In an accommodative stance, central banks may lower interest rates or inject liquidity into the banking system to promote borrowing, investment and economic activity. This policy is typically used during periods of economic slowdown or recession.
- **Pair 4 is correct: Dovish monetary policy involves reducing interest rates to encourage borrowing and spending.** A dovish approach prioritises stimulating economic growth and employment over controlling inflation. By lowering interest rates, the central bank aims to make borrowing cheaper for consumers and businesses, thereby boosting spending, and investment. Dovish policies are often implemented during periods of low inflation or economic stagnation.

**Therefore, the correct answer is (d) All four pairs.**

**24.** *(b)* To control inflation and maintain price stability

**The primary goal of the monetary policy framework adopted by the Reserve Bank of India (RBI) is to control inflation and maintain price stability.** Price stability ensures that inflation remains within a target range, preventing extreme fluctuations in the cost of goods and services. Keeping inflation under control is crucial

**Thus, option (b) is the correct answer.**

**25.** *(b)* Only two

- **Statement 1 is incorrect: The RBI's inflation targeting framework uses the Consumer Price Index (CPI) as the primary measure of** inflation, not the Wholesale Price Index (WPI). The CPI is considered a better reflection of the inflation that affects consumers directly, as it measures the changes in prices of a basket of goods and services typically consumed by households. The WPI, on the other hand, measures price changes at the wholesale level and is less representative of consumer inflation.

- **Statement 2 is correct: The inflation target in India is set by the Government of India in consultation with the RBI**, as part of the **Monetary Policy Framework Agreement.** The inflation target is currently set at 4% with a tolerance band of ±2%, meaning the acceptable inflation range is 2% to 6%. This target guides the RBI's monetary policy decisions aimed at controlling inflation while supporting economic growth.
- **Statement 3 is correct: The RBI is required to provide an explanation to the government if inflation deviates from the target range (2% to 6%) for three consecutive quarters.** If inflation remains persistently outside this band, the RBI must submit a report to the government explaining the reasons for the deviation and outlining the proposed remedial actions to bring inflation back within the target range. This ensures transparency and accountability in the monetary policy process.

**Therefore, the correct answer is (b) Only two.**

**26.** *(d)* 1, 2 and 3

- **Statement 1 is correct: The Monetary Policy Committee (MPC) is responsible for setting the benchmark interest rates,** such as the **repo rate**, which is crucial for controlling inflation and managing the overall monetary policy of India.
- **Statement 2 is correct: The MPC consists of six members: three from the Reserve Bank of India (RBI), including the Governor and three external members appointed by the Government of India.** However, no government official can be a part of the MPC.
- **Statement 3 is correct: The MPC's decision-making process is based on majority voting,** with each of the six members, including those from the RBI and external appointees, having **equal voting rights.** In the event of a tie, the Governor of the RBI has the casting vote, which ensures that decisions are made efficiently.

**Therefore, the correct answer is (d) 1, 2 and 3.**

**27.** *(b)* 1 only

- **Statement 1 is correct: The MPC is chaired by the Governor of the Reserve Bank of India (RBI)**, who presides over its meetings. In the decision-making process, each member has one vote and if there is a tie, the Governor has the casting vote.
- **Statement 2 is incorrect: Not all members of the MPC are appointed by the Government of India.** The MPC consists of six members, three of whom are from the RBI (including the Governor, the Deputy Governor in charge of monetary policy and one RBI official nominated by the central bank). The remaining three external members are appointed by the Government of India.
- **Statement 3 is incorrect: The MPC is required to meet at least four times a year** to make decisions regarding monetary policy, not once every month. While they may meet more frequently if required, the minimum is four meetings per year.

**Therefore, the correct answer is (b) 1 only.**

**28.** *(c)* Only three

- **Option 1 is correct: Open Market Operations (OMO) involve the buying and selling of government securities** by the central bank to regulate the money supply. When the central bank buys securities, it injects liquidity into the economy, increasing the money supply. Conversely, selling securities reduces liquidity and tightens the money supply. OMOs are considered a **quantitative tool** because they directly influence the amount of money circulating in the economy.
- **Option 2 is correct: The Cash Reserve Ratio (CRR) is the percentage of a bank's total deposits that must be maintained as reserves with the central bank.** By adjusting the CRR, the central bank controls how much money banks can lend. A higher CRR reduces the amount of money available for lending, while

a lower CRR increases liquidity. This is also a **quantitative tool** because it affects the volume of money in the banking system.

- **Option 3 is incorrect: Moral suasion is a qualitative tool.** It involves the central bank using persuasion, communication, or informal requests to influence the behavior of commercial banks without enforcing formal directives
- **Option 4 is correct: The Repo Rate is the interest rate at which the central bank lends money to commercial banks.** By raising or lowering the repo rate, the central bank can influence the cost of borrowing for banks, which in turn affects the money supply and overall economic activity. The repo rate is a **quantitative tool** because it directly influences the money supply by adjusting the availability and cost of funds for banks.

**Therefore, the correct answer is (c) Only three.**

**29.** *(d)* 1, 2 and 3

**Statement 1 is correct:** The **Repo Rate** is the interest rate at which the **RBI lends money to commercial banks** in exchange for **government securities.** It is used by the RBI to regulate short-term liquidity and money supply in the economy.

**Statement 2 is correct: A decrease in the repo rate** makes borrowing cheaper for commercial banks, encouraging them to take more loans from the RBI. This increases **liquidity** in the banking system, which can lead to higher lending and investment in the economy.

**Statement 3 is correct:** The **repo rate** is generally higher than the **reverse repo rate.** The reverse repo rate is the rate at which the RBI borrows money from commercial banks, and this difference encourages banks to lend money to the RBI at the reverse repo rate or borrow from the RBI at the repo rate depending on liquidity conditions

**Therefore, the correct answer is (d) 1, 2 and 3.**

**30.** *(c)* 1, 3 and 4 only

- **Option 1 is correct: Commercial banks are eligible to participate in Liquidity Adjustment Facility (LAF) operations conducted by the RBI.** LAF operations, which include repo and reverse repo transactions, allow commercial banks to borrow or park surplus funds with the RBI to manage their short-term liquidity needs. These operations help ensure stability in the banking system and provide the necessary liquidity.
- **Option 2 is incorrect: Non-Banking Financial Companies (NBFCs) are not eligible to participate in LAF operations directly.** LAF is limited to scheduled commercial banks and primary dealers. While NBFCs are important players in the financial system, they do not have direct access to LAF and instead rely on other mechanisms for liquidity, such as borrowing from banks or issuing debt instruments.
- **Option 3 is correct: Primary Dealers, who are market makers in government securities, are also eligible to borrow under LAF operations.** Primary dealers play a key role in ensuring liquidity in the government securities market and by participating in LAF operations, they can manage their short-term funding needs to support their market-making activities.
- **Option 4 is correct:** Scheduled Co-operative Banks are eligible to borrow under the Liquidity Adjustment Facility (LAF) operations, meaning they can access this facility to manage their short-term liquidity needs by buying and selling government securities with the RBI.

**Therefore, the correct answer is (c) 1, 3 and 4 only.**

**31.** *(c)* The interest rate charged by the central bank on long-term loans extended to commercial banks and financial institutions.

The **Bank Rate** refers to the interest rate charged by a country's **central bank** (such as the RBI in India) on **long-term loans** or advances given to **commercial banks** and other financial institutions. It serves as a tool for controlling **liquidity** and **money supply** in the economy. Changes in the bank rate influence the overall interest rate structure in the financial system.

**Thus, option (c) is the correct answer.**

**32.** *(c)* Both 1 and 2

- **Statement 1 is correct: The Standing Deposit Facility (SDF) is a tool used by the RBI to absorb surplus liquidity from the banking system.** Unlike the Reverse Repo Rate, where the RBI provides government securities as collateral in exchange for funds, the SDF does not require any collateral. It is a flexible tool designed to manage excess liquidity without needing the RBI to offer securities, thereby making the liquidity absorption process more efficient.
- **Statement 2 is correct: The SDF allows banks to deposit their excess funds with the RBI and earn interest on these deposits.** This provides banks with a mechanism to manage their excess liquidity efficiently while earning interest, all without the need for government securities as collateral. This flexibility in liquidity management helps the RBI control the money supply without collateral constraints.

**Therefore, the correct answer is (c) Both 1 and 2.**

**33.** *(c)* All three

- **Statement 1 is correct: The Marginal Standing Facility (MSF) was introduced by the Reserve Bank of India (RBI) in 2011** as part of its monetary policy framework. The MSF provides banks with a mechanism to borrow overnight funds from the RBI against approved government securities. This facility helps banks address short-term liquidity mismatches and maintain financial stability. The MSF acts as a safety valve for the banking system during times of liquidity stress, ensuring that banks can meet their short-term funding needs.
- **Statement 2 is correct: The MSF rate serves as the upper bound of the Liquidity Adjustment Facility (LAF) corridor,** with the repo rate acting as the mid-point and the reverse repo rate as the lower bound. The LAF corridor is a key component of the RBI's monetary policy framework, influencing short-term interest rates in the economy. The MSF rate, being the highest in the corridor, represents the most expensive borrowing option for banks and helps control excessive liquidity.
- **Statement 3 is correct: Banks can typically borrow up to 2% of their Net Demand and Time Liabilities (NDTL) under the MSF.** The NDTL is a measure of a bank's total liabilities, and the MSF provides banks with access to emergency funds when needed. The RBI may adjust this borrowing limit depending on economic conditions or to address specific liquidity challenges in the banking system.

**Therefore, the correct answer is (c) All three.**

**34.** *(a)* 1 and 2 only

- **Statement 1 is correct: Banks can indeed borrow funds under the Repo Rate using securities that are above the SLR requirement.** The Statutory Liquidity Ratio (SLR) mandates banks to hold a certain percentage of their deposits in the form of government securities. However, when borrowing under the Repo Rate, banks can use additional securities (above the required SLR holdings) as collateral to obtain liquidity without affecting their statutory reserves. This allows banks to manage their liquidity without compromising on the mandatory reserves.
- **Statement 2 is correct: The MSF Rate allows banks to borrow funds overnight even if they need to use their excess holdings beyond the SLR requirements.** The **Marginal Standing Facility (MSF)** provides a safety net for banks that face sudden or unexpected liquidity needs. Under the MSF, banks can borrow funds from the RBI by dipping into their excess SLR holdings, which ensures that banks can continue to operate smoothly even in the face of short-term liquidity crises.
- **Statement 3 is incorrect: The MSF Rate provides a ceiling for the Liquidity Adjustment Facility (LAF) corridor, while the Reverse Repo Rate provides a floor.** The **Repo Rate** serves as the mid-point of the LAF corridor, not the floor. The corridor is structured with the **MSF Rate** at the upper end (ceiling), the **Reverse Repo Rate** at the lower end (floor) and the **Repo Rate** in between. This framework helps the RBI manage liquidity and interest rates effectively.

**Therefore, the correct answer is (a) 1 and 2 only.**

**35.** *(c)* Both 1 and 2

- **Statement 1 is correct: The RBI conducts Open Market Operations (OMO) primarily through auctions where government securities are bought or sold.** OMOs help the central bank control the money supply by either injecting or absorbing liquidity from the banking system.
- **Statement 2 is correct: When the RBI purchases government securities under OMO, it injects liquidity into the banking system.** This means that the RBI pays banks for the government securities they sell, increasing the cash reserves available to those banks. With more liquidity, banks have additional funds to lend, which can lead to increased borrowing, investment, and economic activity. This is a common measure used to stimulate the economy, especially during periods of low growth.

**Therefore, the correct answer is (c) Both 1 and 2.**

**36.** *(b)* Only two

- **Statement 1 is correct: The Market Stabilisation Scheme (MSS) is used by the Reserve Bank of India (RBI) to manage excess liquidity in the economy.** When there is an abundance of liquidity in the banking system, it can lead to inflationary pressures by increasing the money supply. The MSS allows the RBI to mop up this excess liquidity, helping to maintain price stability and control inflation.
- **Statement 2 is correct: Under the MSS, the government issues treasury bills and bonds to absorb surplus liquidity from the banking system.** These instruments are issued specifically for sterilisation purposes, which means they are not intended to finance government expenditures.
- **Statement 3 is incorrect: The funds raised through MSS are not used by the government for public spending or investment.** The proceeds from MSS operations are held in a separate account called the MSS account. These funds are solely used for liquidity management purposes by the RBI and are not available for government expenditure.

**Therefore, the correct answer is (b) Only two.**

**37.** *(a)* 1 and 2 only

- **Statement 1 is correct: The Cash Reserve Ratio (CRR) and Statutory Liquidity Ratio (SLR) ensure that banks maintain a buffer of cash, and liquid assets,** which acts as a safeguard against unexpected withdrawals, and liquidity demands. By requiring banks to hold a portion of their deposits in reserve (CRR) and invest in liquid assets like government securities (SLR), the central bank ensures that banks can meet their obligations and maintain financial stability even during periods of stress.
- **Statement 2 is correct: CRR and SLR control the money supply by regulating the amount of funds banks can lend.** When the central bank increases the CRR or SLR, banks have to hold more funds in reserve or in liquid assets, reducing the amount available for lending. This reduces the money supply in the economy, which can help control inflation. Conversely, lowering the CRR or SLR allows banks to lend more, increasing the money supply and stimulating economic activity.
- **Statement 3 is incorrect: Reserve requirements (CRR and SLR) are not intended to provide funds for the RBI's operational expenses.** These requirements are regulatory measures aimed at ensuring liquidity and stability in the financial system. They are designed to control how much money banks can lend and to ensure that banks have enough reserves to meet unexpected liquidity demands, not to generate revenue for the central bank.

**Therefore, the correct answer is (a) 1 and 2 only.**

**38.** *(b)* Bank can lend out a portion of their deposits while keeping a fraction as reserves.

- **Fractional reserve banking is a system in which banks are required to keep only a fraction of their deposits as reserves.** This means that banks do not need to hold the full amount of a depositor's funds at any given time. The required reserves are typically held in cash or deposits with the central bank. The fraction that banks are required to hold as reserves is determined by the central bank through regulations such as the **Cash Reserve Ratio (CRR)** or other reserve requirements.

- **The remaining funds, after reserves are held, can be used for lending or investment purposes.** When banks lend out these funds to borrowers, the money is deposited back into the banking system, either with the same bank or with another bank. These deposits can then be lent out again, creating a multiplier effect. Through this process, banks effectively create money by expanding the amount of funds in circulation.
- **This system allows banks to create money through lending, thereby increasing the money supply.** The money creation process is facilitated by the **money multiplier** effect, which depends on the reserve ratio. The lower the reserve requirement, the greater the money multiplier, as banks can lend out more of their deposits. The increase in money supply resulting from fractional reserve banking plays a key role in promoting economic activity and investment.

**Thus, option (b) is the correct answer.**

***39.*** *(b)* 1 and 3 only

- **Statement 1 is correct: The Cash Reserve Ratio (CRR) is maintained as cash with the Reserve Bank of India (RBI).** Banks are required to keep a specific percentage of their deposits as CRR, which must be in the form of cash, held with the central bank. **Statutory Liquidity Ratio (SLR), on the other hand, can be maintained in the form of cash, gold, or government securities.** This allows banks to fulfill the SLR requirement with more flexibility by holding liquid assets that also yield some return.
- **Statement 2 is incorrect: Banks do not earn interest on the funds kept as CRR with the RBI.** The CRR is a mandatory reserve that banks must hold, but it does not generate any income. These reserves are non-interest bearing, which means that the banks are not compensated for keeping this money idle. The purpose of the CRR is to control liquidity and ensure financial stability, not to provide a return on reserves.
- **Statement 3 is correct: CRR helps control inflation by regulating the amount of money banks can lend.** A higher CRR means that banks have to hold more money with the RBI, reducing the funds available for lending. This reduction in lending capacity decreases the money supply, which helps control inflation. Conversely, lowering the CRR increases the money supply, stimulating borrowing and economic activity.

**Therefore, the correct answer is (b) 1 and 3 only.**

***40.*** *(a)* 1 and 2 only

- **Statement 1 is correct: Increasing the Cash Reserve Ratio (CRR) reduces the money supply** by requiring banks to keep a higher proportion of their deposits as reserves with the Reserve Bank of India (RBI). When the CRR is raised, banks have less money available to lend, which reduces the liquidity in the economy. This can help curb inflation by decreasing the money supply, as less money is circulated for loans and investments.
- **Statement 2 is correct: Reducing the Statutory Liquidity Ratio (SLR) decreases the amount of money banks must hold in liquid assets,** such as government securities, cash, or gold. By lowering the SLR, banks are required to hold fewer liquid assets, freeing up more funds for lending and investment. This increase in lending capacity can stimulate economic activity by increasing the flow of money in the economy.
- **Statement 3 is incorrect:** While both **CRR and SLR can be used to control inflation** by managing liquidity and regulating the money supply, they are **not used exclusively for this purpose.** CRR and SLR also play a crucial role in **maintaining the stability of the banking system.** By ensuring that banks hold sufficient reserves and liquid assets, these measures help protect against sudden liquidity crises, and support the overall soundness of the financial system.

**Therefore, the correct answer is (a) 1 and 2 only.**

**41.** *(d)* None

- **Pair A is incorrect: Moral suasion involves persuading banks to follow certain guidelines without enforcing them legally.** It is a qualitative tool used by the central bank to influence the behavior of financial institutions through requests and recommendations rather than through mandatory regulations or legal actions. Therefore, matching moral suasion to any form of enforcement or credit rationing is incorrect.
- **Pair B is incorrect: Credit rationing involves allocating credit limits to specific banks or financial institutions based on certain criteria,** usually to control excessive lending and manage risk. It is a quantitative measure and is often enforced by the central bank. Credit rationing is not related to moral suasion or selective credit control but focuses on limiting the amount of credit banks can provide.
- **Pair C is incorrect: Selective credit controls involve imposing lending restrictions on certain sectors** of the economy rather than on specific banks. The central bank may restrict credit flow to speculative sectors or high-risk industries while encouraging lending in productive sectors. Therefore, matching selective credit controls to restrictions on individual banks is incorrect.

**Therefore, the correct answer is (d) None.**

**42.** *(b)* Only two

- **Option 1 (Advising banks to increase lending to the agriculture sector) is correct: This is an example of moral suasion,** which is a **qualitative tool.** In this case, the central bank uses informal persuasion to encourage banks to direct more credit toward priority sectors, like agriculture, without legally enforcing the action. It involves requests or recommendations that guide banks' behavior in lending, especially to areas that are deemed critical for economic development.
- **Option 2 (Imposing credit ceilings on loans to speculative real estate projects) is correct: This is an example of selective credit controls,** another **qualitative tool.** By imposing credit ceilings, the central bank restricts the amount of credit available for specific non-essential or speculative sectors, such as real estate, to avoid inflationary pressures or financial instability. This measure helps control credit flow into high-risk sectors.
- **Option 3 (Changing the repo rate) is incorrect: Changing the repo rate is a quantitative tool,** not a qualitative one.

**Therefore, the correct answer is (b) Only two.**

**43.** *(a)* 1 and 3 only

- **Option 1 is correct: Lowering the repo rate reduces the cost of borrowing,** which encourages spending and investment by businesses and consumers. By lowering the repo rate, the central bank makes it cheaper for commercial banks to borrow funds.
- **Option 2 is incorrect: Increasing the Statutory Liquidity Ratio (SLR) would restrict the amount of money banks can lend.** When the SLR is increased, banks are required to hold more funds in liquid assets like government securities, leaving less money available for lending.
- **Option 3 is correct: Announcing a moratorium on loan repayments would provide financial relief to borrowers,** helping them manage their finances during tough economic times. During a recession, businesses and consumers may struggle with cash flow issues.
- **Option 4 is incorrect: Selling government securities is a contractionary measure that absorbs liquidity from the banking system.** By selling government securities, the central bank removes money from the economy, reducing the funds available for lending.

**Therefore, the correct answer is (a) 1 and 3 only.**

**44.** *(b)* 2, 3 and 4 only

- **To combat high inflation, the central bank should increase the Repo Rate** to make borrowing more expensive. By raising the **Repo Rate,** the cost of borrowing for commercial banks increases, which leads to higher interest rates for consumers and businesses. This discourages borrowing and reduces spending, and investment, helping to slow down inflation by curbing demand in the economy.

- **Conducting Open Market Operations (OMO) by selling government securities helps absorb liquidity** from the banking system. When the central bank sells government securities, it withdraws money from circulation, reducing the available funds for lending and spending.
- **Implementing Selective Credit Controls to limit loans for non-essential consumer goods** is another tool used to control inflation. By restricting the flow of credit to sectors that drive inflation, such as luxury or non-essential consumer goods, the central bank ensures that resources are directed to more essential and productive areas of the economy.
- **Lowering the Cash Reserve Ratio (CRR) would increase liquidity and potentially worsen inflation**, so it is **not suitable** in this scenario.

**Therefore, the correct answer is (b) 2, 3 and 4 only.**

***45.*** *(d)* The mechanism through which changes in the central bank's monetary policy (such as interest rates) affect the broader economy, particularly inflation and output.

**Monetary policy transmission** refers to the **mechanism** by which changes in the central bank's policy rates, such as the **repo rate**, influence various economic variables such as **inflation, employment and economic growth.** It affects interest rates, credit availability, and ultimately consumer spending, and investment in the economy.

**Thus, option (d) is the correct answer.**

***46.*** *(c)* Only three

- **Statement 1 is correct: Reduction in non-performing assets (NPAs)** helps banks improve their financial health, enabling them to pass on policy rate changes more effectively to borrowers, thereby smoothing monetary policy transmission.
- **Statement 2 is correct: Greater use of external benchmarks** for lending rates, such as linking rates to the **repo rate**, ensures that banks adjust their lending rates in line with changes in monetary policy, leading to quicker and more transparent transmission.
- **Statement 3 is correct: Increased competition among banks** encourages banks to quickly adjust lending rates in line with monetary policy changes to attract customers, thereby improving transmission.
- **Statement 4 is incorrect: Government interventions in fixing lending rates** for specific sectors can distort market-determined rates and reduce the effectiveness of monetary policy transmission, as it prevents banks from adjusting rates based on central bank policies.

**Therefore, the correct answer is (c) Only three.**

***47.*** *(b)* To lower long-term interest rates by selling short-term government securities and buying long-term government securities.

**Operation Twist** is a monetary policy tool where a central bank, like the **RBI** or the **Federal Reserve, simultaneously sells short-term government securities and buys long-term government securities.**

**Thus, option (b) is the correct answer.**

## Past Learning (Answers)

| | | | | | | | | | |
|---|---|---|---|---|---|---|---|---|---|
| 1 (d) | 2 (a) | 3 (a) | 4 (a) | 5 (d) | 6 (a) | 7 (b) | 8 (b) | 9 (d) | 10 (b) |
| 11 (b) | 12 (a) | 13 (b) | 14 (c) | 15 (c) | | | | | |

# CHAPTER 07 Inflation

## Assessment Round

### Topic 1 : Meaning and Causes

**1.** With reference to the 'Inflation', consider the following statements:

1. It is the sustained increase in the general price level of goods and services in an economy over a period of time.
2. It erodes the purchasing power of money.
3. Ideal inflation rate beneficial for an economy is 0%.

Which of the statements given above is/are correct?

(a) 1 and 2 only (b) 1 and 3 only
(c) 2 and 3 only (d) 1, 2 and 3

**2.** Why is inflation often measured on a year-on-year (YoY) basis?

(a) To smooth out short-term price volatility and seasonal variations.
(b) To adjust for changes in government policies affecting prices.
(c) To capture the impact of international trade on domestic prices.
(d) To calculate inflation based on quarterly economic performance.

**3.** Consider the following types of inflation with their corresponding inflation rates:

| | Types of Inflation | Description |
|---|---|---|
| 1. | Creeping Inflation | Inflation rate exceeds 50% per month |
| 2. | Hyperinflation | Inflation rate is between 1% to 3% annually |
| 3. | Galloping Inflation | Inflation rate is in double digits annually |
| 4. | Moderate Inflation | Inflation rate is slightly above 3% but remains below 10% annually |

How many of the above pairs is/are correctly matched?

(a) Only one pair (b) Only two pairs
(c) Only three pairs (d) All four pairs

**4.** Consider the following statements:

1. Cost-push inflation is often caused by supply shocks such as a sudden increase in oil prices.
2. Stagflation refers to a situation where high inflation occurs alongside high unemployment.
3. Creeping inflation is characterised by a sudden and rapid increase in the price level.

Which of the statements given above are correct?

(a) 1 and 2 only (b) 1 and 3 only
(c) 2 and 3 only (d) 1, 2 and 3

**5.** Consider the following factors:

1. Rise of wages due to strong labour unions.
2. Cartelisation of essential commodities like oil.
3. Increase in government spending on infrastructure.
4. Supply chain disruptions due to Israel-Hamas conflict.

Which of the given above factors can result into 'Cost-Push Inflation'?

(a) 1 and 3 only (b) 1, 2 and 4 only
(c) 2, 3 and 4 only (d) 1, 2, 3 and 4

**6.** Which of the following factors are commonly considered causes of 'Demand-Pull Inflation'?

1. Increased consumer spending due to higher disposable income.
2. Expansionary monetary policy by the central bank.
3. Rising production costs, such as higher wages.
4. Government fiscal stimulus measures.

Select the correct answer from the codes given below:

(a) 1 and 4 only (b) 2 and 3 only
(c) 1, 2 and 4 only (d) 1, 2, 3 and 4

**7.** Consider the following causes of inflation with their corresponding types:

| Causes | Type of Inflation |
|---|---|
| 1. Excessive government spending | Demand-pull Inflation |
| 2. Supply chain bottlenecks | Cost-push Inflation |
| 3. Central bank lowering interest rates | Cost-push Inflation |
| 4. A sudden increase in commodity prices | Demand-pull Inflation |

How many of the above pairs is/are correctly matched?

(a) Only one pair
(b) Only two pairs
(c) Only three pairs
(d) All four pairs

**8.** Which of the following best describes the concept of 'Food Inflation'?

(a) A general increase in the prices of all goods and services across the economy.
(b) A sustained rise in the prices of essential food items, including cereals, fruits, vegetables and dairy products.
(c) A situation where food prices decline due to improved agricultural productivity and supply.
(d) A temporary increase in food prices caused by seasonal factors.

**9.** Consider the following factors:

1. Increased consumer preference for healthier, protein-rich diets.
2. Supply constraints in the production of protein-rich foods such as pulses, eggs and meat.
3. Rising Per Capita Income.
4. Decreased demand for cereals and grains in the economy.

How many of the given above factors could contribute to 'Protein Inflation'?

(a) Only one (b) Only two
(c) Only three (d) All four

## Topic 2 : Indices to Measure Inflation

**10.** With reference to the indices used to measure inflation in India, consider the following statements:

1. Consumer Price Index (CPI) measures the change in prices of a basket of goods and services at the retail level.
2. Wholesale Price Index (WPI) captures the average price changes at the wholesale level, primarily for goods sold in bulk.
3. The GDP deflator is a broad measure of inflation that includes both goods and services produced domestically.

How many of the statements given above is/are correct?

(a) Only one (b) Only two
(c) All three (d) None

**11.** With reference to the measurement of inflation, consider the following statements:

1. CPI is often considered a better measure of inflation for consumers than the WPI because it reflects the prices of goods and services purchased by households.
2. WPI includes the prices of services, making it more comprehensive than the CPI.
3. GDP deflator is less frequently updated compared to the CPI and WPI.

Which of the statements given above is/are correct?

(a) 1 only (b) 1 and 3 only
(c) 2 and 3 only (d) 1, 2 and 3

**12.** Consider the following inflation indices with their corresponding publishing agency:

| | Inflation Index | Publishing Agency |
|---|---|---|
| 1. | Consumer Price Index (CPI) | National Statistical Office (NSO) |
| 2. | Wholesale Price Index (WPI) | Ministry of Commerce and Industry |
| 3. | GDP Deflator | Reserve Bank of India (RBI) |
| 4. | Consumer Food Price Index | Labour Bureau |

How many of the above pairs is/are correctly matched?

(a) Only one pair
(b) Only two pairs
(c) Only three pairs
(d) All four pairs

**13.** Consider the following statements:

1. In the Consumer Price Index (CPI), food items typically have a higher weightage compared to fuel.
2. The Wholesale Price Index (WPI) assigns a higher weightage to fuel than to food items.

Which of the given above statements is/are correct?

(a) 1 only
(b) 2 only
(c) Both 1 and 2
(d) Neither 1 nor 2

**14.** With reference to the weightage of food and fuel in inflation measurement, consider the following statements:

1. The high weightage of food in the CPI reflects the significant proportion of consumer expenditure on food items in India.
2. The WPI places more emphasis on fuel prices due to their impact on industrial production costs.
3. The difference in weightage between food and fuel in CPI, and WPI can lead to varying inflation rates reported by these indices.

How many of the statements given above is/are correct?

(a) Only one (b) Only two
(c) All three (d) None

**15.** Consider the following statements about 'GDP Deflator':

1. GDP deflator reflects changes in the price level of all goods and services included in Gross Domestic Product (GDP).
2. It is calculated as the ratio of nominal GDP to real GDP.
3. Unlike CPI and WPI, the GDP deflator is not based on a fixed basket of goods, and services, making it a more comprehensive measure of inflation.

Which of the statements given above are correct?

(a) 1 and 2 only (b) 2 and 3 only
(c) 1 and 3 only (d) 1, 2 and 3

**16.** Consider the following Consumer Price Index (CPI) indices with their corresponding utility or purpose:

| | CPI Index | | Utility or Purpose |
|---|---|---|---|
| 1. | CPI for Industrial Workers (CPI-IW) | A. | Used for revising Dearness Allowance (DA) for government employees |
| 2. | CPI for Agricultural Labourers (CPI-AL) | B. | Reflects the cost of living for rural agricultural workers |
| 3. | CPI for Rural Labourers (CPI-RL) | C. | Used to measure inflation specifically for urban non-manual workers |
| 4. | CPI for Urban Non-Manual Employees (CPI-UNME) | D. | Captures inflation experienced by rural labour households |

How many of the given above pairs is/are correctly matched?

(a) Only one pair
(b) Only two pairs
(c) Only three pairs
(d) All four pairs

**17.** With reference to the Consumer Price Index for Industrial Workers (CPI-IW), consider the following statements:

1. CPI-IW includes a basket of goods and services consumed by industrial workers, including food, clothing, housing, and education.
2. The base year for calculating CPI-IW is 2016, reflecting current consumption patterns.
3. Labour Bureau under the Ministry of Labour and Employment is responsible for compiling and publishing CPI-IW.

Which of the statements given above are correct?

(a) 1 and 2 only (b) 2 and 3 only
(c) 1 and 3 only (d) 1, 2 and 3

**18.** How do imported goods affect the measurement of inflation in CPI and GDP Deflator?

(a) Imported goods influence both CPI and GDP deflator equally as both measure the prices of all goods consumed within a country.
(b) Imported goods have a direct impact on the CPI but are excluded from the GDP deflator, which focuses only on domestic production.
(c) Both CPI and GDP deflator are designed to exclude imported goods to avoid external price fluctuations.
(d) Imported goods do not affect either CPI or GDP deflator since both focus on domestic products.

**19.** With reference to the Producer Price Index (PPI), consider the following statements:

1. PPI measures the average change in selling prices received by domestic producers for their output.
2. PPI is considered a more accurate measure of inflation at the production level compared to WPI.
3. The Goldar Committee recommended the introduction of PPI to replace the Wholesale Price Index (WPI) for better inflation measurement in India.

How many of the above statements is/are correct?

(a) Only one (b) Only two
(c) All three (d) None

**20.** With reference to the 'NHB Residex', consider the following statements:

1. It is India's first official housing price index.
2. It tracks the movement of residential property prices in different cities across India.
3. The index is compiled by the National Housing Bank (NHB) and captures data on both primary, and secondary property markets.

How many of the given above statements is/are correct?

(a) Only one
(b) Only two
(c) All three
(d) None

**21.** Which of the following best describes the 'All India Housing Price Index (HPI)'?

(a) An index that tracks the rental rates of residential properties across major Indian cities.
(b) An index that measures changes in the prices of residential properties in major cities, compiled by the Reserve Bank of India (RBI).
(c) A quarterly survey of the housing preferences of urban households in India.
(d) An index that measures the cost of constructing new housing units in rural India.

**22.** Consider List I with List II and select the correct answer from the codes given below:

| List I (Terms) | List II (Meaning) |
|---|---|
| 1. Deflation | government policies aimed at increasing demand |
| 2. Disinflation | Persistent rise in the price of goods and services |
| 3. Inflation | General fall in the level of prices |
| 4. Reflation | Reduction of the rate of Inflation |

How many pairs given above is/are correctly matched?

(a) Only one pair
(b) Only two pairs
(c) All the four pairs
(d) None

**23.** With reference to headline and core inflation, consider the following statements:

1. Headline inflation includes the total inflation within an economy, including volatile items such as food and fuel.
2. Core inflation excludes certain volatile items like food and fuel to provide a more stable measure of long-term inflation trends.
3. Headline inflation is less responsive to short-term shocks in food and energy prices compared to core inflation.

How many of the statements given above is/are correct?

(a) Only one
(b) Only two
(c) All three
(d) None

**24.** Which of the following statement(s) is/are correct about 'Core Inflation'?

1. It reflects the impact of global commodity price fluctuations on domestic prices.
2. It is typically used to assess the effectiveness of a central bank's monetary policy.
3. It includes prices of essential commodities like food and energy.

Select the correct answer from the codes given below:

(a) 3 only
(b) 2 and 3 only
(c) 1 and 2 only
(d) 2 only

**25.** Consider the following items:

1. Petrol/Diesel for a vehicle
2. Lubricants and other fuels for vehicles
3. Health services
4. Food and beverages

How many of the given above items is/are excluded from 'Refined Core Inflation'?

(a) Only one
(b) Only two
(c) Only three
(d) All four

**26.** Consider the following statements about 'Imported Inflation':

**Statement I:** Imported inflation occurs when the prices of goods and services imported from other countries increase, leading to higher overall price levels in the domestic economy.

**Statement II:** A weaker domestic currency can exacerbate the effects of imported inflation by making imports more expensive.

Which one of the following is correct in respect of the above statements?

(a) Both Statement I and Statement II are correct, and Statement II is the correct explanation for Statement I.
(b) Both Statement I and Statement II are correct, and Statement II is not the correct explanation for Statement I.
(c) Statement I is correct, but Statement II is incorrect.
(d) Statement I is incorrect, but Statement II is correct.

**27.** Consider the following economic scenarios:

1. An increase in import duties on essential goods
2. Rising global prices of raw materials
3. Stronger domestic currency against foreign currencies
4. Trade disruptions leading to higher costs for imported goods

How many of the above scenarios is/are likely to result in imported inflation?

(a) Only one (b) Only two
(c) Only three (d) All four

**28.** What does the term 'base effect' refer to in the context of inflation measurement?

(a) The influence of a high or low base year price level on the current inflation rate.
(b) The impact of core inflation on the overall inflation rate.
(c) The seasonal adjustment made to inflation data to reflect cyclical changes.
(d) The effect of changes in the monetary base on the inflation rate.

**29.** With reference to the base effect in inflation measurement, consider the following statements:

1. The base effect can cause inflation rates to appear higher or lower depending on the price level in the base year.
2. A low base year inflation rate can lead to a higher inflation rate in the current year, even if the price increase is moderate.
3. The base effect is not considered when calculating core inflation.

How many of the statements given above is/are correct?

(a) Only one (b) Only two
(c) All three (d) None

**30.** What does the Phillips Curve illustrate in economics?

(a) The relationship between inflation and unemployment.
(b) The trade-off between interest rates and economic growth.
(c) The connection between money supply and inflation.
(d) The impact of exchange rates on trade balances.

**31.** Consider the following statements about 'Shrinkflation'.

1. It occurs when companies reduce the size or quantity of a product while keeping the price the same.
2. It is a form of hidden inflation, as consumers pay the same price for less quantity.
3. It directly affects the CPI by increasing the recorded inflation rate.

How many of the statements given above is/are correct?

(a) Only one (b) Only two
(c) All three (d) None

**32.** Which of the following factors are typically associated with structural inflation?

1. Supply-side constraints, such as inadequate infrastructure and logistics.
2. Rigidities in the labour market, including wage stickiness.
3. Excessive government regulation that hinders market efficiency.
4. Short-term demand shocks that cause temporary price increases.

Select the correct answer using the codes given below:

(a) 1 and 2 only
(b) 2 and 4 only
(c) 1, 2 and 3 only
(d) 1, 3 and 4 only

**33.** Which of the following best describes 'Skewflation'?

(a) A situation where prices of all goods and services increase uniformly across the economy.
(b) A situation where the prices of certain goods rise sharply while others remain stable or decrease.
(c) A type of inflation where wages rise faster than the prices of goods and services.
(d) A condition where inflation occurs only in luxury goods, while essential goods remain unaffected.

**34.** What is an inflation spiral?

(a) A situation where inflation decreases continuously over time due to falling demand.
(b) A process where rising prices lead to higher wages, which in turn lead to further price increases.
(c) A scenario where inflation remains constant despite changes in monetary policy.
(d) A phenomenon where inflation only affects certain sectors of the economy.

**35.** Which of the following factors are likely to contribute to food inflation?

1. Poor agricultural output due to adverse weather conditions.
2. Increased demand for protein-rich foods like meat and dairy products.
3. Rising transportation costs due to higher fuel prices.
4. Government subsidies on food production.

Select the correct answer from the codes given below:

(a) 1 and 3 only (b) 2 and 4 only
(c) 1, 2 and 3 only (d) 1, 2, 3 and 4

**36.** What is the key difference between the concept of 'Stagflation' and the 'Phillips Curve'?

(a) The Phillips Curve suggests that inflation and unemployment have an inverse relationship, while stagflation describes a situation where both high inflation, and high unemployment occur simultaneously.

(b) The Phillips Curve indicates that inflation is always caused by high unemployment, whereas stagflation occurs when low inflation and low unemployment happen together.

(c) The Phillips Curve shows the direct relationship between economic growth and inflation, while stagflation involves high economic growth with high inflation.

(d) The Phillips Curve is relevant only in long -term economic analysis, whereas stagflation is a short-term economic phenomenon.

**37.** In the context of economics, which of the following statements best describes the 'Fisher Effect'?

(a) It refers to the relationship between the change in the general price level and the change in prices in the current year.

(b) It suggests that a free-market economy will automatically recover from recession and high unemployment without external intervention.

(c) It posits that the remaining lifespan of durable goods like technology is proportional to their current age.

(d) It asserts that the real interest rate is equal to the nominal interest rate adjusted for inflation.

**38.** Which of the following best describes the difference between an Inflationary Gap and a Deflationary Gap?

(a) An inflationary gap occurs when aggregate demand exceeds aggregate supply, while a deflationary gap occurs when aggregate supply exceeds aggregate demand.

(b) An inflationary gap occurs when the economy is operating below its potential output, while a deflationary gap occurs when the economy is operating above its potential output.

(c) An inflationary gap is associated with high unemployment rates, while a deflationary gap is associated with rising inflation.

(d) An inflationary gap leads to lower prices, while a deflationary gap results in higher prices.

**39.** Consider the following statements regarding inflation and the real interest rate:

**Statement I:** The real interest rate is calculated by subtracting the inflation rate from the nominal interest rate.

**Statement II:** Higher inflation leads to a lower real interest rate if the nominal interest rate remains unchanged.

Which one of the following is correct in respect of the above statements?

(a) Both Statement I and Statement II are correct, and Statement II is the correct explanation for Statement I.

(b) Both Statement I and Statement II are correct, and Statement II is not the correct explanation for Statement I.

(c) Statement I is correct, but Statement II is incorrect.

(d) Statement I is incorrect, but Statement II is correct.

**40.** With reference to the effects of inflation, consider the following statements:

1. Inflation erodes the purchasing power of money.
2. Inflation leads to an increase in the real interest rate, benefiting savers.
3. Inflation generally benefits creditors at the expense of debtors.
4. Moderate inflation is often associated with economic growth.

How many of the statements given above is/are correct?

(a) Only one

(b) Only two

(c) Only three

(d) All four

**41.** Consider the following groups:

1. Fixed-income earners, such as pensioners.
2. Creditors, including banks and financial institutions.
3. Debtors, such as mortgage holders.
4. Investors in fixed-rate bonds.

Which of the given above groups are likely to be negatively affected by high inflation?

(a) 1 and 4 only (b) 1, 2 and 4 only
(c) 1, 3 and 4 only (d) 2 and 3 only

**42.** How many of the following measures can be used to control Demand-Pull Inflation?

1. Raising the central bank's policy interest rate.
2. Increasing government subsidies on essential commodities.
3. Reducing government spending on public projects.

Select the correct answer from the codes given below:

(a) Only one (b) Only two
(c) All three (d) None

**43.** With reference to the Inflation Targeting Framework in India, consider the following statements:

1. RBI's monetary policy is primarily aimed at maintain price stability while supporting economic growth.
2. Inflation Targeting framework allows for a flexible approach, enabling the RBI to address short-term economic fluctuations.
3. If inflation consistently stays outside the tolerance band, the RBI is required to submit a report to the Parliament explaining the reasons and corrective measures.

How many of the statements given above is/are correct?

(a) Only one (b) Only two
(c) All three (d) None

**44.** Which of the following are potential effects of using contractionary monetary policy to control inflation?

1. Higher unemployment rates due to reduced economic activity.
2. Strengthening of the domestic currency as higher interest rates attract foreign capital.
3. Increased consumer spending due to higher interest income on savings.
4. Slower economic growth as borrowing costs rise.

Select the correct answer from the codes given below:

(a) 1 and 4 only (b) 2 and 3 only
(c) 1, 2 and 4 only (d) 1, 3 and 4 only

**45.** Consider the following statements about the 'Inflation Targeting Framework' adopted by the RBI:

1. RBI targets a headline inflation rate measured by the CPI to maintain price stability in the economy.
2. The inflation target set is set by the RBI in every 5 years.

Which of the statements given above is/are correct?

(a) 1 only (b) 2 only
(c) Both 1 and 2 (d) Neither 1 nor 2

**46.** In the context of Indian economy, which of the following measures are likely to be adopted by the Government/RBI to tackle Inflation?

1. Increasing Cash Reserve Ratio (CRR)
2. Increased indirect taxes
3. Increasing the irrigation coverage
4. Reduction of Repo rate

Select the correct answer from the codes given below:

(a) 1 and 3 only (b) 3 and 4 only
(c) 1, 2 and 4 only (d) 1, 2, 3 and 4

# OMR SHEET

**Assessment Round**

| | | | | | | | |
|---|---|---|---|---|---|---|---|
| 1 | (a) (b) (c) (d) | 31 | (a) (b) (c) (d) | 61 | (a) (b) (c) (d) | 91 | (a) (b) (c) (d) |
| 2 | (a) (b) (c) (d) | 32 | (a) (b) (c) (d) | 62 | (a) (b) (c) (d) | 92 | (a) (b) (c) (d) |
| 3 | (a) (b) (c) (d) | 33 | (a) (b) (c) (d) | 63 | (a) (b) (c) (d) | 93 | (a) (b) (c) (d) |
| 4 | (a) (b) (c) (d) | 34 | (a) (b) (c) (d) | 64 | (a) (b) (c) (d) | 94 | (a) (b) (c) (d) |
| 5 | (a) (b) (c) (d) | 35 | (a) (b) (c) (d) | 65 | (a) (b) (c) (d) | 95 | (a) (b) (c) (d) |
| 6 | (a) (b) (c) (d) | 36 | (a) (b) (c) (d) | 66 | (a) (b) (c) (d) | 96 | (a) (b) (c) (d) |
| 7 | (a) (b) (c) (d) | 37 | (a) (b) (c) (d) | 67 | (a) (b) (c) (d) | 97 | (a) (b) (c) (d) |
| 8 | (a) (b) (c) (d) | 38 | (a) (b) (c) (d) | 68 | (a) (b) (c) (d) | 98 | (a) (b) (c) (d) |
| 9 | (a) (b) (c) (d) | 39 | (a) (b) (c) (d) | 69 | (a) (b) (c) (d) | 99 | (a) (b) (c) (d) |
| 10 | (a) (b) (c) (d) | 40 | (a) (b) (c) (d) | 70 | (a) (b) (c) (d) | 100 | (a) (b) (c) (d) |
| 11 | (a) (b) (c) (d) | 41 | (a) (b) (c) (d) | 71 | (a) (b) (c) (d) | 101 | (a) (b) (c) (d) |
| 12 | (a) (b) (c) (d) | 42 | (a) (b) (c) (d) | 72 | (a) (b) (c) (d) | 102 | (a) (b) (c) (d) |
| 13 | (a) (b) (c) (d) | 43 | (a) (b) (c) (d) | 73 | (a) (b) (c) (d) | 103 | (a) (b) (c) (d) |
| 14 | (a) (b) (c) (d) | 44 | (a) (b) (c) (d) | 74 | (a) (b) (c) (d) | 104 | (a) (b) (c) (d) |
| 15 | (a) (b) (c) (d) | 45 | (a) (b) (c) (d) | 75 | (a) (b) (c) (d) | 105 | (a) (b) (c) (d) |
| 16 | (a) (b) (c) (d) | 46 | (a) (b) (c) (d) | 76 | (a) (b) (c) (d) | 106 | (a) (b) (c) (d) |
| 17 | (a) (b) (c) (d) | 47 | (a) (b) (c) (d) | 77 | (a) (b) (c) (d) | 107 | (a) (b) (c) (d) |
| 18 | (a) (b) (c) (d) | 48 | (a) (b) (c) (d) | 78 | (a) (b) (c) (d) | 108 | (a) (b) (c) (d) |
| 19 | (a) (b) (c) (d) | 49 | (a) (b) (c) (d) | 79 | (a) (b) (c) (d) | 109 | (a) (b) (c) (d) |
| 20 | (a) (b) (c) (d) | 50 | (a) (b) (c) (d) | 80 | (a) (b) (c) (d) | 110 | (a) (b) (c) (d) |
| 21 | (a) (b) (c) (d) | 51 | (a) (b) (c) (d) | 81 | (a) (b) (c) (d) | 111 | (a) (b) (c) (d) |
| 22 | (a) (b) (c) (d) | 52 | (a) (b) (c) (d) | 82 | (a) (b) (c) (d) | 112 | (a) (b) (c) (d) |
| 23 | (a) (b) (c) (d) | 53 | (a) (b) (c) (d) | 83 | (a) (b) (c) (d) | 113 | (a) (b) (c) (d) |
| 24 | (a) (b) (c) (d) | 54 | (a) (b) (c) (d) | 84 | (a) (b) (c) (d) | 114 | (a) (b) (c) (d) |
| 25 | (a) (b) (c) (d) | 55 | (a) (b) (c) (d) | 85 | (a) (b) (c) (d) | 115 | (a) (b) (c) (d) |
| 26 | (a) (b) (c) (d) | 56 | (a) (b) (c) (d) | 86 | (a) (b) (c) (d) | 116 | (a) (b) (c) (d) |
| 27 | (a) (b) (c) (d) | 57 | (a) (b) (c) (d) | 87 | (a) (b) (c) (d) | 117 | (a) (b) (c) (d) |
| 28 | (a) (b) (c) (d) | 58 | (a) (b) (c) (d) | 88 | (a) (b) (c) (d) | 118 | (a) (b) (c) (d) |
| 29 | (a) (b) (c) (d) | 59 | (a) (b) (c) (d) | 89 | (a) (b) (c) (d) | 119 | (a) (b) (c) (d) |
| 30 | (a) (b) (c) (d) | 60 | (a) (b) (c) (d) | 90 | (a) (b) (c) (d) | 120 | (a) (b) (c) (d) |

## Calculate Your Score

| | |
|---|---|
| **Correct (✓)** | |
| **Incorrect (✓)** | |
| **Unattempted** | |
| **Total Score** | |
| **Accuracy (%)** | |

## Reasons for Incorrect Answers?

| | |
|---|---|
| 1. Lack of Knowledge/Existing Source Insufficient | |
| 2. Lack of Multiple Revision | |
| 3. Common Sense Mistakes | |

**Note :**

1. Calculate total score as correct answers carry 2 marks each 1/3rd marks will deducted for **Incorrect** Answers.
2. Calculate Accuracy (%) by dividing the number of correct answers to the total number of attempted questions.

## Past Learning

**1.** With reference to the Indian economy, consider the following statements: **(2022)**

1. If the inflation is too high, Reserve Bank of India (RBI) is likely to buy government securities.
2. If the rupee is rapidly depreciating, RBI is likely to sell dollars in the market.
3. If interest rates in the USA or European Union were to fall, that is likely to induce RBI to buy dollars.

Which of the statements given above are correct?

(a) 1 and 2 only (b) 2 and 3 only
(c) 1 and 3 only (d) 1, 2 and 3

**2.** With reference to the Indian economy, demand-pull inflation can be caused/increased by which of the following? **(2021)**

1. Expansionary policies
2. Fiscal stimulus
3. Inflation-indexing wages
4. Higher purchasing power
5. Rising interest rates

Select the correct answer using the codes given below:

(a) 1, 2 and 4 only (b) 3, 4 and 5 only
(c) 1, 2, 3 and 5 only (d) 1, 2, 3, 4 and 5

**3.** Consider the following statements: **(2020)**

1. The weightage of food in Consumer Price Index (CPI) is higher than that in Wholesale Price Index (WPI).
2. The WPI does not capture changes in the prices of services, which CPI does.
3. The Reserve Bank of India has now adopted WPI as its key measure of inflation and to decide on changing the key policy rates.

Select the correct answer using the codes given below:

(a) 1 and 2 only (b) 2 only
(c) 3 only (d) 1, 2 and 3

**4.** Which of the following factors/policies were affecting the price of rice in India in the recent past? **(2020)**

1. Minimum Support Price
2. Government's trading
3. Government's stockpiling
4. Consumer subsidies

Select the correct answer using the codes given below:

(a) 1, 2 and 4 only (b) 1, 3 and 4 only
(c) 2 and 3 only (d) 1, 2, 3 and 4

**5.** With reference to inflation in India, which of the following statements is correct? **(2015)**

(a) Controlling the inflation in India is the responsibility of the Government of India only
(b) The Reserve Bank of India has no role in controlling the inflation
(c) Decreased money circulation helps in controlling the inflation
(d) Increased money circulation helps in controlling the inflation

**6.** Which of the following brings out the 'Consumer Price Index Number for Industrial Workers'? **(2015)**

(a) The Reserve Bank of India
(b) The Department of Economic Affairs
(c) The Labour Bureau
(d) The Department of Personnel and Training

**7.** Consider the following statements: **(2013)**

1. Inflation benefits the debtors.
2. Inflation benefits the bond-holders.

Select the correct answer using the codes given below:

(a) 1 only (b) 2 only
(c) Both 1 and 2 (d) Neither 1 nor 2

**8.** A rise in general level of prices may be caused by? **(2013)**

1. An increase in the money supply
2. A decrease in the aggregate level of output
3. An increase in the effective demand

Select the correct answer using the codes given below.

(a) 1 only (b) 1 and 2 only
(c) 2 and 3 only (d) 1, 2 and 3

# Detailed Solutions

## Assessment Round

**1.** *(a)* 1 and 2 only

- **Statement 1 is correct: Inflation** refers to a **sustained increase in the general price level** of goods and services over a period of time. As prices rise, the same amount of money buys fewer goods, and services, reflecting a general decrease in purchasing power.
- **Statement 2 is correct: Inflation erodes the purchasing power of money,** meaning that as prices increase, each unit of currency buys fewer goods and services than before. This can reduce the real value of money held by individuals and businesses.
- **Statement 3 is incorrect:** An **ideal inflation** rate is not 0%. Most central banks aim for a moderate inflation rate (typically around 2%) because it encourages spending and investment, rather than hoarding money. **Zero inflation** or deflation can lead to economic stagnation and decreased consumer spending.

**Thus, the correct answer is (a) 1 and 2 only.**

**2.** *(a)* To smooth out short-term price volatility and seasonal variations.

Inflation is often measured on a **year-on-year basis** to compare the general price level of goods and services in the current month to the same month in the previous year. This method **helps to smooth out short-term price volatility and seasonal variations,** providing a more stable, and comparable measure of inflation over time.

**Thus, option (a) is the correct answer.**

**3.** *(b)* Only two pairs

- **Pair 1 is incorrect : Creeping inflation,** also known as mild inflation, occurs when prices rise slowly, usually within the range of 1% to 3% per year. This level of inflation is generally considered manageable and can be beneficial for economic growth.
- **Pair 2 is incorrect : Hyperinflation** is an extremely high and typically accelerating inflation, often exceeding 50% per month. It is usually associated with a **collapse in the value of a country's currency.**
- **Pair 3 is correct : Galloping inflation** refers to an inflation rate that is in the double digits (10% or more but less than 50% per year). It is higher than moderate inflation and can cause significant economic disruptions.
- **Pair 4 is correct : Moderate inflation** occurs when the inflation rate is more than 3% but remains below 10% per year. **It is faster than creeping inflation but is still considered manageable for an economy.**

**Therefore, the correct answer is (b) Only two pairs.**

**4.** *(a)* 1 and 2 only

- **Statement 1 is correct: Cost-push inflation** occurs when the overall price level rises due to an increase in the cost of production. This can be caused by supply shocks such as a sudden increase in the price of oil, which raises production costs for businesses and, consequently, the prices of goods, and services.
- **Statement 2 is correct: Stagflation** refers to a situation where an economy experiences **high inflation and high unemployment** simultaneously, along with stagnant demand. This is a challenging economic condition because the standard tools to fight inflation (like raising interest rates) can worsen unemployment and vice versa.
- **Statement 3 is incorrect: Creeping inflation** is not characterised by a sudden and rapid increase in the price level. Instead, creeping inflation refers to a slow and gradual increase in prices.

**Therefore, the correct answer is (a) 1 and 2 only.**

**5.** *(b)* 1, 2 and 4 only

- **Rise of wages due to strong labour unions: Correct.** When strong labour unions negotiate higher wages, production costs increase. Businesses may pass these increased labour costs onto consumers through higher prices, resulting in cost-push inflation.

- **Cartelisation of essential commodities like oil: Correct.** When a group of producers (like OPEC for oil) forms a cartel and decides to limit production, the reduced supply can lead to higher prices. This increase in essential commodity prices, such as oil, can raise production and transportation costs across the economy, contributing to cost-push inflation.
- **Increase in government spending on infrastructure: Incorrect.** While increased government spending on infrastructure can lead to **demand-pull inflation (where increased demand leads to higher prices)**, it does not directly lead to cost-push inflation, which is specifically related to increases in the cost of production.
- **Supply chain disruptions due to Israel-Hamas conflict: Correct.** Supply chain disruptions can cause shortages of goods and materials, leading to increased production costs. When these higher costs are passed on to consumers, it results in cost-push inflation.

**Therefore, the correct answer is (b) 1, 2 and 4 only.**

**6.** *(c)* 1, 2 and 4 only

- **Statement 1 is correct**: Increased consumer spending due to **higher disposable income** directly boosts demand in the economy, contributing to demand-pull inflation.
- **Statement 2 is correct: Expansionary monetary policy**, such as lowering interest rates or increasing the money supply, leads to **higher borrowing and spending**, which boosts demand, and can result in demand-pull inflation.
- **Statement 3 is incorrect**: Rising production costs, such as higher wages, typically contribute to cost-push inflation, not demand-pull inflation.
- **Statement 4 is correct: Government fiscal stimulus** are government spending and tax policies measures such as tax-cut, that increase disposable income or spending in the economy, thereby raising demand and contributing to demand-pull inflation.

**Thus, the correct answer is (c) 1, 2 and 4 only.**

**7.** *(b)* Only two pairs

- **Pair 1 is correctly matched**: When the **government spends excessively**, it increases aggregate demand, which can lead to demand-pull inflation as the demand for goods and services outstrips supply.
- **Pair 2 is correctly matched: Supply chain disruptions** reduce the supply of goods, increasing production costs, which can lead to cost-push inflation as companies raise prices to cover higher costs.
- **Pair 3 is incorrectly matched**: As **lowering interest rates** increases the money supply and encourages borrowing, and spending, leading to **demand-pull inflation** rather than hyperinflation, which is characterised by extremely rapid and uncontrollable price increases.
- **Pair 4 is incorrectly matched**: Sharp rise in commodity prices (e.g., oil) increases the cost of production, leading to **cost-push inflation.** Stagflation is a combination of stagnant economic growth and high inflation, which is not necessarily tied to a sudden increase in commodity prices.

**Therefore, the correct answer is (b) Only two pairs.**

**8.** *(b)* A sustained rise in the prices of essential food items, including cereals, fruits, vegetables and dairy products.

**Food Inflation** refers to a **sustained increase** in the prices of essential **food items**, such as cereals, fruits, vegetables, and dairy products. It can be driven by supply-side factors like poor agricultural productivity, adverse weather conditions, or higher demand for food items. Food inflation directly affects the cost of living and can lead to overall inflationary pressures in the economy.

**Thus, option (b) is the correct answer.**

**9.** *(c)* Only three

**Protein Inflation** refers to the increase in the prices of **protein-rich food items** such as meat, fish, eggs, dairy products and pulses.

- **Statement 1 is correct: Increased consumer preference for healthier, protein-rich diets** drives up demand for foods such as pulses, eggs and meat. As demand increases without a corresponding rise in supply, prices for these items can rise, contributing to **Protein Inflation**.

- **Statement 2 is correct: Supply constraints** in the production of protein-rich foods, such as reduced output of eggs, meat, or pulses due to factors like weather conditions or production issues, lead to a limited supply of these items. This shortage in supply results in higher prices, contributing to protein inflation.
- **Statement 3 is correct**: As **income levels increase**, especially in developing economies, people tend to shift their diets towards more **nutrient-dense foods**, including protein-rich items like meat, eggs and dairy. This increased demand puts upward pressure on prices, especially if supply does not grow proportionately.
- **Statement 4 is incorrect: Decreased demand for cereals and grains** does not directly contribute to protein inflation. A reduction in the demand for cereals may shift consumption patterns but does not cause a direct increase in the prices of protein-rich foods.

**Therefore, the correct answer is (c) Only three.**

**10.** *(c)* All three

- **Statement 1 is correct**: The Consumer Price Index (CPI) measures the change in prices of a basket of **goods and services** at the **retail level**, reflecting the cost of living for consumers.
- **Statement 2 is correct**: The Wholesale Price Index (WPI) captures the average price changes at the wholesale level, primarily for **goods** sold in bulk before they reach the retail market.
- **Statement 3 is correct**: The GDP deflator is a broad measure of inflation that includes both goods and services produced **domestically**, as it compares the nominal GDP to the real GDP.
- Unlike the Consumer Price Index (CPI) and Wholesale Price Index (WPI), which track the price changes of a specific basket of goods and services, the GDP deflator covers all goods and services produced domestically.
- **The GDP deflator** is a measure of inflation that reflects the change in the overall price level of all goods and services produced in an economy. It is used to adjust the nominal Gross Domestic Product (GDP) to arrive at real GDP, which is a more accurate representation of an economy's size and growth over time by removing the effects of inflation.

**Thus, the correct answer is (c) All three.**

**11.** *(b)* 1 and 3 only

- **Statement 1 is correct**: The Consumer Price Index (CPI) is considered a better measure of inflation for consumers because it reflects the prices of goods and services that households typically purchase, including food, clothing, and services like healthcare and education.
- **Statement 2 is incorrect**: The Wholesale Price Index (WPI) **does not include the prices of services.** It primarily tracks the price changes of goods at the wholesale level, focusing on bulk goods rather than retail services. The CPI includes services, making it more reflective of consumer-level inflation.
- **Statement 3 is correct: The GDP deflator is less frequently updated compared to the CPI and WPI.** While CPI and WPI are updated monthly, the GDP deflator is updated quarterly, as it is derived from GDP data, which is released less frequently.

**Therefore, the correct answer is (b) 1 and 3 only.**

**12.** *(b)* Only two pairs

- **Pair 1 is correctly matched**: CPI is published by the **NSO**, which is part of the **Ministry of Statistics and Programme Implementation (MoSPI).**
  - The base year for the Consumer Price Index (CPI) in India is **2012**
- **Pair 2 is correctly matched**: The WPI is published by the **Office of the Economic Adviser** under the Ministry of Commerce and Industry.
  - The base year for the Wholesale Price Index (WPI) in India is **2011-12.**
- **Pair 3 is incorrectly matched**: The GDP deflator is derived from GDP data provided

by the **Ministry of Statistics and Programme Implementation (MoSPI)**, not the RBI.
– Currently, India uses **2011-12** as the base year for calculating **real GDP**.

- **Pair 4 is incorrectly matched**: The CFPI is published by the **National Statistical Office (NSO)**, as it is a sub-index of the CPI.

**Thus, the correct answer is (b) Only two pairs.**

**13.** *(a)* 1 only

- **Statement 1 is correct**: The CPI reflects the consumption basket of households, where **food items typically have a higher weightage** compared to fuel.
- **Statement 2 is incorrect**: In the Wholesale Price Index (WPI), fuel typically has a higher weightage compared to food items. The WPI measures the price of goods at the wholesale level and fuel plays a major role in influencing wholesale prices due to its impact on transportation, and industrial production costs.

**Thus, the correct answer is (a) 1 only.**

**14.** *(c)* All three

- **Statement 1 is correct**: The **Consumer Price Index (CPI)** assigns a **high weightage to food items** because food constitutes a significant portion of household expenditure in India, especially in low-income households. This high weight reflects the importance of food in daily consumption patterns.
- **Statement 2 is correct**: The **Wholesale Price Index (WPI)** places more emphasis on **fuel prices**, as they have a considerable impact on **industrial production costs.** Fuel prices affect transportation, manufacturing and energy costs, which are critical components of the industrial sector.
- **Statement 3 is correct**: The **difference in weightage** between food and fuel in CPI, and WPI can lead to **different inflation rates** being reported by these indices.

**Thus, the correct answer is (c) All three.**

**15.** *(d)* 1, 2 and 3

- **Statement 1 is correct**: The **GDP deflator** measures the changes in the overall price level of all goods and services produced in an economy, and included in the GDP. It provides a broader view of inflation as it accounts for all sectors of the economy.
- **Statement 2 is correct**: The **GDP deflator** is calculated as the ratio of **nominal GDP** (which includes current prices) to **real GDP** (which is adjusted for inflation).
- **Statement 3 is correct**: Unlike the **Consumer Price Index (CPI)** and the **Wholesale Price Index (WPI)**, which are based on a **fixed basket of goods, and services**, the GDP deflator reflects price changes for all goods, and services that are currently being produced.

**Therefore, the correct answer is (d) 1, 2 and 3.**

**16.** *(b)* Only two pairs

- **Pair 1 is correctly matched with A**: CPI-IW is used to revise **Dearness Allowance (DA)** for government employees and industrial workers. It reflects changes in the cost of living for industrial workers.
- **Pair 2 is correctly matched with B**: CPI-AL reflects the cost of living for **rural agricultural workers** and is used to measure inflation in this sector.
- **Pair 3 is incorrectly matched with C**: CPI-RL captures the inflation experienced by **rural labour households**, particularly those engaged in casual labour.
- **Pair 4 is incorrectly matched with D**: CPI-UNME measures inflation specifically for **urban non-manual workers,** but this index is no longer in use.

**Thus, the correct answer is (b) Only two pairs.**

**17.** *(d)* 1, 2 and 3

- **Statement 1 is correct**: CPI-IW includes a comprehensive basket of goods and services that reflect the consumption patterns of industrial workers, covering essentials such as food, clothing, housing, and education.
- **Statement 2 is correct**: **The base year for CPI-IW is 2016**, which is periodically revised to reflect the current consumption patterns of industrial workers. This base year for calculating was updated from the earlier base year of 2001.

- **Statement 3 is correct:** The Labour Bureau under the **Ministry of Labour and Employment** is responsible for compiling and publishing the CPI-IW. The index is crucial for revising dearness allowance (DA) for government employees and industrial workers.

**Thus, the correct answer is (d) 1, 2 and 3.**

**18.** *(b)* Imported goods have a direct impact on the CPI but are excluded from the GDP deflator, which focuses only on domestic production.

- The **CPI** includes the prices of **imported goods** since it measures the cost of a fixed basket of consumer goods, which may include imports.
- The **GDP deflator,** however, only reflects the prices of goods and services **produced domestically,** so imported goods do not influence its calculation.

**Thus, option (b) is the correct answer.**

**19.** *(c)* All three

- **Statement 1 is correct:** The **PPI** tracks the **average change** in **selling prices** that domestic producers receive for their output. It measures price changes at the **producer level,** which can indicate early inflationary trends before they are reflected at the consumer level.
- **Statement 2 is correct: PPI** is considered a **more accurate measure** of price changes at the **production level** compared to **WPI,** as it excludes taxes and subsidies that affect retail prices.
- **Statement 3 is correct:** The **Goldar Committee** recommended introducing the **PPI** to replace the **WPI** for a more **accurate measurement of inflation** in India.

**Thus, the correct answer is (c) All three.**

**20.** *(c)* All three

- **Statement 1 is correct: NHB Residex** is India's first official **housing price index.** Launched by the **National Housing Bank (NHB),** it was created to provide an official measure of residential property price trends in India.
- **Statement 2 is correct:** NHB Residex tracks the **movement of residential property prices** across different **cities** in India. It reflects price changes and trends in the housing sector, helping to provide insights into the real estate market.
- **Statement 3 is correct:** The index is compiled by the **National Housing Bank** (NHB) and uses data from multiple sources to capture price changes in both the **primary (new homes)** and **secondary (resale homes)** markets, making it a comprehensive tool for tracking housing price trends.

**Thus, the correct answer is (c) All three.**

**21.** *(b)* An index that measures changes in the prices of residential properties in major cities, compiled by the Reserve Bank of India (RBI).

The **All India Housing Price Index** (HPI) is a measure of the **changes in residential property prices** in **major cities** across India. It is compiled by the **Reserve Bank of India (RBI)** based on data from housing loan transactions. The index helps track real estate price trends and offers insights into the housing market's movement over time.

**Thus, option (b) is the correct answer.**

**22.** *(d)* None

- **Pair 1 is incorrectly matched:** Deflation refers to a **general fall in the level of prices** in an economy. It is the opposite of inflation.
- **Pair 2 is incorrectly matched:** Disinflation refers to a **reduction in the rate of inflation,** meaning prices are still rising but at a slower rate.
- **Pair 3 is incorrectly matched:** Inflation refers to the **persistent rise in the price of goods and services** over time, reducing the purchasing power of money.
- **Pair 4 is incorrectly matched:** Reflation refers to **government policies aimed at increasing demand** to boost economic activity, not related to unemployment and recession.

**Thus, the correct answer is (d) None.**

**23.** *(b)* Only two

- **Statement 1 is correct: Headline inflation** includes the total inflation within an economy, encompassing all items, including **volatile items** like food and fuel. It captures the overall inflation rate.

- **Statement 2 is correct: Core inflation excludes certain volatile items** such as **food and fuel** to provide a more stable measure of long-term inflation trends. By removing these items, core inflation gives a better sense of underlying inflationary pressures.
- **Statement 3 is incorrect: Headline inflation** is **more responsive** to short-term shocks in food and energy prices because it includes these volatile components. **Core inflation** is less responsive to such shocks because it excludes these items.

**Thus, the correct answer is (b) Only two.**

***24.*** *(d)* 2 only

- **Statement 1 is incorrect**: Core inflation excludes volatile items such as food and energy, which are often subject to global commodity price fluctuations. Therefore, core inflation is not directly affected by short-term global commodity price changes.
- **Statement 2 is correct**: Core inflation is often used by central banks to gauge underlying inflationary pressures and to assess the effectiveness of monetary policy.
- **Statement 3 is incorrect**: Core inflation deliberately excludes essential commodities like food and energy to avoid short-term price volatility

**Thus, the correct answer is (d) 2 only.**

***25.*** *(c)* Only three

- **Option 1 is correct: Petrol/Diesel for a vehicle** is **excluded** from Refined Core Inflation because fuel prices are highly volatile and subject to global oil price fluctuations.
- **Option 2 is correct: Lubricants and other fuels for vehicles** are also **excluded** from Refined Core Inflation for similar reasons, as they fall under volatile fuel items.
- **Option 3 is incorrect: Health services** are generally **included** in Refined Core Inflation because they tend to have stable pricing and are not subject to the same volatility as fuel and food.
- **Option 4 is correct: Food and beverages** are **excluded** from Refined Core Inflation because they exhibit high price volatility due to factors like seasonality, weather, and supply chain disruptions.

**Thus, the correct answer is (c) Only three.**

***26.*** *(a)* Both Statement I and Statement II are correct, and Statement II is the correct explanation for Statement I.

- **Imported inflation** refers to the increase in the general price level in a country due to the rising costs of imported goods and services. This type of inflation occurs when a country relies on imports for certain commodities like fuel, which can be caused by various factors such as:
  - Exchange rate depreciation
  - Global price increases
  - Trade disruptions or supply chain issues
- **Statement I is correct**: Imported inflation indeed occurs when the prices of goods and services that are imported from other countries increase, which leads to a rise in the overall price levels within the domestic economy.
- **Statement II is correct**: A weaker domestic currency can exacerbate imported inflation by making foreign goods more expensive. When the domestic currency depreciates in relation to foreign currencies, the cost of importing goods and services rises, even if their foreign prices remain unchanged. This increased cost is passed on to domestic consumers, resulting in higher inflationary pressure.

**Thus, option (a) is the correct answer.**

***27.*** *(c)* Only three

- **Scenario 1 is correct: An increase in import duties on essential goods** - This scenario is likely to result in imported inflation because higher import duties increase the cost of imported goods, which is passed on to consumers in the form of higher prices, contributing to inflation.
- **Scenario 2 is correct: Rising global prices of raw materials** - As the increased cost of raw materials globally will make imports more expensive for the domestic economy. This, in turn, raises the overall price levels domestically.
- **Scenario 3 is incorrect: Stronger domestic currency against foreign currencies** - A

stronger domestic currency is unlikely to lead to imported inflation. In fact, it may reduce inflationary pressures, as a **stronger currency makes imports cheaper**, thus lowering the cost of imported goods and services.

- **Scenario 4 is correct: Trade disruptions leading to higher costs for imported goods** - Trade disruptions can lead to imported inflation, as they can increase the cost of transporting goods or limit supply, driving up the prices of imports and thereby contributing to inflation.

**Thus, the correct answer is (c) Only three.**

***28.*** *(a)* The influence of a high or low base year price level on the current inflation rate.

- The base effect refers to how the price level in the previous year (the base year) influences the inflation rate in the current year. A low or high base can either exaggerate or understate the current inflation rate.
- **High base effect**: If the inflation rate was high in the base period (previous year), the current inflation rate may appear lower, even if there is a significant rise in prices, simply because it is being compared to a high base.
- **Low base effect**: If the inflation rate was low in the base period, the current inflation rate may appear higher, as prices are being compared to a relatively low base.

**Thus, option (a) is the correct answer.**

***29.*** *(b)* Only two

- **Statement 1 is correct**: The **base effect** refers to the impact that the price level in the **base year** has on the calculation of inflation rates. If prices were unusually high or low in the base year, it can cause inflation rates in the current year to appear **higher or lower**, even if the current price changes are moderate.
- **Statement 2 is correct**: If inflation was **low in the base year**, even a **moderate price increase** in the current year can result in a **higher inflation rate**. This happens because the previous year's low price level makes the percentage change in prices seem larger in comparison.
- **Statement 3 is incorrect**: The **base effect** is relevant to all forms of inflation measurement, including core inflation. Core inflation, which excludes volatile items like food and fuel, can still be influenced by the base effect if there were significant price changes in the base year.

**Thus, the correct answer is (b) Only two.**

***30.*** *(a)* The relationship between inflation and unemployment.

The Phillips Curve illustrates the **inverse relationship** between inflation and unemployment, suggesting that as inflation rises, unemployment tends to fall, and vice versa, in the short run.

**Thus, option (a) is the correct answer.**

***31.*** *(b)* Only two

- **Statement 1 is correct: Shrinkflation** occurs when companies **reduce the size or quantity** of a product but keep the **price the same.** This is a common practice used to maintain profitability without directly raising prices.
- **Statement 2 is correct**: Shrinkflation is considered a form of **hidden inflation** because consumers are **paying the same price** but receiving **less quantity**, which reduces the value they get for their money, even though the price per unit of quantity has effectively increased.
- **Statement 3 is incorrect**: Shrinkflation does not **directly affect the Consumer Price Index (CPI)**, as the CPI typically tracks **price changes** rather than changes in product size or quantity. Since the price remains the same, shrinkflation can go unnoticed in CPI calculations, although it still impacts consumer purchasing power.

**Therefore, the correct answer is (b) Only two.**

***32.*** *(c)* 1, 2 and 3 only

- **Structural inflation refers to a type of inflation** that arises due to inherent or fundamental imbalances and inefficiencies within the economy's structure, rather than from demand-pull or cost-push factors.
- **Statement 1 is correct**: Structural inflation often arises from supply-side constraints, such as inadequate infrastructure, which limit the economy's ability to meet demand.
- **Statement 2 is correct**: Rigidity in the labour market, including wage stickiness, can contribute to structural inflation by

preventing wages from adjusting to economic conditions.

- **Statement 3 is correct:** Excessive government regulation can reduce market efficiency, leading to persistent inflationary pressures.
- **Statement 4 is incorrect:** Short-term demand shocks typically cause temporary price increases, which are not considered structural inflation but rather a result of cyclical or demand-pull inflation.

**Thus, the correct answer is (c) 1, 2 and 3 only.**

***33.*** *(b)* A situation where the prices of certain goods rise sharply while others remain stable or decrease.

**Skewflation** refers to a condition where there is **uneven inflation**, meaning that the prices of certain goods or sectors increase sharply, while the prices of other goods remain stable or even decrease. This leads to a **skewed price increase** in specific parts of the economy rather than across the board.

**Thus, option (b) is the correct answer.**

***34.*** *(b)* A process where rising prices lead to higher wages, which in turn lead to further price increases.

An inflationary spiral refers to a situation in which inflation feeds on itself, causing a continuous rise in prices. This spiral can occur through a **vicious cycle of wage-price or cost-price increases**, where rising prices lead to higher wages and higher wages in turn lead to further price increases.

**Thus, option (b) is the correct answer.**

***35.*** *(c)* 1, 2 and 3 only

- **Statement 1 is correct: Poor agricultural output due to adverse weather conditions:** When agricultural output falls due to poor weather (e.g., droughts, floods), the supply of food decreases, pushing prices higher.
- **Statement 2 is correct: Increased demand for protein-rich foods like meat and dairy products:** A shift in consumer preferences toward protein-rich foods can increase demand, especially in developing countries, leading to higher prices for these items and contributing to food inflation.
- **Statement 3 is correct: Rising transportation costs due to higher fuel prices:** Higher fuel prices increase transportation costs, which directly impact the cost of moving food products from farms to markets.
- **Statement 4 is incorrect: Government subsidies on food production:** Subsidies are generally designed to reduce the cost of food production and keep prices stable. Therefore, government subsidies are **unlikely to contribute to food inflation**; instead, they often have a **moderating effect.**

**Hence, the correct answer is (c) 1, 2 and 3 only.**

***36.*** *(a)* The Phillips Curve traditionally shows an **inverse relationship between inflation and unemployment**, where low unemployment is associated with high inflation and vice-versa. However, **stagflation is an exception to this relationship**, where an economy experiences both high inflation and high unemployment at the same time, challenging the traditional Phillips Curve concept.

**Thus, option (a) is the correct answer.**

***37.*** *(d)* It asserts that the real interest rate is equal to the nominal interest rate adjusted for inflation.

- The **Fisher Effect** is an economic theory proposed by economist Irving Fisher, which describes the relationship between nominal interest rates, real interest rates and inflation.
- **Real Interest Rate = Nominal Interest Rate - Expected Inflation Rate**
- The Fisher Effect states that the real interest rate is derived by subtracting the inflation rate from the nominal interest rate, illustrating the relationship between inflation and interest rates.

**Thus, option (d) is the correct answer.**

***38.*** *(a)* An inflationary gap occurs when aggregate demand exceeds aggregate supply, while a deflationary gap occurs when aggregate supply exceeds aggregate demand.

An **Inflationary Gap** occurs when **aggregate demand** in the economy exceeds **aggregate supply**, leading to upward pressure on prices, which can cause inflation. In contrast, a **Deflationary Gap** occurs when **aggregate supply** exceeds **aggregate demand**, resulting in excess production capacity and downward pressure on prices, which can cause deflation or stagnation.

**Thus, option (a) is the correct answer.**

**39.** *(a)* Both Statement I and Statement II are correct and Statement II is the correct explanation for Statement I.

- **Statement I is correct:** The real interest rate is indeed calculated by subtracting the inflation rate from the nominal interest rate (Real Interest Rate = Nominal Interest Rate - Inflation Rate).
- **Statement II is correct:** When inflation increases while the nominal interest rate remains the same, the real interest rate decreases, reducing the actual purchasing power of the interest earned.

**Hence, the correct answer is (a).**

**40.** *(b)* Only two

- **Statement 1 is correct:** As inflation rises, the value of money declines, meaning that a given amount of money buys fewer goods and services than before. This reduction in purchasing power is a key effect of inflation.
- **Statement 2 is incorrect: Inflation typically reduces the real interest rate** if the nominal interest rate does not rise in proportion to inflation. This hurts savers, as the returns on their savings diminish in real terms.
- **Statement 3 is incorrect: Inflation typically benefits debtors** because they can repay their loans with money that has less purchasing power. Conversely, creditors lose out because the real value of the repayments they receive is reduced.
- **Statement 4 is correct:** Moderate inflation is a sign of increasing demand and can be associated with healthy economic growth, as it indicates a growing economy, and rising prices at a manageable level.

**Hence, the correct answer is (b) Only two.**

**41.** *(b)* 1, 2 and 4 only

- **Statement 1 is correct: Fixed-income earners negatively affected** since their income remains constant, the rising prices erode their purchasing power, meaning they can afford fewer goods and services over time.
- **Statement 2 is correct: Creditors, including banks and financial institutions are negatively affected** by high inflation because the value of the money they receive in repayment is reduced. The real value of the debt decreases, meaning they get back less purchasing power than they lent out.
- **Statement 3 is incorrect:** Debtors generally **benefit** from high inflation, as they can repay their loans with money that has less purchasing power, effectively reducing the real value of their debt.
- **Statement 4 is correct: Investors in fixed-rate bonds** is **negatively affected** by high inflation because the fixed interest payments they receive lose value in real terms, meaning their returns are worth less in an inflationary environment.

**Thus, the correct answer is (b) 1, 2 and 4 only.**

**42.** *(b)* Only two

- **Statement 1 is correct:** By **raising the central bank's policy interest** rate, borrowing becomes more expensive, which reduces consumer spending and business investment, thus cooling down demand.
- **Statement 2 is incorrect: Increasing subsidies does not directly control demand-pull inflation.** In fact, it can increase demand by making essential commodities cheaper, which could worsen inflationary pressures rather than reduce them.
- **Statement 3 is correct: Reducing government spending on public projects** can help control **demand-pull inflation.** By reducing government spending, overall demand in the economy is decreased, which can help bring down inflationary pressures.

**Thus, the correct answer is (b) Only two.**

**43.** *(b)* Only two

- Under the Inflation Targeting Framework, the RBI's primary goal is to maintain price stability (keeping inflation within the target range), but it also aims to support economic growth, as explicitly stated in its objectives.

- **Statement 1 is correct**: RBI's monetary policy aims to maintain the inflation target while also supporting the broader goal of economic growth.
- **Statement 2 is correct**: The Inflation Targeting Framework in India allows for flexibility to address short-term economic changes without deviating from the long-term inflation target.
- **Statement 3 is incorrect**: The RBI is required to explain any significant deviations from the inflation target to the Central government, not Parliament, outlining the causes and proposed corrective actions.

**Thus, the correct answer is (b) Only two.**

***44.*** *(c)* 1, 2 and 4 only

**Contractionary monetary policy** is a type of monetary policy used by central banks to reduce the money supply in the economy and curb inflation.

- **Statement 1 is correct**: Contractionary monetary policy typically reduces overall economic activity by making borrowing more expensive and reducing consumer, and business spending. As demand falls, businesses may cut jobs, leading to higher unemployment.
- **Statement 2 is correct: Higher interest rates** can make a country's **financial assets more attractive** to foreign investors, leading to an inflow of capital. This can increase demand for the domestic currency, causing it to appreciate i.e. Strengthening of domestic currency.
- **Statement 3 is incorrect**: When there are higher interest rates consumers tend to reduce overall consumer spending because borrowing becomes more expensive and consumers tend to save more rather than spend more when interest rates rise.
- **Statement 4 is correct**: Contractionary monetary policy raises borrowing costs for consumers and businesses, leading to a reduction in spending, and investment, which slows down economic growth.

**Thus, the correct answer is (c) 1, 2 and 4 only.**

***45.*** *(a)* 1 only

- **Statement 1 is correct**: The **Inflation Targeting Framework** in India focuses on the **Consumer Price Index (CPI)** as the primary measure of inflation. The RBI's goal is to maintain inflation within a target range to ensure price stability while supporting economic growth.
- **Statement 2 is incorrect**: The inflation target is **set by the Government of India**, in consultation with the RBI, for a period of 5 years. The RBI is responsible for implementing the policy to achieve this target but does not set the target on its own.

**Thus, the correct answer is (a) 1 only.**

***46.*** *(a)* 1 and 3 only

- **Option 1 is correct: Increasing Cash Reserve Ratio (CRR)** is a **contractionary monetary policy** measure. By increasing CRR, the RBI reduces the amount of money banks can lend, which decreases aggregate demand and helps curb inflation.
- **Option 2 incorrect: Increased indirect taxes like GST and excise duty increase the cost** of goods, and services, leading to inflation. Therefore, increasing indirect taxes is not a measure to tackle inflation.
- **Option 3 correct**: Increasing irrigation coverage, while increasing irrigation coverage can **improve agricultural production and supply**, it takes time to have a significant impact on prices. This is a long-term measure and not a quick fix for inflation.
- **Option 4 incorrect**: Reduction of Repo rate is an **expansionary monetary policy measure.** By reducing the repo rate, the RBI makes it cheaper for banks to borrow money from it, which encourages them to lend more to the public. This increases aggregate demand and can lead to inflation.

**Thus, the correct answer is (a) 1 and 3 only.**

## Past Learning (Answers)

| | | | | | | | |
|---|---|---|---|---|---|---|---|
| 1 (b) | 2 (a) | 3 (a) | 4 (d) | 5 (c) | 6 (c) | 7 (a) | 8 (d) |

CHAPTER 08

# Banking System

## Assessment Round

### Topic 1 : Classification of Banking System

**1.** Consider the following statements:

1. Scheduled banks are those included in the Second Schedule of the Reserve Bank of India (RBI) Act, 1934.
2. Non-scheduled banks are exempt from maintaining the CRR with the Reserve Bank of India.
3. Both scheduled and non-scheduled banks are eligible to borrow money from the RBI under Liquidity Adjustment Facility (LAF).

How many of the statements given above is/are correct?

(a) Only one (b) Only two
(c) All three (d) None

**2.** Which of the following benefits do Scheduled Banks in India enjoy due to their status?

1. Access to refinance facilities from the Reserve Bank of India (RBI).
2. Higher public trust and confidence due to being regulated under the RBI Act.
3. Exemption from reporting compliance and financial statements to the RBI.
4. Eligible to participate in the government's borrowing programme through Open Market Operations (OMOs).

Select the correct answer from the codes given below:

(a) 1, 2 and 4 only (b) 1 and 2 only
(c) 2 and 3 only (d) 1, 3 and 4 only

**3.** Consider the following categories of banks:

1. Foreign Banks operating in India
2. Payment Banks
3. Small Finance Banks
4. Non-Banking Financial Companies (NBFCs)

How many of the above is/are classified as 'Scheduled Commercial Banks (SCBs)' in India?

(a) Only one (b) Only two
(c) Only three (d) All four

**4.** Consider the following statements:

1. Cooperative banks are member-owned institutions while commercial banks are owned by shareholders.
2. The main motive of commercial banks is to earn profit while cooperative banks focus on serving their members.
3. Commercial banks are regulated solely by the RBI while cooperative banks are regulated by both the RBI and the respective State Governments.

Which of the statements given above are correct?

(a) 1 and 2 only (b) 1 and 3 only
(c) 2 and 3 only (d) 1, 2 and 3

**5.** Consider the following statements:

1. Commercial banks have a centralised structure of management while cooperative banks have a democratic structure where each member has equal voting rights.
2. Both commercial and cooperative banks are mainly regulated by the Banking Regulation Act, 1949.

Which of the statements given above is/are correct?

(a) 1 only (b) 2 only
(c) Both 1 and 2 (d) Neither 1 nor 2

**6.** Consider the following laws:
1. Banking Regulation Act, 1949
2. Multi-State Cooperative Societies Act, 2002
3. Companies Act, 2013
4. Reserve Bank of India Act, 1934

How many of the above laws is/are directly involved in regulating cooperative banks in India?

(a) Only one (b) Only two
(c) Only three (d) All four

**7.** Consider the following statements:
1. Primary Agricultural Credit Societies (PACS) are at the grassroots level of the cooperative credit structure.
2. District Central Cooperative Banks (DCCBs) provide financial support to PACS and link them to State Cooperative Banks (SCBs).
3. State Cooperative Banks (SCBs) directly provide credit to individual farmers and rural enterprises.

Which of the statements given above are correct?

(a) 1 and 2 only
(b) 1 and 3 only
(c) 2 and 3 only
(d) 1, 2 and 3

## Topic 2 : Different types of Banks

**8.** Consider the following functions:
1. Providing credit to small and marginal farmers
2. Issuance of credit cards
3. Supporting rural development by providing loans to small businesses and artisans
4. Serving as a channel for implementing government-sponsored schemes

How many of the above functions can be undertaken by Regional Rural Banks in India?

(a) Only one
(b) Only two
(c) Only three
(d) All four

**9.** Consider the following statements about the 'Regional Rural Banks (RRBs)':
1. RRBs are jointly owned by the Government of India, the concerned State Government and a sponsoring bank.
2. RRBs are regulated by the RBI and the NABARD.
3. RRBs can provide both short-term and long-term credit to the agricultural sector and rural artisans.

Which of the statements given above are correct?

(a) 1 and 2 only
(b) 1 and 3 only
(c) 2 and 3 only
(d) 1, 2 and 3

**10.** With reference to the 'Regional Rural Banks (RRBs)' in India, consider the following statements:
1. These banks are required to provide 75% of their total credit as Priority Sector Lending (PSL).
2. The sponsor bank mandatorily has to be the public sector bank.
3. RRBs can have branches in the urban areas.

Which of the statements given above are correct?

(a) 1 and 2 only (b) 1 and 3 only
(c) 2 and 3 only (d) 1, 2 and 3

**11.** Consider the following statements about 'Local Area Banks (LABs)':
1. These banks are permitted to operate in multiple states across India.
2. Each LAB is registered as a public limited company under the Companies Act, 2013.
3. They are regulated by the Reserve Bank of India (RBI).

How many of the statements given above is/are correct?

(a) Only one
(b) Only two
(c) All three
(d) None

**12.** Consider the following statements:

1. Small Finance Banks (SFBs) can provide both loans and accept deposits from the public.
2. Both SFBs and Payment Banks are required to comply with the CRR and SLR requirements set by the RBI.
3. Both Small Finance Banks and Payment Banks are regulated by the Reserve Bank of India (RBI).

How many of the statements given above is/are correct?

(a) Only one (b) Only two
(c) All three (d) None

**13.** With reference to the 'Payment Banks in India', consider the following statements:

1. These banks can accept demand deposits but cannot accept time deposits.
2. These banks can provide loans to small businesses and farmers.
3. These banks are allowed to offer internet banking and mobile banking services.

Which of the statements given above are correct?

(a) 1 and 2 only (b) 1 and 3 only
(c) 2 and 3 only (d) 1, 2 and 3

**14.** Consider the following statements about 'Small Finance Banks (SFBs)':

1. SFBs are required to extend minimum 75% loans to the priority sector.
2. They are required to allocate a minimum of 50% of their loan portfolio to loans and advances up to ₹ 25 lakh.
3. SFBs are permitted to engage in foreign exchange transactions and offer international banking services.

Which of the statements given above are correct?

(a) 1 and 2 only (b) 2 and 3 only
(c) 1 and 3 only (d) 1, 2 and 3

**15.** Consider the following types of borrowers:

1. Agricultural labourers
2. Small business units
3. Urban low-income groups
4. Infrastructure companies

How many of the above is/are typically eligible to borrow from Small Finance Banks (SFBs) in India?

(a) Only one (b) Only two
(c) Only three (d) All four

**16.** With reference to the 'Neo Banks', consider the following statements:

1. These banks operate entirely online without any physical branch network.
2. These banks are required to partner with traditional banks for their operations.
3. They are directly regulated by the Reserve Bank of India (RBI) and hold a banking license.

Which of the statements given above are correct?

(a) 1 and 2 only (b) 1 and 3 only
(c) 2 and 3 only (d) 1, 2 and 3

## Topic 3 : Banking Parameters

**17.** With reference to 'Priority Sector Lending (PSL)' in India, consider the following statements:

1. All Scheduled Commercial Banks (SCBs) in India are mandated to allocate minimum 40% of their Adjusted Net Bank Credit (ANBC) to priority sectors.
2. RRBs have the same priority sector lending targets as SCBs.
3. UCBs are exempted from meeting the priority sector lending targets.

Which of the statements given above is/are correct?

(a) 1 and 2 only (b) 1 only
(c) 2 and 3 only (d) 1, 2 and 3

**18.** Consider the following sectors:

1. Agriculture
2. Renewable Energy
3. Export Credit
4. Micro, Small and Medium Enterprises (MSMEs)

How many of the above sectors is/are eligible for Priority Sector Lending (PSL) by banks in India?

(a) Only one (b) Only two
(c) Only three (d) All four

**19.** Consider the following types of banks:
1. Regional Rural Banks
2. Foreign Banks
3. Small Finance Banks
4. Urban Cooperative Banks

Which of the given above banks in India have the same PSL targets?
(a) 1 and 2 only (b) 2 and 3 only
(c) 1, 2 and 4 only (d) 1, 3 and 4 only

**20.** Consider the following statements about 'Priority Sector Lending Certificates (PSLCs)' in India:
1. Banks that have surplus lending in the priority sector can sell PSLCs to banks that are deficient.
2. PSLCs can only be traded within a financial year and cannot be carried forward to the next year.
3. The price of PSLCs is determined by the market forces based on demand and supply.

Which of the statements given above are correct?
(a) 1 and 2 only
(b) 2 and 3 only
(c) 1 and 3 only
(d) 1, 2 and 3

**21.** With reference to the 'Priority Sector Lending Certificates (PSLCs)', consider the following statements:
1. PSLCs are issued and traded on a trading platform known as E-Kuber provided by the RBI.
2. There is no transfer of risk or loan assets between banks when PSLCs are traded.

Which of the statements given above is/are correct?
(a) 1 only
(b) 2 only
(c) Both 1 and 2
(d) Neither 1 nor 2

**22.** Consider the following statements about the 'External Benchmark Lending Rate (EBLR)' adopted by banks in India:

**Statement I:** RBI mandated that all new floating rate loans to retail and micro, small and medium enterprises (MSMEs) be linked to an external benchmark from 1st October, 2019.

**Statement II:** The adoption of the EBLR by banks in India is intended to improve transparency and ensure quicker transmission of monetary policy rates to borrowers.

Which one of the following is correct in respect of the above statements?
(a) Both Statement I and Statement II are correct and Statement II is the correct explanation for Statement I.
(b) Both Statement I and Statement II are correct and Statement II is not the correct explanation for Statement I.
(c) Statement I is correct, but Statement II is incorrect.
(d) Statement I is incorrect, but Statement II is correct.

**23.** Consider the following rates:
1. Repo Rate
2. Base Rate
3. Marginal Cost of Funds-Based Lending Rate (MCLR)

How many of the above rates is/are associated with the Internal Benchmark Lending Rate Regime in India?
(a) Only one
(b) Only two
(c) Only three
(d) None

**24.** What is the primary goal of the Basel III norms introduced by the Basel Committee on Banking Supervision?
(a) To increase the profitability of banks
(b) To reduce capital requirements for banks
(c) To enhance the ability of banks to absorb shocks arising from financial and economic stress
(d) To standardise accounting practices across banks

**25.** With reference to the Basel Committee on Banking Supervision (BCBS), consider the following statements:

1. It was established in response to the global financial crisis of 2008.
2. BCBS sets minimum standards for capital adequacy, stress testing and market liquidity risk for banks worldwide.
3. BCBS can impose fines on banks that fail to comply with its standards.

How many of the statements given above is/are correct?

(a) Only one
(b) Only two
(c) All three
(d) None

**26.** Consider the following statements about the 'Basel Committee on Banking Supervision (BCBS)':

1. BCBS identifies Globally Systemically Important Banks (G-SIBs) and imposes additional capital requirements on them.
2. It is headquartered at the Bank for International Settlements (BIS) in Basel, Switzerland.

Which of the statements given above is/are correct?

(a) 1 only
(b) 2 only
(c) Both 1 and 2
(d) Neither 1 nor 2

**27.** With reference to the 'Capital Adequacy Ratio (CAR)', consider the following statements:

1. It is a measure of a bank's capital, expressed as a percentage of its risk-weighted assets.
2. It is set by each individual bank.
3. Higher CAR requirements are imposed on banks Deemed Domestic Systemically Important Banks (D-SIBs).

Which of the statements given above are correct?

(a) 1 and 2 only
(b) 1 and 3 only
(c) 2 and 3 only
(d) 1, 2 and 3

**28.** Which of the following statements best describes the purpose of maintaining a high Capital Adequacy Ratio (CAR)?

(a) To maximise the bank's profitability
(b) To ensure the bank can absorb a reasonable amount of loss and protect depositors
(c) To decrease the cost of capital for the bank
(d) To allow banks to lend without any regulatory oversight

**29.** Consider the following financial institutions:

1. Scheduled Commercial Banks (SCBs)
2. Small Finance Banks (SFBs)
3. Urban Cooperative Banks (UCBs)
4. Non-Banking Finance Companies (NBFCs)

How many of the given above financial institutions is/are required to adhere to CAR norms as per the RBI regulations?

(a) Only one
(b) Only two
(c) Only three
(d) All four

**30.** With reference to 'Additional Tier-1 (AT-1) Bonds', consider the following statements:

1. These bonds can be issued by banks to meet their capital requirements under Basel III norms.
2. These are perpetual in nature as they do not have a maturity date unlike the other bonds.
3. These bonds offer higher yields compared to traditional bonds due to their higher risk profile.

How many of the statements given above is/are correct?

(a) Only one
(b) Only two
(c) All three
(d) None

**31.** Which component introduced by Basel III helps banks to manage short-term liquidity risks, ensuring they can survive a 30-day stress scenario?

(a) Leverage Ratio
(b) Net Stable Funding Ratio (NSFR)
(c) Liquidity Coverage Ratio (LCR)
(d) Risk-Weighted Assets (RWA)

**32.** Which of the following best explains the purpose of the Net Stable Funding Ratio (NSFR) introduced under Basel III norms?
(a) To ensure that banks maintain a balance between their long-term assets and liabilities to promote resilience over a one-year time horizon.
(b) To enhance the risk-weighted capital adequacy of banks in periods of economic stress.
(c) To calculate the total market risk exposure of a bank's trading book.
(d) To set a minimum standard for operational risk management in global banks.

**33.** What is the primary purpose of the Capital Conservation Buffer (CCB) introduced under Basel III norms?
(a) To ensure banks can meet short-term liquidity needs during financial stress.
(b) To require banks to hold additional capital to absorb losses during periods of financial stability and prevent depletion of capital during periods of stress.
(c) To provide banks with funds to invest in high-risk assets.
(d) To eliminate the need for maintaining a minimum capital ratio.

**34.** How does the Counter-cyclical Capital Buffer (CCyB) mechanism operate to reduce the pro-cyclicality of the banking sector under Basel III norms?
(a) By mandating that banks reduce lending activities during economic downturns.
(b) By automatically lowering the capital requirements during periods of economic stability.
(c) By requiring banks to accumulate additional capital during periods of high credit growth and allowing this buffer to be released during downturns.
(d) By setting a fixed buffer percentage that does not change regardless of economic conditions.

**35.** What is the primary purpose of the Leverage Ratio introduced under Basel III norms?
(a) To increase the risk-weighted capital requirements for banks.
(b) To limit the total leverage a bank can use relative to its equity, preventing excessive leverage.
(c) To ensure banks have sufficient high-quality liquid assets.
(d) To regulate the minimum reserve requirements for banks.

## Topic 4 : Non-Performing Assets (NPA's)

**36.** With reference to Non-Performing Assets (NPAs) in the banking sector, consider the following statements:
1. An asset is classified as non-performing if the interest or principal amount remains overdue for more than 90 days.
2. NPAs have no impact on a bank's profitability and capital adequacy.
3. The provisioning for NPAs is mandatory for all banks as per the RBI guidelines.

How many of the statements given above is/are correct?
(a) Only one
(b) Only two
(c) All three
(d) None

**37.** What is the primary purpose of categorising an account as a Special Mention Account (SMA) by banks?
(a) To indicate a successful loan repayment history
(b) To monitor accounts showing early signs of stress and prevent them from becoming Non-Performing Assets (NPAs)
(c) To classify loans that are exempt from regulatory scrutiny
(d) To categorise accounts with no credit activity

**38.** With reference to 'Special Mention Accounts (SMAs)' in the banking sector, consider the following statements:

1. SMA-0 accounts are those where the principal or interest payment is overdue for 1 to 30 days.
2. SMA-2 accounts are those where the principal or interest payment is overdue for more than 60 days but less than 90 days.
3. An account is classified as a NPA immediately after it is categorised as SMA-2.

How many of the statements given above is/are correct?

(a) Only one (b) Only two
(c) All three (d) None

**39.** Consider the following statements about the 'Provisioning Coverage Ratio (PCR)':

1. PCR is a measure of the funds set aside by banks to cover potential losses from their non-performing assets (NPAs).
2. A higher PCR indicates a bank's lower ability to absorb losses from NPAs.
3. PCR is directly related to the interest rates offered by the bank on its deposits.

Which of the statements given above is/are correct?

(a) 1 and 2 only
(b) 1 only
(c) 2 and 3 only
(d) 1, 2 and 3

**40.** Which of the following actions are likely to increase a bank's Provisioning Coverage Ratio (PCR)?

1. Writing off bad loans from the bank's books
2. Increasing provisions against doubtful and bad debts
3. Reducing the gross amount of non-performing assets (NPAs) through recovery

Select the correct answer from the codes given below:

(a) 1 and 2 only
(b) 1 and 3 only
(c) 2 and 3 only
(d) 1, 2 and 3

**41.** Which of the following measures are specifically targeted at resolving the issue of NPAs in the Indian banking sector?

1. Asset Quality Review (AQR)
2. Corporate Debt Restructuring (CDR)
3. Implementation of External Benchmark Lending Rate (EBLR)
4. Prompt Corrective Action (PCA) framework

Select the correct answer from the codes given below:

(a) 1 and 3 only (b) 1, 2 and 4 only
(c) 2, 3 and 4 only (d) 1, 2, 3 and 4

**42.** Consider the following statements about 'Debt Recovery Tribunals (DRTs)':

1. These are statutory bodies which are established to facilitate the speedy recovery of debts due to banks and financial institutions.
2. They have the authority to handle cases involving debts of all amounts including small loans and microfinance.
3. DRTs are empowered to initiate insolvency proceedings against defaulting borrowers.

Which of the statements given above is/are correct?

(a) 1 only (b) 1 and 3 only
(c) 2 and 3 only (d) 1, 2 and 3

**43.** Consider the following statements with reference to the 'SARFAESI Act, 2002':

1. The Act allows banks and financial institutions to auction residential or commercial properties to recover loans.
2. The Act allows banks to seize and sell only secured collateral without court's intervention.
3. SARFAESI Act applies to all categories of borrowers, including farmers with agricultural land.

Which of the statements given above are correct?

(a) 1 and 2 only
(b) 1 and 3 only
(c) 2 and 3 only
(d) 1, 2 and 3

**44.** Consider the following actions that taken by the banks:

1. Issuing a demand notice to the borrower for the repayment of the loan.
2. Taking possession of the secured asset if the borrower fails to repay.
3. Banks to sell their loan assets to ARCs.

How many of the above actions is/are specifically authorised under the SARFAESI Act, 2002?

(a) Only one (b) Only two
(c) All three (d) None

**45.** Consider the following statements with reference to the 'Asset Reconstruction Companies (ARCs)':

1. ARCs purchase NPAs from banks and financial institutions to manage and recover them.
2. ARCs are allowed to acquire both secured and unsecured loans from banks.
3. ARCs are required to register with the RBI to operate legally in India.

How many of the statements given above is/are correct?

(a) Only one (b) Only two
(c) All three (d) None

**46.** What is the primary purpose of the Prompt Corrective Action (PCA) framework introduced by the Reserve Bank of India (RBI)?

(a) To encourage banks to expand their branch network.
(b) To impose regulatory actions to prevent further deterioration in the financial health of banks showing signs of stress.
(c) To provide tax incentives to banks for reducing their Non-Performing Assets (NPAs).
(d) To mandate that banks increase interest rates to improve profitability.

**47.** Consider the following measures that might be imposed on banks:

1. Restriction on dividend distribution
2. Limitations on the expansion of branch networks
3. Mandatory capital infusion by the government
4. Prohibition on non-core activities

How many of the above measures can be imposed under the PCA framework?

(a) Only one (b) Only two
(c) Only three (d) All four

**48.** Consider the following triggers:

1. Capital Adequacy Ratio (CAR) falling below the minimum regulatory requirements
2. Gross Non-Performing Assets (NPAs) exceeding a certain threshold
3. Negative Return on Assets (RoA) for consecutive years
4. High exposure to unsecured loans

How many of the given above triggers is/are specifically recognised under the 'PCA Framework'?

(a) Only one (b) Only two
(c) Only three (d) All four

**49.** Which of the following types of financial institutions are subject to the PCA framework by the RBI?

1. Urban Cooperative Banks
2. Private Sector Banks
3. Small Finance and Payment Banks
4. Systemically Important Non-Deposit Taking Non-Banking Financial Companies (NBFC-ND-SI)

Select the correct answer from the codes given below:

(a) 1 and 2 only (b) 3 and 4 only
(c) 1, 2 and 4 only (d) 1, 2, 3 and 4

**50.** With reference to Domestic Systemically Important Banks (D-SIBs) in India, consider the following statements:

1. The classification of D-SIBs by the RBI is reviewed annually.
2. RBI requires D-SIBs to maintain additional capital requirements beyond the standard regulatory norms.
3. Only public sector banks can be classified as D-SIBs by the RBI.

How many of the statements given above is/are correct?

(a) Only one (b) Only two
(c) All three (d) None

**51.** With reference to the 'Financial Services Institution Bureau (FSIB)', consider the following statements:

1. FSIB has taken over the functions of the former Bank Board Bureau (BBB).
2. It also handles appointments for top management positions in insurance companies owned by the government.
3. It was created to improve the financial health of all private sector banks in India.

Which of the statements given above are correct?

(a) 1 and 2 only
(b) 1 and 3 only
(c) 2 and 3 only
(d) 1, 2 and 3

**52.** With reference to the 'Insolvency and Bankruptcy Code (IBC), 2016', consider the following statements:

1. It allows for the resolution of insolvency cases through a corporate insolvency resolution process (CIRP) and liquidation.
2. It provides a framework for both corporate and individual insolvency resolution.
3. IBC mandates that the corporate insolvency resolution process (CIRP) must be completed within 330 days, including any extensions or litigation time.

Which of the statements given above are correct?

(a) 1 and 2 only
(b) 1 and 3 only
(c) 2 and 3 only
(d) 1, 2 and 3

**53.** Consider the following statements about the IBC, 2016:

1. Under the IBC, the Insolvency Professional (IP) has the power to replace the existing management of the debtor company.
2. Insolvency and Bankruptcy Board of India (IBBI) regulates the insolvency professionals and information utilities under the IBC.
3. Committee of Creditors (CoC) has the authority to approve or reject the resolution plan during the corporate insolvency resolution process.

Which of the statements given above are correct?

(a) 1 and 2 only (b) 2 and 3 only
(c) 1 and 3 only (d) 1, 2 and 3

**54.** Consider the following bodies:

1. Insolvency and Bankruptcy Board of India (IBBI)
2. National Company Law Tribunal (NCLT)
3. Debt Recovery Tribunal (DRT)
4. National Company Law Appellate Tribunal (NCLAT)

How many of the above bodies was/were created under the IBC Code, 2016 to manage insolvency resolution processes in India?

(a) Only one (b) Only two
(c) Only three (d) All four

**55.** Consider the following steps involved in the Corporate Insolvency Resolution Process (CIRP) under the Insolvency and Bankruptcy Code (IBC), 2016:

1. Initiation of the insolvency process by the creditor or debtor
2. Appointment of an Interim Resolution Professional (IRP)
3. Approval of the resolution plan by the Committee of Creditors (CoC)
4. Liquidation of the debtor's assets

How many of the above steps is/are mandatory in every CIRP under the IBC?

(a) Only one
(b) Only two
(c) Only three
(d) All four

**56.** What is the primary objective of introducing Pre-Packaged Insolvency Resolution Processes (Pre-Packs) under the Insolvency and Bankruptcy Code (IBC), 2016?

(a) To liquidate companies as quickly as possible.
(b) To allow companies to merge with their competitors without regulatory oversight.
(c) To provide a faster and more cost-effective insolvency resolution process, particularly for MSMEs.
(d) To enable banks to directly take over debtor companies without a resolution process.

**57.** With reference to the 'Insolvency and Bankruptcy Board of India (IBBI)', consider the following statements:

1. It is responsible for setting standards and guidelines for insolvency professionals and the conduct of insolvency proceedings.
2. It has the authority to impose penalties and disciplinary actions against the insolvency professionals.
3. It can adjudicate insolvency cases under the Insolvency and Bankruptcy Code (IBC).

Which of the statements given above are correct?

(a) 1 and 2 only (b) 1 and 3 only
(c) 2 and 3 only (d) 1, 2 and 3

**58.** What is the primary rationale behind using recapitalisation as a tool to address the problem of Non-Performing Assets (NPAs) in public sector banks?

(a) To provide banks with immediate liquidity to cover operational costs.
(b) To improve the capital adequacy of banks, allowing them to absorb losses from NPAs and continue lending.
(c) To increase the number of branches and expand banking services in rural areas.
(d) To mandate that banks, reduce interest rates on loans.

**59.** Which of the following potential outcomes is a major risk associated with repeated rounds of bank recapitalisation without structural reforms?

(a) Permanent reduction in interest rates for borrowers
(b) Encouragement of moral hazard among bank management, leading to continued poor lending practices
(c) Increase in the number of foreign banks in the domestic market
(d) Mandatory reduction in the size of public sector banks

**60.** With reference to the 'Project Sashakt', consider the following statements:

1. It was designed based on the recommendations of the Sunil Mehta Committee.
2. It recommended the creation of an Asset Management Company (AMC) for large Non-Performing Assets (NPAs).
3. The committee suggested a five-pronged strategy for resolution of stressed assets, categorised by the size of the loan.

How many of the statements given above is/are correct?

(a) Only one (b) Only two
(c) All three (d) None

**61.** Consider the following statements about the 'Inter-Creditor Agreement (ICA)' under the Project Sashakt:

1. It is a collective agreement among all creditors of a borrower to cooperate in the resolution of stressed assets.
2. It requires unanimous consent from all lenders before any resolution plan can be implemented.
3. It is a legally binding document that outlines the rights and obligations of all participating creditors.

Which of the statements given above are correct?

(a) 1 and 2 only
(b) 1 and 3 only
(c) 2 and 3 only
(d) 1, 2 and 3

**62.** With reference to the Bad Bank structure in India, consider the following statements:

1. National Asset Reconstruction Company Limited (NARCL) is responsible for purchasing stressed assets from banks while India Debt Resolution Company Limited (IDRCL) is responsible for resolving these assets.
2. IDRCL holds a majority stake in NARCL to ensure efficient resolution of assets.
3. NARCL issues government-backed securities to banks as a part of the asset purchase process.

How many of the statements given above is/are correct?

(a) Only one
(b) Only two
(c) All three
(d) None

**63.** Consider the following statements about the 'National Asset Reconstruction Company Limited (NARCL)':

1. Public sector banks hold a majority stake in NARCL.
2. NARCL is funded entirely through equity contributions from public sector banks.
3. The primary role of NARCL is to directly manage and resolve the stressed assets it acquires.

Which of the statements given above is/are correct?

(a) 1 and 2 only (b) 1 only
(c) 2 and 3 only (d) 1, 2 and 3

## Topic 5 : Non-Banking Financial Institutions (NBFIs)

**64.** With reference to the differences between Non-Banking Financial Companies (NBFCs) and banks, consider the following statements:

1. NBFCs are allowed to accept demand deposits from the public.
2. NBFCs do not form part of the payment and settlement system and cannot issue cheques drawn on themselves.
3. Banks are required to maintain a Cash Reserve Ratio (CRR) with the Reserve Bank of India, while NBFCs are not.

Which of the statements given above are correct?

(a) 1 and 2 only
(b) 1 and 3 only
(c) 2 and 3 only
(d) 1, 2 and 3

**65.** Consider the following statements:

1. Deposit-taking NBFCs are allowed to accept public deposits up to a certain limit prescribed by the Reserve Bank of India (RBI).
2. Systemically important NBFCs are those with an asset size of INR 500 crore or more.
3. All NBFCs are required to maintain a minimum Capital Adequacy Ratio (CAR) of 9%.

Which of the statements given above are correct?

(a) 1 and 2 only (b) 1 and 3 only
(c) 2 and 3 only (d) 1, 2 and 3

**66.** Consider the following regulatory requirements:

1. Maintenance of a minimum Capital Adequacy Ratio (CAR)
2. Adherence to the Liquidity Coverage Ratio (LCR) requirements similar to banks.
3. Mandatory adherence to the PSL norms

How many of the above regulatory requirements is/are mandatory for NBFCs in India?

(a) Only one (b) Only two
(c) All three (d) None

**67.** Consider the following regulatory bodies in India:

1. Reserve Bank of India (RBI)
2. Securities and Exchange Board of India (SEBI)
3. Ministry of Corporate Affairs (MCA)
4. Insurance Regulatory and Development Authority of India (IRDAI)

How many of the above regulatory bodies is/are involved in the regulation of Non-Banking Financial Companies (NBFCs) in India?

(a) Only one
(b) Only two
(c) Only three
(d) All four

**68.** Consider the following institutions:

1. National Bank for Agriculture and Rural Development (NABARD)
2. Export-Import Bank of India (EXIM Bank)
3. National Housing Bank (NHB)
4. Small Industries Development Bank of India (SIDBI)

How many of the given above institutions is/are classified as All India Financial Institutions (AIFIs)?

(a) Only one (b) Only two
(c) Only three (d) All four

## Topic 6 : Other Concepts and Initiatives

**69.** Which of the following best describes the Lead Bank Scheme?
(a) A scheme where a designated bank leads all financial institutions in a state to distribute loans to large corporate borrowers.
(b) A scheme where a designated bank coordinates the efforts of all banks and financial institutions in a district to enhance banking services and promote financial inclusion.
(c) A programme where the Reserve Bank of India provides direct loans to rural areas to promote agricultural development.
(d) A government initiative to provide interest-free loans to small and medium enterprises in underserved regions.

**70.** Consider the following statements about the 'Lead Bank Scheme':
1. The Service Area Approach under the Lead Bank Scheme assigns specific villages to bank branches for focused financial inclusion.
2. RBI is the regulatory authority overseeing the Lead Bank Scheme.
3. The Lead Bank Scheme applies only to rural areas and is not implemented in urban regions.

How many of the given statements is/are correct?
(a) Only one
(b) Only two
(c) All three
(d) None

**71.** Consider the following statements about Digital Banking Units (DBUs):
1. DBUs offer fully digital services and do not require physical bank branches for operations.
2. DBUs are focused on delivering specific digital services such as opening bank accounts, loan applications and fund transfers.
3. DBUs can offer all services that traditional banks provide, including cash withdrawal and deposits.

How many of the given statements is/are correct?
(a) Only one (b) Only two
(c) All three (d) None

**72.** Which of the following services are typically available at Digital Banking Units (DBUs)?
1. Cash withdrawal through ATMs
2. Cash deposit through BNA machines
3. In-person banking assistance from tellers
4. Online loan application processing

Select the correct answer from the codes given below:
(a) 1, 2 and 4 only
(b) 1, 3 and 4 only
(c) 2 and 3 only
(d) 1, 2, 3 and 4

**73.** Which of the following best describes Core Banking Solution (CBS)?
(a) A centralised banking system where customers can access their bank accounts and conduct transactions only at their home branch.
(b) A banking solution that allows customers to access their bank accounts and perform transactions from any branch of the bank.
(c) A system designed exclusively for interbank transactions that allows financial institutions to settle cross-border payments.
(d) A platform that provides only internet banking services to retail customers for day-to-day transactions.

**74.** Which of the following best describes a White Label ATM (WLA)?
(a) An ATM operated by a non-banking entity that allows customers of multiple banks to withdraw money and perform other banking services.
(b) An ATM exclusively set up by the government to provide financial services to rural areas.
(c) An ATM installed by a bank that only serves its own customers for cash withdrawals and balance inquiries.
(d) An ATM that allows customers to exchange foreign currencies and make international transactions.

# OMR SHEET

**Assessment Round**

| | | | | | | | | | | | | | | | | | | | |
|---|---|---|---|---|---|---|---|---|---|---|---|---|---|---|---|---|---|---|---|
| 1 | a | b | c | d | 31 | a | b | c | d | 61 | a | b | c | d | 91 | a | b | c | d |
| 2 | a | b | c | d | 32 | a | b | c | d | 62 | a | b | c | d | 92 | a | b | c | d |
| 3 | a | b | c | d | 33 | a | b | c | d | 63 | a | b | c | d | 93 | a | b | c | d |
| 4 | a | b | c | d | 34 | a | b | c | d | 64 | a | b | c | d | 94 | a | b | c | d |
| 5 | a | b | c | d | 35 | a | b | c | d | 65 | a | b | c | d | 95 | a | b | c | d |
| 6 | a | b | c | d | 36 | a | b | c | d | 66 | a | b | c | d | 96 | a | b | c | d |
| 7 | a | b | c | d | 37 | a | b | c | d | 67 | a | b | c | d | 97 | a | b | c | d |
| 8 | a | b | c | d | 38 | a | b | c | d | 68 | a | b | c | d | 98 | a | b | c | d |
| 9 | a | b | c | d | 39 | a | b | c | d | 69 | a | b | c | d | 99 | a | b | c | d |
| 10 | a | b | c | d | 40 | a | b | c | d | 70 | a | b | c | d | 100 | a | b | c | d |
| 11 | a | b | c | d | 41 | a | b | c | d | 71 | a | b | c | d | 101 | a | b | c | d |
| 12 | a | b | c | d | 42 | a | b | c | d | 72 | a | b | c | d | 102 | a | b | c | d |
| 13 | a | b | c | d | 43 | a | b | c | d | 73 | a | b | c | d | 103 | a | b | c | d |
| 14 | a | b | c | d | 44 | a | b | c | d | 74 | a | b | c | d | 104 | a | b | c | d |
| 15 | a | b | c | d | 45 | a | b | c | d | 75 | a | b | c | d | 105 | a | b | c | d |
| 16 | a | b | c | d | 46 | a | b | c | d | 76 | a | b | c | d | 106 | a | b | c | d |
| 17 | a | b | c | d | 47 | a | b | c | d | 77 | a | b | c | d | 107 | a | b | c | d |
| 18 | a | b | c | d | 48 | a | b | c | d | 78 | a | b | c | d | 108 | a | b | c | d |
| 19 | a | b | c | d | 49 | a | b | c | d | 79 | a | b | c | d | 109 | a | b | c | d |
| 20 | a | b | c | d | 50 | a | b | c | d | 80 | a | b | c | d | 110 | a | b | c | d |
| 21 | a | b | c | d | 51 | a | b | c | d | 81 | a | b | c | d | 111 | a | b | c | d |
| 22 | a | b | c | d | 52 | a | b | c | d | 82 | a | b | c | d | 112 | a | b | c | d |
| 23 | a | b | c | d | 53 | a | b | c | d | 83 | a | b | c | d | 113 | a | b | c | d |
| 24 | a | b | c | d | 54 | a | b | c | d | 84 | a | b | c | d | 114 | a | b | c | d |
| 25 | a | b | c | d | 55 | a | b | c | d | 85 | a | b | c | d | 115 | a | b | c | d |
| 26 | a | b | c | d | 56 | a | b | c | d | 86 | a | b | c | d | 116 | a | b | c | d |
| 27 | a | b | c | d | 57 | a | b | c | d | 87 | a | b | c | d | 117 | a | b | c | d |
| 28 | a | b | c | d | 58 | a | b | c | d | 88 | a | b | c | d | 118 | a | b | c | d |
| 29 | a | b | c | d | 59 | a | b | c | d | 89 | a | b | c | d | 119 | a | b | c | d |
| 30 | a | b | c | d | 60 | a | b | c | d | 90 | a | b | c | d | 120 | a | b | c | d |

## Calculate Your Score

| | |
|---|---|
| **Correct (✓)** | |
| **Incorrect (✓)** | |
| **Unattempted** | |
| **Total Score** | |
| **Accuracy (%)** | |

## Reasons for Incorrect Answers?

| | |
|---|---|
| 1. Lack of Knowledge/Existing Source Insufficient | |
| 2. Lack of Multiple Revision | |
| 3. Common Sense Mistakes | |

**Note :**

1. Calculate total score as correct answers carry 2 marks each 1/3rd marks will deducted for **Incorrect** Answers.
2. Calculate Accuracy (%) by dividing the number of correct answers to the total number of attempted questions.

## Past Learning

1. Consider the following statements: **(2024)**

**Statement I :** Syndicated lending spreads the risk of borrower default across multiple lenders.

**Statement II :** The syndicated loan can be fixed amount/lump sum of funds, but cannot be a credit line.

Which one of the following is correct in respect of the above statements?

(a) Both Statement I and Statement II are correct, and Statement II explains Statement I.

(b) Both Statement I and Statement II are correct, but Statement II does not explains Statement I.

(c) Statement I is correct, but Statement II incorrect.

(d) Statement I is incorrect, but Statement II is correct.

2. With reference to the rule/rules imposed by the Reserve Bank of India while treating foreign banks, consider the following statements: **(2024)**

1. There is no minimum capital requirement for wholly owned banking subsidiaries in India.
2. For wholly owned banking subsidiaries in India, at least 50% of the board members should be Indian nationals.

Which of the statements given above is/are correct?

(a) 1 only (b) 2 only

(c) Both 1 and 2 (d) Neither 1 nor 2

3. With reference to the 'Banks Board Bureau (BBB)', which of the following statements are correct? **(2022)**

1. The Governor of RBI is the Chairman of BBB.
2. BBB recommends for the selection of heads for Public Sector Banks.
3. BBB helps the Public Sector Banks in developing strategies and capital raising plans.

Select the correct answer from the codes given below:

(a) 1 and 2 only

(b) 2 and 3 only

(c) 1 and 3 only

(d) 1, 2 and 3

4. With reference to 'Urban Cooperative Banks' in India, consider the following statements: **(2021)**

1. They are supervised and regulated by local boards set up by the State Governments.
2. They can issue equity shares and preference shares.
3. They were brought under the purview of the Banking Regulation act, 1949 through an amendment in 1966.

Which of the statements given above is/are correct?

(a) 1 only

(b) 2 and 3 only

(c) 1 and 3 only

(d) 1,2 and 3

5. The Chairman of public sector banks are selected by the: **(2019)**

(a) Banks Board Bureau

(b) Reserve Bank of India

(c) Union Ministry of Finance

(d) Management of concerned bank

6. The Service Area Approach was implemented under the purview of: **(2019)**

(a) Integrated Rural Development Programme

(b) Lead Bank Scheme

(c) Mahatma Gandhi National Rural Employment Guarantee Scheme

(d) National Skill Development Mission

7. Which of the following is not included in the assets of a commercial bank in India? **(2019)**

(a) Advances

(b) Deposits

(c) Investments

(d) Money at call and short notice

**8.** What was the purpose of the Inter Creditor Agreement signed by Indian banks and financial institutions recently? **(2019)**

(a) To lessen the Government of India's perennial burden of fiscal deficit and current account deficit.
(b) To support the infrastructure projects of Central and State Governments.
(c) To act as independent regulator in case of applications for loans of ₹ 50 crore or more.
(d) To aim at faster resolution of stressed assets of ₹ 50 crore or more which are-under consortium lending.

**9.** Consider the following statements: **(2018)**

1. Capital Adequacy Ratio (CAR) is the amount that banks have to maintain in the form of their own funds to offset any loss that banks incur if the account-holders fail to repay dues.
2. CAR is decided by each individual bank.

Which of the statements given above is/are correct?

(a) 1 only
(b) 2 only
(c) Both 1 and 2
(d) Neither 1 nor 2

**10.** Which one of the following links all the ATMs in India? **(2018)**

(a) Indian Banks' Association
(b) National Securities Depository Limited
(c) National Payments Corporation of India
(d) Reserve Bank of India

**11.** What is the purpose of setting up Small Finance Banks (SFBs) in India? **(2017)**

1. To supply credit to small business units.
2. To supply credit to small and marginal farmers.
3. To encourage young entrepreneurs to set up business particularly in rural areas.

Select the correct answer using the codes given below:

(a) 1 and 2 only
(b) 2 and 3 only
(c) 1 and 3 only
(d) 1, 2 and 3

**12.** The term 'Core Banking Solutions' is sometimes seen in the news. Which of the following statements best describes/ describe this term? **(2016)**

1. It is a networking of a bank's branches which enables customers to operate their accounts from any branch of the bank on its network regardless of where they open their accounts.
2. It is an effort to increase RBI's control over commercial banks through computerisation.
3. It is a detailed procedure by which a bank with huge non-performing assets is taken over by another bank.

Select the correct answer using the codes given below:

(a) 1 only (b) 2 and 3 only
(c) 1 and 3 only (d) 1, 2 and 3

**13.** What is/are the purpose/purposes of the 'Marginal Cost of Funds based Lending Rate (MCLR)' announced by RBI? **(2016)**

1. These guidelines help improve the transparency in the methodology followed by banks for determining the interest rates on advances.
2. These guidelines help ensure availability of bank credit at interest rates which are fair to the borrowers as well as the banks.

Select the correct answer using the codes given below:

(a) 1 only (b) 2 only
(c) Both 1 and 2 (d) Neither 1 nor 2

**14.** The establishment of 'Payment Banks' is being allowed in India to promote financial inclusion. Which of the following statements is/are correct in this context? **(2016)**

1. Mobile telephone companies and supermarket chains that are owned and controlled by residents are eligible to be promoters of Payment Banks.
2. Payment Banks can issue both credit cards and debit cards.
3. Payment Banks cannot undertake lending activities.

Select the correct answer using the codes given below:

(a) 1 and 2 only (b) 1 and 3 only
(c) 2 only (d) 1, 2 and 3

**15.** 'Basel III Accord' or simply 'Basel III', often seen in the news, seeks to: **(2015)**

(a) develop national strategies for the conservation and sustainable use of biological diversity.
(b) improve banking sector's ability to deal with financial and economic stress and improve risk management.
(c) reduce the greenhouse gas emissions but places a heavier burden on developed countries.
(d) transfer technology from developed countries to poor countries to enable them to replace the use of chlorofluorocarbons in refrigeration with harmless chemicals.

**16.** What is/are the facility/facilities the beneficiaries can get from the services of Business Correspondent (Bank Saathi) in branchless areas? **(2014)**

1. It enables the beneficiaries to draw their subsidies and social security benefits in their villages.
2. It enables the beneficiaries in the rural areas to make deposits and withdrawals.

Select the correct answer using the codes given below:

(a) 1 only
(b) 2 only
(c) Both 1 and 2
(d) Neither 1 nor 2

**17.** Priority Sector Lending by banks in India constitutes the lending to: **(2013)**

(a) Agriculture
(b) Micro and small enterprises
(c) Weaker sections
(d) All of the above

# Detailed Solutions

## Assessment Round

**1.** *(b)* Only two

- **Statement 1 is correct: Scheduled banks** are indeed those that are included in the **Second Schedule of the Reserve Bank of India (RBI) Act, 1934.** They meet certain criteria laid down by the RBI.
- **Statement 2 is correct:** Non-scheduled banks in India are **exempt from maintaining the CRR** with the RBI as they are not listed in the Second Schedule of the RBI Act, 1934 and therefore not subject to the same regulations regarding CRR maintenance as scheduled banks are. **These banks can have CRR fund with themselves as no compulsion has been made by the RBI to deposit it in the RBI.**
- **Statement 3 is incorrect:** While both scheduled and non-scheduled banks can theoretically borrow from the RBI, scheduled banks have easier access to various RBI facilities, including borrowing for liquidity needs under the Liquidity Adjustment Facility (LAF). Non-scheduled banks can only borrow in emergency situations due to their limited access to the central bank's facilities.

**Therefore, the correct answer is (b) Only two.**

**2.** *(a)* 1, 2 and 4 only

- **Statement 1 is correct:** Scheduled banks have access to refinance facilities from the Reserve Bank of India (RBI), allowing them to obtain funds for lending and other financial activities, enhancing their liquidity position.
- **Statement 2 is correct:** Being regulated under the RBI Act and included in the Second Schedule gives scheduled banks a higher level of public trust and confidence, as they are perceived to be more stable and reliable.
- **Statement 3 is incorrect:** Scheduled banks are **not exempt from reporting compliance and financial statements to the RBI.** In fact, they are required to regularly report their financial health and comply with various regulations set by the RBI to ensure transparency and sound banking practices.
- **Statement 4 is correct:** Scheduled banks are eligible to participate in the government's borrowing programme through Open Market Operations, allowing them to buy and sell government securities, which aids in liquidity management and investment.

**Therefore, the correct answer is (a) 1, 2 and 4 only.**

**3.** *(c)* Only three

- **Option 1 is correct: Foreign Banks operating in India** are classified as **Scheduled Commercial Banks (SCBs).** They are included in the RBI's schedule and operate under the same regulatory framework as domestic SCBs, provided they meet specific criteria.
- **Option 2 is correct: Payment Banks** are a type of **Scheduled Commercial Bank.** They are licensed to accept deposits and provide certain financial services, but they cannot provide loans or issue credit cards. Examples include **Airtel Payments Bank** and **Paytm Payments Bank.**
- **Option 3 is correct: Small Finance Banks** are also classified as **Scheduled Commercial Banks.** They are primarily focused on providing financial inclusion by offering loans and accepting deposits from underserved sections of the society. Examples include **Ujjivan Small Finance Bank.**
- **Option 4 is incorrect: Non-Banking Financial Companies (NBFCs)** are **not classified as SCBs.** Although they provide financial services similar to banks, such as loans and asset financing, they do not hold a banking license and are not included in the RBI's schedule of SCBs.

**Thus, the correct answer is (c) Only three.**

**4.** *(d)* 1, 2 and 3

- **Statement 1 is correct:** Commercial banks are owned by shareholders who invest capital in the bank, while cooperative banks are owned by their members, who are also the customers of the bank.

- **Statement 2 is correct**: The main motive of commercial banks is to earn profits for their shareholders, whereas cooperative banks aim to serve the financial needs of their members, often at lower costs.
- **Statement 3 is correct**: Commercial banks are regulated solely by the Reserve Bank of India (RBI). Cooperative banks, however, are regulated by both the RBI and the respective State Governments in which they operate.

**Thus, the correct answer is (d) 1, 2 and 3.**

**5.** *(c)* Both 1 and 2

- **Statement 1 is correct**: Commercial banks typically have a **centralised management structure** where decisions are made by a Board of Directors or senior management. In contrast, cooperative banks have a **democratic structure where each member has one vote**, regardless of their shareholding, ensuring equal participation in decision-making.
- **Statement 2 is correct**: Both types of banks are regulated under the Banking Regulation Act, 1949, while cooperative banks are also subject to state cooperative laws and additional oversight from the respective State Governments.

**Thus, the correct answer is (c) Both 1 and 2.**

**6.** *(b)* Only two

- **Option 1 is correct**: The **Banking Regulation Act, 1949** plays a crucial role in regulating cooperative banks in India. It governs the banking operations of cooperative banks, especially after the amendments that brought these banks under stricter oversight by the **Reserve Bank of India (RBI)**.
- **Option 2 is correct**: The **Multi-State Cooperative Societies Act, 2002** applies to cooperative banks that operate in more than one state. This law governs their formation, management and functioning, making it essential for **multi-state cooperative banks**.
- **Option 3 is incorrect**: The **Companies Act, 2013** governs the corporate sector and **does not directly regulate cooperative banks.** Cooperative banks are formed under specific cooperative laws, not the Companies Act.
- **Option 4 is incorrect**: While the **Reserve Bank of India Act, 1934** governs the overall functioning of the **Reserve Bank of India**, it does not directly regulate cooperative banks. The regulation of cooperative banks is primarily through the **Banking Regulation Act, 1949**, though RBI plays a supervisory role.

**Thus, the correct answer is (b) Only two.**

**7.** *(a)* 1 and 2 only

- **Statement 1 is correct**: Primary Agricultural Credit Societies (PACS) are indeed at the grassroots level of the cooperative credit structure. They operate at the village level and provide short-term credit to farmers for agriculture and related activities.
- **Statement 2 is correct**: District Central Cooperative Banks (DCCBs) serve as intermediaries between PACS and State Cooperative Banks (SCBs). They provide financial support to PACS and help link them to SCBs for broader financial resources.
- **Statement 3 is incorrect**: State Cooperative Banks (SCBs) **do not directly provide credit** to individual farmers. They primarily provide financial support to DCCBs and act as the apex body in the cooperative credit structure, handling state-level finances and policy matters.

**Thus, the correct answer is (a) 1 and 2 only.**

**8.** *(d)* All four

- **Statement 1 is correct**: One of the primary functions of Regional Rural Banks (RRBs) is to provide credit to small and marginal farmers. This helps support agricultural activities in rural areas, which is a key focus of RRBs.
- **Statement 2 is correct**: RRBs issue credit cards, including Kisan Credit Cards (KCC), to farmers for agricultural and related expenses. This facility is aimed at providing farmers with easy and timely credit.

- **Statement 3 is correct:** RRBs also extend credit to small businesses, artisans and rural entrepreneurs, supporting rural development and promoting livelihood opportunities in rural areas.
- **Statement 4 is correct:** RRBs are often used as a conduit for implementing various government-sponsored schemes such as PM Kisan, MGNREGA and others aimed at rural development.

**All four functions listed are correct for Regional Rural Banks (RRBs) in India. Therefore, the correct answer is (d) All four.**

**9.** *(d)* 1, 2 and 3

- **Statement 1 is correct:** RRBs are jointly owned by the Government of India (50%), the concerned State Government (15%) and a sponsoring bank (35%) which can be public or private sector bank.
- **Statement 2 is correct:** RRBs are regulated by both the **Reserve Bank of India (RBI)** and the **National Bank for Agriculture and Rural Development (NABARD)**. While RBI acts as the primary regulatory authority, NABARD supervises the functioning of RRBs to ensure they meet their objectives.
- **Statement 3 is correct:** RRBs are empowered to provide both **short-term credit** for seasonal agricultural operations and **long-term credit** for agricultural development and rural artisans to support a range of rural economic activities.

**Thus, the correct answer is (d) 1, 2 and 3.**

**10.** *(b)* 1 and 3 only

- **Statement 1 is correct:** RRBs are required to allocate **75% of their total credit** towards Priority Sector Lending (PSL), which includes sectors such as agriculture, micro-enterprises, education, housing and other priority sectors that are crucial for rural development.
- **Statement 2 is incorrect:** While many RRBs are sponsored by public sector banks, it is **not mandatory** for the sponsor bank to always be a public sector bank.
- **All the Public Sector Banks except Punjab and Sind Bank sponsored one or more RRBs.**
- **Jammu and Kashmir Bank is the only private-sector bank to sponsor an RRB.**
- **Statement 3 is correct:** Although RRBs primarily operate in rural areas, they are allowed to have branches in **urban and semi-urban areas** to support rural-to-urban migration and cater to customers with rural linkages.
- Around 92 per cent of the RRB branches are located in rural and semi-urban areas.

**Therefore, statements 1 and 3 are correct, so the answer is (b) 1 and 3 only.**

**11.** *(b)* Only two

- **Statement 1 is incorrect: Local Area Banks (LABs)** are permitted to operate in a limited area comprising two-three contiguous districts, allowing them to focus on regional banking needs.
- **Statement 2 is correct:** LABs are **registered as public limited companies** under the Companies Act, 2013, which provides the framework for their incorporation and operation as corporate entities.
- **Statement 3 is correct:** LABs are regulated by the Reserve Bank of India (RBI) and must adhere to the guidelines set forth by the RBI. Additionally, as public limited companies, they are also governed by the Ministry of Corporate Affairs under the Companies Act, 2013.

**Therefore, the correct answer is (b) Only two.**

**12.** *(c)* All three

- **Statement 1 is correct:** Small Finance Banks (SFBs) can provide loans and accept deposits from the public. They are established to serve underserved sections of society, including small businesses and low-income households.
- **Statement 2 is correct:** Both SFBs and Payment Banks must comply with the Cash Reserve Ratio (CRR) and Statutory Liquidity Ratio (SLR) requirements as set by the RBI to ensure liquidity and financial stability.
- **Statement 3 is correct:** Both Small Finance Banks (SFBs) and Payment Banks are regulated by the Reserve Bank of India (RBI).

**Therefore, the correct answer is (c) All three.**

**13.** *(b)* 1 and 3 only

- **Statement 1 is correct**: Payment Banks can accept demand deposits up to ₹ 200,000 per customer, but they are not permitted to accept time deposits.
- **Statement 2 is incorrect**: Payment Banks are **not permitted to provide loans or credit facilities**. They focus on providing transactional and deposit services. They are not allowed to issue credit cards.
- **Statement 3 is correct**: Payment Banks are allowed to offer internet banking and mobile banking services to facilitate easy access to banking services for their customers.

**Thus, the correct answer is (b) 1 and 3 only.**

**14.** *(d)* 1, 2 and 3

- **Statement 1 is correct**: Small Finance Banks (SFBs) must allocate **75% of their Adjusted Net Bank Credit (ANBC)** towards **Priority Sector Lending (PSL)**, which is a key requirement for these banks to ensure financial inclusion.
- **Statement 2 is correct**: SFBs are required to ensure that at least **50% of their loan portfolio** consists of loans and advances of up to **₹ 25 lakh**. This helps them focus on small borrowers and micro-enterprises.
- **Statement 3 is correct**: In a notification dated 8th August, 2022, the **Reserve Bank of India (RBI)expanded the scope of operations for a small finance bank by permitting them to operate as an Authorised Dealer Category I in foreign exchange (forex) business.** The RBI has also prescribed eligibility criteria for the same. This step will offer more flexibility to such small finance banks to cater to their customers' forex business requirements.
  - **Ujjivan Small Finance Bank** in 2024 received approval from **RBI** and secured an **AD 1 Licence** from RBI to offer full-fledged bouquet of forex products and services.
  - With this license, Ujjivan SFB can offer a full range of **forex transactions** - buying, selling and borrowing foreign currencies—for customers in India and abroad.
  - In **retail banking**, services will include **remittances, FCNR/RFC deposits, Forex cards, currency exchange**, and capital transactions like **ECB, ODI and FDI.**

**Thus, the correct answer is (d) 1, 2 and 3.**

**15.** *(c)* Only three

- **Option 1 is correct: Agricultural labourers are among the primary target groups for SFBs,** which focus on providing financial services to underserved rural and low-income populations.
- **Option 2 is correct**: SFBs are **designed to serve small and micro-businesses**. They provide loans to small business units, which is a key part of their mandate to promote financial inclusion.
- **Option 3 is correct**. SFBs are allowed to **cater to urban low-income groups**, providing them with access to banking services, including loans and credit facilities, which are often difficult for these groups to obtain from traditional commercial banks.
- **Option 4 is incorrect**: SFBs are not designed to serve large infrastructure companies; they focus on small borrowers and micro-enterprises.

**Three of the above types are eligible borrowers for SFBs, so the correct answer is (c) Only three.**

**16.** *(a)* 1 and 2 only

- **Statement 1 is correct**: Neo banks **operate entirely online without any physical branch network**, offering all their services through digital platforms such as mobile apps and websites.
- **Statement 2 is correct**: In India, neo banks do not hold independent banking licenses and are required to **partner with traditional banks** to offer banking services, as they cannot operate independently under current regulations.
- **Statement 3 is incorrect**: Neo banks do not have a **direct banking license** from the RBI. Instead, they rely on their partnerships with traditional banks, which are regulated by the RBI. Neo banks themselves are not directly regulated by the RBI as independent banks.

**Hence, statements 1 and 2 are correct, so the answer is (a) 1 and 2 only.**

**17.** *(b)* 1 only

- **Statement 1 is correct:** All Scheduled Commercial Banks in India are required **to allocate 40%** of their Adjusted Net Bank Credit (ANBC) or Credit Equivalent Amount of Off-Balance Sheet Exposure (whichever is higher) to priority sectors.
- **Statement 2 is incorrect:** Regional Rural Banks (RRBs) have different PSL targets compared to scheduled commercial banks. **RRBs are required to allocate 75% of their ANBC or Credit Equivalent Amount of Off-Balance Sheet Exposure (whichever is higher) to priority sectors.**
- **Statement 3 is incorrect:** Urban Cooperative Banks (UCBs) are **not exempted** from meeting priority sector lending targets. UCBs are also required to adhere to specific PSL targets as prescribed by the RBI which currently stands at 75%.

**Therefore, the correct answer is (b) 1 only.**

**18.** *(d)* All four

**Priority Sectors under PSL** are Agriculture, MSMEs, Export Credit, Education, Housing, Social Infrastructure, Renewable Energy, Weaker Sections.

- **Option 1 is correct:** Agriculture is a significant category under Priority Sector Lending (PSL) in India, with a focus on providing credit to farmers for crop production, equipment purchase and other agriculture-related activities.
- **Option 2 is correct:** Renewable energy projects are included under PSL to encourage investments in sustainable and eco-friendly energy solutions.
- **Option 3 is correct:** Export credit is eligible for PSL to promote exports and enhance foreign exchange earnings for the country.
- **Option 4 is correct:** MSMEs are a crucial category under PSL to promote entrepreneurship and economic development at the grassroots level.

**Therefore, the correct answer is (d) All four.**

**19.** *(d)* 1, 3 and 4 only

The banks that have the same PSL target of 75% are Regional Rural Banks (RRBs), Small Finance Banks (SFBs) and Urban Cooperative Banks (UCBs).

**Foreign Banks** are also required to meet a **PSL target of 40%** of ANBC or Credit Equivalent Amount of Off-Balance Sheet Exposure (whichever is higher).

**Therefore, the correct answer is (d) 1, 3 and 4 only.**

**20.** *(d)* 1, 2 and 3

**Priority Sector Lending Certificates** (PSLCs) are **financial instruments** introduced by the Reserve Bank of India (RBI) to help banks meet their Priority Sector Lending (PSL) targets. It allows banks to sell excess credits to banks that are falling short, providing flexibility and efficiency in achieving PSL requirements.

- **Statement 1 is correct:** Banks that have surplus lending in the priority sector can sell PSLCs to banks that are deficient, enabling the latter to meet their PSL requirements.
- **Statement 2 is correct:** PSLCs are **generally valid for one financial year** and must be used within that period. They cannot be carried forward to meet PSL requirements for the next financial year.
- **Statement 3 is correct:** The price of PSLCs is determined by market forces based on the demand and supply for these certificates, which reflects the PSL shortfalls or surpluses among banks.

**Therefore, the correct answer is (d) 1, 2 and 3.**

**21.** *(c)* Both 1 and 2

- **Statement 1 is correct: E-Kuber** is the **core banking solution platform** of the Reserve Bank of India (RBI) and it facilitates the issuance and trading of **Priority Sector Lending Certificates** (PSLCs) among banks.
- **Statement 2 is correct:** PSLCs involve only the sale of the certificate and do not transfer the underlying loan assets or associated risks. The bank selling the PSLC retains the loan on its balance sheet, while the purchasing bank uses the certificate to meet its Priority Sector Lending (PSL) targets.

**Therefore, the correct answer is (c) Both 1 and 2.**

**22.** *(a)* Both Statement I and Statement II are correct and Statement II is the correct explanation for Statement I.

**The External Benchmark Lending Rate (EBLR)** is the interest rate that banks use to determine the interest rates for loans. The Reserve Bank of India (RBI) requires all banks to link their loans to an external benchmark, such as the repo rate, to better transmit policy rate changes.

- **Statement I is correct:** The Reserve Bank of India (RBI) mandated that all new floating rate loans to retail and MSME borrowers be linked to an external benchmark, such as the RBI's repo rate, the 3-month or 6-month Treasury Bill rate, or any other benchmark market interest rate published by the Financial Benchmarks India Pvt. Ltd (FBIL), starting from 1st October, 2019.
- **Statement II is correct:** The adoption of the EBLR aims to improve transparency in loan pricing and ensure that changes in the RBI's policy rates are quickly reflected in the lending rates charged to borrowers.

**Thus, option (a) is the correct answer.**

**23.** *(b)* Only two

- **Option 1 is incorrect:** The repo rate is an **external benchmark**, set by the Reserve Bank of India (RBI), and is not part of the Internal Benchmark Lending Rate Regime.
- **Option 2 is correct:** The Base Rate is an internal benchmark rate that was used by banks to determine the minimum interest rate for lending, which is part of the Internal Benchmark Lending Rate Regime.
- **Option 3 is correct: Marginal Cost of Funds-Based Lending Rate** (MCLR) is a more recent internal benchmark rate used by banks to determine interest rates for loans. It is part of the Internal Benchmark Lending Rate Regime.

**Thus, two of the above rates are associated with the Internal Benchmark Lending Rate Regime, so the answer is (b) Only two.**

**24.** *(c)* To enhance the ability of banks to absorb shocks arising from financial and economic stress.

The primary goal of Basel III is to improve the regulation, supervision, and risk management within the banking sector. By increasing capital requirements and introducing new regulatory standards such as the leverage ratio and liquidity coverage ratio, **Basel III aims to strengthen banks' ability to withstand financial stress and avoid the kind of systemic crises that occurred during the global financial crisis of 2008.**

**Thus, option (c) is the correct answer.**

**25.** *(a)* Only one

- **Statement 1 is incorrect:** The Basel Committee on Banking Supervision (BCBS) was established in 1974 by the central bank Governors of the G10 countries in response to disturbances in the international financial markets, not specifically the 2008 financial crisis.
  - Basel III norms were introduced after the 2008 crisis, but the BCBS itself predates that.
- **Statement 2 is correct:** The BCBS sets **minimum standards for various aspects of banking regulation,** including capital adequacy, stress testing and market liquidity risk, to strengthen the regulation, supervision, and practices of banks worldwide.
- **Statement 3 is incorrect:** The BCBS does not have the authority to impose fines or enforce compliance. It is an **advisory body** that sets standards, with enforcement left to national regulators.

**Thus, the correct answer is (a) Only one.**

**26.** *(c)* Both 1 and 2

**Statement 1 is correct:** The BCBS, in collaboration with the **Financial Stability Board (FSB),** identifies Globally Systemically Important Banks (G-SIBs) and suggests additional capital requirements to enhance their resilience against potential financial shocks.

**Statement 2 is correct:** The BCBS is **headquartered** at the **Bank for International Settlements (BIS) in Basel, Switzerland,** which serves as a forum for central banks and provides a space for cooperation on international financial and banking matters.

**Therefore, the correct answer is (c) Both 1 and 2.**

**27.** *(b)* 1 and 3 only

- **Statement 1 is correct:** The **Capital Adequacy Ratio (CAR)**, also known as the Capital to Risk-Weighted Assets Ratio (CRAR), is a measure used to evaluate a bank's financial strength by **assessing its capital reserves relative to its risk-weighted assets.** It ensures that banks have sufficient capital to absorb potential losses and remain solvent during periods of financial stress.
- **Statement 2 is incorrect:** CAR requirements are set by **regulatory authorities,** such as the **Reserve Bank of India (RBI) in India and not by individual banks.** Banks are required to meet these regulatory standards.
- **Statement 3 is correct:** Higher CAR requirements, known as additional capital surcharges, are imposed on banks that are identified as Globally Systemically Important Banks (G-SIBs) to mitigate the risks they pose to the global financial system.

**Thus, the correct answer is (b) 1 and 3 only.**

**28.** *(b)* To ensure the bank can absorb a reasonable amount of loss and protect depositors.

A high Capital Adequacy Ratio (CAR) is maintained to ensure that a bank can absorb a reasonable amount of loss arising from operational and financial risks. It protects depositors and promotes the overall stability of the banking system by ensuring that banks have sufficient capital to cover unexpected losses.

**Thus, option (b) is the correct answer.**

**29.** *(d)* All four

- **Option 1 is correct:** CBs are required to maintain a minimum **Capital Adequacy Ratio (CAR)** as per the **Basel III** norms and **RBI regulations.** In India, the minimum CAR for SCBs is 9%.
- **Option 2 is correct:** SFBs, like other banks, are required to adhere to CAR norms to ensure they have sufficient capital to absorb financial risks. **Minimum CAR = 15%.**
- **Option 3 is correct:** Urban Cooperative Banks (UCBs) are required to adhere to specific CAR norms prescribed by the RBI to maintain financial stability. **Minimum CAR = 12%.**
- **Option 4 is correct:** NBFCs have their own capital adequacy requirements set by the RBI, though they differ from those of commercial banks. **Minimum CAR = 15%.**

**Therefore, the correct answer is (d) All four.**

**30.** *(c)* All three

- **Statement 1 is correct:** AT-1 Bonds are a type of capital instrument that banks can issue to meet their capital requirements under Basel III norms. They are **part of the additional tier-1 capital,** which helps banks absorb losses while remaining a going concern.
- **Statement 2 is correct:** AT-1 Bonds **do not have a fixed maturity date.** They are **perpetual in nature,** meaning they do not have a set end date and can theoretically exist indefinitely. This characteristic makes them different from traditional bonds with defined maturity dates.
- **Statement 3 is correct: AT-1 Bonds offer higher yields compared to traditional bonds** due to their higher risk profile. This is because they have loss-absorbing features, such as being written down or converted into equity if the issuing bank's capital ratio falls below a certain threshold.

**Therefore, the correct answer is (c) All three.**

**31.** *(c)* **Liquidity Coverage Ratio (LCR)**

The Liquidity Coverage Ratio (LCR) was introduced by Basel III to help banks manage **short-term liquidity risks.** It requires banks to hold enough **high-quality liquid assets (HQLA)** to cover their **net cash outflows** over a **30-day stress period.** This ensures that banks have the liquidity to survive short-term financial stress.

**Thus, option (c) is the correct answer.**

**32.** *(a)* The **Net Stable Funding Ratio (NSFR)** is designed to promote the stability of a bank's funding structure by requiring it to maintain a stable funding profile in relation to the composition of its assets and off-balance-sheet activities. This ratio aims to reduce the likelihood that disruptions to a bank's regular sources of funding will erode its liquidity position, increasing overall banking sector resilience over a longer time horizon, specifically one year.

**Thus, option (a) is the correct answer.**

**33.** *(b)* The **Capital Conservation Buffer (CCB)** is a regulatory requirement introduced under the Basel III norms to ensure that **banks build up extra capital during periods of stability,** which can be drawn upon in times of financial stress. The Capital Conservation Buffer (CCB) is an **additional layer of common equity Tier 1 capital.**

**Thus, option (b) is the correct answer.**

**34.** *(c)* The **Counter-cyclical Capital Buffer (CCyB)** is designed to counteract the natural pro-cyclicality of the banking sector, where **lending tends to increase during economic booms and decrease during downturns.** The CCyB requires banks to accumulate additional capital when credit growth is deemed excessive, which helps to absorb potential losses if economic conditions deteriorate. This buffer can then be released during economic downturns, allowing banks to continue lending and supporting the economy without breaching capital requirements.

**Thus, option (c) is the correct answer.**

**35.** *(b)* The primary purpose of the Leverage Ratio under Basel III is to **limit the amount of debt a bank can take on relative to its equity.** By doing so, it prevents banks from becoming excessively leveraged, which can increase the risk of insolvency during periods of financial stress.

Unlike risk-weighted capital requirements, the Leverage Ratio is a simple, **non-risk-based measure that serves as a backstop to risk-weighted capital requirements.**

Basel III requires banks to maintain a minimum Tier 1 Leverage Ratio of 3%. This ratio ensures that a bank's core capital is sufficiently high relative to its overall exposure, including both on-balance-sheet and off-balance-sheet items.

**Thus, option (b) is the correct answer.**

**36.** *(b)* Only two

- **Statement 1 is correct:** An asset is classified as a Non-Performing Asset (NPA) when the interest or principal payment remains overdue for more than 90 days. This classification is used to identify loans that are not performing as expected. **Stages of Non-Performing Assets (NPAs):**
  – **Standard Assets:** Performing loans with timely payments.
  – **Sub-Standard Assets:** Overdue for more than 90 days but less than 12 months.
  – **Doubtful Assets:** Sub-standard for more than 12 months, high recovery risk.
  – **Loss Assets:** Uncollectible loans, considered a total loss.

  These stages reflect increasing risk as loans become overdue.
- **Statement 2 is incorrect:** NPAs significantly impact a bank's profitability and capital adequacy. When an asset becomes non-performing, the bank is unable to earn interest on the loan, reducing profitability. Additionally, **NPAs require higher provisioning,** which affects the bank's capital adequacy.
- **Statement 3 is correct:** The Reserve Bank of India (RBI) mandates provisioning for NPAs to ensure that banks have sufficient capital to cover potential losses arising from non-performing assets.

**Thus, the correct answer is (b) Only two.**

**37.** *(b)* **Special Mention Accounts (SMAs)** are used by banks to identify and monitor accounts that show early signs of stress or potential default. The primary purpose of this categorisation is to take preventive measures to address the issues and prevent these accounts from turning into Non-Performing Assets (NPAs).

**Thus, option (b) is the correct answer.**

**38.** *(b)* Only two

- **Statement 1 is correct: SMA-0** accounts are those where the principal or interest payment is overdue for 1 to 30 days. This classification helps banks identify early signs of financial stress.
- **Statement 2 is correct: SMA-2** accounts are those where the principal or interest payment is overdue for 61 to 90 days. This classification indicates a higher risk of the account becoming an NPA.

- **Statement 3 is incorrect:** An account is **not automatically classified as an NPA** immediately after being categorised as SMA-2. It is classified as an NPA if the overdue status exceeds 90 days.

**Thus, the correct answer is (b) Only two.**

***39.*** *(b)* 1 only

**The Provisioning Coverage Ratio (PCR)** is a financial metric used by banks to measure the proportion of bad loans (Non-Performing Assets or NPAs) that a bank has covered with provisions. It reflects the bank's ability to absorb potential losses due to loan defaults.

- **Statement 1 is correct:** The Provisioning Coverage Ratio (PCR) is indeed a measure of the funds that banks set aside to cover potential losses from their non-performing assets (NPAs). It represents the ratio of provisions to gross NPAs.
- **Statement 2 is incorrect:** A higher PCR indicates a bank's higher ability to absorb potential losses from NPAs, not a lower ability. It means the bank has more funds reserved to cover the bad loans.
- **Statement 3 is incorrect:** The PCR is not directly related to the interest rates offered by the bank on its deposits. The **PCR is related to the bank's asset quality and risk management practices**, while interest rates on deposits are influenced by market conditions, liquidity and monetary policy.

**Therefore, the correct answer is (b) 1 only.**

***40.*** *(d)* 1, 2 and 3

- **Statement 1 is correct: Writing off bad loans** helps increase the **Provisioning Coverage Ratio (PCR)**. When a bank writes off bad loans, it removes the non-performing assets (NPAs) from its books, reducing the burden of NPAs and improving the overall provisioning ratio. Although the loans are written off, the provisions made against them are retained, thus increasing the PCR.
- **Statement 2 is correct: Increasing provisions against doubtful and bad debts** directly increases the PCR, as it enhances the amount of funds set aside to cover potential losses from NPAs. The higher the provisions, the better the bank's capacity to absorb future losses, thereby improving the PCR.
- **Statement 3 is correct: Reducing the gross amount of NPAs** through recovery also boosts the PCR. When a bank recovers bad debts, it reduces its NPAs without necessarily reducing the provisions already made. This leads to a higher proportion of provisions compared to the outstanding NPAs, thereby increasing the PCR.

**Thus, the correct answer is (d) 1, 2 and 3.**

***41.*** *(b)* 1, 2 and 4 only

- **Option 1 is correct: The Asset Quality Review (AQR)** was initiated by the RBI in 2015 to identify and clean up the stressed assets (NPAs) in the banking system. It aimed at improving the quality of bank balance sheets by recognising NPAs more transparently.
- **Option 2 is correct: Corporate Debt Restructuring (CDR)** was a mechanism that aimed to provide restructuring solutions for distressed corporate borrowers to reduce NPAs.
- **Option 3 is incorrect: EBLR is a regulatory measure that determines the minimum interest rate below which banks are not permitted to lend**, but it is not specifically targeted at addressing NPAs.
- **Option 4 is correct: The Prompt Corrective Action (PCA)** framework is a supervisory tool used by the RBI to address the deteriorating financial health of banks, including those with high levels of NPAs. Under PCA, banks are subject to certain restrictions to restore financial stability.

**Thus, the correct answer is (b) 1, 2 and 4 only.**

***42.*** *(a)* 1 only

- **Statement 1 is correct: Debt Recovery Tribunals (DRTs)** were established under the **Recovery of Debts Due to Banks and Financial Institutions Act** (RDDBFI Act), 1993. Their primary purpose is to ensure the speedy recovery of debts owed to banks and financial institutions.
- **Statement 2 is incorrect:** DRTs do not handle cases involving small loans and microfinance. They only handle cases where the debt amount is ₹ 20 lakh (2 million) or more.

- **Statement 3 is incorrect:** DRTs are not empowered to initiate insolvency proceedings against defaulting borrowers. **Insolvency proceedings** are handled under the **Insolvency and Bankruptcy Code (IBC) by the National Company Law Tribunal (NCLT).**

**Therefore, the correct answer is (a) 1 only.**

**43.** *(a)* 1 and 2 only

- **Statement 1 is correct:** The SARFAESI Act allows banks and financial institutions to auction residential or commercial properties that have been pledged as collateral to recover loans in case of a default.
- **Statement 2 is correct:** The SARFAESI Act allows banks and financial institutions to seize and sell secured collateral, such as property or assets pledged as security for a loan, without the need for court intervention. This helps expedite the recovery process.
- **Statement 3 is incorrect:** The SARFAESI Act **does not apply to agricultural land.** Agricultural loans given against the security of agricultural land are exempt from the provisions of the Act.

**So, the correct answer is (a) 1 and 2 only.**

**44.** *(c)* All three

- **Statement 1 is correct:** Under the **SARFAESI Act, 2002,** banks must first issue a **demand notice** to the borrower, giving them 60 days to repay the loan before any further action is taken.
- **Statement 2 is correct:** If the borrower fails to repay the loan within the 60-days notice period, banks are authorised to **take possession of the secured asset** under the SARFAESI Act without requiring court intervention.
- **Statement 3 is correct:** The SARFAESI Act allows banks to **sell their loan assets to Asset Reconstruction Companies (ARCs)**, which specialise in recovering bad debts.

**Therefore, the correct answer is (c) All three.**

**45.** *(c)* All three

- **Statement 1 is correct: Asset Reconstruction Companies (ARCs)** purchase Non-Performing Assets (NPAs) from banks and financial institutions to manage and recover them. This helps banks clean up their balance sheets and focus on core banking activities.
- **Statement 2 is correct:** ARCs can acquire **both secured and unsecured loans** from banks. However, the focus is often on secured loans, as they have underlying collateral that can be liquidated to recover dues.
- **Statement 3 is correct:** ARCs are **registered under the RBI** to operate legally in India and **regulated** under the Securitisation and Reconstruction of Financial Assets and Enforcement of Securities Interest Act, 2002 (SARFAESI Act, 2002).

**Thus, the correct answer is (c) All three.**

**46.** *(b)* The **PCA framework** is an RBI tool to monitor banks' financial health. It triggers corrective actions when key indicators like **capital, NPAs, or profitability** fall below required levels, helping prevent bank failures through restrictions on lending and operations. The primary purpose of the Prompt Corrective Action (PCA) framework is to **impose regulatory actions to prevent further deterioration in the financial health of banks** that show signs of financial stress, such as low capital adequacy or high levels of non- performing assets.

**Thus, option (b) is the correct answer.**

**47.** *(c)* Only three

- **Option 1 is correct:** One of the measures under the PCA framework is restricting banks from distributing dividends to conserve capital and improve their financial position.
- **Option 2 is correct:** Banks under the PCA framework may face limitations on opening new branches or expanding their operations to ensure focus on financial recovery.
- **Option 3 is incorrect:** The PCA framework does **not mandate capital infusion** by the government; it focuses on internal measures and restrictions for banks to restore financial health.
- **Option 4 is correct:** The PCA framework may prohibit banks from engaging in non-core activities, which could distract from their focus on improving financial health and stability.

**Therefore, the correct answer is (c) Only three.**

**48.** *(b)* Only two

**PCA Framework got revised in 2021 which came into effect from 1st January, 2022.**

- **Option 1 is correct:** The PCA framework uses the Capital Adequacy Ratio (CAR) as a key indicator to trigger corrective actions. If a bank's CAR falls below a certain level, it can be placed under PCA.
- **Option 2 is correct:** The PCA framework considers Gross NPAs as a critical factor. If a bank's Gross NPAs exceed the threshold set by the RBI, it may invoke PCA.
- **Option 3 is incorrect: Negative RoA** for two consecutive years is no more a recognised trigger for the PCA framework after the revision of PCA framework.
- **Option 4 is incorrect:** High exposure to unsecured loans is not specifically mentioned as a trigger for the PCA framework. The PCA framework focuses on overall asset quality and capital adequacy, rather than exposure to specific types of loans.

**Therefore, the correct answer is (b) Only two.**

**49.** *(c)* 1, 2 and 4 only

- **Option 1 is correct:** Urban Cooperative Banks (UCBs) are included under the PCA framework as of the latest update from the RBI, effective from April 2025, aimed at enabling timely supervisory interventions for UCBs experiencing financial stress.
- **Option 2 is correct:** Private Sector Banks are also subject to the PCA framework. The RBI monitors these banks using the same criteria as public sector banks, such as capital adequacy, asset quality and profitability.
- **Option 3 is incorrect:** RBI's revised PCA framework in 2021 **excludes Small Finance Banks (SFBs) Payment Banks and Regional Rural Banks (RRBs)** from the list of lenders where prompt corrective action can be initiated.
- **Option 4 is correct:** Systemically Important Non-Deposit Taking Non-Banking Financial Companies (NBFC-ND-SI) are subject to a variant of the PCA framework introduced by the RBI to address their specific risks and ensure financial stability.

**Thus, the correct answer is (c) 1, 2 and 4 only.**

**50.** *(b)* Only two

- **Statement 1 is correct:** The **Reserve Bank of India (RBI) reviews the classification of Domestic Systemically Important Banks (D-SIBs) annually** to determine which banks meet the criteria for systemic importance based on their size, interconnectedness and other factors. They are often referred to as 'Too Big To Fail (TBTF)'.
- **Statement 2 is correct:** The Reserve Bank of India (RBI) requires D-SIBs to maintain additional capital requirements, known as the **Additional Common Equity Tier 1 (CET1) capital**, over and above the standard regulatory norms to enhance their resilience and ensure they can absorb potential losses.
- **Statement 3 is incorrect:** Both public and private sector banks can be classified as D-SIBs by the RBI, based on criteria such as size, interconnectedness, lack of substitutability and complexity. It is not limited to public sector banks only. At present, RBI has identified 3 banks as D-SIB in India - **State Bank of India (SBI); HDFC Bank** and **ICICI Bank.**

**Thus, the correct answer is (b) Only two.**

**51.** *(a)* 1 and 2 only

- **Statement 1 is correct:** The FSIB was established **to take over the functions of the former Bank Board Bureau (BBB)**, including the selection of top executives for public sector banks and financial institutions.
- **Statement 2 is correct:** The FSIB also **handles appointments for top management positions in government-owned insurance companies,** thereby expanding its mandate beyond public sector banks.
- **Statement 3 is incorrect:** The FSIB is focused on public sector banks and financial institutions, **not private sector banks.** Its creation aims to enhance governance and professional management in these public institutions.

**Therefore, the correct answer is (a) 1 and 2 only.**

**52.** *(d)* 1, 2 and 3

- **Statement 1 is correct:** The IBC allows for the resolution of insolvency cases through mechanisms such as the corporate insolvency resolution process (CIRP) and if resolution is not possible, liquidation.

- **Statement 2 is correct:** The IBC provides a comprehensive framework for resolving both corporate and individual insolvency, ensuring a uniform process across different types of debtors.
- **Statement 3 is correct:** The IBC mandates that the corporate insolvency resolution process (CIRP) should be completed within 330 days, which includes any extensions granted by the tribunal and the time taken for litigation.

**Therefore, the correct answer is (d) 1, 2 and 3.**

**53.** *(d)* 1, 2 and 3

- **Statement 1 is correct:** The Insolvency Professional (IP), once appointed, takes over the management of the debtor company and has the authority to replace the existing management to ensure a fair and unbiased insolvency resolution process.
- **Statement 2 is correct:** The Insolvency and Bankruptcy Board of India (IBBI) is the regulatory body responsible for overseeing the conduct of insolvency professionals and information utilities, ensuring compliance with the IBC.
- **Statement 3 is correct:** The **Committee of Creditors** (CoC) comprises the financial creditors of the debtor and has the authority to approve or reject the resolution plan proposed during the corporate insolvency resolution process.

**Thus, the correct answer is (d) 1, 2 and 3.**

**54.** *(a)* Only one

- **Option 1 is correct:** **The IBBI was established under the IBC** to regulate insolvency professionals, insolvency pro-fessional agencies, and information utilities.
- **Option 2 incorrect: NCLT created under the Companies Act, 2013** is designated under the IBC as the adjudicating authority for corporate insolvency resolution processes.
- **Option 3 is incorrect:** The DRT **established under the RDB Act, 1993** is the adjudicating authority under the IBC for individual and partnership insolvency cases, not corporate insolvency.
- **Option 4 is incorrect:** National Company Law Appellate Tribunal (NCLAT) constituted **under the Companies Act, 2013,** it hears appeals against the orders of the NCLT **and also** serves as the appellate authority under the IBC.

**Therefore, the correct answer is (a) Only one.**

**55.** *(c)* Only three

- **Option 1 is correct:** The insolvency process begins with a petition by either the creditor or the debtor.
- **Option 2 is correct:** An Interim Resolution professional (IRP) is appointed to take control of the debtor's assets and operations immediately after the insolvency process is initiated.
- **Option 3 is correct:** The Committee of Creditors (CoC) must approve a resolution plan by a majority vote before it is implemented.
- **Option 4 is incorrect: Liquidation is not mandatory in every CIRP.** It occurs only if no viable resolution plan is approved by the CoC or if the resolution process fails to resolve the debtor's financial distress within the prescribed time frame.

**Therefore, only three of these steps are mandatory in every CIRP under the IBC, so the answer is (c) Only three.**

**56.** *(c)* The primary objective of introducing Pre-Packaged Insolvency Resolution Processes (Pre-Packs) under the IBC is to provide a faster and more cost-effective mechanism for resolving insolvency, especially for Micro, Small, and Medium Enterprises (MSMEs). Pre-Packs allow for an agreement between creditors and the debtor on a resolution plan before formal proceedings, streamlining the process and reducing time and costs associated with traditional insolvency proceedings.

**Thus, option (c) is the correct answer.**

**57.** *(a)* 1 and 2 only

- **Statement 1 is correct:** IBBI is the regulatory authority responsible for overseeing the functioning of insolvency professionals, insolvency professional agencies and information utilities under the Insolvency and Bankruptcy Code (IBC).

- It is responsible for setting standards and guidelines for insolvency professionals and ensuring that insolvency proceedings are conducted according to the regulations under the IBC. This includes setting the ethical and professional standards for those involved in insolvency processes.
- **Statement 2 is correct**: The IBBI has the authority to impose penalties and take disciplinary actions against insolvency professionals who do not comply with the rules and regulations under the IBC. This ensures that insolvency processes are conducted ethically and efficiently.
- **Statement 3 is incorrect: The IBBI does not have the authority to adjudicate insolvency cases.** The adjudication of insolvency cases is handled by the National Company Law Tribunal (NCLT) for corporate insolvency and the Debt Recovery Tribunal (DRT) for individual insolvency cases.

**Therefore, the correct answer is (a) 1 and 2 only.**

**58.** *(b)* The primary rationale behind using recapitalisation to address NPAs is **to improve the capital adequacy of banks**. By injecting capital, banks are better positioned to absorb losses from existing NPAs, maintain capital ratios above regulatory requirements, and continue lending to support economic growth. This helps stabilise the banking system by ensuring that banks have sufficient capital buffers to handle bad loans and other financial stresses.

**Government's 4R's strategy of recognising NPAs** transparently, **resolving and recovering** value from Stressed Accounts through clean and effective laws and processes, **recapitalising banks,** and **reforming banks** through the PSB Reforms Agenda.

**Thus, option (b) is the correct answer.**

**59.** *(b)* Repeated rounds of bank recapitalisation without addressing underlying structural issues can create a **moral hazard**, where bank management continues poor lending practices, knowing that the government will bail them out in case of financial trouble. This can lead to a cycle of bad loans and recapitalisation, ultimately weakening the banking sector and increasing the fiscal burden on the government. It is important for recapitalisation efforts to be accompanied by structural reforms that improve risk management and governance in banks.

**Thus, option (b) is the correct answer.**

**60.** *(c)* All three

- **Statement 1 is correct: Project Sashakt** was developed based on the recommendations of the **Sunil Mehta Committee**, which was formed to address the problem of Non-Performing Assets (NPAs) in the Indian banking sector.
- **Statement 2 is correct:** The Sunil Mehta Committee recommended the formation of an **Asset Management Company** (AMC) to resolve large NPAs (greater than ₹ 500 crore) through a market-driven approach.
- **Statement 3 is correct:** The **Sunil Mehta Committee's five-pronged strategy** under **Project Sashakt:**
  - **SME Resolution**: For loans up to ₹ 50 crore, a bank-led resolution within 90 days.
  - **Mid-Sized Loans:** For loans between ₹ 50 crore and ₹ 500 crore, use the **Inter-Creditor Agreement** (ICA) for faster resolution.
  - **Large Loans:** For loans above ₹ 500 crore, create an **Asset Management Company** (AMC) and work with **Alternate Investment Funds (AIFs)** to resolve large NPAs.
  - **Asset Trading Platform**: Establish a marketplace for selling stressed assets to improve price discovery.
  - **Alternative Investment Fund (AIF)**: Use AIFs to raise and invest capital in resolving large NPAs.

This strategy addresses NPAs based on loan size for effective recovery.

**Thus, option (c) is the correct answer.**

**61.** *(b)* 1 and 3 only

- **Statement 1 is correct: The Inter-Creditor Agreement** (ICA) is a framework under which all creditors of a borrower agree to work together to resolve stressed assets. It aims to provide a structured mechanism for cooperative resolution, reducing the time and complexity involved in resolving such assets.

- **Statement 2 is incorrect**: The ICA does not require unanimous consent from all lenders. Typically, the agreement specifies that a majority of creditors (based on a percentage of total debt) must agree on a resolution plan for it to be implemented. This majority rule helps avoid situations where a single dissenting lender could block a resolution.
- **Statement 3 is correct**: The ICA is a **legally binding** document that outlines the rights and obligations of all participating creditors, ensuring that all parties adhere to the terms of the agreement and cooperate in the resolution process.

**Therefore, the correct answer is (b) 1 and 3 only.**

***62.*** *(b)* Only two

**Statement 1 is correct**: The **NARCL** purchases stressed assets (NPAs) from banks, and the **IDRCL** manages the resolution process of these assets to maximise recovery.

**Statement 2 is incorrect: NARCL** is primarily owned by **public sector banks** and **IDRCL** does not hold a majority stake in NARCL. Instead, IDRCL operates independently to manage the resolution process.

**Statement 3 is correct**: NARCL issues **government-backed security receipts** to banks as part of the asset purchase process, which helps cover potential losses in the resolution of stressed assets.

**Therefore, the correct answer is (b) Only two.**

***63.*** *(b)* 1 only

- **Statement 1 is correct**: Public sector banks hold a majority stake in NARCL, which aligns with its purpose to aid in resolving stressed assets in the public banking sector.
- **Statement 2 is incorrect**: While public sector banks are major stakeholders, NARCL is not funded entirely through equity contributions. It also raises funds through other mechanisms such as issuing securities.
- **Statement 3 is incorrect**: The primary role of NARCL is **not to directly** manage and resolve the stressed assets it acquires. Instead, NARCL focuses on purchasing NPAs, while the actual management and resolution of these assets are handled by the India Debt Resolution Company Limited (IDRCL).

**Therefore, the correct answer is (b) 1 only.**

***64.*** *(c)* 2 and 3 only

- **Statement 1 is incorrect**: NBFCs are not allowed to accept demand deposits from the public, which is a key differentiator between them and banks. NBFCs can accept time deposits.
- **Statement 2 is correct**: NBFCs do not form part of the payment and settlement system, meaning they cannot issue cheques or provide demand deposit services like banks.
- **Statement 3 is correct**: Banks are required to maintain a Cash Reserve Ratio (CRR) with the RBI, whereas NBFCs are not subject to CRR requirements. This is one of the regulatory differences between banks and NBFCs.

**Therefore, the correct answer is (c) 2 and 3 only.**

***65.*** *(a)* 1 and 2 only

- **Statement 1 is correct**: Deposit-taking NBFCs (NBFCs-D) are allowed to accept public deposits but are subject to certain limits and regulations prescribed by the RBI to ensure financial stability and consumer protection.
- **Statement 2 is correct**: Systemically important NBFCs are classified based on their asset size. NBFCs with an asset size of INR 500 crore or more are considered systemically important and are subject to stricter regulatory norms to mitigate systemic risk.
- **Statement 3 is incorrect**: The minimum Capital Adequacy Ratio (CAR) required for NBFCs is higher than 9%. As per RBI guidelines, NBFCs are required to maintain a CAR of at least 15% to ensure sufficient capital buffer against potential losses.

**Thus, the correct answer is (a) 1 and 2 only.**

***66.*** *(a)* Only one

- **Option 1 is correct**: NBFCs in India are required to maintain a minimum **CAR of** **15%** to ensure they have sufficient capital to absorb potential losses and protect depositors and creditors.

- **Option 2 is incorrect:** While banks must adhere to Liquidity Coverage Ratio (LCR) requirements, **NBFCs are not required to meet the same LCR standards as banks.** However, larger NBFCs are subject to specific liquidity management requirements to ensure they have sufficient liquidity to meet short-term obligations.
- **Option 3 is incorrect:** Unlike banks, **NBFCs are not mandated to adhere to Priority Sector Lending (PSL) norms.** PSL requirements are specifically applicable to banks to ensure a portion of their lending goes towards sectors that are considered priority by the government.

**Therefore, the correct answer is (a) Only one.**

***67.*** *(c)* Only three
- **Option 1 is correct:** The **RBI** is the primary regulator for **Non-Banking Financial Companies (NBFCs)** in India, overseeing their licensing, capital adequacy, and other regulatory requirements.
- **Option 2 is correct: SEBI** regulates NBFCs that are involved in activities related to the securities market, such as mutual funds and stockbroking.
- **Option 3 is correct:** The MCA oversees the incorporation, governance, and compliance of all companies in India, including NBFCs. It ensures NBFCs adhere to the Companies Act, 2013.
- **Option 4 is incorrect:** IRDAI regulates the insurance sector, not NBFCs. NBFCs are not involved in the direct provision of insurance services, hence IRDAI does not regulate them.

**Three of the bodies (RBI, SEBI, MCA) are involved in regulating NBFCs, while IRDAI is not. Therefore, the correct answer is (c) Only three.**

***68.*** *(d)* All four

There are five prominent **All India Financial Institutions (AIFIs)**, namely **Export-Import Bank of India (EXIM) Bank, National Bank for Agriculture and Rural Development (NABARD), National Bank for Financing Infrastructure and Development (NABFID), National Housing Bank (NHB)** and **Small Industries Development Bank of India (SIDBI).**

These institutions are responsible for providing long-term financial support to various sectors of the Indian economy, such as agriculture, export, housing and small industries, playing a key role in the country's economic development.

**Therefore, the correct answer is (d) All four.**

***69.*** *(b)* **A scheme where a designated bank coordinates the efforts of all banks and financial institutions in a district to enhance banking services and promote financial inclusion.**
- **The Lead Bank Scheme** was introduced to improve banking services and promote financial inclusion in underdeveloped regions of India.
- Under this scheme, a designated lead bank is assigned to each district and is responsible for **coordinating the efforts of all banks and financial institutions** in that district to ensure the availability of banking services, credit distribution and the promotion of various financial initiatives.
- The scheme focuses particularly on **rural and semi-urban areas** where banking penetration is low.

**Thus, option (b) is the correct answer.**

***70.*** *(b)* Only two
- **Statement 1 is correct:** The **Service Area Approach** assigns specific villages or areas to each bank branch, making them responsible for extending **financial services** and ensuring **credit deployment** in those areas.
- **Statement 2 is correct:** The **Reserve Bank of India (RBI)** regulates and oversees the implementation of the **Lead Bank Scheme** to ensure efficient banking and credit services in under-banked regions.
- **Statement 3 is incorrect:** The **Lead Bank Scheme** is not limited to rural areas; it applies to both **rural** and **urban areas** to promote financial inclusion and ensure access to credit to priority sectors like **agriculture, small-scale industries** and **weaker sections of society.**

**Thus, the correct answer is (b) Only two.**

***71.*** *(b)* Only two
- **Statement 1 is correct: Digital Banking Units (DBUs)** are designed to provide fully digital

services **without the need for physical infrastructure** like traditional branches. They focus on offering online and mobile banking solutions.

- **Statement 2 is correct**: DBUs focus on offering specific digital services, such as account opening, loan applications, and fund transfers, through online platforms without the need for physical paperwork.
- **Statement 3 is incorrect**: While DBUs can offer a wide range of digital banking services, they typically **do not handle cash transactions such as deposits and withdrawals**, which are core services of traditional bank branches.

**Thus, the correct answer is (b) Only two.**

**72.** *(a)* 1, 2 and 4 only

**It must be noted that, DBUs do** provide **cash withdrawal** and **cash deposit** services, but these are offered through **ATMs** for withdrawals and **BNA Machines** (Bulk Note Acceptors) for cash deposits.

- **Option 1 is correct: DBUs offer cash withdrawals** through **ATMs** located at the unit.
- **Option 2 is correct**: Customers can deposit cash using **BNA machines** installed at DBUs.
- **Option 3 is incorrect**: DBUs are designed to be **fully digital** with limited or no in-person assistance from human tellers. Instead, they provide automated or self-service options.
- **Option 4 is correct**: DBUs facilitate **online loan applications**, allowing customers to apply and get approvals digitally without visiting a physical branch.

**Thus, the correct answer is (a) 1, 2 and 4 only.**

**73.** *(b)* A banking solution that allows customers to access their bank accounts and perform transactions from any branch of the bank, while also enabling real-time settlement of government transactions through platforms like e-Kuber.

- **Core Banking Solution (CBS)** is a **centralised banking system** that allows customers to access their accounts and conduct transactions from **any branch of the bank, enhancing convenience and efficiency.**
- In India, systems like **e-Kuber**, which is the RBI's Core Banking Solution, provide real-time settlement for government transactions, ensuring smooth and timely fund transfers between government accounts and commercial banks.

**Thus, option (b) is the correct answer.**

**74.** *(a)* An ATM operated by a non-banking entity that allows customers of multiple banks to withdraw money and perform other banking services.

- **A White Label ATM (WLA)** is operated by **non-banking entities** rather than banks themselves. These ATMs provide services such as **cash withdrawals, balance inquiries and fund transfers** to customers of multiple banks.
- The WLAs do not display the branding of any particular bank and allow customers from various banks to access basic banking services using their debit or credit cards. These ATMs are particularly important in enhancing financial inclusion, especially in underserved or rural areas.

**Thus, option (a) is the correct answer.**

## Past Learning (Answers)

| | | | | | | | | | |
|---|---|---|---|---|---|---|---|---|---|
| 1 (c) | 2 (d) | 3 (b) | 4 (b) | 5 (a) | 6 (b) | 7 (b) | 8 (d) | 9 (a) | 10 (c) |
| 11 (a) | 12 (a) | 13 (c) | 14 (b) | 15 (b) | 16 (c) | 17 (d) | | | |

CHAPTER 09

# Financial Markets

## Assessment Round

### Topic 1 : Financial Market

**1.** With reference to the concept of financial markets, consider the following statements:

1. It facilitates the transfer of funds from savers to borrowers.
2. Both money markets and capital markets are subcategories of financial markets.
3. Financial markets only deal with the trading of stocks and bonds.

Which of the statements given above are correct?

(a) 1 and 2 only (b) 1 and 3 only
(c) 2 and 3 only (d) 1, 2 and 3

**2.** Consider the following statements:

1. Financial securities represent claims on the assets or income of the issuer.
2. Bonds are examples of debt securities while stocks represent ownership in a corporation.
3. All financial securities are issued by governments and public sector enterprises only.

Which of the statements given above are correct?

(a) 1 and 2 only
(b) 2 and 3 only
(c) 1 and 3 only
(d) 1, 2 and 3

**3.** Consider the following participants in the financial market:

1. Commercial Banks
2. Insurance Companies
3. Central Banks
4. Pension Funds

How many of the above is/are considered institutional participants in the financial market?

(a) Only one (b) Only two
(c) Only three (d) All four

**4.** Match the following financial markets with the financial securities they typically trade:

| List I (Financial Markets) | List II (Financial Securities) |
|---|---|
| 1. Capital Market | A. Derivatives |
| 2. Money Market | B. Treasury Bills |
| 3. Derivatives Market | C. Bonds and Equity Shares |
| 4. Forex Market | D. Currencies |

Select the correct answer from the codes given below:

(a) 1-A, 2-C, 3-D, 4-B (b) 1-C, 2-B, 3-A, 4-D
(c) 1-B, 2-D, 3-C, 4-A (d) 1-D, 2-A, 3-B, 4-C

**5.** Consider the following statements:

1. The capital market deals with long-term financial instruments such as bonds and equities.
2. The money market is primarily concerned with short-term borrowing and lending.
3. The derivatives market operates separately from the capital market and does not involve stocks or bonds.

How many of the above statements is/are correct?

(a) Only one (b) Only two
(c) All three (d) None

**6.** Which of the following features best describe the 'Money Market'?

1. Provides short-term financing for businesses and governments.
2. Instruments traded are highly liquid and have low default risk.
3. The interest rates in the money market are fixed by the Central Government.
4. Typically have a maturity period of less than one year.

Select the correct answer from the codes given below:

(a) 1, 2 and 4 only (b) 2 and 3 only
(c) 1 and 4 only (d) 1, 2, 3 and 4

**7.** Which of the following best highlights the regulatory difference between the money market and the capital market?

(a) The capital market is regulated by the SEBI while the money market is regulated by the RBI.
(b) The money market is regulated by international financial institutions, while the capital market is regulated by domestic institutions.
(c) Both the money market and capital market are regulated by the RBI.
(d) SEBI regulates both the money market and capital market in India.

## Topic 2 : Money Market

**8.** Consider the following instruments:

1. Treasury Bills
2. Certificate of Deposits
3. Commercial Papers
4. Repurchase Agreements (Repo)

How many of the above instruments is/are included in the Money Market?

(a) Only one (b) Only two
(c) Only three (d) All four

**9.** Which of the following money market instruments are available only to the government?

1. Treasury Bills
2. Call Money
3. Dated Government Securities (G-Secs)
4. State Development Loans

Select the correct answer from the codes given below:

(a) 1 only (b) 1 and 3 only
(c) 2 and 4 only (d) 1, 3 and 4 only

**10.** With reference to the 'Treasury Bills (T-Bills)' in India, consider the following statements:

1. These are non-interest bearing instruments issued by the RBI on behalf of the Central Government.
2. They are issued at a discount and redeemed at face value upon maturity.
3. Treasury Bills in India have maturity periods ranging from 30 days to 365 days.

How many of the above statements is/are correct?

(a) Only one (b) Only two
(c) All three (d) None

**11.** Which of the following best distinguishes Cash Management Bills (CMBs) from Treasury Bills (T-Bills) in India?

(a) CMBs are used to meet temporary mismatches in the government's cash flow, while T-Bills are issued to finance long-term projects.
(b) CMBs are issued only during periods of fiscal crisis, while T-Bills are part of the government's regular borrowing programme.
(c) CMBs have maturities that are typically shorter than T-Bills and are issued irregularly to address short-term liquidity needs, while T-Bills are issued regularly with fixed maturities.
(d) CMBs can be issued by both the Central and State Governments, while T-Bills are only issued by the Central Government.

**12.** Consider the following types of securities:

1. Treasury Bills (T-Bills)
2. Dated Government Securities (G-Secs)
3. Cash Management Bills (CMBs)
4. Corporate Bonds

How many of the given above securities is/are eligible to qualify for SLR?

(a) Only one (b) Only two
(c) Only three (d) All four

**13.** With reference to the Call Money Market in India, consider the following statements:

1. It refers to short-term loans with a maturity of one day.
2. RBI sets a fixed interest rate for the call money market.
3. It is an unsecured market and does not require any collateral required for the transactions.

Which of the statements given above is/are correct?

(a) 1 and 2 only (b) 1 and 3 only
(c) 2 only (d) 1, 2 and 3

**14.** Which of the following can participate in the Call Money Market in India both as borrowers and lenders?

1. Scheduled Commercial Banks (SCBs)
2. Co-operative Banks
3. Primary Dealers
4. Non-Banking Financial Companies (NBFCs)

Select the correct answer from the codes given below:

(a) 1 and 3 only
(b) 1, 2 and 3 only
(c) 1, 2,3 and 4
(d) 2 and 4 only

**15.** With reference to the Certificate of Deposit (CD) in India, consider the following statements:

1. It is a negotiable money market instrument issued by banks and financial institutions.
2. The minimum maturity period of a CD issued by banks is 7 days.
3. CDs are issued at a discount to face value and redeemed at face value upon maturity.

How many of the above statements is/are correct?

(a) Only one (b) Only two
(c) All three (d) None

**16.** Consider the following statements about 'Certificates of Deposit (CDs)':

1. RBI regulates the issuance of Certificates of Deposit.
2. It can be held in either physical or dematerialised form.
3. CDs are non-transferable and the original investor must hold them until maturity.

Which of the statements given above are correct?

(a) 1 and 2 only (b) 1 and 3 only
(c) 2 and 3 only (d) 1, 2 and 3

**17.** With reference to the 'Commercial Paper (CP)' in India, consider the following statements:

1. It can be issued by all companies regardless of their credit rating.
2. The maturity period for Commercial Paper can extend up to 1 year.
3. It is a short-term unsecured promissory note issued by corporates, primary dealers and financial institutions.

How many of the above statements is/are correct?

(a) Only one (b) Only two
(c) All three (d) None

**18.** Consider the following statements about 'Commercial Bills':

1. They are generally issued for periods ranging from 30 to 90 days.
2. Only financial institutions can issue Commercial Bills in India.
3. Commercial Bills can be discounted by banks before maturity to provide liquidity.

Which of the above statements are correct?

(a) 1 and 2 only (b) 1 and 3 only
(c) 2 and 3 only (d) 1, 2 and 3

**19.** With reference to the Bill Discounting in India, consider the following statements:

1. It is used as a short-term financing tool for businesses to manage working capital needs.
2. The Reserve Bank of India (RBI) regulates the discount rate for all commercial bills in the market.
3. Only scheduled commercial banks are permitted to offer bill discounting services in India.

Which of the above statements is/are correct?

(a) 1 and 2 only
(b) 2 and 3 only
(c) 1 only
(d) 1, 2 and 3

**20.** Which of the following best differentiates Secured Overnight Financing Rate (SOFR) from London Inter-bank Offered Rate (LIBOR)?

(a) SOFR is based on secured overnight lending backed by US Treasury securities, while LIBOR is based on unsecured interbank lending rates submitted by banks.

(b) SOFR is calculated based on estimates submitted by banks, while LIBOR is derived from actual repo transactions in the market.

(c) SOFR is a fixed rate for long-term lending, while LIBOR fluctuates daily.

(d) SOFR is an international rate used globally, while LIBOR is only used in the United States.

**21.** What is the Mumbai Interbank Offer Rate (MIBOR) primarily used for in India?

(a) It is the rate at which the Reserve Bank of India lends money to commercial banks.

(b) It is the rate at which Indian banks borrow from each other in the interbank market for short-term loans.

(c) It is the rate set by international banks for lending to Indian companies in foreign currency.

(d) It is the rate at which Indian corporations can borrow funds from international financial institutions.

## Topic 3 : Capital Market : Debt Based Instruments

**22.** Consider the following statements with respect to the various terminologies of Bond:

1. Coupon rate refers to the periodic interest paid to bondholders.
2. Maturity date is the date when the bond issuer repays the principal amount to the bondholders.
3. Yield to Maturity (YTM) is the annual return an investor will receive if the bond is held until maturity.

How many of the above statements is/are correct?

(a) Only one (b) Only two
(c) All three (d) None

**23.** Which of the following factors can affect the yield of a bond?

1. Interest rates in the economy
2. Credit rating of the bond issuer
3. Inflation expectations
4. Maturity of the bond

Select the correct answer from the codes given below:

(a) 1 and 3 only (b) 2 and 4 only
(c) 1, 2 and 3 only (d) 1, 2, 3 and 4

**24.** Consider the following instances:

1. Rising inflation in the economy
2. Increase in central bank interest rates
3. Improvement in the government's fiscal deficit
4. Tightening of monetary policy by the RBI

How many of the given above is/are likely to increase bond yields in India?

(a) Only one (b) Only two
(c) Only three (d) All four

**25.** With reference to the 'Government Securities (G-Secs)', consider the following statements:

1. These are considered risk-free instruments because they are backed by the government.
2. These can be short-term or long-term.
3. Both Central Government and State Governments can issue Treasury Bills.

Which of the statements given above are correct?

(a) 1 and 2 only (b) 2 and 3 only
(c) 1 and 3 only (d) 1, 2 and 3

**26.** Consider the following statements:

1. Both Treasury Bills and Government Bonds pay periodic interest to investors.
2. Government Bonds can have fixed or floating interest rates depending on the issuance terms.

Which of the statements given above is/are correct?

(a) 1 only (b) 2 only
(c) Both 1 and 2 (d) Neither 1 nor 2

**27.** With reference to the 'State Development Loans (SDLs)', consider the following statements:

1. SDLs are issued by State Governments to meet their budgetary requirements.
2. SDLs are riskier compared to Central Government Bonds because they carry state-specific risks.
3. Interest earned on SDLs is exempt from taxes.

Which of the statements given above are correct?

(a) 1 and 2 only (b) 2 and 3 only
(c) 1 and 3 only (d) 1, 2 and 3

**28.** With reference to the 'RBI's Retail Direct Scheme', consider the following statements:

1. It offers individual investors an option to participate in both the primary and secondary markets for government securities.
2. Retail investors can purchase only long-term government securities under the scheme.
3. The government securities available under the scheme include both Central and State Government bonds.

How many of the given above statements is/ are correct?

(a) Only one (b) Only two
(c) All three (d) None

**29.** Which of the following securities can be bought by retail investors under the Retail Direct Scheme?

1. Treasury Bills (T-Bills)
2. Sovereign Gold Bonds (SGBs)
3. Inflation-Indexed Bonds
4. Corporate Bonds

Select the correct answer from the codes given below:

(a) 1 and 4 only (b) 1, 2 and 3 only
(c) 1, 2 and 4 only (d) 1, 2, 3 and 4

**30.** Which of the following entities are typically allowed to subscribe to India's government securities (public debt)?

1. Commercial banks
2. Insurance companies
3. Foreign Institutional Investors (FIIs)
4. Non-Resident Indians (NRIs)

Select the correct answer from the codes given below:

(a) 1 and 4 only
(b) 2 and 3 only
(c) 1, 2 and 4 only
(d) 1, 2, 3 and 4

**31.** What is the primary objective of the Negotiated Dealing System-Order Matching (NDS-OM) platform?

(a) To enable real-time trading of corporate bonds.
(b) To provide a platform for trading government securities with real-time matching of buy and sell orders.
(c) To facilitate retail investors' direct purchase of mutual funds.
(d) To enable the trading of gold and commodity derivatives.

**32.** Who can access the Negotiated Dealing System-Order Matching (NDS-OM) platform for trading government securities?

(a) Only institutional investors like banks and insurance companies
(b) Only the Reserve Bank of India
(c) Institutional investors and retail investors through indirect access
(d) Only non-resident investors through offshore markets

**33.** With reference to the differences between bonds and debentures, consider the following statements:

1. Bonds generally offer lower interest rates as compared to the debentures.
2. Bonds are a form of equity financing while debentures are a form of debt financing.
3. Debenture holders have a higher claim on assets compared to bondholders in case of liquidation.

How many of the above statements is/are correct?

(a) Only one
(b) Only two
(c) All three
(d) None

**34.** Consider the following statements about 'Convertible Debentures':

1. These can be converted into equity shares at a future date.
2. These usually offer a lower interest rate than non-convertible debentures.
3. The conversion of convertible debentures into equity shares is at the discretion of the company and not the investor.

Which of the statements given above are correct?

(a) 1 and 2 only (b) 1 and 3 only
(c) 2 and 3 only (d) 1, 2 and 3

**35.** Consider the following statements about 'External Commercial Borrowings (ECBs)':

1. It can only be raised in foreign currency and cannot be raised in Indian Rupees.
2. It can only be raised from foreign banks and financial institutions.
3. ECBs raised under the approval route require clearance from the Ministry of Finance.

Which of the statements given above is/are correct?

(a) 1 and 2 only (b) 1 only
(c) 2 and 3 only (d) None of these

**36.** Consider the following:

1. Lower interest rates compared to domestic borrowing.
2. Access to a broader pool of international lenders.
3. ECBs provide more flexibility in repayment terms.
4. ECBs are subject to fewer regulatory constraints than domestic borrowings.

How many of the given above is/are the benefits of borrowing under ECBs?

(a) Only one (b) Only two
(c) Only three (d) All four

**37.** Which of the following uses of ECB proceeds are included in the negative list and hence not permitted?

1. Investment in real estate
2. On-lending to other entities for further lending
3. Investment in capital market
4. Purchase of land for speculative purposes

Select the correct answer from the codes given below:

(a) 1, 2 and 3 only (b) 1 and 4 only
(c) 2, 3 and 4 only (d) 1, 2, 3 and 4

**38.** What is the primary difference between Foreign Currency Denominated Bonds and Rupee Denominated Bonds in terms of currency risk?

(a) Foreign Currency Denominated Bonds carry no currency risk for Indian issuers, while Rupee Denominated Bonds carry significant currency risk for foreign investors.
(b) Foreign Currency Denominated Bonds carry currency risk for Indian issuers, while Rupee Denominated Bonds shift the currency risk to the foreign investors.
(c) Both types of bonds carry currency risk for Indian issuers.
(d) Both types of bonds carry currency risk for foreign investors.

**39.** With reference to the 'Masala Bonds', consider the following statements:

1. These are rupee-denominated bonds issued to overseas investors.
2. The currency risk of Masala Bonds is borne by the Indian issuer.
3. These bonds were first launched by the International Finance Corporation (IFC).

Which of the statements given above is/are correct?

(a) 1 and 3 only (b) 2 and 3 only
(c) 1 only (d) 1, 2 and 3

**40.** With reference to the 'Inflation-Indexed Bonds (IIBs)', consider the following statements:

1. It provides protection against inflation by adjusting both the principal and interest payments.
2. These bonds are available for retail investors as well as institutional investors.
3. In India, Inflation-Indexed Bonds are linked to the Wholesale Price Index (WPI).

Which of the statements given above are correct?

(a) 1 and 2 only (b) 2 and 3 only
(c) 1 and 3 only (d) 1, 2 and 3

***41.*** Consider the following statements about 'Inflation-Indexed Bonds (IIBs)':

1. The interest income earned from IIBs in India is exempt from income tax and capital gain tax.
2. These bonds qualify for the SLR requirement for banks.
3. These bonds in India have a floating coupon rate based on inflation-adjusted principal.

Which of the statements given above are correct?

(a) 1 and 2 only
(b) 2 and 3 only
(c) 1 and 3 only
(d) 1, 2 and 3

***42.*** Which of the following statements about 'Foreign Currency Convertible Bonds (FCCBs)' in India are correct?

1. These are issued by Indian companies in foreign currency.
2. These bonds can be converted into equity shares of the issuing company.
3. They are typically used to raise short-term capital for Indian companies.
4. FCCBs are subject to regulation by the Reserve Bank of India (RBI).

Select the correct answer from the codes given below:

(a) 1, 2 and 4 only
(b) 2 and 3 only
(c) 1 and 4 only
(d) 1, 2, 3 and 4

***43.*** With reference to the Green Bonds in India, consider the following statements:

1. These are debt instruments used to raise funds for environmental projects.
2. The proceeds from Green Bonds can be used to finance renewable energy projects, waste management and sustainable transport initiatives.
3. These bonds in India are regulated by the Securities and Exchange Board of India (SEBI).

How many of the above statements is/are correct?

(a) Only one (b) Only two
(c) All three (d) None

***44.*** Consider the following projects:

1. Energy efficiency projects
2. Sustainable water and waste management
3. Nuclear power generation
4. Biodiversity conservation

How many of the above projects is/are eligible to use the proceeds raised from Sovereign Green Bonds under the India's 'Sovereign Green Bonds Framework'?

(a) Only one
(b) Only two
(c) Only three
(d) All four

***45.*** Consider the following statements with reference to the 'Blue Bonds':

1. These bonds are debt instruments issued to finance projects related to ocean and water-based resources.
2. These bonds were first issued by the United Nations Development Programme (UNDP).

Which of the statements given above is/are correct?

(a) 1 only (b) 2 only
(c) Both 1 and 2 (d) Neither 1 nor 2

***46.*** With reference to Sovereign Gold Bonds (SGBs), consider the following statements:

1. These bonds are government securities denominated in grams of gold.
2. The investor receives the market value of the gold along with periodic interest upon maturity.
3. These bonds are exempt from capital gains tax if held till maturity.

Which of the statements given above are correct?

(a) 1 and 2 only (b) 2 and 3 only
(c) 1 and 3 only (d) 1, 2 and 3

**47.** With reference to the 'Surety Bonds' launched in India, consider the following statements:

1. These bonds are primarily used in infrastructural projects to reduce the reliance on bank guarantees.
2. These are debt instruments like traditional bonds to help contractors in meeting their financial obligations.
3. These were launched by the RBI as part of its regulatory measures.

Which of the statements given above is/are correct?

(a) 1 and 2 only
(b) 2 and 3 only
(c) 1 only
(d) 1, 2 and 3

**48.** Match the following parties in a Surety Bond with their description:

| List I (Parties) | List II (Description) |
|---|---|
| 1. Principal | A. The party that provides the surety, guaranteeing the performance or obligations. |
| 2. Obligee | B. The party for whom the bond is issued, receiving protection against default. |
| 3. Surety | C. The party who has the primary responsibility to perform or fulfil the contract obligations. |

Which of the pairs given above is/are correctly matched?

(a) 1-A, 2-B, 3-C
(b) 1-C, 2-B, 3-A
(c) 1-B, 2-C, 3-A
(d) 1-C, 2-A, 3-B

**49.** With reference to the 'Municipal Bonds' in India, consider the following statements:

1. These bonds are debt securities issued by urban local bodies to fund infrastructure projects.
2. SEBI regulates the issuance of Municipal Bonds in India.
3. These bonds enjoy tax-free status.

How many of the given above statements is/are correct?

(a) Only one (b) Only two
(c) All three (d) None

**50.** What is the primary purpose of Elephant Bonds as proposed in India?

(a) To provide a source of funding for the agricultural sector.
(b) To allow individuals to invest in international stocks.
(c) To encourage disclosure of undisclosed wealth and channel it into infrastructure projects.
(d) To support the Indian tourism industry.

## Topic 4 : Capital Market : Equity Based Instruments

**51.** Consider the following statements:

1. Preference shareholders have a higher claim on assets during the liquidation of a company compared to equity shareholders.
2. Equity shareholders receive a fixed dividend while preference shareholders receive dividends based on company profits.

Which of the statements given above is/are correct?

(a) 1 only
(b) 2 only
(c) Both 1 and 2
(d) Neither 1 nor 2

**52.** Which of the following are features of the Primary Market?

1. Securities are issued for the first time by companies or governments.
2. Funds raised from this market go directly to the issuing entity.
3. Securities can be bought and sold multiple times between investors in this market.
4. Instruments like IPOs and bonds are common in this market.

Select the correct answer using the codes given below:

(a) 1, 2 and 3 only (b) 1, 3 and 4 only
(c) 1, 2 and 4 only (d) 1, 2, 3 and 4

**53.** Identify the market described by the following characteristics:

1. This market facilitates the trading of previously issued securities between investors.
2. It provides liquidity to securities by allowing investors to buy and sell after the initial issue.
3. The transactions in this market do not provide direct funds to the issuing company.
4. Stock exchanges such as the NSE and BSE are examples of this market.

Which market does this describe?

(a) Primary Market (b) Commodity Market
(c) Secondary Market (d) Derivatives Market

**54.** Match the following primary market instruments with their descriptions:

| List I (Instruments) | List II (Descriptions) |
|---|---|
| 1. Initial Public Offering (IPO) | A. Issue of additional shares by a company already listed. |
| 2. Rights Issue | B. Issue of shares to the public for the first time by a company. |
| 3. Follow-on Public Offering (FPO) | C. Offering new shares to existing shareholders in proportion to their holdings. |

Which of the pairs given above is/are correctly matched?

(a) 1-A, 2-B, 3-C (b) 1-B, 2-C, 3-A
(c) 1-C, 2-A, 3-B (d) 1-B, 2-A, 3-C

**55.** Which of the following statements best describes a Draft Red Herring Prospectus (DRHP)?

(a) It is a final document filed after the Initial Public Offering (IPO) process to disclose the results.
(b) It is a preliminary document that contains detailed information about the company's operations and financials, but does not mention the offer price or issue size.
(c) It is a mandatory filing required only for the issuance of debt securities.
(d) It is a confidential document that is not made public during the IPO process.

**56.** With reference to the 'American Depository Receipts (ADRs)', consider the following statements:

1. These are financial instruments that represent shares of a foreign company traded on U.S. stock exchanges.
2. Investors holding ADRs receive dividends in U.S. Dollars.
3. The price of ADRs is linked to the price of the foreign company's shares in its home market.

Which of the statements given above are correct?

(a) 1 and 2 only
(b) 2 and 3 only
(c) 1 and 3 only
(d) 1, 2 and 3

**57.** Consider the following Depository Receipts:

1. Indian Depository Receipts (IDRs)
2. Global Depository Receipts (GDRs)
3. American Depository Receipts (ADRs)
4. Singapore Depository Receipts (SDRs)

How many of the given above can be used by Indian companies to raise funds from outside India?

(a) Only one
(b) Only two
(c) Only three
(d) All four

**58.** Which of the following statements best describes Dematerialisation?

(a) It is the process of converting physical securities into electronic form, which can be held in a demat account with a depository participant.
(b) It is the issuance of new shares by a company to raise capital.
(c) It is the process of holding physical share certificates without converting them into digital form.
(d) It is the method of issuing securities to investors through Initial Public Offerings (IPOs).

**59.** Which of the following statements about Dematerialisation are correct?

1. Dematerialisation was introduced in India in the year 1996 under SEBI's regulations.
2. Securities held in dematerialised form cannot be transferred between investors.
3. Dematerialised securities are held in accounts with depository participants.

Select the correct answer using the codes given below:

(a) 1 and 2 only (b) 1 and 3 only
(c) 2 and 3 only (d) 1, 2 and 3

**60.** Consider the following statements about 'Depositories' in India:

1. It facilitates the dematerialisation of physical securities into electronic form.
2. The two major depositories in India are National Securities Depository Limited (NSDL) and Central Depository Services Limited (CDSL).
3. Depositories directly buy and sell shares on behalf of investors.

Which of the statements given above are correct?

(a) 1 and 2 only (b) 2 and 3 only
(c) 1 and 3 only (d) 1, 2 and 3

**61.** Which of the following statements best describes a key difference between NSDL and CDSL?

(a) NSDL is regulated by SEBI, while CDSL is regulated by the Reserve Bank of India (RBI).
(b) NSDL primarily serves as a depository for shares issued by companies, whereas CDSL only handles government securities.
(c) NSDL provides dematerialisation services primarily for corporate securities, while CDSL focuses on government securities.
(d) NSDL is linked to the NSE (National Stock Exchange), while CDSL is linked to the BSE (Bombay Stock Exchange).

**62.** Which of the following best describes demutualisation in the context of stock exchanges?

(a) A process where ownership and management of the exchange are separated, allowing public trading of exchange shares.
(b) The merger of two or more stock exchanges to form a larger entity.
(c) A method of making stock exchanges exclusive to brokerage firms.
(d) A strategy for increasing government control over stock exchanges.

**63.** Consider the following stock exchanges:

1. Bombay Stock Exchange (BSE)
2. National Stock Exchange (NSE)
3. India International Exchange (INX)
4. Multi Commodity Exchange (MCX)

How many of the given above is/are stock exchanges that deal primarily with Equities?

(a) Only one (b) Only two
(c) Only three (d) All four

**64.** What is the primary objective of the Social Stock Exchange (SSE) in India?

(a) To enable companies to issue shares directly to social workers.
(b) To create a platform where non-profit and for-profit social enterprises can raise funds through equity or debt instruments.
(c) To invest in only public sector organisations working on social causes.
(d) To provide tax-free income to investors in non-profit organisations.

**65.** Which of the following best describes the primary difference between SENSEX and NIFTY50?

(a) SENSEX represents 50 companies, while NIFTY50 represents 30 companies
(b) SENSEX is the index for the Bombay Stock Exchange (BSE), whereas NIFTY50 is the index for the National Stock Exchange (NSE)
(c) SENSEX includes only small-cap companies, while NIFTY50 includes large-cap companies
(d) SENSEX tracks financial sector stocks exclusively, whereas NIFTY50 includes all sectors

**66.** Which of the following best describes insider trading?
(a) Insider trading refers to buying or selling securities based on public financial reports of a company.
(b) Insider trading refers to the buying or selling of securities by someone who has access to non-public, material information about the company.
(c) Insider trading refers to any trade made by a company's employees, regardless of the information they have.
(d) Insider trading is a legal activity that involves trading based on any type of information, public or private.

**67.** Match the following stock market regulations with their descriptions:

| List I (Regulations) | List II (Descriptions) |
|---|---|
| 1. Depositories Act, 1996 | A. Deals with dematerialisation of securities and their transfer in electronic form. |
| 2. Companies Act, 2013 | B. Establishes guidelines for corporate governance, transparency and accountability. |
| 3. SEBI (Prohibition of Insider Trading) Regulations, 2015 | C. Regulates trading activities based on non-public, material information. |

Which of the pairs given above is/are correctly matched?
(a) 1-A, 2-B, 3-C (b) 1-B, 2-A, 3-C
(c) 1-C, 2-A, 3-B (d) 1-A, 2-C, 3-B

**68.** With reference to Participatory Notes (P-Notes), consider the following statements:
1. These are financial instruments used by foreign investors to invest in Indian securities without having to register with SEBI.
2. SEBI has no regulations or oversight on P-Notes, making them unregulated financial instruments.
3. The use of P-Notes has raised concerns for misuse in money laundering and tax evasion.

Which of the statements given above are correct?
(a) 1 and 3 only
(b) 1 and 2 only
(c) 2 and 3 only
(d) 1, 2 and 3

**69.** With reference to Chit Funds in India, consider the following statements:
1. Chit fund participants receive the chit amount based on a system of bidding.
2. Chit Funds Act, 1982 is the primary law governing chit funds in India.
3. Chit funds are regulated by the RBI.

Which of the statements given above are correct?
(a) 1 and 2 only
(b) 1 and 3 only
(c) 2 and 3 only
(d) 1, 2 and 3

**70.** With reference to the Nidhi Companies, consider the following statements:
1. These companies are regulated by the RBI.
2. These companies are NBFCs that focus on borrowing and lending only among members.
3. These companies are allowed to carry out chit fund and hire-purchase businesses.

Which of the statements given above is/are correct?
(a) 1 and 2 only
(b) 2 only
(c) 1 and 3 only
(d) 1, 2 and 3

**71.** Which of the following best describes the function of a Credit Default Swap (CDS)?
(a) A CDS is a derivative contract where the seller compensates the buyer if a specific borrower defaults on a loan.
(b) A CDS is an insurance policy that provides coverage against natural disasters.
(c) A CDS is a financial instrument that allows companies to raise equity capital through bond issues.
(d) A CDS is a mechanism for banks to insure their stock market investments.

**72.** Which of the following best differentiates Angel Investors from Venture Capitalists (VCs)?

(a) Angel investors typically invest in large, well-established companies, while venture capitalists focus on startups.

(b) Angel investors usually invest their personal funds, while venture capitalists manage pooled funds from multiple investors.

(c) Angel investors provide growth-stage funding, while venture capitalists provide early-stage funding.

(d) Angel investors are primarily interested in public companies, while venture capitalists focus on private companies.

**73.** Arrange the following types of investors in increasing order of the risk they take:

1. Private Equity
2. Venture Capital
3. Angel Investors

Select the correct option from the codes given below:

(a) 3-2-1 (b) 2-3-1
(c) 1-2-3 (d) 1-3-2

**74.** With reference to Credit Rating Agencies (CRAs) in India, consider the following statements:

1. The agencies evaluate the creditworthiness of issuers of debt instruments.
2. SEBI regulates credit rating agencies in India.
3. Credit rating agencies provide ratings for both equity and debt instruments.

How many of the statements given above is/are correct?

(a) Only one
(b) Only two
(c) All three
(d) None

**75.** Which of the following are recognised credit rating agencies in India?

1. CRISIL
2. Fitch Ratings
3. Brickwork Ratings
4. Standard and Poor's (S&P)

Select the correct answer using the codes given below:

(a) 1 and 3 only (b) 1, 2 and 3 only
(c) 2, 3 and 4 only (d) 1, 2, 3 and 4

**76.** Which of the following best describes an Exchange Traded Fund (ETF)?

(a) An ETF is a mutual fund that only invests in government bonds.

(b) An ETF is a financial instrument that tracks the performance of an index, commodity, or a basket of assets and is traded like a stock on an exchange.

(c) ETFs are debt instruments issued by the government to raise capital from the public.

(d) ETFs are exclusively designed for institutional investors and cannot be purchased by retail investors.

**77.** Which of the following is a key difference between Exchange Traded Funds (ETFs) and Mutual Funds?

(a) ETFs are bought and sold only at the end of the trading day, while mutual funds can be traded throughout the day.

(b) ETFs typically have lower expense ratios compared to mutual funds because they are passively managed and traded like stocks.

(c) Mutual funds are always passively managed, while ETFs are actively managed.

(d) Both ETFs and mutual funds require investors to purchase shares in whole units only.

**78.** Which of the following statements is/are correct?

1. Bharat-22 ETF is a diversified exchange-traded fund that invests in shares of Public Sector Enterprises (PSEs) only.
2. Bharat Bond ETF invests in bonds issued by Central Public Sector Enterprises (CPSEs).
3. Bharat-22 ETF is managed by the Life Insurance Corporation of India (LIC).

Select the correct answer using the codes given below:

(a) 1 and 2 only
(b) 2 and 3 only
(c) 1 and 3 only
(d) 1, 2 and 3

**79.** Which of the following best describes the 'Collateralised Borrowing and Lending Obligation (CBLO)'?
(a) CBLO is a short-term money market instrument that allows entities to borrow and lend funds against collateral, without using the repo market.
(b) CBLO is a long-term loan issued by the government to public sector enterprises.
(c) CBLO is a debt instrument used by retail investors to raise capital for real estate projects.
(d) CBLO is a derivative instrument used to hedge against inflation risks.

**80.** Which of the following best describes a key difference between the Spot Market and the Futures Market?
(a) In the spot market, the transaction is settled immediately, whereas in the futures market, the transaction is settled at a predetermined future date.
(b) In the spot market, only commodities are traded, whereas in the futures market, only financial assets are traded.
(c) In the futures market, transactions involve physical delivery of the asset, while in the spot market, all transactions are cash-settled.
(d) In the spot market, prices are fixed for future delivery, while in the futures market, prices fluctuate based on real-time demand and supply.

**81.** Which of the following best describes the concept of short selling in the stock market?
(a) Short selling involves buying shares at a high price and selling them when the price increases further.
(b) Short selling refers to borrowing shares and selling them, with the expectation of repurchasing them at a lower price to return to the lender.
(c) Short selling is the practice of holding shares for a long period to take advantage of dividend payouts.
(d) Short selling is when an investor buys shares on margin, hoping for a future increase in price.

**82.** A high Interest Coverage Ratio (ICR) generally indicates:
(a) the company is struggling to meet its debt obligations.
(b) the company has sufficient earnings to comfortably cover its interest payments.
(c) the company has significant liquidity issues.
(d) the company relies heavily on short-term debt.

**83.** What is the primary purpose of Bilateral Netting in financial transactions?
(a) To increase transaction costs between two parties.
(b) To offset multiple obligations between two parties, reducing the total amount exchanged.
(c) To ensure every obligation is settled individually.
(d) To prioritise transactions with higher interest rates.

**84.** With reference to the 'Voluntary Retention Route (VRR)' introduced by the RBI, consider the following statements:
1. It is designed to encourage long-term investments by FPIs in both government and corporate bonds.
2. Investors under the VRR are exempted from certain regulatory caps on foreign investment in debt instruments.
3. Investments made under VRR can be withdrawn at any time without restrictions.

Which of the statements given above are correct?
(a) 1 and 2 only
(b) 1 and 3 only
(c) 2 and 3 only
(d) 1, 2 and 3

**85.** Which of the following best describes the key difference between the Fully Accessible Route (FAR) and the Voluntary Retention Route (VRR) for foreign investments in Indian debt?
(a) FAR allows unrestricted investment in certain government securities, while VRR requires a minimum retention period.
(b) FAR limits investments to corporate bonds, while VRR is open to all debt instruments.
(c) FAR is only accessible to domestic investors, while VRR is designed exclusively for foreign investors.
(d) FAR mandates investors to retain funds for a long-term period, unlike VRR.

# OMR SHEET

**Assessment Round**

| | | | | | | | | | | | | | | | | | | | |
|---|---|---|---|---|---|---|---|---|---|---|---|---|---|---|---|---|---|---|---|
| 1 | a | b | c | d | 31 | a | b | c | d | 61 | a | b | c | d | 91 | a | b | c | d |
| 2 | a | b | c | d | 32 | a | b | c | d | 62 | a | b | c | d | 92 | a | b | c | d |
| 3 | a | b | c | d | 33 | a | b | c | d | 63 | a | b | c | d | 93 | a | b | c | d |
| 4 | a | b | c | d | 34 | a | b | c | d | 64 | a | b | c | d | 94 | a | b | c | d |
| 5 | a | b | c | d | 35 | a | b | c | d | 65 | a | b | c | d | 95 | a | b | c | d |
| 6 | a | b | c | d | 36 | a | b | c | d | 66 | a | b | c | d | 96 | a | b | c | d |
| 7 | a | b | c | d | 37 | a | b | c | d | 67 | a | b | c | d | 97 | a | b | c | d |
| 8 | a | b | c | d | 38 | a | b | c | d | 68 | a | b | c | d | 98 | a | b | c | d |
| 9 | a | b | c | d | 39 | a | b | c | d | 69 | a | b | c | d | 99 | a | b | c | d |
| 10 | a | b | c | d | 40 | a | b | c | d | 70 | a | b | c | d | 100 | a | b | c | d |
| 11 | a | b | c | d | 41 | a | b | c | d | 71 | a | b | c | d | 101 | a | b | c | d |
| 12 | a | b | c | d | 42 | a | b | c | d | 72 | a | b | c | d | 102 | a | b | c | d |
| 13 | a | b | c | d | 43 | a | b | c | d | 73 | a | b | c | d | 103 | a | b | c | d |
| 14 | a | b | c | d | 44 | a | b | c | d | 74 | a | b | c | d | 104 | a | b | c | d |
| 15 | a | b | c | d | 45 | a | b | c | d | 75 | a | b | c | d | 105 | a | b | c | d |
| 16 | a | b | c | d | 46 | a | b | c | d | 76 | a | b | c | d | 106 | a | b | c | d |
| 17 | a | b | c | d | 47 | a | b | c | d | 77 | a | b | c | d | 107 | a | b | c | d |
| 18 | a | b | c | d | 48 | a | b | c | d | 78 | a | b | c | d | 108 | a | b | c | d |
| 19 | a | b | c | d | 49 | a | b | c | d | 79 | a | b | c | d | 109 | a | b | c | d |
| 20 | a | b | c | d | 50 | a | b | c | d | 80 | a | b | c | d | 110 | a | b | c | d |
| 21 | a | b | c | d | 51 | a | b | c | d | 81 | a | b | c | d | 111 | a | b | c | d |
| 22 | a | b | c | d | 52 | a | b | c | d | 82 | a | b | c | d | 112 | a | b | c | d |
| 23 | a | b | c | d | 53 | a | b | c | d | 83 | a | b | c | d | 113 | a | b | c | d |
| 24 | a | b | c | d | 54 | a | b | c | d | 84 | a | b | c | d | 114 | a | b | c | d |
| 25 | a | b | c | d | 55 | a | b | c | d | 85 | a | b | c | d | 115 | a | b | c | d |
| 26 | a | b | c | d | 56 | a | b | c | d | 86 | a | b | c | d | 116 | a | b | c | d |
| 27 | a | b | c | d | 57 | a | b | c | d | 87 | a | b | c | d | 117 | a | b | c | d |
| 28 | a | b | c | d | 58 | a | b | c | d | 88 | a | b | c | d | 118 | a | b | c | d |
| 29 | a | b | c | d | 59 | a | b | c | d | 89 | a | b | c | d | 119 | a | b | c | d |
| 30 | a | b | c | d | 60 | a | b | c | d | 90 | a | b | c | d | 120 | a | b | c | d |

## Calculate Your Score

| | |
|---|---|
| **Correct (✓)** | |
| **Incorrect (✓)** | |
| **Unattempted** | |
| **Total Score** | |
| **Accuracy (%)** | |

## Reasons for Incorrect Answers?

| | |
|---|---|
| 1. Lack of Knowledge/Existing Source Insufficient | |
| 2. Lack of Multiple Revision | |
| 3. Common Sense Mistakes | |

**Note :**

1. Calculate total score as correct answers carry 2 marks each 1/3rd marks will deducted for **Incorrect** Answers.
2. Calculate Accuracy (%) by dividing the number of correct answers to the total number of attempted questions.

## Past Learning

**1.** Consider the following statements: **(2024)**

1. In India, Non-Banking Financial Companies can access the Liquidity Adjustment Facility window of the Reserve Bank of India.
2. In India, Foreign Institutional Investors can hold the Government Securities (G-Secs).
3. In India, Stock Exchanges can offer separate trading platforms for debts.

Which of the statements given above is/are correct?

(a) 1 and 2 only (b) 3 only
(c) 1, 2 and 3 (d) 2 and 3 only

**2.** In India, which of the following can trade in Corporate Bonds and Government Securities? **(2024)**

1. Insurance Companies 2. Pension Funds
3. Retail Investors

Select the correct answer using the codes given below:

(a) 1 and 2 only (b) 2 and 3 only
(c) 1 and 3 only (d) 1, 2 and 3

**3.** Consider the following: **(2024)**

1. Exchange-Traded Funds (ETF)
2. Motor vehicles 3. Currency swap

Which of the above is/are considered financial instruments?

(a) 1 only (b) 2 and 3 only
(c) 1, 2 and 3 (d) 1 and 3 only

**4.** With reference to the Indian economy, 'Collateral Borrowing and Lending Obligations' are the instruments of: **(2024)**

(a) Bond market (b) Forex market
(c) Money market (d) Stock market

**5.** Consider the following markets : **(2023)**

1. Government Bond Market
2. Call Money Market
3. Treasury Bill Market 4. Stock Market

How many of the above is/are included in capital markets?

(a) Only one (b) Only two
(c) Only three (d) All four

**6.** In the context of finance, the term 'beta' refers to: **(2023)**

(a) the process of simultaneous buying and selling of an asset from different platforms.
(b) an investment strategy of portfolio manager to balance risk versus reward.
(c) a type of systemic risk that arises where perfect hedging is not possible.
(d) a numeric value that measures the fluctuations of a stock to change in the overall stock market.

**7.** Consider the following statements: **(2022)**

1. In India, credit rating agencies are regulated by Reserve Bank of India.
2. The rating agency popularly known as ICRA is a public limited company.
3. Brickwork ratings is an Indian credit rating agency.

Which of the statements given above are correct?

(a) 1 and 2 only (b) 2 and 3 only
(c) 1 and 3 only (d) 1, 2 and 3

**8.** With reference to Convertible Bonds, consider the following statements: **(2022)**

1. As there is an option to exchange the bond for equity, Convertible Bonds pay a lower rate of interest.
2. The option to convert to equity affords the bondholder a degree of indexation to rising consumer prices.

Which of the statements given above is/are correct?

(a) 1 only (b) 2 only
(c) Both 1 and 2 (d) Neither 1 nor 2

**9.** With reference to the Indian economy, what are the advantages of 'Inflation-Indexed Bonds (IIBs)'? **(2022)**

1. Government can reduce the coupon rates on its borrowing by way of IIBs.
2. IIBs provide protection to the investors from uncertainty regarding inflation.
3. The interest received as well as capital gains on IIBs are not taxable.

Which of the statements given above are correct?

(a) 1 and 2 only (b) 2 and 3 only
(c) 1 and 3 only (d) 1, 2 and 3

**10.** With reference to the expenditure made by an organisation or a company, which of the following statements is/are correct? **(2022)**

1. Acquiring new technology is capital expenditure.
2. Debt financing is considered capital expenditure, while equity financing is considered revenue expenditure.

Select the correct answer from the codes given below:

(a) 1 only (b) 2 only
(c) Both 1 and 2 (d) Neither 1 nor 2

**11.** Consider the following: **(2021)**

1. Foreign currency convertible bonds
2. Foreign institutional investment with certain conditions
3. Global depository receipts
4. Non-resident external deposits.

Which of the above can be included in Foreign Direct Investments (FDI)?

(a) 1, 2 and 3 only (b) 3 only
(c) 2 and 4 only (d) 1 and 4 only

**12.** Indian Government bond yields are influenced by which of the following? **(2021)**

1. Action of the United States Federal Reserve.
2. Action of the Reserve Bank of India.
3. Inflation and short-term interest rates.

Select the correct answer from the codes given below:

(a) 1 and 2 only
(b) 2 only
(c) 3 only
(d) 1, 2 and 3

**13.** With reference to India, consider the following statements: **(2021)**

1. Retail investors through demat account can invest in 'Treasury Bills' and 'Government of India Debt Bonds' in primary market.
2. The Negotiated Dealing System Order Matching' is a government securities trading platform of the Reserve Bank of India.
3. The 'Central Depository Services Ltd.' is jointly promoted by the Reserve Bank of India and the Bombay Stock Exchange.

Which of the statements given above is/are correct?

(a) 1 only (b) 1 and 2 only
(c) 3 only (d) 2 and 3 only

**14.** What is the importance of the term 'Interest Coverage Ratio' of a firm in India? **(2020)**

1. It helps in understanding the present risk of a firm that a bank is going to give a loan to.
2. It helps in evaluating the emerging risk of a firm that a bank is going to give a loan to.
3. The higher a borrowing firm's level of Interest Coverage Ratio, the worse is its ability to service its debt.

Select the correct answer using the codes given below:

(a) 1 and 2 only (b) 2 only
(c) 1 and 3 only (d) 1, 2 and 3

**15.** With reference to the Indian economy, consider the following statements: **(2020)**

1. Commercial Paper is a short-term unsecured promissory note.
2. Certificate of Deposit is a long-term Instrument issued by RBI to a corporation.
3. 'Call Money' is short-term finance used for interbank transactions.
4. 'Zero-Coupon Bonds' are the interest- bearing short-term bonds issued by the Scheduled Commercial Banks to corporations.

Which of the statements given above is/are correct?

(a) 1 and 2 only
(b) 4 only
(c) 1 and 3 only
(d) 2, 3 and 4 only

**16.** In the context of the Indian economy, non-financial debt includes which of the following? **(2020)**

1. Housing loans owned by household
2. Amounts outstanding on credit cards
3. Treasury Bills

Select the correct answer using the codes given below:

(a) 1 only (b) 1 and 2 only
(c) 3 only (d) 1, 2 and 3

# Detailed Solutions

## Assessment Round

**1.** *(a)* 1 and 2 only

- **Statement 1 is correct: Financial markets** play a crucial role in the economy by facilitating the flow of funds from **savers** (investors) to borrowers (businesses and governments). They enable individuals, companies, and governments to raise funds and invest in productive activities.
- **Statement 2 is correct:** The **financial market** is broadly divided into the **money market** (for short-term securities) and the **capital market** (for long-term securities such as stocks and bonds).
- **Statement 3 is incorrect:** Financial markets deal with a wide range of financial instruments, not just **stocks and bonds**, but also **derivatives, commodities, currencies** and other financial securities.

**Thus, the correct answer is (a) 1 and 2 only.**

**2.** *(a)* 1 and 2 only

- **Statement 1 is correct: Financial securities** represent a **claim** on the issuer's assets or income. For example, stockholders have a claim on the company's profits (dividends) and bondholders have a claim on the interest payments and principal repayment.
- **Statement 2 is correct: Bonds are debt securities,** which means that the issuer borrows funds from investors and promises to pay interest. **Stocks,** on the other hand, represent **ownership** in a corporation, and shareholders receive dividends based on the company's performance.
- **Statement 3 is incorrect:** Financial securities are issued by a variety of entities, including **private companies, governments and public sector enterprises,** not just governments and public entities.

**Thus, the correct answer is (a) 1 and 2 only.**

**3.** *(d)* All four

- **Commercial Banks:** Play a significant role as institutional participants by providing credit, facilitating transactions and offering financial products like loans and deposits.
- **Insurance Companies:** Act as institutional investors, investing large sums of collected premiums into securities and other investment avenues.
- **Central Banks:** Though primarily regulators, central banks like the **Reserve Bank of India** participate in open market operations (buying/selling government securities) and affect interest rates and liquidity.
- **Pension Funds:** These large institutional investors manage funds for employee pensions and invest in stocks, bonds and other financial assets, contributing to market liquidity and stability.

**Thus, the correct answer is (d) All four.**

**4.** *(b)* 1-C, 2-B, 3-A, 4-D

- **Capital Market** typically deals with **Bonds and equity shares.**
- **Money Market** deals with short-term instruments like **Treasury Bills. Commercial Paper, Certificates of Deposit (CDs)** etc.
- **Derivatives Market** trades instruments like **Futures and Options (Derivatives).**
  - The **derivative market** is a financial market where **derivatives**—financial instruments that derive their value from an underlying asset—are traded. These underlying assets can include **stocks, bonds, commodities, currencies, interest rates,** or **market indexes.**
- **Forex Market is used to trade Currencies.**

**Thus, the correct answer is (b) 1-C, 2-B, 3-A, 4-D.**

**5.** *(b)* Only two

- **Statement 1 is correct:** The **capital market** deals with **long-term financial instruments,** such as **bonds** and **equities.**
- **Statement 2 is correct:** The **money market** is focused on **short-term borrowing and lending,** typically for instruments with

maturities of less than one year, like Treasury Bills and Certificates of Deposit.

- **Statement 3 is incorrect**: The **derivatives market** does not operate entirely separately from the **capital market**. In fact, many **derivatives** are **based on underlying assets** that are traded in the capital market, such as **stocks** (equities) and **bonds**.

**Thus, the correct answer is (b) Only two.**

**6.** *(a)* 1, 2 and 4 only

- **Statement 1 is correct**: The **money market** provides **short-term financing** to businesses, financial institutions and governments to manage their liquidity needs.
- **Statement 2 is correct**: Money market instruments, such as **Treasury Bills** and **Commercial Paper**, are **highly liquid** and generally have **low default risk** due to their short-term nature.
- **Statement 3 is incorrect**: The **interest rates** in the money market are determined by **market forces** (supply and demand for short-term funds) and are not directly set by the Central Government.
- **Statement 4 is correct**: Money market instruments typically have a **maturity period of less than one year**, making them highly liquid.

**Thus, the correct answer is (a) 1, 2 and 4 only.**

**7.** *(a)* The capital market is regulated by the SEBI while the money market is regulated by the RBI.

- In India, the **capital market** is primarily regulated by **SEBI**, which oversees the trading of long-term financial instruments such as stocks and bonds.
- On the other hand, the **money market** is regulated by the **RBI**, which manages short-term instruments like Treasury Bills, Certificates of Deposit, and Commercial Paper to ensure liquidity and financial stability.

**Thus, option (a) is the correct answer.**

**8.** *(d)* All four

- **Treasury Bills, Certificate of Deposits, Repurchase Agreements** and **Commercial Papers** are **Money Market instruments.**
- They are short-term, highly liquid instruments that help to manage liquidity in the market.

**Thus, the correct answer is (d) All four.**

**9.** *(a)* 1 only

- **Treasury Bills: Short-term** debt instruments issued by the **Government of India** to manage its short-term liquidity needs. These are available only to the government.
- **Call Money**: These instruments are available to other financial institutions and companies as well.
- **Dated Government Securities (G-Secs): Long-term** securities issued by the **Government of India**, used to raise long-term funds. These are also only available to the government but included in the **capital market.**
- **State Development Loans (SDLs)**: Issued by **State Governments** to raise funds for development projects but included in the **capital market.**

**Thus, the correct answer is (a) 1 only.**

**10.** *(b)* Only two

- **Statement 1 is correct**: Treasury Bills (T-Bills) are classified as **non-interest- bearing instruments**, also known as **zero-coupon instruments**. This means that unlike bonds or other government securities that pay periodic interest, T-Bills do not have interest payments.
  - T-Bills are issued by the **Reserve Bank of India (RBI)** on behalf of the **Government of India.** The RBI conducts regular auctions for Treasury Bills, making them available for purchase by institutional investors, commercial banks and retail investors.
- **Statement 2 is correct**: T-Bills are issued at a **discount** to face value and redeemed at face value upon maturity, allowing the holder to earn the difference as interest.
- **Statement 3 is incorrect**: The maturity periods for **Treasury Bills** in India are standardised as **91 days, 182 days and 364 days**, meaning these instruments are designed for periods of up to one year.

**Thus, the correct answer is (b) Only two.**

**11.** *(c)* CMBs have maturities that are typically shorter than T-Bills and are issued irregularly to address short-term liquidity needs, while T-Bills are issued regularly with fixed maturities.

- **CMBs** are used to address **temporary mismatches** in the government's cash flow and are issued with **shorter, flexible maturities** than T-Bills. CMBs are issued **irregularly**, depending on the government's immediate cash needs, unlike the more regular issuance of T-Bills.
- **T-Bills** have fixed maturities of **91, 182, and 364 days** and are issued **regularly** as part of the government's structured borrowing program. CMBs often less than 90 days.
- **Also, CMB rates are** determined by the **market demand** during auctions, usually at **slightly higher rates** due to urgent needs. Rates in T-Bills are also market-determined but generally **lower** due to their regular issuance and structured nature.

**Thus, option (c) is the correct answer.**

**12.** *(c)* Only three

**Statutory Liquidity Ratio (SLR)** is the minimum percentage of a bank's net demand and time liabilities (NDTL) that it must maintain in the form of liquid assets. These assets can be held in specific approved securities. The Reserve Bank of India (RBI) defines the types of securities that are eligible to meet SLR requirements.

- **Treasury Bills (T-Bills)**: These short-term government securities issued by the Government of India are **eligible** for SLR purposes.
- **Dated Government Securities (G-Secs)**: Long-term government bonds issued by the Central Government are **eligible** for SLR.
- **Cash Management Bills (CMBs)**: These short-term securities, issued by the Government of India to manage temporary liquidity mismatches, are also **eligible** for SLR.
- **Corporate Bonds**: These are **not eligible** for SLR as they are not government-backed and carry higher risk compared to government securities.

**Thus, the correct answer is (c) Only three.**

**13.** *(b)* 1 and 3 only

- **Statement 1 is correct: Call money** refers to extremely short-term loans, typically for a period of **one day.** These loans help banks manage their short-term liquidity needs and meet reserve requirements.
- **Statement 2 is incorrect:** The **interest rate** in the Call Money Market is referred to as the **call rate.** This rate is highly volatile and fluctuates based on the **demand and supply** of funds between banks. RBI does not set a fixed interest rate for the call money market.
- **Statement 3 is correct:** The call money market is an **unsecured market,** meaning no collateral is required for transactions between participants. The short-term nature of these loans makes collateral unnecessary.

**Thus, the correct answer is (b) 1 and 3 only.**

**14.** *(b)* 1, 2 and 3 only

- **Scheduled Commercial Banks:** These are key participants in the Call Money Market, borrowing funds to manage their short-term liquidity needs.
- **Co-operative Banks:** Co-operative Banks can also borrow funds in the Call Money Market to manage their cash flow requirements.
- **Primary Dealers:** These are institutions designated to participate in the government securities market and they can borrow funds in the Call Money Market.
- **Non-Banking Financial Companies (NBFCs): Non-Banking Financial Companies (NBFCs)** in India are allowed to participate in the **Call Money Market** only as **borrowers,** not as lenders.

**Thus, the correct answer is (b) 1, 2 and 3 only.**

**15.** *(c)* All three

- **Statement 1 is correct:** A **Certificate of Deposit (CD)** is a **negotiable, unsecured money market** issued by **banks** and other eligible **financial institutions** to raise short-term funds.
- **Statement 2 is correct:** The **minimum maturity period** for CDs issued by banks is **7 days,** while for financial institutions, it is **1 year.** For financial institutions, the minimum maturity is **one year** and the maximum is **three years.**

- **Statement 3 is correct**: CDs are typically issued at a **discount** to their **face value** and redeemed at face value on maturity, similar to treasury bills, making them attractive for short-term investments.

**Therefore, the correct answer is (c) All three.**

**16.** *(a)* 1 and 2 only

- **Statement 1 is correct: Reserve Bank of India** (RBI) regulates the issuance of CDs, including the rules governing their tenure, issuance and transferability.
- **Statement 2 is correct**: CDs can be held in **physical form** (as certificates) or in **dematerialised form**, making them accessible and transferable through the **demat** system.
- **Statement 3 is incorrect**: CDs are **transferable instruments** and can be sold in the secondary market, making them attractive for investors looking for liquidity/flexibility i.e., the original investor does not need to hold them until maturity. This instrument typically purchased by **corporates, mutual funds and high-net-worth individuals** looking for short-term investments.

**Therefore, the correct answer is (a) 1 and 2 only.**

**17.** *(b)* Only two

- **Statement 1 is incorrect: Commercial Paper** (CP) instrument typically purchased by **corporates, mutual funds, and high-net-worth individuals** looking for short-term investments that is companies with a **good credit rating** from a credit rating agency can issue **Commercial Paper**. It is an unsecured instrument, and therefore, only entities with strong creditworthiness can access this form of short-term borrowing.
- **Statement 2 is correct**: The maturity period for **Commercial Paper** can range from **7 days** to a maximum of **1 year**.
- **Statement 3 is correct: Commercial Paper (CP)** is an **unsecured, short-term debt instrument** issued by **corporates, primary dealers** and **financial institutions** to meet short-term liquidity needs. It is one of the key money market instruments.

**Thus, the correct answer is (b) Only two.**

**18.** *(b)* 1 and 3 only

- **Statement 1 is correct: Commercial Bills** are part of the **money market**, where they are used as a short-term financing tool to manage liquidity for businesses, especially in trade transactions. The maturity period for Commercial Bills generally ranges from **30 to 90 days**.
- **Statement 2 is incorrect**: Commercial Bills are primarily issued by **businesses, not just financial institutions**, to raise funds for working capital needs related to trade.
- **Statement 3 is correct**: Commercial Bills can be **discounted by banks**, which means that the bill holder can sell it to a bank before maturity at a discount. The bank provides immediate liquidity to the holder while the bank itself receives full payment when the bill matures.

**Thus, the correct answer is (b) 1 and 3 only.**

**19.** *(c)* 1 only

- **Statement 1 is correct: Bill discounting** is a widely used **short-term financing tool** that helps businesses meet their immediate cash flow needs by converting their sales invoices or bills of exchange into liquid funds.
  - When businesses discount a bill, the **bank purchases the bill at a discount** and pays the business immediately. The bank then recovers the full amount from the debtor on the bill's maturity date.
- **Statement 2 is incorrect**: RBI does not regulate the **discount rate** for all commercial bills. Discount rates are generally determined by market forces, such as the demand for funds, creditworthiness of the party and prevailing interest rates.
- **Statement 3 is incorrect**: In India, **bill discounting services** are offered by various financial institutions, not just scheduled commercial banks. This includes Non-Banking Financial Companies (NBFCs) and other lending institutions.

**Thus, the correct answer is (c) 1 only.**

**20.** *(a)* SOFR is based on secured overnight lending backed by U.S. Treasury securities, while LIBOR is based on unsecured interbank lending rates submitted by banks.

- The Secured Overnight Financing Rate (SOFR) is a benchmark interest rate for dollar-denominated derivatives and loans that **replaced** the London Interbank Offered Rate (LIBOR).
- **SOFR** is based on **secured transactions** in the US Treasury repo market, which involves lending backed by **collateral** (US Treasury securities).
  - In contrast, **LIBOR** is based on **unsecured interbank lending** and relies on estimates submitted by participating banks. This makes SOFR more reliable and transparent, as it reflects actual transactions rather than estimates.

**Thus, option (a) is the correct answer.**

**21.** *(b)* It is the rate at which Indian banks borrow from each other in the interbank market for short-term loans.

- The **Mumbai Interbank Offer Rate (MIBOR)** is the rate at which **banks in India** lend and borrow from one another for **short-term loans** in the **interbank market.**
- It is India's equivalent of LIBOR and serves as a key benchmark for short-term interest rates in the money market.
- It is calculated based on **actual short-term transactions** between **Indian banks** in the inter-bank market. This makes it a reliable reflection of the true cost of borrowing in the Indian money market.
- The rate is published by the **National Stock Exchange (NSE)** and is widely used as a benchmark for various financial products.

**Thus, option (b) is the correct answer.**

**22.** *(c)* All three

- **Statement 1 is correct:** The **coupon rate** refers to the **fixed interest rate** that is periodically paid to bondholders, usually annually or semi-annually.
- **Statement 2 is correct:** The **maturity date** is when the bond **expires** and the **principal amount** is repaid by the issuer to the bondholders.
- **Statement 3 is correct:** The **Yield to Maturity** (YTM) represents the total **annual return** an investor would earn if the bond is held until it matures, taking into account both the interest payments and any difference between the purchase price and the face value.

**Thus, the correct answer is (c) All three.**

**23.** *(d)* 1, 2, 3 and 4

- **Interest rates in the economy:** Bond yields are **inversely related** to interest rates. **When interest rates rise,** existing bond prices fall, and **yields rise. When interest rates fall,** existing bond prices rise, and **yields decrease.**
- **Credit rating of the bond issuer:** A **lower credit rating** indicates higher default risk, which results in **higher yields** to compensate investors for the increased risk.
- **Inflation expectations:** Rising **inflation** erodes the purchasing power of future interest payments, so investors demand **higher yields** to offset this risk. Conversely, lower inflation expectations lead to lower yields.
- **Maturity of the bond:** Generally, **longer-term bonds** tend to have higher yields than short-term bonds due to the greater uncertainty over longer periods (known as the **term premium**) such as changes in interest rates and inflation over time.

**Thus, the correct answer is (d) 1, 2, 3 and 4.**

**24.** *(c)* Only three

- **Option 1 is correct: Rising inflation:** Assume a bond with a **coupon rate of 5%**. If inflation increases from 2% to 5%, the **real return** on the bond (adjusted for inflation) becomes zero. Investors would demand a higher yield to offset this, leading to a **drop in the bond's price** and a corresponding **increase in yield.**
- **Option 2 is correct: Increase in central bank interest rates:** If the central bank increases interest rates from **4% to 5%**, new bonds will be issued with higher coupon rates. Existing bonds with lower coupon rates (say 4%) will see a **decline in price** in the secondary market because investors prefer the higher-yielding new bonds. This leads to an **increase in the yield** of the existing bonds as the price drops.
- **Option 3 is incorrect: Improvement in the government's fiscal deficit:** If the government improves its fiscal deficit from **5% of GDP to 3%**, it signals **better financial stability** and a **lower need for borrowing.** As a result, bond

demand may increase, pushing **bond prices up** and **yields down**. This is because investors see less risk in government debt when fiscal management improves.

- **Option 4 is correct: Tightening of monetary policy by the RBI**: If the RBI tightens monetary policy by raising rates or conducting open market operations to reduce liquidity, bond prices will fall due to **increased interest rates** in the market. For example, a bond with a **4% coupon rate** will become less valuable compared to new bonds with higher rates, leading to an **increase in yields.**

**Thus, the correct answer is (c) Only three.**

***25.*** *(a)* 1 and 2 only

- **Statement 1 is correct**: Government securities are **risk-free** instruments as they are backed by the **government's creditworthiness**, which implies a very low default risk.
- **Statement 2 is correct: Treasury Bills (T-Bills)** are **short-term securities** with maturities of less than one year. Long-term government securities are called **Government Bonds.**
- **Statement 3 is incorrect**: G-Secs are issued by both the **Central Government** and **State Governments**. While Central Government can issue both short-term (Treasury Bills) and long-term government securities (Dated G-Secs); **State Governments can only issue long-term State Development Loans (SDLs).**

**Thus, the correct answer is (a) 1 and 2 only.**

***26.*** *(b)* 2 only

- **Statement 1 is incorrect**: The **coupon rate** is the **fixed interest rate** that is periodically paid to bondholders, usually annually or semi-annually. Here, **Treasury Bills** are **zero-coupon instruments**, where the return comes from the difference between the purchase price and the redemption value. **Government Bonds**, on the other hand, typically pay periodic interest (coupons).
- **Statement 2 is correct**: Government Bonds may have either **fixed interest rate** (where the coupon rate is constant) or **floating interest rates** (where the coupon rate varies based on a reference rate).

**Thus, the correct answer is (b) 2 only.**

***27.*** *(a)* 1 and 2 only

- **Statement 1 is correct: State Development Loans (SDLs)** are issued by **State Governments** in India to fund their budgetary needs and are a way for states to raise long-term funds to meet budgetary requirements, such as financing development projects and managing fiscal deficits.
- **Statement 2 is correct**: While SDLs are backed by State Governments, they are seen as slightly **riskier** than **Central Government Bonds** because the financial health of states can vary, leading to state-specific risks.
- **Statement 3 is incorrect**: Interest earned on SDLs is **not exempt** from taxes. Like other bonds, the interest earned is taxable unless specified otherwise.

**Thus, the correct answer is (a) 1 and 2 only.**

***28.*** *(b)* Only two

**RBI's Retail Direct Scheme** was launched in November 2021, which enables investment in **government securities** by individual investors. Under this scheme, investors can open a Gilt Securities Account—Retail Direct Gilt account with the RBI.

- **Statement 1 is correct**: Under the **Retail Direct Scheme**, investors can indeed open a **Retail Direct Gilt (RDG) account** through the RBI's **online platform** to participate in government securities' primary and secondary markets.
  - Investors can buy and **sell government securities** in the **secondary market** using the Retail Direct platform.
  - The **Retail Direct platform** allows investors to hold **government securities in dematerialised form**, ensuring digital access and ease of transactions.
- **Statement 2 is incorrect**: Retail investors can purchase **a wide range of government securities**, including both **short-term instruments** like Treasury Bills and **long-term bonds** such as government securities and State Development Loans (SDLs).

- **Statement 3 is correct:** The scheme allows investment in both **Central Government bonds** and **State Development Loans (SDLs)** issued by State Governments.

**Thus, the correct answer is (b) Only two.**

**29.** *(b)* 1, 2 and 3 only

**The Retail Direct Scheme by the Reserve Bank of India (RBI) allows retail investors to directly invest in government securities (G-Secs) through a dedicated online platform.**

- **Treasury Bills (T-Bills) are short-term government securities** that can be bought by retail investors under the Retail Direct Scheme.
- **Sovereign Gold Bonds (SGBs)** are **government securities** denominated in grams of gold. They are substitutes of physical gold. Investors have to pay the issue price in cash and the bonds will be redeemed in cash on maturity. The Bond is issued by Reserve Bank on behalf of Government of India.
- **Inflation-Indexed Bonds,** which provide protection against inflation, can also be bought by retail investors through the platform.
- **Corporate Bonds** are **not part** of the Retail Direct Scheme, as the scheme focuses on government securities only.

**Thus, the correct answer is (b) 1, 2 and 3 only.**

**30.** *(d)* 1, 2, 3 and 4

- **Option 1 is correct: Commercial banks** are the significant participant in India, allowed to subscribe to government securities as part of their Statutory Liquidity Ratio (SLR) requirements.
- **Option 2 is correct: Insurance companies** are key institutional investors in government securities, using them as safe investment avenues to match long-term liabilities that is returns for policyholders.
- **Option 3 is correct: Foreign Institutional Investors (FIIs)** can invest in government securities, subject to limits set by the Reserve Bank of India (RBI) under specific frameworks. These limits are to ensure financial stability and to manage foreign capital inflows in the economy.
- **Option 4 is correct: Non-Resident Indians (NRIs)** can also subscribe to certain categories of government securities under specific schemes like Fully Accessible Route (FAR) which allows them to invest in specified government bonds.

**Thus, the correct answer is (d) 1, 2, 3 and 4.**

**31.** *(b)* To provide a platform for trading government securities with real-time matching of buy and sell orders.

- **The Negotiated Dealing System-Order Matching** (NDS-OM) is an electronic trading platform introduced by the Reserve Bank of India (RBI) in August 2005. It is specifically designed for trading in government securities (G-Secs). It operates under the management of the Clearing Corporation of India Ltd. (CCIL).
- The **NDS-OM** platform is known for its **real-time order matching** system for the trading of **government securities.** This electronic platform ensures that buy and sell orders are matched automatically, improving efficiency in the **government securities** market.
- The platform primarily caters to government securities and is **not** designed for commodities or corporate bonds.

**Thus, option (b) is the correct answer.**

**32.** *(c)* Institutional investors and retail investors through indirect access.

- The **NDS-OM platform** is primarily used by **institutional investors** such as banks, financial institutions and insurance companies.
- However, **retail investors** can also access the platform **indirectly** through brokers or other intermediaries, enabling them to participate in government securities trading.

**Thus, option (c) is the correct answer.**

**33.** *(a)* Only one

- **Statement 1 is correct: Bonds** generally offer **lower interest rates** because they are secured by collateral, whereas **debentures** offer **higher interest rates** to compensate for the risk of being unsecured.

- **Statement 2 is incorrect**: Both **bonds** and **debentures** are forms of **debt financing**, not equity financing.
- **Statement 3 is incorrect: Bondholders typically have a higher claim on assets** than **debenture holders** in the event of liquidation because bonds are more likely to be secured by assets.

**Thus, the correct answer is (a) Only one.**

**34.** *(a)* 1 and 2 only

- **Statement 1 is correct: Convertible debentures** can indeed be converted into **equity shares** at a pre-specified future date, offering investors the option to convert their debt into equity.
- **Statement 2 is correct**: Convertible debentures usually offer a **lower interest rate** compared to non-convertible debentures because they provide the additional benefit of conversion to equity.
- **Statement 3 is incorrect**: The conversion of convertible debentures into equity shares is usually at the discretion of the investor, not the company. The terms of conversion, such as the conversion price and the conversion period, are predefined at the time of issuance.

**Thus, the correct answer is (a) 1 and 2 only.**

**35.** *(d)* None of these

- **Statement 1 is incorrect**: ECBs can be raised in **foreign currency** as well as in **Indian Rupees**, depending on the specific guidelines of the ECB framework. **There are 2 types of ECBs:**
  - **Foreign Currency Denominated ECBs:** Borrowings raised in foreign currencies such as US Dollars or Euros.
  - **Rupee Denominated ECBs (Masala Bonds)**: Borrowings raised in Indian Rupees but issued abroad. The exchange rate risk is borne by the lender and interest payments are made in rupees.
- **Statement 2 is incorrect**: While **foreign banks and financial institutions** are common lenders, ECBs can also be raised from **export credit agencies, suppliers, foreign collaborators** and even **overseas corporate bodies.**
- **Statement 3 is incorrect**: ECBs raised under the **approval route** require clearance from the **RBI** and not directly from the **Ministry of Finance.**

**Thus, the correct answer is (d) None of these.**

**36.** *(c)* Only three

- **Statement 1 is correct: Lower interest rates** in international market are one of the significant advantages of ECBs. It typically offers lower **interest rates** compared to domestic loans, especially in global markets with lower inflation rates.
- **Statement 2 is correct**: ECBs provide access to a **broader pool of international lenders**, including foreign banks, multilateral institutions and export credit agencies.
- **Statement 3 is correct**: ECBs often offer **flexible repayment terms**, including longer tenures for infrastructure and capital-intensive projects. This allowing companies to tailor the borrowing to their specific needs.
- **Statement 4 is incorrect**: ECBs are subject to **strict regulations** from the Reserve Bank of India (RBI) and Ministry of Finance regarding the end-use, tenure and lenders involved for which specific guidelines are provided.

**Thus, the correct answer is (c) Only three.**

**37.** *(d)* 1, 2, 3 and 4

External Commercial Borrowing (ECB) proceeds are included in the **negative list** as per guidelines issued by the Reserve Bank of India (RBI). This means that the funds raised through ECBs cannot be used for specific purposes.

- **Investment in real estate** (except for affordable housing) is on the **negative list**, so ECB proceeds cannot be used for this purpose.
- **On-lending to other entities** is also restricted under ECB guidelines.
- Investment in **capital market is prohibited.**
- **Purchase of land for speculative purposes** is **prohibited** under the negative list of ECB usage.

**Thus, the correct answer is (d) 1, 2, 3 and 4.**

**38.** *(b)* Foreign Currency Denominated Bonds carry currency risk for Indian issuers, while Rupee Denominated Bonds shift the currency risk to the foreign investors.

- **Foreign Currency Denominated Bonds** are issued in foreign currency (such as USD or EUR), which exposes Indian issuers to **currency fluctuation risk**. Any depreciation of the rupee increases the repayment burden for Indian issuers.
- **Rupee Denominated Bonds** (also known as **Masala Bonds**) are issued in Indian Rupees and the **currency risk** is **borne by the foreign investors** who buy these bonds. If the rupee depreciates, foreign investors receive fewer returns in their local currency.

**Thus, option (b) is the correct answer.**

**39.** *(a)* 1 and 3 only

- **Statement 1 is correct: Masala Bonds** are **rupee-denominated bonds** issued by Indian entities to raise funds from **foreign investors.** The bonds are issued in Indian Rupees (INR), but the investment comes from overseas markets.
- **Statement 2 is incorrect:** The **currency risk** for Masala Bonds is borne by the **foreign investors,** not the Indian issuer. This is the key feature of Masala Bonds, as foreign investors take on the risk of any fluctuation in the value of the Indian Rupee.
- **Statement 3 is correct:** The first **Masala Bonds** were issued by the **International Finance Corporation (IFC)** in **2014**, which is an arm of the World Bank. This issuance marked the beginning of rupee-denominated bonds in the international market. Following this, Indian companies like **HDFC, NTPC** and **Indiabulls Housing Finance** have issued Masala Bonds to raise funds from overseas markets.

**Thus, the correct answer is (a) 1 and 3 only.**

**40.** *(a)* 1 and 2 only

**Inflation-Indexed Bonds (IIBs)** are **debt instruments** where the principal and interest payments are linked to an inflation index, typically the **Consumer Price Index (CPI).** These bonds are designed to protect investors from the erosion of purchasing power due to inflation by adjusting their returns in line with inflation rates.

- **Statement 1 is correct: Inflation-Indexed Bonds** (IIBs) are designed to provide protection against inflation by adjusting both the **principal** and **interest** payments based on inflation rates.
  - Interest on IIBs is paid on the inflation-adjusted principal. As inflation increases, the principal amount increases and consequently, the interest payments also rise.
- **Statement 2 is correct:** IIBs are available for both **retail investors** and **institutional investors,** providing a hedge against inflation for various types of investors.
- **Statement 3 is incorrect:** In India, IIBs are generally linked to the **Consumer Price Index (CPI)**, not the Wholesale Price Index (WPI).

**Thus, the correct answer is (a) 1 and 2 only.**

**41.** *(b)* 2 and 3 only

- **Statement 1 is incorrect:** The interest income earned from **Inflation-Indexed Bonds (IIBs)** in India is **not exempt from income tax.** It is subject to the same tax treatment as other fixed-income instruments like other bonds, the interest income is subject to regular taxation. Capital gains from the sale of these bonds may also be subject to taxation depending on the holding period and tax rules.
- **Statement 2 is correct: Inflation-Indexed Bonds (IIBs)** do qualify for the **Statutory Liquidity Ratio (SLR)** requirement for banks, making them attractive for financial institutions to meet their regulatory requirements.
- **Statement 3 is correct:** The coupon on IIBs is **floating** and is paid on the **inflation-adjusted principal**. This ensures that the real value of the interest payments remains protected against inflation.

**Thus, the correct answer is (b) 2 and 3 only.**

**42.** *(a)* 1, 2 and 4 only

**Foreign Currency Convertible Bonds (FCCBs)** are a type of **hybrid financial instrument**

that combine the **features of both debt and equity**. These bonds are issued by Indian companies in foreign currency and they offer investors the option to convert the bonds into equity shares of the issuing company at a predetermined conversion price and time.

- **Statement 1 is correct: Foreign Currency Convertible Bonds (FCCBs)** are **issued in foreign currency** by Indian companies to raise capital from overseas markets. The **interest payments** on FCCBs are made in **foreign currency**, as the bonds are issued in international markets.
- **Statement 2 is correct**: FCCBs have the option to be **converted into equity shares** of the issuing company at a later date, providing flexibility to both the issuer and the investor.
- **Statement 3 is incorrect**: FCCBs are typically issued for **long-term capital needs** rather than short-term financing.
- **Statement 4 is correct**: FCCBs are subject to regulation by the **Reserve Bank of India (RBI)** under India's external borrowing guidelines.

**Thus, the correct answer is (a) 1, 2 and 4 only.**

***43.*** *(c)* All three

- **Statement 1 is correct: Green Bonds** are indeed **debt instruments** that allow issuers to raise funds for **environmental projects** aimed at sustainability and combating climate change.
- **Statement 2 is correct**: The proceeds from Green Bonds can be used to fund various **green projects**, including **renewable energy**, **waste management** and **sustainable transportation**.
- **Statement 3 is correct**: In 2017, the **Securities and Exchange Board of India (SEBI)** issued guidelines to regulate the issuance of Green Bonds in India, ensuring transparency and proper use of proceeds for environmentally friendly projects.

**Thus, the correct answer is (c) All three.**

***44.*** *(c)* Only three

- **Renewable energy projects** are a primary use of Green Bond proceeds, supporting projects like solar, wind and geothermal energy.
- **Sustainable water management** projects are eligible, including water treatment, conservation and infrastructure.
- **Nuclear power generation is excluded.**
- **Biodiversity conservation is included.**

The Sovereign Green Bonds Framework explicitly excludes projects related to:

- Fossil fuel-based projects
- **Nuclear energy**
- Projects that involve **large-scale hydropower plants** exceeding a specified capacity
- Activities that could have a **negative environmental impact**

**Thus, the correct answer is (c) Only three.**

***45.*** *(a)* 1 only

- **Statement 1 is correct: Blue Bonds** are debt instruments issued to raise capital for **ocean and water-related projects**, focusing on sustainable use and conservation of marine resources.
  - The primary objectives of Blue Bonds include supporting **marine conservation, sustainable fisheries** and projects aimed at improving access to **clean water.**
  - One of the key goals of Blue Bonds is to **reduce marine pollution** and promote the **sustainable use of ocean resources,** aligning with global marine conservation objectives.
- **Statement 2 is incorrect**: While Blue Bonds are backed by various international organisations, the **first Blue Bond** was issued by the **Republic of Seychelles** in 2018, not by the UNDP.

**Thus, the correct answer is (a) 1 only.**

***46.*** *(d)* 1, 2 and 3

- **Statement 1 is correct: Sovereign Gold Bonds (SGBs)** are government securities issued by the Reserve Bank of India (RBI) and are denominated in **grams of gold.** Investors can buy these bonds instead of holding physical gold.
- **Statement 2 is correct**: Upon **maturity**, the investor receives the market value of the gold and earns a fixed interest rate, which is

typically around **2.5% per annum**, paid semi-annually on the initial investment.

- **Statement 3 is correct**: SGBs are exempt from **capital gains tax** if held until maturity, making them a tax-efficient investment for those seeking exposure to gold.

**Thus, the correct answer is (d) 1, 2 and 3.**

**47.** *(c)* 1 only

**Surety Bonds** are a **type of guarantee** provided by a **surety company** usually an insurance company to ensure that the obligations of a **principal** such as a contractor or business to a third party, known as the **obligee** such as a government entity or private client, are fulfilled. If the principal fails to meet their contractual obligations, the surety steps in to compensate the obligee for any financial losses, up to the bond's value.

- **Statement 1 is correct: Surety Bonds** are used in **infrastructure projects** and act as a substitute for **bank guarantees**, providing contractors with an alternative way to meet their project-related financial requirements.
- **Statement 2 is incorrect**: These bonds operate as a **tripartite agreement** between the **principal** (contractor), the **obligee** (project owner) and the **surety** (insurance company) ensuring that the contractor meets their contractual obligations.
- **Statement 3 is incorrect**: The **Surety Bonds** were launched in India by **insurance companies**, not the Reserve Bank of India (RBI).

**Thus, the correct answer is (c) 1 only.**

**48.** *(b)* 1-C, 2-B, 3-A

- The **Principal** is the party that has the **primary responsibility** to perform or fulfil the contract obligations like a contractor in a construction project.
- The **Obligee** is the party that requires the bond and **receives protection against default**. This is the party for whom the bond is issued (like a government agency or project owner).
- The **Surety** is the party that provides the guarantee or **guarantees the performance or obligations** of the principal. Typically, this is an insurance company or a financial institution.

**Thus, the correct matching is 1-C, 2-B, 3-A, which corresponds to option (b).**

**49.** *(c)* All three

**Municipal Bonds** are debt instruments issued by municipal bodies or urban local governments to raise funds for public projects. These projects often involve infrastructure development, such as water supply, sewage systems, transport and other public utilities. The tenure ranging from 3 to 10 years, and the returns are dependent on the performance of the project or the overall financial health of the municipal body.

- **Statement 1 is correct: Municipal Bonds** are issued by **urban local bodies** (such as municipalities) to raise funds for infrastructure and development projects.
- **Statement 2 is correct**: SEBI regulates the issuance of **Municipal Bonds** in India, ensuring transparency and compliance with market rules.
- **Statement 3 is correct**: The interest earned on municipal bonds can be **tax-free** in some cases, which makes them attractive to investors.

**Thus, the correct answer is (c) All three.**

**50.** *(c)* To encourage disclosure of undisclosed wealth and channel it into infrastructure projects.

The primary purpose of **Elephant Bonds** is to allow individuals with previously undisclosed wealth to declare their assets, often referred to as 'black money,' with limited tax penalties or amnesty. In return, a significant portion of the disclosed wealth is invested in **infrastructure projects** in India. This policy aims to boost economic development while bringing more assets into the formal economy.

**Thus, option (c) is the correct answer.**

**51.** *(a)* 1 only

- **Statement 1 is correct: Preference shareholders** have a **higher claim on company assets** during liquidation as compared to equity shareholders. They are paid off before equity shareholders in case of dissolution. The general **hierarchy of claims** is as follows:

1. **Secured Creditors** (Bondholders)-These creditors have claims backed by specific assets (collateral)
2. **Unsecured Creditors** (Debenture holders, Trade creditors)- Creditors without specific collateral
3. **Subordinated Debt Holders**-Creditors whose claims are subordinate to other debts.
4. **Preferred Shareholders**- Preferred shareholders have a higher claim than common shareholders
5. **Common Shareholders**- Equity holders or common shareholders are the last to be paid.

- **Statement 2 is incorrect: Preference shares** usually carry a **fixed rate of dividend**, whereas dividends for **equity shareholders** can **fluctuate** based on the company's profits and financial condition. **Preference shareholders** are paid **before equity shareholders** in terms of dividends, giving them a priority in income distribution.

**Thus, the correct answer is (a) 1 only.**

**52.** *(c)* 1, 2 and 4 only

- **Statement 1 is correct**: The **primary market** is where companies or governments issue securities for the **first time** to raise capital.
- **Statement 2 is correct**: The **funds** raised from the primary market go **directly to the issuer**, such as a company or government, for their use.
- **Statement 3 is incorrect**: In the primary market, securities are **not traded between investors**. This feature belongs to the **secondary market**.
- **Statement 4 is correct**: Common instruments in the primary market include **Initial Public Offerings (IPOs), bonds and rights issues.**

**Thus, the correct answer is (c) 1, 2 and 4 only.**

**53.** *(c)* Secondary Market

- The **secondary market** is where investors **trade previously issued securities** such as stocks, bonds, or debentures. It provides **liquidity** for these securities, allowing investors to easily enter and exit positions.
- Stock exchanges such as the NSE and BSE are examples of the secondary market, where trading occurs among investors.

**Thus, option (c) is the correct answer.**

**54.** *(b)* 1-B, 2-C, 3-A

- **Initial Public Offering (IPO)** is the process by which a private company offers its shares to the public for the **first time, transitioning into a publicly-traded company.** The purpose of an IPO is to raise capital from public investors.
- A **Rights Issue** is a method used by companies to raise additional capital by **offering existing shareholders** the opportunity to purchase **additional shares** at a discounted price, in proportion to their current shareholding. This offer is made before the company opens the shares to the general public.
- A **Follow-on Public Offering (FPO)** is a process through which a publicly listed company issues **additional shares to investors after its initial public offering (IPO)**. FPOs are used by companies to raise more capital from the market, either to fund expansion, reduce debt, or meet other corporate needs.

**Thus, the correct answer is (b) 1-B, 2-C, 3-A.**

**55.** *(b)* It is a preliminary document that contains detailed information about the company's operations and financials, but does not mention the offer price or issue size.

- The company and its underwriters conduct **due diligence** to ensure the company complies with legal and financial standards. The company files a **Draft Red Herring Prospectus (DRHP)** with the **Securities and Exchange Board of India (SEBI)**. This document contains detailed information about the company, its financials, risk factors, and the IPO.
- Therefore, the Draft Red Herring Prospectus (DRHP) is a **preliminary document** that provides detailed information about the company's business, risks, and financial performance. However, the **offer price and issue size are not mentioned** in the DRHP, as these are determined later after assessing investor interest.
- The DRHP is made **publicly available** for review by potential investors before the IPO.

**Thus, option (b) is the correct answer.**

**56.** *(d)* 1, 2 and 3

**Depository Receipts (DRs)** are negotiable financial instruments issued by a bank representing a company's shares that are traded on foreign stock exchanges. DRs allow investors to hold shares in a foreign company while trading in the investor's local market and currency. This simplifies cross-border investment.

- **Statement 1 is correct: ADRs** represent shares of a **foreign company** that are traded on **U.S. stock exchanges,** making it easier for U.S. investors to invest in foreign firms. ADRs are issued by **U.S. depository banks.**
- **Statement 2 is correct**: Investors receive **dividends in U.S. Dollars** when holding ADRs, simplifying the investment process.
- **Statement 3 is correct**: The price of ADRs is typically **linked** to the price of the company's shares in its **home market** and it can fluctuate accordingly based on the exchange rate and stock price movements.

**Thus, the correct answer is (d) 1, 2 and 3.**

**57.** *(b)* Only two

- **IDRs: Indian Depository Receipts (IDRs) are issued by foreign companies in India,** so they are not used by Indian companies to raise funds **from outside India.**
- **GDRs**: Indian companies can use **Global Depository Receipts (GDRs)** to raise funds from **international markets** (except the U.S.), especially in Europe and other regions.
- **ADRs: American Depository Receipts (ADRs)** are a tool for Indian companies to raise capital from **U.S. investors.**
- **SDRs: Singapore Depository Receipts (SDRs)** do not exist as a recognised financial instrument for Indian companies.

**Thus, the correct answer is (b) Only two.**

**58.** *(a)* It is the process of converting physical securities into electronic form, which can be held in a demat account with a depository participant.

- **Dematerialisation** introduced under the Depositories Act, 1996 which refers to the conversion of **physical securities** like share certificates into **electronic form.** These digital securities are held in a **demat account** with depository participants (such as banks or financial institutions), making it easier to trade and manage them.
- In India, the two main depositories that facilitate the dematerialisation process are: **NSDL (National Securities Depository Limited)** and **CDSL (Central Depository Services Limited).** These depositories work through Depository Participants (DPs) like banks and brokerage firms to provide services to investors.

**Thus, option (a) is the correct answer.**

**59.** *(b)* 1 and 3 only

- **Statement 1 is correct: Dematerialisation** refers to the process of converting **physical share certificates** into an **electronic form** to simplify trading and reduce the risk of fraud or theft. **Dematerialisation** was introduced in India in **1996,** allowing investors to hold securities in electronic form through depositories like NSDL and CDSL.
- **Statement 2 is incorrect**: Dematerialised securities can be easily **transferred between investors** through electronic systems, making transactions more efficient and secure.
- **Statement 3 is correct**: Once dematerialised, securities are held in **demat accounts** with **depository participants** (DPs), who act as intermediaries between investors and depositories.

**Thus, the correct answer is (b) 1 and 3 only.**

**60.** *(a)* 1 and 2 only

- **Statement 1 is correct: Depositories** hold securities (such as shares, bonds and debentures) in **electronic form** and enable their **transfer** ***via*** **a book-entry** system. It enable the **dematerialisation** of physical securities into **electronic form,** which simplifies the handling of securities.
- **Statement 2 is correct:** The two main depositories in India are **NSDL (National Securities Depository Limited)** and **CDSL (Central Depository Services Limited).**
- **Statement 3 is incorrect:** Depositories do not directly buy and sell shares. They **act as intermediaries** that hold and facilitate the transfer of securities, while the buying and selling are done through brokers.

**Thus, the correct answer is (a) 1 and 2 only.**

**61.** *(d)* NSDL is linked to the NSE (National Stock Exchange), while CDSL is linked to the BSE (Bombay Stock Exchange).

- **NSDL** is older, larger, and more focused on **institutional investors**, with a stronger association with **NSE. CDSL** caters more to **retail investors**, with a simpler platform and a growing base through its association with BSE. However, both depositories serve the same function of holding securities in electronic form.
- Both NSDL and CDSL are regulated by **SEBI**.

**Thus, option (d) is the correct answer.**

**62.** *(a)* A process where ownership and management of the exchange are separated, allowing public trading of exchange shares.

**Demutualisation** is a structural transformation in which a stock exchange changes from being a member-owned mutual organisation to a shareholder-owned corporation. Through this process, **ownership, management** and **trading rights** are separated, allowing the exchange to raise capital by issuing public shares. This change opens up participation to investors outside traditional brokerage firms and enhances operational transparency.

**Thus, option (a) is the correct answer.**

**63.** *(c)* Only three

- **Option 1 is correct: Bombay Stock Exchange** (BSE) is one of India's primary stock exchanges dealing with **equities**.
- **Option 2 is correct: National Stock Exchange** (NSE) also primarily deals with **equities** and is one of the major stock exchanges in India.
- **Option 3 is correct: India International Exchange** (INX) offers trading in various asset classes, including equities, currencies, and commodities. It operates for 22 hours a day, allowing investors from different time zones to trade at their convenience.
- **Option 4 is incorrect: Multi Commodity Exchange** (MCX) is a **commodity exchange**, not a stock exchange dealing in equities.

**Thus, the correct answer is (c) Only three.**

**64.** *(b)* To create a platform where non-profit and for-profit social enterprises can raise funds through equity or debt instruments.

- The **Social Stock Exchange** (SSE) in India was established as a unique platform to address the funding needs of **social enterprises**. It allows **non-profits and for-profit entities with social objectives** to raise capital via equity or debt instruments, facilitating the inflow of private investment into social impact sectors. This helps in mobilising resources for projects related to health, education, poverty alleviation, and other areas of social benefit.
- **Option (a) is incorrect**: SSE is not a platform for issuing shares directly to social workers; it is intended for social impact enterprises to raise funds from institutional and retail investors.
- **Option (c) is incorrect**: The exchange is open to both public and private entities with social goals, not only to public sector organisations.
- **Option (d) is incorrect**: The SSE does not provide tax-free income but is structured to allow organisations that create social impact to access funding.

**Thus, option (b) is the correct answer.**

**65.** *(b)* SENSEX is the index for the Bombay Stock Exchange (BSE), whereas NIFTY50 is the index for the National Stock Exchange (NSE)

- **Option (a) is incorrect: SENSEX** consists of **30 companies**, while **NIFTY50** represents 50 **companies**. This gives NIFTY50 a broader base, as it includes more companies and provides a wider sectoral representation than SENSEX.
- **Option (b) is correct**: The **primary difference** lies in the exchanges they represent. **SENSEX** is the **benchmark index for the Bombay Stock Exchange** (BSE), tracking 30 leading companies listed on the BSE, while **NIFTY50** is the **benchmark index for the National Stock Exchange** (NSE), representing 50 top companies from diverse sectors. This makes **option (b) correct.**
- **Option (c) is incorrect**: Both SENSEX and NIFTY50 include **large-cap companies** rather than focusing on only small-cap or

mid-cap stocks. These indices are composed of companies with significant market capitalisation that represent the Indian economy's growth and strength.

- **Option (d) is incorrect:** Neither index is limited to a single sector. **SENSEX** and **NIFTY50** both cover a wide array of sectors such as financial services, IT, consumer goods, and energy, providing a comprehensive outlook of the Indian economy.

**Thus, option (b) is the correct answer.**

**66.** *(b)* Insider trading refers to the buying or selling of securities by someone who has access to non-public, material information about the company.

- **Insider trading** occurs when individuals with **material non-public information** about a company trade its securities for personal profit, taking advantage of information not yet available to the public.
- This practice is illegal under the provision of SEBI (Prohibition of Insider Trading) Regulations, 2015 as it provides an unfair advantage to those with access to confidential company data.

**Thus, the correct answer is (b).**

**67.** *(a)* 1-A, 2-B, 3-C

- **Depositories Act, 1996:** This Act introduced the concept of **dematerialisation** of securities and their transfer in **electronic form.**
- **Companies Act, 2013:** This Act includes provisions for **corporate governance** to ensure transparency and accountability to protect shareholder rights.
- **SEBI (Prohibition of Insider Trading) Regulations, 2015:** These regulations aim to prevent **insider trading** by prohibiting trading based on **non-public, material information.**

**Thus, the correct answer is (a) 1-A, 2-B, 3-C.**

**68.** *(a)* 1 and 3 only

- **Statement 1 is correct: Participatory Notes (P-Notes)** are used by foreign investors to invest in **Indian markets** without registering with SEBI.
- **Statement 2 is incorrect:** SEBI has introduced **regulations** to monitor and control the use of P-Notes, particularly in addressing issues of money laundering.
- **Statement 3 is correct:** There are concerns that **P-Notes** may be used for **money laundering** and **tax evasion** due to the anonymity they offer.

**Thus, the correct answer is (a) 1 and 3 only.**

**69.** *(a)* 1 and 2 only

- **Statement 1 is correct:** Chit funds act as a **hybrid savings and borrowing scheme** where members pool money, and one member receives the total pool each period. The chit amount is determined through a system of **bidding**, where the lowest bid wins, and the winning participant receives the chit amount after deductions.
- **Statement 2 is correct:** These chit funds are **regulated** by the **Chit Funds Act, 1982.**
- **Statement 3 is incorrect:** Chit funds are regulated by the respective **State Governments** and are not under the direct regulation of the Reserve Bank of India (RBI).

**Thus, the correct answer is (a) 1 and 2 only.**

**70.** *(b)* 2 only

- **Statement 1 is incorrect:** Nidhi companies are **not regulated** by the **RBI**. Instead, they are governed by the **Ministry of Corporate Affairs (MCA)** under the Companies Act, 2013. Nidhi companies must be incorporated under the **Companies Act, 2013,** and obtain the necessary certification from the MCA to operate.
- **Statement 2 is correct:** Nidhi companies are a type of **Non-Banking Financial Company (NBFC)** that focus on accepting deposits from and lending to their **members only.**
- **Statement 3 is incorrect:** Nidhi companies are **not allowed** to engage in **chit fund, hire-purchase,** or **leasing activities.** They are only permitted to accept deposits and provide loans to their members.

**Thus, the correct answer is (b) 2 only.**

**71.** *(a)* A CDS is a derivative contract where the seller compensates the buyer if a specific borrower defaults on a loan.

A **Credit Default Swap (CDS)** is a **financial derivative** that acts like insurance for lenders. The buyer of a CDS makes regular payments to the seller, and in return, the seller agrees to compensate the buyer if the borrower defaults on a loan. It helps manage credit risk in financial markets.

**Thus, the correct answer is (a).**

**72.** *(b)* Angel investors usually invest their personal funds, while venture capitalists manage pooled funds from multiple investors.

- **Angel Investors** typically invest **their own money** into startups at an **early stage**, while **Venture Capitalists (VCs)** manage funds from multiple investors to invest in **growth-stage or later-stage** companies.
- **Venture Capitalists** pool capital from institutions and individuals and their investments are significantly larger compared to **angel investments.**

**Thus, the correct answer is (b).**

**73.** *(a)* 3-2-1

- **Angel Investors** typically take the **highest risk** as they invest in **early-stage startups,** which are more prone to failure but also have high potential returns.
- **Venture Capitalists** invest in **startups and growth-stage companies,** usually with more structure and development than those targeted by angel investors, but still involve significant risk.
- **Private Equity** investors take the **lowest risk** among the three, as they generally invest in **established companies** that require capital for growth or restructuring, making their investments more secure.

**Thus, the correct order is (a) 3-2-1.**

**74.** *(b)* Only two

- **Statement 1 is correct:** Credit rating agencies evaluate the **creditworthiness** of entities issuing **debt instruments** like bonds and debentures, helping investors assess the risk.
- **Statement 2 is correct: SEBI** is the regulatory authority overseeing credit rating agencies in India, ensuring they follow proper guidelines.
- **Statement 3 is incorrect:** Credit rating agencies **primarily rate debt instruments,** not equity instruments as equity represents ownership in a company, not debt.

**Thus, the correct answer is (b) Only two.**

**75.** *(b)* 1, 2 and 3 only

- **CRISIL (Credit Rating Information Services of India Limited):** One of the major **Indian credit rating agencies.**
- **Fitch Ratings:** A **global rating agency** that operates in India.
- **Brickwork Ratings: An Indian credit rating agency.**
- **Standard and Poor's (S&P):** While it is a global rating agency, its operations are not specific to India's domestic credit rating agencies.

**Other credit rating agencies in India:**

- ICRA (Investment Information and Credit Rating Agency of India Limited)
- CARE (Credit Analysis and Research Limited)
- Moody's Investors Service

**These agencies assess the creditworthiness of companies, financial institutions and governments, providing investors with insight into the risk associated with investing in debt instruments issued by these entities.**

**Thus, the correct answer is (b) 1, 2 and 3 only.**

**76.** *(b)* An ETF is a financial instrument that tracks the performance of an index, commodity, or a basket of assets and is traded like a stock on an exchange.

- **Exchange Traded Funds (ETFs)** are investment funds that track the performance of **indices, commodities, or a basket of assets** and are traded on stock exchanges, similar to individual stocks meaning they can be **bought and sold throughout the trading day.**
- ETFs offer investors the opportunity to diversify their portfolio by investing in multiple assets through a single financial instrument.

**Thus, the correct answer is (b).**

**77.** *(b)* ETFs typically have lower expense ratios compared to mutual funds because they are passively managed and traded like stocks.

- ETFs and stocks **trade throughout the day**, whereas mutual funds can only be bought or sold at the **end of the trading day based on their Net Asset Value** (NAV).
- ETFs are generally **passively managed**, tracking an index, whereas mutual funds can be either **actively or passively managed**.
- ETFs offer **better liquidity** and can be traded anytime during market hours, while mutual funds can only be redeemed at the end of the day.
- **Since, ETFs** are generally passively managed and have **lower expense ratios** because they track an index or asset. **Mutual funds** are often actively managed, requiring frequent trading, which leads to **higher costs**.

**Thus, the correct answer is (b).**

**78.** *(a)* 1 and 2 only

- **Statement 1 is correct: Bharat-22** ETF is a diversified ETF comprising shares of **Public Sector Enterprises** (**PSEs**), but it also includes some private companies where the government holds significant stakes.
- **Statement 2 is correct: Bharat Bond ETF** invests in bonds issued by **Central Public Sector Enterprises** (**CPSEs**) and other government entities.
- **Statement 3 is incorrect:** The **Bharat-22** ETF is not managed by LIC but is managed by **ICICI Prudential Asset Management Company.**

**Thus, the correct answer is (a) 1 and 2 only.**

**79.** *(a)* CBLO is a short-term money market instrument that allows entities to borrow and lend funds against collateral, without using the repo market.

The **Collateralised Borrowing and Lending Obligation** (CBLO) is a short-term money market instrument that enables borrowing and lending against **collateral** such as government securities, primarily used by institutional participants like banks, mutual funds, and financial institutions. It operates as an alternative to the repo market, allowing participants to meet their short-term funding needs with relatively low risk.

**Thus, the correct answer is (a).**

**80.** *(a)* In the spot market, the transaction is settled immediately, whereas in the futures market, the transaction is settled at a predetermined future date.

- In the **spot market**, transactions involve the **immediate settlement** (on the spot) of the trade, meaning that the asset or commodity is delivered and paid for right away.
- In the **futures market**, the transaction is an agreement to buy or sell an asset at a **predetermined future date** and price, allowing participants to hedge against future price fluctuations.

**Thus, the correct answer is (a).**

**81.** *(b)* Short selling refers to borrowing shares and selling them, with the expectation of repurchasing them at a lower price to return to the lender.

- **Short selling** occurs when an investor **borrows shares** from a broker and sells them immediately, hoping to **repurchase the shares at a lower price** in the future.
- The investor profits if the stock price drops and can return the shares to the lender at a lower cost. It is a strategy used to benefit from **falling stock prices.**

**Thus, the correct answer is (b).**

**82.** *(b)* The company has sufficient earnings to comfortably cover its interest payments.

A high Interest Coverage Ratio signifies that a company's earnings are well above its interest expenses, indicating financial health and a low risk of default. This high ratio reassures investors and creditors about the company's stability.

**Thus, the correct answer is (b).**

**83.** *(b)* To offset multiple obligations between two parties, reducing the total amount exchanged

- **Option (b) is correct:** The primary purpose of **Bilateral Netting** is to **consolidate and offset multiple financial obligations** between two parties. By calculating the net payable or receivable amount, it significantly reduces the number of individual transactions and the total amount exchanged, enhancing financial efficiency and reducing exposure.

- **Option (a) is incorrect**: Bilateral Netting **reduces transaction costs** by consolidating multiple obligations into a single net payable or receivable, which minimises the need for multiple transactions.
- **Option (c) is incorrect**: Bilateral Netting does not settle each obligation individually. Instead, it combines multiple obligations into a **single net amount** for settlement, streamlining the process.
- **Option (d) is incorrect**: Bilateral Netting does not focus on prioritising higher interest transactions but rather aims to **reduce the total exposure** by offsetting obligations.

**Thus, option (b) is the correct answer.**

***84.*** *(a)* 1 and 2 only

- **Statement 1 is correct**: The **Voluntary Retention Route (VRR)** was introduced by the **Reserve Bank of India (RBI)** to attract **long-term foreign portfolio investments (FPIs)** in India's debt markets, including **both government and corporate bonds**. The VRR allows FPIs to invest in these sectors with certain benefits, encouraging stable capital inflow.
- **Statement 2 is correct**: Under the VRR, investors enjoy **exemptions from certain regulatory limits** that usually apply to foreign investments in Indian debt instruments.
- **Statement 3 is incorrect**: Unlike standard investment routes, VRR requires investors to retain their investments for a **minimum retention period**, which restricts immediate withdrawals. This condition ensures long-term commitment, reducing the volatility associated with short-term capital flows.

**Thus, option (a) is the correct answer.**

***85.*** *(a)* FAR allows unrestricted investment in certain government securities, while VRR requires a minimum retention period.

- **Option (a) is correct**: The **Fully Accessible Route (FAR)** allows **foreign investors unrestricted access to specific government securities**, enabling them to invest without any cap. In contrast, the **Voluntary Retention Route (VRR)** requires foreign investors to retain a specified portion of their investments in Indian debt markets for a **minimum retention period**, ensuring long-term commitment and reducing capital volatility. This is the key difference, as **FAR provides unrestricted investment** without retention constraints, making this option correct.
- **Option (b) is incorrect**: FAR is not limited to corporate bonds but focuses on **designated government securities**. VRR, on the other hand, includes both **government and corporate bonds** but enforces a retention period.
- **Option (c) is incorrect**: FAR and VRR are both intended for **foreign investors** to invest in Indian debt markets. Domestic investors have separate provisions for investing in government and corporate securities.
- **Option (d) is incorrect**: VRR is the one that mandates a **minimum retention period** for investments, while FAR does not enforce any such retention requirement, allowing unrestricted participation in designated government securities.

**Thus, option (a) is the correct answer.**

## Past Learning (Answers)

| | | | | | | | | | |
|---|---|---|---|---|---|---|---|---|---|
| **1** (c) | **2** (d) | **3** (d) | **4** (c) | **5** (b) | **6** (d) | **7** (b) | **8** (c) | **9** (a) | **10** (a) |
| **11** (a) | **12** (d) | **13** (b) | **14** (a) | **15** (c) | **16** (d) | | | | |

CHAPTER 10

# Financial Regulatory Bodies

## Assessment Round

### Topic 1 : Financial Stability and Development Council (FSDC)

**1.** With reference to the Financial Stability and Development Council (FSDC), consider the following statements:

1. The council meets annually to assess the stability of the Indian financial sector.
2. The council is chaired by the RBI Governor.
3. It is responsible for the inter-regulatory coordination between financial sector regulators in India.

How many of the statements given above is/are correct?

(a) Only one (b) Only two
(c) All three (d) None

**2.** Which of the following regulatory bodies are members of the Financial Stability and Development Council (FSDC)?

1. Pension Fund Regulatory and Development Authority (PFRDA)
2. Competition Commission of India (CCI)
3. Reserve Bank of India (RBI)
4. National Housing Bank (NHB)

Select the correct answer from the codes given below:

(a) 3 only (b) 1 and 4 only
(c) 1 and 3 only (d) 1, 3 and 4 only

**3.** Consider the following statements about the 'Financial Stability and Development Council (FSDC)':

1. It has a sub-committee, which is chaired by the RBI Governor.
2. It is responsible for monitoring the regulation of credit rating agencies in India.
3. FSDC also addresses issues related to the regulation of microfinance institutions in India.

Which of the statements given above are correct?

(a) 1 and 2 only (b) 1 and 3 only
(c) 2 and 3 only (d) 1, 2 and 3

### Topic 2 : Reserve Bank of India

**4.** With reference to the Reserve Bank of India (RBI), consider the following statements:

1. The RBI was established based on the recommendations of the Hilton Young Commission.
2. The RBI is the sole authority for the issuance of currency in India, except for one-rupee notes and coins.
3. The RBI regulates both banking and non-banking financial companies (NBFCs).

How many of the statements given above is/are correct?

(a) Only one (b) Only two
(c) All three (d) None

**5.** Consider the following statements:

1. RBI Governor is appointed by the Government of India.
2. RBI is governed by a Central Board of Directors which consists of both full-time and part-time directors.
3. The RBI Act, 1934, provides clear grounds for the removal of the RBI Governor.

Which of the statements given above are correct?

(a) 1 and 2 only (b) 1 and 3 only
(c) 2 and 3 only (d) 1, 2 and 3

**6.** Under Section 7 of the Reserve Bank of India (RBI) Act, 1934, which of the following powers are conferred upon the Central Government?

(a) The power to issue directions to the RBI Governor in matters of public interest.
(b) The power to directly control the monetary policy decisions of the RBI.
(c) The power to appoint the RBI Governor without consultation with the RBI Board.
(d) The power to dismiss the RBI Governor without explanation.

**7.** Consider the following functions:

1. Formulating monetary policy
2. Regulation of the banking sector
3. Managing the foreign exchange reserves
4. Debt management of both Central Government and State Government

How many of the above functions is/are performed by the RBI?

(a) Only one (b) Only two
(c) Only three (d) All four

**8.** Which of the following statements are correct regarding the RBI's role in currency management?

1. It is responsible for issuing and managing the circulation of currency notes.
2. RBI directly manages the design of coins used in India.
3. RBI must maintain a reserve backing for the currency issued in the form of gold and foreign securities.

Select the correct answer from the codes given below:

(a) 1 and 2 only (b) 1 and 3 only
(c) 2 and 3 only (d) 1, 2 and 3

**9.** Consider the following locations with the RBI printing presses:

| | List I (Location) | | List II (RBI Printing Press) |
|---|---|---|---|
| 1. | Salboni, West Bengal | A. | Bharatiya Reserve Bank Note Mudran Pvt. Ltd. (BRBNMPL) |
| 2. | Dewas, Madhya Pradesh | B. | Currency Note Press (CNP) |
| 3. | Nashik, Maharashtra | C. | Bank Note Press (BNP) |
| 4. | Mysuru, Karnataka | D. | Bharatiya Reserve Bank Note Mudran Pvt. Ltd. (BRBNMPL) |

How many of the above pairs is/are correctly matched?

(a) Only one (b) Only two
(c) Only three (d) All four

**10.** What is the purpose of the Minimum Reserve System (MRS) adopted by the Reserve Bank of India (RBI) for currency issuance?

(a) To ensure that the government has enough funds to issue new currency
(b) To maintain a minimum level of reserves in gold and foreign exchange to back currency issuance
(c) To regulate the amount of liquidity in the banking system
(d) To manage foreign investments in India

**11.** Which of the following acts is/are administered by the RBI to regulate the banking sector in India?

1. Banking Regulation Act, 1949
2. Foreign Exchange Management Act (FEMA), 1999
3. Payment and Settlement Systems Act, 2007
4. Companies Act, 2013

Select the correct answer using the codes given below:

(a) 1, 2 and 3 only (b) 1, 3 and 4 only
(c) 2 and 4 only (d) 1, 2 and 4 only

**12.** Consider the following types of institutions:

1. Scheduled Commercial Banks (SCBs)
2. Non-Banking Financial Companies (NBFCs)
3. Housing Finance Companies (HFCs)

How many of the above institutions is/are regulated by the Reserve Bank of India (RBI)?

(a) Only one (b) Only two
(c) All three (d) None

**13.** What does the term 'Lender of Last Resort' primarily refer to in the context of central banking?
(a) A commercial bank that lends to individuals during financial crises
(b) The government providing funds to bail out failing companies
(c) The central bank offering emergency loans to financial institutions facing liquidity shortages
(d) Private investors lending money to distressed companies

**14.** With reference to the E-Kuber platform of the RBI, consider the following statements:
1. It is the Core Banking Solution (CBS) platform used by the RBI for handling government transactions.
2. It allows commercial banks to access government securities, fund management and auction platforms.
3. It is exclusively used for the transactions between RBI and the government, and no other entities are allowed to participate.

Which of the statements given above are correct?
(a) 1 and 2 only
(b) 1 and 3 only
(c) 2 and 3 only
(d) 1, 2 and 3

**15.** Consider the following statements with reference to the RBI's role as the debt manager for the government:
1. RBI manages the public debt for both the Central Government and State Governments.
2. RBI manages both domestic and external debt for the Government of India.
3. RBI can independently decide the borrowing limits for both the Central and State Governments

How many of the statements given above is/are correct?
(a) Only one
(b) Only two
(c) All three
(d) None

**16.** Which of the following tasks are undertaken by the Reserve Bank of India (RBI) in managing the public debt of the government?
1. Conducting auctions for government securities
2. Issuing State Development Loans (SDLs) on behalf of State Governments
3. Deciding the interest rates for all government bonds
4. Facilitating secondary market transactions in government bonds

Select the correct answer from the codes given below:
(a) 1, 2 and 4 only
(b) 2 and 3 only
(c) 1, 3 and 4 only
(d) 1, 2 and 3 only

**17.** With reference to the 'Public Debt Management Cell (PDMC)', consider the following statements:
1. It is responsible for formulating India's fiscal policy.
2. One of the key roles of PDMC is to facilitate the smooth issuance of government bonds through auctions.
3. PDMC is an independent body set up under the RBI to manage public debt.

Which of the statement(s) given above is/are correct?
(a) 1 and 2 only (b) 2 only
(c) 1 and 3 only (d) 1, 2, and 3

**18.** Consider the following statements:
1. RBI regulates all inter-bank and retail payment systems under the Payment and Settlement Systems Act, 2007.
2. RBI has the power to issue licenses for the operation of payment systems in India.
3. Mobile wallets and prepaid payment instruments operate independently of RBI regulation.

Which of the statements given above are correct?
(a) 1 and 2 only (b) 1 and 3 only
(c) 2 and 3 only (d) 1, 2 and 3

**19.** Consider the following statements in the context of digital payments:

1. RBI mandates two-factor authentication (2FA) for all card-based online transactions.
2. Payment systems such as the Unified Payments Interface (UPI) and Immediate Payment Service (IMPS) are regulated by the RBI.
3. The RBI is not responsible for setting the interchange fees for digital payment transactions.

Which of the statements given above are correct?

(a) 1 and 2 only (b) 2 and 3 only
(c) 1 and 3 only (d) 1, 2 and 3

**20.** With reference to the Board for Regulation and Supervision of Payment and Settlement Systems (BPSS), consider the following statements:

1. It is a sub-committee of the Central Board of the RBI and is responsible for regulating and supervising payment and settlement systems in India.
2. BPSS has the power to oversee the functioning of the National Payments Corporation of India (NPCI), which manages the Unified Payments Interface (UPI).
3. BPSS is chaired by the Finance Minister of India.

Which of the statements given above are correct?

(a) 1 and 2 only
(b) 2 and 3 only
(c) 1 and 3 only
(d) 1, 2 and 3

**21.** With reference to the concept of a regulatory sandbox, consider the following statements:

1. A regulatory sandbox is designed to test innovative financial products and services in a controlled environment.
2. Entities participating in a regulatory sandbox are exempt from all regulatory requirements during the testing phase.
3. RBI oversees the operation of the regulatory sandbox in India.

How many of the statements given above is/are correct?

(a) Only one (b) Only two
(c) All three (d) None

**22.** With reference to the RBI's regulatory sandbox, consider the following statements:

1. Only startups are allowed to participate in the regulatory sandbox.
2. It is exclusively designed for blockchain-based projects.
3. The regulatory sandbox reduces the time to market for innovative financial products.

How many of the statements given above is/are correct?

(a) Only one (b) Only two
(c) All three (d) None

**23.** Consider the following organisations/institutions:

1. Deposit Insurance and Credit Guarantee Corporation (DICGC)
2. National Payments Corporation of India (NPCI)
3. Bharatiya Reserve Bank Note Mudran Private Limited (BRBNMPL)
4. Indian Financial Technology and Allied Services (IFTAS)

How many of the given above is/are subsidiaries of the Reserve Bank of India (RBI)?

(a) Only one
(b) Only two
(c) Only three
(d) All four

**24.** Consider the following:

1. Government securities
2. Foreign exchange reserves
3. Currency in circulation
4. Gold reserves

How many of the given above is/are included in the asset side of the RBI's balance sheet?

(a) Only one
(b) Only two
(c) Only three
(d) All four

**25.** Which of the following are considered liabilities of the RBI?

1. Currency in circulation
2. Deposits held by commercial banks with the RBI
3. Foreign exchange reserves
4. Gold reserves

Select the correct answer using the codes given below:

(a) 1 and 2 only (b) 3 and 4 only
(c) 1, 2 and 3 only (d) 1, 2, 3 and 4

**26.** What is the primary purpose of the Economic Capital Framework (ECF) adopted by the Reserve Bank of India (RBI)?

(a) To regulate fiscal policy for the Government of India
(b) To determine the optimal amount of reserves the RBI should maintain to meet risks and contingencies
(c) To manage government borrowings and debt levels
(d) To set guidelines for foreign exchange market interventions

**27.** With reference to the 'Economic Capital Framework (ECF)', consider the following statements:

1. It governs the distribution of surplus reserves from the RBI to the Government of India.
2. The framework was designed to ensure the RBI has sufficient capital buffers to handle potential risks.
3. The ECF mandates that at least 50% of the RBI's profits must be transferred to the government annually.

Which of the statements given above are correct?

(a) 1 and 2 only (b) 2 and 3 only
(c) 1 and 3 only (d) 1, 2 and 3

**28.** Which of the following are considered major contributors to the income generated by the Reserve Bank of India (RBI)?

1. Investment in government securities
2. Earnings from foreign exchange reserves
3. Interest income from loans to the Central and State Governments.
4. Seigniorage (profit from currency issuance)

Select the correct answer using the codes given below:

(a) 1 and 2 only (b) 2 and 3 only
(c) 1 and 4 only (d) 1, 2 and 3 only

## Topic 3 : Securities and Exchange Board of India (SEBI)

**29.** With reference to the structure of the Securities and Exchange Board of India (SEBI), consider the following statements:

1. SEBI functions under the Ministry of Finance with its Board members appointed by the Central Government.
2. The Board of SEBI includes representatives from the Ministry of Finance, Ministry of Corporate Affairs and the Reserve Bank of India (RBI).
3. SEBI was established as a non-statutory body in 1988 and later gained statutory status in 1992.

Which of the statements given above are correct?

(a) 1 and 2 only (b) 1 and 3 only
(c) 2 and 3 only (d) 1, 2 and 3

**30.** Consider the following statements:

1. SEBI regulates the stock exchanges in India.
2. SEBI is responsible for the registration of stockbrokers and sub-brokers.
3. SEBI has the authority to regulate mutual funds in India.

How many of the statements given above is/are correct?

(a) Only one (b) Only two
(c) All three (d) None

**31.** With reference to the powers of SEBI, consider the following statements:

1. SEBI can conduct investigations and impose penalties for violations of securities laws.
2. SEBI has the authority to regulate and approve initial public offerings (IPOs) in India.
3. SEBI can directly intervene in the monetary policy of the Reserve Bank of India (RBI).

How many of the statements given above is/are correct?

(a) Only one (b) Only two
(c) All three (d) None

**32.** Consider the following statements about 'Securities Appellate Tribunal (SAT)':

1. It is a statutory body established under the SEBI Act, 1992.
2. It can hear appeals against decisions made by SEBI, PFRDA and IRDAI.
3. Decisions of SAT are final and cannot be challenged in any higher court.

Which of the statements given above are correct?

(a) 1 and 2 only (b) 2 and 3 only
(c) 1 and 3 only (d) 1, 2 and 3

**33.** Which of the following powers are granted to SEBI under the SEBI Act of 1992?

1. Regulating mergers and acquisitions of listed companies.
2. Issuing guidelines for insider trading.
3. Regulating the issuance of securities in the primary market.

Select the correct answer using the codes given below:

(a) 1 and 2 only (b) 2 and 3 only
(c) 1, 2 and 3 (d) 1 and 3 only

**34.** Consider the following statements:

1. SEBI has the power to conduct searches and seize documents related to securities law violations.
2. SEBI has the authority to ban individuals or companies from trading in the securities market for fraudulent practices.
3. SEBI can regulate the activities of Foreign Portfolio Investors (FPIs) in the Indian market.

Which of the statements given above are correct?

(a) 1 and 2 only
(b) 2 and 3 only
(c) 1, 2 and 3
(d) 1 and 3 only

**35.** Consider the following institutions:

1. National Stock Exchange (NSE)
2. Central Depository Services (India) Ltd. (CDSL)
3. Clearing Corporation of India Ltd. (CCIL)
4. Reserve Bank of India (RBI)

How many of the given above is/are considered Market Infrastructure Institutions (MIIs)?

(a) Only one
(b) Only two
(c) Only three
(d) All four

**36.** With reference to 'Market Infrastructure Institutions (MIIs)', consider the following statements:

1. MIIs include stock exchanges, clearing corporations, and depositories.
2. MIIs play a crucial role in maintaining the stability and transparency of financial markets.
3. MIIs are regulated by the Securities and Exchange Board of India (SEBI).

How many of the statements given above is/are correct?

(a) Only one (b) Only two
(c) All three (d) None

## Topic 4 : Insurance and Regulatory Development Authority (IRDAI)

**37.** Arrange the following events in the evolution of insurance sector in India in correct chronological order:

1. Establishment of the Life Insurance Corporation of India (LIC)
2. Nationalisation of General Insurance Companies
3. Passage of the Insurance Regulatory and Development Authority (IRDA) Act
4. Liberalisation of the Insurance Sector and entry of private players

Select the correct order using the codes given below:

(a) 1-2-3-4
(b) 2-1-3-4
(c) 1-2-4-3
(d) 2-1-4-3

**38.** With reference to the Insurance Regulatory and Development Authority of India (IRDAI), consider the following statements:

1. IRDAI was established by an Act of Parliament in 1999.
2. IRDAI regulates both life and general insurance companies in India.
3. IRDAI is empowered to issue licenses to new insurance companies but cannot revoke them once issued.

How many of the statements given above is/are correct?

(a) Only one
(b) Only two
(c) All three
(d) None

**39.** Consider the following insurance companies:

1. Life Insurance Corporation of India (LIC)
2. New India Assurance
3. General Insurance Corporation of India (GIC Re)
4. United India Insurance Company

How many of the above is/are categorised as Domestic Systemically Important Insurers (D-SIIs)?

(a) Only one
(b) Only two
(c) Only three
(d) All four

**40.** With reference to the Deposit Insurance and Credit Guarantee Corporation (DICGC), consider the following statements:

1. DICGC insures deposits in cooperative banks along with commercial banks.
2. The maximum deposit insurance cover provided by DICGC is ₹ 5 lakh per depositor per bank.
3. DICGC operates under the RBI.

How many of the statements given above is/are correct?

(a) Only one
(b) Only two
(c) All three
(d) None

**41.** Which of the following deposit types are covered by the Deposit Insurance and Credit Guarantee Corporation (DICGC)?

1. Fixed deposits
2. Savings deposits
3. Inter-bank deposits
4. Recurring deposits

Select the correct answer from the codes given below:

(a) 1 and 2 only (b) 2 and 4 only
(c) 1, 2 and 4 only (d) 1, 2, 3 and 4

**42.** With reference to the Export Credit Guarantee Corporation of India (ECGC), consider the following statements:

1. ECGC provides credit insurance to exporters to cover risks related to non-payment by foreign buyers.
2. ECGC is a government-owned corporation under the Ministry of Commerce and Industry.
3. ECGC provides insurance only for exports to high-risk countries.

Which of the statements given above are correct?

(a) 1 and 2 only
(b) 2 and 3 only
(c) 1 and 3 only
(d) 1, 2 and 3

**43.** Consider the following statements:

1. Insurance penetration refers to the percentage of insurance premium to the Gross Domestic Product (GDP).
2. Insurance density is the ratio of total insurance premiums to the total population of a country.
3. Economic Survey highlighted that India's insurance penetration remains below the global average.

How many of the statements given above is/are correct?

(a) Only one
(b) Only two
(c) All three
(d) None

## Topic 5 : Pension Fund Regulatory and Development Authority of India (PFRDA)

**44.** With reference to the 'Pension Fund Regulatory and Development Authority (PFRDA)', consider the following statements:

1. It was first established in 2013 under the Pension Fund Regulatory and Development Authority Act.
2. PFRDA is responsible for regulating the National Pension System (NPS) and other pension schemes in India.
3. The PFRDA is under the direct control of the Ministry of Labour and Employment.

How many of the statements given above is/are correct?

(a) Only one
(b) Only two
(c) All three
(d) None

**45.** Consider the following statements:

1. PFRDA manages both voluntary and mandatory pension schemes in India.
2. PFRDA is empowered to set investment guidelines for pension funds in India.
3. PFRDA directly administers pension payouts to all government employees in India.

How many of the statements given above is/are correct?

(a) Only one (b) Only two
(c) All three (d) None

**46.** Consider the following features of the 'National Pension System (NPS)':

1. It is a voluntary retirement savings scheme.
2. It offers both Tier I and Tier II accounts for subscribers.
3. Withdrawals from the Tier I account are fully tax-exempt at the time of retirement.
4. It is regulated by the Pension Fund Regulatory and Development Authority (PFRDA).

How many of the above features is/are correct?

(a) Only one
(b) Only two
(c) Only three
(d) All four

**47.** With reference to the National Pension System (NPS), consider the following statements:

1. The NPS is open to both Indian citizens and NRIs (Non-Resident Indians).
2. It is mandatory for all Indian citizens above 18 years of age.
3. The minimum contribution required for the NPS Tier I account is ₹ 10,000 per year.

Which of the statements given above are incorrect?

(a) 1 and 2 only
(b) 2 and 3 only
(c) 1 and 3 only
(d) 1, 2 and 3

**48.** Please consider the given below hypothetical scenario and answer the question given below:

Ravi, a 35-year-old Indian citizen, is currently working as a private-sector employee in India. He is interested in joining the National Pension System (NPS) to save for his retirement. However, Ravi plans to move to the United States in a few months and is unsure whether he can continue his NPS contributions as a Non-Resident Indian (NRI) once he relocates.

Considering Ravi's situation, is he eligible to join the NPS and continue his contributions if he moves abroad as an NRI?

(a) Yes, he can join NPS and continue contributing as an NRI.
(b) No, NPS is only available to Indian citizens residing in India.
(c) Yes, he can join NPS, but he cannot contribute once he becomes an NRI.
(d) No, only government employees are eligible for NPS.

## Topic 6 : International Financial Services Centers Authority (IFSCA)

**49.** With reference to the 'International Financial Services Centres Authority (IFSCA)', consider the following statements:
1. IFSCA is empowered to regulate all financial institutions operating in IFSCs in India.
2. The primary function of the IFSCA is to facilitate cross-border trading between financial markets in India and other countries.

Which of the statements given above is/are correct?
(a) 1 only
(b) 2 only
(c) Both 1 and 2
(d) Neither 1 nor 2

**50.** Consider the following statements:
1. IFSCA can regulate trading in securities, commodities and derivatives within IFSCs.
2. IFSCA has the power to levy fines and penalties on financial institutions that violate its guidelines.
3. The IFSCA can issue licenses to new banks and insurance companies to operate in India.

How many of the statements given above is/are correct?
(a) Only one (b) Only two
(c) All three (d) None

**51.** Consider the following regulatory bodies:
1. Reserve Bank of India (RBI)
2. Insurance Regulatory and Development Authority of India (IRDAI)
3. Pension Fund Regulatory and Development Authority (PFRDA)
4. Ministry of External Affairs (MEA)

How many of the above is/are part of the IFSCA composition?
(a) Only one
(b) Only two
(c) Only three
(d) All four

**52.** With reference to International Financial Service Centres (IFSC), consider the following statements:
1. IFSCs in India provide services related to banking, capital markets and insurance for non-residents only.
2. IFSCs are regulated by the International Financial Services Centres Authority (IFSCA).
3. GIFT City in Gujarat is India's first IFSC.

How many of the statements given above is/are correct?
(a) Only one (b) Only two
(c) All three (d) None

**53.** Which of the following services are offered by an International Financial Service Centre (IFSC) in India?
1. Fund management for global investors
2. Cross-border banking services
3. Local retail banking for Indian citizens
4. Insurance and reinsurance for global entities

Select the correct answer using the codes given below:
(a) 1, 2 and 4 only (b) 2 and 3 only
(c) 1 and 4 only (d) 1, 2, 3 and 4

# OMR SHEET

**Assessment Round**

| | | | | | | | | | | | | | | | | | | | |
|---|---|---|---|---|---|---|---|---|---|---|---|---|---|---|---|---|---|---|---|
| 1 | a | b | c | d | 31 | a | b | c | d | 61 | a | b | c | d | 91 | a | b | c | d |
| 2 | a | b | c | d | 32 | a | b | c | d | 62 | a | b | c | d | 92 | a | b | c | d |
| 3 | a | b | c | d | 33 | a | b | c | d | 63 | a | b | c | d | 93 | a | b | c | d |
| 4 | a | b | c | d | 34 | a | b | c | d | 64 | a | b | c | d | 94 | a | b | c | d |
| 5 | a | b | c | d | 35 | a | b | c | d | 65 | a | b | c | d | 95 | a | b | c | d |
| 6 | a | b | c | d | 36 | a | b | c | d | 66 | a | b | c | d | 96 | a | b | c | d |
| 7 | a | b | c | d | 37 | a | b | c | d | 67 | a | b | c | d | 97 | a | b | c | d |
| 8 | a | b | c | d | 38 | a | b | c | d | 68 | a | b | c | d | 98 | a | b | c | d |
| 9 | a | b | c | d | 39 | a | b | c | d | 69 | a | b | c | d | 99 | a | b | c | d |
| 10 | a | b | c | d | 40 | a | b | c | d | 70 | a | b | c | d | 100 | a | b | c | d |
| 11 | a | b | c | d | 41 | a | b | c | d | 71 | a | b | c | d | 101 | a | b | c | d |
| 12 | a | b | c | d | 42 | a | b | c | d | 72 | a | b | c | d | 102 | a | b | c | d |
| 13 | a | b | c | d | 43 | a | b | c | d | 73 | a | b | c | d | 103 | a | b | c | d |
| 14 | a | b | c | d | 44 | a | b | c | d | 74 | a | b | c | d | 104 | a | b | c | d |
| 15 | a | b | c | d | 45 | a | b | c | d | 75 | a | b | c | d | 105 | a | b | c | d |
| 16 | a | b | c | d | 46 | a | b | c | d | 76 | a | b | c | d | 106 | a | b | c | d |
| 17 | a | b | c | d | 47 | a | b | c | d | 77 | a | b | c | d | 107 | a | b | c | d |
| 18 | a | b | c | d | 48 | a | b | c | d | 78 | a | b | c | d | 108 | a | b | c | d |
| 19 | a | b | c | d | 49 | a | b | c | d | 79 | a | b | c | d | 109 | a | b | c | d |
| 20 | a | b | c | d | 50 | a | b | c | d | 80 | a | b | c | d | 110 | a | b | c | d |
| 21 | a | b | c | d | 51 | a | b | c | d | 81 | a | b | c | d | 111 | a | b | c | d |
| 22 | a | b | c | d | 52 | a | b | c | d | 82 | a | b | c | d | 112 | a | b | c | d |
| 23 | a | b | c | d | 53 | a | b | c | d | 83 | a | b | c | d | 113 | a | b | c | d |
| 24 | a | b | c | d | 54 | a | b | c | d | 84 | a | b | c | d | 114 | a | b | c | d |
| 25 | a | b | c | d | 55 | a | b | c | d | 85 | a | b | c | d | 115 | a | b | c | d |
| 26 | a | b | c | d | 56 | a | b | c | d | 86 | a | b | c | d | 116 | a | b | c | d |
| 27 | a | b | c | d | 57 | a | b | c | d | 87 | a | b | c | d | 117 | a | b | c | d |
| 28 | a | b | c | d | 58 | a | b | c | d | 88 | a | b | c | d | 118 | a | b | c | d |
| 29 | a | b | c | d | 59 | a | b | c | d | 89 | a | b | c | d | 119 | a | b | c | d |
| 30 | a | b | c | d | 60 | a | b | c | d | 90 | a | b | c | d | 120 | a | b | c | d |

## Calculate Your Score

| | |
|---|---|
| **Correct (✓)** | |
| **Incorrect (✓)** | |
| **Unattempted** | |
| **Total Score** | |
| **Accuracy (%)** | |

## Reasons for Incorrect Answers?

| | |
|---|---|
| 1. Lack of Knowledge/Existing Source Insufficient | |
| 2. Lack of Multiple Revision | |
| 3. Common Sense Mistakes | |

**Note :**

1. Calculate total score as correct answers carry 2 marks each 1/3rd marks will deducted for **Incorrect** Answers.
2. Calculate Accuracy (%) by dividing the number of correct answers to the total number of attempted questions.

## Past Learning

**1.** Consider the following statements: **(2021)**

1. The Governor of the Reserve Bank of India (RBI) is appointed by the Central Government.
2. Certain provisions in the Constitution of India give the Central Government the right to issue directions to the RBI in the public interest.
3. The Governor of the RBI draws his power from the RBI Act.

Which of the statements given above are correct?

(a) 1 and 2 only (b) 2 and 3 only
(c) 1 and 3 only (d) 1, 2 and 3

**2.** In India, the Central Bank's function as the 'lender of last resort' usually refers to which of the following? **(2021)**

1. Lending to trade and industry bodies when they fail to borrow from other sources
2. Providing liquidity to the banks having a temporary crisis
3. Lending to governments to finance budgetary deficits.

Which of the statements given above is/are correct?

(a) 1 and 2 only
(b) 2 only
(c) 2 and 3 only
(d) 3 only

**3.** Consider the following statements: **(2018)**

1. The Reserve Bank of India manages and services Government of India Securities but not any State Government Securities.
2. Treasury bills are issued by the Government of India and there are no treasury bills issued by the State Governments.
3. Treasury bills offered are issued at a discount from the par value.

Which of the statements given above is/are correct?

(a) 1 and 2 only
(b) 3 only
(c) 2 and 3 only
(d) 1, 2 and 3

**4.** Who among the following can join the National Pension System (NPS)? **(2017)**

(a) Resident Indian citizens only
(b) Persons of age from 21 to 55 only
(c) All State Government employees joining the services after the date of notification by the respective State Governments
(d) All Central Governments Employees including those of Armed Forces joining the services on or after 1st April, 2004

**5.** With reference to 'Financial Stability and Development Council', consider the following statements: **(2016)**

1. It is an organ of NITI Aayog.
2. It is headed by the Union Finance Minister.
3. It monitors macroprudential supervision of the economy.

Which of the statements given above is/are correct?

(a) 1 and 2 only (b) 3 only
(c) 2 and 3 only (d) 1, 2 and 3

**6.** The Reserve Bank of India regulates the commercial banks in matters of: **(2013)**

1. Liquidity of assets 2. Branch expansion
3. Merger of banks 4. Winding-up of banks

Select the correct answer from the codes given below:

(a) 1 and 4 only (b) 2, 3 and 4 only
(c) 1, 2 and 3 only (d) 1, 2, 3 and 4

**7.** The Reserve Bank of India (RBI) acts as a bankers' bank. This would imply which of the following? **(2012)**

1. Other bank retains their deposits with the RBI.
2. The RBI lends funds to the commercial banks in times of need.
3. The RBI advises the commercial banks on monetary matters.

Select the correct answer from the codes given below:

(a) 2 and 3 only (b) 1 and 2 only
(c) 1 and 3 only (d) 1, 2 and 3

# Detailed Solutions

## Assessment Round

**1.** *(a)* Only one

The Financial Stability and Development Council (FSDC) is an **apex body** established by the GOI in 2010 with to strengthen the financial stability framework, maintain macroeconomic stability, and ensure financial sector development.

- **Statement 1 is incorrect**: The Financial Stability and Development Council (FSDC) **meets as needed**, not necessarily annually.
- **Statement 2 is incorrect**: The FSDC is chaired by the **Union Finance Minister**, not the Governor of the RBI.
- **Statement 3 is correct**: One of the key roles of the FSDC is to ensure **inter-regulatory coordination** among the various financial sector regulators in India, such as the RBI, SEBI, IRDAI and PFRDA.

**Thus, the correct answer is (a) Only one.**

**2.** *(c)* 1 and 3 only

The Financial Stability and Development Council (FSDC) is an apex body chaired by the Union Finance Minister. It comprises the following members:

– **Governor, Reserve Bank of India (RBI)**
– Finance Secretary and/or Secretary, Department of Economic Affairs (DEA)
– Secretary, Department of Financial Services (DFS)
– Chief Economic Adviser, Ministry of Finance
– Chairman, Securities and Exchange Board of India (SEBI)
– Chairman, Insurance Regulatory and Development Authority of India (IRDAI)
– **Chairman, Pension Fund Regulatory and Development Authority (PFRDA)**

- **Option 1 is correct**: PFRDA is a part of the FSDC and contributes to the financial stability framework by regulating pension funds.
- **Option 2 is incorrect**: CCI, which regulates competition and anti-trust issues, is not a part of FSDC.
- **Option 3 is correct**: The RBI is a member of the FSDC and plays a key role in maintaining financial stability in the country.
- **Option 4 is incorrect**: NHB, though important for housing finance, is not a direct member of the FSDC.

**Thus, the correct answer is (c) 1 and 3 only.**

**3.** *(d)* 1, 2 and 3

- **Statement 1 is correct**: The FSDC has a **sub-committee** chaired by the **Governor of the Reserve Bank of India**. This sub-committee focuses on the technical and operational aspects of financial sector stability and development.
- **Statement 2 is correct**: FSDC is involved in **monitoring the regulation of credit rating agencies** in India as part of its mandate to oversee the financial system.
- **Statement 3 is correct**: FSDC also deals with issues related to the regulation of **microfinance institutions**, as they play a key role in financial inclusion and impact financial stability, especially in the rural sector.

**Thus, the correct answer is (d) 1, 2 and 3.**

**4.** *(c)* All three

- **Statement 1 is correct**: The RBI was established in 1935 based on the recommendations of the Hilton Young Commission.
- **Statement 2 is correct**: The RBI is the sole authority for the issuance of currency in India, **except for one-rupee notes and coins**, which are issued by the **Minister of Finance** but are managed by the RBI.
- **Statement 3 is correct**: The RBI regulates both banking and Non-Banking Financial Companies (NBFCs) in India, ensuring financial stability across sectors. NBFCs are

regulated by the **Reserve Bank of India (RBI)** under the Reserve Bank of India Act, 1934 and provide financial services similar to banks but are restricted in certain activities.

**All three statements are correct, so the answer is (c) All three.**

**5.** *(a)* 1 and 2 only

- **Statement 1 is correct:** The **RBI Governor** is appointed by the Government of India, typically for a tenure of three years, which can be extended for another two years. This decision typically made by the Cabinet's Appointments Committee.
- **Statement 2 is correct:** The **RBI** is governed by a **Central Board of Directors**. This board includes both **full-time directors**, such as the Governor and Deputy Governors, and **part-time directors**, who are appointed by the Government of India.
  - The **Central Board of Directors** is the governing body of the **Reserve Bank of India**, as established under the **RBI Act, 1934**. The Central Board is responsible for the overall direction and management of the RBI's affairs.
- **Statement 3 is incorrect:** The **RBI Act, 1934**, does not explicitly outline the grounds for the removal of the RBI Governor. The act is silent on specific reasons for removal, and any decision regarding the removal of the Governor is at the discretion of the Government of India.

**Thus, the correct answer is (a) 1 and 2 only.**

**6.** *(a)* **Section** 7 **of the Reserve Bank of India (RBI) Act, 1934**, grants the **Central Government** certain powers concerning the functioning of the RBI.

This section gives the **Central Government** the authority to consult with the Governor of the RBI and issue directions in matters of public interest, after consultation. However, this provision is rarely invoked as it would interfere with the autonomy of the central bank.

**Hence, option (a) is the correct answer.**

**7.** *(d)* All four

- **Formulating monetary policy:** This involves setting interest rates and controlling the money supply in the economy to achieve specific objectives like price stability, growth, and employment.
- **Regulation of the banking sector:** This includes overseeing the operations of banks, ensuring their financial soundness, and protecting depositors' interests.
- **Managing foreign exchange reserves:** This involves buying and selling foreign currencies to maintain the value of the rupee and ensure the country has sufficient reserves to meet its international obligations.
- **Debt management of both Central Government and State Government:** This involves advising the government on borrowing and lending, issuing government bonds, and managing public debt.

**Therefore, the correct answer is (d) All four.**

**8.** *(b)* 1 and 3 only

- **Statement 1 is correct:** The RBI is responsible for issuing and managing the circulation of currency notes in India.
- **Statement 2 is incorrect:** The **design of coins** is managed by the **Ministry of Finance**, not the RBI.
- **Statement 3 is correct:** The **Reserve Bank of India (RBI)** maintains a reserve backing for the currency it issues under the **Minimum Reserve System (MRS)**. This reserve is composed of the following:

**Gold:** The RBI is required to hold a certain amount of gold as part of its reserve to back the currency issued. **Foreign Securities:** The RBI also holds foreign currencies and securities as part of the reserve backing the currency issuance.

**Thus, the correct answer is (b) 1 and 3 only.**

**9.** *(b)* Only two

The correct matches for the RBI printing presses are:

- **Pair 1 is correct:** Salboni, West Bengal – A. Bharatiya Reserve Bank Note Mudran Pvt. Ltd. (BRBNMPL)
- **Pair 2 is incorrect:** Dewas, Madhya Pradesh – C. Bank Note Press (BNP), not Currency Note Press (CNP).

- **Pair 3 is incorrect**: Nashik, Maharashtra – B. Currency Note Press (CNP), not Bank Note Press (BNP).
- **Pair 4 is correct**: Mysuru, Karnataka – A. Bharatiya Reserve Bank Note Mudran Pvt. Ltd. (BRBNMPL)

**So, two pairs are correctly matched. The correct answer is (b) Only two.**

***10.*** *(b)* To maintain a minimum level of reserves in gold and foreign exchange to back currency issuance.

- The **Minimum Reserve System (MRS)** requires the RBI to hold a **minimum reserve of gold and foreign exchange** to back the issuance of currency notes, ensuring stability in the value of the currency.
- Under the Minimum Reserve System, the RBI has to keep a minimum reserve of ₹ 200 crore comprising of gold coin and gold bullion and foreign currencies. Out of the total ₹ 200 crores, ₹ 115 crore should be in the form of gold coins or gold bullion.
- The purpose of shifting to MRS was to expand **money supply** to meet the needs of increasing transactions in the economy

**Thus, option (b) the correct answer.**

***11.*** *(a)* 1, 2 and 3 only

- **Banking Regulation Act, 1949** is the key legislation that provides the RBI with the powers to regulate and supervise banks in India.
- **Foreign Exchange Management Act (FEMA), 1999** is administered by the RBI to manage and regulate foreign exchange transactions and ensure external stability.
- **Payment and Settlement Systems Act, 2007** is administered by the RBI to regulate and oversee payment and settlement systems in India, ensuring smooth and secure transactions.
- **The Companies Act, 2013**, is primarily concerned with the **regulation of companies,** including their formation, governance and financial reporting. While it has some relevance to banking companies, it is not specifically administered by the RBI for the purpose of regulating the banking sector. It is regulated by **Ministry of Corporate Affairs.**

**Hence, the correct answer is (a) 1, 2 and 3 only.**

***12.*** *(c)* All three

The RBI's role is to provide the best facilities to all banks in India and to safeguard public trust in the national financial system.

The Reserve Bank of India (RBI) regulates many institutions, including:

- **Scheduled Commercial Banks:** All scheduled commercial banks are regulated by the RBI.
- **Non-Banking Financial Companies (NBFCs):** The RBI regulates all NBFCs, including All India Financial Institutions (AIFIs), Primary Dealers (PDs), and Credit Information Companies (CICs).
- **RBI regulates HFCs** that provide loans for residential housing. Previously under the National Housing Bank (NHB), regulation of these companies was transferred to the RBI in 2019.
- **Payment Banks:** The RBI regulates all payment banks.
- **Select all-India financial institutions:** The RBI supervises and regulates ten all-India financial institutions, including IDBI, ICICI, IFCI, IIBI, Exim Bank, NABARD, NHB, SIDBI, IDFC and TFCI.

**All three types of institutions are regulated by the RBI, so the correct answer is (c) All three.**

***13.*** *(c)* The 'Lender of Last Resort' refers to the role of central banks, like the Reserve Bank of India (RBI), in providing **emergency loans to financial institutions** that are facing liquidity crises, ensuring stability in the financial system. This is to done to;

- **Protect depositors:** This will protect people who have deposited money in banks.
- **Prevent bank runs:** This will prevent customers from withdrawing their money in panic from banks that are temporarily short on liquidity.
- **Act as a safety net:** This will provide emergency funding to prevent liquidity crises and bank runs.

**Hence, option (c) is the correct answer.**

**14.** *(a)* 1 and 2 only

The **E-Kuber platform** is a core banking solution introduced by the Reserve Bank of India (RBI). It is used for various financial operations and services offered by the central bank to the government and other financial institutions.

- **Statement 1 is correct:** E-Kuber is the Core Banking Solution platform of the RBI used to handle various government-related transactions, including payments and receipts.
- **Statement 2 is correct:** E-Kuber provides access to commercial banks, enabling them to participate in auctions for government securities and manage their funds with the RBI.
- **Statement 3 is incorrect:** E-Kuber is **not exclusively used for transactions between the RBI and the government**; it is also accessible to commercial banks and financial institutions for various functions, including managing liquidity and participating in auctions of government securities

**Therefore, the correct answer is (a) 1 and 2 only.**

**15.** *(a)* Only one

- **Statement 1 is correct:** The RBI acts as the **debt manager for both the Central and State Governments**, managing the issuance of government securities and bonds. RBI helps the Central Government raise funds by issuing Treasury Bills (short-term) and dated securities (long-term). Also, RBI facilitates the issuance of State Development Loans (SDLs) on behalf of State Governments.
- **Statement 2 is incorrect: The RBI mainly manages domestic debt.** External debt management typically falls under the purview of the Ministry of Finance.
- **Statement 3 is incorrect:** The borrowing limits for the Central and State Governments are decided by the governments themselves, in consultation with the RBI, but the RBI cannot independently set these limits.

**Thus, one statement is correct, so the correct answer is (a) Only one.**

**16.** *(a)* 1, 2 and 4 only

- **Statement 1 is correct:** The RBI conducts regular auctions for government securities including Treasury Bills and managing the issuance of bonds on behalf of the government.
- **Statement 2 is correct:** The RBI issues **State Development Loans (SDLs)** on behalf of State Governments to raise funds for their financial need.
- **Statement 3 is incorrect:** The interest rates for government bonds are determined by the market through the auction process, not by the RBI.
- **Statement 4 is correct:** The RBI facilitates secondary market transactions in government bonds through its systems, ensuring liquidity in the government securities market.

**Thus, the correct answer is (a) 1, 2 and 4 only.**

**17.** *(b)* 2 only

Public Debt Management Cell is an interim arrangement before setting up an independent and statutory debt management agency namely the Public Debt Management Agency (PDMA). It has the **advisory** functions to the government.

- **Statement 1 is incorrect:** PDMC does not formulate fiscal policy. It is focused on debt management whereas fiscal policy is decided by the government.
- **Statement 2 is correct:** One of the functions of PDMC is to ensure the smooth issuance of government securities through auctions and other debt instruments. This is essential for managing the government's borrowing program and ensuring adequate liquidity in the market for government securities.
- **Statement 3 is incorrect:** The **PDMC** is not an independent body. It was set up as a **transitional arrangement** under the **Department of Economic Affairs** in the **Ministry of Finance.** While it works closely with the RBI, it is not under the RBI's direct authority. The long-term goal is to establish a statutory **Public Debt Management Agency (PDMA).**

**Thus, the correct answer is (b) 2 only.**

**18.** *(a)* 1 and 2 only

- **Statement 1 is correct:** The Reserve Bank of India (RBI) regulates all inter-bank and retail payment systems in India under the **Payment and Settlement Systems Act, 2007.** This act gives the RBI the authority to regulate, supervise, and manage the payment and settlement systems.

- **Statement 2 is correct**: The RBI has the power to issue licenses for the operation of payment systems in India. Any entity that operates a payment system must obtain authorisation from the RBI under the **Payment and Settlement Systems Act, 2007**.
- **Statement 3 is incorrect**: Mobile wallets and prepaid payment instruments (PPIs) are **regulated by the RBI**. They do not operate independently of RBI regulation. The RBI issues guidelines and regulates these instruments to ensure the safety, efficiency, and security of payments.

**Thus, the correct answer is (a) 1 and 2 only.**

**19.** *(b)* 2 and 3 only

- **Statement 1 is incorrect**: While the RBI has encouraged the use of two-factor authentication (2FA) for online transactions to enhance the security of digital payments and reduce fraud, **it hasn't mandated it for all card-based transactions.** RBI has tabled a new draft of Framework on Alternative Authentication Mechanisms for Digital Payment Transactions, focussing on various authentication forms required while making payments online.

**Two-factor authentication (2FA)** is a security process in which a user provides two different authentication factors to verify their identity. This method adds an extra layer of security to the authentication process by requiring not only a password and username but also something that the user has on them. The two factors typically used are:

**Something you know**: This is usually a password or PIN.

**Something you have**: This could be a physical device like a mobile phone, a security token, or a One-Time Password (OTP) sent *via* SMS or email.

**Examples: ATM transactions**: You need your ATM card (something you have) and a PIN (something you know).

- **Statement 2 is correct**: The **RBI regulates digital payment systems** such as UPI and IMPS to ensure security, efficiency, and reliability in the payments ecosystem.
- **Statement 3 is correct**: The **RBI does not set interchange fees** for digital payment transactions. Interchange fees are typically set by the payment networks (such as Visa, Mastercard) or by the market through commercial negotiations between banks, payment processors, and merchants.

**Thus, Statements 2 and 3 are correct, so the correct answer is (b) 2 and 3 only.**

**20.** *(a)* 1 and 2 only

**The Board for Regulation and Supervision of Payment and Settlement Systems (BPSS)** is a committee of the Reserve Bank of India (RBI) that oversees payment systems in India. The BPSS is the **highest policy-making body for payment systems in the country.** The Governor of the RBI chairs the BPSS.

**The Payment and Settlement Systems Act,** 2007 (PSS Act) authorised the RBI to create the BPSS. The RBI also created a Department of Payment and Settlement Systems (DPSS) in 2005 to focus on payment and settlement systems.

- **Statement 1 is correct**: The BPSS is a sub-committee of the RBI's Central Board and is responsible for overseeing the regulation and supervision of payment and settlement systems in India.
- **Statement 2 is correct**: BPSS has the power to oversee the functioning of the National Payments Corporation of India (NPCI), which manages key payment systems like Unified Payments Interface (UPI), RuPay, and others.
- **Statement 3 is incorrect**: BPSS is chaired by the Governor of the Reserve Bank of India, not the Finance Minister.
- **Therefore, Statements 1 and 2 are correct, so the correct answer is (a) 1 and 2 only.**

**21.** *(b)* Only two

A **regulatory sandbox** is a framework set up by a financial sector regulator to allow small-scale, live testing of innovations by private firms in a controlled environment under the regulator's supervision.

- **Statement 1 is correct:** A regulatory sandbox allows fintech firms and other entities to test innovative financial products and services in a controlled environment under the supervision of the regulator.
- **Statement 2 is incorrect:** Entities participating in a regulatory sandbox **are not exempt from all regulatory requirements.** They are given specific exemptions or relaxations for the duration of the testing phase, but they still must comply with core regulatory safeguards, especially those related to consumer protection and financial integrity.
- **Statement 3 is correct:** The RBI oversees the operation of the regulatory sandbox in India.

**Thus, two statements are correct, so the answer is (b) Only two.**

**22.** *(a)* Only one

- **Statement 1 is incorrect:** The regulatory sandbox is open to a **wide range of entities,** including startups, established companies, and financial institutions that have innovative solutions to test.
- **Statement 2 is incorrect:** The RBI's regulatory sandbox is **not limited to blockchain-based projects.** It is designed to accommodate a wide range of innovative financial products and services, including those leveraging emerging technologies like artificial intelligence, machine learning, and big data.
- **Statement 3 is correct:** By providing a controlled environment for testing and experimentation, the sandbox can help reduce the time it takes for new products to reach the market.

**Hence, only Statement 3 is correct. The correct answer is (a) Only one.**

**23.** *(c)* Only three

The Reserve Bank of India (RBI) has established several subsidiaries to carry out various specialised functions.

- **Deposit Insurance and Credit Guarantee Corporation** (DICGC) is a wholly owned subsidiary of the RBI. Provides insurance to depositors in case of bank failure and guarantees credit to promote financial stability.
  - **Establishment:** 1978
  - **Role:** Insures bank deposits up to a certain limit per depositor per bank
- **Bharatiya Reserve Bank Note Mudran Private Limited (BRBNMPL)** is also a subsidiary of the RBI. It engages in printing banknotes for the Reserve Bank of India.
  - **Establishment:** 1995
  - **Role:** It operates two currency printing presses, one in Mysuru, Karnataka and the other in Salboni, West Bengal.
- **National Payments Corporation of India (NPCI):** is not a subsidiary of the RBI. NPCI is an umbrella organisation for retail payments and settlement systems in India, established by a consortium of major banks and regulated by the RBI, but it is not directly owned by the RBI.
- **Indian Financial Technology and Allied Services (IFTAS)** is a wholly owned subsidiary of the RBI.
- It provides technology services, including payment systems infrastructure and communication networks, to banks and financial institutions.
  - **Establishment:** 2015
  - **Role:** Develops and maintains IT systems for secure financial transactions
- **Other subsidiaries of RBI:** Reserve Bank Information Technology Private Limited (ReBIT); National Housing Bank (NHB) and Clearing Corporation of India Ltd. (CCIL)

**Therefore, three of the listed entities are RBI subsidiaries, so the answer is (c) Only three.**

**24.** *(c)* Only three

The Reserve Bank of India's (RBI) balance sheet includes assets such as gold, foreign currency assets, and loans and advances.

- **Option 1 is correct: Government securities** are part of the **asset side** of the RBI's balance sheet. These represent the investments made by the RBI in government bonds, which are used to manage liquidity and influence interest rates in the economy.
- **Option 2 is correct: Foreign exchange reserves** are also recorded on the asset side of the RBI's

balance sheet. These reserves consist of foreign currencies, foreign securities, and other assets held by the RBI to manage the exchange rate and support the Indian rupee.

- **Option 3 is incorrect: Currency in circulation** is not an asset but a **liability** on the RBI's balance sheet. It represents the currency issued by the RBI that is held by the public and banks.
- **Option 4 is correct: Gold reserves** are included in the **asset side** of the RBI's balance sheet. The RBI holds gold as part of its reserves to provide financial stability and backing for the currency.

**Thus, the correct answer is (c) Only three.**

***25.*** *(a)* 1 and 2 only

- **Option 1 is correct: Currency in circulation** is a liability because it represents the currency issued by the RBI that is used by the public.
- **Option 2 is correct: Deposits held by commercial banks with the RBI** are also liabilities because they are the reserves held by banks with the central bank.
- **Option 3 and 4 are incorrect: Foreign exchange reserves** and **gold reserves** are assets, not liabilities, as they represent the holdings of the RBI.

**Thus, the correct answer is (a) 1 and 2 only.**

***26.*** *(b)* The **Economic Capital Framework** (ECF) was adopted by the Reserve Bank of India (RBI) to assess the appropriate level of **reserves** or **capital** that the RBI should maintain. These reserves help the RBI manage various risks, including **market risk, credit risk, operational risk**, and **contingencies** related to its operations. This framework ensures that the RBI maintains a sufficient capital buffer to handle any financial shocks while also determining how much surplus can be transferred to the government.

**Therefore, option (b) is the correct answer.**

***27.*** (a) 1 and 2 only

- **Statement 1 is correct**: The Economic Capital Framework (ECF) governs the distribution of surplus reserves from the RBI to the Government of India. It determines how much of the RBI's surplus capital can be transferred to the government while ensuring that the RBI maintains adequate reserves.
- **Statement 2 is correct**: The ECF ensures that the RBI maintains adequate capital buffers to manage risks such as monetary, financial and operational risks.
- **Statement 3 is incorrect**: The ECF does **not mandate a specific percentage of profits** to be transferred to the government. The amount of surplus transferred depends on the available reserves and the required risk buffer.

**Therefore, the correct answer is (a) 1 and 2 only.**

***28.*** *(a)* 1 and 2 only

- **Statement 1 is correct: Investment in government securities** generates significant income for the RBI, as it invests in long-term and short-term bonds issued by the government. The interest earned from holding government bonds contributes significantly to the RBI's income.
- **Statement 2 is correct**: The **earnings from foreign exchange reserves** are another significant contributor to the RBI's income. These reserves are invested in foreign assets like bonds and securities, which generate interest income.
- **Statement 3 is incorrect**: The RBI does not directly earn **interest income from loans to the Central and State Governments.** Instead, it earns income from the management of government debt and its investments, not from direct loans to the government.
- **Statement 4 is incorrect: Seigniorage** refers to the profit made from **issuing currency**; however, it is not a major contributor to the RBI's income compared to other sources like investments and foreign reserves.

**Thus, the correct answer is (a) 1 and 2 only.**

***29.*** *(c)* 2 and 3 only

- **Statement 1 is incorrect**: While SEBI was initially established under the Ministry of Finance, it gained statutory autonomy in 1992. Its Board members are now appointed by the Central Government, but SEBI functions independently of any ministry.
- **Statement 2 is correct**: The Board of SEBI includes members from the Ministry of

Finance, Ministry of Corporate Affairs and the Reserve Bank of India to ensure coordination across regulatory and financial bodies.

- **Statement 3 is correct:** SEBI was initially established as a non-statutory body in 1988 to regulate the securities market. It gained statutory powers through the SEBI Act, 1992, granting it more authority and legal standing to regulate the market.

**Therefore, Statements 2 and 3 are correct, so the correct answer is (c) 2 and 3 only.**

**30.** *(c)* All three

- **Statement 1 is correct:** The **Securities and Exchange Board of India (SEBI)** is the primary regulatory body for stock exchanges in India. SEBI's role includes ensuring that stock exchanges operate in a fair and transparent manner, protecting investor interests.
- **Statement 2 is correct:** SEBI is also responsible for the **registration and regulation of stockbrokers and sub-brokers.** This ensures that only qualified and authorized individuals and entities participate in the securities market, promoting transparency and accountability.
- **Statement 3 is correct:** SEBI has the authority to **regulate mutual funds** in India, setting guidelines for their operation, protecting investor interests, and ensuring proper disclosures by mutual fund companies.

**Therefore, the correct answer is (c) All three.**

**31.** *(b)* Only two

- **Statement 1 is correct: SEBI can conduct investigations and impose penalties for violations of securities laws.** SEBI has the authority to investigate suspected violations of securities laws and impose penalties on individuals and entities found guilty of wrongdoing.
- **Statement 2 is correct:** SEBI regulates the issuance of Initial Public Offerings (IPOs) to protect investor interests.
- **Statement 3 is incorrect: SEBI does not have the authority to directly intervene in the monetary policy of the Reserve Bank of India (RBI).** Monetary policy, which involves setting interest rates and controlling the money supply, is primarily the responsibility of the RBI. SEBI does not have the authority to intervene in the monetary policy of the RBI.

**Thus, the correct answer is (b) Only two.**

**32.** *(a)* 1 and 2 only

The **Securities Appellate Tribunal (SAT)** is a **quasi-judicial body** established in 2005 under the Securities and Exchange Board of India (SEBI) Act, 1992. It serves as the **appellate authority** for decisions made by the Securities and Exchange Board of India (SEBI).

- **Statement 1 is correct:** The Securities Appellate Tribunal (SAT) was established under the SEBI Act, 1992, as a statutory body to hear appeals against SEBI's decisions. It was set up to provide an independent platform for appeals against SEBI's decisions.
- **Statement 2 is correct:** SAT has the authority to hear appeals against decisions made not only by **SEBI** but also by the **Pension Fund Regulatory and Development Authority (PFRDA)** and the **Insurance Regulatory and Development Authority of India (IRDAI).**
- **Statement 3 is incorrect:** While SAT's decisions are generally considered final, they **can be challenged in the Supreme Court** under limited circumstances, such as when there is a violation of fundamental rights or a question of law of national importance. Therefore, SAT is not the last appellate authority, and parties can seek further appeal in a higher court.

**Thus, the correct answer is (a) 1 and 2 only.**

**33.** *(c)* 1, 2 and 3

- **Statement 1 is correct: Regulating mergers and acquisitions of listed companies:** SEBI has the power to regulate mergers and acquisitions of listed companies through the SEBI (Substantial Acquisition of Shares and Takeovers) Regulations, which provides rules for corporate takeovers.
- **Statement 2 is correct: Issuing guidelines for insider trading:** SEBI issues guidelines and regulations to prevent insider trading under the SEBI (Prohibition of Insider Trading) Regulations, 2015.

- **Statement 3 is correct: Regulating the issuance of securities in the primary market:** SEBI regulates the primary market, ensuring companies issuing securities to the public comply with the necessary regulations under SEBI's jurisdiction.

**Thus, the correct answer is (c) 1, 2 and 3.**

***34.*** *(c)* 1, 2 and 3

- **Statement 1 is correct: SEBI has the power to conduct searches and seize documents related to securities law violations.** SEBI has the authority to investigate suspected violations of securities laws and conduct searches to gather evidence.
- **Statement 2 is correct:** SEBI has authority to impose penalties, including bans on trading, on individuals or companies found guilty of fraudulent practices.
- **Statement 3 is correct:** SEBI regulates the activities of FPIs in India, ensuring that they comply with Indian securities laws and that their investments do not pose a threat to market stability.

**Thus, the correct answer is (c) 1, 2 and 3.**

***35.*** *(c)* Only three

- **National Stock Exchange** (NSE): This is a stock exchange, which is a type of Market Infrastructure Institution (MII). It provides a platform for buying and selling securities.
- **Central Depository Services (India) Ltd.** (CDSL): This is a depository, another type of MII. It holds securities in electronic form and provides related services.
- **Clearing Corporation of India Ltd. (CCIL):** This is a clearing house, yet another type of MII. It settles transactions and manages counterparty risks.
- **Reserve Bank of India (RBI):** While the RBI plays a crucial role in the financial system, it is not considered a Market Infrastructure Institution. It is the central bank of India and has a broader mandate of regulating the banking system and monetary policy.

**Therefore, the correct answer is (c) Only three.**

***36.*** *(c)* All three

- **Statement 1 is correct: Market Infrastructure Institutions (MIIs)** encompass **stock exchanges, clearing corporations, and depositories.** These institutions form the foundational infrastructure for the securities market, facilitating efficient trading, clearing, and settlement of transactions.
- **Statement 2 is correct:** MIIs play a **crucial role in maintaining the stability and transparency** of financial markets. By providing a structured and regulated environment for transactions, MIIs enhance investor confidence and uphold the integrity of financial systems.
- **Statement 3 is correct:** MIIs are regulated by the **Securities and Exchange Board of India** (SEBI), which oversees their operations to ensure they comply with regulatory standards, protect investor interests, and maintain market stability.

**All three statements are correct, so the correct answer is (c) All three.**

***37.*** *(a)* 1-2-3-4

- **The Life Insurance Corporation** (LIC) was established in **1956** when the government nationalised all life insurance companies in India through the **LIC Act, 1956.**
- **Nationalisation of General Insurance Companies–1972** Following the nationalisation of life insurance, the government nationalised the general insurance sector in **1972** under the **General Insurance Business (Nationalisation) Act, 1972.**
- **The Insurance Regulatory and Development Authority (IRDA) Act was passed in 1999** to provide a regulatory framework for the insurance sector.
- **Liberalisation of the Insurance Sector and Entry of Private Players - 2000** In the year 2000, after the liberalisation of the Indian economy in the 1990s, the insurance sector was opened to private players.

**Therefore, the correct chronological order is (a) 1-2-3-4.**

***38.*** *(b)* Only two

- **Statement 1 is correct:** The **Insurance Regulatory and Development Authority of India (IRDAI)** was established by an Act of

Parliament in 1999 through the **IRDA Act, 1999.** It was set up to regulate and develop the insurance industry in India.

- **Statement 2 is correct: IRDAI regulates both life and general insurance companies** in India. It ensures that these companies adhere to regulatory standards, maintain transparency, and protect the interests of policyholders.
- **Statement 3 is incorrect:** While IRDAI has the authority to **issue licenses to new insurance companies,** it also has the power to **revoke licenses** if companies fail to comply with regulatory norms or violate guidelines.

**Therefore, only two statements are correct. So, the correct answer is (b) Only two.**

**39.** *(c)* Only three

- **Life Insurance Corporation of India (LIC):** LIC is indeed a Domestic Systemically Important Insurer (D-SII). It is the largest life insurance company in India and plays a crucial role in the financial system.
- **New India Assurance:** This is also a D-SII, being one of the leading general insurance companies in India.
- **General Insurance Corporation of India (GIC Re):** GIC Re is the reinsurer of last resort in India and is also classified as a D-SII.
- **United India Insurance Company:** While United India Insurance is a large and well-established insurance company, it is **not currently classified as a D-SII.**
- Therefore, three out of the four insurance companies listed are categorised as Domestic Systemically Important Insurers (D-SIIs).

**Thus, the correct answer is (c) Only three.**

**40.** *(c)* All three

- **Statement 1 is correct:** The **DICGC** insures deposits held in both **commercial banks** and **cooperative banks.** This ensures that depositors are protected in case these banks fail or face insolvency. The coverage applies uniformly across different types of banks to protect small depositors.
- **Statement 2 is correct:** The DICGC provides a maximum insurance cover of ₹ 5 lakh per depositor per bank. This means if a bank goes into liquidation, depositors can claim up to ₹ 5 lakh (including both principal and interest). This limit was raised from ₹ 1 lakh to ₹ 5 lakh in 2020 to offer better security to depositors.
- **Statement 3 is correct:** The **DICGC** operates as a subsidiary of the **Reserve Bank of India (RBI).** It is responsible for managing deposit insurance and credit guarantee schemes, with the primary function of protecting depositors' money in case of bank failure.

**Thus, the correct answer is (c) All three.**

**41.** *(c)* 1, 2 and 4 only

Deposits Covered by the Deposit Insurance and Credit Guarantee Corporation (DICGC):

- **Fixed Deposits** – DICGC covers fixed deposit which are deposits made for a fixed period of time and earn a fixed interest rate.
- **Savings Deposits** – DICGC also covers savings deposits, which are typically more flexible and allow for frequent withdrawals.
- **Inter-bank Deposits – Not covered** by DICGC. The insurance does not extend to deposits made by one bank into another.
- **Recurring Deposits** – Recurring deposits, where a fixed amount is deposited regularly, are also covered by DICGC.

**Thus, correct answer is (c) 1, 2 and 4 only.**

**42.** *(a)* 1 and 2 only

**The Export Credit Guarantee Corporation of India (ECGC)** is a government-owned company that provides insurance and guarantees to Indian exporters against risks associated with exporting goods and services. It helps to mitigate the risks faced by exporters, such as non-payment by buyers, political risks, and currency fluctuations.

- **Statement 1 is correct:** ECGC offers credit insurance to exporters, protecting them from risks of non-payment by foreign buyers.
- **Statement 2 is correct:** ECGC is a government-owned corporation, operating under the Ministry of Commerce and Industry, with the aim of promoting exports.
- **Statement 3 is incorrect:** ECGC provides coverage for exports to various countries, not just high-risk countries, but the premium may

vary based on the risk associated with each country.

**Thus, the correct answer is (a) 1 and 2 only.**

***43.*** *(c)* All three

- **Statement 1 is correct:** Insurance penetration is defined as the ratio of total insurance premiums (both life and non-life) to the GDP of the country.
- **Statement 2 is correct:** Insurance density is a metric that measures the level of insurance penetration within a country by dividing the total insurance premiums collected by the total population, which represent the average per capita insurance premium.
- **Statement 3 is correct: Economic Survey 2023-24 indicates that India's insurance penetration decreased from 4.2% in 2022 to 4% in 2023.** It has frequently noted that India's insurance penetration (both life and non-life) remains below the global average. As of 2023, **India's insurance penetration rate remains below the global average (6.8%).** This means that the proportion of insurance premiums to the Gross Domestic Product (GDP) in India is lower than in many other countries.

**Thus, the correct answer is (c) All three.**

***44.*** *(b)* Only two

- **Statement 1 is correct:** The **Pension Fund Regulatory and Development Authority (PFRDA)** was formally established in **2013** under the **Pension Fund Regulatory and Development Authority Act.** Although it was initially set up in 2003 as a regulatory body, it gained statutory status through the Act passed in 2013.
- **Statement 2 is correct: PFRDA** is responsible for regulating the **National Pension System** (NPS) as well as other pension schemes designed to ensure retirement income for subscribers.
- **Statement 3 is incorrect:** The **PFRDA** functions under the oversight of the **Ministry of Finance**, not the Ministry of Labour and Employment. The Ministry of Finance manages policies related to pension regulation, with PFRDA as the regulatory authority for pension schemes.

**Therefore, the correct answer is (b) Only two.**

***45.*** *(b)* Only two

- **Statement 1 is correct:** The Pension Fund Regulatory and Development Authority (PFRDA) manages both voluntary and mandatory pension schemes in India.
  - **Voluntary schemes:** These schemes are open to individuals who choose to participate, such as the National Pension System (NPS) for individuals and the Atal Pension Yojana (APY).
  - **Mandatory schemes:** These schemes are mandatory for certain categories of individuals, such as government employees and employees of certain private sector organisations.
- **Statement 2 is correct:** Under the PFRDA Act, 2013, the PFRDA was established as the regulatory authority overseeing the NPS and all related intermediaries.
- **Statement 3 is incorrect:** The PFRDA does **not directly administer pension payouts;** these are handled by pension fund managers and other entities under its supervision.

**Thus, two statements are correct, so the answer is (b) Only two.**

***46.*** *(c)* Only three

The **National Pension System** (NPS) is a voluntary, defined-contribution pension scheme in India, regulated by the Pension Fund Regulatory and Development Authority (PFRDA).

- **Statement 1 is correct:** The **National Pension System (NPS)** is indeed a **voluntary retirement savings scheme** that allows individuals to systematically save for retirement. It is open to all Indian citizens and is particularly beneficial for individuals looking to build a retirement corpus.
- **Statement 2 is correct: NPS offers both Tier I and Tier II accounts.** Tier I is the primary pension account with restrictions on withdrawal, while Tier II is a voluntary savings account with greater liquidity and no lock-in period, offering flexibility to subscribers.
- **Statement 3 is incorrect:** Withdrawals from the **Tier I account** are **partially tax-exempt** at the time of retirement. Currently, up to 60%

of the corpus withdrawn from Tier I is tax-free, while the remaining 40% must be used to purchase an annuity, which is subject to tax.

- **Statement 4 is correct:** The NPS is **regulated by the Pension Fund Regulatory and Development Authority (PFRDA)**, which oversees its functioning and ensures compliance with regulatory standards to safeguard subscribers' interests.

**Threrefore, the correct answer is (c) Only three.**

**47.** *(b)* 2 and 3 only

- **Statement 1 is correct:** The **NPS is available to both Indian citizens and NRIs (Non-Resident Indians)**. This allows a broader range of participants to join the scheme and benefit from systematic retirement savings, regardless of their residency status.
- **Statement 2 is incorrect:** The **NPS is not mandatory for all citizens.** It is a **voluntary scheme** for most individuals, although it is mandatory for **central government employees who joined after 2004.** Private individuals can choose to participate in the scheme at their discretion.
- **Statement 3 is incorrect:** The **minimum contribution required for the Tier I account** is not ₹ 10,000 per year; it is **typically around ₹ 1,000 per year,** making it affordable for a wide range of contributors.

**Therefore, the correct answer is (b) 2 and 3 only.**

**48.** *(a)* Yes, he can join NPS and cantinue contributing as an NRI.

Indian citizens between the ages of 18 and 70 can join NPS, and it is open to both residents and Non-Resident Indians (NRIs). Ravi can continue contributing to NPS even after relocating abroad as an NRI.

**Therefore, option (a) is the correct answer.**

**49.** *(a)* 1 only

- **Statement 1 is correct:** The IFSCA regulates financial institutions and services operating in India's International Financial Services Centres.
- **Statement 2 is incorrect:** While the IFSCA facilitates international financial services, its primary focus is on regulating financial institutions and services operating within IFSCs in India.

**Thus, the correct answer is (a) 1 only.**

**50.** *(b)* Only two

- **Statement 1 is correct:** IFSCA has the authority to regulate trading in securities, commodities, and derivatives within IFSCs to maintain transparency and stability.
- **Statement 2 is correct:** IFSCA has the authority to impose fines and penalties for non-compliance with its rules and regulations.
- **Statement 3 is incorrect:** IFSCA can issue licenses for entities to operate within IFSCs, but it does not issue licenses for banks and insurance companies to operate across India.

**Thus, the correct answer is (b) Only two.**

**51.** *(c)* Only three

- **Chairperson:** Appointed by the Government of India
- The authority comprises one member each nominated by the **Reserve Bank of India**, the **Securities and Exchange Board of India**, the **Insurance Regulatory and Development Authority**, and the **Pension Fund Regulatory and Development Authority.**
- In addition to that, 2 members from the **Ministry of Finance** will be appointed by the central government and 2 members will be appointed by the Central Government on the recommendation of a Selection Committee.
- **Option 1, 2 and 3 are correct:** Representatives from the **RBI, IRDAI** and **PFRDA** are part of the IFSCA.
- **Option 4 is incorrect:** The **Ministry of External Affairs (MEA)** is not represented in the composition of IFSCA.

**Three of the listed regulatory bodies are part of IFSCA, so the correct answer is (c) Only three.**

**52.** *(b)* Only two

- **Statement 1 is incorrect:** IFSC as envisaged under the Indian context 'is a jurisdiction that provides financial services to **non-residents and residents (Institutions)**, in foreign currency other than Indian Rupee (INR)'.
- **Statement 2 is correct:** IFSCs are regulated by the **International Financial Services Centres Authority** (IFSCA), which is a unified regulatory body created to oversee all financial services activities in IFSCs, including banking, insurance, and capital markets.
- **Statement 3 is correct: GIFT City** (Gujarat International Finance Tec-City) located in **Gujarat** is India's **first** IFSC. It was established as a hub for international financial transactions and is the pioneering project of its kind in India.

**Thus, the correct answer is (b) Only two.**

**53.** *(a)* 1, 2 and 4 only

- **Statement 1 is correct:** IFSCs provide a platform for global investors to manage their funds in India. This includes services like portfolio management, investment advisory, and fund administration
- **Statement 2 is correct:** IFSCs provide cross-border banking services, enabling international banking transactions, including lending, trade financing, and more.
- **Statement 3 is incorrect: FSCs are primarily focused on serving global investors and financial institutions. They do not typically offer local retail banking services to Indian citizens. This is primarily handled by domestic banks.**
- **Statement 4 is correct:** IFSCs offer reinsurance services for global, facilitating risk management on an international scale.

**Thus, the correct answer is (a) 1, 2 and 4 only.**

## Past Learning (Answers)

1 (c) 2 (b) 3 (c) 4 (c) 5 (c) 6 (d) 7 (d)

CHAPTER

# 11 External Sector

## Assessment Round

### Topic 1 : Current Account

**1.** Which of the following measures are typically taken by a country to open its economy?
1. Reducing tariffs and trade barriers.
2. Liberalising Foreign Direct Investment (FDI) rules.
3. Increasing state control over industries.
4. Allowing free movement of capital and goods across borders.

Select the correct answer from the codes given below:
(a) 1, 2 and 3 only (b) 1, 2 and 4 only
(c) 2 and 3 only (d) 1, 2, 3 and 4

**2.** Consider the following statements:
1. The trade-to-GDP ratio is commonly used to measure the openness of an economy.
2. India's trade-to-GDP ratio was approximately 45% in 2023 indicating moderate openness to international trade.
3. Economies with higher trade-to-GDP ratios are generally considered more open to global markets.

How many of the statements given above is/are correct?
(a) Only one (b) Only two
(c) All three (d) None

**3.** Consider the following hypothetical examples:
1. An Indian IT company provides software development services to a U.S. based firm.
2. An Indian educational institution offers online courses to international students.
3. A tourist from Germany avails spa and wellness services at a resort in Kerala.
4. An Indian consultancy firm offers management advice to a company in the United Kingdom.

How many of the above examples fall under the definition of 'Export of Services'?
(a) Only one (b) Only two
(c) Only three (d) All four

**4.** Which of the following items are recorded under the Current Account of a country?
1. Net trade in goods
2. Net earnings on cross-border investments
3. Net trade in services
4. Net transfer payments

Select the correct answer using the codes given below:
(a) 1 and 3 only (b) 1, 2 and 4 only
(c) 2 and 4 only (d) 1, 2, 3 and 4

**5.** Consider the following examples of transactions:
1. Remittances sent by Indian workers abroad to their families in India.
2. Grants provided to the Indian government by World Bank.
3. Profits earned by a foreign company and sent back to its home country.

How many of the above examples fall under 'Transfer Payments' in the Balance of Payments?
(a) Only one (b) Only two
(c) All three (d) None

**6.** Consider the following statements:
1. India accounts for approximately 2.4% of global exports and around 3% of global imports.
2. India's top import items include crude oil and electronic goods.

Which of the statement(s) given above is/are correct?

(a) 1 only (b) 2 only
(c) Both 1 and 2 (d) Neither 1 nor 2

**7.** Which of the following is a potential implication of a negative Current Account Deficit (CAD) for an economy?

(a) Increased dependence on foreign capital to finance the deficit, leading to higher external debt.
(b) An appreciation of the domestic currency due to higher exports.
(c) Reduction in foreign exchange reserves, strengthening the domestic economy.
(d) Higher domestic savings, reducing the need for foreign capital.

**8.** With reference to the trends of Current Account Deficit (CAD) in India, consider the following statements:
1. India experienced a Current Account Surplus in the FY 2020-21 primarily due to reduced imports and a fall in oil prices.
2. India has typically recorded a Current Account Deficit due to high imports of oil and gold.
3. India's trade deficit in goods has consistently been higher than its trade surplus in services.

Which of the statements given above are correct?

(a) 1 and 2 only (b) 2 and 3 only
(c) 1 and 3 only (d) 1, 2 and 3

**9.** Trade in services includes both Factor and Non-Factor income. Which of the following constitute the 'Non-Factor Income'?
1. Rent from the land given on lease in Germany.
2. Earning from shipping and banking services.
3. Profits of an Indian company established in US.
4. Tourism services.

Select the correct answer from the codes given below:

(a) 2, 3 and 4 only (b) 1 and 4 only
(c) 2 and 4 only (d) 1 and 3 only

**10.** Consider the following events that could impact India's Current Account Deficit (CAD):
1. Implementation of Foreign Trade Policy (FTP) 2023
2. Introduction of merchanting trade reforms
3. Increasing global crude oil prices
4. Expansion of Production-Linked Incentive (PLI) schemes

How many of the above is/are likely to reduce India's CAD?

(a) Only one (b) Only two
(c) Only three (d) All four

## Topic 2 : Capital Account

**11.** Which of the following constitute capital account of the Balance of Payments?
1. Remittances
2. External Assistance
3. Commercial Borrowings
4. Non-Resident Banking Deposits

Select the correct answer from the codes given below:

(a) 1 and 4 only (b) 2 and 3 only
(c) 2, 3 and 4 only (d) 1, 2, 3 and 4

**12.** With reference to the Capital Account in India's Balance of Payments (BoP), consider the following statements:
1. It includes non-debt capital receipts such as equity investments.
2. A capital outflow occurs when Indian residents increase their ownership of foreign assets, leading to a reduction in India's foreign exchange reserves.
3. Grants for disaster relief from foreign governments are recorded in the Capital Account.

Which of the statement(s) given above is/are correct?

(a) 1 and 2 only (b) 2 and 3 only
(c) 1 only (d) 1, 2 and 3

**13.** Which of the following is a key distinction between Foreign Direct Investment (FDI) and Foreign Portfolio Investment (FPI)?
(a) FDI involves a long-term interest and control in the management of a company, whereas FPI only involves short-term financial investment.
(b) FDI is typically made in the form of bonds, while FPI is made in equities and real estate.
(c) FPI allows investors to have managerial control, whereas FDI investors do not.
(d) FDI involves the purchase of stocks and bonds, while FPI involves the establishment of new companies.

**14.** With reference to Foreign Direct Investment (FDI) and Foreign Portfolio Investment (FPI), consider the following statements:
1. FDI refers to investments in physical assets like land and factories.
2. FPI involves investments in financial assets such as stocks and bonds.
3. FDI investors typically gain managerial control of the company.
4. FPI investors aim for long-term ownership of the company.

How many of the statements given above is/are correct?
(a) Only one (b) Only two
(c) Only three (d) All four

**15.** Which of the following best describes Hot Money in the context of international finance?
(a) Short-term capital that moves quickly across markets, often seeking higher returns or arbitrage opportunities.
(b) Long-term foreign investment focused on developing infrastructure in emerging markets.
(c) Capital that is invested in bonds and long-term equities to avoid risks in volatile markets.
(d) Funds invested exclusively in real estate for long-term gains.

**16.** Consider the following statements about the Foreign Portfolio Investment (FPI):
1. The FPI consists of securities and other financial assets held by the investors in another country.
2. The FPI provides the investor with direct ownership of a company's assets.
3. The ADRs and the GDRs are FPI holdings.
4. The FPI is a part of a country's Capital Account.

Which of the statements given above are correct?
(a) 1, 2 and 3 only (b) 1, 3 and 4 only
(c) 2 and 4 only (d) 1, 2, 3 and 4

**17.** Which of the following is a potential economic risk associated with 'Hot Money'?
(a) Increased long-term economic stability due to consistent investment flows.
(b) Higher foreign exchange reserves, reducing currency volatility.
(c) Rapid capital outflows that can destabilise a country's currency and financial markets.
(d) Stable inflows of foreign direct investment, boosting industrial development.

**18.** Which of the following sectors fall under the '100% Automatic Route' category of the Foreign Direct Investment (FDI)?
1. Agriculture and Animal Husbandry
2. Tourism and Hospitality
3. Pension
4. Banking (Public sector)
5. Nidhi Company

Select the correct answer using the codes given below:
(a) 1, 2 and 5 only
(b) 1 and 2 only
(c) 2 and 4 only
(d) 1, 3 and 5 only

**19.** Which of the following phenomena is/are the likely consequence(s) of large capital inflow into a country?
1. High inflation
2. Increasing real effective exchange rate
3. Declining competitiveness of the export sector

Select the correct answer using the codes given below:
(a) 1 and 2 only
(b) 2 and 3 only
(c) 3 only
(d) 1, 2 and 3

**20.** Consider the following statements:

1. Computer software and hardware sector attracted the highest FDI equity inflows.
2. Singapore is the top investing country in India, followed by USA and Mauritius.
3. The top destination for FDI inflows is Delhi, followed by Maharashtra and Karnataka.

How many of the statements given above is/are correct?

(a) Only one (b) Only two
(c) All three (d) None

**21.** With reference to FDI routes in India, consider the following statements:

1. FDI through the Government route requires an application *via* the Foreign Investment Facilitation Portal.
2. Under the Automatic route, FDI is allowed without government approval.
3. The Government route requires the approval of the Ministry of Finance after consultation with the DPIIT.

How many of the statements given above is/are correct?

(a) Only one (b) Only two
(c) All three (d) None

**22.** Consider the following sectors:

1. Lottery business
2. Atomic energy
3. Railway infrastructure
4. Chit funds

How many of the sectors listed above is/are prohibited for FDI in India?

(a) Only one (b) Only two
(c) Only three (d) All four

**23.** Consider the following statements about the External Commercial Borrowings (ECB):

1. The ECB is a loan availed from non-resident lenders with a minimum average maturity of 10 years.
2. The ECB can be availed by both automatic route and by approval route.
3. The ECB dilutes stake in the company.
4. The corporate can raise the ECBs from international capital markets.

Which of the statements given above are correct?

(a) 1, 2 and 3 only
(b) 2, 3 and 4 only
(c) 2 and 4 only
(d) 1, 2, 3 and 4

**24.** With reference to the 'External Debt in India', consider the following statements:

1. The sovereign debt of India is much higher than the non-sovereign debt.
2. External Commercial Borrowings (ECBs) constitute the highest component of the external debt in India.
3. The share of long-term external debt is much higher than short-term external debt.

Which of the statements given above is/are correct?

(a) 1 only (b) 2 and 3 only
(c) 2 only (d) None of these

**25.** Which of the following form(s) part of the External Debt of the country?

1. Multilateral Debt
2. Bilateral Debt
3. NRI Deposits
4. Commercial Borrowings

Choose the correct answer from the codes given below:

(a) 1 only
(b) 1 and 2 only
(c) 1, 2 and 4 only
(d) 1, 2, 3 and 4

**26.** Which of the following statements is/are correct about India's external debt?

1. US Dollar remains the leading currency of denomination for external debt.
2. Commercial lenders were the biggest contributors to external debt, followed by NRI deposits and short-term trade credits.

Select the correct answer using the codes given below:

(a) 1 only
(b) 2 only
(c) Both 1 and 2
(d) Neither 1 nor 2

**27.** Consider the following components:
1. Multilateral loans
2. Treasury bills held by Foreign Portfolio Investors (FPIs)
3. SDR allocation by IMF
4. Bilateral loans from foreign governments

How many of the above components is/are included in Sovereign External Debt?
(a) Only one (b) Only two
(c) Only three (d) All four

**28.** Consider the following possible implications:
1. Increased borrowing costs in international markets
2. Loss of investor confidence leading to capital outflows
3. Strengthening of the country's currency due to restricted imports
4. Downgrade in the country's sovereign credit rating

How many of the given above implications is/are likely outcomes of an external debt default?
(a) Only one (b) Only two
(c) Only three (d) All four

## Topic 3 : BoP Surplus or Deficit

**29.** Consider the following statements about 'India's Balance of Payments (BoP)':
1. National Statistical Office (NSO) compiles and publishes BoP data for India.
2. BoP records all economic transactions between residents of a country and rest of the world.
3. Capital account balance comprises the balance of trade of goods and services, factor incomes and net cash transfers.
4. Current account balance reflects net change in ownership of national assets.

Which of the statements given above is/are correct?
(a) 2 only (b) 1 and 3 only
(c) 2, 3 and 4 only (d) 1, 2, 3 and 4

**30.** Consider the following events:
1. Capital flight from the country
2. A large increase in foreign debt repayment obligations
3. A sharp increase in global oil prices
4. Global interest rate hikes

How many of the given above events is/are likely to worsen the Balance of Payments (BoP) of a country?
(a) Only one (b) Only two
(c) Only three (d) All four

**31.** Which of the following are included in India's Forex Reserves?
1. Foreign Currency
2. Gold Holdings of the RBI
3. Loans from the World Bank
4. Special Drawing Rights
5. Reserve Tranche Position

Select the correct answer from the codes given below:
(a) 1 and 4 only (b) 2 and 4 only
(c) 1, 3 and 4 only (d) 1, 2, 4 and 5 only

**32.** Consider the following statements with reference to 'India's Foreign Exchange Reserve':
1. It consists only of Foreign Currencies, Gold and Special Drawing Rights (SDRs).
2. SDRs have highest share of foreign exchange reserves.
3. India has more foreign exchange reserves than USA.

Which of the statement(s) given above is/are correct?
(a) 1 only (b) 1 and 2 only
(c) 2 and 3 only (d) None of these

**33.** Which of the following foreign assets are counted under Foreign Currency Assets (FCA) of India?
1. Deposits in foreign central banks and commercial banks abroad
2. Investment in US Treasury Bills
3. Indian Rupee denominated bonds
4. Foreign exchange balances held with foreign institutions

Select the correct answer using the codes given below:
(a) 1 and 2 only (b) 1, 2 and 4 only
(c) 1 and 4 only (d) 2, 3 and 4 only

**34.** Which of the following best describes the concept of Reserve Tranche Position (RTP) with the IMF?

(a) The amount of foreign currency reserves that a member country must keep with the IMF as a safety cushion.

(b) A portion of a country's quota with the IMF that is accessible to the country without stringent conditions, considered as part of its foreign exchange reserves.

(c) A mechanism that allows a member country to borrow funds from the IMF in the event of a Balance of Payments crisis.

(d) A facility used to impose additional financial contributions on member countries during periods of global financial instability.

**35.** Which of the following best describes the term 'Import Cover'?

(a) The total number of months a country can finance its imports using its foreign exchange reserves.

(b) The insurance provided by the government to cover importers from price fluctuations.

(c) A limit imposed by the central bank on the amount of imports a country can handle annually.

(d) A trade agreement between two countries to set quotas for importing goods.

**36.** What would happen if a country's Import Cover falls below a critical threshold?

(a) The country would experience an economic boom due to surplus reserves.

(b) The country could face a currency crisis or balance of payments crisis due to insufficient foreign reserves to cover imports.

(c) The central bank would immediately increase interest rates to boost the import cover.

(d) The country's currency would strengthen as a result of reduced imports.

**37.** Arrange the following events in the correct order :

1. Excessive current account deficit
2. Depletion of foreign exchange reserves
3. Capital flight from the country
4. Currency depreciation

Select the correct answer using the codes given below:

(a) 1 - 2 - 3 - 4
(b) 1 - 3 - 2 - 4
(c) 1 - 4 - 2 - 3
(d) 1 - 2 - 4 - 3

**38.** Which of the following is a common consequence of a Balance of Payments (BoP) crisis for a developing country?

(a) Rapid appreciation of the national currency due to increased foreign investments.

(b) Increased foreign debt as the country borrows to stabilise its economy.

(c) Decline in import costs due to a stronger domestic currency.

(d) Surge in domestic employment due to improved trade conditions.

**39.** Which of the following factors contributed to India's 1991 Balance of Payments (BoP) Crisis?

1. High fiscal deficit
2. Rising oil prices due to the Gulf War
3. Significant foreign exchange reserves
4. Overvaluation of the Indian Rupee

Select the correct answer:

(a) 1, 2 and 3 only (b) 3 and 4 only
(c) 1, 2 and 4 only (d) 1, 2, 3 and 4

## Topic 4 : Exchange Rate

**40.** Consider the following factors:

1. Huge Inflows of Foreign Portfolio Investments (FPI).
2. Hike in the interest rate by US Federal Reserves.
3. Increase in the International Oil Price.
4. Buying of US Dollars by the RBI from the market.

Which of the given factors might lead to the depreciation of Rupee?

(a) 2, 3 and 4 only
(b) 1, 2, 3 and 4
(c) 2 and 3 only
(d) 3 and 4 only

**41.** Consider the following interventions by the RBI:

1. Buying government securities in the open market
2. Selling dollars in the forex market
3. Tightening of monetary policy

How many of the given above actions is/are likely to lead to currency appreciation?

(a) Only one (b) Only two
(c) All three (d) None

**42.** In which of the following cases, India's exchange rate will increase?

1. Indians going to US for tourism activity.
2. American people visiting India for leisure.
3. Demand for foreign goods drops in Indian market.

Select the correct answer using the codes given below:

(a) 1 and 3 only (b) 2 and 3 only
(c) 1 only (d) 1, 2 and 3

**43.** Which of the following could be the possible impact(s) from the 'Depreciation of Currency'?

1. Decline in the exports of Indian goods and services.
2. Increase in the tourists' arrivals to India.
3. Going abroad for holiday becomes cheaper.

Select the correct answer from the codes given below:

(a) 2 only (b) 1 and 2 only
(c) 1 and 3 only (d) None of these

**44.** Consider the following:

1. Clean floating
2. Dirty floating
3. Gold standard

Which of the given above is/are 'Currency Exchange Rate' systems?

(a) 1 and 3 only (b) 2 only
(c) 2 and 3 only (d) 1, 2 and 3

**45.** Which of the following statements best describes the difference between a fixed exchange rate and a floating exchange rate?

(a) In a fixed exchange rate system, the value of the currency is determined by supply and demand in the foreign exchange market, while in a floating exchange rate system, the central bank actively intervenes to maintain a fixed value.
(b) A fixed exchange rate system requires the central bank to maintain the currency at a predetermined level, whereas in a floating exchange rate system, the currency's value fluctuates freely based on market forces.
(c) Both fixed and floating exchange rate systems require regular central bank intervention to stabilise the currency.
(d) In both systems, the currency's value is determined entirely by market forces with no central bank intervention.

**46.** With reference to the 'Fixed Exchange Rate System', consider the following statements:

1. It provides greater certainty for importers and exporters regarding the exchange rate.
2. The central bank does not need to intervene regularly to maintain the exchange rate.
3. A fixed exchange rate system can lead to a depletion of foreign exchange reserves during a currency crisis.

How many of the statements given above is/are correct?

(a) Only one
(b) Only two
(c) All three
(d) None

**47.** Which of the following best explains the difference between Depreciation and Devaluation of a currency?

(a) Depreciation refers to a deliberate reduction in the value of a currency by the government, while devaluation occurs due to market forces.
(b) Depreciation occurs due to market forces, while devaluation is a deliberate reduction in the value of a currency by the government or central bank under a fixed exchange rate system.
(c) Depreciation increases the purchasing power of a currency in international markets, while devaluation decreases it.
(d) Both depreciation and devaluation are used to strengthen a country's currency in global markets.

**48.** Which of the following is a major disadvantage of a floating exchange rate system?

(a) It requires constant intervention by the central bank to maintain the value of the currency.

(b) It exposes a country to excessive currency volatility, which can create uncertainty for international trade and investment.

(c) It eliminates the ability of the country to use monetary policy effectively.

(d) It fixes the currency value, leading to a lack of flexibility in responding to economic conditions.

**49.** In which of the following exchange rates, official reserve transactions are equal to zero?

1. Fixed Exchange Rate
2. Flexible Exchange Rate
3. Managed Floating Exchange Rate
4. Pegged Exchange Rate

Choose the correct answer from the codes given below:

(a) 2 only
(b) 2 and 3 only
(c) 1, 2 and 3 only
(d) 1, 2, 3 and 4

**50.** Which of the following best describes the managed floating exchange rate system followed by many countries, including India?

(a) The exchange rate is fixed by the government, and there is no market influence on the currency's value.

(b) The exchange rate is determined entirely by market forces without any central bank intervention.

(c) The exchange rate is primarily determined by market forces, but the central bank intervenes occasionally to stabilise the currency.

(d) The central bank continuously intervenes to maintain a fixed exchange rate against a foreign currency.

**51.** Consider the following statements with regard to the 'Real Exchange Rate':

1. Real Exchange Rate measures the prices abroad relative to those at home.
2. If the Real Exchange Rate rises above one, it will boost India's export competitiveness.

Which of the statements given above is/are correct?

(a) 1 only (b) 2 only
(c) Both 1 and 2 (d) Neither 1 nor 2

**52.** Which of the following best describes the concept of 'Purchasing Power Parity (PPP)'?

(a) A theory that suggests that exchange rates between two currencies are determined solely by the market forces of supply and demand.

(b) A theory that states that in the long run, exchange rates should adjust so that the price of an identical basket of goods in two different countries is the same when expressed in a common currency.

(c) A measure used by central banks to stabilise their currency by comparing inflation rates across countries.

(d) A financial mechanism used by countries to hedge against foreign exchange risks.

**53.** With reference to the Nominal Effective Exchange Rate (NEER) and Real Effective Exchange Rate (REER), consider the following statements:

1. NEER is a weighted average of a country's currency in relation to a basket of other major currencies.
2. REER adjusts NEER for differences in inflation rates between the home country and its trading partners.
3. An increase in NEER indicates an appreciation of a country's currency relative to a basket of other currencies.

How many of the statements given above is/are correct?

(a) Only one (b) Only two
(c) All three (d) None

**54.** With reference to the 'International Comparison Programme (ICP)', which of the following statement(s) is/are correct?

1. It is a worldwide statistical initiative coordinated by the International Monetary Fund (IMF).
2. ICP helps to calculate Purchasing Power Parities (PPPs) to compare the economic performance of countries.
3. India ranked as the third-largest economy in the world under the ICP 2017 cycle.

Select the correct answer from the codes given below:

(a) 1 and 2 only (b) 2 and 3 only
(c) 1 and 3 only (d) 2 only

**55.** Consider the following statements:

1. NEER and REER data are published by the Ministry of Finance to track India's export competitiveness.
2. NEER-40 provides a more comprehensive view of the Rupee's external value compared to NEER-6 due to its wider basket of currencies.
3. The base year for the RBI's NEER and REER calculations is 2004-05.

Which of the statements given above is/are correct?

(a) 1 and 2 only (b) 2 only
(c) 1 and 3 only (d) 2 and 3 only

## Topic 5 : Currency Convertibility

**56.** Which of the following statements best describes capital account convertibility?

(a) It allows for the free exchange of domestic currency for international trade in goods and services.
(b) It permits unrestricted movement of investments and capital across borders without any regulatory control.
(c) It limits the flow of capital to protect the domestic economy from speculative investments.
(d) It restricts the convertibility of the domestic currency only for essential imports and exports.

**57.** Consider the following statements about 'Currency Convertibility':

1. Indian rupee is not fully convertible on current and capital account transactions.
2. RBI puts certain restrictions on the convertibility of Indian rupee using the powers conferred under FERA 1973.
3. S.S. Tarapore Committee was set up to look into the matter of capital account convertibility in India.

Which of the statements given above are correct?

(a) 1 and 2 only (b) 2 and 3 only
(c) 1 and 3 only (d) 1, 2 and 3

**58.** Consider the following:

1. Increased speculative capital flows.
2. Greater vulnerability to external economic shocks.
3. High dependence on foreign capital inflows.
4. Currency instability and volatility.

How many of the given above is/are the risks associated with capital account convertibility?

(a) Only one
(b) Only two
(c) Only three
(d) All four

**59.** Which of the following would be the effects of full Capital Account Convertibility in India?

1. No cap on the debt that Indian company can raise in foreign currency through ECBs or some other ways.
2. No limit to export and import of capital goods.
3. No restrictions on Foreign Direct Investment in all the sectors.
4. Will be able to access foreign currency for travel, education, medical or other designated purposes.

Select the correct answer from the codes given below:

(a) 1 and 4 only
(b) 1, 2 and 3 only
(c) 1, 3 and 4 only
(d) 2, 3 and 4 only

**60.** Consider the following hypothetical scenario: The Indian Rupee is experiencing significant depreciation due to large capital outflows triggered by global uncertainty and rising inflation. This has led to a sharp increase in the country's Current Account Deficit (CAD) and the Indian government is concerned about a potential currency crisis. As a policy advisor to the government, which of the following measures should be taken to prevent a future currency crisis?

1. Increase foreign exchange reserves by entering into currency swap agreements with major economies.
2. Impose temporary restrictions on capital outflows
3. Promote bilateral trade agreements to settle trade in local currencies rather than the U.S. dollar.
4. Enhance export competitiveness through production-linked incentives (PLIs).

Select the correct answer from the codes given below:

(a) 1, 2 and 4 only (b) 1 and 3 only
(c) 1, 3 and 4 only (d) 2, 3 and 4 only

## Topic 6 : Other Concepts

**61.** Which of the following best describes the process of de-dollarisation?

(a) The gradual replacement of the U.S. dollar as the world's primary reserve currency by the Euro.
(b) The efforts by countries to reduce their reliance on the U.S. dollar for international trade and foreign exchange reserves.
(c) The elimination of the U.S. dollar from global financial markets due to inflationary pressures.
(d) The shift from using paper money to digital currencies by central banks worldwide.

**62.** Consider the following:

1. Reduced exposure to foreign exchange risk.
2. Greater demand for Indian goods and services.
3. Increased influence of India's monetary policy on the global economy.
4. Dependence on U.S. dollars for trade transactions.

How many of the given above is/are benefits of the internationalisation of the Indian Rupee?

(a) Only one (b) Only two
(c) Only three (d) All four

**63.** Arrange the following currencies in the correct order of their global usage and internationalisation from the most to the least internationalised:

1. Euro (EUR) 2. US Dollar (USD)
3. Japanese Yen (JPY) 4. Chinese Yuan (CNY)

Select the correct answer from the codes given below:

(a) 1-2-3-4 (b) 2-1-3-4
(c) 2-1-4-3 (d) 1-3-2-4

**64.** Which of the following best describes the concept of internationalisation of the Indian Rupee?

(a) The process of allowing Indian citizens to freely invest in foreign markets without any restrictions.
(b) The use of the Indian Rupee for international trade, investments, and as a global reserve currency by foreign countries.
(c) The replacement of the U.S. dollar with the Indian Rupee as the dominant global reserve currency.
(d) The mandatory use of the Indian Rupee by Indian citizens for all international transactions.

**65.** Which of the following measures have been taken by the Indian government and the RBI to promote the internationalisation of the Rupee?

1. Allowing Indian banks to offer Rupee-denominated loans to foreign entities.
2. Permitting trade settlements with certain countries in Indian Rupees.
3. Introducing Rupee-denominated bonds, known as Masala Bonds, for international investors.

Select the correct answer using the codes given below:

(a) 1 and 2 only (b) 2 and 3 only
(c) 1 and 3 only (d) 1, 2 and 3

**66.** Consider the following pairs:

| Account Type | Description |
|---|---|
| 1. Nostro | An account a domestic bank holds in a foreign bank in the foreign currency. |
| 2. Vostro | An account held by a foreign bank in a domestic bank in the local currency of the domestic bank. |
| 3. Loro | An account managed by a third-party bank on behalf of other banks. |

How many of the above pairs is/are correctly matched?

(a) Only one (b) Only two
(c) All three (d) None

**67.** Consider the following pairs:

| Currency Type | Description |
|---|---|
| 1. Hard currency | Currency that is widely accepted around the world and has a stable exchange rate. |
| 2. Soft currency | Currency that fluctuates greatly and is generally accepted only within its home country. |
| 3. Hot money | Short-term capital flows that move quickly in and out of financial markets in search of profit. |

How many of the above pairs is/are correctly matched?

(a) Only one (b) Only two
(c) All three (d) None

**68.** Which of the following best describes a 'Reverse Currency War'?

(a) A situation where countries deliberately devalue their currencies to boost exports.
(b) A situation where countries actively try to strengthen their currencies to control inflation.
(c) A scenario where central banks lower interest rates to stimulate economic growth.
(d) A financial strategy where countries purchase foreign currencies to stabilise domestic markets.

**69.** The Reserve Bank of India (RBI) conducts Forex Swaps for specific purposes. In this context, which of the following are the objective of these Forex Swaps?

1. Providing short-term liquidity in foreign currency
2. Stabilising the Indian Rupee during volatile periods
3. Supporting long-term investment in infrastructure
4. Managing foreign exchange reserves efficiently

Select the correct answer from the codes given below:

(a) 1 and 2 only
(b) 1, 2 and 4 only
(c) 2, 3 and 4 only
(d) 1, 2, 3 and 4

**70.** Which of the following is a primary reason for the countries to engage in a 'Currency War'?

(a) To devalue their currency in order to boost exports and make their products more competitive internationally.
(b) To increase the value of their currency and reduce inflation.
(c) To attract foreign investment by raising interest rates.
(d) To accumulate large foreign exchange reserves by selling domestic currency.

**71.** Which of the following can be considered the benefits of 'Currency Swap Agreements'?

1. Stabilising a country's foreign exchange reserves.
2. Reducing dependence on the US dollar in international trade.
3. Facilitating trade and investment between countries in their local currencies.
4. Protecting against exchange rate volatility.

Select the correct answer from the codes given below:

(a) 1 and 3 only
(b) 2, 3 and 4 only
(c) 1, 2 and 3 only
(d) 1, 2, 3 and 4

**72.** Which of the following best describes Dutch Disease?

(a) A situation where a country experiences economic growth due to the discovery of natural resources, leading to increased exports and balanced economic development.

(b) A strategy adopted by countries to devalue their currency to boost exports.

(c) A condition where high levels of foreign investment lead to economic diversification.

(d) A phenomenon where the rapid expansion of one sector, usually natural resources, leads to a decline in other sectors, especially manufacturing.

**73.** With reference to the 'Net International Investment Position (NIIP)', consider the following statements:

1. NIIP is the difference between a country's foreign assets and foreign liabilities.
2. A positive NIIP indicates that a country owes more to the world than it owns.
3. India's NIIP has consistently remained negative in the last 5 years.

Which of the given above statement(s) is/are correct?

(a) 1, 2 and 3 (b) 1 only
(c) 2 and 3 only (d) 1 and 3 only

**74.** Which of the following best describes the 'J-Curve effect' in economics?

(a) The phenomenon where a country's trade balance initially worsens after a devaluation of its currency, but improves over time.

(b) A situation where an economy experiences sustained growth followed by a sudden collapse.

(c) The rapid appreciation of a country's currency after a prolonged period of depreciation.

(d) The immediate positive impact of currency devaluation on a country's trade balance.

**75.** Which of the following best describes 'Official Reserve Transactions' in the context of international economics?

(a) Transactions related to a country's export and import of goods and services.

(b) Private transactions conducted by individuals and corporations in foreign markets.

(c) Financial assistance provided by international organisations to developing countries.

(d) Transactions conducted by the central bank involving foreign currency reserves, gold or special drawing rights (SDRs).

**76.** Which of the following regulatory aspects are typically associated with Bilateral Investment Treaties (BITs)?

1. BITs are primarily negotiated and signed between the governments of two countries.
2. BITs are regulated by the World Trade Organisation (WTO).
3. BITs can be amended or terminated by mutual consent of the contracting countries.

Select the correct answer from the codes given below:

(a) 1 and 3 only (b) 2 and 3 only
(c) 1 and 2 only (d) 1, 2 and 3

## Topic 7 : Foreign Trade

**77.** Consider the following statements:

1. Tariff barriers are easier to quantify compared to Non-Tariff Barriers.
2. Non-Tariff Barriers (NTBs) are used only by developing countries to protect their industries.
3. Tariff barriers can generate revenue for the government while Non-Tariff Barriers primarily aim to control the quantity or quality of imports.

How many of the statements given above is/are correct?

(a) Only one (b) Only two
(c) All three (d) None

**78.** Consider the following:

1. Anti-Dumping Duty 2. Import quotas
3. Export bans 4. Rules of Origin

How many of the given above is/are examples of Non-Tariff Barriers?

(a) Only one (b) Only two
(c) Only three (d) All four

**79.** Which of the following best describes about 'Rules of Origin' in international trade?
(a) Rules that define the national source of a product and determine which country's products qualify for preferential treatment under trade agreements.
(b) Guidelines for setting import tariffs based on a product's market demand.
(c) Regulations governing the quality standards that products must meet for international trade.
(d) Laws dictating the procedures for customs clearance of imported goods.

**80.** Consider the following statements:
1. Anti-Dumping Duty (ADD) is imposed when imported goods are priced below their fair market value in the domestic market.
2. Countervailing Duty (CVD) is imposed to counteract subsidies provided by foreign governments to their exporters.
3. Ministry of Finance imposes ADD and CVD based on the recommendations from the Directorate General of Trade Remedies (DGTR).

Which of the given statements are correct?
(a) 1 and 2 only (b) 2 and 3 only
(c) 1 and 3 only (d) 1, 2 and 3

**81.** With reference to the Foreign Trade Policy 2023 of India, consider the following statements:
1. It introduces the concept of districts as export hubs to promote exports from every district of India.
2. The policy aims to reach the export target of USD 2 trillion by 2030.
3. It emphasises digitisation and reduction of regulatory burden to facilitate ease of doing business.

Which of the given statements are correct?
(a) 1 and 2 only (b) 2 and 3 only
(c) 1 and 3 only (d) 1, 2 and 3

**82.** With reference to the Directorate General of Foreign Trade (DGFT), consider the following statements:
1. DGFT is responsible for implementing and managing the Foreign Trade Policy of India.
2. It functions under the Ministry of Commerce and Industry in India.
3. It works in coordination with the World Trade Organisation (WTO) to regulate trade disputes between India and other nations.

Which of the given statements is/are correct?
(a) 1 and 2 only (b) 2 and 3 only
(c) 1 and 3 only (d) 1, 2 and 3

**83.** Which of the following best describes about the 'Harmonised System of Nomenclature (HSN) Code'?
(a) A classification system used to categorise industries based on their economic output.
(b) A system used by countries to monitor foreign investments.
(c) A set of codes used by banks to process international financial transactions.
(d) An internationally standardised system for classifying traded products.

**84.** Arrange the following levels of economic integration in the correct order of their depth, starting from the least integrated to the most integrated:
1. Free Trade Area 2. Customs Union
3. Economic Union 4. Common Market

Select the correct answer from the codes given below:
(a) 1 - 2 - 4 - 3 (b) 2 - 1 - 3 - 4
(c) 4 - 1 - 2 - 3 (d) 1 - 4 - 2 - 3

**85.** With reference to 'Free Trade Agreements (FTA)' and 'Preferential Trade Agreements (PTA)', consider the following statements:
1. An FTA eliminates or reduces tariffs on goods across all sectors, while a PTA grants partial tariff reductions on specific goods.
2. FTAs generally have a negative list of goods that are excluded from tariff concessions, while PTAs have a positive list of goods eligible for tariff concessions.
3. FTAs are more comprehensive in scope compared to PTAs, often covering services, investment and intellectual property rights.

How many of the statements given above is/are correct?
(a) Only one (b) Only two
(c) All three (d) None

**86.** Which of the following is a key feature that distinguishes a Comprehensive Economic Partnership Agreement (CEPA) from a Comprehensive Economic Cooperation Agreement (CECA)?

(a) CEPA covers intellectual property rights, while CECA focus exclusively on tariffs and trade quotas.

(b) CECA includes broader economic cooperation measures, while CEPA focuses only on trade and investment.

(c) CEPA includes cooperation in sectors like investment, services and dispute resolution mechanisms, while CECA primarily focus on tariff reductions on goods.

(d) CECA focuses on reducing non-tariff barriers, while CEPA only addresses tariff barriers.

**87.** The Eurasian Customs Union is an economic integration initiative aimed at fostering trade and economic cooperation among its member states. In this context, which of the following countries are part of the Eurasian Customs Union?

1. Russia
2. Kazakhstan
3. Ukraine
4. Belarus

Select the correct answer using the codes given below:

(a) 1, 2 and 3 only
(b) 1, 2 and 4 only
(c) 2, 3 and 4 only
(d) 1, 3 and 4 only

**88.** MERCOSUR is a regional trade bloc that promotes economic cooperation among its member countries. In this context, which of the following countries are founding members of MERCOSUR?

1. Argentina 2. Brazil
3. Chile 4. Uruguay

Select the correct answer using the codes given below:

(a) 1, 2 and 3 only (b) 2, 3 and 4 only
(c) 1, 2 and 4 only (d) 1, 3 and 4 only

**89.** Which of the following best describes the Early Harvest Scheme (EHS) in the context of trade agreements?

(a) A preliminary agreement between two countries focusing on reducing tariffs on select goods before a comprehensive trade deal is finalised.

(b) A programme that provides subsidies to farmers for early harvesting of crops to prevent wastage.

(c) A strategy used by countries to devalue their currencies to boost exports.

(d) A scheme aimed at promoting early Foreign Direct Investments (FDI) in agriculture.

**90.** Consider the following countries:

1. Japan 2. Australia
3. United States 4. Sri Lanka

How many of the given above countries has/have an FTA with India?

(a) Only one (b) Only two
(c) Only three (d) All four

**91.** Arrange the following trade agreements of India in the correct chronological order of their implementation:

1. India-Malaysia Comprehensive Economic Cooperation Agreement (CECA)
2. India-UAE Comprehensive Economic Partnership Agreement (CEPA)
3. India-ASEAN Free Trade Agreement
4. India-Mauritius Comprehensive Economic Cooperation and Partnership Agreement (CECPA)

Select the correct answer using the codes given below:

(a) 3 - 1 - 4 - 2 (b) 2 - 3 - 4 - 1
(c) 3 - 2 - 4 - 1 (d) 1 - 2 - 3 - 4

# OMR SHEET

**Assessment Round**

| | | | | | | | |
|---|---|---|---|---|---|---|---|
| 1 | (a) (b) (c) (d) | 31 | (a) (b) (c) (d) | 61 | (a) (b) (c) (d) | 91 | (a) (b) (c) (d) |
| 2 | (a) (b) (c) (d) | 32 | (a) (b) (c) (d) | 62 | (a) (b) (c) (d) | 92 | (a) (b) (c) (d) |
| 3 | (a) (b) (c) (d) | 33 | (a) (b) (c) (d) | 63 | (a) (b) (c) (d) | 93 | (a) (b) (c) (d) |
| 4 | (a) (b) (c) (d) | 34 | (a) (b) (c) (d) | 64 | (a) (b) (c) (d) | 94 | (a) (b) (c) (d) |
| 5 | (a) (b) (c) (d) | 35 | (a) (b) (c) (d) | 65 | (a) (b) (c) (d) | 95 | (a) (b) (c) (d) |
| 6 | (a) (b) (c) (d) | 36 | (a) (b) (c) (d) | 66 | (a) (b) (c) (d) | 96 | (a) (b) (c) (d) |
| 7 | (a) (b) (c) (d) | 37 | (a) (b) (c) (d) | 67 | (a) (b) (c) (d) | 97 | (a) (b) (c) (d) |
| 8 | (a) (b) (c) (d) | 38 | (a) (b) (c) (d) | 68 | (a) (b) (c) (d) | 98 | (a) (b) (c) (d) |
| 9 | (a) (b) (c) (d) | 39 | (a) (b) (c) (d) | 69 | (a) (b) (c) (d) | 99 | (a) (b) (c) (d) |
| 10 | (a) (b) (c) (d) | 40 | (a) (b) (c) (d) | 70 | (a) (b) (c) (d) | 100 | (a) (b) (c) (d) |
| 11 | (a) (b) (c) (d) | 41 | (a) (b) (c) (d) | 71 | (a) (b) (c) (d) | 101 | (a) (b) (c) (d) |
| 12 | (a) (b) (c) (d) | 42 | (a) (b) (c) (d) | 72 | (a) (b) (c) (d) | 102 | (a) (b) (c) (d) |
| 13 | (a) (b) (c) (d) | 43 | (a) (b) (c) (d) | 73 | (a) (b) (c) (d) | 103 | (a) (b) (c) (d) |
| 14 | (a) (b) (c) (d) | 44 | (a) (b) (c) (d) | 74 | (a) (b) (c) (d) | 104 | (a) (b) (c) (d) |
| 15 | (a) (b) (c) (d) | 45 | (a) (b) (c) (d) | 75 | (a) (b) (c) (d) | 105 | (a) (b) (c) (d) |
| 16 | (a) (b) (c) (d) | 46 | (a) (b) (c) (d) | 76 | (a) (b) (c) (d) | 106 | (a) (b) (c) (d) |
| 17 | (a) (b) (c) (d) | 47 | (a) (b) (c) (d) | 77 | (a) (b) (c) (d) | 107 | (a) (b) (c) (d) |
| 18 | (a) (b) (c) (d) | 48 | (a) (b) (c) (d) | 78 | (a) (b) (c) (d) | 108 | (a) (b) (c) (d) |
| 19 | (a) (b) (c) (d) | 49 | (a) (b) (c) (d) | 79 | (a) (b) (c) (d) | 109 | (a) (b) (c) (d) |
| 20 | (a) (b) (c) (d) | 50 | (a) (b) (c) (d) | 80 | (a) (b) (c) (d) | 110 | (a) (b) (c) (d) |
| 21 | (a) (b) (c) (d) | 51 | (a) (b) (c) (d) | 81 | (a) (b) (c) (d) | 111 | (a) (b) (c) (d) |
| 22 | (a) (b) (c) (d) | 52 | (a) (b) (c) (d) | 82 | (a) (b) (c) (d) | 112 | (a) (b) (c) (d) |
| 23 | (a) (b) (c) (d) | 53 | (a) (b) (c) (d) | 83 | (a) (b) (c) (d) | 113 | (a) (b) (c) (d) |
| 24 | (a) (b) (c) (d) | 54 | (a) (b) (c) (d) | 84 | (a) (b) (c) (d) | 114 | (a) (b) (c) (d) |
| 25 | (a) (b) (c) (d) | 55 | (a) (b) (c) (d) | 85 | (a) (b) (c) (d) | 115 | (a) (b) (c) (d) |
| 26 | (a) (b) (c) (d) | 56 | (a) (b) (c) (d) | 86 | (a) (b) (c) (d) | 116 | (a) (b) (c) (d) |
| 27 | (a) (b) (c) (d) | 57 | (a) (b) (c) (d) | 87 | (a) (b) (c) (d) | 117 | (a) (b) (c) (d) |
| 28 | (a) (b) (c) (d) | 58 | (a) (b) (c) (d) | 88 | (a) (b) (c) (d) | 118 | (a) (b) (c) (d) |
| 29 | (a) (b) (c) (d) | 59 | (a) (b) (c) (d) | 89 | (a) (b) (c) (d) | 119 | (a) (b) (c) (d) |
| 30 | (a) (b) (c) (d) | 60 | (a) (b) (c) (d) | 90 | (a) (b) (c) (d) | 120 | (a) (b) (c) (d) |

## Calculate Your Score

| | |
|---|---|
| **Correct (✓)** | |
| **Incorrect (✓)** | |
| **Unattempted** | |
| **Total Score** | |
| **Accuracy (%)** | |

## Reasons for Incorrect Answers?

| | |
|---|---|
| 1. Lack of Knowledge/Existing Source Insufficient | |
| 2. Lack of Multiple Revision | |
| 3. Common Sense Mistakes | |

**Note :**

1. Calculate total score as correct answers carry 2 marks each 1/3rd marks will deducted for **Incorrect** Answers.
2. Calculate Accuracy (%) by dividing the number of correct answers to the total number of attempted questions.

## Past Learning

**1.** Consider, the following statements: **(2023)**

**Statement I:** India accounts for 3.2% of global export of goods.

**Statement II:** Many local companies and some foreign companies operating in India have taken advantage of India's 'Production-linked Incentive' scheme.

Which one of the following is correct in respect of the above statements?

(a) Both Statement I and Statement II are correct and Statement II is the correct explanation for Statement I.

(b) Both Statement I and Statement II are correct and Statement II is not the correct explanation for Statement I.

(c) Statement I is correct, but Statement II is incorrect.

(d) Statement I is incorrect, but Statement II is correct.

**2.** Consider the following statements: **(2023)**

**Statement I:** Switzerland is one of the leading exporters of gold in terms of value.

**Statement II:** Switzerland has the second largest gold reserves in the world.

Which one of the following is correct in respect of the above statements?

(a) Both Statement I and Statement II are correct, and Statement II is the correct explanation for Statement I.

(b) Both Statement I and Statement II are correct, and Statement II is not the correct explanation for Statement I.

(c) Statement I is correct, but Statement II is incorrect.

(d) Statement I is incorrect, but Statement II is correct.

**3.** With reference to the Indian economy, consider the following statements: **(2022)**

1. An increase in Nominal Effective Exchange Rate (NEER) indicates the appreciation of rupee.
2. An increase in the Real Effective Exchange Rate (REER) indicates an improvement in trade competitiveness.
3. An increasing trend in domestic inflation relative to inflation in other countries is likely to cause an increasing divergence between NEER and REER.

Which of the statements given above are correct?

(a) 1 and 2 only

(b) 2 and 3 only

(c) 1 and 3 only

(d) 1, 2 and 3

**4.** Consider the following statements: **(2022)**

1. Tight monetary policy of US Federal Reserve could lead to capital flight.
2. Capital flight may increase the interest cost of firms with existing External Commercial Borrowings (ECBs).
3. Devaluation of domestic currency decreases the currency risk associated with ECBS.

Which of the statements given above are correct?

(a) 1 and 2 only

(b) 2 and 3 only

(c) 1 and 3 only

(d) 1, 2 and 3

**5.** Consider the following statements: **(2021)**

The effect of the devaluation of a currency is that it necessarily

1. Improves the competitiveness of the domestic exports in the foreign markets
2. Increase the foreign value of the domestic currency
3. Improves the trade balance

Which of the above statements is/are correct?

(a) 1 only

(b) 1 and 2

(c) 3 only

(d) 2 and 3

**6.** With reference to the international trade of India at present, which of the following statements is/are correct? **(2020)**

1. India's merchandise exports are less than its merchandise imports.
2. India's imports of iron and steel, chemicals, fertilisers and machinery have decreased in recent years.
3. India's exports of services are more than its imports of services.
4. India suffers from an overall trade/current account deficit.

Select the correct answer from the codes given below:

(a) 1 and 2 only (b) 2 and 4 only
(c) 3 only (d) 1, 3 and 4 only

**7.** If another global financial crisis happens in the near future, which of the following actions/policies are most likely to give some immunity to India? **(2020)**

1. Not depending on short-term foreign borrowings
2. Opening up to more foreign banks
3. Maintaining full capital account convertibility

Select the correct answer from the codes given below:

(a) 1 only (b) 1 and 2 only
(c) 3 only (d) 1, 2 and 3

**8.** The term 'West Texas Intermediate', sometimes found in news, refers to a grade of: **(2020)**

(a) Crude Oil
(b) Bullion
(c) Rare Earth Elements
(d) Uranium

**9.** With reference to Foreign Direct Investment in India, which one of the following is considered its major characteristic? **(2020)**

(a) It is the investment through capital instruments essentially in a listed company.
(b) It is a largely non-debt creating capital flow.
(c) It is the investment which involves debt-servicing.
(d) It is the investment made by foreign institutional investors in the Government securities.

**10.** Consider the following statements: **(2019)**

1. Purchasing Power Parity (PPP) exchange rates are calculated by comparing the prices of the same basket of goods and services in different countries.
2. In terms of PPP dollars, India is the sixth-largest economy in the world.

Which of the statements given above is/are correct?

(a) 1 only (b) 2 only
(c) Both 1 and 2 (d) Neither 1 nor 2

**11.** Which one of the following is not the most likely measure the Government/RBI takes to stop the slide of Indian rupee? **(2019)**

(a) Curbing imports of non-essential goods and promoting exports
(b) Encouraging Indian borrowers to issue rupee-denominated Masala Bonds
(c) Easing conditions relating to external commercial borrowing
(d) Following an expansionary monetary policy

**12.** In the context of India, which of the following factors is/are contributors to reducing the risk of a currency crisis? **(2019)**

1. The foreign currency earnings of India's IT sector
2. Increasing the government expenditure
3. Remittances from Indians abroad

Select the correct answer using the codes given below:

(a) 1 only (b) 1 and 3 only
(c) 2 only (d) 1, 2 and 3

**13.** Consider the following statements: **(2019)**

1. Most of India's external debt is owed by governmental entities.
2. All of India's external debt is denominated in US dollars.

Which of the statements given above is/are correct?

(a) 1 only (b) 2 only
(c) Both 1 and 2 (d) Neither 1 nor 2

**14.** 'Broad-based Trade and Investment Agreement (BTIA)' is sometimes seen in the news in the context of negotiations held between India and **(2017)**
(a) European Union
(b) Gulf Cooperation Council
(c) Organisation for Economic Cooperation and Development
(d) Shanghai Cooperation Organisation

**15.** What is/are the purpose/purposes of the Government's 'Sovereign Gold Bond Scheme' and 'Gold Monetisation Scheme'? **(2016)**
1. To bring the idle gold lying with Indian households into the economy
2. To promote FDI in the gold and jewelery sector
3. To reduce India's dependence on gold imports.

Select the correct answer from the codes given below:
(a) 1 only (b) 2 and 3 only
(c) 1 and 3 only (d) 1, 2 and 3

**16.** The problem of international liquidity is related to the non-availability of: **(2015)**
(a) goods and services
(b) gold and silver
(c) dollars and other hard currencies
(d) exportable surplus

**17.** Convertibility of rupee implies: **(2015)**
(a) being able to convert rupee notes into gold
(b) allowing the value of the rupee to be fixed by market forces
(c) freely permitting the conversion of rupee to other currencies and vice-versa
(d) developing an international market for currencies in India

**18.** The balance of payments of a country is a systematic record of: **(2015)**
(a) all import and transactions of a during a given period normally a year
(b) goods exported from a country during a year
(c) economic transaction between the government of one country to another
(d) capital movements from one country to another

**19.** Which of the following best describes the term 'import cover', sometimes seen in the news? **(2014)**
(a) It is the ratio of value of imports to the Gross Domestic Product of a country.
(b) It is the total value of imports of a country in a year.
(c) It is the ratio between the value of exports and that of imports between two countries.
(d) It is the number of months of imports that could be paid for by a country's international reserves.

**20.** With reference to Balance of Payments, which of the following constitutes/constitute the Current Account? **(2014)**
1. Balance of trade
2. Foreign assets
3. Balance of invisibles
4. Special Drawing Rights

Select the correct answer from the codes given below:
(a) 1 only (b) 2 and 3 only
(c) 1 and 3 only (d) 1, 2 and 4 only

**21.** Which of the following constitute Capital Account? **(2013)**
1. Foreign Loans
2. Foreign Direct Investment
3. Private Remittances
4. Portfolio Investment

Select the correct answer from the codes given below:
(a) 1, 2 and 3 only (b) 1, 2 and 4 only
(c) 2, 3 and 4 only (d) 1, 3 and 4 only

**22.** Which one of the following groups of items is included in India's foreign-exchange reserves? **(2013)**
(a) Foreign-currency assets, Special Drawing Rights (SDRs) and loans from foreign countries
(b) Foreign-currency assets, gold holdings of the RBI and SDRs
(c) Foreign-currency assets, loans from the World Bank and SDRs
(d) Foreign-currency assets, gold holdings of the RBI and loans from the World Bank

# Detailed Solutions

## Assessment Round

**1.** *(b)* 1, 2 and 4 only

- **Statement 1 is correct: Reducing tariffs and trade barriers** is a common measure taken to open an economy. Lower tariffs and fewer trade restrictions promote cross-border trade by making it easier and more affordable to import and export goods.
- **Statement 2 is correct: Liberalising Foreign Direct Investment (FDI) rules** is another important step in opening up an economy. By relaxing restrictions on FDI, a country attracts more foreign capital and encourages global companies to invest, leading to greater economic integration and growth.
- **Statement 3 is incorrect: Increasing state control over industries** typically signifies a move toward a more closed or regulated economy. Opening up an economy generally involves reducing state control to allow for more market-driven operations and competition.
- **Statement 4 is correct: Allowing free movement of capital and goods across borders** is a hallmark of an open economy. This measure facilitates global trade, investment and financial flows, integrating the country's economy with international markets.

**Thus, the correct answer is (b) 1, 2 and 4 only.**

**2.** *(c)* All three

- **Statement 1 is correct:** The **trade-to-GDP ratio** measures the proportion of an economy's total trade (exports and imports) in relation to its GDP, serving as a key indicator of economic openness.
- **Statement 2 is correct:** India's trade-to-GDP ratio has been increasing in recent years, reflecting its growing integration into the global economy. This trade openness indicator, which rose from 37.5 in FY05 to 45.9 in FY24, has contributed significantly to economic growth as it facilitated an efficient allocation of resources through comparative advantage.
  - Thus, India's trade-to-GDP ratio has been around 45%, reflecting a moderate level of integration into global trade but there is still room for further liberalisation.
- **Statement 3 is correct:** A higher **trade-to-GDP ratio** generally signals greater openness, as it shows that trade forms a significant part of the economy.

**Thus, the correct answer is (c) All three.**

**3.** *(d)* All four

- **Statement 1 is correct:** An Indian IT company providing software development services to a U.S.-based firm consider as an export of services because the Indian company is delivering software services to a foreign client.
- **Statement 2 is correct:** An Indian educational institution offering online courses to international students is an export of services because the institution in India provides educational services to students outside India.
- **Statement 3 is correct:** A tourist from Germany availing spa and wellness services at a resort in Kerala here even though the services are consumed within India, they are considered export of services because they are provided to a foreign national, which contributes to foreign exchange earnings for India.
- **Statement 4 is correct:** An Indian consultancy firm offering management advice to a company in the United Kingdom is an export of services because the Indian consultancy is offering professional services to a foreign company.

**Thus, the correct answer is (d) All four.**

**4.** *(d)* 1, 2, 3 and 4

**Current Account** reflect the records of the flow of **goods, services, income and current transfers.** This account shows whether a country is a net lender or borrower with the rest of the world in terms of real goods and services and it has the following components:

1. **Trade in Goods and Services:** This includes exports and imports of goods (e.g., cars, oil) and services (e.g., IT services, tourism).
2. **Income:** Earnings from investments abroad, like dividends or interest, and payments to foreign investors.
3. **Current Transfers:** Transfers without any counterpart, such as remittances sent by migrants, foreign aid, and gifts.

- **Option 1 is correct: Net trade in goods** refers to the difference between the value of a country's exports and imports of goods.
- **Option 2 is correct: Net earnings on cross-border investments** refers to **income** from foreign investments, such as dividends, interest and profits from foreign subsidiaries.
- **Option 3 is correct: Net trade in services** refers to the difference between the value of a country's exports and imports of services, such as transportation, tourism and financial services.
- **Option 4 is correct: Net transfer payments also called as current transfers are the** unilateral transfers, such as remittances from foreign workers, foreign aid and grants to the country.

**Therefore, the correct answer is (d) 1, 2, 3 and 4.**

**5.** *(b)* Only two

- **Statements 1 and 2 are correct: Remittances** and **grants** are examples of **unilateral transfers,** meaning they are one-way transfers of money without receiving any goods or services in return. This classified as **Transfer Payments** in the **Current Account** of the Balance of Payments.
- **Statement 3 is incorrect: Profits** repatriated by a foreign company fall under **primary income** (investment income) in the **Current Account,** not Transfer Payments.

**Thus, the correct answer is (b) Only two.**

**6.** *(c)* Both 1 and 2

- **Statement 1 is correct:** India's global share in exports is around 2.4%, while its share in imports stands at 3%, reflecting its significant role in global trade.
- **Statement 2 is correct:** India's **top imports** include **crude oil** (to meet its energy demands) and **electronic goods,** which are in high demand domestically.

**Thus, the correct answer is (c) Both 1 and 2.**

**7.** *(a)* Increased dependence on foreign capital to finance the deficit, leading to higher external debt.

A **negative CAD** means that a country's imports and payments abroad exceed its exports and receipts, necessitating external borrowing or foreign capital inflows to finance the deficit.

- This can lead to an increase in external debt and make the economy more vulnerable to global financial fluctuations.

**Thus, option (a) is the correct answer.**

**8.** *(d)* 1, 2 and 3

- **Statement 1 is correct:** India has a current account surplus of 2% of GDP in FY21, a historic high after 17 years mainly due to a sharp reduction in imports caused by the pandemic and a decrease in global oil prices.
- **Statement 2 is correct:** Historically, India has run a **Current Account Deficit (CAD)** due to its reliance on imports of **crude oil** and **gold,** which constitute a large portion of its import bill.
- **Statement 3 is correct:** India's **trade deficit** in goods (especially oil and gold imports) has been larger than its **trade surplus** in services, contributing to a persistent CAD. India's strong services sector earnings not been sufficient to offset the large deficits in goods trade, which include high imports of oil, machinery, electronics and gold.

**Thus, the correct answer is (d) 1, 2 and 3.**

**9.** *(c)* 2 and 4 only

**Non-Factor income** refers to earnings from services such as **tourism, shipping, banking** and other services that do not involve factors of production like labour, land or capital.

- **Option 1 is incorrect: Rent from the land given on lease in Germany is Factor Income** because it involves income derived from land, a factor of production.

- **Option 2 is correct: Earning from shipping and banking services is Non-Factor Income** as it involves services provided without using factors of production like labour or land directly. It is a part of trade in services.
- **Option 3 is incorrect: Profits of an Indian company established in the US is Factor Income** as it involves profits earned from capital investments abroad (a factor of production).
- **Option 4 is correct: Tourism services** is **Non-Factor Income** as it involves providing services to tourists, which is part of the trade in services without directly involving factors of production.

**Thus, the correct answer is (c) 2 and 4 only.**

**10.** *(c)* Only three

- **Statement 1 is correct**: One of the major objects of **Foreign Trade Policy (FTP) 2023** is to increase India's exports to **$2 trillion** by 2030 by promoting domestic industries and improving trade facilitation. This increase in exports can help reduce India's **Current Account Deficit (CAD)** by bringing in more foreign exchange, thus positively impacting the balance of payments.
- **Statement 2 is correct: Merchanting trade reforms** refer to changes in trade practices where goods are bought and sold by Indian traders without physically entering the country. This encourages more trade activity, which can lead to higher foreign exchange inflows, helping to **reduce the CAD**.
- **Statement 3 is incorrect: Increasing global crude oil prices** would raise India's import bill, as India is heavily reliant on imported crude oil. Higher oil prices increase the outflow of foreign exchange, thereby **worsening the CAD**, not reducing it.
- **Statement 4 is correct**: The **expansion of Production-Linked Incentive (PLI) schemes** promotes domestic manufacturing in key sectors. This reduces the need for imports of goods that can be produced domestically, while potentially boosting exports. Both factors can help in **reducing the CAD** by lowering imports and increasing exports.

**Therefore, the correct answer is (c) Only three.**

**11.** *(c)* 2, 3 and 4 only

**Capital Account** focus on records the flow of capital, including investments and loans, between a country and the rest of the world and this account tracks the net change in ownership of a country's assets and liabilities, showing how much a country is borrowing or lending to finance its current account deficits or surpluses. It has following components:

- **Option 1 is incorrect: Remittances** are the part of the **current account** under 'current transfers' because they represent money sent by individuals working abroad to their home country.
- **Option 2 is correct: External assistance** refers to **foreign aid or loans** received from other countries or international organisations. These transactions affect the capital flows and are recorded in the **capital account**.
- **Option 3 is correct: Commercial borrowings**, including loans from foreign financial institutions, are a form of capital inflow and are recorded in the capital account.
- **Option 4 is correct: Deposits made by non-residents** in Indian banks represent financial inflows and are therefore part of the capital account.

**Thus, the correct answer is (c) 2, 3 and 4 only.**

**12.** *(a)* 1 and 2 only

- **Statement 1 is correct**: The **Capital Account** includes **non-debt capital receipts such as Sovereign Loans**, External Assistance, Non-Resident Banking Deposits, etc. and **equity investments** such as FDI and FPI.
- **Statement 2 is correct**: When Indian residents invest abroad, it leads to **capital outflows** and a reduction in foreign exchange reserves, reflecting changes in asset ownership.
- **Statement 3 is incorrect: Grants for disaster relief** are recorded in the **Current Account**, not in the Capital Account.

**Thus, the correct answer is (a) 1 and 2 only.**

**13.** *(a)* FDI involves a long-term interest and control in the management of a company, whereas FPI only involves short-term financial investment.

| Aspect | FDI | FPI |
|---|---|---|
| Definition | Long-term physical investment in a business | Investment in financial assets (stocks, bonds) |
| Control | Provides management control or influence | No control over the company |
| Nature | Involves ownership of real assets (factories, etc.) | Involves purchase of financial instruments |
| Duration | Long-term investment | Short-term investment |
| Risk | Higher due to long-term commitment | Lower, but subject to market volatility |
| Economic Impact | Direct impact through job creation and technology transfer | Indirect impact on financial markets |

**Thus, the correct answer is (a).**

**14.** *(c)* Only three

- **Statement 1 is correct: FDI (Foreign Direct Investment)** involves investment in **physical assets**, such as land, buildings, factories and other infrastructure. It is a type of investment focused on establishing a long-term interest in a foreign business or sector.
- **Statement 2 is correct: FPI (Foreign Portfolio Investment)** includes investments in **financial assets** like **stocks, bonds, and other securities.** FPI is typically associated with shorter-term investments compared to FDI, with investors primarily seeking returns rather than control.
- **Statement 3 is correct: FDI investors** often acquire **managerial control** or a significant degree of influence over the operations of the company they invest in. This control is one of the key distinctions between FDI and FPI.
- **Statement 4 is incorrect: FPI investors** generally do not seek long-term ownership or control of the company. Instead, FPI is associated with **short-tomedium-term investments** aimed at generating returns, rather than achieving long-term involvement or control.

**Thus, the correct answer is (c) Only three.**

**15.** *(a)* Short-term capital that moves quickly across markets, often seeking higher returns or arbitrage opportunities.

- **Hot money** refers to **short-term capital flows** that rapidly move across countries and financial markets to seek quick returns or exploit interest rate differentials. These investments are typically in liquid assets and can be withdrawn quickly, contributing to financial market volatility.
- For example, if a country raises its interest rates, it may attract hot money from foreign investors seeking higher returns. However, if the interest rates fall or financial conditions worsen, this money can quickly leave the country, causing economic disruptions.

**Thus, option (a) is the correct answer.**

**16.** *(b)* 1, 3 and 4 only

- **Statement 1 is correct but 2 is incorrect:** The Foreign Portfolio Investment (FPI) consists of securities and other financial assets held by the investors in another country. **It does not provide the investor with direct ownership of a company's assets** and is relatively liquid, depending on the volatility of the market.
  - Along with the Foreign Direct Investment (FDI), the FPI is one of the common ways to invest in an overseas economy. The FDI and the FPI are both important sources of funding for most economies.
- **Statement 3 is correct:** The FPI holdings can include stocks, ADRs (the American Depositary Receipts), GDRs (the Global Depositary Receipts), bonds, mutual funds and exchange traded funds
- **Statement 4 is correct:** On a macro-level, the FPI is a part of a country's Capital Account and is shown on its Balance of Payments (BOP). The BOP calculates the amount of money flowing from one country to other countries over a financial year.

**Thus, the correct answer is option (b) 1, 3 and 4 only.**

**17.** *(c)* Rapid capital outflows that can destabilise a country's currency and financial markets.

**Hot money** can cause economic instability as these short-term capital flows are highly volatile. If investors rapidly withdraw their funds, it can lead to a sudden **capital flight**, destabilizing the currency and financial markets, particularly in developing countries.

**Therefore, the correct answer is option (c).**

**18.** *(b)* 1 and 2 only

- The 100% Automatic Route allows foreign investors to invest in a sector without prior approval from the Government of India. Some sectors under this route are:
- **Option 1 is correct: Agriculture and Animal Husbandry - 100% FDI** is allowed under the automatic route for specific activities like floriculture, horticulture, animal husbandry and pisciculture.
- **Option 2 is correct: Tourism and Hospitality - 100% FDI** is allowed under the automatic route in the tourism and hospitality sector.
- **Option 3 is incorrect: Pension - FDI** in the pension sector is allowed up to **49%** under the **Government approval route**, not 100% automatic.
- **Option 4 is incorrect: Banking (Public Sector) - FDI** in public sector banks is allowed up to **20%** and it requires approval. This is not under the 100% automatic route.
- **Option 5 is incorrect: Nidhi Company**: FDI in **Nidhi Companies** is **not permitted** under the automatic route.

**Thus, the correct answer is (b) 1 and 2 only.**

**19.** *(d)* 1, 2 and 3

- **Option 1 is correct: High capital inflow** into a country can led to **high inflation.** Capital inflow increases the supply of money and demand for goods and services. This can lead to inflationary pressures as the increased demand pushes up prices, especially if the productive capacity of the economy does not grow at the same pace.
- **Option 2 is correct:** A large capital inflow often leads to an **increase in the real effective exchange rate (REER).** The foreign capital flows indicate that the demand for the domestic currency increases, leading to an appreciation of the currency. This makes domestic goods more expensive in the international market, reflected in a higher REER.
- **Option 3 is correct:** An **increasing REER** due to capital inflows can lead to a **decline in export competitiveness.** As the domestic currency appreciates, it becomes more expensive for foreign buyers to purchase goods and services from the country, making exports less competitive in global markets. This can hurt the export sector over time, leading to a **decline in competitiveness.**

**Therefore, the correct answer is (d) 1, 2 and 3.**

**20.** *(b)* Only two

- **Statement 1 is correct:** The **computer software and hardware sector** attracted the highest FDI inflows, followed by other sectors. The top 5 sectors receiving highest FDI Equity Inflow during FY 2021-22 are
  - Computer Software & Hardware (24.60%);
  - Services Sector (Fin., Banking, Insurance, Non-Fin/Business, Outsourcing, R&D, Courier, Tech. Testing and Analysis, Other) (12.13%);
  - Automobile Industry (11.89%);
  - Trading 7.72% and;
  - Construction (Infrastructure) Activities (5.52%).
- **Statement 2 is correct:** Singapore (27.01%) and USA (17.94%) have emerged as top 2 sourcing nations in FDI equity flows into India in FY2021-22 followed by Mauritius (15.98%), Netherland (7.86%) and Switzerland (7.31%).
- **Statement 3 is incorrect:** The top 5 states receiving highest FDI Equity Inflow during FY 2021-22 are Karnataka (37.55%), Maharashtra (26.26%), Delhi (13.93%), Tamil Nadu (5.10%) and Haryana (4.76%)

**Therefore, the correct answer is (b) Only two.**

**21.** *(b)* Only two

Foreign Direct Investment (FDI) in India can enter through two primary routes: **the Automatic Route and the Government Approval Route.** These routes determine how foreign investment in Indian companies or sectors is regulated and approved by the government.

- **Statement 1 is correct: FDI through the Government route** requires an application to be submitted *via* the **Foreign Investment Facilitation Portal.** This portal streamlines the process for foreign investors who need government approval to invest in certain sectors.
- **Statement 2 is correct:** Under the **Automatic route,** FDI is permitted **without requiring government approval.** Investors can directly invest in sectors under this route as long as they comply with sectoral caps and regulatory guidelines.
- **Statement 3 is incorrect:** For FDI through the Government route, the **Department for Promotion of Industry and Internal Trade (DPIIT)** consults with the relevant ministry associated with the sector in question, not necessarily the **Ministry of Finance.** The approval process involves the ministry overseeing the specific sector, not the Ministry of Finance.

**Therefore, the correct answer is (b) Only two.**

***22.*** *(c)* Only three

Foreign Direct Investment (FDI) in India is prohibited in certain sectors due to national security, public interest, or regulatory concerns and the government does not allow foreign capital inflows into those areas. Below is a list of sectors where FDI is prohibited:

1. **Lottery business** is prohibited for FDI in India.
2. **Atomic energy** is also a sector where FDI is prohibited.
3. Gambling and Betting (including Casinos)
4. **Chit Funds and Nidhi Companies**
5. Trading in Transferable Development Rights
6. Real Estate Business (speculative trading)
7. Manufacturing of Cigars, Cigarettes, Tobacco
8. Atomic Energy
9. Railway Operations however **railway infrastructure is not prohibited** for FDI and FDI is allowed in certain segments like **high-speed rail projects.**
10. Certain agriculture activities

**Thus, the correct answer is (c) Only three.**

***23.*** *(c)* 2 and 4 only

**External Commercial Borrowings (ECB)** refer to the borrowing of funds by Indian companies from foreign sources in the form of loans, bonds, or other financial instruments.

- **Statement 1 is incorrect:** The minimum average maturity period for ECBs depends on the type of ECB. For most cases, the minimum average maturity is **3 years,** but in some cases like infrastructure projects, it can be longer.
- **Statement 2 is correct:** ECBs can be raised under both the **automatic route** (no prior approval required) and the **approval route** (prior approval from RBI needed), depending on the type and amount of borrowing.
- **Statement 3 is incorrect: ECBs** are debt instruments and unlike equity financing, they do **not dilute the stake** of existing shareholders. Debt financing such as ECBs does not involve issuing shares.
- **Statement 4 is correct:** Corporates can raise ECBs from international markets, including from foreign banks, international financial institutions and capital markets.

**Thus, the correct answer is (c) 2 and 4 only.**

***24.*** *(b)* 2 and 3 only

- **Statement 1 is incorrect:** The **sovereign debt** of India, which includes debt taken by the government, is **much lower** than the **non-sovereign debt,** which comprises loans and borrowings by private entities, banks, and other financial institutions. In India's external debt composition, non-sovereign debt (private sector debt) typically forms a larger portion compared to sovereign debt.
  - **Sovereign debt constitutes around** 4.1% of India's GDP and Non-Sovereign debt constitutes around 14.7% of the GDP.
  - **The external debt to GDP ratio was 18.8% at end-June 2024** as compared with 18.9% at end-March 2024.
- **Statement 2 is correct: External Commercial Borrowings (ECBs),** which refer to loans taken by Indian companies from foreign lenders, constitute a significant component of India's external debt. ECBs have consistently formed **the largest share of India's external**

debt, reflecting the reliance on foreign loans for corporate and infrastructure investments.

- **The share of outstanding debt of non-financial corporations in total external debt was the highest at 37.4%, followed by deposit-taking corporations (except the central bank) (28.4%), general government (21.9%) and other financial corporations (7.5%).**

- **Statement 3 is correct:** The share of **long-term external debt** (with a maturity of more than one year) is much higher than **short-term external debt** (which matures within one year). This is due to India's preference for long-term borrowing to finance infrastructure and development projects, reducing refinancing risks associated with short-term borrowing.
  - **The share of short-term debt (with original maturity of up to one year) in total external debt increased to 19.4% at end-June 2024 from 19.1% at end-March 2024.**

**Therefore, the correct answer is (b) 2 and 3 only.**

**25.** *(d)* 1, 2, 3 and 4

- **Option 1 is correct: Multilateral debt** refers to loans and borrowings from international financial institutions such as the World Bank, IMF, and Asian Development Bank (ADB). These loans are a part of the country's external debt.
- **Option 2 is correct: Bilateral debt** refers to loans taken by the country from foreign governments. This is also classified under the external debt of the country, as it involves borrowing from another nation.
- **Option 3 is correct: NRI (Non-Resident Indian) Deposits** are included in external debt as they represent foreign currency deposits made by Indians living abroad in Indian banks. These deposits are a liability for the country and are counted as part of external debt.
- **Option 4 is correct: Commercial borrowings**, including External Commercial Borrowings (ECBs) by private companies and other entities, form a major component of the country's external debt. These borrowings are taken from foreign lenders for various corporate and infrastructure purposes.

**Therefore, the correct answer is (d) 1, 2, 3 and 4.**

**26.** *(c)* Both 1 and 2

- **Statement 1 is correct: US dollar-denominated debt remained the largest component of India's external debt**, with a share of 54.6% at end-June 2024, followed by debt denominated in the Indian rupee (31.2%), yen (5.4%), SDR (5.1%), and euro (2.9%).
- **Statement 2 is correct: Commercial lenders** contribute the largest portion of the external debt, followed by **NRI deposits** and **short-term trade credits**, comprising 79.1% of total external debt.

**Therefore, the correct answer is (c) Both 1 and 2.**

**27.** *(d)* All four

- **Option 1 is correct: Multilateral loans** are the loans provided by international financial institutions like the **World Bank, IMF** which form the part of India's **Sovereign External Debt** as they are government borrowings from external multilateral agencies.
- **Option 2 is correct:** While FPIs invest in Indian treasury bills, these investments are **domestic debt** and are not classified as **Sovereign External Debt**. FPI investments in treasury bills are part of the domestic financial market.
- **Option 3 is correct: Special Drawing Rights (SDRs)** allocated by the **IMF** to member countries are included in the **Sovereign External Debt**. SDRs represent a claim to foreign currencies and form part of a country's external obligations.
- **Option 4 is correct:** Loans from foreign governments to India are part of India's **Sovereign External Debt**. These are bilateral loans taken by the Indian government from other nations, such as Japan or Germany, and are included in external debt calculations.

**Therefore, the correct answer is (d) All four.**

**28.** *(c)* Only three

- **Statement 1 is correct: Increased borrowing costs** are a common outcome following a default, as international lenders demand higher interest rates to compensate for heightened risks.

- **Statement 2 is correct:** An external debt default typically results in a **loss of investor confidence**, leading to **capital outflows** as investors seek more stable markets.
- **Statement 3 is incorrect: Strengthening of the currency** is unlikely; instead, currency depreciation is more common due to reduced investor confidence and capital flight.
- **Statement 4 is correct:** A default can lead to a **downgrade in the country's sovereign credit rating**, further impacting its ability to secure affordable credit.

**Therefore, the correct answer is (c) Only three.**

***29.*** *(a)* 2 only

- **Statement 1 is incorrect:** The **Reserve Bank of India (RBI)**, not the National Statistical Office (NSO), is responsible for compiling and publishing India's Balance of Payments (BoP) data.
- **Statement 2 is correct:** The **Balance of Payments (BoP)** is a comprehensive record of all economic transactions between residents of a country and the rest of the world, including trade in goods and services, investment flows and financial transfers.
- **Statement 3 is incorrect:** The **current account**, not capital account, reflects the balance of trade in goods and services, factor incomes and transfers. The capital account which deals with the financial transactions, such as foreign investments and loans, not goods and services.
- **Statement 4 is incorrect:** The current account primarily reflects the net flow of income and transfers into or out of a country, including trade in goods and services, income from investments, and remittances. The capital account records the net change in ownership of national assets, such as foreign investments and loans.

**Thus, the correct answer is (a) 2 only.**

***30.*** *(d)* All four

- **Option 1 is correct: Capital flight** refers to to **rapid outflow of financial assets or capital from a country due to economic or political instability**. This leads to a reduction in foreign reserves and worsens the **Balance of Payments (BoP)**, as it increases pressure on the current account and capital account.
- **Option 2 is correct:** When a country has **large foreign debt repayments**, it needs to use its foreign reserves to repay external debts, leading to an outflow of foreign currency. This worsens the **BoP**, especially the capital account, as foreign debt payments deplete reserves.
- **Option 3 is correct:** A **sharp increase in global oil prices** can worsen the BoP as it leads to higher import costs, increasing the current account deficit that is increases the trade deficit which worsening the overall **BoP** condition.
- **Option 4 is correct: Global interest rate hikes** particularly in major economies like the US, make investments in those countries more attractive which would **cause capital outflows** as investors seek better returns elsewhere, worsening the BoP.

**Therefore, the correct answer is (d) All four.**

***31.*** *(d)* 1, 2, 4 and 5 only

- **Option 1 is correct: Foreign currency assets** (FCA) form **the largest component** of India's forex reserves. These are holdings in major international currencies such as the US dollar, euro, yen, and pound sterling, and are managed by the Reserve Bank of India (RBI).
- **Option 2 is correct:** The **gold holdings of the RBI** are also a part of India's forex reserves. The RBI holds a significant amount of gold, which adds to the stability and value of the country's reserves.
- **Option 3 is incorrect: Loans from the World Bank** are not part of India's forex reserves. Forex reserves consist of highly liquid assets that can be used to settle international transactions, whereas loans from institutions like the World Bank are obligations rather than assets.
- **Option 4 is correct: Special Drawing Rights** (SDRs), which are international reserve assets allocated by the International Monetary Fund (IMF), are part of India's forex reserves. SDRs can be exchanged for freely usable currencies in times of need.

- **Option 5 is correct:** The **Reserve Tranche Position (RTP)** with the IMF is also included in India's forex reserves. The RTP represents the portion of a member country's quota in the IMF that can be accessed without any conditions, essentially functioning as a reserve asset.

**Therefore, the correct answer is (d) 1, 2, 4 and 5 only.**

**32.** *(d)* None of these

Forex reserves refer to the assets which are held by the central bank in foreign currencies, gold reserves, SDRs with IMF etc. and act as buffer against challenging and difficult times.

- **Statement 1 is incorrect:** India's foreign exchange reserves are made up of **four major components:** Foreign Currency Assets (FCA), Gold reserves, SDRs and the Reserve Tranche Position with the IMF.
- **Statement 2 is incorrect:** SDRs do not have the highest share of India's foreign exchange reserves. The **largest component of the reserves is Foreign Currency Assets** (FCA), which constitutes the majority portion. SDRs form only a small part of the total reserves.
- **Statement 3 is incorrect:** India does not have more foreign exchange reserves than the USA. The United States has a much larger economy and holds a significant number of foreign reserves through various institutions, although it often relies more on its own currency due to the dollar's status as the world's reserve currency.

**Therefore, the correct answer is (d) None of these.**

**33.** *(b)* 1, 2 and 4 only

**Foreign Currency Assets** (FCA) are a major component of India's foreign exchange reserves, managed by the Reserve Bank of India (RBI). FCAs consist of foreign currency assets held in foreign currencies, foreign central banks, and other institutions.

- **Option 1 is correct: Deposits in foreign central banks and commercial banks abroad** are part of Foreign Currency Assets (FCA).
- **Option 2 is correct: Securities of foreign governments** like US treasury bonds are also included under FCA.
- **Option 3 is incorrect: Indian Rupee denominated bonds** are not foreign currency assets, as they are denominated in INR, not foreign currency.
- **Option 4 is correct: Foreign exchange balances held with foreign institutions** are part of **FCA** as they contribute to foreign currency reserves.

**Therefore, the correct answer is (b) 1, 2 and 4 only.**

**34.** *(b)* A portion of a country's quota with the IMF that is accessible to the country without stringent conditions, considered as part of its foreign exchange reserves.

- The **Reserve Tranche Position (RTP)** is a part of a member country's **quota** with the IMF that can be **freely accessed** by the country when needed. It is counted as part of a country's foreign exchange reserves because there are no stringent conditions attached to its use. It is essentially the amount of foreign exchange a country has contributed to the IMF that can be readily accessed.
- For India, the **Reserve Tranche Position** with the IMF is a part of its foreign exchange reserves, which also include Foreign Currency Assets (FCA), Special Drawing Rights (SDRs), and gold reserves. In times of external financial stress, India can utilise its RTP to obtain foreign exchange without any conditions from the IMF.

**Therefore, the correct answer is (b).**

**35.** *(a)* The total number of months a country can finance its imports using its foreign exchange reserves.

- **Import Cover** refers to the number of months a country's foreign exchange reserves can cover the cost of imports if no new foreign exchange earnings are made. It is a measure of a country's external vulnerability and economic stability.
- **For example,** If India's foreign exchange reserves can finance 10 months of imports, it indicates that India has a comfortable import

cover and is well-positioned to handle external pressures on its currency and trade.

**Therefore, the correct answer is (a).**

**36.** *(b)* The country could face a currency crisis or balance of payments crisis due to insufficient foreign reserves to cover imports.

A **low import cover** signals that a country has insufficient foreign exchange reserves to finance its import needs, which could lead to a **currency crisis** or **balance of payments issues**, making the country more vulnerable to external shocks. This situation can lead to the following risks:

- **Currency Crisis**: Insufficient reserves may erode investor confidence, causing the currency to depreciate sharply. As reserves fall, the country might struggle to support its currency, leading to a rapid decline in its value.
- **Balance of Payments Crisis**: The country may face difficulties meeting its foreign debt obligations or paying for essential imports (such as oil, food, and raw materials). This can lead to a **balance of payments crisis**, where the country is unable to finance its current account deficit.

**Therefore, the correct answer is (b).**

**37.** *(a)* 1 - 2 - 3 - 4

The correct order that typically led to a Balance of Payments (BoP) crisis are:

- **Option 1**: The process typically begins with an **excessive current account deficit**, which means the country is importing far more than it exports, leading to a significant outflow of foreign exchange.
- **Option 2**: Know to finance this current account deficit, the country uses its **foreign exchange reserves**. Over time these reserves get **depleted.**
- **Option 3: Due to depletion of foreign exchange, both domestic and foreign** Investors may lose confidence, resulting in capital flight (rapid withdrawal of investments).
- **Option 4**: The depletion of reserves and capital flight puts downward pressure on the domestic currency, leading to **currency depreciation** as demand for foreign currency exceeds the supply of the domestic currency.

**Therefore, the correct answer is (a) 1 - 2 - 3 - 4.**

**38.** *(b)* Increased foreign debt as the country borrows to stabilise its economy

- **Option (b) is correct : A BoP crisis** occurs when a country faces a large **current account deficit** (excessive imports over exports) and sees a **rapid depletion of foreign exchange reserves**, often due to capital flight, leading to an inability to finance imports or service external debt. This forces the country to borrow from external sources like the **International Monetary Fund (IMF)** to stabilise its economy, leading to increased foreign debt.
- **Option (a) is incorrect: Rapid appreciation of the national currency** is unlikely, as a BoP crisis typically leads to **currency depreciation**, not appreciation.
- **Option (c) is incorrect: Decline in import costs** is incorrect because a BoP crisis generally leads to **higher import costs** due to currency depreciation.
- **Option (d) is incorrect: Surge in domestic employment** is also unlikely during a BoP crisis, as economic instability, reduced investments and higher costs may actually worsen employment conditions.

**Therefore, the correct answer is (b).**

**39.** *(c)* 1, 2 and 4 only

- **Option 1 is correct**: India faced a **high fiscal deficit**, which meant the government was spending more than it was earning, leading to heavy borrowing and exacerbating the BoP crisis.
- **Option 2 is correct: The Gulf War led to a sharp rise in oil prices**, increasing India's import bill and depleting foreign exchange reserves, worsening the BoP situation.
- **Option 3 is incorrect**: India did not have **significant foreign exchange reserves** during the crisis. In fact, its reserves had dwindled to dangerously low levels, which was a key factor behind the crisis.
- **Option 4 is correct**: The Indian rupee was **overvalued**, which made Indian exports expensive and non-competitive in the global market, contributing to a decline in export earnings.

**Thus, the correct answer is (c) 1, 2 and 4 only.**

**40.** *(a)* 2, 3 and 4 only

- **Statement 1 is incorrect: FPI inflows brings capital in the country which** indicate increase demand for the Indian rupee as foreign investors convert their foreign currency to rupees to invest in Indian assets. This generally leads to the **appreciation** of the rupee, not depreciation.
- **Statement 2 is correct:** When US Federal Reserve **increases interest rates,** US assets become more attractive to global investors. This often leads to **capital outflows** from emerging markets like India as investors seek higher returns in the US. This reduces the demand for the Indian rupee, leading to **depreciation.**
- **Statement 3 is correct:** India is a major importer of oil this make it vulnerable to exchange market as when international oil prices rise, it increases India's import bill, which puts pressure on the rupee. More rupees are needed to purchase foreign currency to pay for the higher-priced oil, leading to the rupee's **depreciation.**
- **Statement 4 is correct:** The RBI policy is to protect domestic currency from market volatility; to do this it buys US dollars from the market; it increases the demand for US dollars and decreases the supply of Indian rupees. This action causes the rupee to **depreciate** as the dollar becomes stronger relative to the rupee.

**Therefore, the correct answer is (a) 2, 3 and 4 only.**

**41.** *(b)* Only two

- **Option 1 is incorrect:** When the **RBI buys government securities** through **Open Market Operations (OMO),** it injects liquidity into the economy, increasing the money supply. This action tends to **depreciate** the currency as there is more domestic currency in circulation. Therefore, this is **not likely to lead to currency appreciation.**
- **Option 2 is correct:** The **RBI sells dollars** in the foreign exchange market; it increases the supply of dollars and reduces the supply of the Indian rupee. This action can lead to **appreciation of the rupee** as it strengthens due to reduced availability in the market.
- **Option 3 is correct:** A **tightening of monetary policy** (such as raising interest rates) makes borrowing more expensive, reduces inflationary pressures and attracts foreign investment due to higher returns. This increases the demand for the domestic currency, leading to **currency appreciation.**

**Therefore, the correct answer is (b) Only two.**

**42.** *(b)* 2 and 3 only

- **Statement 1 is incorrect:** Indians going to US for tourism activity will lead to the increased demand for dollars and thus, the value of dollar increased with respect to rupee. This results in depreciation of Indian currency and thus, **the exchange rate declines.**
- **Statement 2 is correct:** American people visiting India will lead to the increased demand of rupees and lessen the demand of dollars. The consequence of this will be the increased value of rupee or appreciation of Indian currency. **Thus, the exchange rate increases.**
- **Statement 3 is correct:** Declining demand of foreign goods in Indian market activity will lead to the decreased demand for dollars and thus, the value of dollar decreases with respect to rupee. **This results in appreciation of Indian currency or higher exchange rate.**

**Thus, option (b) is the correct answer.**

**43.** *(a)* 2 only

- **Statement 1 is incorrect:** Depreciation of the Indian currency typically leads to an **increase in exports** as Indian goods and services become **cheaper** for foreign buyers which led to increasing exports. Exporters benefit because their products become more competitive in global markets due to the lower value of the rupee.
- **Statement 2 is correct:** Depreciation of the Indian rupee makes India a **cheaper destination** for foreign tourists, as their home currency will buy more rupees. This can lead to an **increase in tourist arrivals** to India as it becomes more affordable for foreigners to visit.

- **Statement 3 is incorrect**: Depreciation of the rupee makes travelling abroad **more expensive** for Indian tourists because they need more rupees to purchase foreign currency. Hence, going abroad for a holiday becomes costlier, not cheaper.

**Therefore, the correct answer is (a) 2 only.**

**44.** *(d)* 1, 2 and 3

**Currency Exchange Rate Systems** are the policies through which countries manage the value of their currency relative to other currencies. There are several exchange rate systems, each with its own features, advantages, and disadvantages. Broadly, these systems can be categorised as fixed, floating or hybrid systems.

- **Option 1 is correct**: Under **Clean floating as called as flexible exchange rates or floating exchange rate**, the exchange rate is **market-determined** without any central bank intervention. This option can only exist where there is no **government interference**, as would be the case in a purely capitalistic economy. Clean floats are a result of Laissez-Faire or free market economics.
- **Option 2 is correct**: In case of **managed floating** also called **dirty floating** is the hybrid rate system, the central banks intervene to buy and sell foreign currencies in an attempt to moderate exchange rate movements whenever they feel that such actions are appropriate.
- **Option 3 is correct**: From around 1870 to 1914, the prevailing system was the **gold standard** which was **fixed exchange rate system** in which each participant country committed itself to convert freely its currency into gold at a fixed price.

**Thus, option (d) is the correct answer.**

**45.** *(b)* A fixed exchange rate system requires the central bank to maintain the currency at a predetermined level, whereas in a floating exchange rate system, the currency's value fluctuates freely based on market forces.

- In a **fixed exchange rate system,** the central bank must intervene to keep the currency pegged to a specific value, usually against another currency or a basket of currencies.
- In contrast, a **floating exchange rate system** allows the currency to fluctuate based on **market supply and demand,** with minimal central bank intervention.

**Thus, option (b) is the correct answer.**

**46.** *(b)* Only two

- **Statement 1 is correct**: One of the key advantages of a **fixed exchange rate system** is that it provides **certainty and stability** for international trade. Importers and exporters benefit because they know the exact exchange rate they will get when conducting international transactions. This reduces exchange rate risk, which can be a major concern in international trade under a floating exchange rate system.
- **Statement 2 is incorrect**: The central bank in a fixed exchange rate system must **regularly intervene** to maintain the exchange rate. This involves buying or selling foreign currencies to ensure that the domestic currency stays at its fixed value. Unlike a floating exchange rate, where market forces determine the exchange rate, a fixed system requires constant monitoring and intervention to counter any upward or downward pressure on the currency.
- **Statement 3 is correct**: One of the challenges of maintaining a fixed exchange rate is the **risk of reserve depletion**. If a country is under significant external pressure, such as during a balance of payments crisis or a speculative attack on the currency, the central bank may have to use its foreign exchange reserves to defend the currency's value. In extreme cases, this can lead to a **depletion of reserves,** forcing the country to devalue its currency or abandon the fixed exchange rate system altogether.

**Thus, option (b) is the correct answer.**

**47.** *(b)* Depreciation occurs due to market forces, while devaluation is a deliberate reduction in the value of a currency by the government or central bank under a fixed exchange rate system.

- **Depreciation** refers to a **decrease in the value of a currency** due to market forces such as supply and demand, often under a floating exchange rate system.

- **Devaluation**, on the other hand, is a **deliberate action taken by the government or central bank to reduce the value of a currency** under a fixed exchange rate system. Both reduce the purchasing power of a currency, but the mechanisms behind them differ significantly.

**Thus, option (b) is the correct answer.**

**48.** *(b)* It exposes a country to excessive currency volatility, which can create uncertainty for international trade and investment.

One of the primary disadvantages of a floating exchange rate system is that the currency's value fluctuates based on market forces, which can lead to volatility. This can create uncertainty for businesses engaged in international trade, as it becomes harder to predict future exchange rates, and may affect both trade and investment decisions.

**Thus, option (b) is the correct answer.**

**49.** *(a)* 2 only

- **Option 1 is incorrect**: In a **fixed exchange rate** system, the **central bank actively intervenes** in the foreign exchange market to maintain the currency at a fixed value relative to another currency. These interventions **require official reserve**, meaning the central bank buys or sells foreign currency to keep the exchange rate stable. Therefore, official reserve transactions are **not equal to zero** in a fixed exchange rate system.
- **Option 2 is correct**: In a **flexible exchange rate** system under which value of the currency is determined by market forces of supply and demand so, central bank does not intervene in the foreign exchange market, and there are no official reserve transactions. Therefore, **official reserve transactions are equal to zero** in a flexible exchange rate system.
- **Option 3 is incorrect**: In a **managed floating exchange rate** system, the central bank intervenes occasionally to stabilise or influence the exchange rate. Because of this intervention, official reserve transactions are **not equal to zero.**
- **Option 4 is incorrect**: In a **pegged exchange rate** system, the currency is fixed to another currency or basket of currencies. The central bank must intervene in the forex market to maintain the peg, leading to official reserve transactions. Therefore, official reserve transactions are **not equal to zero.**

**Thus, the correct answer is (a) 2 only.**

**50.** *(c)* The exchange rate is primarily determined by market forces, but the central bank intervenes occasionally to stabilise the currency.

In a **managed floating exchange rate system**, the exchange rate is generally allowed to fluctuate according to **market forces** such as supply and demand. However, central banks, such as the **RBI** in India, may intervene in the foreign exchange market to prevent excessive volatility and ensure currency stability during times of economic uncertainty.

**Thus, option (c) is the correct answer.**

**51.** *(a)* 1 only

- **Statement 1 is correct**: The **Real Exchange Rate (RER) system** measures the **prices abroad relative to those at home adjusted for the nominal exchange rate and inflation**. It reflects the purchasing power of one country's currency in relation to another after accounting for price level differences.
- **Statement 2 is incorrect**: If **RER is greater than 1**, it means foreign goods are cheaper relative to domestic goods, which makes exports less competitive and imports more attractive. If **RER** is **less than** 1, it means domestic goods are cheaper relative to foreign goods, potentially boosting exports.

Here, If the **real exchange rate rises above one**, it indicates that **domestic goods** have become relatively more expensive compared to foreign goods. This would make India's exports **less competitive**, as foreign buyers would find Indian goods more expensive. Therefore, a rising real exchange rate generally **hurts** export competitiveness rather than boosting it.

**Therefore, the correct answer is (a) 1 only.**

**52.** *(b)* A theory that states that in the long run, exchange rates should adjust so that the price of an identical basket of goods in two different countries is the same when expressed in a common currency.

**Purchasing Power Parity** (PPP) is an economic theory that suggests that the **exchange rate** between two currencies should adjust over time so that a **basket of goods** costs the same in both countries when priced in a common currency. This concept helps compare the cost of living between countries and is often used to measure the **real value** of a currency.

**Thus, option (b) is the correct answer.**

**53.** *(c)* All three

- **Statement 1 is correct:** NEER is indeed a weighted average of a country's currency compared to a basket of major foreign currencies, typically weighted by the trade significance of each currency. It provides an overall measure of the value of the currency in nominal terms without adjusting for inflation.
- **Statement 2 is correct:** REER adjusts NEER by taking into account **inflation differentials** between the home country and its major trading partners, reflecting the true purchasing power of the currency.
- **Statement 3 is correct:** An increase in NEER indicates an **appreciation** of the domestic currency compared to a basket of foreign currencies.

**Therefore, the correct answer is (c) All three.**

**54.** *(b)* 2 and 3 only

**The International Comparison Programme** (ICP) is a global statistical initiative led by the **World Bank** in partnership with other international and regional organisations. Its primary objective is to produce internationally comparable measures of economic indicators, such as Gross Domestic Product (GDP), by calculating Purchasing Power Parities (PPPs) across countries.

- **Statement 1 is incorrect:** The **International Comparison Programme** (ICP) is coordinated by the **World Bank**, not by the IMF.
- **Statement 2 is correct:** The ICP helps calculate **Purchasing Power Parities (PPPs)**, which are used to compare the real size of economies and the relative price levels of goods and services across countries.
- **Statement 3 is correct:** According to the **2017 ICP cycle**, India ranked as the **third-largest economy** in the world based on **PPP-based GDP**.

**Therefore, the correct answer is (b) 2 and 3 only.**

**55.** *(b)* 2 only

NEER-6 uses a smaller basket of 6 major currencies (such as the US dollar, Euro, Yen, Pound Sterling, etc.) to calculate the exchange rate. **NEER-40**, on the other hand, uses a broader basket of **40 currencies** that are representative of a wider range of trading partners.

- **Statement 1 is incorrect:** NEER and REER are not published by the **Ministry of Finance** but by the **RBI** to measure the external value of the Indian Rupee relative to a basket of major currencies.
- **Statement 2 is correct: NEER-40** provides a broader measure of India's exchange rate competitiveness as it considers a larger set of currencies, compared to **NEER-6**, which only includes 6 currencies.
- **Statement 3 is incorrect:** NEER and REER are published **monthly**, not quarterly, by the RBI. The **base year** for the **NEER** and **REER** indices, as published by the RBI is **2015-16**.

**Therefore, the correct answer is (b) 2 only.**

**56.** *(b)* It permits unrestricted movement of investments and capital across borders without any regulatory control.

- **Capital account convertibility** allows for the free and unrestricted movement of capital across countries for **investment purposes.**
- This includes the ability to buy foreign assets, shares, and investments without any regulatory control. It is distinct from current account convertibility, which pertains to trade in goods and services.

**Thus, option (b) is the correct answer.**

**57.** *(c)* 1 and 3 only

**Currency convertibility** refers to the freedom to convert a country's currency into another currency at market-determined exchange rates and it can be full Convertibility or partial Convertibility. Also, types of Currency

Convertibility can be Current Account Convertibility or Capital Account Convertibility.

- **Statement 1 is correct**: The **Indian rupee** is **partially convertible** on the **current account** but not fully convertible on the capital account. This means that while individuals and companies can freely convert the rupee for transactions related to trade and services (current account). However, there are restrictions on the convertibility of the rupee for capital account transactions, such as investments and loans.
- **Statement 2 is incorrect**: Any restrictions on currency convertibility are governed by FEMA, not FERA as **Foreign Exchange Regulation Act (FERA), 1973** was replaced by the **Foreign Exchange Management Act (FEMA), 1999**. Therefore, FEMA provides a more liberal framework compared to FERA and governs the exchange of foreign currencies in India.
- **Statement 3 is correct**: The **S.S. Tarapore Committee** was set up to make recommendations for gradually moving toward full convertibility of the Indian rupee in the **capital account**, addressing concerns such as inflation, fiscal deficit and exchange rate volatility.

**Therefore, the correct answer is (c) 1 and 3 only.**

**58.** *(d)* All four

- **Option 1 is correct: Increased speculative capital flows** are a risk associated with capital account convertibility, as unrestricted capital movement can attract speculative investments, increasing volatility in financial markets.
- **Option 2 is correct**: With an open capital account, fluctuations in the global economy can impact the domestic economy more directly and therefore, economies with full capital account convertibility are more exposed to **global financial crises** or external economic fluctuations.
- **Option 3 is correct: High dependence on foreign capital inflows** can develop as convertibility allows greater access to international funds, which can become a challenge if foreign investment decreases.
- **Option 4 is correct: Currency instability and volatility** can result from unrestricted capital movement, as capital flows in and out rapidly, impacting exchange rates.

**Therefore, the correct answer is (d) All four.**

**59.** *(b)* 1, 2 and 3 only

- **Statement 1 is correct: Full capital account convertibility** would mean there would be **no cap on the debt** that Indian companies can raise in foreign currency through mechanisms like **External Commercial Borrowings (ECBs)** or other forms of foreign capital.
- **Statement 2 is correct**: Also, with full capital account convertibility, there would be **no limit on the export and import of capital goods** as it allowing companies to freely engage in cross-border capital transactions for investments in infrastructure, technology, or machinery without government-imposed restrictions.
- **Statement 3 is correct**: It would also mean the **removal of restrictions on Foreign Direct Investment (FDI)** across all sectors, enabling foreign investors to invest freely in any sector.
- **Statement 4 is incorrect: Access to foreign currency for travel, education, medical or other designated purposes falls under current account convertibility**, which India already allows.

**Therefore, the correct answer is (b) 1, 2 and 3 only.**

**60.** *(c)* 1, 3 and 4 only

- **Statement 1 is correct: Increasing foreign exchange reserves** helps provide a buffer against speculative attacks and short-term volatility.
- **Statement 2 is incorrect**: Impose temporary restrictions on capital outflows might provide short-term relief, but such measures can undermine investor confidence and trigger further capital flight when restrictions are lifted.
- **Statement 3 is correct: Bilateral trade agreements** using local currencies reduce reliance on the U.S. dollar, decreasing vulnerability to exchange rate fluctuations.
- **Statement 4 is correct: Enhancing export competitiveness** will help reduce the trade deficit, thus improving the **Current Account**

Balance, which is crucial for stabilising the currency.

**Therefore, the correct answer is (c) 1, 3 and 4 only.**

**61.** *(b)* The efforts by countries to reduce their reliance on the U.S. dollar for international trade and foreign exchange reserves.

- **De-dollarisation** refers to the deliberate efforts by countries to reduce their dependence on the **U.S. dollar** in international trade, foreign exchange reserves and financial transactions.
- This process is driven by concerns over U.S. monetary policy, geopolitical tensions, and a desire for greater autonomy in international trade.

**Thus, option (b) is the correct answer.**

**62.** *(c)* Only three

Internationalisation of the Indian Rupee refers to the process by which the Indian Rupee (INR) gains acceptance and is used in global trade and financial transactions outside of India, similar to how major currencies like the U.S. dollar, Euro, or Japanese yen are used internationally.

- **Statement 1 is correct: Reduced exposure to foreign exchange risk:** If the Rupee is used more widely in global trade, Indian companies and the government will face **less risk from currency fluctuations.**
- **Statement 2 is correct: Greater demand for Indian goods and services:** Internationalisation can improve **trade competitiveness** as Indian businesses trade more in Rupees.
- **Statement 3 is correct: Increased influence of India's monetary policy:** A widely used Rupee would give India greater control over its **monetary policy** in influencing global financial markets.
- **Statement 4 is incorrect:** Internationalisation aims to **reduce reliance** on foreign currencies like the U.S. dollar.

**Therefore, the correct answer is (c) Only three.**

**63.** *(b)* 2-1-3-4

- The **US Dollar (USD)** is the most widely used and internationalised currency, serving as the world's primary **reserve currency.**
- The **Euro (EUR)** is the second-most internationalised currency, used extensively within the European Union and globally for trade and reserves.
- The **Japanese Yen (JPY)** is the third-most internationalised currency due to Japan's economic size.
- The **Chinese Yuan (CNY)** is gaining internationalisation but still ranks below the other major currencies in terms of global usage.

**Therefore, the correct answer is (b) 2-1-3-4.**

**64.** *(b)* The use of the Indian Rupee for international trade, investments and as a global reserve currency by foreign countries.

**Internationalisation of the Rupee** refers to the process of making the Rupee widely used for **global trade, investment,** and as a **reserve currency** by other countries, allowing it to be used in international financial markets just like the U.S. dollar or the Euro.

**Thus, option (b) is the correct answer.**

**65.** *(d)* 1, 2 and 3

- **Statement 1 is correct:** Indian banks have been permitted to offer **Rupee-denominated loans** to foreign entities, allowing Indian currency to be used more extensively in cross-border financial transactions. For example, **Exim Bank of India** offers **Rupee-denominated loans** to foreign companies, especially in neighbouring countries like **Bangladesh** and **Sri Lanka,** to fund projects or imports from India.
- **Statement 2 is correct:** The RBI has allowed **trade settlements** with countries like Russia and Iran in **Indian Rupees,** promoting its use in international trade. **For example,** India has established **trade agreements** with countries like **Russia and Iran** to settle transactions in **Indian Rupees.**
- **Statement 3 is correct: Masala Bonds** are Rupee-denominated bonds issued in foreign markets, allowing foreign investors to invest in Indian projects without exposure to currency risk.

**Therefore, the correct answer is (d) 1, 2 and 3.**

**66.** *(c)* All three

- **Pair 1 is correctly matched:** A **Nostro account** is one that a domestic bank holds in a foreign bank in the foreign currency of that country.

- **Pair 2 is correctly matched:** A **Vostro account** is held by a foreign bank in a domestic bank and it is maintained in the local currency of the domestic bank.
- **Pair 3 is correctly matched: A Loro account** is managed by a third-party bank on behalf of other banks, facilitating transactions where direct relationships do not exist.

**All three pairs are correctly matched; therefore, the correct answer is (c) All three.**

**67.** *(c)* All three

- **Pair 1 is correctly matched: A hard currency** is one that is stable, widely accepted globally, and maintains its value over time. Examples include the US Dollar (USD) and Euro (EUR).
- **Pair 2 is correctly matched: A soft currency** tends to fluctuate in value and is not widely accepted outside its home country due to economic instability. It is typically more volatile.
- **Pair 3 is correctly matched: Hot money** refers to short-term capital that moves quickly in and out of markets, often driven by speculation or interest rate changes.

**All three pairs are correctly matched; therefore, the correct answer is (c) All three.**

**68.** *(b)* A situation where countries actively try to strengthen their currencies to control inflation.

A **Reverse Currency War** refers to a situation where countries attempt to **strengthen** their currencies rather than devalue them. This is often done to **control inflation** and stabilise the economy, in contrast to the typical currency war where countries devalue their currency to boost exports.

**Thus, option (b) is correct answer.**

**69.** *(b)* 1, 2 and 4 only

- **Statement 1 is correct:** One of the key purposes of RBI's Forex Swaps is to **provide short-term liquidity** in foreign currency, which is essential during periods of limited foreign exchange availability in the banking sector.
- **Statement 2 is correct:** Forex Swaps also help in **stabilising the Indian Rupee** during volatile periods by allowing RBI to manage currency flows and prevent excessive fluctuation.
- **Statement 3 is incorrect: Supporting long-term infrastructure investment** is not a typical objective of Forex Swaps. This purpose is generally addressed through other financial mechanisms and long-term funding sources.
- **Statement 4 is correct:** **Managing foreign exchange reserves efficiently** is another objective, as Forex Swaps allow the RBI to maintain adequate reserves without making permanent adjustments to holdings.

**Thus, option (b) is the is correct answer.**

**70.** *(a)* To devalue their currency in order to boost exports and make their products more competitive internationally.

Countries often engage in **Currency Wars** by deliberately devaluing their currencies. This makes their exports cheaper and more competitive on the global market, thus boosting economic growth through increased demand for their goods and services. It is a strategy used to gain a trade advantage over other nations.

**Thus, option (a) is the correct answer.**

**71.** *(d)* 1, 2, 3 and 4

A **Currency Swap Agreement** is a financial arrangement between two countries or institutions to exchange a specific amount of their currencies at a predetermined exchange rate for a specified period. These agreements are designed to enhance financial stability, provide liquidity support and manage currency fluctuations in international trade and finance.

All four items describe benefits of a Currency Swap Agreement:

1. It helps to **stabilise foreign exchange reserves** by enabling countries to exchange currencies directly.
2. It reduces **dependence on the US dollar** by facilitating trade in local currencies.
3. It facilitates **trade and investment** between countries, making it easier to transact using their respective currencies.

4. It protects against **exchange rate volatility**, allowing parties to avoid fluctuations in global currency markets.

**Therefore, the correct option is (d) 1, 2, 3 and 4.**

**72.** *(d)* A phenomenon where the rapid expansion of one sector, usually natural resources, leads to a decline in other sectors, especially manufacturing.

**Dutch Disease** refers to the negative economic consequences that can occur when the discovery or exploitation of natural resources leads to the rise of one sector (often resource-based), causing other sectors, particularly **manufacturing**, to decline due to factors like an appreciating currency and reduced competitiveness.

**Thus, option (d) is the correct answer.**

**73.** *(d)* 1 and 3 only

- **Statement 1 is correct**: The **NIIP** is the difference between a country's foreign assets and foreign liabilities. It reflects the net balance of external assets and liabilities.
- **Statement 2 is incorrect**: A **positive NIIP** indicates that a country **owns** more abroad than it owes i.e., it is a net creditor to the world. A **negative NIIP** means that a country **owes more** to the world than it owns i.e., it is a net debtor.
- **Statement 3 is correct**: **India's NIIP** has consistently been negative, indicating that India has more foreign liabilities than foreign assets, mainly due to foreign investments and borrowings. India has been a **net debtor** to the world.

**Therefore, the correct answer is (d) 1 and 3 only.**

**74.** *(a)* The phenomenon where a country's trade balance initially worsens after a devaluation of its currency, but improves over time.

- The **J-Curve** describes the **initial worsening of a trade balance** following a **currency devaluation**, as the country continues to pay higher prices for imports.
- Over time, as exports become more competitive and import volumes adjust, the trade balance improves, forming a shape similar to the letter 'J' on a graph.

**Thus, option (a) is the correct answer.**

**75.** *(d)* Transactions conducted by the central bank involving foreign currency reserves, gold or Special Drawing rights (SDRs).

- **Official Reserve Transactions** refer to the transactions made by a country's central bank or monetary authority to manage its **foreign currency reserves, gold reserves** and **SDRs.**
- These transactions are crucial for maintaining exchange rate stability and managing the country's international liquidity. These transactions are critical in influencing the **balance of payments** and stabilizing the country's currency in the foreign exchange market.

**Thus, option (d) is the correct answer.**

**76.** *(a)* 1 and 3 only

- **Statement 1 is correct: Bilateral Investment Treaties (BITs)** are agreements negotiated directly between two countries to provide protections for foreign investors and their investments. These agreements are legally binding on both countries.
- **Statement 2 is incorrect**: While the WTO regulates international trade, **BITs are not under its purview.** BITs are independent agreements between two countries, not governed by multilateral organisations like the WTO.
- **Statement 3 is correct**: Countries that are parties to a BIT **can choose to amend or terminate the agreement by mutual consent,** often following a renegotiation or change in their policy stance.

**Thus, the correct answer is (a) 1 and 3 only.**

**77.** *(b)* Only two

- **Statement 1 is correct**: Tariff barriers such as customs duties or taxes on imports are easier to quantify because they involve a clear percentage or fixed fee imposed on goods crossing borders.
- **Statement 2 is incorrect: Non-Tariff Barriers** are not used only by developing countries; both developed and developing countries use NTBs to regulate trade.

- **Statement 3 is correct:** Tariff barriers generate revenue for the government by taxing imports. In contrast, Non-Tariff Barriers (NTBs) are primarily designed to control the quantity or quality of imports rather than generating revenue and they often focus on protecting domestic industries through measures like health and safety standards, quotas, or technical regulations.

**Therefore, the correct answer is (b) Only two.**

**78.** *(d)* All four

Non-Tariff Barriers (NTBs) refer to restrictions or measures other than tariffs that countries use to control the amount or value of trade across borders.

- **Option 1 is correct: Anti-Dumping Duty** is a **tariff measure** imposed on imports that are sold below fair market value to protect domestic industries from unfair competition. It is a tariff-based measure, not a non-tariff barrier.
- **Option 2 is correct: Import quotas** are a type of Non-Tariff Barrier that limits the quantity of certain goods that can be imported into a country. It limits imports without using direct tariffs, making it a classic **non-tariff barrier.**
- **Option 3 is correct: Export bans** are a form of NTB used to control the supply of certain goods, typically to protect domestic industries or ensure sufficient domestic supply.
- **Option 4 is correct: Rules of Origin** are regulations that determine the country of origin of a product, used to apply certain trade preferences or restrictions. These rules are often used in free trade agreements and are a type of non-tariff barrier.

**Thus, the correct answer is (d) All four.**

**79.** *(a)* Rules that define the national source of a product and determine which country's products qualify for preferential treatment under trade agreements.

**Rules of Origin** are the criteria used to define where a product was made. These rules are essential in determining whether a product qualifies for preferential treatment under trade agreements, such as lower tariffs or exemptions.

**Thus, option (a) is the correct answer.**

**80.** *(d)* 1, 2 and 3

- **Statement 1 is correct: Anti-Dumping Duty** is imposed to protect domestic industries from goods being sold at unfairly low prices by foreign exporters. This duty is levied when imported goods are sold below their fair market value, which can harm domestic producers.
- **Statement 2 is correct: Countervailing Duty** is imposed to counterbalance subsidies that foreign exporters receive from their governments, ensuring fair competition.
- **Statement 3 is correct:** Both **ADD** and **CVD** are imposed by the **Ministry of Finance** in India, but the process is based on **recommendations from the Directorate General of Trade Remedies** (**DGTR**), which investigates the cases of dumping and subsidies and suggests appropriate duties.

**Therefore, the correct answer is (d) 1, 2 and 3.**

**81.** *(d)* 1, 2 and 3

- **Statement 1 is correct:** The **Foreign Trade Policy** 2023 focuses on making districts **export hubs** by identifying and promoting products with export potential from every district.
- **Statement 2 is correct:** The policy sets an ambitious goal of reaching **USD 2 trillion** in exports by 2030 with $1 trillion in goods exports and $1 trillion in services exports.
- **Statement 3 is correct:** The policy places a strong emphasis on **digitisation** and easing the regulatory burden to improve the ease of doing business, with initiatives such as electronic certificates of origin.

**Thus, the correct answer is (d) 1, 2 and 3.**

**82.** *(a)* 1 and 2 only

- **Statement 1 is correct:** The DGFT is responsible for formulating and implementing the **Foreign Trade Policy (FTP)** of India, as well as promoting India's exports. It plays a key role in regulating and promoting international trade by ensures the proper application of trade-related policies.
- **Statement 2 is correct:** DGFT operates under the **Ministry of Commerce and**

Industry and oversees India's international trade practices. It provides policy inputs, issues export/import licenses and works to promote India's exports.

- **Statement 3 is incorrect**: The DGFT does not directly regulate trade disputes with the WTO. Dispute resolution under the WTO is handled by the Ministry of Commerce and Industry in coordination with India's representatives at the WTO.

**Therefore, the correct answer is (a) 1 and 2 only.**

**83.** *(d)* An internationally standardised system for classifying traded products.

The **HSN Code** is an **internationally standardised system** developed by the **World Customs Organisation** (WCO) for classifying goods traded across borders. It helps streamline customs procedures and ensures uniformity in product classification. It standardises the process across countries, which helps customs officials identify products and apply appropriate tariffs and taxes.

In India, the **HSN Code** is used to calculate **excise duty, customs tariffs** and **GST**.

**Thus, option (d) is the correct answer.**

**84.** *(a)* 1 - 2 - 4 - 3

The correct order of economic integration from least to most integrated is:

- **Free Trade Area**: Countries remove tariffs on trade between themselves but maintain individual trade policies with non-members.
- **Customs Union**: Member countries adopt a common external tariff on non-members.
- **Common Market**: In addition to removing trade barriers and adopting a common external tariff, there is free movement of factors of production like labour and capital.
- **Economic Union**: Member countries integrate their economies further by coordinating fiscal and monetary policies.

**Thus, option (a) is the correct answer.**

**85.** *(c)* All three

- **Statement 1 is correct**: **FTAs** aim for full or near-full elimination of tariffs across all sectors, while **PTAs** offer **partial tariff reductions** on a select list of goods.
- **Statement 2 is correct**: **FTAs** typically operate on a **negative list**, where only a few goods are excluded from tariff reductions, meaning most goods are included except those on the list, while **PTAs** work on a **positive list**, where only specific goods receive tariff reductions, meaning only the listed goods receive preferential treatment.
- **Statement 3 is correct**: FTAs tend to be **broader in scope**, covering areas such as services, investment and intellectual property rights, while PTAs are often limited to goods.

**Therefore, the correct answer is (c) All three.**

**86.** *(c)* CEPA includes cooperation in sectors like investment, services and dispute resolution mechanisms, while CECA primarily focuses on tariff reductions on goods.

**CEPA** covers a **wider range of sectors**, including **investment, services** and mechanisms for **dispute resolution**, making it a more comprehensive agreement with the aims to deepen overall economic integration between the countries. In contrast, **CECA** is mainly concerned with **reducing tariffs on goods**, with limited scope on services and investment.

**Thus, option (c) is the correct answer.**

**87.** *(b)* 1, 2 and 4 only

The **Eurasian Customs Union** is a regional economic integration initiative designed to facilitate trade and economic cooperation among its member states by establishing a common customs area and eliminating trade barriers. The Eurasian Customs Union was established by **Russia, Kazakhstan** and **Belarus** to create a single market for goods, with a unified customs policy and external tariff. **Ukraine** is not a member of the Eurasian Customs Union, although it has participated in trade discussions with the union.

**Thus, option (b) is the correct answer.**

**88.** *(c)* 1, 2 and 4 only

**MERCOSUR** (Southern Common Market) is a regional trade bloc in South America aimed at promoting economic integration, free trade, and the movement of goods, people, and capital among its member states. It was founded in 1991 by **Argentina, Brazil, Paraguay** and **Uruguay** under the Treaty of Asunción. **Chile** is not a founding member but is an associate member of the bloc.

**Thus, option (c) is the correct answer.**

**89.** *(a)* A preliminary agreement between two countries focusing on reducing tariffs on select goods before a comprehensive trade deal is finalised.

- The **Early Harvest Scheme** (EHS) is a trade mechanism where countries agree to reduce or eliminate tariffs on certain goods early in the negotiation process, before a full **Free Trade Agreement** (FTA) is finalised. It is designed to provide immediate benefits and build momentum for more comprehensive trade negotiations.
- The goal of EHS is to provide **early trade benefits and build trust** between the negotiating countries, laying the groundwork for a more extensive trade agreement.

**Thus, option (a) is the correct answer.**

**90.** *(c)* Only three

- **Option 1 is correct:** **Japan** and India have signed the **Comprehensive Economic Partnership Agreement (CEPA) in 2011**, which is a form of FTA.
- **Option 2 is correct**: India and Australia have recently signed the **India-Australia Economic Cooperation and Trade Agreement** (ECTA) in 2022. This is a form of a **free trade agreement** focused on boosting trade in goods and services, along with reducing tariffs.
- **Option 3 is incorrect**: India does not have a full-fledged FTA with the United States, though the two countries engage in bilateral trade agreements and discussions. However, no comprehensive trade agreement exists.
- **Option 4 is correct**: India has an FTA with **Sri Lanka**, known as the **Indo-Sri Lanka Free Trade Agreement (ISFTA)** which was signed in 1998.

**Thus, India has FTAs with three of the countries listed. So, the correct answer is (c).**

**91.** *(a)* 3 - 1 - 4 - 2

- **India-ASEAN Free Trade Agreement** – Signed in **2009** and implemented in **2010**.
- **India-Malaysia Comprehensive Economic Cooperation Agreement (CECA)** – Signed in **2011** and implemented the same year.
- **India-Mauritius Comprehensive Economic Cooperation and Partnership Agreement (CECPA)** – Signed in 2021.
- **India-UAE Comprehensive Economic Partnership Agreement (CEPA) Signed in 2022**, this agreement covers a wide range of sectors, including goods, services and investments, and aims to significantly increase bilateral trade between India and the UAE.

**Therefore, the correct answer is (a) 3 - 1 - 4 - 2.**

## Past Learning (Answers)

| | | | | | | | | | |
|---|---|---|---|---|---|---|---|---|---|
| 1 (d) | 2 (c) | 3 (c) | 4 (a) | 5 (a) | 6 (d) | 7 (a) | 8 (a) | 9 (b) | 10 (a) |
| 11 (d) | 12 (b) | 13 (d) | 14 (a) | 15 (c) | 16 (c) | 17 (c) | 18 (a) | 19 (d) | 20 (c) |
| 21 (b) | 22 (b) | | | | | | | | |

# CHAPTER 12 Multilateral Financial Institutions

## Assessment Round

### Topic 1 : World Trade Organisation (WTO)

**1.** Which of the following correctly differentiates between General Agreement on Tariffs and Trade (GATT) and World Trade Organisation (WTO)?

1. GATT was a provisional legal agreement, whereas the WTO is an international organization with a legal entity.
2. GATT's dispute resolution mechanism was informal, while the WTO has a formal and binding dispute settlement process.
3. The GATT covered trade in goods while the WTO covers trade in goods, services, and intellectual property rights.

Select the correct answer using the codes given below:

(a) 1 and 3 only (b) 1 and 2 only
(c) 2 and 3 only (d) 1, 2 and 3

**2.** Which of the following accurately describes the purpose of a 'round' in the context of international trade negotiations under GATT/WTO?

(a) A round refers to a single meeting held annually by WTO member countries to discuss trade issues.

(b) A round is a multi-year negotiation process among member countries aimed at reducing trade barriers and updating trade rules.

(c) A round is the term used for bilateral agreements between two countries under WTO.

(d) A round refers to the dispute resolution process initiated by any member country against another in the WTO.

**3.** With reference to the structure of the WTO, consider the following statements:

1. The Ministerial Conference is the highest decision-making body of the WTO and meet at least once every two years.
2. The General Council operates only as a dispute settlement body within the WTO.
3. The WTO Secretariat is responsible for implementing trade policies of member countries.

How many of the statements given above is/are correct?

(a) Only one (b) Only two
(c) All three (d) None

**4.** Consider the following statements:

1. WTO's Ministerial Conference is composed of representatives from all member countries.
2. The Council for Trade in Goods, Council for Trade in Services and Council for Trade-Related Aspects of Intellectual Property Rights (TRIPS) report directly to the General Council.
3. Trade Policy Review Body (TPRB) is responsible for monitoring and examining the trade policies of WTO member countries.

How many of the statements given above is/are correct?

(a) Only one (b) Only two
(c) All three (d) None

**5.** Which of the following statements accurately describe about WTO's Appellate Body?

1. It consists of seven members who are appointed for four-year term.
2. Decisions of the appellate body are final and binding on WTO member countries.
3. The Appellate Body reports directly to the General Council.
4. The Appellate Body primarily handles disputes related to intellectual property rights.

Select the correct answer from the codes given below:

(a) 1 and 2 only (b) 2 and 3 only
(c) 1, 3 and 4 only (d) 1, 2 and 4 only

**6.** Which of the following statements are correct regarding the structure and mechanism of the WTO Dispute Settlement System?

1. The Dispute Settlement Body (DSB) is composed of all WTO members and is responsible for overseeing the entire dispute resolution process.
2. The Appellate Body has the power to review panel reports and can modify, reverse or uphold the panel's legal findings.
3. The process of dispute settlement begins directly with the formation of a Dispute Settlement Panel, without prior consultations.

Which of the statements given above are correct?

(a) 1 and 2 only (b) 2 and 3 only
(c) 1 and 3 only (d) 1, 2 and 3

**7.** Which of the following statements best describes the 'Most Favoured Nation (MFN)' principle under the WTO agreements?

(a) It allows member countries to charge higher tariffs on goods from countries they have trade disputes with.
(b) It ensures that any trade advantage or benefit granted to one WTO member country must be extended to all other member countries.
(c) It permits countries to negotiate exclusive trade agreements with selected trading partners without offering the same terms to others.
(d) It provides preferential treatment to developing countries in all trade agreements.

**8.** With reference to the Most Favoured Nation (MFN) principle under WTO, consider the following statements:

1. All WTO member countries are required in general to grant MFN status to each other.
2. India granted MFN status to Pakistan in 1996 but has been revoked in 2019.
3. The MFN principle allows member countries to impose higher tariffs on imports from countries with which they have political disputes.

How many of the statements given above is/are correct?

(a) Only one
(b) Only two
(c) All three
(d) None

**9.** Which of the following are valid exceptions to the Most Favoured Nation (MFN) principle under WTO rules?

1. Free Trade Agreements (FTAs) allow members to offer preferential treatment to participating countries.
2. Developing countries are permitted to receive special and differential treatment under the Generalised System of Preferences (GSP).
3. Countries can impose trade restrictions against members with whom they have ongoing disputes.

Select the correct answer using the codes given below:

(a) 1, 2 and 3
(b) 1 and 2 only
(c) 2 and 3 only
(d) 1 and 3 only

**10.** Which of the following statements best describes the 'National Treatment' principle under the WTO agreements?

(a) It allows member countries to apply different taxes and regulations on imported goods compared to domestically produced goods.

(b) It ensures that imported goods must be treated no less favourably than domestically produced goods once they have cleared customs.

(c) It permits countries to provide subsidies exclusively to domestically produced goods.

(d) It allows countries to impose higher tariffs on imported goods to protect domestic industries.

**11.** Consider the following statements about the 'Generalised System of Preferences (GSP)':

1. GSP is a unilateral trade programme that allows developed countries to grant preferential tariff treatment to developing countries.
2. It allows beneficiary countries to export goods to the donor countries at reduced or zero tariffs.
3. United States and the European Union are among the countries that offer GSP benefits to developing countries.

How many of the above statements is/are correct?

(a) Only one (b) Only two
(c) All three (d) None

## Topic 2 : WTO Agreements

**12.** Consider the following WTO agreements:

1. Agreement on Agriculture (AoA)
2. Trade-Related Aspects of Intellectual Property Rights (TRIPS)
3. Agreement on Trade-Related Investment Measures (TRIMs)
4. General Agreement on Trade in Services (GATS)

How many of the above agreements specifically address non-goods aspects of trade, such as services or intellectual property rights?

(a) Only one (b) Only two
(c) Only three (d) All four

**13.** With reference to the 'Agreement on Agriculture (AoA)', consider the following statements :

1. AoA emerged from the Uruguay Round negotiations.
2. It aimed to limit trade-distorting agricultural subsidies.
3. It covers only the trade of raw agricultural products and not processed agricultural products.

How many of the statements given above is/are correct?

(a) Only one (b) Only two
(c) All three (d) None

**14.** Which of the following product categories are covered under the WTO Agreement on Agriculture (AoA)?

1. Livestock products 2. Fisheries
3. Fruits and vegetables 4. Alcoholic beverages

Select the correct answer using the codes given below:

(a) 1 and 2 only (b) 1 and 3 only
(c) 2 and 4 only (d) 1, 3 and 4 only

**15.** Consider the following pillars of the WTO Agreement on Agriculture (AoA) with their correct description:

| List I (Pillars of AoA) | List II (Descriptions) |
|---|---|
| 1. Market Access | A. Reducing government support and subsidies that distort agricultural trade. |
| 2. Domestic Support | B. Converting non-tariff barriers to tariffs and committing to tariff reductions. |
| 3. Export Subsidies | C. Reducing the volume and financial value of subsidies provided for agricultural exports. |

How many of the given above pairs is/are correctly matched?

(a) Only one pair (b) Only two pairs
(c) All three pairs (d) None

**16.** Consider the following examples of agricultural subsidies:
1. Minimum Support Price (MSP)
2. Fertiliser subsidies
3. Research and development grants
4. Subsidies for electricity used in farming.

How many of the above subsidies is/are classified under the 'Amber Box' according to the WTO Agreement on Agriculture (AoA)?
(a) Only one
(b) Only two
(c) Only three
(d) All four

**17.** Consider the following types of subsidies with their correct classification under the AoA:

| List I (Examples of Subsidies) | List II (Subsidy Box Classification) |
|---|---|
| 1. Minimum Support Price (MSP) | Amber Box |
| 2. Subsidies for environmental protection | Green Box |
| 3. Direct payments under production limits | Blue Box |

How many pairs given above is/are correctly matched?
(a) Only one pair
(b) Only two pairs
(c) All three pairs
(d) None

**18.** Consider the following statements about 'De-minimis provision':
1. The provision applies to all types of agricultural subsidies, whether they are trade-distorting or not.
2. It applies only to the developed countries under the AoA.

Which of the statement(s) given above is/are correct?
(a) 1 only
(b) 2 only
(c) Both 1 and 2
(d) Neither 1 nor 2

**19.** What is the primary purpose of the Bali Peace Clause agreed upon at the WTO Bali Ministerial Conference 2013?
(a) To allow developed countries to exceed their domestic support limits for agricultural subsidies.
(b) To provide temporary protection for developing countries against legal challenges if they exceed their domestic support limits for public stockholding programmes.
(c) To impose trade sanctions on countries violating WTO trade rules.
(d) To eliminate all forms of agricultural subsidies globally.

**20.** Which of the following statement(s) is/are correct about the TRIPs Agreement?
1. It was one of the original agreements negotiated under the GATT in 1947.
2. It was fully implemented by all WTO members in 1995.
3. The Doha Declaration (2001) acknowledged the right to protect public health.

Select the correct answer using the codes given below:
(a) 1 and 3 only
(b) 3 only
(c) 1, 2 and 3
(d) 1 and 2 only

**21.** Consider the following statements with reference to the various features of TRIPs Agreement:
1. The TRIPs Agreement obligates WTO members to provide protection for industrial designs for at least 10 years.
2. The Agreement includes provisions for safeguarding confidential information, known as trade secrets.
3. It requires all WTO members to establish a uniform system for IP enforcement without any flexibility.

Which of the statements given above is/are correct?
(a) 1 and 2 only
(b) 2 only
(c) 1 and 3 only
(d) 1, 2 and 3

**22.** With reference to the concept of 'Compulsory Licensing', consider the following statements:

1. Compulsory licensing allows a government to permit someone else to produce a patented product without the consent of the patent owner.
2. Under the TRIPs Agreement, compulsory licenses can be issued only for life-saving drugs.
3. In India, the first compulsory license was issued for a cancer drug in 2012.

How many of the statements given above is/are correct?

(a) Only one
(b) Only two
(c) All three
(d) None

**23.** With reference to the 'National IPR Policy (2016)', consider the following statements:

1. The policy aims to create an awareness of intellectual property rights among all sections of society.
2. It establishes the DPIIT as the nodal agency for IPR policy implementation in India.
3. The policy promotes commercialisation of intellectual property assets to boost economic growth.

How many of the statements given above is/are correct?

(a) Only one (b) Only two
(c) All three (d) None

**24.** With reference to the National IPR Policy 2016, consider the following statements:

1. The policy proposes setting up specialised IP courts for faster adjudication of IPR disputes.
2. The policy is intended to encourage the development of Traditional Knowledge Digital Libraries.
3. The policy mandates all public-funded research organisations to register their IP assets with the government.

Which of the statements given above is/are correct?

(a) 1 and 2 only
(b) 2 only
(c) 1 and 3 only
(d) 1, 2 and 3

**25.** With reference to the 'General Agreement on Trade in Services (GATS)', consider the following statements:

1. It is the first multilateral agreement that covers trade in services under the WTO.
2. GATS mandates that all member countries must fully liberalise their service sectors without any exceptions.
3. The Agreement follows the MFN principle.

How many of the statements given above is/are correct?

(a) Only one
(b) Only two
(c) All three
(d) None

**26.** Consider the modes of service supply with their corresponding examples:

| List I (Mode of Service) | List II (Examples) |
|---|---|
| 1. Mode 1: Cross-border supply | A. A university offering online courses to students abroad |
| 2. Mode 2: Consumption abroad | B. A tourist receiving hotel services in another country |
| 3. Mode 3: Commercial presence | C. A foreign bank opening a branch in the host country |
| 4. Mode 4: Presence of natural persons | D. An engineer travelling abroad for a temporary project |

How many pairs given above is/are correctly matched?

(a) Only one pair (b) Only two pairs
(c) Only three pairs (d) All four pairs

**27.** With reference to the Trade-Related Investment Measures (TRIMs) Agreement, consider the following statements:

1. It prohibits measures that are inconsistent with national treatment and quantitative restrictions on trade.
2. It only applies to the trade in goods and excludes service industries.
3. The agreement is not concerned with the regulation of foreign investment.

How many of the statements given above is/are correct?

(a) Only one (b) Only two
(c) All three (d) None

**28.** Which of the following statements correctly describe measures prohibited under the TRIMs Agreement?

1. Measures that require enterprises to purchase a certain number of local products.
2. Measures that restrict the importation of goods based on the value of exports.
3. Measures that mandate foreign investors to establish joint ventures with local companies.
4. Measures that impose trade-balancing requirements on imported goods.

Select the correct answer using the codes given below:

(a) 1 and 3 only (b) 1, 2 and 4 only
(c) 2 and 3 only (d) 1, 3 and 4 only

**29.** With reference to the WTO Agreement on Fisheries Subsidies, consider the following statements:

1. The Agreement aims to prohibit subsidies that contribute to Illegal, Unreported and Unregulated (IUU) fishing.
2. It allows for subsidies that promote the sustainable management of fish stocks.
3. The Agreement mandates the complete elimination of all forms of fisheries subsidies by 2030.

How many of the statements given above is/are correct?

(a) Only one (b) Only two
(c) All three (d) None

**30.** Consider the following statements about 'WTO Agreement on Fisheries Subsidies':

1. The Agreement applies to both marine and inland fisheries.
2. It provides flexibility for developing countries to maintain certain subsidies for small-scale fisheries operating within their Exclusive Economic Zones (EEZs).
3. The Agreement requires annual reporting by member countries on the status of fish stocks within their territories.

Which of the statements given above is/are correct?

(a) 1 and 2 only (b) 2 and 3 only
(c) 1 and 3 only (d) 2 only

**31.** With reference to the Trade Facilitation Agreement (TFA), consider the following statements:

1. It is the first multilateral trade agreement concluded since the establishment of the WTO.
2. The agreement aims to expedite the movement, release and clearance of goods including goods in transit.
3. India has set up a National Committee on Trade Facilitation (NCTF) chaired by the Cabinet Secretary to coordinate the implementation of TFA provisions.

Which of the statements given above is/are correct?

(a) 1 and 2 only (b) 2 only
(c) 1 and 3 only (d) 1, 2 and 3

## Topic 3 : WTO Terminologies/Groupings

**32.** Which of the following measures are covered under the Agreement on Sanitary and Phytosanitary (SPS) Measures?

1. Measures to protect animal or plant life from the entry, establishment, or spread of pests
2. Measures to protect human or animal life from risks arising from additives, contaminants, toxins, or disease-causing organisms in food
3. Measures to ensure labelling requirements for imported goods
4. Measures to prevent deceptive practices in trade

Select the correct answer using the codes given below:

(a) 1 and 2 only (b) 2 and 4 only
(c) 1, 2 and 3 only (d) 1, 3 and 4 only

**33.** Which of the following are examples of sanitary and phytosanitary measures allowed under the SPS Agreement?

1. Banning the import of meat products from regions affected by foot-and-mouth disease
2. Imposing tariffs on imported fruits
3. Setting maximum pesticide residue levels in food products
4. Requiring a certificate of origin for agricultural products

Select the correct answer using the codes given below:

(a) 1 and 3 only (b) 2 and 4 only
(c) 1, 2 and 3 only (d) 1, 3 and 4 only

**34.** Consider the following statements about the Information Technology Agreement (ITA) :

1. It is a plurilateral agreement under the WTO that applies to both hardware and software technology products.
2. Only developed countries are signatories to the ITA.
3. India is a signatory to this agreement.

How many of the statements given above is/are correct?

(a) Only one (b) Only two
(c) All three (d) None

**35.** Under the Information Technology Agreement (ITA 2.0) Agreement of the WTO, which of the following product categories is most likely to benefit?

(a) Agricultural machinery and fertilizers
(b) Consumer electronics and semiconductors
(c) Textile and apparel products
(d) Automotive spare parts and components

**36.** Which of the following best describes the concept of Special and Differential Treatment (SDT) under WTO agreements?

(a) It allows developed countries to impose higher tariffs on imports from developing countries.
(b) It provides developing countries with longer time periods to implement commitments and greater flexibility in meeting trade obligations.
(c) It grants exclusive trade benefits to least developed countries (LDCs) at the expense of other member nations.
(d) It exempts all developing countries from any trade commitments under WTO agreements.

**37.** Which of the following statements best describes the purpose of the 'Special Safeguard Mechanism (SSM)' under the WTO Agreement on Agriculture?

(a) It allows developing countries to impose additional tariffs in response to import surges or price declines.
(b) It permits developed countries to increase subsidies for their agricultural products.
(c) It allows all WTO member countries to exempt themselves from trade liberalisation commitments.
(d) It restricts developing countries from using any trade protection measures.

**38.** Which of the following WTO groupings include India as a member?

1. G-20
2. Cairns Group
3. G-33
4. African Group

Select the correct answer using the codes given below:

(a) 1 and 2 only
(b) 1 and 3 only
(c) 2 and 4 only
(d) 1, 3 and 4 only

**39.** Which of the following is a key objective of the Cotton-4 (C-4) grouping within the WTO framework?

(a) To establish a common cotton trading bloc for African countries
(b) To advocate for the elimination of cotton subsidies and tariffs in developed countries
(c) To increase cotton production through shared technology among C-4 members
(d) To create a uniform cotton pricing mechanism among all WTO member countries

**40.** Consider the following statements with reference to the concept of 'Developing Country status' in the WTO:

1. WTO members can self-declare themselves as developing countries to avail special and differential treatment.
2. Once declared, a country's developing status cannot be challenged by any other WTO member.
3. Developing countries are given longer transition periods to implement trade agreements.

How many of the statements given above is/are correct?

(a) Only one
(b) Only two
(c) All three
(d) None

## Topic 4 : International Monetary Fund (IMF)

**41.** With reference to the Bretton Woods Conference of 1944, consider the following statements:

1. The conference led to the establishment of the International Monetary Fund (IMF) and the World Bank.
2. It was held with the objective of rebuilding the economies of war-torn European countries.
3. The Bretton Woods Conference laid the foundation for a fixed exchange rate system.

How many of the statements given above is/are correct?

(a) Only one (b) Only two
(c) All three (d) None

**42.** Consider the following statements:

1. IMF was designed to provide short-term financial assistance to member countries facing balance of payments problems.
2. World Bank was initially created to provide long-term loans for infrastructure projects in war-torn Europe.
3. Both institutions were designed to regulate international trade directly.

How many of the statements given above is/are correct?

(a) Only one
(b) Only two
(c) All three
(d) None

**43.** Consider the following statements about the 'International Monetary Fund (IMF)':

1. Each member country's voting power in the IMF is determined solely by its economic size.
2. The IMF's Board of Governors is the highest decision-making body within the organisation.
3. All member countries have an equal number of votes in the IMF's decision-making process.

Which of the statements given above is/are correct?

(a) 1 and 2 only (b) 2 only
(c) 1 and 3 only (d) 1, 2 and 3

**44.** Consider the following statements:

1. Any country that wishes to join the IMF must first be a member of the United Nations.
2. A country must agree to pay a quota subscription as part of its membership.
3. All member countries of the IMF have an equal voting power regardless of their financial contributions.

How many of the statements given above is/are correct?

(a) Only one (b) Only two
(c) All three (d) None

**45.** Consider the following aspects:

1. Voting power in the IMF
2. Access to financial resources
3. Contribution to the IMF's general resources
4. Representation in the IMF's Board of Governors

How many of the given above aspects is/are influenced by a member country's IMF quota?

(a) Only one (b) Only two
(c) Only three (d) All four

**46.** Which of the following factors determine a member country's quota in the IMF?
1. Gross Domestic Product (GDP)
2. Population
3. Foreign exchange reserves
4. Trade volume

Select the correct answer using the codes given below:
(a) 1, 2 and 3 only (b) 1, 3 and 4 only
(c) 1 and 4 only (d) 1, 2, 3 and 4

**47.** With reference to the 'IMF Quota', consider the following statements:
1. India is among the top 10 countries with the highest IMF quotas.
2. The quota is reviewed and adjusted every two years by the IMF.
3. The quota allocated to each member determines the extent of its access to IMF financial resources.

How many of the statements given above is/are correct?
(a) Only one (b) Only two
(c) All three (d) None

**48.** Consider the following features of 'Special Drawing Rights (SDRs)':
1. SDRs are used as the unit of account by the IMF.
2. The value of SDRs is determined daily based on market exchange rates.
3. Countries are required to repay the allocated SDRs to the IMF within a specified time frame.
4. SDRs are allocated to IMF member countries based on their quota.

How many of the above features is/are correct?
(a) Only one (b) Only two
(c) Only three (d) All four

**49.** Which of the following currencies are used in the calculation of the SDR value?
1. US Dollar
2. Chinese Yuan (Renminbi)
3. Japanese Yen
4. Indian Rupee

Select the correct answer using the codes given below:
(a) 1, 2 and 3 only
(b) 2 and 4 only
(c) 1, 2, 3, and 4
(d) 1 and 3 only

**50.** Consider the following functions:
1. Providing short-term financial assistance to member countries facing balance of payments problems
2. Acting as a lender of last resort for the global banking system
3. Issuing currency to member countries for international trade
4. Offering technical assistance and training to member countries

How many of the given above is/are the functions carried out by the IMF?
(a) Only one (b) Only two
(c) Only three (d) All four

**51.** Consider the following types of IMF lending facilities:
1. Extended Fund Facility (EFF)
2. Stand-By Arrangement (SBA)
3. Extended Credit Facility (ECF)
4. Rapid Credit Facility (RCF)

How many of the above facilities is/are considered concessional lending by the IMF?
(a) Only one
(b) Only two
(c) Only three
(d) All four

**52.** Which of the following best describes the primary objective of the IMF's 'Resilience and Sustainability Facility (RSF)'?
(a) To provide emergency financing to countries facing sudden balance of payments crises
(b) To support long-term structural reforms aimed at addressing climate change and pandemic preparedness
(c) To offer concessional loans exclusively for low-income countries
(d) To fund infrastructure projects in developing countries

**53.** Consider the following reports:
1. World Economic Outlook (WEO)
2. Global Financial Stability Report (GFSR)
3. Doing Business Report
4. Fiscal Monitor

How many of the given above reports is/are released by the IMF?

(a) Only one (b) Only two
(c) Only three (d) All four

**54.** With reference to India's relationship with the IMF, consider the following statements:
1. India is a founding member of the IMF.
2. IMF provided financial assistance to India during the balance of payments crisis in 1991.
3. India has never borrowed from the IMF in this 21st century.

How many of the statements given above is/are correct?

(a) Only one (b) Only two
(c) All three (d) None

## Topic 5 : World Bank

**55.** Consider the following statements with respect to the World Bank:
1. Each member country has equal voting power regardless of its financial contributions.
2. World Bank's Board of Governors meets once a year to make major policy decisions.
3. To become a member of the World Bank, a country must first join the IMF.

Which of the statements given above is/are correct?

(a) 2 only (b) 2 and 3 only
(c) 1 and 3 only (d) 1, 2 and 3

**56.** Arrange the following countries in descending order of their shareholding in the World Bank (IBRD):
1. China 2. Japan
3. India 4. United States

Select the correct answer using the codes given below.

(a) 4 - 2 - 1 - 3 (b) 1 - 4 - 2 - 3
(c) 4 - 1 - 2 - 3 (d) 2 - 4 - 3 - 1

**57.** Which of the following reports are published by the World Bank?
1. World Development Report
2. Ease of Doing Business Report
3. Global Economic Prospects
4. World Investment Report

Select the correct answer using the codes given below:

(a) 1, 2 and 3 only (b) 1 and 4 only
(c) 2, 3 and 4 only (d) 1, 2, 3 and 4

**58.** Consider the following institutions:
1. International Bank for Reconstruction and Development (IBRD)
2. International Development Association (IDA)
3. International Finance Corporation (IFC)
4. International Fund for Agricultural Development (IFAD)

How many of the above institutions is/are part of the World Bank Group?

(a) Only one (b) Only two
(c) Only three (d) All four

**59.** Consider the following institutions of the World Bank Group:
1. International Bank for Reconstruction and Development (IBRD)
2. International Development Association (IDA)
3. International Finance Corporation (IFC)
4. International Centre for Settlement of Investment Disputes (ICSID)

How many of the above institutions is/are India a member of?

(a) Only one (b) Only two
(c) Only three (d) All four

**60.** Consider the following statements:
1. IDA is the concessional lending arm of the World Bank, providing loans to the poorest countries.
2. IFC focuses on the private sector development in developing countries.
3. MIGA provides political risk insurance to investors and lenders.

How many of the statements given above is/are correct?

(a) Only one (b) Only two
(c) All three (d) None

**61.** Consider the following statements:

1. IBRD can directly finance private sector projects without any government guarantee.
2. All IBRD loans to member countries are backed by sovereign guarantees from their respective governments.
3. Membership in the IBRD is mandatory for all members of the IDA.

How many of the statements given above is/are correct?

(a) Only one (b) Only two
(c) All three (d) None

**62.** With reference to the 'International Finance Corporation (IFC)', consider the following statements:

1. It provides loans and equity investments to promote private sector development in developing countries.
2. IFC provides direct financial assistance to governments for poverty reduction programmes.

Which of the statements given above is/are correct?

(a) 1 only (b) 2 only
(c) Both 1 and 2 (d) Neither 1 nor 2

## Topic 6 : Regional Development Banks

**63.** Consider the following regional development banks:

1. Asian Development Bank (ADB)
2. African Development Bank (AfDB)
3. New Development Bank (NDB)
4. European Bank for Reconstruction and Development (EBRD)

How many of the above regional development banks is/are India a member of?

(a) Only one (b) Only two
(c) Only three (d) All four

**64.** Consider the following regional development banks with their respective headquarters:

| Regional Development Bank | Headquarters |
|---|---|
| 1. Asian Development Bank (ADB) | Beijing, China |
| 2. New Development Bank (NDB) | Manila, Philippines |
| 3. European Bank for Reconstruction and Development (EBRD) | London, United Kingdom |
| 4. African Development Bank (AfDB) | Abidjan, Côte d'Ivoire |

How many pairs given above is/are correctly matched?

(a) Only one pair (b) Only two pairs
(c) Only three pairs (d) All four pairs

**65.** Consider the following countries:

1. Egypt 2. Brazil
3. Bangladesh 4. India

How many of the given above countries is/are members of the New Development Bank (NDB)?

(a) Only one (b) Only two
(c) Only three (d) All four

**66.** With reference to the 'Asian Infrastructure Investment Bank (AIIB)', consider the following statements:

1. AIIB focuses on funding infrastructure projects across both Asia and other regions outside Asia.
2. The voting power of member countries in AIIB is based on their economic size.
3. China and India are the largest shareholders in the AIIB.

Which of the statements given above are correct?

(a) 1 and 2 only (b) 2 and 3 only
(c) 1 and 3 only (d) 1, 2 and 3

**67.** Consider the following statements about 'Asian Development Bank (ADB)':

1. ADB provides both financial assistance and technical assistance to its member countries to support development projects.
2. The voting power in the ADB is equally distributed among all member countries.
3. ADB focuses exclusively on infrastructure projects in developing countries.

How many of the statements given above is/are correct?

(a) Only one (b) Only two
(c) All three (d) None

**68.** With reference to the New Development Bank (NDB), consider the following statements:

1. It was established by the BRICS nations during the Fortaleza Summit in 2014.
2. All BRICS countries hold equal voting power in the NDB, regardless of their economic size.
3. The primary objective of the NDB is to finance infrastructure and sustainable development projects exclusively in the BRICS countries.

Which of the statements given above are correct?

(a) 1 and 2 only (b) 2 and 3 only
(c) 1 and 3 only (d) 1, 2 and 3

## Topic 7 : Other Groupings

**69.** Which of the following statements are correct about the 'Financial Action Task Force (FATF)'?

1. It was established in 1989 to combat money laundering and terrorism financing.
2. Its recommendations are legally binding on all member countries.
3. The FATF works with other international organizations like the IMF and World Bank to ensure global financial stability.

Which of the statements given above are correct?

(a) 1 and 2 only (b) 2 and 3 only
(c) 1 and 3 only (d) 1, 2 and 3

**70.** Match the following FATF lists with their correct descriptions:

| List I (FATF Lists) | List II (Descriptions) |
|---|---|
| 1. FATF Blacklist | A. Jurisdictions under increased monitoring for AML/CFT deficiencies but working with FATF to improve. |
| 2. FATF Grey list | B. Countries considered high-risk and non-cooperative, subject to potential countermeasures. |
| 3. Non-Cooperative Countries | C. Countries flagged for severe deficiencies and recommended for significant countermeasures. |
| 4. Jurisdictions under Review | D. Countries being evaluated for their compliance with FATF recommendations. |

Select the correct answer from the codes given below:

(a) 1-B, 2-A, 3-C, 4-D
(b) 1-A, 2-B, 3-D, 4-C
(c) 1-C, 2-D, 3-A, 4-B
(d) 1-D, 2-C, 3-B, 4-A

**71.** Which of the following countries are part of the G-7 (Group of Seven)?

1. Canada 2. Russia
3. Japan 4. Italy

Select the correct answer from the codes given below:

(a) 1, 3 and 4 only (b) 2, 3 and 4 only
(c) 1, 3 and 4 only (d) 1, 2, 3 and 4

**72.** With reference to the G-20, consider the following statements:

1. It comprises a mix of both developed and emerging economies, representing diverse global interests.
2. It was initially established in response to the 2008 global financial crisis to stabilise the world economy.
3. The G-20 meetings occur exclusively in member nations located in the Northern Hemisphere.

Which of the statements given above is/are correct?

(a) 1 and 2 only (b) 2 and 3 only
(c) 1 only (d) 1, 2 and 3

**73.** In which one of the following groups are all the four countries members of G20?

(a) Argentina, Mexico, South Africa and Turkey
(b) Australia, Canada, Malaysia and New Zealand
(c) Brazil, Iran, Saudi Arabia and Vietnam
(d) Indonesia, Japan, Singapore and South Korea

# OMR SHEET

**Assessment Round**

| | | | | | | | | | | | | | | | | | | | |
|---|---|---|---|---|---|---|---|---|---|---|---|---|---|---|---|---|---|---|---|
| 1 | a | b | c | d | 31 | a | b | c | d | 61 | a | b | c | d | 91 | a | b | c | d |
| 2 | a | b | c | d | 32 | a | b | c | d | 62 | a | b | c | d | 92 | a | b | c | d |
| 3 | a | b | c | d | 33 | a | b | c | d | 63 | a | b | c | d | 93 | a | b | c | d |
| 4 | a | b | c | d | 34 | a | b | c | d | 64 | a | b | c | d | 94 | a | b | c | d |
| 5 | a | b | c | d | 35 | a | b | c | d | 65 | a | b | c | d | 95 | a | b | c | d |
| 6 | a | b | c | d | 36 | a | b | c | d | 66 | a | b | c | d | 96 | a | b | c | d |
| 7 | a | b | c | d | 37 | a | b | c | d | 67 | a | b | c | d | 97 | a | b | c | d |
| 8 | a | b | c | d | 38 | a | b | c | d | 68 | a | b | c | d | 98 | a | b | c | d |
| 9 | a | b | c | d | 39 | a | b | c | d | 69 | a | b | c | d | 99 | a | b | c | d |
| 10 | a | b | c | d | 40 | a | b | c | d | 70 | a | b | c | d | 100 | a | b | c | d |
| 11 | a | b | c | d | 41 | a | b | c | d | 71 | a | b | c | d | 101 | a | b | c | d |
| 12 | a | b | c | d | 42 | a | b | c | d | 72 | a | b | c | d | 102 | a | b | c | d |
| 13 | a | b | c | d | 43 | a | b | c | d | 73 | a | b | c | d | 103 | a | b | c | d |
| 14 | a | b | c | d | 44 | a | b | c | d | 74 | a | b | c | d | 104 | a | b | c | d |
| 15 | a | b | c | d | 45 | a | b | c | d | 75 | a | b | c | d | 105 | a | b | c | d |
| 16 | a | b | c | d | 46 | a | b | c | d | 76 | a | b | c | d | 106 | a | b | c | d |
| 17 | a | b | c | d | 47 | a | b | c | d | 77 | a | b | c | d | 107 | a | b | c | d |
| 18 | a | b | c | d | 48 | a | b | c | d | 78 | a | b | c | d | 108 | a | b | c | d |
| 19 | a | b | c | d | 49 | a | b | c | d | 79 | a | b | c | d | 109 | a | b | c | d |
| 20 | a | b | c | d | 50 | a | b | c | d | 80 | a | b | c | d | 110 | a | b | c | d |
| 21 | a | b | c | d | 51 | a | b | c | d | 81 | a | b | c | d | 111 | a | b | c | d |
| 22 | a | b | c | d | 52 | a | b | c | d | 82 | a | b | c | d | 112 | a | b | c | d |
| 23 | a | b | c | d | 53 | a | b | c | d | 83 | a | b | c | d | 113 | a | b | c | d |
| 24 | a | b | c | d | 54 | a | b | c | d | 84 | a | b | c | d | 114 | a | b | c | d |
| 25 | a | b | c | d | 55 | a | b | c | d | 85 | a | b | c | d | 115 | a | b | c | d |
| 26 | a | b | c | d | 56 | a | b | c | d | 86 | a | b | c | d | 116 | a | b | c | d |
| 27 | a | b | c | d | 57 | a | b | c | d | 87 | a | b | c | d | 117 | a | b | c | d |
| 28 | a | b | c | d | 58 | a | b | c | d | 88 | a | b | c | d | 118 | a | b | c | d |
| 29 | a | b | c | d | 59 | a | b | c | d | 89 | a | b | c | d | 119 | a | b | c | d |
| 30 | a | b | c | d | 60 | a | b | c | d | 90 | a | b | c | d | 120 | a | b | c | d |

## Calculate Your Score

| | |
|---|---|
| **Correct (✓)** | |
| **Incorrect (✓)** | |
| **Unattempted** | |
| **Total Score** | |
| **Accuracy (%)** | |

## Reasons for Incorrect Answers?

| | |
|---|---|
| 1. Lack of Knowledge/Existing Source Insufficient | |
| 2. Lack of Multiple Revision | |
| 3. Common Sense Mistakes | |

**Note :**

1. Calculate total score as correct answers carry 2 marks each 1/3rd marks will deducted for **Incorrect** Answers.
2. Calculate Accuracy (%) by dividing the number of correct answers to the total number of attempted questions.

## Past Learning

**1.** Consider the following statements about G-20: **(2023)**

1. The G-20 group was originally established as a platform for the Finance Ministers and Central Bank Governors to discuss the international economic and financial issues.
2. Digital public infrastructure is one of India's G-20 priorities.

Which of the statements given above is/are correct?

(a) 1 only (b) 2 only
(c) Both 1 and 2 (d) Neither 1 nor 2

**2.** With reference to the 'G-20 Common Framework', consider the following statements: **(2022)**

1. It is an initiative endorsed by the G20 together with the Paris Club.
2. It is an initiative to support Low Income Countries with unsustainable debt.

Which of the statements given above is/are correct?

(a) 1 only (b) 2 only
(c) Both 1 and 2 (d) Neither 1 nor 2

**3.** 'Rapid Financing Instrument' and 'Rapid Credit Facility' are related to the provisions of lending by which of the following? **(2022)**

(a) Asian Development Bank
(b) International Monetary Fund
(c) United Nations Environment Programme Finance Initiative
(d) World Bank

**4.** With reference to Trade-Related Investment Measures (TRIMS), which of the following statements is/are correct? **(2020)**

1. Quantitative restrictions on imports by foreign investors are prohibited.
2. They apply to investment measures related to trade in both goods and services.
3. They are not concerned with the regulation of foreign investment.

Select the correct answer from the codes given below:

(a) 1 and 2 only (b) 2 only
(c) 1 and 3 only (d) 1, 2 and 3

**5.** 'Golden Tranche' (Reserve Tranche) refers to: **(2020)**

(a) a loan system of the World Bank
(b) one of the operations of a Central Bank
(c) a credit system granted by WTO to its members
(d) a credit system granted by IMF to its members

**6.** The Global Competitiveness Report is published by the: **(2019)**

(a) International Monetary Fund
(b) United Nations Conference on Trade and Development
(c) World Economic Forum
(d) World Bank

**7.** With reference to Asian Infrastructure Investment Bank (AIIB), consider the following statements: **(2019)**

1. AIIB has more than 80 member nations.
2. India is the largest shareholder in AIIB.
3. AIIB does not have any members from outside Asia.

Select the correct answer from the codes given below:

(a) 1 only (b) 2 and 3 only
(c) 1 and 3 only (d) 1, 2 and 3

**8.** With reference to the 'National Intellectual Property Rights Policy', consider the following statements: **(2017)**

1. It reiterates India's commitment to the Doha Development Agenda and the TRIPS Agreement.
2. Department of Industrial Policy and Promotion is the nodal agency for regulating intellectual property rights in India.

Select the correct answer from the codes given below:

(a) 1 only (b) 2 only
(c) Both 1 and 2 (d) Neither 1 nor 2

**9.** Consider the following statements: **(2017)**
1. India has ratified the Trade Facilitation Agreement (TFA) of WTO.
2. TFA is a part of WTO's Bali Ministerial Package of 2013.
3. TFA came into force in January 2016.

Which of the statements given above is/are correct?
(a) 1 and 2 only (b) 1 and 3 only
(c) 2 and 3 only (d) 1, 2 and 3

**10.** India enacted The Geographical Indications of Goods (Registration and Protection) Act, 1999 in order to comply with the obligations to: **(2016)**
(a) ILO (b) IMF
(c) UNCTAD (d) WTO

**11.** Recently, which one of the following currencies has been proposed to be added to the basket of the IMF's SDR? **(2016)**
(a) Rouble (b) Rand
(c) Indian Rupee (d) Renminbi

**12.** In the context of which of the following do you sometimes find the terms 'amber box', 'blue box' and 'green box' in the news? **(2016)**
(a) WTO affairs
(b) SAARC affairs
(c) UNFCCC affairs
(d) India-EU negotiations on FTA

**13.** With reference to the International Monetary and Financial Committee (IMFC), consider the following statements: **(2016)**
1. IMFC discusses matters of concern affecting the global economy, and advises the International Monetary Fund (IMF) on the direction of its work.
2. The World Bank participates as observer in MFC's meetings.

Which of the statements given above is/are correct?
(a) 1 only
(b) 2 only
(c) Both 1 and 2
(d) Neither 1 nor 2

**14.** Consider the following statements: **(2016)**
1. New Development Bank has been set up by APEC.
2. The headquarters of New Development Bank is in Shanghai.

Which of the statements given above is/are correct?
(a) 1 only (b) 2 only
(c) Both 1 and 2 (d) Neither 1 nor 2

**15.** 'Global Financial Stability Report' is prepared by the **(2016)**
(a) European Central Bank
(b) International Monetary Fund
(c) International Bank for Reconstruction and Development
(d) Organisation for Economic Cooperation and Development

**16.** The terms 'Agreement on Agriculture', 'Agreement on the Application of Sanitary and Phytosanitary Measures' and Peace Clause' appear in the news frequently in the context of the affairs of the: **(2015)**
(a) Food and Agriculture Organisation
(b) United Nations Framework Conference on Climate Change
(c) World Trade Organisation
(d) United Nations Environment Programme

**17.** Which one of the following issues the 'Global Economic Prospects' report periodically? **(2015)**
(a) The Asian Development Bank
(b) The European Bank for Reconstruction and Development
(c) The US Federal Reserve Bank
(d) The World Bank

**18.** Which of the following organisations brings out the publication known as 'World Economic Outlook'? **(2014)**
(a) The International Monetary Fund
(b) The United Nations Development Programme
(c) The World Economic Forum
(d) The World Bank

# Detailed Solutions

## Assessment Round

**1.** *(d)* 1, 2 and 3

- **Statement 1 is correct: GATT** was established as a **provisional agreement** with no legal entity, mainly aiming to reduce tariffs and trade barriers. In contrast, the **WTO** is a **permanent international organisation** with a legal structure, established in 1995, and responsible for governing global trade rules.
- **Statement 2 is correct: GATT's dispute resolution mechanism** was **informal and lacked binding authority**, leading to prolonged disputes. The **WTO**, however, introduced a **formal and binding dispute settlement process**, ensuring that trade conflicts are resolved efficiently and equitably.
- **Statement 3 is correct:** The **GATT** was limited to **trade in goods** only, focusing on reducing tariffs and quotas. The WTO expanded this scope to include **trade in services** and **intellectual property rights**, reflecting the evolving global economy.

**Thus, the correct answer is (d) 1, 2 and 3.**

**2.** *(b)* A round is a multi-year negotiation process among member countries aimed at reducing trade barriers and updating trade rules.

In the context of GATT/WTO, a 'round' is a series of multiyear negotiations where member countries discuss and agree on reducing trade barriers, tariff reductions and updating trade rules.

**For example**, Uruguay Round (1986–1994) which led to the creation of the WTO and expanded negotiations to include services (GATS) and intellectual property (TRIPS).

**Thus, option (b) is the correct answer.**

**3.** *(a)* Only one

- **Statement 1 is correct:** The Ministerial Conference, includes representatives from all member countries, acts as the highest decision-making body and meets at least **once every two years**.
- **Statement 2 is incorrect:** The General Council performs multiple functions, including acting as a dispute settlement body and a **trade policy review body**.
- **Statement 3 is incorrect:** The WTO Secretariat does **not implement trade policies** of member countries. Its role is to provide administrative and technical support, conduct research, and offer assistance to developing countries. It has no decision-making power and does not enforce trade policies.

**Thus, the correct answer is (a) Only one.**

**4.** *(c)* All three

- **Statement 1 is correct:** The Ministerial Conference includes representatives from all member countries and serves as the highest decision-making body, which is required to meet at least every two years and which can take decisions on all matters under any of the multilateral trade agreements.
- **Statement 2 is correct:** These three councils report directly to the General Council and handle their respective areas of trade.
- **Statement 3 is correct:** The Trade Policy Review Body (TPRB) is responsible for reviewing and monitoring the trade policies of WTO member countries.

**Thus, the correct answer is (c) All three.**

**5.** *(a)* 1 and 2 only

- **Statement 1 is correct:** The Appellate Body of the WTO under Dispute Settlement Body comprises seven members who are appointed for four-year term.
- **Statement 2 is correct:** The **decisions of the Appellate Body** are indeed **final and binding** on all WTO member countries, ensuring compliance and resolution in trade disputes.
- **Statement 3 is incorrect:** The Appellate Body is a standing body formed under the Dispute Settlement Body (DSB) which directly reports to the WTO General Council.

**Therefore, while the Appellate Body operates under the DSB, it does not report directly to the General Council.**

- **Statement 4 is incorrect:** The Appellate Body handles disputes across various aspects of WTO agreements, not solely **intellectual property rights;** it addresses disputes in areas like trade in goods, services, and other WTO agreements.

**Therefore, the correct answer is (a) 1 and 2 only.**

**6.** *(a)* 1 and 2 only

- **Dispute Settlement Body (DSB) (Correct):** The DSB consists of all **WTO members** and is responsible for managing and overseeing the entire dispute settlement process. It establishes panels, adopts panel and Appellate Body reports, and authorizes sanctions or compensation if necessary.
- **Appellate Body's role (Correct):** The Appellate Body reviews legal aspects of the panel's findings when a party appeals. It has the power to modify, reverse, or uphold the panel's legal conclusions. It consists of **seven members** who serve four-year terms.
- **Direct formation of the panel without consultations (Incorrect):** The dispute settlement process begins with consultations between the disputing parties, which last up to 60 days. Only if these consultations fail does the process move to the formation of a Dispute Settlement Panel.

**Thus, the correct answer is (a) 1 and 2 only.**

**7.** *(b)* The Most Favoured Nation (MFN) principle is a core concept of the WTO agreements. It requires that if a member country grants any trade advantage (such as lower tariffs) to one member, it must extend the same benefit to all other WTO member countries, ensuring non-discrimination in international trade. This principle helps to stabilise the free trade system, which increases predictability and trade and investment.

- **Option (a) is incorrect:** The MFN principle prohibits discriminatory treatment of member countries, even in the context of trade disputes.
- **Option (c) is incorrect:** The MFN principle generally prohibits preferential treatment for certain countries. However, there are some exceptions, such as regional trade agreements.
- **Option (d) is incorrect:** While the WTO does have provisions for special and differential treatment for developing countries, these are not part of the MFN principle. The MFN principle applies equally to all member countries, regardless of their level of development.

**Thus, option (b) is the correct answer.**

**8.** *(b)* Only two

- **Statement 1 is correct:** The MFN principle requires WTO members to extend the same trade advantages to all other members unless exemptions apply.
- **Statement 2 is correct:** India granted MFN status to Pakistan in 1996, but Pakistan has not reciprocated by granting India MFN status. India revoked Pakistan's MFN status in 2019 after the Pulwama attack, resulting in an increased tariffs on Pakistani imports.
- **Statement 3 is incorrect:** The MFN principle does not allow countries to impose higher tariffs due to political disputes; it promotes non-discriminatory trade practices.

  Therefore, any discriminatory treatment based on political factors would violate the MFN principle and could lead to trade disputes.

**Thus, the correct answer is (b) Only two.**

**9.** *(b)* 1 and 2 only

- **Statement 1 is correct:** Free Trade Agreements (FTAs) are recognised as exceptions where countries can grant preferential treatment to members within the agreement.
- **Statement 2 is correct:** Developing countries receive preferential treatment under the Generalised System of Preferences (GSP), allowing them special concessions.
- **Statement 3 is incorrect:** The MFN principle does not permit countries to impose trade restrictions against members simply because they have ongoing disputes. While the WTO allows for dispute resolution and may permit

retaliation under specific circumstances, this does not constitute a general exception to the MFN principle.

**Therefore, the correct answer is (b) 1 and 2 only**

**10.** *(b)* The **National Treatment** principle means that once imported goods enter a country, they should be treated the same as locally produced goods regarding taxes, regulations, and other requirements. This prevents discrimination against foreign goods in favour of domestic products.

- **Option (a) is incorrect:** The National Treatment principle prohibits any such discriminatory treatment.
- **Option (c) is incorrect:** The National Treatment principle also extends to subsidies. If a country provides a subsidy to a domestic industry, it must offer the same subsidy to imported goods as well.
- **Option (d) is incorrect:** If a country imposes higher tariffs on imported goods based on the origin would violate the principle of National Treatment.

**Thus, option (b) is the correct answer.**

**11.** *(c)* All three

**The Generalised System of Preferences (GSP)** was first adopted as a concept by the **United Nations Conference on Trade and Development (UNCTAD)** in **1968.** The aim was to promote economic growth and development in developing countries by providing them with **preferential access to the markets of developed countries.** This initiative was seen as a way to **reduce trade barriers** and enable developing countries to increase their exports, thereby fostering their economic development.

- **Statement 1 is correct:** GSP is a **unilateral trade preference scheme,** meaning that developed countries provide tariff concessions to developing countries without requiring reciprocal treatment.
- **Statement 2 is correct:** The GSP allows beneficiary countries to export goods to donor countries at **reduced or zero tariffs.** This makes easier for developing or underdeveloped countries to access the markets of developed countries.
- **Statement 3 is correct:** Both the United States and the European Union offer GSP benefits to developing countries.

**Therefore, the correct answer is (c) All three.**

**12.** *(b)* Only two

- **Agreement on Agriculture (AoA)** focuses on trade in **goods,** specifically agricultural products.
- **Trade-Related Aspects of Intellectual Property Rights (TRIPS)** address intellectual property rights, a **non-goods** aspect.
- **Agreement on Trade-Related Investment Measures (TRIMs)** were primarily focuses on investment measures affecting **trade in goods, not directly** related to services or intellectual property rights.
- **General Agreement on Trade in Services (GATS)** specifically addresses trade in services, a **non-goods** aspect.

**Therefore, the correct answer is (b) Only two.**

**13.** *(b)* Only two

**Statement 1 is correct:** The AoA was indeed introduced as part of the Uruguay Round negotiations which was concluded in 1994 of the General Agreement on Tariffs and Trade (GATT) and came into force with the establishment of the WTO in 1995.

**Statement 2 is correct:** One of the primary objectives of the AoA was to limit trade-distorting agricultural subsidies by focuses on reducing tariffs and import barriers for agricultural products.

**Statement 3 is incorrect:** The AoA's scope includes **both raw and processed agricultural products,** ensuring comprehensive coverage across the agricultural sector, not limited to raw goods alone.

**Therefore, the answer is (b) Only two.**

**14.** *(d)* 1, 3 and 4 only

**Livestock products** and **fruits and vegetables** are covered under the AoA as they fall under the category of agricultural products also alcoholic and non alcoholic.

- The **Agreement on Agriculture (AoA) excludes** the following product categories:
- **Fish and Fish Products**: Fisheries and related products are treated as non-agricultural under WTO agreements.
- **Forestry Products**: Timber, wood, and other forestry products **do not** fall under the AoA.
- **Mineral Products**: These products, including those derived from minerals, are excluded from the scope of the AoA.
- **Rubber and Jute Products**: Although agricultural in nature, processed rubber and jute products are excluded.
- **Alcoholic Beverages**: Although some ingredients (e.g., grains) are agricultural, the final products (e.g., beer, wine, spirits) are **included** in the AoA.

  These exclusions mean that the AoA primarily focuses on products like crops, livestock, and other directly related agricultural items.

**Therefore, the correct answer is (d) 1, 3 and 4 only.**

***15.*** *(a)* Only one pair

- **Pair 1 incorrect : Market Access is correctly matched with (B). Market Access** under the AoA involves converting non-tariff barriers to tariffs (a process called "tariffication") and committing to **reduce these tariffs** over time to open up agricultural markets.
- **Pair 2 incorrect : Domestic Support is correctly matched with (A). Domestic Support** focuses on **reducing trade-distorting subsidies** and government support that can artificially affect production and prices in the agricultural sector.

**(classifies subsidies into** three categories:**)**

- **Green Box**: These subsidies are considered **minimal trade-distorting** and do not affect production. They are allowed without limits. Examples include environmental programs, research, disaster relief, and infrastructure services.
- **Amber Box**: These subsidies are **trade-distorting** and are subject to **reduction commitments** by WTO members. They include measures like price support and direct payments that influence production levels.
- **Blue Box**: These subsidies are a middle ground and are **linked to production-limiting programs**. They are allowed under the condition that farmers limit production, aiming to reduce surplus while still supporting farmers' incomes.
- **Pair 3 correct : Export Subsidies is correctly matched with (C).** The **Export Subsidies** pillar aims to limit the **volume and financial value of subsidies for agricultural exports,** reducing their impact on global agricultural trade competitiveness.

**Therefore, the correct answer is (a) Only one pair.**

***16.*** *(c)* Only three

- **Amber Box subsidies** are those that **distort production and trade.** They include the Minimum Support Price (MSP), fertiliser subsidies and power subsidies which directly affect production decisions.
- **Research and development grants** are typically classified under the **Green Box** as they do not directly distort trade and fall under Green Box.

**Therefore, the correct answer is (c) Only three.**

***17.*** *(c)* All three pairs

- **Pair 1 is correct: Minimum Support Price (MSP)** is a floor price set by the government for certain agricultural products. It ensures that farmers receive a minimum price for their crops, even if market prices are lower. This can distort trade by making domestic products artificially cheaper. Therefore, it falls under the Amber Box as it distorts trade by influencing production of certain agriculture goods.
- **Pair 2 is correct: Subsidies for environmental protection fall** under the Green Box since they do not distort trade.
- **Pair 3 is correct: Direct payments under production limits are** classified under the Blue Box. The Blue Box includes subsidies that are linked to production limits, which can reduce trade distortions.

**Thus, the correct answer is (c) All three pairs.**

***18.*** *(d)* Neither 1 nor 2

- **Statement 1 is incorrect**: The De-minimis provision **applies only to trade-distorting subsidies** (i.e., those classified under the Amber Box) and **not to all types of agricultural subsidies**. It sets a threshold below which these trade-distorting subsidies are considered minimal and, therefore, are exempt from reduction commitments.
- **Statement 2 is incorrect**: The De-minimis provision **applies to both developed and developing countries** under the Agreement on Agriculture (AoA). However, the allowable thresholds differ:

For developed countries, it is set at 5% of the total value of agricultural production, while for developing countries, it is 10%.

**Therefore, the answer is (d) Neither 1 nor 2.**

***19.*** *(b)* To provide temporary protection for developing countries against legal challenges if they exceed their domestic support limits for public stockholding programmes.

The **Bali Peace Clause** at the Ninth WTO Ministerial Conference held in Bali, Indonesia, in December 2013. It relates to the issue of **food security and subsidies provided by developing countries** under the Agreement on Agriculture (AoA).

Key Points of the Bali Peace Clause:

- **Temporary Protection**: The Peace Clause provides **temporary protection** for developing countries, allowing them to exceed their **agricultural subsidy limits** under the WTO Agreement on Agriculture (AoA) without facing legal challenges from other WTO members.
- **Applicability**: It applies to **public stockholding programmes** for food security purposes, where governments purchase food from farmers at administered prices (e.g., Minimum Support Price in India) and distribute it to the poor.
- **Duration**: The Peace Clause is intended to be a **temporary measure** until a **permanent solution** is negotiated at the WTO. It is in place as long as no final agreement on public stockholding is reached.
- **Conditions**: To avail of the Peace Clause, countries must provide **transparent reporting** and **ensure that the programmes do not distort trade** or negatively affect the food security of other countries.

**Thus, option (b) is the correct answer.**

***20.*** *(b)* 3 only

- **Statement 1 is incorrect**: The TRIPs Agreement was not part of the original GATT in 1947; it was negotiated during the **Uruguay Round (1986-1994)**.
- **Statement 2 is incorrect**: There was a **transition period** for developing and least-developed countries to implement the TRIPs Agreement.
  - **Developing countries were given transition periods of 10 years** to implement patent protection, especially for pharmaceutical products.
  - A 2005 amendment allowed least-developed countries to delay implementing pharmaceutical patent protection until 2033.
- **Statement 3 is correct**: The **Doha Declaration** on TRIPs and Public Health in 2001 recognised members' rights to protect public health, allowing for measures like **compulsory licensing**.

**Therefore, the correct answer is (b) 3 only.**

***21.*** *(a)* 1 and 2 only

- **Statement 1 is correct**: The **TRIPs Agreement** requires WTO members to provide protection for **industrial designs** for a minimum term of **10 years**. This helps to safeguard the unique designs of industrial products and maintain fair competition.
- **Statement 2 is correct**: The Agreement includes **provisions for the protection of trade secrets**, or confidential information, which are considered part of intellectual property rights under TRIPs.
- **Statement 3 is incorrect**: The TRIPs Agreement allows **flexibility** for member countries in how they implement IP enforcement. Countries can adapt enforcement mechanisms to suit their legal

and economic circumstances, so it does not mandate a **uniform system.**

**Therefore, the correct answer is (a) 1 and 2 only.**

**22.** *(b)* Only two

- **Statement 1 is correct:** Compulsory licensing allows the government to authorise the production of a patented product without the patent holder's consent.
- **Statement 2 is incorrect:** Under the TRIPs Agreement, compulsory licenses can be issued for various reasons, not just for life-saving drugs, such as to address public health crises or national emergencies.
- **Statement 3 is correct:** India issued its first compulsory license in 2012 for the cancer drug Nexavar (Sorafenib Tosylate) which is used to treat liver and kidney cancer.

**Thus, the correct answer is (b) Only two.**

**23.** *(c)* All three

- **Statement 1 is correct:** The National IPR Policy (2016) aims to create awareness about intellectual property rights among all sections of society, enhancing respect for IP in the interests of economic growth.
- **Statement 2 is correct:** The policy designates the Department for Promotion of Industry and Internal Trade (DPIIT) as the nodal agency responsible for the implementation, coordination, and promotion of intellectual property rights in India.
- **Statement 3 is correct:** The policy encourages the commercialisation of intellectual property assets to promote economic growth and transform IP assets into marketable products, thereby driving innovation and entrepreneurship.

**Thus, the correct answer is (c) All three.**

**24.** *(d)* 1, 2 and 3

- **Statement 1 is correct:** The **National IPR Policy (2016)** proposes the establishment of **specialised IP** courts or **IPR cells** within existing courts to ensure **faster adjudication** of IPR disputes, thereby reducing the pendency of cases.
- **Statement 2 is correct:** The policy aims to **promote the development and use of Traditional Knowledge Digital Libraries (TKDL)** to protect India's traditional knowledge and prevent its misappropriation by unauthorized parties.
- **Statement 3 is correct:** The **National IPR Policy** mandates that all publicly funded research organisations register their IP assets with the government and aims to promote the commercialisation and protection of research outputs generated with public funds.

**Thus, the correct answer is (d) 1, 2 and 3.**

**25.** *(b)* Only two

- **Statement 1 is correct:** The General Agreement on Trade in Services (GATS) is the first multilateral agreement that covers trade in services under the framework of the World Trade Organisation (WTO).
- **Statement 2 is incorrect:** GATS does not mandate that all member countries must fully liberalise their service sectors without exceptions. Instead, member countries have the flexibility to choose the sectors they wish to liberalise, and they can specify limitations and exceptions.
- **Statement 3 is correct:** The GATS Agreement follows the Most Favoured Nation (MFN) principle, which means that any favourable treatment provided to one member country must be extended to all other WTO member countries, subject to some exceptions.

**Thus, the correct answer is (b) Only two.**

**26.** *(d)* All four pairs

- **Pair 1 is correct: Mode 1 (Cross-border supply)** - A: Online education across borders.
- **Pair 2 is correct: Mode 2 (Consumption abroad)** - B: A tourist using hotel services in another country.
- **Pair 3 is correct: Mode 3 (Commercial presence)** - C: A foreign bank setting up a branch.
- **Pair 4 is correct: Mode 4 (Presence of natural persons)** - D: A professional working temporarily abroad.

| Mode | Criteria | Suplier Presence |
|---|---|---|
| Mode-1 Cross-border supply | Service delivered within the territory of the Member from the territory of another Member.<br>Example: Tele-Medicine or Tele-education. | Service supplier **not present within the territory** of the Member. |
| Mode-2 Consumption abroad | Refers to situations where a **service consumer moves into another** Member's territory to obtain a service.<br>Example: Tourism, Hospitality, etc. | |
| Mode-3 Commerical presence | Service supplier of one member establishes a **territorial presence**, including through ownership or lease of premises, in another Member's territory to provide a service companies or hotel chains. | Service supplier **present within the territory** of the Member. |
| Mode-4 Presence of a natural person | Persons of **one Member** entering the territory of another Member to supply a service.<br>Example: Accountants, Doctors or Teachers. | |

**Thus, the correct answer is (d) All four pairs.**

**27.** *(b)* Only two

- **Statement 1 is correct:** The **TRIMs Agreement prohibits measures** that are **inconsistent with the national treatment** principle i.e., treating foreign and domestic products equally and **quantitative restrictions** on trade like local content requirements or trade-balancing requirements.
- **Statement 2 is correct:** The TRIMs Agreement **applies only to trade in goods** and **excludes service industries.** It focuses on **investment measures that can affect trade in goods.**
- **Statement 3 is incorrect:** While the TRIMs Agreement does not directly regulate foreign investment policies, it is **concerned with investment measures** that have an impact on **trade in goods.** Thus, it addresses how certain investment-related measures can distort trade.

**Therefore, the correct answer is (b) Only two.**

**28.** *(b)* 1, 2 and 4 only

The TRIMs Agreement prohibits investment measures that are inconsistent with the **principles of national treatment (non-discrimination)** and **prohibits quantitative restrictions** on trade. Here's how each measure aligns with the TRIMs Agreement:

- **Statement 1 is correct: Local content requirements** that mandate enterprises to purchase or use a certain number of local products **violate the TRIMs Agreement.** For example, a local content requirement imposed in a non-discriminatory manner on domestic and foreign enterprises is inconsistent with the TRIMs Agreement because it involves discriminatory treatment of imported products in favour of domestic products.
- **Statement 2 is correct:** Measures that restrict the importation of goods based on the value of exports are prohibited, as they impose quantitative restrictions inconsistent with WTO rules.
- **Statement 3 is incorrect:** The TRIMs Agreement does not explicitly prohibit measures requiring foreign investors to establish joint ventures with local companies. Such requirements are typically addressed in broader investment agreements, not specifically under TRIMs.
- **Statement 4 is correct:** Measures that impose trade-balancing requirements (e.g., ensuring that imports do not exceed a certain value compared to exports) are prohibited under the TRIMs Agreement.

**Therefore, the correct answer is (b) 1, 2 and 4 only.**

**29.** *(b)* Only two

- **Statement 1 is correct:** The WTO Agreement aims to prohibit subsidies that contribute to **Illegal, Unreported and Unregulated (IUU)** fishing, which is a key aspect of the agreement to promote sustainable fishing practices.
- **Statement 2 is correct:** It allows subsidies that promote sustainable management, provided they do not contribute to overfishing, meaning subsidies that support responsible fishing practices and conservation efforts are permitted.
- **Statement 3 is incorrect:** The Agreement does not mandate the complete elimination of all subsidies but focuses on harmful subsidies. It focuses on eliminating harmful subsidies, especially those that contribute to overfishing, overcapacity, and IUU fishing, rather than a complete ban on all subsidies.

**Therefore, the correct answer is (b) Only two.**

**30.** *(d)* 2 only

- **Statement 1 is incorrect:** The Agreement primarily focuses on marine fisheries and **not inland fisheries**. It prohibits subsidies that support fishing activities in areas beyond national jurisdiction (e.g., the high seas).
- **Statement 2 is correct:** The Agreement provides **flexibility for developing countries**, allowing them to maintain certain subsidies for **small-scale fisheries** operating within their **Exclusive Economic Zones (EEZs)**. This provision supports the livelihoods of small-scale fishers in developing nations.
- **Statement 3 is incorrect:** While the Agreement promotes **transparency** in fisheries subsidies, it does not specifically mandate **annual reporting** on the status of fish stocks within member countries' territories. Reporting requirements focus more on subsidy practices rather than fish stock assessments.
- Under the Agreement on Fisheries Subsidies, as part of these notifications members will be required to notify the type or kind of fishing activity being subsidised and, to the extent possible, to provide information on stock status, conservation measures, fleets and vessels being subsidised, along with catch data.

**Therefore, the correct answer is (d) 2 only.**

**31.** *(d)* 1, 2 and 3

- **Statement 1 is correct:** The Trade Facilitation Agreement (TFA) is indeed the first multilateral **trade agreement** concluded since the establishment of the WTO in 1995. It was adopted at the WTO's **Ninth Ministerial Conference in Bali in 2013.**
- **Statement 2 is correct:** The TFA aims to **expedite the movement, release, and clearance of goods, including goods in transit.** It focuses on streamlining customs procedures, reducing trade barriers, and improving transparency to facilitate international trade.
- **Statement 3 is correct:** India has established a **National Committee on Trade Facilitation** (NCTF), chaired by the **Cabinet Secretary,** to oversee and coordinate the implementation of TFA provisions. This committee includes representatives from various ministries and stakeholders involved in trade facilitation.

**Therefore, the correct answer is (d) 1, 2 and 3.**

**32.** *(a)* 1 and 2 only

The purpose of the SPS Agreement is to ensure that measures established by governments to protect human, animal and plant life and health are consistent with obligations prohibiting arbitrary or unjustifiable discrimination on trade between countries where the same conditions prevail.

- **Statement 1 is correct:** The **Agreement on Sanitary and Phytosanitary (SPS) Measures** covers **measures to protect animal or plant life** from the entry, establishment, or spread of **pests.** This is to prevent the spread of harmful organisms that could damage agriculture and ecosystems.
- **Statement 2 is correct:** The SPS Agreement includes **measures to protect human or animal life** from risks due to **additives, contaminants, toxins, or disease-causing organisms in food.** It aims to ensure food safety and reduce health risks arising from unsafe food sources.
- **Statement 3 is incorrect:** While labelling requirements may relate to product information, they are generally covered under the **Agreement on Technical Barriers to**

Trade (TBT), not the SPS Agreement, which focuses on health and safety standards for protecting life and health.

- **Statement 4 is incorrect:** Measures to **prevent deceptive practices in trade** are outside the scope of the SPS Agreement and are also more relevant to the TBT Agreement, which covers broader trade practices and product standards.

**Therefore, the correct answer is (a) 1 and 2 only.**

**33.** *(a)* 1 and 3 only

Sanitary (human and animal health) and phytosanitary (plant health) measures apply to domestically produced food or local animal and plant diseases, as well as to products coming from other countries.

Countries may take measures to ensure that food is safe for consumers, and to prevent the spread of pests or diseases among animals and plants. These sanitary and phytosanitary measures can take many forms, such as requiring **products to come from a disease-free area**, inspection of products, specific treatment or processing of products, **setting of allowable maximum levels of pesticide residues** or permitted use of only certain additives in food.

- **Statement 1 is correct:** The SPS Agreement permits **banning the import of meat products** from regions affected by diseases such as **foot-and-mouth disease** to protect human and animal health from contagious diseases that could spread through trade.
- **Statement 2 is incorrect: Imposing tariffs on imported fruits** is a **trade measure** and does not fall under sanitary and phytosanitary measures. Tariffs are a form of economic protection and are not used to address health or safety risks, so they fall outside the scope of the SPS Agreement.
- **Statement 3 is correct: Setting maximum pesticide residue levels** in food products is an example of an SPS measure. Such regulations are designed to protect human health from potentially harmful substances in food, aligning with SPS standards.
- **Statement 4 is incorrect: Requiring a certificate of origin** is not a sanitary or phytosanitary measure. This requirement typically pertains to verifying the source of the product for trade purposes rather than ensuring health or safety, making it outside the SPS Agreement's provisions

**Therefore, the correct answer is (a) 1 and 3 only.**

**34.** *(b)* Only two

- **Statement 1 is correct:** ITA is a **plurilateral agreement** under the **WTO**, focused on eliminating tariffs on certain information technology products, promoting free trade in this sector among WTO members.
  - The ITA covers a **large number of high technology products**, including computers, telecommunication equipment, semi-conductors, semiconductor manufacturing and testing equipment, software, scientific instruments, as well as most of the parts and accessories of these products.
- **Statement 2 is incorrect:** The ITA is not restricted to **developed countries.** It is a **plurilateral agreement**, meaning it is open to both **developed and developing countries,** many of whom have joined the agreement to benefit from reduced tariffs on IT products.
- **Statement 3 is correct:** India is a signatory to the Information Technology Agreement (ITA) (now also known as ITA-1), a plurilateral agreement of WTO. As on date, there are altogether 75 member signatories, including 27 EU member countries, accounting for about 97 percent of the world trade in Information Technology (IT) products. **India joined the ITA on 25th March, 1997.**

**Thus, the correct answer is (b) Only two.**

**35.** *(b)* Consumer electronics and semiconductors

The **ITA 2.0 Agreement** primarily covers products in the **information technology sector,** including items like **consumer electronics, semiconductors, and other high-tech goods.** By reducing tariffs on these products, the agreement promotes freer trade and benefits countries specialising in the production and export of IT goods.

**Thus, option (b) is the correct answer.**

**36.** *(b)* It provides developing countries with longer time periods to implement commitments and greater flexibility in meeting trade obligations.

- **Special and Differential Treatment (SDT) provisions** under WTO agreements are designed to provide developing and least-developed countries (LDCs) more time and flexibility to implement their trade commitments, recognising their economic challenges and development needs. The aim is to help these countries integrate more effectively into the global trading system.

Here are the key aspects of SDT for developing countries:

- **Longer Time Periods for Implementation** of WTO agreements and commitments.
- **Lower Commitments and Obligations** as compared to developed countries.
- Developed countries are encouraged to provide **technical assistance, training, and capacity-building** support to help developing countries and LDCs implement WTO agreements.
- Developed countries are expected to provide **greater market access** to exports from developing countries and LDCs, often through preferential trade schemes like the Generalised System of Preferences (GSP).
- In cases involving disputes, developing countries and LDCs are given **special consideration**, including more time to prepare and respond in WTO dispute settlement proceedings.
- Under the Agreement on Agriculture (AoA), developing countries have more **flexibility in using domestic support measures** and export subsidies for agriculture.

**Thus, option (b) is the correct answer.**

**37.** *(a)* It allows developing countries to impose additional tariffs in response to import surges or price declines.

The **Special Safeguard Mechanism** (SSM) under the WTO Agreement on Agriculture enables developing countries to temporarily impose additional tariffs on agricultural imports when there are sudden import surges or a significant drop in import prices to protect their domestic farmers.

**Thus, option (a) is the correct answer.**

**38.** *(b)* 1 and 3 only

- **G-20: India is a member of the G-20 developing nations**, a coalition formed to negotiate on agricultural issues in the WTO.
- **Cairns Group: India is not a member.** This group includes agricultural exporting countries that advocate for agricultural trade liberalisation.
- **G-33: India is a member.** This group represents developing countries advocating for flexibility in the WTO's agricultural negotiations, particularly concerning food security and rural livelihoods.
- **African Group**: This group comprises African nations within the WTO framework. India is not a member of these groups. 52.

**Therefore, the correct answer is (b) 1 and 3 only.**

**39.** *(b)* To advocate for the elimination of cotton subsidies and tariffs in developed countries

- The **Cotton-4 (C-4)** grouping focuses on advocating for the reduction and elimination of subsidies and tariffs imposed by developed countries on cotton, which they believe distort global trade and harm the competitiveness of cotton producers in these African countries.
- The Cotton-4 (C-4) grouping consists of **Benin, Burkina Faso, Chad and Mali.** These countries are significant cotton producers and have been actively advocating for the reduction of subsidies and trade barriers in the global cotton trade within the WTO framework.

**Thus, option (b) is the correct answer.**

**40.** *(b)* Only two

There are no **WTO definitions of 'developed' and 'developing' countries.** Members announce for themselves whether they are 'developed' or 'developing' countries. However, other members can challenge the decision of a member to make use of provisions available to developing countries.

- **Statement 1 is correct**: WTO members can self-declare themselves as developing countries, which allows them to access special and differential treatment (SDT) provisions.

- **Statement 2 is incorrect:** A country's developing status can be challenged by other WTO members, as has been done by some developed countries.
- **Statement 3 is correct:** Developing countries are indeed granted longer transition periods to implement WTO agreements. This gives them more time to adjust their domestic policies and regulations to comply with international trade rules.

**Therefore, the correct answer is (b) Only two.**

**41.** *(b)* Only two

- **Statement 1 is correct:** The Bretton Woods Conference resulted in the creation of the International Monetary Fund (IMF) and the International Bank for Reconstruction and Development (IBRD), which later became part of the World Bank Group.
- **Statement 2 is incorrect:** Although the conference aimed to ensure economic stability and avoid future financial crises, it wasn't specifically focused only on rebuilding war-torn European countries but on establishing a global financial order.
- **Statement 3 is correct:** The conference laid the foundation for a fixed exchange rate system where currencies were pegged to the US dollar, which was in turn linked to gold.

**Therefore, the correct answer is (b) Only two.**

**42.** *(b)* Only two

- **Statement 1 is correct:** The IMF was established to provide short-term financial assistance to countries with balance of payments issues and helping them to stabilise their economies.
- **Statement 2 is correct:** The World Bank (initially known as the International Bank for Reconstruction and Development - IBRD) was created to provide long-term loans for rebuilding war-torn economies, particularly Europe after World War II.
- **Statement 3 is incorrect:** The **IMF** and **World Bank** was not designed to regulate **international trade directly**. Their primary focus was on **monetary stability** and **development financing**, respectively, not trade regulation. Trade-related issues were addressed by the **GATT** (General Agreement on Tariffs and Trade) in 1947, which later evolved into the **WTO** (World Trade Organisation).

**Therefore, the correct answer is (b) Only two.**

**43.** *(b)* 2 only

The **voting power** is determined by a **quota system**. This system reflects each member country's **financial contribution** to the IMF, which is based on factors such as the country's **GDP**, **trade volume**, **financial reserves**, and **economic stability**. For example, the United States has the largest voting share due to its substantial quota, giving it more influence in IMF decisions.

- **Statement 1 is incorrect:** A member country's **voting power in the IMF** is primarily determined by its **quota**, which reflects the country's **economic size** and contributions to the IMF. Larger economies have greater voting power due to their higher quotas.
- **Statement 2 is correct:** The Board of Governors, which consists of representatives from all member countries, is the highest decision-making body within the IMF.
- **Statement 3 is incorrect:** Voting power is not equal among member countries; it depends on the size of each country's quota in the IMF. Each member country receives basic votes plus additional votes proportional to its quota.

**Thus, the correct answer is (b) 2 only.**

**44.** *(a)* Only one

- **Statement 1 is incorrect:** While most IMF members are also United Nations members, it is not a strict requirement for a country to be a UN member to join the IMF. For example, Switzerland, which joined the IMF in 1992 but was not a UN member at that time. It only became a member of the United Nations later, in 2002.
- **Statement 2 is correct:** Each member country is required to pay a quota subscription, which represents its financial commitment to the IMF.

- **Statement 3 is incorrect**: Voting power in the IMF is not equal; it is based on each country's quota, which reflects their financial contributions and economic size.

**Thus, the correct answer is (a) Only one.**

**45.** *(c)* Only three

**The IMF Quota determines a country's voting power, access to financial resources, and contribution to the IMF's resources.** It **does not directly influence representation in the IMF's Board of Governors,** as every member country has representation regardless of its quota.

**Therefore, the correct answer is (c) Only three.**

**46.** *(b)* 1, 3 and 4 only

The **IMF quota** for each member country is determined by taking into **account** the following **key factors:**

- **GDP (Gross Domestic Product):** Represents the economic size of a country and carries the most weight in the formula. It indicates the country's capacity to contribute to the IMF.
- **Openness:** Measures a country's **involvement in international** trade. It considers both exports and imports, reflecting how integrated the country is with the global economy.
- **Economic Variability:** Assesses the variability in a country's income, reflecting economic fluctuations. This factor captures the country's susceptibility to balance of payments problems.
- **International Reserves:** Represents a country's holdings of foreign exchange reserves, gold, and SDRs (Special Drawing Rights). It indicates a country's ability to deal with external shocks.

These factors combinedly determine the **quota subscription** for each member, which influences the country's financial contributions, access to IMF resources, and voting power within the organisation.

**Option 2 is incorrect: Population** is not directly considered in the IMF quota formula.

**Thus, the correct answer is (b) 1, 3 and 4 only.**

**47.** *(b)* Only two

- **Statement 1 is correct**: India is the 8th largest quota holding country.
- **Statement 2 is incorrect**: The IMF quota reviews take place **periodically** but not every two years; they typically occur every five years.
- **Statement 3 is correct**: The quota subscription for each member, which influences the country's financial contributions, access to IMF resources, and voting power within the organisation. Thus, the quota determines the extent of access a member country has to IMF financial resources, such as borrowing limits.

**Thus, the correct answer is (b) Only two.**

**48.** *(c)* Only three

- **Feature 1 is correct**: SDRs serve as an international reserve asset and are used as the unit of account by the IMF and some other international organisations.
- **Feature 2 is correct**: The value of SDRs is determined daily based on the **market exchange rates** of the currencies in the SDR basket of five major currencies: the US dollar, euro, Japanese yen, British pound sterling, and Chinese yuan.
- **Feature 3 is incorrect**: Countries are not required to repay SDRs since they are not loans but rather allocations made by the IMF. They are supplementary reserve assets that can be used by member countries to meet their balance of payments needs.
- **Feature 4 is correct**: SDR allocations are based on a member country's IMF quota, reflecting its size in the global economy.

**Thus, the correct answer is (c) Only three.**

**49.** *(a)* 1, 2 and 3 only

The SDR value is calculated based on a basket of **five major international currencies:**

- **US Dollar (USD)**
- **Euro (EUR)**
- **Japanese Yen (JPY)**
- **British Pound Sterling (GBP)**
- **Chinese Yuan (Renminbi - CNY)**

The **Indian Rupee** is **not a part of the SDR basket.**

**Thus, the correct answer is (a) 1, 2 and 3 only.**

**50.** *(b)* Only two

- **Function 1 is correct:** The IMF provides short-term financial assistance to member countries facing balance of payments difficulties.
- **Function 2 is incorrect:** The IMF is **not a lender of last resort** for the global banking system; this function is typically performed by central banks in their respective countries.
- **Function 3 is incorrect:** The IMF does not issue currency for trade; it **only provides financial resources and assistance** to its members.
- **Function 4 is correct:** The IMF offers technical assistance and training in areas such as fiscal policy, monetary policy, and exchange rate management to help them strengthen their economic condition and implement sound economic policies.

**Therefore, the correct answer is (b) Only two.**

**51.** *(b)* Only two

**Concessional lending of IMF** refers to loans provided at lower interest rates or more favourable terms.

- **Option 1 is incorrect:** The **Extended Fund Facility** (EFF) provides non-concessional financial support to countries with longer-term balance of payments issues. It is typically used for countries with structural economic issues and does not offer concessional terms.
- **Option 2 is incorrect:** The **Stand-By Arrangement (SBA)** is another non-concessional facility aimed at addressing short-term or temporary balance of payments needs. It is often used by middle-income and emerging-market countries.
- **Option 3 is correct:** The **Extended Credit Facility (ECF)** is a concessional lending facility provided to low-income countries with prolonged balance of payments issues, offering favourable terms and low-interest rates.
- **Option 4 is correct:** The **Rapid Credit Facility (RCF)** is also concessional, providing quick financial support to low-income countries facing urgent balance of payments needs, such as natural disasters or sudden economic shocks.

**Thus, the correct answer is (b) Only two.**

**52.** *(b)* To support long-term structural reforms aimed at addressing climate change and pandemic preparedness

The **Resilience and Sustainability Facility (RSF)**, introduced by the IMF in 2022, aims to assist countries in addressing long-term challenges, such as **climate change** and **pandemic preparedness.** The RSF provides **affordable financing** to help countries implement **structural reforms** that enhance resilience and sustainability, focusing on issues that can impact macroeconomic stability.

- **Option** (a) refers more to the Rapid Financing Instrument (RFI), which deals with sudden crises.
- **Option** (c) and **option** (d) are not accurate, as the RSF is not limited to low-income countries or specifically aimed at infrastructure projects.

**Thus, option (b) is the correct answer.**

**53.** *(c)* Only three

- The **IMF** releases the **World Economic Outlook (WEO),** the **Global Financial Stability Report (GFSR),** and the **Fiscal Monitor.** These reports provide insights into the global economy, financial stability, and fiscal policy.

| | **World Economic Outlook** | **Global Financial Stability Report** |
|---|---|---|
| **Published by** | International Monetary Fund (IMF) | International Monetary Fund (IMF) |
| **Frequency** | Twice a year (April and October) | Twice a year (April and October) |

| | | |
|---|---|---|
| **Focus** | Global economic outlook, including growth forecasts | State of global financial systems, markets and risks |
| **Key Aspects** | Macroeconomic trends, fiscal policies, trade balances, risks | Financial market developments, banking stability, systemic risks |
| **Importance** | Used for assessing economic trends and policy decisions | Promotes financial stability by highlighting vulnerabilities |

- The **Doing Business Report** is published by the **World Bank**, not the IMF. It was publisher annually until it was discontinued in 2021. Other major report published by World Bank are **Human Capital Index, Global Economic Prospects** and **World Development Report.**

**Thus, the correct answer is (c) Only three.**

**54.** *(c)* All three

- **Statement 1 is correct: India is a founding member** of the International Monetary Fund (IMF), joining in 1945 when the organisation was created to promote global monetary cooperation. India has actively participated in the IMF's activities since its inception.
- **Statement 2 is correct:** The **IMF provided crucial financial assistance to India** in 1991 during its **balance of payments crisis.** This support helped India stabilise its economy and initiate major economic liberalisation and reform measures, which transformed the Indian economy and integrated it with the global market.
- **Statement 3 is correct:** India borrowed SDR 3.9 billion during the period 1981-84. Again during 1991 to 1993, India borrowed an amount of SDR 3.56 billion (SDR 1351.98 million under the Compensatory and Contingency Financing Facility and SDR 2207.925 million under Standby Arrangement). **Repayment of all the loans taken from International Monetary Fund has been completed on 31st May, 2000. India is now a contributor to the IMF.**
  - India has not taken major financial loans in the 21st century, indicating improved self-reliance.

**Therefore, the correct answer is (c) All three.**

**55.** *(b)* 2 and 3 only

- **Statement 1 is incorrect:** In the **World Bank,** voting power is **not equal** among member countries. Instead, it is based on the **financial contributions** or the shareholding of each country. Countries that contribute more capital to the World Bank, such as the United States and Japan, have more voting power compared to countries with smaller contributions. The shareholders in World Bank are:
- **Statement 2 is correct:** The Board of Governors, consisting of representatives from all member countries, meets once a year to discuss major policy issues.
- **Statement 3 is correct:** To become a member of the **World Bank,** a country must first join the **International Monetary Fund (IMF).** Membership in the IMF is a prerequisite for becoming a member of the World Bank, as both institutions work closely together to ensure global financial stability and development.

**Thus, the correct answer is (b) 2 and 3 only.**

**56.** *(a)* 4 - 2 - 1 - 3

The **United States** holds the largest share in the World Bank (IBRD), followed by **Japan, China** and then **India.**

| | Country | Capital Share | Percentage Share | Voting Power | Percentage Share |
|---|---|---|---|---|---|
| 1. | United Staes | 31,964.5 | 16.84 | 265,219 | 16.38 |
| 2. | Japan | 15,320.6 | 8.07 | 127,250 | 7.86 |
| 3. | Germany | 8,733.9 | 4.60 | 72,649 | 4.49 |
| 4. | France | 8,371.7 | 4.41 | 69,647 | 4.30 |
| 5. | United Kingdom | 8,371.7 | 4.41 | 69,647 | 4.30 |
| 6. | China | 5,404.3 | 2.85 | 45,049 | 2.78 |

| | | | | | |
|---|---|---|---|---|---|
| 7. | Canada | 5,403.8 | 2.85 | 45,045 | 2.78 |
| 8. | India | 5,403.8 | 2.85 | 45,045 | 2.78 |
| 9. | Italy | 5,403.8 | 2.85 | 45,045 | 2.78 |
| 10. | Russia | 5,403.8 | 2.85 | 45,045 | 2.78 |
| 11. | Turkey | 1,004.6 | 0.53 | 8,578 | 0.53 |
| | Other | 89,014.5 | 46.89 | 781,380 | 48.24 |
| | **Total** | **189,801.0** | **100.00** | **1,619,599** | **100.00** |

**Thus, option (a) is the correct answer.**

**57.** *(a)* 1, 2 and 3 only

- The **World Bank** publishes the **World Development Report**, the **Ease of Doing Business Report** (discontinued), and the **Global Economic Prospects.**
- The **World Investment Report** is published by the **United Nations Conference on Trade and Development** (**UNCTAD**), not by the World Bank.

**Therefore, the correct answer is (a) 1, 2 and 3 only.**

**58.** *(c)* Only three

- The **World Bank Group** consists of five institutions:
  1. **International Bank for Reconstruction and Development (IBRD)**
  2. **International Development Association (IDA)**
  3. **International Finance Corporation** (**IFC**)
  4. Multilateral Investment Guarantee Agency (MIGA)
  5. International Centre for Settlement of Investment Disputes (ICSID)
- **International Fund for Agricultural Development (IFAD)** is a separate organisation and is not a part of the World Bank Group. It is a **specialised agency of the United Nations** that works to address poverty and hunger in rural areas of developing countries
- Also, note that India is a member of only four and the **exception** is **ICSID.**

**Therefore, the correct answer is (c) Only three.**

**59.** *(c)* Only three

- India is a member of the **International Bank for Reconstruction and Development (IBRD), International Development Association (IDA), Multilateral Investment Guarantee Agency (MIGA)** and **International Finance Corporation (IFC).**
- However, India **is not a member** of the **International Centre for Settlement of Investment Disputes (ICSID).**

**Therefore, the correct answer is (c) Only three.**

**60.** *(c)* All three

- **Statement 1 is correct:** The **International Development Association (IDA)** is a development finance institution which offers concessional loans and grants to the world's poorest developing countries. The IDA is a member of the World Bank Group and is headquartered in Washington, DC in the United States.
- **Statement 2 is correct: International Finance Corporation (IFC)** focuses on private sector development, offering investment and advisory services to businesses in developing countries.
- **Statement 3 is correct: Multilateral Investment Guarantee Agency** (**MIGA**) provides political risk insurance to help encourage investment in developing countries.

**Therefore, the correct answer is (c) All three.**

**61.** *(b)* Only two

- **Statement 1 is incorrect:** The IBRD does not finance private sector projects directly; its loans are typically provided to sovereign governments or that are backed by government guarantees.
- **Statement 2 is correct:** IBRD loans are backed by sovereign guarantees from the borrowing member countries.
- **Statement 3 is correct:** The International Development Association (IDA) is the concessional arm of the World Bank that offers low-interest loans and grants to the world's poorest countries. For a country to become a member of the IDA, it must first be

a member of the IBRD. This membership requirement ensures that IDA members are also part of the broader World Bank Group framework.

**Therefore, the correct answer is (b) Only two.**

**62.** *(a)* 1 only

- **Statement 1 is correct**: IFC provides loans, equity investments, and advisory services to help stimulate private sector growth in developing countries.
- **Statement 2 is incorrect**: The IFC does not provide direct financial assistance to governments; it focuses on investments in the private sector. It providing financial resources to private companies and projects that can contribute to poverty reduction through economic development.

**Thus, the correct answer is (a) 1 only.**

**63.** *(d)* All four

- **Asian Development Bank (ADB)** was established in 1966 to promote economic development and cooperation in Asia and the Pacific. India is a **founding** member of the ADB.
- **African Development Bank (AfDB)** was established in 1964 with the objective to promote sustainable economic development and social progress of African countries. India became a member of the African Development Bank in **1983**.
- **New Development Bank (NDB)**: The NDB, also known as the BRICS Bank, was established in 2014 by the BRICS countries (Brazil, Russia, India, China and South Africa). India is a **founding** member of the NDB.
- **European Bank for Reconstruction and Development (EBRD): The EBRD was established in 1991 to promote market economy and private sector investment in countries in economic transition, mainly in Central and Eastern Europe.** India became the EBRD's 69th shareholder when it joined the Bank in July 2018.

**Therefore, the correct answer is (d) All four.**

**64.** *(b)* Only two pairs

- **Pair 1 is incorrect: ADB** is headquartered in **Manila, Philippines.**
- **Pair 2 is incorrect: NDB** is headquartered in **Shanghai, China.** Therefore, Pair 2 should be Shanghai, not Beijing.
- **Pair 3 is correct: EBRD** is headquartered in **London, United Kingdom.**
- **Pair 4 is correct: AfDB** is headquartered in **Abidjan, Côte d'Ivoire.**

**Therefore, two pairs are correctly matched, so the answer is (b) Only two pairs.**

**65.** *(d)* All four

The New Development Bank (NDB) is a multilateral development bank established by Brazil, Russia, India, China and South Africa (BRICS) with the purpose of mobilising resources for infrastructure and sustainable development projects in emerging markets and developing countries (EMDCs).

- **Egypt** and **Bangladesh** are recent additions to the NDB membership, while **Brazil** and **India** are among the founding BRICS members.

**Thus, the correct answer is (d) All four.**

**66.** *(d)* 1, 2 and 3

- **Statement 1 is correct**: The AIIB focuses on funding infrastructure projects not only in Asia but also in other regions outside Asia. It expanding its reach beyond the continent and also funds projects in other regions, such as Africa and Europe.
- **Statement 2 is correct**: Voting power in the AIIB is based on the economic size and financial contributions of the member countries.
- **Statement 3 is correct**: China and India are the two largest shareholders in the AIIB, reflecting their economic size and importance in the region i.e., China is the AIIB's largest shareholder with a 26.5% voting share. India is the second-largest, with 7.5%, followed by Russia, which has a 5.97% voting share.

**Thus, the correct answer is (d) 1, 2 and 3.**

**67.** *(a)* Only one

- **Statement 1 is correct**: The ADB provides both concessional and non-concessional loans to its member countries to support various development projects.
- **Statement 2 is incorrect**: Voting power in the ADB is based on the financial contributions of member countries, not equally distributed. Japan and the United States are the largest shareholders of the ADB.
- **Statement 3 is incorrect**: While the ADB focuses significantly on infrastructure projects, it also supports other sectors such as health, education and finance.

**Thus, the correct answer is (a) Only one.**

**68.** *(a)* 1 and 2 only

- **Statement 1 is correct**: The New Development Bank (NDB) was established by the BRICS countries (Brazil, Russia, India, China and South Africa) during the **Fortaleza Summit in 2014.**
- **Statement 2 is correct**: Unlike many other international financial institutions, the NDB operates on an equal voting power model, where **each BRICS country has equal influence** regardless of economic size.
- **Statement 3 is incorrect**: Although the NDB was established by the BRICS countries, it finances infrastructure and sustainable development projects not only in BRICS countries, but also in other developing nations.

**Therefore, the correct answer is (a) 1 and 2 only.**

**69.** *(c)* 1 and 3 only

- **Statement 1 is correct**: The Financial Action Task Force (FATF) was indeed established in **1989 by the G7 countries** to develop policies to combat money laundering. Later, its mandate was expanded to include terrorism financing.
- **Statement 2 is incorrect**: The FATF's recommendations are **not legally binding**, but they carry significant weight. Non-compliance can lead to sanctions, economic consequences, and damage to a country's reputation.
- **Statement 3 is correct**: The FATF **works closely with other global organisations** like the International Monetary Fund (IMF), the World Bank, and others to ensure effective measures are in place to combat money laundering and terrorism financing.

**Thus, the correct answer is (c) 1 and 3 only.**

**70.** *(a)* 1-B, 2-A, 3-C, 4-D

- **The FATF Blacklist (1-B)**: includes high-risk and non-cooperative countries that fail to meet international anti-money laundering (AML) and countering the financing of terrorism (CFT) standards. Countries on this list are subject to possible countermeasures, which may include stricter financial scrutiny or sanctions.
- **The FATF Grey list (2-A)**: includes jurisdictions under increased monitoring. These countries have strategic deficiencies in their AML/CFT frameworks but are actively working with the FATF to address these shortcomings. Grey listed countries face reputational risks and enhanced scrutiny from global financial systems but are not subject to immediate sanctions.
- **Countries in Non-Cooperative Countries category (3-C)**: is flagged for severe deficiencies and recommended for strong countermeasures by FATF. These countries often fail to take meaningful steps to improve their compliance with FATF standards, prompting the global community to apply economic or financial pressure.
- **Jurisdictions under Review list (4-D)**: includes countries that are being evaluated by the FATF for their compliance with international AML/CFT standards. These reviews determine whether countries meet FATF requirements or if they need to be placed under increased monitoring or other measures.

**Thus, the correct answer is (a) 1-B, 2-A, 3-C, 4-D.**

**71.** *(a)* 1, 3 and 4 only

- **Option 1 is correct: Canada** is one of the G-7 members, which includes the most advanced economies in the world. It has been a part of the group since the formation of the G-7.

- **Option 2 is incorrect: Russia** was a part of the G-8 until 2014, but it was suspended from the group after its annexation of Crimea. Since then, the group reverted to the G-7 and Russia is no longer a participant.
- **Option 3 is correct: Japan** is a key member of the G-7 and is one of the world's largest and most advanced economies. It plays an important role in global economic discussions and policy coordination within the group.
- **Option 4 is correct: Italy is one of the founding members of the G-7.** The country contributes to the group's discussions on economic policies, trade and global governance.

**Thus, the correct answer is (a) 1, 3 and 4 only.**

**72.** *(c)* 1 only

- **Statement 1 is correct**: The G-20 is a unique grouping of both developed and emerging economies, including countries from Asia, Africa, Europe, and the Americas, which allows it to address a range of global issues affecting diverse economic conditions.
- **Statement 2 is incorrect**: While the G-20 took on a prominent role during the 2008 financial crisis, it was actually formed in **1999** to bring together finance ministers and central bank governors to discuss global economic stability.
- **Statement 3 is incorrect**: The G-20 does not restrict meetings to the **Northern Hemisphere**; for example, Australia and Indonesia, both located in the Southern Hemisphere, have hosted G-20 summits.

**Thus, the correct answer is (c) 1 only.**

**73.** *(a)* Argentina, Mexico, South Africa and Turkey

- **Option (a) is correct**: Argentina, Mexico, South Africa and Turkey are all members of the G20. These countries are part of this global platform, which includes both developed and emerging economies.
- **Option (b) is incorrect**: While Australia and Canada are members of the G20, Malaysia and New Zealand are not members.
- **Option (c) is incorrect**: Although Brazil and Saudi Arabia are G20 members, Iran and Vietnam are not part of the G20.
- **Option (d) is incorrect**: While Indonesia, Japan and South Korea are G20 members, Singapore is not a G20 member.

**Thus, option (a) is the correct answer.**

## Past Learning (Answers)

| | | | | | | | | | |
|---|---|---|---|---|---|---|---|---|---|
| 1 (c) | 2 (c) | 3 (b) | 4 (c) | 5 (d) | 6 (c) | 7 (a) | 8 (c) | 9 (a) | 10 (d) |
| 11 (d) | 12 (a) | 13 (c) | 14 (b) | 15 (b) | 16 (c) | 17 (d) | 18 (a) | | |

CHAPTER 13

# Indian Agriculture

## Assessment Round

### Topic 1 : Overview of Indian Agriculture

**1.** Arrange the following sub-sectors of Agriculture and Allied Activities according to their contribution to the agricultural Gross Value Added (GVA) in India in recent years (from highest to lowest):

1. Livestock
2. Fisheries
3. Forestry and Logging
4. Crop Production

Select the correct answer using the codes below:

(a) 4-1-2-3 (b) 1-4-2-3
(c) 4-1-3-2 (d) 1-2-3-4

**2.** With reference to the trends in agricultural production in India, consider the following statements:

1. The production of foodgrains in India has consistently crossed 300 million tonnes in recent years.
2. India's horticulture production has consistently surpassed foodgrain production in recent years.

Which of the statements given above is/are correct?

(a) 1 only (b) 2 only
(c) Both 1 and 2 (d) Neither 1 nor 2

**3.** Match the following agricultural revolutions with the commodities they are associated with:

| Agricultural Revolution | Commodity |
|---|---|
| 1. Green Revolution | A. Wheat and Rice |
| 2. White Revolution | B. Milk |
| 3. Blue Revolution | C. Fish and Aquaculture |
| 4. Yellow Revolution | D. Oilseeds |

Select the correct match from the codes given below:

(a) 1-A, 2-B, 3-C, 4-D
(b) 1-B, 2-A, 3-D, 4-C
(c) 1-A, 2-C, 3-B, 4-D
(d) 1-D, 2-C, 3-A, 4-B

**4.** With reference to India's rank in the production of various commodities, consider the following statements:

1. India is the largest producer of milk in the world.
2. India ranks second in the production of wheat.
3. India is the third-largest producer of sugarcane globally.

How many of the statements given above is/are correct?

(a) Only one (b) Only two
(c) All three (d) None

**5.** Arrange the following food grains based on their production volume in India (from highest to lowest) according to recent data:

1. Rice
2. Wheat
3. Coarse Cereals
4. Pulses

Select the correct answer using the codes below:

(a) 1-2-3-4 (b) 2-1-3-4
(c) 1-3-2-4 (d) 3-1-4-2

**6.** With reference to the 10th Agricultural Census (2015-16), consider the following statements:

1. It is conducted every five years to assess the structure of operational holdings in the country.
2. The census noted an increase in the number of female-operated agricultural holdings.
3. The census recorded that over 85% of agricultural holdings in India are categorised as small and marginal holdings.

Which of the statements given above are correct?

(a) 1 and 2 only
(b) 2 and 3 only
(c) 1 and 3 only
(d) 1, 2 and 3

**7.** With reference to the findings of 10th Agricultural Census (2015-16), consider the following statements:

1. Rajasthan recorded the highest average size of operational holdings in India.
2. Bihar and West Bengal recorded the highest number of marginal and small landholdings.
3. Uttar Pradesh has the largest number of operational holdings among all Indian states.

Which of the statements given above are correct?

(a) 1 and 2 only
(b) 1 and 3 only
(c) 2 and 3 only
(d) 1, 2 and 3

**8.** Consider the following types of farmers with their operational landholding sizes:

| Type of Farmer | Operational Landholding Size |
|---|---|
| 1. Marginal Farmer | Less than 1 hectare |
| 2. Small Farmer | 1 to 2 hectares |
| 3. Large Farmer | Above 10 hectares |

How many pairs given above is/are correctly matched?

(a) Only one pair (b) Only two pairs
(c) All three pairs (d) None

## Topic 2 : Farm Credit

**9.** Arrange the following steps taken by the government in the correct chronological order of their introduction to boost agricultural credit:

1. Launch of the Kisan Credit Card (KCC) scheme
2. Introduction of the Interest Subvention Scheme
3. Introduction of the PSL mandate by the RBI
4. Setting up of NABARD

Select the correct answer from the codes given below:

(a) 3-4-1-2 (b) 1-4-3-2
(c) 3-4-2-1 (d) 4-1-3-2

**10.** With reference to the RBI report on agricultural credit, consider the following statements:

1. The share of short-term crop loans in total agricultural credit increased from 51% in 2000 to 75% in 2018.
2. The report observed that 72% of the agricultural households' credit needs were met through institutional sources in 2016-17.
3. Credit for allied activities like livestock and fisheries was adequately proportional to their contribution to agricultural output.

How many of the above statements is/are correct?

(a) Only one (b) Only two
(c) All three (d) None

**11.** Arrange the following sources of farm credit in the correct order based on their contribution to total agricultural credit in India (from highest to lowest):

1. Regional Rural Banks (RRBs)
2. Cooperative Banks
3. Scheduled Commercial Banks
4. Non-Banking Financial Companies (NBFCs)

Select the correct answer using the codes below:

(a) 3-2-1-4 (b) 2-3-1-4
(c) 3-1-2-4 (d) 1-3-2-4

**12.** With reference to NABARD (National Bank for Agriculture and Rural Development), consider the following statements:

1. It was established in 1982 to increase the flow of credit to agriculture and rural development.
2. NABARD manages the Rural Infrastructure Development Fund (RIDF).
3. NABARD refinances regional rural banks (RRBs) and cooperative banks.

How many of the statements given above is/are correct?

(a) Only one
(b) Only two
(c) All three
(d) None

**13.** Consider the following statements about NABARD:

1. It supports watershed development to improve water management in agriculture.
2. It manages the SHG-Bank linkage programme.
3. It is responsible for rural housing under Pradhan Mantri Awas Yojana (PMAY).

Which of the statements given above are correct?

(a) 1 and 2 only
(b) 2 and 3 only
(c) 1 and 3 only
(d) 1 and 2 only

**14.** Consider the following funds:

1. Rural Infrastructure Development Fund (RIDF)
2. National Adaptation Fund for Climate Change (NAFCC)
3. Micro Irrigation Fund (MIF)
4. National Investment and Infrastructure Fund (NIIF)

How many of the given above funds is/are managed by NABARD?

(a) Only one
(b) Only two
(c) Only three
(d) All four

**15.** With reference to the 'Rural Infrastructure Development Fund (RIDF)', consider the following statements:

1. It was set up by the Government of India in 1995-96 to support the creation of rural infrastructure.
2. State Governments are the primary beneficiaries of RIDF funding for infrastructure projects.
3. RIDF is primarily funded by contributions from domestic commercial banks as part of their priority sector lending shortfalls.

Which of the statements given above are correct?

(a) 1 and 2 only
(b) 1 and 3 only
(c) 2 and 3 only
(d) 1, 2 and 3

**16.** With reference to the 'Kisan Credit Card (KCC)', consider the following statements:

1. Only commercial banks are eligible to issue Kisan Credit Cards under the scheme.
2. Farmers can use the KCC for investment credit to purchase farm equipment like tractors.
3. It can be used for both short-term crop loans and for allied activities like animal husbandry or fisheries.

Which of the statements given above are correct?

(a) 1 and 2 only (b) 2 and 3 only
(c) 1 and 3 only (d) 1, 2 and 3

**17.** Consider the following purposes:

1. Construction of farmhouses for residential purposes.
2. Meeting short-term credit needs for crop production.
3. Investment credit for irrigation infrastructure including tubewells.
4. Purchase of tractors and farm machinery.

How many of the given above is/are covered under the KCC scheme?

(a) Only one (b) Only two
(c) Only three (d) All four

**18.** With reference to the 'Modified Interest Subvention Scheme (MISS)', consider the following statements:

1. The scheme offers a 2% annual interest subvention for short-term crop loans up to ₹ 3 lakh.
2. Loans for allied agricultural activities, such as dairy and fisheries, are also covered under the scheme.
3. The scheme is available to both commercial banks and cooperative banks for issuing agricultural loans.

Which of the statements given above are correct?

(a) 1 and 2 only (b) 1 and 3 only
(c) 2 and 3 only (d) 1, 2 and 3

## Topic 3 : Agricultural Insurance

**19.** With reference to the Pradhan Mantri Fasal Bima Yojana (PMFBY), consider the following statements:

1. Under the PMFBY, insurance is mandatory for farmers availing loans from financial institutions.
2. The premium paid by farmers for commercial and horticultural crops is 1.5% of the sum insured.
3. The scheme provides coverage for pre-sowing and post-harvest losses due to natural calamities.

How many of the statements given above is/are correct?

(a) Only one (b) Only two
(c) All three (d) None

**20.** Consider the following statements about the 'Pradhan Mantri Fasal Bima Yojana (PMFBY)':

1. The scheme includes coverage for localised calamities such as hailstorms, landslides and inundation.
2. The subsidy for the premium is shared equally by the Central and State Governments.
3. PMFBY provides insurance coverage for the damage caused by wild animal attacks on crops.

Which of the statements given above is/are correct?

(a) 1 only (b) 1 and 3 only
(c) 2 and 3 only (d) 1, 2 and 3

**21.** Which of the following categories of farmers are eligible for coverage under the Pradhan Mantri Fasal Bima Yojana (PMFBY)?

1. Loanee farmers
2. Non-loanee farmers
3. Sharecroppers and tenant farmers
4. Farmers engaged in allied activities like fisheries

Select the correct answer using the codes given below:

(a) 1 and 3 only (b) 1, 2 and 3 only
(c) 2 and 3 only (d) 1, 2, 3 and 4

**22.** Which of the following technological advancements are being utilised under the Pradhan Mantri Fasal Bima Yojana (PMFBY) to improve the efficiency of crop insurance?

1. Remote sensing technology for crop loss assessment
2. Use of drones for real-time monitoring of crops
3. Blockchain technology for claim settlement
4. Smartphones for direct data collection from farmers

Select the correct answer from the codes given below:

(a) 1 and 3 only (b) 1, 2 and 4 only
(c) 2 and 3 only (d) 1, 2, 3 and 4

## Topic 4 : Irrigation

**23.** Which of the following correctly describes about 'Water Use Efficiency (WUE)'?

(a) Water use efficiency refers to the amount of crop yield produced per unit of water consumed.
(b) Water use efficiency measures the total water usage in agricultural irrigation systems.
(c) WUE emphasises reducing the overall water availability for irrigation without considering crop productivity.
(d) WUE applies exclusively to drip irrigation systems and not to any other irrigation methods.

**24.** Consider the following irrigation methods with the regions in India where they are predominantly practiced:

| | Irrigation Method | Region |
|---|---|---|
| 1. | Tubewell Irrigation | Punjab and Haryana |
| 2. | Canal Irrigation | Uttar Pradesh and Rajasthan |
| 3. | Tank Irrigation | Tamil Nadu and Karnataka |

How many pairs given above is/are correctly matched?

(a) Only one pair (b) Only two pairs
(c) All three pairs (d) None

**25.** With reference to the Pradhan Mantri Krishi Sinchayee Yojana (PMKSY), consider the following statements:

1. It is a centrally sponsored scheme aimed at improving irrigation coverage and water use efficiency in agriculture.
2. Accelerated Irrigation Benefit Programme (AIBP) under PMKSY focuses on completing long-pending micro-irrigation projects.
3. It is solely implemented by the Ministry of Agriculture and Farmers' Welfare.

Which of the statements given above is/are correct?

(a) 1 only
(b) 2 and 3 only
(c) 1 and 3 only
(d) 1, 2 and 3

**26.** Consider the following components of the Pradhan Mantri Krishi Sinchayee Yojana (PMKSY) with their descriptions:

| | Component of PMKSY | Description |
|---|---|---|
| 1. | Har Khet Ko Pani | Focuses on micro-irrigation and water-use efficiency at the farm level |
| 2. | Per Drop More Crop | Ensures water access to every farm through various water resources |
| 3. | Watershed Development | Focuses on conserving soil and moisture through watershed management |

How many pairs given above is/are correctly matched?

(a) Only one pair
(b) Only two pairs
(c) All three pairs
(d) None

**27.** Consider the following components of the Pradhan Mantri Krishi Sinchayee Yojana (PMKSY) with their respective nodal ministries:

| | Component of PMKSY | Nodal Ministry |
|---|---|---|
| 1. | Har Khet Ko Pani | Ministry of Jal Shakti |
| 2. | Per Drop More Crop | Ministry of Agriculture and Farmers' Welfare |
| 3. | Watershed Development | Ministry of Rural Development |
| 4. | Accelerated Irrigation Benefit Programme (AIBP) | Ministry of Jal Shakti |

How many pairs given above is/are correctly matched?

(a) Only one pair
(b) Only two pairs
(c) Only three pairs
(d) All four pairs

**28.** With reference to the Micro-Irrigation Fund (MIF), which of the following statements is correct?

(a) The Micro-Irrigation Fund is entirely financed by the Central Government.
(b) The fund aims to promote surface irrigation projects across the country.
(c) The Micro-Irrigation Fund is operated by NABARD and aims to support the adoption of micro-irrigation technologies.
(d) The Micro-Irrigation Fund only focuses on small and marginal farmers.

## Topic 5 : Fertilizer Sector

**29.** Consider the following statements:

1. India is the second-largest consumer of fertilizers in the world after China.
2. India imports both raw materials for fertilizer production, such as ammonia, and finished fertilizers like urea and potash.
3. A significant portion of India's phosphatic fertilizers is imported from countries like Morocco and China.

How many of the statements given above is/are correct?

(a) Only one (b) Only two
(c) All three (d) None

**30.** With reference to India's fertilizer subsidy regime, consider the following statements:

1. The government fixes the Maximum Retail Price (MRP) for urea while phosphatic and potassic fertilizers have largely decontrolled prices.
2. Nutrient-Based Subsidy (NBS) scheme was introduced in 2010 to encourage the balanced use of fertilizers.
3. Under the NBS scheme, the government directly sets the retail prices of all fertilizers, including phosphatic and potassic (P&K) fertilizers.

Which of the statements given above are correct?

(a) 1 and 2 only (b) 1 and 3 only
(c) 2 and 3 only (d) 1, 2 and 3

**31.** Which of the following fertilisers are subsidised under the 'Nutrient-Based Subsidy (NBS)' regime in India?

1. Ammonium Sulphate
2. Di-Ammonium Phosphate (DAP)
3. Urea
4. NPK Complex Fertilizers

Select the correct answer from the codes given below:

(a) 1, 2 and 4 only (b) 2 and 4 only
(c) 1 and 3 only (d) 1, 2, 3 and 4

**32.** Arrange the following fertilizer categories in decreasing order of subsidy allocation based on the recent data:

1. Nutrient-Based Subsidy (P&K Fertilizers)
2. Urea subsidy
3. Organic fertilizer subsidy

Select the correct answer from the codes given below:

(a) 1-2-3 (b) 2-1-3
(c) 1-3-2 (d) 3-2-1

**33.** With reference to the 'Soil Health Card Scheme', consider the following statements:

1. The scheme provides farmers with detailed information about soil nutrient status and recommendations for improving soil fertility.
2. The scheme is implemented by the Ministry of Agriculture and Farmers' Welfare in collaboration with State Governments.
3. Only farmers from rainfed areas are eligible for the Soil Health Card under this scheme.

Which of the statements given above is/are correct?

(a) 1 and 2 only (b) 2 and 3 only
(c) 1 and 3 only (d) 1, 2 and 3

**34.** Which of the following nutrients are included in the soil testing process under the Soil Health Card Scheme?

1. Organic Carbon 2. Sulphur
3. Iron 4. Magnesium

Select the correct answer from the codes given below:

(a) 1 and 2 only (b) 1, 2 and 3 only
(c) 1, 2, 3 and 4 (d) 3 and 4 only

**35.** With reference to the 'PM-PRANAM scheme', consider the following statements:

1. The scheme aims to incentivise states for reducing the use of chemical fertilizers.
2. Under the scheme, the savings from reduced fertilizer use are shared with farmers directly.
3. The scheme encourages the use of organic and bio-fertilizers as alternatives to chemical fertilizers.

How many of the statements given above is/are correct?

(a) Only one (b) Only two
(c) All three (d) None

**36.** Consider the following:
1. Increased nutrient use efficiency
2. Reduced fertilizer usage
3. Improved crop productivity
4. Increased nitrogen emissions

How many of the above is/are correct benefits of 'Nano Liquid Urea'?
(a) Only one (b) Only two
(c) Only three (d) All four

**37.** Which of the following statements best describes the 'Urea Gold'?
(a) Urea Gold is a specialised fertilizer containing a blend of urea and micronutrients to enhance soil health and crop productivity.
(b) Urea Gold is a premium-priced urea variant designed specifically for industrial use, not agricultural purposes.
(c) Urea Gold contains only urea with no additional nutrients, aiming to replace traditional urea completely.
(d) Urea Gold is a natural organic fertilizer made from bio-degradable waste used primarily for organic farming.

**38.** Consider the following:
1. Reduced fertilizer consumption
2. Enhanced crop yield
3. Increased Nitrogen Use Efficiency (NUE)
4. Prevents diversion for industrial use

How many of the given above is/are correct benefits of 'Neem Coated Urea'?
(a) Only one (b) Only two
(c) Only three (d) All four

## Topic 6 : Minimum Support Prices (MSP)

**39.** With reference to the Minimum Support Price (MSP), consider the following statements:
1. It is announced by the Cabinet Committee on Economic Affairs at the beginning of each sowing season.
2. MSP guarantees that farmers will always receive a price higher than the market rate for their crops.
3. MSP is declared for both Kharif and Rabi crops.

Which of the statements given above is/are correct?
(a) 1 and 3 only (b) 2 only
(c) 1 and 2 only (d) 3 only

**40.** Consider the following crops:
1. Wheat
2. Maize
3. Cotton
4. Sugarcane

How many of the given above is/are covered under the MSP?
(a) Only one (b) Only two
(c) Only three (d) All four

**41.** Which of the following best explains the difference between Minimum Support Prices (MSP) and Fair and Remunerative Price (FRP)?
(a) MSP ensures farmers are paid a minimum price even when the market price is lower, while FRP sets a price for sugarcane based on recovery of sugar content.
(b) MSP guarantees farmers a profit, while FRP ensures that sugarcane farmers do not face any losses.
(c) MSP is designed for long-term sustainability of all crops, while FRP is aimed solely at regulating sugarcane prices during a crisis.
(d) Both MSP and FRP guarantee prices for all crops based on the global market price.

**42.** With reference to the 'Fair and Remunerative Price (FRP)', consider the following statements:
1. It is the minimum price at which sugar mills must purchase sugarcane from farmers.
2. It is revised annually by the Commission for Agricultural Costs and Prices (CACP).
3. The State Governments can set a higher price than the FRP called the State Advised Price (SAP).

Which of the statements given above are correct?
(a) 1 and 2 only (b) 1 and 3 only
(c) 2 and 3 only (d) 1, 2 and 3

**43.** What legal mechanism enforces the payment of the Fair and Remunerative Price (FRP) to sugarcane farmers?

(a) The Sugarcane (Control) Order, 1966, legally enforces sugar mills to pay FRP to farmers within a specified time.
(b) The Essential Commodities Act, mandates that all agricultural commodities, including sugarcane, be sold at FRP.
(c) The Agricultural Produce Marketing Committee Act regulates FRP payments for sugarcane farmers.
(d) The Competition Commission of India enforces FRP to prevent unfair trade practices in the sugar market.

**44.** Consider the following types of costs with their descriptions used by the Commission for Agricultural Cost and Prices (CACP) for recommending MSP:

| Type of Cost | Description |
|---|---|
| 1. A2 | Only includes paid-out expenses such as seeds, fertilizers and hired labour. |
| 2. A2+FL | Covers paid-out costs plus the imputed value of family labour. |
| 3. C2 | Covers A2+FL plus imputed rent on owned land and interest on fixed capital. |

How many pairs given above is/are correctly matched?

(a) Only one (b) Only two
(c) All three (d) None

**45.** Which of the following are components of the PM-AASHA Scheme?

1. Price Support Scheme (PSS)
2. Price Deficiency Payment Scheme (PDPS)
3. Market Intervention Scheme (MIS)
4. Private Procurement and Stockist Scheme (PPSS)

Select the correct answer using the codes below:

(a) 1, 2 and 3 only (b) 1, 2 and 4 only
(c) 2, 3 and 4 only (d) 1, 2, 3 and 4

**46.** Which of the following best describes the Price Deficiency Payment Scheme (PDPS) under PM-AASHA?

(a) PDPS compensates farmers for the difference between the Minimum Support Price (MSP) and the actual market price of crops without any physical procurement of crops by the government.
(b) PDPS ensures direct government procurement of all surplus crops at market prices.
(c) PDPS is aimed at encouraging private players to procure crops from farmers at market prices.
(d) PDPS compensates farmers only when the market price is higher than the MSP.

**47.** Consider the following agencies:

1. Food Corporation of India (FCI)
2. Cotton Corporation of India (CCI)
3. National Cooperative Development Corporation (NCDC)
4. National Agricultural Cooperative Marketing Federation (NAFED)

How many of the given above is/are involved in the procurement of crops?

(a) Only one (b) Only two
(c) Only three (d) All four

## Topic 7 : Agricultural Marketing and Exports

**48.** With reference to the Agricultural Produce Market Committee (APMC) Acts, consider the following statements:

1. Regulation of agricultural markets falls under the State List in the Seventh Schedule of the Indian Constitution.
2. State Governments have the power to notify mandis (regulated markets) under the APMC Act for the sale of agricultural produce.
3. The APMC Acts mandate farmers to sell their produce only within state-controlled mandis without direct sale options.

Which of the statements given above are correct?

(a) 1 and 2 only (b) 1 and 3 only
(c) 2 and 3 only (d) 1, 2 and 3

**49.** With reference to the National Agriculture Market (e-NAM), consider the following statements:

1. The e-NAM platform is implemented by the Small Farmers' Agribusiness Consortium (SFAC).
2. It is a centrally sponsored scheme that helps farmers access markets across India using a single, unified online platform.
3. It facilitates the online trading of all agricultural produce at guaranteed MSP prices.

How many of the statements given above is/are correct?

(a) Only one (b) Only two
(c) All three (d) None

**50.** Which of the following best describes the Agri-Market Infrastructure Fund (AMIF)?

(a) A fund established to upgrade and modernise existing agricultural markets and infrastructure.
(b) A fund that provides loans to farmers for setting up private mandis and cold storage facilities.
(c) A fund aimed at promoting direct exports of agricultural commodities from farmers.
(d) A scheme designed to guarantee Minimum Support Price (MSP) for all crops traded in agricultural markets.

**51.** With reference to the 'Agriculture Infrastructure Fund (AIF)', consider the following statements:

1. The fund provides an interest subvention of 3% per annum for loans up to ₹ 2 crore.
2. The AIF scheme aims to build post-harvest infrastructure, such as processing units and cold chains, at the farm-gate level.
3. The scheme is implemented by the Ministry of Agriculture and Farmers' Welfare.

Which of the statements given above are correct?

(a) 1 and 2 only (b) 1 and 3 only
(c) 2 and 3 only (d) 1, 2 and 3

**52.** With reference to the 'Farmer Producer Organisations (FPOs)', consider the following statements:

1. FPOs are legal entities which can be registered as companies or cooperative societies.
2. Small Farmers' Agri-business Consortium (SFAC) plays a key role in the promotion and development of FPOs.
3. Small and marginal farmers are not eligible to become members of an FPO.

Which of the statements given above are correct?

(a) 1 and 2 only (b) 2 and 3 only
(c) 1 and 3 only (d) 1, 2 and 3

**53.** Which of the following are features of a 'Negotiable Warehouse Receipt (NWR)'?

1. NWRs allow farmers to use stored commodities as collateral for loans from banks.
2. These are issued only by government-regulated warehouses under the supervision of the Warehousing Development and Regulatory Authority (WDRA).
3. These can be traded or transferred from one party to another.

Select the correct answer using the codes given below:

(a) 1 and 2 only (b) 1 and 3 only
(c) 2 and 3 only (d) 1, 2 and 3

**54.** With reference to India's agricultural exports, consider the following statements:

1. India has been a trade surplus country in agricultural products for several years.
2. India's agricultural exports have been dominated by low-value commodities such as bulk grains and raw sugar.
3. India's share of high-value and value-added agricultural products is significantly lower than that of China and the United States.

How many of the statements given above is/are correct?

(a) Only one (b) Only two
(c) All three (d) None

**55.** Consider the following statements:

1. India is the world's second-largest agricultural producer with the largest arable land area and the second-largest irrigated area after China.
2. The share of India's agricultural exports in global Agri-exports was 2.4% in 2022.
3. India ranks in the top 5 globally in terms of agricultural exports.

Which of the statements given above is/are correct?

(a) 1 and 2 only (b) 3 only
(c) 1 only (d) 1, 2 and 3

**56.** Arrange the following agricultural commodities by their export value from India in recent years, from highest to lowest:

1. Rice (other than basmati)
2. Marine products
3. Sugar
4. Fresh fruits

Select the correct answer from the codes given below:

(a) 1-2-3-4 (b) 2-1-3-4
(c) 3-2-1-4 (d) 2-3-1-4

**57.** Consider the following countries:

1. United States
2. China
3. Bangladesh
4. United Arab Emirates (UAE)

How many of the given above is/are among the top export destinations for India's agricultural products in recent years?

(a) Only one (b) Only two
(c) Only three (d) All four

**58.** With reference to the Agricultural and Processed Food Products Export Development Authority (APEDA), consider the following statements:

1. It is responsible for promoting the export of both agricultural and processed food products from India.
2. It operates under the Ministry of Agriculture and Farmers' Welfare.
3. It provides financial assistance for the development of export-oriented infrastructure.

Which of the statements given above are correct?

(a) 1 and 2 only
(b) 1 and 3 only
(c) 2 and 3 only
(d) 1, 2 and 3

**59.** With reference to the Essential Commodities Act, consider the following statements:

1. The Act empowers the Central Government to control the supply and distribution of essential commodities.
2. Only food items can be declared as essential commodities under this Act.
3. The Act is intended to prevent hoarding and black marketing of essential items.

Which of the statements given above are correct?

(a) 1 and 2 only
(b) 1 and 3 only
(c) 2 and 3 only
(d) 1, 2 and 3

**60.** Consider the following actions:

1. Setting of maximum retail prices for specific commodities
2. Imposition of stock limits to prevent hoarding
3. Control the quality standards for non-essential luxury items
4. Regulation of the distribution of essential items

How many of the given above actions can be enforced under the 'Essential Commodities Act'?

(a) Only one
(b) Only two
(c) Only three
(d) All four

# OMR SHEET

**Assessment Round**

| | | | | | | | | | | | | | | | | | | | |
|---|---|---|---|---|---|---|---|---|---|---|---|---|---|---|---|---|---|---|---|
| 1 | a | b | c | d | 31 | a | b | c | d | 61 | a | b | c | d | 91 | a | b | c | d |
| 2 | a | b | c | d | 32 | a | b | c | d | 62 | a | b | c | d | 92 | a | b | c | d |
| 3 | a | b | c | d | 33 | a | b | c | d | 63 | a | b | c | d | 93 | a | b | c | d |
| 4 | a | b | c | d | 34 | a | b | c | d | 64 | a | b | c | d | 94 | a | b | c | d |
| 5 | a | b | c | d | 35 | a | b | c | d | 65 | a | b | c | d | 95 | a | b | c | d |
| 6 | a | b | c | d | 36 | a | b | c | d | 66 | a | b | c | d | 96 | a | b | c | d |
| 7 | a | b | c | d | 37 | a | b | c | d | 67 | a | b | c | d | 97 | a | b | c | d |
| 8 | a | b | c | d | 38 | a | b | c | d | 68 | a | b | c | d | 98 | a | b | c | d |
| 9 | a | b | c | d | 39 | a | b | c | d | 69 | a | b | c | d | 99 | a | b | c | d |
| 10 | a | b | c | d | 40 | a | b | c | d | 70 | a | b | c | d | 100 | a | b | c | d |
| 11 | a | b | c | d | 41 | a | b | c | d | 71 | a | b | c | d | 101 | a | b | c | d |
| 12 | a | b | c | d | 42 | a | b | c | d | 72 | a | b | c | d | 102 | a | b | c | d |
| 13 | a | b | c | d | 43 | a | b | c | d | 73 | a | b | c | d | 103 | a | b | c | d |
| 14 | a | b | c | d | 44 | a | b | c | d | 74 | a | b | c | d | 104 | a | b | c | d |
| 15 | a | b | c | d | 45 | a | b | c | d | 75 | a | b | c | d | 105 | a | b | c | d |
| 16 | a | b | c | d | 46 | a | b | c | d | 76 | a | b | c | d | 106 | a | b | c | d |
| 17 | a | b | c | d | 47 | a | b | c | d | 77 | a | b | c | d | 107 | a | b | c | d |
| 18 | a | b | c | d | 48 | a | b | c | d | 78 | a | b | c | d | 108 | a | b | c | d |
| 19 | a | b | c | d | 49 | a | b | c | d | 79 | a | b | c | d | 109 | a | b | c | d |
| 20 | a | b | c | d | 50 | a | b | c | d | 80 | a | b | c | d | 110 | a | b | c | d |
| 21 | a | b | c | d | 51 | a | b | c | d | 81 | a | b | c | d | 111 | a | b | c | d |
| 22 | a | b | c | d | 52 | a | b | c | d | 82 | a | b | c | d | 112 | a | b | c | d |
| 23 | a | b | c | d | 53 | a | b | c | d | 83 | a | b | c | d | 113 | a | b | c | d |
| 24 | a | b | c | d | 54 | a | b | c | d | 84 | a | b | c | d | 114 | a | b | c | d |
| 25 | a | b | c | d | 55 | a | b | c | d | 85 | a | b | c | d | 115 | a | b | c | d |
| 26 | a | b | c | d | 56 | a | b | c | d | 86 | a | b | c | d | 116 | a | b | c | d |
| 27 | a | b | c | d | 57 | a | b | c | d | 87 | a | b | c | d | 117 | a | b | c | d |
| 28 | a | b | c | d | 58 | a | b | c | d | 88 | a | b | c | d | 118 | a | b | c | d |
| 29 | a | b | c | d | 59 | a | b | c | d | 89 | a | b | c | d | 119 | a | b | c | d |
| 30 | a | b | c | d | 60 | a | b | c | d | 90 | a | b | c | d | 120 | a | b | c | d |

## Calculate Your Score

| | |
|---|---|
| **Correct (✓)** | |
| **Incorrect (✓)** | |
| **Unattempted** | |
| **Total Score** | |
| **Accuracy (%)** | |

## Reasons for Incorrect Answers?

| | |
|---|---|
| 1. Lack of Knowledge/Existing Source Insufficient | |
| 2. Lack of Multiple Revision | |
| 3. Common Sense Mistakes | |

**Note :**

1. Calculate total score as correct answers carry 2 marks each 1/3rd marks will deducted for **Incorrect** Answers.
2. Calculate Accuracy (%) by dividing the number of correct answers to the total number of attempted questions.

## Past Learning

**1.** With reference to the Digital India Land Records Modernisation Programme, consider the following statements: **(2024)**

1. To implement the scheme, the Central Government provides 100% funding.
2. Under the Scheme, Cadastral Maps are digitised.
3. An initiative has been undertaken to transliterate the Records of Rights from local language to any of the languages recognised by the Constitution of India.

Which of the statements given above are correct?

(a) 1 and 2 only
(b) 2 and 3 only
(c) 1 and 3 only
(d) 1, 2 and 3

**2.** Which one of the following best describes the concept of 'Small Farmer Large Field'? **(2023)**

(a) Resettlement of a large number of people, uprooted from their countries due to war, by giving them a large cultivable land which they cultivate collectively and share the produce.
(b) Many marginal farmers in an area organise themselves into groups and synchronise and harmonise selected agricultural operations.
(c) Many marginal farmers in an area together make a contract with a corporate body and surrender their land to the corporate body for a fixed term for which the corporate body makes a payment of agreed amount to the farmers.
(d) A company extends loans, technical knowledge and material inputs to a number of small farmers in an area so that they produce the agricultural commodity required by the company for its manufacturing process and commercial production.

**3.** Consider the following statements: **(2023)**

1. The Government of India provides Minimum Support Price for niger (Guizotia abyssinica) seeds.
2. Niger is cultivated as a Kharif crop.
3. Some tribal people in India use niger seed oil for cooking.

How many of the given above statements is/are correct?

(a) Only one
(b) Only two
(c) All three
(d) None

**4.** Among the following, which one is the least water-efficient crop? **(2021)**

(a) Sugarcane
(b) Sunflower
(c) Pearl millet
(d) Red gram

**5.** With reference to chemical fertilizers in India, consider the following statements: **(2020)**

1. At present, the retail price of chemical fertilizers is market-driven and not administered by the Government.
2. Ammonia, which is an input of urea, is produced from natural gas.
3. Sulfur, which is a raw material for phosphoric acid fertilizer is a by-product of oil refineries.

Which of the statements given above is/are correct?

(a) 1 only
(b) 2 and 3 only
(c) 2 only
(d) 1, 2 and 3

**6.** Under the Kisan Credit Card scheme, short-term credit support is given to farmers for which of the following purposes? **(2020)**

1. Working capital for maintenance of farm assets harvesters
2. Purchase of combine tractors and mini trucks requirements of farm
3. Consumption households
4. Post-harvest expenses
5. Construction of family house and setting up of village cold storage facility.

Select the correct answer using the codes given below:

(a) 1, 2 and 5 only
(b) 1, 3 and 4 only
(c) 2, 3, 4 and 5 only
(d) 1, 2, 3, 4 and 5

**7.** In India, which of the following can be considered as public investment in agriculture? **(2020)**

1. Fixing Minimum Support Price for agricultural produce of all crops
2. Computerisation of Primary Agricultural Credit Societies
3. Social Capital development
4. Free electricity supply to farmers
5. Waiver of agricultural loans by the banking system
6. Setting up of cold storage facilities by the governments.

Select the correct answer using the codes given below:

(a) 1, 2 and 5 only (b) 1, 3, 4 and 5 only
(c) 2, 3 and 6 only (d) 1, 2, 3, 4, 5 and 6

**8.** Consider the following statements: **(2020)**

1. In the case of all cereals, pulses, and oil seeds, the procurement at Minimum Support Price (MSP) is unlimited in any State/UT of India.
2. In the case of cereals and pulses, the MSP is fixed in any State/UT at a level to which the market price will never rise.

Which of the statements given above is/are correct?

(a) 1 only
(b) 2 only
(c) Both 1 and 2
(d) Neither 1 and 2

**9.** Consider the following statements: **(2020)**

1. In terms of short-term credit delivery to the agriculture sector, District Central Cooperative Banks (DCCBs) deliver more credit in comparison to Scheduled Commercial Banks and Regional Rural Banks.
2. One of the most important functions of DCCBs is to provide funds to the Primary Agricultural Credit Societies.

Which of the statements given above is/are correct?

(a) 1 only
(b) 2 only
(c) Both 1 and 2
(d) Neither 1 and 2

**10.** With reference to the land reforms in independent India, which one of the following statements is correct? **(2019)**

(a) The ceiling laws were aimed at family holdings and not individual holdings.
(b) The major aim of land reforms was providing agricultural land to all the landless.
(c) It resulted in cultivation of cash crops as a predominant form of cultivation.
(d) Land reforms permitted no exemptions to the ceiling limits.

**11.** Among the agricultural commodities imported by India, which one of the following accounts for the highest imports in terms of value in the last five years? **(2019)**

(a) Spices (b) Fresh fruits
(c) Pulses (d) Vegetable oils

**12.** Among the following, which one is the largest exporter of rice in the world in the last five years? **(2019)**

(a) China (b) India
(c) Myanmar (d) Vietnam

**13.** The economic cost of food grains to the Food Corporation of India is Minimum Support Price and bonus (if any) paid to the farmers plus: **(2019)**

(a) transportation cost only
(b) interest cost only
(c) procurement incidentals and distribution cost
(d) procurement incidentals and charges for godowns

**14.** Consider the following statements: **(2018)**

1. The quantity of imported edible oils is more than the domestic production of edible oils in the last five years.
2. The Government does not impose any customs duty on all imported edible oils as a special case.

Which of the statements given above is/are correct?

(a) 1 only
(b) 2 only
(c) Both 1 and 2
(d) Neither 1 and 2

**15.** With reference to the provisions made under the National Food Security Act, 2013, consider the following statements: **(2018)**

1. The families coming under the category of 'below poverty line (BPL)' only are eligible to receive subsidised food grains.
2. The eldest woman in a household, of age 18 years or above, shall be the head of the household for the purpose of issuance of a ration card.
3. Pregnant women and lactating mothers are entitled to a 'take-home ration' of 1600 calories per day during pregnancy and for six months thereafter.

Which of the statements given above is/are correct?

(a) 1 and 2 only
(b) 2 only
(c) 1 and 3 only
(d) 3 only

**16.** Consider the following: **(2018)**

1. Areca nut
2. Barley
3. Coffee
4. Finger millet
5. Groundnut
6. Sesamum
7. Turmeric

The Cabinet Committee on Economic Affairs has announced the Minimum Support Price for which of the above?

(a) 1, 2, 3 and 7 only
(b) 2, 4, 5 and 6 only
(c) 1, 3, 4, 5 and 6 only
(d) 1, 2, 3, 4, 5, 6 and 7

**17.** What is/are the advantage/advantages of implementing the 'National Agriculture Market' scheme? **(2017)**

1. It is a pan-India electronic trading portal for agricultural commodities.
2. It provides the farmers access to nationwide market, with prices commensurate with the quality of their produce.

Select the correct answer using the codes given below.

(a) 1 only (b) 2 only
(c) Both 1 and 2 (d) Neither 1 and 2

**18.** Which of the following is/are the advantage/advantages of practicing drip irrigation? **(2016)**

1. Reduction in weed
2. Reduction in soil salinity
3. Reduction in soil erosion

Select the correct answer using the codes given below:

(a) 1 and 2 only (b) 3 only
(c) 1 and 3 only (d) None of these

**19.** With reference to 'Pradhan Mantri Fasal Bima Yojana', consider the following statements: **(2016)**

1. Under this scheme, farmers will have to pay a uniform premium of two percent for any crop they cultivate in any season of the year.
2. This scheme covers post-harvest losses arising out of cyclones and unseasonal rains.

Which of the statements given above is/are correct?

(a) 1 only (b) 2 only
(c) Both 1 and 2 (d) Neither 1 and 2

**20.** The Fair and Remunerative Price (FRP) of sugarcane is approved by the: **(2015)**

(a) Cabinet Committee on Economic Affairs
(b) Commission for Agricultural Costs and Prices
(c) Directorate of Marketing and Inspection, Ministry of Agriculture
(d) Agricultural Produce Market Committee

**21.** In India, markets in agricultural products are regulated under the: **(2015)**

(a) Essential Commodities Act, 1955
(b) Agricultural Produce Market Committee Act enacted by States
(c) Agricultural Produce (Grading and Marking) Act, 1937
(d) Food Products Order, 1956 and Meat and Food Products Order, 1973

# Detailed Solutions

## Assessment Round

**1.** *(a)* 4-1-2-3

- **Crops: Crops** are the **largest contributor** to Agricultural GVA, accounting for approximately 55-60%. This includes cereals, pulses, oilseeds, fruits, vegetables and other crop cultivation. Crop production remains the backbone of India's agriculture sector.
- **Livestock: Livestock** is the **second-largest contributor**, with a share of about 25-28%. This sub-sector includes dairy farming, poultry and animal husbandry. The growth in livestock is due to increasing demand for animal products and livelihood opportunities it provides.
- **Fisheries: Fisheries** contribute around 7-8% to Agricultural GVA. The fisheries sector has been growing due to enhanced focus on aquaculture and increasing domestic and export demand for fish and seafood.
- **Forestry and Logging: Forestry and Logging** account for approximately 7-8% of Agricultural GVA. This includes timber production and non-timber forest products. While important for ecological balance, its contribution to GVA is relatively smaller.

**Thus, the correct answer is (a) 4-1-2-3.**

**2.** *(c)* Both 1 and 2

- **Statement 1 is correct:** In recent years, India's **foodgrain production** has consistently surpassed **300 million tonnes**, reflecting improvements in agricultural practices and favourable monsoon conditions.
- **Statement 2 is correct:** In recent years, **horticulture production** in India has exceeded foodgrain production, driven by increasing demand for fruits and vegetables.
  - As per the 2nd advance estimates for 2022-23, the total horticulture production is estimated to be 351.92 million Tonne, surpassing the total foodgrain production of 329.69 million Tonne during the year. At present, India is the second largest producer of vegetables and fruits in the world. Country ranks first in the production of number of crops like banana, lime and lemon, papaya, okra.

**Thus, the correct answer is (c) Both 1 and 2.**

**3.** *(a)* 1-A, 2-B, 3-C, 4-D

- **Green Revolution:** The **Green Revolution** led to a significant increase in **wheat and rice** production in India during the 1960s-70s. As a result, India is currently the **second-largest producer of wheat** globally and **the largest exporter of rice.**
- **White Revolution:** The **White Revolution** (Operation Flood) turned India into the **world's largest producer** of milk, a position it continues to hold today. The initiative transformed the dairy industry, ensuring milk self-sufficiency.
- **Blue Revolution:** The **Blue Revolution** focused on **fisheries and aquaculture**. India is now the **second-largest fish producer** in the world, with a significant focus on **aquaculture** development.
- **Yellow Revolution:** The **Yellow Revolution** targeted the production of **oilseeds**, such as mustard and sunflower. India is one of the largest importers of edible oils but also produces oilseeds domestically as part of this revolution.

**Thus, the correct answer is (a) 1-A, 2-B, 3-C, 4-D.**

**4.** *(b)* Only two

- **Statement 1 is correct:** India is indeed the **largest producer of milk** globally due to initiatives like the **White Revolution.** India accounts for around **22% of global milk production**, making it the **top milk-producing country** in the world. This success is largely due to India's strong dairy sector and programmes like the **White Revolution** (Operation Flood), which began in the 1970s and transformed India into a global leader in milk production.

- **Statement 2 is correct:** India is the **second-largest producer of wheat** after China. India's wheat production saw a significant boost after the **Green Revolution** in the 1960s, which introduced high-yielding varieties of wheat, improved irrigation, and modern farming techniques.

**Note:** globally, India ranks first with 13.9% share in world's wheat area, while in terms of production, it stands second after China with almost 39% lesser production and productivity lag of about 52% (NBS, 2014).

The major wheat-producing states in India include **Uttar Pradesh, Punjab, Haryana, Madhya Pradesh, Rajasthan, and Bihar.**

- **Statement 3 is incorrect:** India is the **largest producer** of sugarcane, not the third-largest. It is the largest producer of sugarcane globally, followed by **Brazil** and **China.**

**Thus, the correct answer is (b) Only two.**

**5.** *(a)* 1-2-3-4

- Rice is the **largest** produced food grain in India, with annual production **exceeding 100 million tonnes.**
- **Wheat** is the **second-largest** crop, with production around **100 million tonnes.**
- Coarse cereals like **millets, maize, sorghum,** etc., have a significant production but are lower than rice and wheat.
- While India is the **largest producer of pulses,** the total production is lower than other food grains, around **25 million tonnes.**

As per Final Estimates, the estimated production of major crops during 2022-23 is as under:

**Foodgrains** – 3296.87 lakh tonnes

1. Rice – 1357.55 lakh tonnes
2. Wheat – 1105.54 lakh tonnes
3. Nutri / Coarse Cereals – 573.19 lakh tonnes
4. Maize – 380.85 lakh tonnes
5. Pulses – 260.58 lakh tonnes
6. Tur – 33.12 lakh tonnes
7. Gram – 122.67 lakh tonnes
8. Oilseeds – 413.55 lakh tonnes.

The Final Estimates of production of major crops for the year 2022-23 have been released by the Department of Agriculture and Farmers Welfare.

**Thus, the correct order from highest to lowest production is Rice > Wheat > Coarse Cereals > Pulses, making the answer (a) 1-2-3-4.**

**6.** *(d)* 1, 2 and 3

The Department of Agriculture and Farmers Welfare under **Ministry of Agriculture and Farmers Welfare** conducts Agriculture Censuses in India in collaboration with States/UTs.

**The first Agriculture Census in 1970-71,** India has conducted **ten Agriculture Censuses** so far and the present census with reference year 2020-21 is the **11th Census**

- **Statement 1 is correct:** The **Agricultural Census** is conducted every **five years** to gather data on the **structure of operational holdings** and other key indicators in the agriculture sector.
  - The census provides detailed information on the **ownership patterns** of agricultural holdings, including gender distribution, allowing insights into how many agricultural holdings are managed by women.
- **Statement 2 is correct:** The census recorded an increase in the number of **female-operated agricultural holdings,** reflecting a positive trend in women's participation in agriculture.
  - The **southern states** such as **Kerala** and **Tamil Nadu** have a relatively higher proportion of **female-operated agricultural holdings** compared to the northern states, reflecting changing gender roles in agriculture.
- **Statement 3 is correct:** The **10th Agricultural Census** revealed that more than 85% of agricultural holdings in India are **small and marginal** (less than 2 hectares in size).

**Therefore, the correct answer is (d) 1, 2 and 3.**

**7.** *(d)* 1, 2 and 3

- **Statement 1 is correct: Rajasthan** has the **highest average size** of operational holdings, with large landholdings being common due to extensive arid and semi-arid farming.

- **Statement 2 is correct: Bihar** and **West Bengal** recorded a very high number of **marginal and small landholdings**, primarily due to dense population and land fragmentation.
- **Statement 3 is correct: Uttar Pradesh** has the largest number of operational holdings among Indian states, contributing significantly to national agricultural activity.

**Therefore, the correct answer is (d) 1, 2 and 3.**

**8.** *(c)* All three pairs

- **Pair 1 is correct**: A marginal farmer operates **less than 1 hectare** of land, which makes up the majority of holdings in India.
- **Pair 2 is correct**: A small farmer operates between **1 to 2 hectares** of land.
- **Pair 3 is correct**: A large farmer operates **more than 10 hectares** of land, which is rare in India compared to marginal and small holdings.
  - **Medium Farmer**: A medium farmer operates between **2 to 10 hectares** of land.

**Thus, the correct answer is (c) All three pairs.**

**9.** *(a)* 3 - 4 - 1 - 2

- **The Priority Sector Lending** (PSL) norms were first introduced in **1969** as part of the nationalisation of banks in India and was the initiative by the **Reserve Bank of India (RBI)** aimed at providing adequate and timely credit to specific sectors like agriculture that are considered important for overall economic development, but often face credit shortages.
  - Under the PSL guidelines, banks are mandated to allocate a certain portion of their lending to these identified priority sectors.
- **NABARD** is an apex development financial institution in India, established on 12th July, 1982 by an act of Parliament. It was created with a mandate to promote sustainable and equitable agriculture and rural development. NABARD provides financial support and services to boost **agricultural productivity**, enhance **rural livelihoods** and promote **rural infrastructure development.**
- **The Kisan Credit Card** (KCC) scheme was launched in **1998** to provide farmers with timely and adequate credit support from the banking system. It was launched by the **NABARD** to meet the comprehensive credit needs of the agricultural sector.
- It provides **short-term credit for crop production** and other needs related to agriculture, such as buying seeds, fertilizers, pesticides, etc. and **also supports post-harvest expenses**, maintenance of farm assets, consumption needs and working capital requirements for allied agricultural activities like dairy, poultry, fisheries and more.
- **The Interest Subvention Scheme (ISS)** was introduced by the **Government of India** in the year **2006-07**. It was launched with the aim of providing **short-term credit** to farmers at **subsidised interest rates** to help them meet their agricultural needs and reduce their dependence on informal sources of credit.

**Thus, the correct answer is (a) 3 - 4 - 1 - 2.**

**10.** *(b)* Only two

- **Statement 1 is correct**: The **RBI report** highlighted that the **Interest Subvention Scheme** increased the share of short-term crop loans in agricultural credit from **51% to 75%** between 2000 and 2018.
- **Statement 2 is correct**: The report highlighted that 72% of agricultural households' credit needs were met by **institutional sources** such as banks while **28%** came from non-institutional sources like moneylenders.
- **Statement 3 is incorrect**: The **RBI report** pointed out that allied activities like **livestock and fisheries** received **only 10%** of agricultural credit, despite contributing **40%** to agricultural output.

**Thus, the correct answer is (b) Only two.**

**11.** *(a)* 3-2-1-4

- **Commercial Banks** contribute the largest share of total agricultural credit, given their widespread network and resources.
- **Cooperative Banks** also play a significant role in rural credit, particularly at the local level.
- **Regional Rural Banks (RRBs)** are important but contribute less compared to Commercial and Cooperative Banks.

- **Non-Banking Financial Companies (NBFCs)** provide credit but contribute the smallest share among the listed institutions.

**Thus, the correct answer is (a) 3-2-1-4.**

***12.*** *(c)* All three

- **Statement 1 is correct: NABARD** was established in **1982** following the recommendations of the **B. Sivaraman Committee**, specifically to promote agriculture and rural development by improving access to credit. The bank plays a crucial role in policy formulation and financial assistance for the agricultural sector.
- **Statement 2 is correct: NABARD** manages the **Rural Infrastructure Development Fund** (RIDF), which was set up to finance rural infrastructure projects. This fund is crucial for financing projects such as roads, bridges, irrigation and drinking water supply, improving the overall rural economy.
- **Statement 3 is correct: NABARD** provides **refinancing** to various institutions like **Regional Rural Banks (RRBs)** and **cooperative banks** to ensure the smooth flow of credit to agriculture and rural sectors, enhancing their ability to lend to farmers and rural enterprises.

**Thus, the correct answer is (c) All three.**

***13.*** *(a)* 1 and 2 only

- **Statement 1 is correct: NABARD** has been actively involved in **watershed development programmes** aimed at improving the management of water resources in rural areas, especially in rain-fed regions. The programmes focus on conserving water and enhancing soil productivity, leading to better agricultural outcomes and sustainability.
- **Statement 2 is correct: NABARD** spearheads the **Self-Help Group (SHG)-Bank linkage programme**, which connects self-help groups with formal financial institutions. It is regarded as the largest microfinance initiative globally, offering women and small communities' access to credit for entrepreneurial activities and rural development.
- **Statement 3 is incorrect:** NABARD is not directly responsible for rural housing initiatives under **Pradhan Mantri Awas Yojana (PMAY)**. While NABARD may support related rural infrastructure projects, PMAY is managed primarily by the **Ministry of Housing and Urban Affairs.**

**Thus, the correct answer is (a) 1 and 2 only.**

***14.*** *(c)* Only three

- **Rural Infrastructure Development Fund** (RIDF): Managed by **NABARD** to fund rural infrastructure projects.
- **National Adaptation Fund for Climate Change (NAFCC)**: Managed by **NABARD** to support adaptation measures to climate change in rural areas.
- **Micro Irrigation Fund (MIF)**: Managed by **NABARD** to support State Governments for expanding micro-irrigation coverage.
- **National Investment and Infrastructure Fund (NIIF)** is not managed by NABARD; it is managed by a separate entity, called National Investment and Infrastructure Fund Limited (NIIFL) to boost infrastructure funding.

**Thus, the correct answer is (c) Only three.**

***15.*** *(d)* 1, 2 and 3

- **Statement 1 is correct:** The **Rural Infrastructure Development Fund** (RIDF) was established in **1995-96** by the Government of India to provide funds for **rural infrastructure projects**, addressing gaps in areas like irrigation, roads, bridges and social infrastructure.
- **Statement 2 is correct: State Governments** are the **primary beneficiaries** of RIDF funds, using them to implement rural infrastructure projects that benefit the local population. **RIDF funds** are not provided directly to individual farmers.
- **Statement 3 is correct:** RIDF is funded by **contributions from commercial banks** that fall short of their **priority sector lending** targets. These funds are then used to finance rural infrastructure projects.

**Thus, the correct answer is (d) 1, 2 and 3.**

**16.** *(b)* 2 and 3 only

- **Statement 1 is incorrect:** The Kisan Credit Card can be issued by **commercial banks, Regional Rural Banks (RRBs)**, and **cooperative banks**, not just by commercial banks.
- **Statement 2 is correct:** The KCC can be used for **investment credit** to purchase **farm equipment** like tractors, irrigation pumps, etc.
- **Statement 3 is correct:** The KCC can be used for both **short-term crop loans** and for **allied activities** like **animal husbandry, fisheries** and **dairy farming.**

**Thus, the correct answer is (b) 2 and 3 only.**

**17.** *(c)* Only three

- **Construction of farmhouses:** KCC is not meant for financing the **construction of farmhouses** for residential purposes.
- **Crop production:** KCC can be used for **short-term credit** for crop production, helping farmers meet their immediate financial needs during the growing season.
- **Irrigation infrastructure:** KCC can be utilised for **investment credit** to improve **irrigation infrastructure**, including the construction of **tubewells.**
- **Farm machinery:** KCC allows the purchase of **tractors and farm machinery** to enhance productivity.

**Thus, the correct answer is (c) Only three.**

**18.** *(d)* 1, 2 and 3

The **Modified Interest Subvention Scheme (MISS)** an updated version of the traditional Interest Subvention Scheme (ISS) to provide financial assistance in the form of interest subvention to eligible sectors. The key goal of this scheme is to ensure that farmers, particularly small and marginal farmers, have access to affordable credit at reduced interest rates, while also extending benefits to other allied sectors.

**Statement 1 is correct:** Under the **Modified Interest Subvention Scheme,** farmers receive a **2% interest subvention** on short-term crop loans up to ₹ 3 lakh, reducing their interest burden.

- An **additional 3% subvention** is provided for **prompt repayment,** further lowering the effective interest rate for farmers who repay their loans on time.

**Statement 2 is correct:** The scheme covers loans for **allied agricultural activities,** such as **dairy, fisheries** and **animal husbandry,** supporting a broader spectrum of rural livelihoods.

**Statement 3 is correct:** The scheme applies to loans provided by **commercial banks, Regional Rural Banks (RRBs)** and **cooperative banks,** supporting a broad range of rural financial institutions.

**Thus, the correct answer is (d) 1, 2 and 3.**

**19.** *(a)* Only one

- **Statement 1 is incorrect:** Under PMFBY (launched in 2016), it is **mandatory for farmers** availing loans from financial institutions to take crop insurance. **PMFBY 2.0 (revised in 2020) made complete voluntary for all farmers in 2020.**
- **Statement 2 is incorrect:** Premium is paid as % of the sum assured or Actuarial Premium Rate (APR), whichever is less. APR is the premium rate set by insurance companies. Premium by farmers: 2% for Kharif crops, 1.5% for Rabi crops and **5% for commercial horticulture crops.**
  - The remaining premium is **subsidized by the government** (shared between the Central and State Governments), making the scheme affordable for farmers.
- **Statement 3 is correct:** PMFBY provides coverage for **pre-sowing and post-harvest losses caused by natural calamities such as** floods, drought and cyclones.

**Thus, the correct answer is (a) Only one.**

**20.** *(a)* 1 only

- **Statement 1 is correct:** PMFBY provides coverage for **localised calamities** such as **hailstorms, landslides** and **inundation.**
- **Statement 2 is incorrect:** When PMFBY launched in 2016, the **premium subsidy** under PMFBY is shared between the **Central** and **State Governments,** usually in equal proportions but the revised guidelines of

PMFBY in 2020 the Central Government provides a **larger share** of the subsidy, especially for northeastern states where the Central Government contributes **90%** and in other states, the ratio is **50:50**.

- **Statement 3 is incorrect:** Currently, **wild animal attacks** are **not covered** under the PMFBY scheme.

**Thus, the correct answer is (a) 1 only.**

**21.** *(b)* 1, 2 and 3 only

- **Option 1 is correct: Loanee farmers** are **mandatorily covered** under PMFBY as part of their loan agreements with banks.
- **Option 2 is correct: Non-loanee farmers** can voluntarily opt for coverage under PMFBY.
- **Option 3 is correct: Sharecroppers and tenant farmers** are also eligible for coverage.
- **Option 4 is incorrect:** The **PMFBY** specifically provides **crop insurance** for farmers growing **notified food crops, oilseeds,** and certain **commercial** and **horticultural crops**. It does not cover allied agricultural activities such as **fisheries, animal husbandry** or **dairy farming**.
  - For allied activities, other government programmes like the **Modified Interest Subvention Scheme (MISS)** may provide financial support, but they are not covered under PMFBY.

**Therefore, the correct answer is (b) 1, 2 and 3 only.**

**22.** *(b)* 1, 2 and 4 only

- **Statement 1 is correct: Remote sensing technology** is widely used for **crop loss assessment**, enabling accurate and efficient identification of areas affected by natural calamities.
- **Statement 2 is correct:** Drones are increasingly being used for **real-time crop monitoring**, providing a detailed assessment of crop health and losses.
- **Statement 3 is incorrect:** Although **blockchain technology** could be explored to streamline the claim settlement process, making it more transparent and efficient but its usage in **claim settlement** under PMFBY is not yet implemented.
- **Statement 4 is correct: Smartphones** are used for **direct data collection** from farmers, improving the accuracy of information and speeding up processes like registration and claim filing.

**Therefore, the correct answer is (b) 1, 2 and 4 only.**

**23.** *(a)* **Water Use Efficiency (WUE)** refers to the **crop yield per unit of water used**, emphasising maximising crop production while minimising water consumption. It is not limited to any particular irrigation system and applies broadly across various techniques, including surface, sprinkler and drip irrigation.

- The focus of WUE is **optimising water usage** rather than merely reducing it, ensuring that crop productivity is maintained or improved.

**Thus, the correct answer is (a).**

**24.** *(c)* All three pairs

- **Pair 1 is correctly matched: Tubewell irrigation** requires the construction of **deep wells** to access underground water resources. It is widely used method in India (Punjab and Haryana regions) for extracting groundwater to irrigate agricultural fields.
- **Pair 2 is correctly matched: Canal Irrigation** works best in regions with abundant **river flow** and large **reservoir systems** like Upper Ganges Canal (Uttar Pradesh), Sutlej-Yamuna Link Canal (Punjab and Haryana).
- **Pair 3 is correctly matched: Tank irrigation** is a traditional method of water storage, commonly used in **southern India.**

**Thus, the correct answer is (c) All three pairs.**

**25.** *(a)* 1 only

- **Statement 1 is correct:** PMKSY is a **centrally sponsored scheme (CSS)** with funding shared between the Central and State Governments, focusing on improving irrigation and water-use efficiency in agriculture. PMKSY is implemented with a **funding pattern of 60:40 between the Central Government** and **State Governments** for general states. For **North- eastern** states and **Himalayan regions,** the funding pattern is **90:10** between the centre and the state. **Union Territories** are fully funded by the **Central Government.**

- **Statement 2 is incorrect:** The **Accelerated Irrigation Benefit Programme (AIBP)** focuses on **completing long-pending major and medium irrigation projects** to increase water availability. The **Per Drop More Crop** component promotes **micro-irrigation techniques** like drip and sprinkler irrigation to ensure efficient water usage at the farm level.
- **Statement 3 is incorrect:** PMKSY is implemented by **multiple ministries,** including the **Ministry of Jal Shakti, Ministry of Agriculture and Farmers' Welfare** and the **Ministry of Rural Development,** in a convergent manner.

**Thus, the correct answer is (a) 1 only.**

**26.** *(a)* Only one pair

Components of PMKSY:

PMKSY has **four major components** designed to cover different aspects of irrigation and water management:

- **Accelerated Irrigation Benefits Programme (AIBP):** This component focuses on accelerating the completion of major and medium irrigation projects that have been pending for a long time.
- **Har Khet Ko Pani (HKKP):** The focus of this component is to ensure that every farm gets water.
- **Per Drop More Crop (PDMC):** This component promotes water-saving technologies such as drip irrigation, sprinkler irrigation and other micro-irrigation methods.
- **Watershed Development:** This component focuses on improving the rain-fed areas by developing watersheds, promoting soil conservation, recharging groundwater and building water-harvesting structures.
- **Pair 1 is incorrect matched: Har Khet Ko Pani** ensures water access to every farm using surface and groundwater resources.
- **Pair 2 is incorrectly matched: Per Drop More Crop** aims at improving **water-use efficiency** through technologies like **drip and sprinkler irrigation.**
- **Pair 3 is correctly matched: Watershed Development** focuses on **soil and water conservation** through **watershed management** techniques.

**Therefore, the correct answer is (a) Only one pair.**

**27.** *(d)* All four pairs

The Pradhan Mantri Krishi Sinchayee Yojana (PMKSY) involves multiple components that are coordinated and implemented by different ministries.

- **Pair 1 is correctly matched: Har Khet Ko Pani** component of PMKSY aims to ensure water access to every farm and is implemented by the **Ministry of Jal Shakti.**
- **Pair 2 is correctly matched: Per Drop More Crop** component focuses on improving water use efficiency at the farm level and is under the **Ministry of Agriculture and Farmers' Welfare.**
- **Pair 3 is correctly matched: Watershed Development** component focuses on soil and water conservation and is handled by the **Ministry of Rural Development.**
- **Pair 4 is correctly matched: Accelerated Irrigation Benefit Programme (AIBP)** is aimed at expediting irrigation projects and is under the **Ministry of Jal Shakti.**

Thus, these ministries work together to ensure the effective implementation of PMKSY, focusing on irrigation expansion, water-use efficiency, and sustainable water management practices across India.

**Therefore, the correct answer is (d) All four pairs.**

**28.** *(c)* The Micro-Irrigation Fund is operated by NABARD and aims to support the adoption of micro-irrigation technologies.

- The Micro-Irrigation Fund (MIF) was set up in 2018 to promote the adoption and expansion of micro-irrigation practices, particularly drip and sprinkler irrigation, across the country.
- The fund aims to boost water-use efficiency in agriculture and ensure sustainable agricultural practices, especially in water-scarce regions.
- The MIF is managed by **NABARD** (National Bank for Agriculture and Rural Development) to promote the expansion and adoption of **micro-irrigation technologies** like drip and sprinkler systems, primarily

under the **Per Drop More Crop** component of the **PMKSY.**

- It is not entirely financed by the Central Government alone and it covers all categories of farmers, not just small and marginal farmers.

**Thus, option (c) is the correct answer.**

**29.** *(c)* All three

- **Statement 1 is correct**: India is indeed the **second-largest consumer** of fertilizers globally, after China. Fertilizers play a crucial role in Indian agriculture due to the country's large agricultural sector and population. Fertilizer consumption is concentrated on crops like **rice, wheat, sugarcane and cotton,** which are heavily dependent on chemical fertilizers for higher yields.
- **Statement 2 is correct**: India imports raw materials such as **ammonia** and **phosphoric acid** for domestic fertilizer production, as well as finished fertilizers like **urea, potash,** and **DAP (Diammonium Phosphate)**. India imports a large quantity of **Muriate of Potash** (MoP), primarily from countries like **Belarus, Canada** and **Jordan.**
- **Statement 3 is correct**: India imports a significant amount of **phosphatic fertilizers,** with major suppliers including **Morocco and China**. In fact, Morocco is a leading exporter of phosphate rock, which is a key component in producing phosphatic fertilizers.

**Thus, the correct answer is (c) All three.**

**30.** *(a)* 1 and 2 only

- **Statement 1 is correct**: The **Maximum Retail Price (MRP)** of urea is fixed by the government, while the prices of **phosphatic and potassic (P&K) fertilizers** are **decontrolled** under the **Nutrient-Based Subsidy (NBS)** scheme.
- **Statement 2 is correct: NBS scheme introduced in 2010** to encourage the balanced use of fertilizers. This scheme covers **phosphatic** and **potassic fertilizers,** where the government provides a fixed subsidy per nutrient (N, P, K, S) basis and manufacturers are allowed to determine the selling price.
- The subsidy for **urea,** however, is still determined separately, and its price remains fully controlled by the government.
- **Statement 3 is incorrect:** Under the NBS scheme, the **government does not set retail prices** of P&K fertilizers, as they are decontrolled.

**Thus, the correct answer is (a) 1 and 2 only.**

**31.** *(a)* 1, 2 and 4 only

- **Option 1 is correct: Ammonium Sulphate** is a **nitrogenous fertilizer** and is covered under the Nutrient-Based Subsidy (NBS) regime, where subsidies are provided based on its nitrogen (N) and sulphur (S) content.
- **Option 2 is correct:** DAP is a major **phosphatic fertilizer** subsidised under the NBS regime. The subsidy is provided based on its nitrogen (N) and phosphorus (P) content.
- **Option 3 is incorrect: Urea** is not included under the NBS scheme and is subsidised separately under price control.
- **Option 4 is correct:** NPK complex fertilizers are subsidised under the **Nutrient-Based Subsidy (NBS)** regime based on their nitrogen (N), phosphorus (P) and potassium (K) content.

Thus, only **Ammonium Sulphate, Di-Ammonium Phosphate (DAP)** and **NPK Complex Fertilisers** are covered under the **Nutrient-Based Subsidy** (NBS) regime.

**Therefore, the correct answer is (a) 1, 2 and 4 only.**

**32.** *(b)* 2-1-3

In the Union Budget for FY 2024-25, the government has **allocated ₹ 1.64 trillion for fertilizer subsidies,** which is lower than the revised estimate of ₹ 1.88 trillion for FY 2023-24.

- The **Urea subsidy** has been allocated ₹ 1.22 trillion for FY 2024-25, making it the highest allocation.
- The **Nutrient-Based Subsidy (NBS)** for **P&K fertilizers** has been allocated ₹ 45,000 crore.
- The **organic fertilizer subsidy** has a comparatively smaller allocation.

Thus, based on the recent data for fertilizer subsidy allocation:

- **Urea subsidy:** 71%
- **Nutrient-Based Subsidy (P&K Fertilizers):** 25%
- **Organic fertiliser subsidy:** 4%

**Thus, the correct answer is (b) 2-1-3.**

**33.** *(a)* 1 and 2 only

**The Soil Health Card Scheme** was in 2015 with the objective of promoting **balanced use of fertilizers and improving soil health across the country.** The scheme provides farmers with Soil Health Cards (SHCs) that contain information about the nutrient status of their soil and specific recommendations to improve soil productivity.

- **Statement 1 is correct:** The **Soil Health Card Scheme** provides farmers with information on the **nutrient status of their soil** along with **recommendations** on how to improve fertility by using the right amount of fertilizers.
- **Statement 2 is correct:** The scheme is implemented by the **Ministry of Agriculture and Farmers' Welfare** in collaboration with **state governments,** making it a joint initiative.
- **Statement 3 is incorrect:** The scheme covers **all farmers,** not just those from **rainfed areas.**

By 2022, the government had issued **22 crore Soil Health Cards** to farmers across India in two phases. This has been instrumental in improving awareness among farmers about soil health management practices.

**Therefore, the correct answer is (a) 1 and 2 only.**

**34.** *(c)* 1, 2, 3 and 4

The collected soil samples are tested in a soil testing laboratory for various parameters including:

- **Macro-nutrients** like Nitrogen (N), Phosphorus (P), and Potassium (K)
- **Secondary** nutrients like **Sulphur** (S): It is essential for the synthesis of amino acids and proteins in plants.
- **Micro-nutrients** like Zinc (Zn), **Iron (Fe),** Copper (Cu), **Manganese (Mn),** and Boron (B): Iron is a crucial micronutrient that aids in chlorophyll synthesis and overall plant metabolism and Magnesium is a part of the chlorophyll molecule and is vital for photosynthesis.
- **Soil pH and Electrical Conductivity** (EC)
- **Organic Carbon (OC) content:** It is an indicator of soil fertility and plays a key role in improving soil structure and water retention.

This test result of the Soil Health Card is valid for **two years,** after which the soil is retested and updated recommendations are provided.

**Therefore, the correct answer is (c) 1, 2, 3 and 4.**

**35.** *(b)* Only two

The **PM-PRANAM Scheme** (Prime Minister Programme for Restoration, Awareness, Nourishment and Amelioration of Mother Earth) was announced as part of the **2023-24 Union Budget** with the primary objective of reducing the use of chemical fertilisers and promoting balanced and sustainable agriculture practices across the country.

- **Statement 1 is correct:** The **PM-PRANAM scheme** to promote sustainable agricultural practices. The scheme encourages states to reduce their consumption of chemical fertilizers, such as urea and DAP. The states that show a reduction in the use of these fertilizers compared to previous years are provided with **incentives** by the Central Government.
- **Statement 2 is incorrect:** The savings from reduced fertilizer use are not shared **directly with farmers** but are distributed to State Governments as an incentive.
- **Statement 3 is correct:** The scheme promotes the use of **organic and bio-fertilizers** as alternatives to chemical fertilizers, thereby reducing the dependency on synthetic fertilizers and ensuring sustainable farming practices that are environmentally friendly.

**Therefore, the correct answer is (b) Only two.**

**36.** *(c)* Only three

Nano Liquid Urea is a new innovation in the agricultural sector aimed at enhancing the **efficiency of nitrogen fertilizers.** It is developed to **address issues of nitrogen loss in conventional urea** applications and to promote more sustainable agricultural practices.

- **Option 1 is correct: Increased nutrient use efficiency**: Nano Liquid Urea has a higher absorption rate, improving the efficiency of nutrient uptake.
- **Option 2 is correct: Reduced fertilizer usage:** Nano Liquid Urea requires lower quantities compared to conventional urea.
- **Option 3 is correct: Improved crop productivity**: The use of Nano Urea results in increased productivity due to efficient nutrient absorption.
- **Option 4 is incorrect: Increased nitrogen emissions are incorrect**: Nano Liquid Urea actually **reduces nitrogen emissions.** It is designed to reduce nitrogen losses through volatilisation and leaching, thereby decreasing nitrogen emissions into the environment.

**Therefore, the correct answer is (c) Only three.**

**37.** *(a)* Urea Gold is a specialised fertilizer containing a blend of urea and micronutrients to enhance soil health and crop productivity.

**Urea Gold** is developed by Rashtriya Chemicals and Fertilizers Ltd (RCF) as new variety of urea fertilizer **to address sulfur deficiencies** in Indian soils and improve nitrogen use efficiency (NUE).

Here are some key features:

- **Urea Gold** is a **fortified fertilizer** that combines **urea** with **sulphur**. This combination not only supplies nitrogen but also provides essential micronutrients like sulphur, which is crucial for plant health.
- The addition of sulphur enhances **nutrient uptake efficiency**, promoting better crop productivity. This also helps address sulphur deficiency in soils, which is common in many agricultural regions of India.
- Unlike traditional urea, Urea Gold ensures **balanced fertilization**, improving soil health and productivity in the long-term.
- **Urea Gold is recognised as a more sustainable option for boosting crop yields while maintaining soil health.**

**Thus, option (a) is the correct answer.**

**38.** *(d)* All four

**Neem Coated Urea** (NCU) is a specialised form of urea that has been coated with neem oil to improve its efficiency and reduce environmental concerns associated with conventional urea. The initiative was introduced **to address issues of excessive urea usage, nutrient loss and environmental degradation.**

- **Reduces fertilizer consumption**: Since nitrogen is used more efficiently, less urea is required for the same crop yield. The slower release of nitrogen means that farmers can use less urea without negatively impacting crop productivity. This helps reduce **over-reliance on urea**, which has been a problem in Indian agriculture.
- **Enhances crop yield**: By ensuring a steady release of nitrogen, Neem Coated Urea improves crop productivity.
- **Increased Nitrogen Use Efficiency** (NUE): Neem Coated Urea reduces the loss of nitrogen to the environment, improving nitrogen use efficiency.
- **Prevents diversion**: The neem coating makes urea unsuitable for industrial purposes, preventing its misuse in non-agricultural sectors.

**Thus, the correct answer is (d) All four.**

**39.** *(a)* 1 and 3 only

- **Statement 1 is correct: The Minimum Support Price (MSP)** is announced by the Cabinet Committee on Economic Affairs (CCEA), based on the recommendations of the Commission for Agricultural Costs and Prices (CACP). This happens before the sowing seasons (Kharif and Rabi) to ensure that farmers are informed in advance about the prices they can expect for their crops.
- **Statement 2 is incorrect**: MSP is the price at which the government guarantees to buy the crops if the market price falls below it. However, it **does not guarantee that the market price will always be lower than MSP.** Sometimes, farmers might sell their produce at a price higher than the MSP in the open market, depending on market conditions.
- **Statement 3 is correct**: MSP is declared for both Kharif and Rabi crops, covering a wide variety of crops such as rice, wheat, pulses and oilseeds.

**Thus, the correct answer is (a) 1 and 3 only.**

**40.** *(c)* Only three

The Minimum Support Price (MSP) covers a variety of crops in India across both Kharif and Rabi seasons, ensuring farmers receive a minimum price for their produce. The following categories of crops are generally **covered under MSP:**

- **Kharif Crops:**

1. **Cereals:** Paddy (Rice), Maize, Jowar (Sorghum), Bajra (Pearl Millet) and Ragi (Finger Millet)
2. **Pulses:** Tur (Arhar or Pigeon Pea), Moong (Green Gram) and Urad (Black Gram)
3. **Oilseeds:** Groundnut, Soybean, Sunflower Seed, Sesamum and Nigerseed
4. **Commercial Crops:** Cotton and Jute

- **Rabi Crops:**

1. **Cereals:** Wheat, Barley
2. **Pulses:** Gram (Chickpea) and Masur (Lentil)
3. **Oilseeds:** Rapeseed and Mustard, Safflower

- **Other Commercial Crops: Sugarcane** is not covered under MSP; instead, its price is set by the Fair and **Remunerative Price (FRP)** system.

**Copra** is covered under the Minimum Support Price (MSP) in India. The MSP is announced for both Ball Copra and Milling Copra.

**Thus, the correct answer is (c) Only three.**

**41.** *(a)* MSP ensures farmers are paid a minimum price even when the market price is lower, while FRP sets a price for sugarcane based on recovery of sugar content.

- **MSP** is designed to ensure that farmers are not affected by low market prices for a variety of crops. It is primarily designed to ensure that farmers receive a **minimum income** for their crops and are protected against market fluctuations.
- FRP is specifically calculated for **sugarcane pricing** and is based on the **recovery rate** of sugar from sugarcane. The recovery rate refers to the amount of sugar extracted from sugarcane during the production process. The higher the recovery rate, the higher the FRP. It ensures that sugarcane farmers receive a fair price for their produce, factoring in production costs, margins and sugar recovery rates.

**Thus, the correct answer is (a).**

**42.** *(b)* 1 and 3 only

**Fair and Remunerative Price (FRP)** is determined by the Central Government based on factors like sugar recovery rates, cost of production and other inputs to ensure a fair return to farmers.

- **Statement 1 is correct: Fair and Remunerative Price (FRP) is a legally binding** price that sugar mills are required to pay to sugarcane farmers. This legal mandate ensures that farmers receive a minimum price for their produce, regardless of fluctuations in market prices.
- **Statement 2 is incorrect:** FRP is revised annually by the **Cabinet Committee on Economic Affairs (CCEA)** based on the recommendations of the CACP.
- **Statement 3 is correct:** The **State Advised Price** (SAP) is a price that some state governments, especially in major sugarcane-growing states like Uttar Pradesh and Tamil Nadu, set over and above the FRP. The SAP is typically higher and takes into consideration local factors, such as higher production costs or regional demands from farmers.

**Thus, the correct answer is (b) 1 and 3 only.**

**43.** *(a)* The **Sugarcane (Control) Order, 1966,** legally enforces sugar mills to pay FRP to farmers within a specified time.

The **Sugarcane (Control) Order, 1966** under the **Essential Commodities Act** mandates the payment of the **Fair and Remunerative Price** (FRP) to sugarcane farmers.

- Sugar mills are legally required to pay FRP to farmers within **14 days** of procurement. Failure to do so results in interest payments for the delayed amount.
- The **APMC Act** governs agricultural markets but does not regulate FRP payments for sugarcane and the **Competition Commission of India** deals with market competition and does not enforce agricultural pricing mechanisms.

**Thus, option (a) is the correct answer.**

**44.** *(c)* All three

The **Commission for Agricultural Costs and Prices** (CACP) recommends the **Minimum Support Price** (MSP) for various crops based on different types of cost calculations.

- **Cost A2**: All the direct costs incurred by farmers for the cultivation of crops. It covers items such as cost of seeds, fertilizers, pesticides, and irrigation, hired labour, Fuel, electricity and other inputs, Interest on working capital etc.
- **Cost A2+FL: Cost A2** plus the **imputed value of family labour.** In addition to the direct expenses, it accounts for the value of the labour provided by family members, even if no actual payment is made.
- Cost C2: This is the most comprehensive cost and includes:
  - **Cost A2+FL**
  - Value of rent on owned land
  - Imputed interest on owned fixed capital assets like machinery
- **Pair 1 is correctly matched:** A2 refers to the actual **paid-out costs** such as seeds, fertilizers, hired labour, etc.
- **Pair 2 is correctly matched:** A2+FL includes the **imputed value of family labour** along with A2 costs.
- **Pair 3 is correctly matched:** C2 is the most comprehensive, adding imputed rent and interest on owned land to A2+FL.

**Thus, the correct answer is (c) All three.**

**45.** *(d)* 1, 2, 3 and 4

- The Pradhan Mantri Annadata Aay Sanrakshan Abhiyan (PM-AASHA) is an umbrella scheme launched in 2018 to ensure fair price realisation for farmers. The scheme is designed to boost the income of farmers by providing a remunerative price for their produce and aims to tackle the issue of distress sales.

**PM-AASHA have the components of Price Support Scheme (PSS), Price Stabilisation Fund (PSF), Price Deficit Payment Scheme (PDPS) and Market Intervention Scheme (MIS) and Pilot of Private Procurement and Stockist Scheme (PPSS).**

- **Price Support Scheme (PSS)**: the government directly procures pulses, oilseeds and copra from farmers at the Minimum Support Price (MSP) through nodal agencies like the Food Corporation of India (FCI) and NAFED.
- **Price Deficiency Payment Scheme (PDPS)**: Under this components farmer are paid the difference between the MSP and the selling price in the open market. The scheme is implemented for crops like oilseeds, where direct procurement may not be feasible.
- **Market Intervention Scheme (MIS)**: This scheme allows the government to procure surplus agricultural commodities at MSP to prevent a sharp decline in prices.
- **Pilot of Private Procurement and Stockist Scheme (PPSS)**: In this, private sector entities are encouraged to procure crops at MSP. This scheme was introduced as a pilot project in selected states to improve market competitiveness.

**Thus, the correct answer is (d) 1, 2, 3 and 4.**

**46.** *(a)* PDPS compensates farmers for the difference between the Minimum Support Price (MSP) and the actual market price of crops, without any physical procurement of crops by the government.

- The **Price Deficiency Payment Scheme (PDPS)** ensures that farmers are compensated for the **difference between the MSP** and the market price. However, unlike the **Price Support Scheme (PSS)**, no physical procurement of crops is involved.
- The scheme primarily targets **oilseeds** under the **PM-AASHA** umbrella. It is aimed at ensuring farmers of oilseeds receive compensation if market prices fall below the MSP.
- This scheme helps protect farmers from adverse price fluctuations in the oilseeds market without the need for direct procurement by the government.
- This helps avoid procurement and storage costs while ensuring that farmers receive the guaranteed price.

**Therefore, the correct answer is (a).**

**47.** *(c)* Only three

- **Food Corporation of India (FCI)**: The Food Corporation of India was setup under the **Food Corporation's Act 1964**, in order to fulfil following objectives of the Food Policy which include **effective price support** operations for safeguarding the interests of the farmers, **distribution of foodgrains** throughout the country for public distribution system and **maintaining satisfactory level of operational and buffer stocks** of foodgrains to ensure National Food Security. FCI is mainly responsible for the procurement of **wheat and rice**.
- **Cotton Corporation of India (CCI)**: CCI is involved in the procurement of **cotton** from farmers.
- **National Agricultural Cooperative Marketing Federation (NAFED)**: NAFED is involved in procuring **pulses, oilseeds and other crops** under schemes like PSS.
- **National Cooperative Development Corporation (NCDC)**: NCDC is **not directly involved** in procurement; its role is more related to providing financial and technical assistance to cooperative societies, including those involved in agricultural marketing and procurement.

**Thus, the correct answer is (c) Only three.**

**48.** *(a)* 1 and 2 only

**The Agricultural Produce Market Committee (APMC) Acts** regulate the buying and selling of agricultural products in designated market areas, commonly referred to as mandis. The purpose of these acts is to ensure fair trade practices, protect farmers from exploitation, and ensure that they receive remunerative prices for their produce.

- **Statement 1 is correct**: The regulation of **agricultural markets** falls under the **State List** in the **Seventh Schedule** of the Indian Constitution, giving State Governments the authority to regulate agricultural trade.
- **Statement 2 is correct**: State Governments can notify **mandis** or regulated markets for the sale of agricultural produce under the APMC Acts.
- **Statement 3 is incorrect**: In recent years, states have introduced reforms to the APMC Acts, allowing farmers to sell their produce outside the mandis through direct sales or private markets.

**Thus, the correct answer is (a) 1 and 2 only.**

**49.** *(b)* Only two

**National Agriculture Market (e-NAM)** is a pan-India electronic trading portal launched by the Government of India in April 2016. It aims to create a unified national market for agricultural commodities by integrating existing Agricultural Produce Market Committee (APMC) markets across the country. The platform facilitates transparent and competitive online trading, ensuring farmers get a better price for their produce.

- **Statement 1 is correct**: e-NAM is implemented by the **Small Farmers' Agribusiness Consortium (SFAC)**, which is under the Ministry of Agriculture and Farmers' Welfare.
- **Statement 2 is correct**: e-NAM is a **centrally sponsored scheme** designed to help farmers access markets across India *via* an online platform.
- **Statement 3 is incorrect**: e-NAM facilitates online trading, but prices are **market- driven** and transactions are not guaranteed at MSP prices.

**Therefore, the correct answer is (b) Only two.**

**50.** *(a)* A fund established to upgrade and modernise existing agricultural markets and infrastructure.

- The **Agri-Market Infrastructure Fund (AMIF)** was set up with the objective of **modernizing and upgrading agricultural markets** (such as APMC mandis), including developing **infrastructure like cold storage, warehousing**, and other market facilities to improve market efficiency and reduce post-harvest losses.
- It does not involve loans for setting up private markets or mandis, nor does it guarantee MSP for all crops.

**Therefore, the correct answer is (a).**

**51.** *(d)* 1, 2 and 3

- **Statement 1 is correct**: The beneficiaries receive a 3% interest subvention on loans up to ₹ 2 crore, with a maximum repayment period of 7 years. Additionally, the scheme covers the reimbursement of credit guarantee fees paid by banks.
- **Statement 2 is correct**: The fund focuses on developing **post-harvest infrastructure,** including **processing units and cold chains,** to reduce post-harvest losses.
- **Statement 3 is correct** The AIF scheme is implemented by the **Ministry of Agriculture and Farmers' Welfare**, which oversees the allocation of funds, monitoring of projects, and ensuring the benefits reach the intended beneficiaries.

**Therefore, the correct answer is (d) 1, 2 and 3.**

**52.** *(a)* 1 and 2 only

- **Statement 1 is correct: FPOs** are legal entities formed by groups of farmers to help them overcome challenges related to inputs, production, marketing and financing. It can be registered as either **companies** or **cooperative societies**, providing flexibility in how farmer groups choose to organise themselves.
- **Statement 2 is correct**: Small Farmers' Agri-business Consortium (SFAC) is instrumental in promoting and facilitating the formation of FPOs in India.
- **Statement 3 is incorrect**: Since, the average farm size declined from 2.3 hectares (ha) in 1970-71 to 1.08 ha in 2015-16. The share of small and marginal farmers increased from 70% in 1980-81 to 86% in 2015-16. FPOs are designed to support **small and marginal farmers** as well, providing them access to inputs and markets collectively.

**Therefore, the correct answer is (a) 1 and 2 only.**

**53.** *(d)* 1, 2 and 3

- **Statement 1 is correct**: NWRs can be used by farmers to **secure loans** from banks by pledging the receipt as collateral. NWRs help farmers avoid distress sales by providing them the flexibility to store their produce and sell when market conditions are more favourable.
- **Statement 2 is correct**: NWRs are issued by warehouses registered with the **Warehousing Development and Regulatory Authority (WDRA)**, ensuring regulatory oversight.
- **Statement 3 is correct**: NWRs are **negotiable instruments**, meaning they can be transferred or traded, providing **liquidity** to farmers and traders.

**Thus, the correct answer is (d) 1, 2 and 3.**

**54.** *(c)* All three

- **Statement 1 is correct**: India has consistently been a **trade surplus country** in terms of agricultural products, meaning its exports exceed its imports.
- **Statement 2 is correct**: India's agricultural exports are still dominated by **low-value commodities**, including **bulk grains** and **raw sugar**, which limits its value-added potential.
- **Statement 3 is correct**: India's share of high-value and value-added agricultural products is lower compared to China and the US, where these products make up a larger portion of exports.

**Thus, the correct answer is (c) All three.**

**55.** *(a)* 1 and 2 only

- **Statement 1 is correct**: India ranks as the **second-largest agricultural producer** with the **largest arable land** and **second-largest irrigated area** after China.
- **Statement 2 is correct**: India's share in global agricultural exports was recorded at **2.4%** in 2022.
- **Statement 3 is incorrect**: India retains eighth position in global agriculture exports in 2023 as per WTO (August 2024).

**Thus, the correct answer is (a) 1 and 2 only.**

**56.** *(b)* 2-1-3-4

- **Marine products** have consistently been the top agricultural export from India.
- **Rice (other than basmati)** follows closely, with high demand in several regions, particularly Africa.
- **Sugar** is also a significant export but lower in value compared to marine products and rice.
- **Fresh fruits** are exported in smaller quantities compared to these bulk commodities.

**Thus, the correct answer is (b) 2-1-3-4.**

**57.** *(d)* All four

The largest importers of India's agricultural products, as of 2023-24 (until January 2024), were the USA, China, UAE and Bangladesh. During this period, the USA was the largest importer of Indian agricultural products at US$ 4.20 billion with a share of 10.89% of the total exports. The USA and China were the major importers of India's marine products.

**Thus, option (d) is the correct answer.**

**58.** *(b)* 1 and 3 only

- **Statement 1 is correct:** The **Agricultural and Processed Food Products Export Development Authority (APEDA)** is responsible for promoting the export of both agricultural and processed food products from India. This includes various categories such as fruits, vegetables, cereals and processed foods like juices and snacks.
- **Statement 2 is incorrect:** APEDA operates under the **Ministry of Commerce and Industry**, not under the Ministry of Agriculture and Farmers' Welfare.
- **Statement 3 is correct:** APEDA provides financial assistance to exporters for developing export-oriented infrastructure like pack houses, cold storage and quality control labs.

**Therefore, the correct answer is (b) 1 and 3 only.**

**59.** *(b)* 1 and 3 only

- **Statement 1 is correct:** The Essential Commodities Act allows the Central Government to regulate the supply, distribution and trade of commodities declared as essential, helping to ensure availability to the public at fair prices.
- **Statement 2 is incorrect:** While food items are commonly listed, the Act also includes other commodities like petroleum, fertilizers, and drugs that can be declared essential when necessary.
- **Statement 3 is correct:** The Act aims to prevent the hoarding and black marketing of essential items, ensuring fair distribution, especially in times of shortage.

**Thus, the correct answer is (b) 1 and 3 only.**

**60.** *(c)* Only three

- **Option 1 is enforceable:** The Essential Commodities Act empowers the government to set maximum retail prices for essential commodities to make them affordable and prevent price manipulation.
- **Option 2 is enforceable:** The Act allows the imposition of stock limits to prevent hoarding and ensure that essential goods remain available in the market.
- **Option 3 is not enforceable:** The Act does not apply to non-essential luxury items, as it primarily focuses on essential goods critical for public welfare.
- **Option 4 is enforceable:** The Act authorises the government to regulate the distribution of essential items to ensure equitable access for the population.

**Thus, the correct answer is (c) Only three.**

## Past Learning (Answers)

| | | | | | | | | | |
|---|---|---|---|---|---|---|---|---|---|
| 1 (d) | 2 (b) | 3 (c) | 4 (a) | 5 (b) | 6 (b) | 7 (c) | 8 (d) | 9 (b) | 10 (b) |
| 11 (d) | 12 (b) | 13 (c) | 14 (a) | 15 (b) | 16 (b) | 17 (c) | 18 (c) | 19 (b) | 20 (a) |
| 21 (b) | | | | | | | | | |

CHAPTER 14

# Industrial Sector

## Assessment Round

### Topic 1 : Indices to Measure Industrial Growth

**1.** Consider the following measures:
1. Index of Industrial Production (IIP)
2. Annual Survey of Industries (ASI)
3. Purchasing Managers' Index (PMI)
4. Gross Domestic Product (GDP) data
5. Index of Core Industries (ICI)

How many of the given above measures are primarily used to estimate industrial production?

(a) Only two (b) Only three
(c) Only four (d) All five

**2.** With reference to the Purchasing Managers' Index (PMI), consider the following statements:
1. It is released on a monthly basis and covers both the manufacturing and services sectors.
2. It is calculated by the Ministry of Finance, Government of India.
3. PMI serves as a leading indicator of economic activity.

How many of the statements given above is/are correct?

(a) Only one (b) Only two
(c) All three (d) None

**3.** Consider the following statements about PMI:
1. It helps in predicting future trends in the manufacturing sector.
2. A PMI value above 50 indicates that the sector is expanding.
3. PMI readings are based on qualitative responses from purchasing managers.

Which of the given statements is/are correct?

(a) 1 and 3 only (b) 1 and 2 only
(c) 2 and 3 only (d) 1, 2 and 3

**4.** Consider the following criteria:
1. New Orders
2. Inflation Rate
3. Production Output
4. Employment
5. Supplier Deliveries

How many of the above criteria is/are actually included in the PMI calculation?

(a) Only two (b) Only three
(c) Only four (d) All five

**5.** With reference to the 'Index of Industrial Production (IIP)', consider the following statements:
1. It is released on a monthly basis by the Ministry of Commerce and Industry.
2. It measures the industrial production in three sectors-Mining, Manufacturing and Electricity.
3. The base year for the IIP calculation is 2011-12.

How many of the statements given above is/are correct?

(a) Only one (b) Only two
(c) All three (d) None

**6.** Which sector has the highest weightage in the Index of Industrial Production (IIP)?

(a) Mining (b) Electricity
(c) Manufacturing (d) Construction

**7.** With reference to the Index of Core Industries (ICI), consider the following statements:

1. It is released by the Ministry of Finance.
2. The Core Industries Index includes eight key sectors.
3. The Core Industries collectively contribute more than 50% to the total Index of Industrial Production (IIP).

Which of the given statements is/are correct?

(a) 1 and 2 only (b) 2 only
(c) 1 and 3 only (d) 2 and 3 only

**8.** Arrange the following sectors under the Index of Core Industries (ICI) in the order of their decreasing weightage:

1. Electricity
2. Coal
3. Refinery Products
4. Steel

Select the correct answer using the codes given below:

(a) 3 - 4 - 1 - 2 (b) 1 - 3 - 2 - 4
(c) 3 - 1 - 4 - 2 (d) 4 - 2 - 3 - 1

**9.** With reference to the 'Annual Survey of Industries (ASI)', consider the following statements:

1. It is the most comprehensive source of industrial statistics in India.
2. The survey covers only manufacturing industries registered under the Factories Act, 1948.
3. ASI is conducted on an annual basis by the Ministry of Commerce and Industry.

How many of the statements given above is/are correct?

(a) Only one (b) Only two
(c) All three (d) None

**10.** Arrange the following sub-sectors of the industrial sector in the correct decreasing order of their GDP contribution:

1. Construction
2. Electricity, Gas and Water Supply
3. Manufacturing
4. Mining

Select the correct answer using the codes given below:

(a) 3 - 1 - 4 - 2 (b) 1 - 3 - 2 - 4
(c) 3 - 1 - 2 - 4 (d) 1 - 4 - 3 - 2

## Topic 2 : Industrial Policies

**11.** With reference to the various Industrial Policies in India since Independence, consider the following statements:

1. Industrial Policy Resolution of 1948 marked the beginning of the mixed economy in India.
2. New Industrial Policy of 1991 introduced the concept of LPG (Liberalisation, Privatisation and Globalisation).
3. Industrial Policy of 1956 was focused primarily on promoting the private sector.

How many of the statements given above is/are correct?

(a) Only one (b) Only two
(c) All three (d) None

**12.** Consider the following statements about the 'Industrial Policy Resolution (IPR), 1956':

1. It divided industries into three schedules based on the level of government control.
2. It emphasised the development of the private sector in all strategic industries.
3. It laid the foundation for India's socialist pattern of industrialisation.

Which of the given statements are correct?

(a) 1 and 2 only (b) 1 and 3 only
(c) 2 and 3 only (d) 1, 2 and 3

**13.** Consider the following:

1. Abolition of industrial licensing for most industries
2. FDI Liberalisation Policy
3. Reduction of the public sector's role in certain industries
4. Introduction of Monopolies and Restrictive Trade Practices (MRTP) Act for regulating business practices

How many of the above changes was/were actually introduced by the Industrial Policy Resolution of 1991?

(a) Only one (b) Only two
(c) Only three (d) All four

**14.** Consider the following sectors:
1. Railways operations
2. Atomic energy production
3. Defence manufacturing
4. Mining of coal
5. Space research

How many of the given above sectors is/are exclusively reserved for the public sector in present times?
(a) Only one (b) Only two
(c) Only three (d) All five

**15.** With reference to 'National Investment and Manufacturing Zones (NIMZs)', consider the following statements:
1. NIMZs are industrial zones aimed at promoting world-class manufacturing activities in India.
2. Each NIMZ will have a minimum area of 50 square kilometres.
3. The development of NIMZs is entirely funded by the Central Government.

Which of the given statements are correct?
(a) 1 and 2 only
(b) 1 and 3 only
(c) 2 and 3 only
(d) 1, 2 and 3

**16.** Consider the following locations:
1. Medak (Telangana)
2. Prakasam (Andhra Pradesh)
3. Kutch (Gujarat)
4. Jabalpur (Madhya Pradesh)
5. Nagpur (Maharashtra)

How many of the above locations have been identified for setting up NIMZs?
(a) Only two (b) Only three
(c) Only four (d) All five

**17.** Which of the following statements correctly highlights a difference in the objectives of NIMZs and SEZs?
(a) NIMZs aim to promote export-oriented growth, while SEZs focus on enhancing domestic manufacturing capabilities.
(b) SEZs primarily target the development of infrastructure, while NIMZs aim to increase the share of the manufacturing sector in GDP to 25%.
(c) NIMZs are designed to create industrial townships with world-class infrastructure, while SEZs aim to provide employment opportunities only.
(d) NIMZs focus on generating employment and enhancing domestic manufacturing, while SEZs focus on promoting exports.

**18.** With reference to Special Economic Zones (SEZs) in India, consider the following statements:
1. SEZs operate as foreign enclaves within India and are treated separately from the customs territory for trade purposes.
2. Goods and services sold from SEZs to the rest of India are treated as imports and subject to customs duty.
3. SEZs were primarily established to promote industrial growth within India's rural areas.

Which of the statements given above are correct?
(a) 1 and 2 only
(b) 1 and 3 only
(c) 2 and 3 only
(d) 1, 2 and 3

**19.** Which of the following statements is correct about the 'National Single Window System (NSWS)'?
(a) The NSWS is designed to cater only to foreign investors interested in investing in India.
(b) The NSWS integrates services from various ministries, departments and states, offering pre-establishment to post-operational approvals.
(c) The NSWS only provides information on regulatory requirements without facilitating any application processes.
(d) The NSWS replaces all existing state-level single window clearance systems.

**20.** With reference to the 'Industrial Corridors in India', consider the following statements:
1. Industrial Corridors are developed with an aim of enhancing the manufacturing and industrial capabilities along designated regions.
2. National Industrial Corridor Development and Implementation Trust (NICDIT) is responsible for coordinating the development of Industrial Corridors.
3. Industrial Corridors are regulated and monitored by the Ministry of Commerce and Industry.

How many of the statements given above is/are correct?
(a) Only one (b) Only two
(c) All three (d) None

**21.** Which of the following statements is/are correct about the development of industrial corridors in India?
1. Chennai-Bengaluru Industrial Corridor (CBIC) is being developed in collaboration with the Japanese government.
2. The East Coast Economic Corridor (ECEC) is entirely funded by the World Bank.
3. Delhi-Mumbai Industrial Corridor (DMIC) is financed exclusively by the Government of India without any foreign assistance.

Select the correct answer from the codes given below:
(a) 1 and 2 only (b) 1 only
(c) 2 and 3 only (d) 1, 2 and 3

**22.** Consider the following States/UTs:
1. Haryana 2. Rajasthan
3. Madhya Pradesh 4. Gujarat

How many of the given above states is/are crossed by the 'Delhi-Mumbai Industrial Corridor (DMIC)'?
(a) Only one (b) Only two
(c) Only three (d) All four

**23.** With reference to the 'Production Linked Incentive (PLI) Scheme', consider the following statements:
1. The scheme aims to increase India's manufacturing capacity by providing financial incentives to selected sectors.
2. The PLI incentives are provided for a period of 10 years for all sectors.
3. The PLI Scheme applies to only export-oriented units.

Which of the given statements is/are correct?
(a) 1 only (b) 1 and 3 only
(c) 2 and 3 only (d) 1, 2, and 3

**24.** Consider the following sectors:
1. Pharmaceuticals
2. Automobiles and Auto Components
3. Solar Photovoltaic (PV) Modules
4. Textiles

How many of the given above sectors is/are covered under the PLI Scheme?
(a) Only one (b) Only two
(c) Only three (d) All four

**25.** With reference to the 'Design Linked Incentive (DLI) Scheme', consider the following statements:
1. The DLI Scheme aims to support both product design and chip design startups in India.
2. The scheme offers financial incentives to startups, MSMEs and large companies engaged in integrated circuit (IC) design.
3. The DLI Scheme is exclusively meant for promoting manufacturing units in India.

How many of the above statements is/are correct?
(a) Only one (b) Only two
(c) All three (d) None

**26.** Consider the following statements about 'Design Linked Incentive (DLI) Scheme':
1. The scheme is implemented by the India Semiconductor Mission (ISM), which operates under the Ministry of Electronics and Information Technology (MeitY).
2. The DLI Scheme offers incentives only for product manufacturing, not for design activities.

Which of the given above statements is/are correct?
(a) 1 only (b) 2 only
(c) Both 1 and 2 (d) Neither 1 nor 2

**27.** Which of the following best describes the primary role of Invest India?

(a) To regulate foreign direct investment (FDI) flows into India
(b) To act as India's national investment promotion and facilitation agency, providing comprehensive services to investors
(c) To manage India's monetary policy and exchange rates
(d) To oversee the taxation policies for multinational corporations

## Topic 3 : MSME Sector

**28.** Consider the following criteria:

1. Investment in Plant and Machinery
2. Annual Turnover
3. Number of Employees
4. Location of the Enterprise

How many of the above criteria is/are officially used to define MSMEs in India?

(a) Only one
(b) Only two
(c) Only three
(d) All four

**29.** With reference to the revised MSME classification in India, consider the following statements:

1. The revised definition applies to both manufacturing and service enterprises.
2. The investment limit for a medium enterprise is set at ₹ 20 crore.
3. A medium enterprise is defined as one with an investment of up to ₹ 50 crore and turnover of up to ₹ 250 crore.

Which of the given statements is/are correct?

(a) 1 only
(b) 1 and 3 only
(c) 2 and 3 only
(d) 1, 2 and 3

**30.** Consider the following statements with reference to the 'MUDRA Yojana':

1. It provides loans up to ₹ 10 lakh to non-corporate, non-farm small/micro enterprises.
2. MUDRA loans are categorised under three schemes: Shishu, Kishor and Tarun.
3. The MUDRA scheme offers subsidies on interest rates for all MSMEs.

How many of the statements given above is/are correct?

(a) Only one (b) Only two
(c) All three (d) None

**31.** Consider the following pairs of MSME schemes and their purpose:

| | MSME Scheme | Purpose |
|---|---|---|
| 1. | Technology Upgradation Fund Scheme (TUFS) | To provide technology upgradation subsidies for textiles |
| 2. | Credit Linked Capital Subsidy Scheme (CLCSS) | Offers subsidies for technology upgradation in MSMEs |
| 3. | Solar Charkha Mission | To promote the use of solar energy in MSME manufacturing |
| 4. | Market Development Assistance (MDA) | To support MSMEs in marketing their products domestically |

How many of the given above pairs is/are correctly matched?

(a) Only one pair (b) Only two pairs
(c) Only three pairs (d) All four pairs

**32.** Consider the following MSME schemes with their implementing authorities:

| | MSME Scheme | Implementing Authority |
|---|---|---|
| 1. | MUDRA Yojana | Small Industries Development Bank of India (SIDBI) |
| 2. | Credit Guarantee Fund Scheme for MSMEs (CGTMSE) | Ministry of MSME |
| 3. | Udyam Registration | Ministry of Commerce and Industry |
| 4. | Coir Udyami Yojana | Coir Board |

How many of the given above pairs is/are correctly matched?

(a) Only one pair (b) Only two pairs
(c) Only three pairs (d) All four pairs

**33.** Match the following MSME digital initiatives with their corresponding purposes:

| MSME Digital Initiative | Purpose |
|---|---|
| 1. MSME Sampark | An online platform for resolving delayed payment issues of MSMEs. |
| 2. MSME Sambandh | To monitor the procurement of goods and services by CPSEs from MSMEs. |
| 3. MSME Samadhaan | A digital platform to connect job seekers with MSMEs. |
| 4. MSME Sambhav | A mass outreach program to promote entrepreneurship and skill development among youth. |

How many of the above pairs is/are correctly matched?
(a) Only one pair
(b) Only two pairs
(c) Only three pairs
(d) All four pairs

## Topic 4 : Mining Sector

**34.** With reference to the regulation of mining industry in India, consider the following statements:
1. Mining leases for major minerals are granted by the State Governments.
2. The regulation of offshore mining activities comes under the jurisdiction of State Governments.
3. The Central Government can intervene in the regulation of mineral leases if the mineral is considered a 'strategic mineral.'

How many of the above statements is/are correct?
(a) Only one (b) Only two
(c) All three (d) None

**35.** Which of the following statements about the regulation of the mining industry in India is/are correct?
1. Indian Bureau of Mines (IBM) maintains a database of mineral resources and mining activities across the country.
2. Ministry of Mines is responsible for the overall regulation of mineral exploration and mining activities, including coal.
3. Environmental Impact Assessment (EIA) process is mandatory for granting mining leases for major minerals.

Select the correct answer from the codes given below:
(a) 1 and 2 only
(b) 1 and 3 only
(c) 2 and 3 only
(d) 1, 2 and 3

**36.** Consider the following minerals:
1. Sand
2. Granite
3. Limestone
4. Coal
5. Marble

How many of the above are classified as 'minor minerals' under Indian laws and regulations?
(a) Only two
(b) Only three
(c) Only four
(d) All five

**37.** Which of the following statements about minor minerals in India is/are correct?
1. The regulation of minor minerals is primarily the responsibility of state governments.
2. Minor minerals include minerals like bauxite, copper and iron ore.
3. The royalty rates for minor minerals are decided by the Central Government.

Select the correct answer from the codes given below:
(a) 1 only
(b) 1 and 3 only
(c) 2 and 3 only
(d) 1, 2 and 3

**38.** Consider the following regulatory authorities with their roles:

| Pair Regulatory Authority | Role |
|---|---|
| 1. Geological Survey of India (GSI) | Conducts mineral exploration and maintains geological data |
| 2. Ministry of Mines | Formulates policies for the exploration and development of non-coal minerals |
| 3. Indian Bureau of Mines (IBM) | Ensures occupational safety and health in mining operations |
| 4. Directorate General of Mines Safety (DGMS) | Oversees sustainable mining practices and mineral exploration |

How many of the above pairs is/are correctly matched?

(a) Only one pair (b) Only two pairs
(c) Only three pairs (d) All four pairs

**39.** With reference to the 'District Mineral Foundation (DMF)' in India, consider the following statements:

1. DMF funds are utilised for the welfare of mining-affected communities in districts where mining activities take place.
2. The establishment of DMFs is mandated under the Mines and Minerals (Development and Regulation) Act, 1957.
3. The funds collected by DMFs are managed directly by the Central Government.

How many of the above statements is/are correct?

(a) Only one (b) Only two
(c) All three (d) None

**40.** Consider the following statements about 'District Mineral Foundation (DMF)' in India:

1. DMFs are established as non-profit trusts in mining-affected districts.
2. Pradhan Mantri Khanij Kshetra Kalyan Yojana (PMKKKY) scheme is linked to the utilisation of DMF funds.
3. DMF funds can only be used for infrastructure development in mining districts.

Which of the given statements are correct?

(a) 1 and 2 only (b) 2 and 3 only
(c) 1 and 3 only (d) 1, 2 and 3

**41.** Which of the following statements about the 'National Mineral Exploration Trust (NMET)' are correct?

1. It is responsible for funding mineral exploration projects in India.
2. The funds for NMET are collected from mining leaseholders in the form of a royalty.
3. NMET is administered by the Geological Survey of India (GSI).

Select the correct answer from the codes given below:

(a) 1 and 2 only (b) 1 and 3 only
(c) 2 and 3 only (d) 1, 2 and 3

**42.** Arrange the following regulatory milestones in the coal industry in the correct chronological order of their implementation:

1. Enactment of the Coal Mines (Nationalisation) Act
2. Introduction of the Coal Mines (Special Provisions) Act
3. Establishment of Coal India Limited (CIL)
4. Opening up of the coal mining sector to private companies for commercial mining

Select the correct answer using the codes given below:

(a) 1 - 3 - 2 - 4 (b) 1 - 3 - 4 - 2
(c) 1 - 4 - 3 - 2 (d) 3 - 2 - 1 - 4

**43.** With reference to the recent participation of the private sector in coal mining in India, consider the following statements:

1. The government has removed the end-use restrictions for coal mined by private companies under the commercial mining policy.
2. Private companies are allowed to sell 100% of their coal production in the open market.
3. Private players are allowed to export coal mined under the commercial mining policy without any restrictions.

Which of the given above statements are correct?

(a) 1 and 2 only (b) 2 and 3 only
(c) 1 and 3 only (d) 1, 2 and 3

# OMR SHEET

**Assessment Round**

| | | | | | | | |
|---|---|---|---|---|---|---|---|
| 1 | ⓐ ⓑ ⓒ ⓓ | 31 | ⓐ ⓑ ⓒ ⓓ | 61 | ⓐ ⓑ ⓒ ⓓ | 91 | ⓐ ⓑ ⓒ ⓓ |
| 2 | ⓐ ⓑ ⓒ ⓓ | 32 | ⓐ ⓑ ⓒ ⓓ | 62 | ⓐ ⓑ ⓒ ⓓ | 92 | ⓐ ⓑ ⓒ ⓓ |
| 3 | ⓐ ⓑ ⓒ ⓓ | 33 | ⓐ ⓑ ⓒ ⓓ | 63 | ⓐ ⓑ ⓒ ⓓ | 93 | ⓐ ⓑ ⓒ ⓓ |
| 4 | ⓐ ⓑ ⓒ ⓓ | 34 | ⓐ ⓑ ⓒ ⓓ | 64 | ⓐ ⓑ ⓒ ⓓ | 94 | ⓐ ⓑ ⓒ ⓓ |
| 5 | ⓐ ⓑ ⓒ ⓓ | 35 | ⓐ ⓑ ⓒ ⓓ | 65 | ⓐ ⓑ ⓒ ⓓ | 95 | ⓐ ⓑ ⓒ ⓓ |
| 6 | ⓐ ⓑ ⓒ ⓓ | 36 | ⓐ ⓑ ⓒ ⓓ | 66 | ⓐ ⓑ ⓒ ⓓ | 96 | ⓐ ⓑ ⓒ ⓓ |
| 7 | ⓐ ⓑ ⓒ ⓓ | 37 | ⓐ ⓑ ⓒ ⓓ | 67 | ⓐ ⓑ ⓒ ⓓ | 97 | ⓐ ⓑ ⓒ ⓓ |
| 8 | ⓐ ⓑ ⓒ ⓓ | 38 | ⓐ ⓑ ⓒ ⓓ | 68 | ⓐ ⓑ ⓒ ⓓ | 98 | ⓐ ⓑ ⓒ ⓓ |
| 9 | ⓐ ⓑ ⓒ ⓓ | 39 | ⓐ ⓑ ⓒ ⓓ | 69 | ⓐ ⓑ ⓒ ⓓ | 99 | ⓐ ⓑ ⓒ ⓓ |
| 10 | ⓐ ⓑ ⓒ ⓓ | 40 | ⓐ ⓑ ⓒ ⓓ | 70 | ⓐ ⓑ ⓒ ⓓ | 100 | ⓐ ⓑ ⓒ ⓓ |
| 11 | ⓐ ⓑ ⓒ ⓓ | 41 | ⓐ ⓑ ⓒ ⓓ | 71 | ⓐ ⓑ ⓒ ⓓ | 101 | ⓐ ⓑ ⓒ ⓓ |
| 12 | ⓐ ⓑ ⓒ ⓓ | 42 | ⓐ ⓑ ⓒ ⓓ | 72 | ⓐ ⓑ ⓒ ⓓ | 102 | ⓐ ⓑ ⓒ ⓓ |
| 13 | ⓐ ⓑ ⓒ ⓓ | 43 | ⓐ ⓑ ⓒ ⓓ | 73 | ⓐ ⓑ ⓒ ⓓ | 103 | ⓐ ⓑ ⓒ ⓓ |
| 14 | ⓐ ⓑ ⓒ ⓓ | 44 | ⓐ ⓑ ⓒ ⓓ | 74 | ⓐ ⓑ ⓒ ⓓ | 104 | ⓐ ⓑ ⓒ ⓓ |
| 15 | ⓐ ⓑ ⓒ ⓓ | 45 | ⓐ ⓑ ⓒ ⓓ | 75 | ⓐ ⓑ ⓒ ⓓ | 105 | ⓐ ⓑ ⓒ ⓓ |
| 16 | ⓐ ⓑ ⓒ ⓓ | 46 | ⓐ ⓑ ⓒ ⓓ | 76 | ⓐ ⓑ ⓒ ⓓ | 106 | ⓐ ⓑ ⓒ ⓓ |
| 17 | ⓐ ⓑ ⓒ ⓓ | 47 | ⓐ ⓑ ⓒ ⓓ | 77 | ⓐ ⓑ ⓒ ⓓ | 107 | ⓐ ⓑ ⓒ ⓓ |
| 18 | ⓐ ⓑ ⓒ ⓓ | 48 | ⓐ ⓑ ⓒ ⓓ | 78 | ⓐ ⓑ ⓒ ⓓ | 108 | ⓐ ⓑ ⓒ ⓓ |
| 19 | ⓐ ⓑ ⓒ ⓓ | 49 | ⓐ ⓑ ⓒ ⓓ | 79 | ⓐ ⓑ ⓒ ⓓ | 109 | ⓐ ⓑ ⓒ ⓓ |
| 20 | ⓐ ⓑ ⓒ ⓓ | 50 | ⓐ ⓑ ⓒ ⓓ | 80 | ⓐ ⓑ ⓒ ⓓ | 110 | ⓐ ⓑ ⓒ ⓓ |
| 21 | ⓐ ⓑ ⓒ ⓓ | 51 | ⓐ ⓑ ⓒ ⓓ | 81 | ⓐ ⓑ ⓒ ⓓ | 111 | ⓐ ⓑ ⓒ ⓓ |
| 22 | ⓐ ⓑ ⓒ ⓓ | 52 | ⓐ ⓑ ⓒ ⓓ | 82 | ⓐ ⓑ ⓒ ⓓ | 112 | ⓐ ⓑ ⓒ ⓓ |
| 23 | ⓐ ⓑ ⓒ ⓓ | 53 | ⓐ ⓑ ⓒ ⓓ | 83 | ⓐ ⓑ ⓒ ⓓ | 113 | ⓐ ⓑ ⓒ ⓓ |
| 24 | ⓐ ⓑ ⓒ ⓓ | 54 | ⓐ ⓑ ⓒ ⓓ | 84 | ⓐ ⓑ ⓒ ⓓ | 114 | ⓐ ⓑ ⓒ ⓓ |
| 25 | ⓐ ⓑ ⓒ ⓓ | 55 | ⓐ ⓑ ⓒ ⓓ | 85 | ⓐ ⓑ ⓒ ⓓ | 115 | ⓐ ⓑ ⓒ ⓓ |
| 26 | ⓐ ⓑ ⓒ ⓓ | 56 | ⓐ ⓑ ⓒ ⓓ | 86 | ⓐ ⓑ ⓒ ⓓ | 116 | ⓐ ⓑ ⓒ ⓓ |
| 27 | ⓐ ⓑ ⓒ ⓓ | 57 | ⓐ ⓑ ⓒ ⓓ | 87 | ⓐ ⓑ ⓒ ⓓ | 117 | ⓐ ⓑ ⓒ ⓓ |
| 28 | ⓐ ⓑ ⓒ ⓓ | 58 | ⓐ ⓑ ⓒ ⓓ | 88 | ⓐ ⓑ ⓒ ⓓ | 118 | ⓐ ⓑ ⓒ ⓓ |
| 29 | ⓐ ⓑ ⓒ ⓓ | 59 | ⓐ ⓑ ⓒ ⓓ | 89 | ⓐ ⓑ ⓒ ⓓ | 119 | ⓐ ⓑ ⓒ ⓓ |
| 30 | ⓐ ⓑ ⓒ ⓓ | 60 | ⓐ ⓑ ⓒ ⓓ | 90 | ⓐ ⓑ ⓒ ⓓ | 120 | ⓐ ⓑ ⓒ ⓓ |

## Calculate Your Score

| | |
|---|---|
| **Correct (✓)** | |
| **Incorrect (✓)** | |
| **Unattempted** | |
| **Total Score** | |
| **Accuracy (%)** | |

## Reasons for Incorrect Answers?

| | |
|---|---|
| 1. Lack of Knowledge/Existing Source Insufficient | |
| 2. Lack of Multiple Revision | |
| 3. Common Sense Mistakes | |

**Note :**

1. Calculate total score as correct answers carry 2 marks each 1/3rd marks will deducted for **Incorrect** Answers.
2. Calculate Accuracy (%) by dividing the number of correct answers to the total number of attempted questions.

## Past Learning

**1.** Consider the following statements with reference to India: **(2023)**

1. According to the 'Micro, Small and Medium Enterprises Development (MSMED) Act, 2006, the 'medium enterprises' are those with investments in plant and machinery between 15 crore and 25 crore.
2. All bank loans to the Micro, Small and Medium Enterprises qualify under the priority sector.

Which of the statements given above is/are correct?

(a) 1 only
(b) 2 only
(c) Both 1 and 2
(d) Neither 1 nor 2

**2.** With reference to foreign-owned e-commerce firms operating in India, which of the following statements is/are correct? **(2022)**

1. They can sell their own goods in addition to offering their platforms as market-places.
2. The degree to which they can own big sellers on their platforms is limited.

Select the correct answer using the codes given below:

(a) 1 only (b) 2 only
(c) Both 1 and 2 (d) Neither 1 nor 2

**3.** Consider the following statements: **(2019)**

1. Coal sector was nationalised by the Government of India under Indira Gandhi.
2. Now, coal blocks are allocated on lottery basis
3. Till recently, India imported coal to meet the shortages of domestic supply, but now India is self-sufficient in coal production.

Which of the statements given above is/are correct?

(a) 1 only (b) 2 and 3 only
(c) 3 only (d) 1, 2 and 3

**4.** With reference to 'Stand Up India Scheme', which of the following statements is/are correct? **(2016)**

1. Its purpose is to promote entrepreneurship among SC/ST and women entrepreneurs.
2. It provides for refinance through SIDBI.

Select the correct answer using the codes given below:

(a) 1 only (b) 2 only
(c) Both 1 and 2 (d) Neither 1 nor 2

**5.** What is/are the purpose/purposes of 'District Mineral Foundations' in India? **(2016)**

1. Promoting mineral exploration activities in mineral-rich districts
2. Protecting the interests of the persons affected by mining operations
3. Authorising State Governments to issue licences for mineral exploration

Select the correct answer using the codes given below:

(a) 1 and 2 only
(b) 2 only
(c) 1 and 3 only
(d) 1, 2 and 3

**6.** In the 'Index of Eight Core Industries', which one of the following is given the highest weight? **(2015)**

(a) Coal production
(b) Electricity generation
(c) Fertiliser production
(d) Steel production

# Detailed Solutions

## Assessment Round

**1.** *(c)* Only four

The measures used to estimate **industrial production** include:

- **Index of Industrial Production (IIP):** A widely used monthly indicator to measure the overall performance of the industrial sector, covering **mining, manufacturing and electricity.** Base year of IIP is 2011-12.
- **Annual Survey of Industries (ASI):** Provides comprehensive data on **registered manufacturing industries** annually, making it an important measure of industrial production. The Annual Survey of Industries (ASI) is the principal source of Industrial Statistics in India.
- The National Statistical Office (NSO), Ministry of Statistics and Programme Implementation (MoSPI) is the publishing agency for both IIP and ASI.
- **Purchasing Managers' Index (PMI):** A survey-based measure that tracks the **manufacturing activity** in the country and serves as an indicator of industrial production trends. PMI is compiled by IHS Markit which is the part of S&P Global.
- **Gross Domestic Product (GDP) data:** Although GDP data includes information from the industrial sector, it is a **broader measure** of the entire economy, not specifically used to estimate industrial production trends.
- **Index of Core Industries (ICI):** Measures the performance of **eight core industries,** which are significant contributors to industrial production. Published by Office of the Economic Adviser, Department for Promotion of Industry and Internal Trade (DPIIT), Ministry of Commerce and Industry having base year 2011-12.

**Therefore, the correct answer is (c) Only four.**

**2.** *(b)* Only two

- **Statement 1 is correct:** The PMI is indeed released on a **monthly basis** and covers both the **manufacturing and services sectors.** The PMI for the manufacturing sector and services sector are often considered as separate indicators, providing insights into each sector's performance.
- **Statement 2 is incorrect:** The PMI is **not calculated by the Ministry of Finance, Government of India.** Instead, it is compiled and released by **private agencies** like **IHS Markit** in collaboration with various business associations. It is a **survey-based index** derived from responses from purchasing managers in respective sectors.
- **Statement 3 is correct:** The PMI is a number from 0 to 100. A print above 50 means expansion, while a score below that denotes contraction. A reading at 50 indicates no change. A rising PMI suggests **improving business conditions,** while a declining PMI indicates **deteriorating conditions.** This makes PMI a valuable tool for economists and policymakers to anticipate **future economic trends.** Thus, PMI serves as a **leading indicator of economic activity.**

**So, the correct answer is (b) Only two.**

**3.** *(d)* 1, 2 and 3

- **Statement 1 is correct:** The PMI is indeed used to **predict future trends in the manufacturing sector** as it serves as a **leading indicator of economic activity.** It provides early signals about changes in business conditions.
- **Statement 2 is correct:** A PMI value **above 50 indicates expansion.** Conversely, a value **below 50** signifies that the sector is contracting.
- **Statement 3 is correct:** The PMI is **calculated based on monthly surveys** conducted among purchasing managers from companies in the manufacturing and services sectors. These surveys assess **various aspects of business activity,** such as new orders, production levels, employment, supplier deliveries and inventory levels.

**Thus, the correct answer is (d) 1, 2 and 3.**

**4.** *(c)* Only four

The PMI is calculated based on the following **five key criteria:**

1. **New Orders:** This measures the level of new demand for goods and services, indicating whether demand is increasing or decreasing.
2. **Production Output:** This criterion reflects the actual level of goods and services produced.
3. **Employment:** It captures the changes in employment levels, showing whether companies are hiring or laying off workers.
4. **Supplier Deliveries:** This measures how fast or slow suppliers are delivering goods, indicating changes in demand and supply chain conditions.
5. **Inventory Levels:** It refers to the quantity of goods and materials a company holds, including both raw materials and finished products

However, **Inflation Rate** is **not directly included** as a criterion in PMI calculations. While inflation may impact PMI components indirectly, it is not a standalone factor used in the PMI calculation.

**Therefore, the correct answer is (c) Only four.**

**5.** *(b)* Only two

- **Statement 1 is incorrect:** The IIP is released on a **monthly basis**, but it is published by the **Ministry of Statistics and Programme Implementation (MoSPI)**, not the Ministry of Commerce and Industry.
- **Statement 2 is correct:** The IIP measures the industrial production in three sectors: **Mining, Manufacturing and Electricity.** The **manufacturing sector** holds the highest weight in the IIP calculation, followed by mining and electricity.
- **Statement 3 is correct:** The base year for the IIP calculation is **2011-12.**

**Therefore, the correct answer is (b) Only two.**

**6.** *(c)* Manufacturing

The **Index of Industrial Production (IIP)** is a composite indicator that measures the short-term changes in the volume of production for a **basket of industrial products.** It tracks the output across three main sectors: **Manufacturing (77.63%), Mining (14.37%) and Electricity (7.99%)**

**Thus, option (c) is the correct answer.**

**7.** *(b)* 2 only

- **Statement 1 is incorrect:** The **Index of Core Industries (ICI)** is released by the **Office of the Economic Adviser, Department for Promotion of Industry and Internal Trade (DPIIT)** under the **Ministry of Commerce and Industry,** not the Ministry of Finance.
- **Statement 2 is correct:** The ICI covers **eight core industries,** which are **Coal, Crude Oil, Natural Gas, Refinery Products, Fertilizers, Steel, Cement and Electricity.** These sectors represent key industries that drive the Indian economy.
- **Statement 3 is incorrect:** The **eight core industries** collectively contribute about **40.27%** to the overall Index of Industrial Production (IIP), making them a significant part of the IIP calculation.

**Therefore, the correct answer is (b) 2 only.**

**8.** *(c)* 3 - 1 - 4 - 2

The sectors under the Index of Core Industries (ICI) are ranked in the following order based on their **decreasing weightage:**

- **Refinery Products** - Highest weightage (28.04%)
- **Electricity** – Second highest (19.85%)
- **Steel** – Third highest (17.92%),
- **Coal** - Lower weightage compared to the others (10.33%)

**Therefore, the correct answer is (c) 3-1-4-2.**

**9.** *(b)* **Only two**

- **Statement 1 is correct:** The Annual Survey of Industries (ASI) is indeed the **most comprehensive source of industrial statistics** in India. It provides detailed data on various aspects of registered manufacturing industries, including employment, wages, productivity and industrial output.

- However, defence establishments, oil storage and distribution depots, departmental units such as railway workshops, RTC workshops, Govt. Mints, sanitary, water supply, gas storage etc. are excluded from the purview of the survey.
- **Statement 2 is correct:** The ASI covers **manufacturing industries registered under the Factories Act, 1948** and also covers Bidi and cigar manufacturing establishments registered under the Bidi and Cigar Workers (Conditions of Employment) Act 1966. It collects data from factories employing 10 or more workers with power and 20 or more workers without power.
- **Statement 3 is incorrect:** The ASI is conducted on an annual basis but is carried out by **the Ministry of Statistics and Programme Implementation (MoSPI)**, not the Ministry of Commerce and Industry.

**Hence, the correct answer is (b) Only two.**

***10.*** *(c)* 3-1-2-4

Within the industrial sector:

- **Manufacturing** has the highest contribution, accounting for around 15-20% of GDP.
- **Construction** follows, contributing approximately 8-9%.
- **Electricity, Gas and Water Supply** contribute around 2-3%.
- **Mining** has a slightly lower contribution compared to the others.

**Therefore, the correct order is Manufacturing > Construction > Electricity, Gas, and Water Supply > Mining, making the correct answer (c) 3-1-2-4.**

***11.*** *(b)* Only two

- **Statement 1 is correct:** The **Industrial Policy Resolution of 1948** marked the beginning of a **mixed economy** in India, where both the **public and private sectors** were expected to coexist and play significant roles in industrial development.
- **Statement 2 is correct:** The **New Industrial Policy of 1991** indeed introduced the concept of **Liberalisation, Privatisation, and Globalization** (LPG). This policy aimed at reducing government intervention, encouraging private investment and integrating the Indian economy with the global market.
- **Statement 3 is incorrect:** The **Industrial Policy of 1956** primarily focused on expanding the **public sector** and categorised industries into three schedules. It laid the foundation for a **socialist pattern of development**, where the government played a dominant role in industrialisation.
- **Therefore, the correct answer is (b) Only two.**

***12.*** *(b)* 1 and 3 only

- **Statement 1 is correct:** The **Industrial Policy Resolution of 1956** divided industries into **three schedules:**
  - **Schedule A:** Industries exclusively under the state/government sector.
  - **Schedule B:** Industries progressively becoming state-owned but with some private sector participation.
  - **Schedule C:** Industries left open to the private sector.
- **Statement 2 is incorrect:** The policy **did not emphasise the development of the private sector** in all strategic industries. Instead, it focused on **public sector dominance** in strategic industries, limiting private sector involvement to a supportive role.
- **Statement 3 is correct:** The resolution laid the foundation for India's **socialist pattern of industrialisation,** where the state took a leading role in economic planning and industrial development.

**Thus, the correct answer is (b) 1 and 3 only.**

***13.*** *(c)* Only three

- **Abolition of industrial licensing** was a key feature of the 1991 policy, but it wasn't abolished for all industries—certain strategic sectors remained under licensing.
- **Introduction of FDI** was an important change introduced, encouraging foreign investment in various sectors.
- **Reduction of the public sector's role** was a significant shift, leading to disinvestment and a greater role for the private sector.

- The **Monopolies and Restrictive Trade Practices (MRTP) Act** was not introduced by the 1991 policy; it had been in existence since **1969**. The 1991 policy, however, modified its applicability by **eliminating the need for MRTP clearance for large firms**. This was done because of the reason that the focus shifted towards promoting competition and reducing regulatory burdens on businesses.

**Therefore, the correct answer is (c) Only three.**

***14.*** *(b)* Only two

- **Railways operations**: Certain aspects of railway operations, such as passenger train services, are reserved for the public sector, but private players are now being allowed to participate in some freight and limited passenger train services.
- **Atomic energy production**: This sector remains **exclusively reserved for the public sector**, as per the Atomic Energy Act, 1962.
- **Defence manufacturing**: While earlier reserved for the public sector, it has now been opened up to private **participation**, with FDI permitted up to a certain extent.
- **Mining of coal**: This sector has been liberalised, and **private players** are allowed to participate, though it was historically reserved for the public sector.
- **Space research**: While the Indian Space Research Organisation (ISRO) remains the primary entity, the sector has seen increasing involvement from **private players**, especially in satellite manufacturing and launch services.

**Therefore, only two sectors (atomic energy production and certain aspects of railway operations) are reserved for the public sector, making option (b) is the correct answer.**

***15.*** *(a)* 1 and 2 only

- **Statement 1 is correct**: The **National Investment and Manufacturing Zones (NIMZs)** are indeed industrial zones that aim to create **world-class manufacturing infrastructure** to boost industrial growth, attract investment and generate employment.
- **Statement 2 is correct**: Each NIMZ is planned to have a **minimum area of 50 square kilometres** (5,000 hectares), ensuring that these zones are large enough to accommodate industrial clusters and provide necessary infrastructure.
- **Statement 3 is incorrect**: The development of NIMZs is **not entirely funded by the Central Government**. It involves a **Public-Private Partnership (PPP) model**, where funding and investment come from **both Central and State Governments** as well as private investors.

**Therefore, the correct answer is (a) 1 and 2 only.**

***16.*** *(b)* Only three

- Government of India also accorded in-principal approval to the **16 NIMZs** under the National Manufacturing Policy (NMP). Out of these, **5 NIMZs**, namely (i) Prakasam District of Andhra Pradesh, (ii) Sangareddy (erstwhile Medak) District of Telangana, (iii) Kalinganagar, Jajpur District of Odisha, (iv) Hyderabad Pharma City NIMZ in Rangareddy District of Telangana and (v) Nagpur (Maharashtra), were accorded final approval.
- **Kutch (Gujarat)** and **Jabalpur (Madhya Pradesh)** have not been officially approved for NIMZ status as per current plans.

**Therefore, the correct answer is (b) Only three.**

***17.*** *(d)* NIMZs focus on generating employment and enhancing domestic manufacturing, while SEZs focus on promoting exports.

The main objective of Special Economic Zones is promotion of exports, while NIMZs are based on the principle of industrial growth in partnership with States and focuses on manufacturing growth and employment generation. NIMZs are different from SEZs in terms of size, level of infrastructure planning, governance structures related to regulatory procedures and exit policies.

- The **objective of NIMZs** is to enhance the **share of manufacturing** in India's GDP to 25% and to create **100 million** jobs by promoting domestic manufacturing.
- The **objective of SEZs** is to create a favourable environment for **export-oriented**

growth, providing incentives and infrastructure specifically for industries engaged in exports.

Thus, while NIMZs are broader and aim to promote both domestic and international market participation, **SEZs are more focused on exports** and foreign exchange earnings.

**Thus, option (d) is the correct answer.**

**18.** *(a)* 1 and 2 only

- **Statement 1 is correct:** SEZs **function as enclaves within the country**, meaning they are designated as separate entities for customs purposes. This allows **goods manufactured in SEZs to be considered 'exports' from India**, even though they are physically located within Indian borders.
- **Statement 2 is correct:** When goods and services produced in **SEZs are sold to the rest of India, they are treated as imports into the domestic market**. These transactions are subject to customs duties and other applicable taxes to maintain trade balance.
- **Statement 3 is incorrect:** SEZs were established to promote **export-oriented growth** rather than specifically targeting rural development. While some SEZs may be located in rural areas, the primary goal is to enhance exports and foreign exchange earnings.

**Thus, option (a) is the correct answer.**

**19.** *(b)* The NSWS integrates services from various ministries, departments and states, offering pre-establishment to post-operational approvals.

- NSWS launched on the 22nd of September 2021 by the **Union Minister of Commerce** and was created by Department for Promotion of Industry and Internal Trade (DPIIT) to provide a **single platform** to enable the **identification and obtaining of approvals and clearances** needed by investors, entrepreneurs, and businesses in India.
- The **NSWS** is designed to be a comprehensive platform that integrates services from various **ministries, departments and states,** providing businesses and investors with access to **pre-establishment to post-operational approvals** required for starting and operating businesses.

This integration helps in **simplifying and expediting the clearance process** at both central and state levels.

**Thus, option (b) is the correct answer.**

**20.** *(c)* All three

- **Statement 1 is correct:** Industrial Corridors are developed with the objective of **enhancing manufacturing and industrial capabilities** by providing integrated infrastructure, boosting economic activity along the corridor regions.
- **Statement 2 is correct:** The **National Industrial Corridor Development and Implementation Trust (NICDIT)** is the apex body responsible for planning, coordinating, and implementing Industrial Corridor projects across India.
- **Statement 3 is correct:** The development of Industrial Corridors is regulated and monitored by the **Department for Promotion of Industry and Internal Trade (DPIIT)** under the **Ministry of Commerce and Industry.**

**Therefore, the correct answer is (c) All three.**

**21.** *(b)* 1 only

- **Statement 1 is correct:** The **Chennai-Bengaluru Industrial Corridor (CBIC)** is being developed with **Japanese collaboration,** aiming to strengthen industrial infrastructure between Chennai and Bengaluru.
- **Statement 2 is incorrect:** The **East Coast Economic Corridor (ECEC)** is **not entirely funded by the World Bank;** the Asian Development Bank (ADB) also plays a significant role in financing and supporting its development.
- **Statement 3 is incorrect:** The **DMIC** is financed with assistance from **both the Government of India and foreign investment,** including **collaboration with the Japanese government.**

**Therefore, the correct answer is (b) 1 only.**

**22.** *(d)* All four

The **Delhi-Mumbai Industrial Corridor (DMIC)** is one of India's largest infrastructure projects, covering a distance of around **1,500 km** between Delhi and Mumbai. It aims to develop **industrial zones** and improve **transportation infrastructure**. The DMIC passes through the following **states**:

- **Haryana**: The corridor covers **industrial regions like Manesar and Bawal**, making Haryana an integral part of the DMIC route.
- **Rajasthan**: The corridor traverses **key industrial areas such as Neemrana and Khushkhera**, promoting industrial development in Rajasthan.
- **Madhya Pradesh**: The DMIC route includes areas like **Pithampur and Neemuch**, making Madhya Pradesh a major beneficiary of the corridor's development.
- **Gujarat**: One of the largest states covered by the DMIC, Gujarat features **Dholera Special Investment Region (DSIR)** as a key part of the corridor.

**The Delhi-Mumbai Industrial Corridor (DMIC) passes through the following states and Union Territories:** Uttar Pradesh; Delhi NCR; Haryana; Rajasthan; Madhya Pradesh; Gujarat and Maharashtra

**Thus, option (d) is the correct answer.**

***23.*** *(a)* 1 only

- **Statement 1 is correct**: The **PLI Scheme** aims to boost India's **manufacturing capacity** by providing **financial incentives** based on increased production levels in selected sectors. It seeks to make Indian products globally competitive and encourage investment in high-growth industries.
- **Statement 2 is incorrect**: The PLI incentives are not uniformly provided for a period of 10 years across all sectors. The incentive duration varies from 5 to 7 years depending on the sector.
- **Statement 3 is incorrect**: The PLI Scheme does not apply **exclusively to export-oriented units**. It provides incentives based on incremental sales of products manufactured in India, whether for the domestic market or for export.
- **Therefore, the correct answer is (a) 1 only.**

***24.*** *(d)* All four

In India's vision of becoming 'Atmanirbhar', Production Linked Incentive (PLI) Schemes for **14 key sectors** have been announced with an outlay of ₹ 1.97 lakh crore (over US$26 billion) to enhance India's Manufacturing capabilities and Exports.

The Production Linked Incentive (PLI) Scheme aims to boost domestic manufacturing by offering incentives to selected sectors to enhance production and promote export competitiveness. The scheme covers the following sectors:

- **Pharmaceuticals**: The PLI scheme incentivises the production of critical bulk drugs and high-value pharmaceutical products.
- **Automobiles and Auto Components**: This sector is covered to promote the manufacturing of advanced automotive technology components.
- **Solar Photovoltaic (PV) Modules**: The scheme encourages the domestic production of high-efficiency solar PV modules to reduce import dependency.
- **Textiles**: The PLI scheme includes the textile sector, focusing on man-made fiber and technical textiles.

**Therefore, the correct answer is (d) All four.**

***25.*** *(b)* Only two

- **Statement 1 is correct**: The **Design Linked Incentive (DLI) Scheme** is designed to promote the growth and development of **semiconductor design companies** in India aiming to establish India as a global hub for semiconductor design and innovation.
  - The DLI Scheme aims to support **both product design and chip design startups** by providing incentives to promote innovation and strengthen India's capabilities in semi-conductor design.
- **Statement 2 is correct**: The scheme provides **financial incentives** to a wide range of participants, including **startups, MSMEs and large companies** involved in the design and development of **integrated circuits (ICs), system-on-chips (SoCs) and semi-conductor packaging.**
- **Statement 3 is incorrect**: The DLI Scheme is not exclusively for manufacturing but primarily focuses on **design and innovation**

in the semiconductor sector, providing support to design-centric activities.

**Therefore, the correct answer is (b) Only two.**

**26.** *(a)* 1 only

- **Statement 1 is correct:** The DLI Scheme is implemented by the **India Semiconductor Mission (ISM)**, which functions under the **Ministry of Electronics and Information Technology (MeitY)**. ISM is responsible for driving initiatives to build a strong semiconductor design ecosystem in India.
- **Statement 2 is incorrect:** The DLI Scheme is not limited to product manufacturing; it specifically promotes **design activities** by providing incentives to companies engaged in the design and development of semiconductors, chips and other related technologies.

**Therefore, the correct answer is (a) 1 only.**

**27.** *(b)* To act as India's national investment promotion and facilitation agency, providing comprehensive services to investors.

- **Option (a) is incorrect:** Invest India does not have regulatory authority over foreign direct investment (FDI). Instead, it acts as a facilitator, assisting investors in understanding FDI policies and processes but not enforcing them.
- **Option (b) is correct: Invest India** is India's national **investment promotion and facilitation agency**. Its primary role is to attract and support both domestic and international investors by providing end-to-end services, from investment advisory to establishing operations. Invest India offers **market insights, regulatory support and connections** with government departments to streamline the investment process in India.
- **Option (c) is incorrect:** Managing India's **monetary policy and exchange rates** is the responsibility of the Reserve Bank of India (RBI), not Invest India.
- **Option (d) is incorrect:** Invest India does not oversee **taxation policies** for multinational corporations; this falls under the Ministry of Finance and other tax authorities. Invest India may, however, guide investors on taxation issues for specific projects or sectors.

**Thus, option (b) is the correct answer.**

**28.** *(b)* Only two

The MSME definition is based on two criteria:

- **Investment in Plant and Machinery:** This criterion sets different investment limits for micro, small and medium enterprises.
- **Annual Turnover:** This criterion specifies turnover limits for categorising MSMEs.
- The **number of employees** and **location of the enterprise** are not part of the official MSME classification.

**Therefore, the correct answer is (b) Only two.**

**29.** *(b)* 1 and 3 only

- **Statement 1 is correct:** The revised MSME definition applies to **both manufacturing and service enterprises**, bringing uniformity in classification.
- **Statement 2 is incorrect:** The investment limit for a medium enterprise is ₹ 50 crore, not ₹ 20 crore.
- **Statement 3 is correct: A medium enterprise** is defined as having an investment up to ₹ 50 crore and turnover up to **₹ 250 crore.**

| Classification | Micro | Small | Medium |
|---|---|---|---|
| Manufacturing Enterprises and Enterprises redering services | Investment in Plant and Machinery or Equipment; | Investment in Plant and Machinery or Equipment; | Investment in Plant and Machinery or Equipment; |
| | Not more than ₹ 1 crore and Annula Turnover; not more than ₹ 5 crore | Not more than ₹ 10 crore and Annual Turnover; not more than ₹ 50 crore | Not more than ₹ 50 crore and Anual Turnover; not more than ₹ 250 crore |

**Therefore, the correct answer is (b) 1 and 3 only.**

**30.** *(b)* Only two

Pradhan Mantri MUDRA Yojana (PMMY) is a scheme launched on 8th April, 2015 with the aim to facilitate easy collateral-free micro credit of up to ₹ 10 lakh to non-corporate, non-farm small and micro entrepreneurs for income generating activities. These loans are classified as MUDRA loans under PMMY. These loans are given by Commercial Banks, RRBs, Small Finance Banks, MFIs and NBFCs.

- **Statement 1 is correct:** The **MUDRA Yojana** offers loans up to **₹ 10 lakh to non-corporate, non-farm small/micro enterprises** to promote entrepreneurship.
- **Statement 2 is correct:** The MUDRA scheme is categorised into three products:
  - **Shishu** (loans up to ₹ 50,000)
  - **Kishor** (loans from ₹ 50,001 to ₹ 5 lakh)
  - **Tarun** (loans from ₹ 5 lakh to ₹ 10 lakh).
- **Statement 3 is incorrect:** The MUDRA scheme does not inherently offer **subsidies on interest rates** for all MSMEs. The interest rates are determined by the lending institutions based on guidelines from the government or the RBI and there are no universal subsidies on interest for all borrowers.

**Therefore, the correct answer is (b) Only two.**

**31.** *(d)* All four pairs

- **Pair 1 is correct:** The **Technology Upgradation Fund Scheme (TUFS)** provides technology upgradation subsidies for the textile sector, including MSMEs.
- **Pair 2 is correct:** The **Credit Linked Capital Subsidy Scheme (CLCSS)** offers subsidies for technology upgradation in MSMEs.
- **Pair 3 is correct:** The **Solar Charkha Mission** aims to promote solar-powered charkhas (spinning wheels) and create employment in rural areas. This mission promotes the use of solar energy in MSME manufacturing, especially in khadi and village industries.
- **Pair 4 is correct:** The **Market Development Assistance** (MDA) scheme helps MSMEs market their products domestically and internationally by participating in trade fairs and exhibitions.

**Thus, the correct answer is (d) All four pairs.**

**32.** *(c)* Only three pairs

- **Pair 1 is correct:** The **MUDRA Yojana** is implemented by the **Small Industries Development Bank of India (SIDBI)**, which provides refinance support to banks and financial institutions lending to MSMEs.
- **Pair 2 is correct:** The **Credit Guarantee Fund Scheme for MSMEs (CGTMSE)** is implemented under the **Ministry of MSME** and offers collateral-free credit to eligible MSMEs.
- **Pair 3 is incorrect:** The **Udyam Registration** process is managed by the **Ministry of MSME**, not the Ministry of Commerce and Industry.
- **Pair 4 is correct:** The **Coir Udyami Yojana** is implemented by the **Coir Board** to promote coir-based MSMEs. (Coir is a natural fiber that comes from the husk of a coconut)

**Therefore, the correct answer is (c) Only three pairs.**

**33.** *(b)* Only two pairs

- **Pair 1 is incorrect: MSME Sampark** is an **online job portal** that connects **job seekers with MSMEs** for employment opportunities, not for resolving delayed payment issues.
- **Pair 2 is correct: MSME Sambandh** is designed to **monitor the procurement of goods and services by Central Public Sector Enterprises (CPSEs)** from MSMEs, ensuring they meet their procurement targets.
- **Pair 3 is incorrect: MSME Samadhaan** is a digital platform that allows MSMEs to **file complaints about delayed payments** from buyers and track the resolution process.
- **Pair 4 is correct: MSME Sambhav** is a **mass outreach programme** to promote **entrepreneurship, skill development and awareness** among students across the country.

**Therefore, the correct answer is (b) Only two pairs.**

**34.** *(b)* Only two

- **Statement 1 is correct:** The **Mines and Minerals (Development and Regulation) Act, 1957 (MMDR Act)** is indeed the **primary legislation** that governs the mining industry in India. It provides guidelines for the granting of mineral concessions and the regulation of mining operations.
- **State governments** have the authority to **grant mining leases for major minerals**, but they do so in accordance with the rules and guidelines set by the Central Government.
- **Statement 2 is incorrect:** The **regulation of offshore mining activities** falls under the jurisdiction of the **Central Government**, not State Governments. State Governments are responsible for the regulation of onshore mining activities within their boundaries.
- **Statement 3 is correct:** The **Central Government** can intervene and regulate leases if the mineral is considered a **'strategic mineral'**, such as uranium or atomic minerals, due to their importance to national security.

**Therefore, the correct answer is (b) Only two.**

**35.** *(b)* 1 and 3 only

- **Statement 1 is correct:** The IBM maintains a **comprehensive database** of mineral resources, reserves, and mining activities across the country, contributing to effective planning and management of the mining sector.
- **Statement 2 is incorrect: Ministry of Mines** is responsible for survey, exploration and mining of all minerals, other than **natural gas, petroleum, atomic minerals and coal.** In the case of atomic minerals and coal, activities of the Ministry are limited to regional exploration.
  - The **Ministry of Mines** is responsible for regulating **non-coal minerals,** while the **Ministry of Coal** regulates the **coal mining sector.**
- **Statement 3 is correct:** The **Environmental Impact Assessment (EIA) process** is mandatory for obtaining mining leases for major minerals to ensure that mining activities are conducted in an environmentally sustainable manner.

**Therefore, the correct answer is (b) 1 and 3 only.**

**36.** *(b)* Only three

According to the **Mines and Minerals (Development and Regulation) Act, 1957,** 'minor minerals' include minerals that have relatively low economic value and are typically used in construction and industrial purposes. The following minerals are classified as 'minor minerals':

- **Sand:** Classified as a minor mineral, commonly used in construction.
- **Granite:** Considered a minor mineral and used extensively for construction and decorative purposes.
- **Marble:** Also classified as a minor mineral, used in construction, flooring and decorative applications.

However:

- **Limestone:** Although it is used in construction, limestone is considered a **major mineral** when used in cement production.
- **Coal:** Classified as a **major mineral** due to its significance as a primary energy source.

**Therefore, the correct answer is (b) Only three.**

**37.** *(a)* 1 only

- **Statement 1 is correct:** Under the **Mines and Minerals (Development and Regulation) Act, 1957,** the state governments are empowered to make rules regarding the regulation and management of minor minerals, including their extraction, transportation and royalty collection.
- **Statement 2 is incorrect: Bauxite, copper and iron ore** are classified as **major minerals** due to their significant industrial and economic importance. Minor minerals generally include minerals like **sand, gravel, clay, marble and granite.** The distinction between minor and major minerals is based on their economic importance and usage.
- **Statement 3 is incorrect:** The **royalty rates for minor minerals** are **determined by state governments,** not the Central Government.

Each state has the authority to fix rates based on local considerations.

**Therefore, the correct answer is (a) 1 only.**

**38.** *(b)* Only two pairs

- **Pair 1 is correct:** The **Geological Survey of India (GSI)** is responsible for **conducting geological surveys and mineral exploration.** It also maintains comprehensive geological and mineral resource data for the country, making it a crucial authority in the field of geology and mineral exploration.
- **Pair 2 is correct:** The **Ministry of Mines is the authority** responsible for **formulating policies for the exploration and development of non-coal minerals** in India. It oversees mineral concessions, development and management.
- **Pair 3 is incorrect:** The **Indian Bureau of Mines (IBM)** is responsible for **overseeing sustainable mining practices, promoting scientific mining and ensuring effective mineral exploration.** It also maintains a database of mineral resources and mining activities in India. The function related to **occupational safety** belongs to Directorate General of Mines Safety (DGMS).
- **Pair 4 is incorrect:** The **Directorate General of Mines Safety (DGMS)** is the authority responsible for **ensuring occupational safety, health and welfare of workers in the mining industry.** It sets safety standards and conducts inspections in mining operations.

**Thus, the correct answer is (b) Only two pairs.**

**39.** *(b)* Only two

DMFs are **non-profit trusts** that were formed under the **Mines and Minerals (Development and Regulation) (MMDR) Amendment Act 2015** with an objective to work in the interest and benefits of persons and areas affected by mining-related operations in a manner as may be prescribed by the State Government.

- **Statement 1 is correct:** The **District Mineral Foundation (DMF)** funds are indeed utilised for the **welfare of mining-affected communities**, with the aim of ensuring that people living in mining areas benefit from the mineral wealth extracted from their regions.
- **Statement 2 is correct:** The establishment of DMFs is mandated under the **Mines and Minerals (Development and Regulation) Act, 1957 (MMDR Act)**, following amendments made in **2015**. This makes it compulsory for mining leaseholders to contribute to the DMF funds.
- **Statement 3 is incorrect:** The funds collected by DMFs are **managed at the district level** by a governing body that typically includes local authorities. The **Central Government** provides guidelines, but the management is not done directly by it.

**Thus, the correct answer is (b) Only two.**

**40.** *(a)* 1 and 2 only

- **Statement 1 is correct:** DMFs are established as **non-profit trusts** in districts where mining operations occur, with the purpose of funding welfare initiatives for people affected by mining activities.
- **Statement 2 is correct: Pradhan Mantri Khanij Kshetra Kalyan Yojana (PMKKKY):** The objective of this programme is to work for the welfare of people and areas affected by mining related operations with the help of the funds generated by DMFs with the aims to ensure that the **DMF funds** are used to implement welfare projects in areas such as healthcare, education and livelihood enhancement for mining-affected communities. In all states' DMF rules, some high-priority areas are identified which are entitled to get at least 60 per cent of the DMF fund.
- **Statement 3 is incorrect:** While DMF funds can be used for **infrastructure development,** they are not restricted to this purpose alone. They can also be utilised for **healthcare, education, drinking water supply, environmental conservation and other welfare measures** for mining-affected communities.

**Therefore, the correct answer is (a) 1 and 2 only.**

**41.** *(a)* 1 and 2 only

- **Statement 1 is correct:** The **National Mineral Exploration Trust** (NMET) was established to **fund mineral exploration** projects across India. It aims to enhance mineral discovery and development, thereby supporting the country's mining sector.

- **Statement 2 is correct:** Funds for NMET are collected as a **percentage of the royalty payments** made by mining leaseholders. This royalty is based on the value of the minerals extracted.
  - Currently, mining leaseholders contribute **2% of the royalty amount** to the NMET fund, which is utilised for exploration activities.
- **Statement 3 is incorrect:** The NMET is **not administered by the Geological Survey of India (GSI).** It is administered by a governing body under the **Ministry of Mines,** which supervises its functioning and approves funding for mineral exploration projects.

**Therefore, the correct answer is (a) 1 and 2 only.**

**42.** *(a)* 1-3-2-4

- **Enactment of the Coal Mines (Nationalisation) Act, 1973:** This act led to the **nationalisation of coal mines,** effectively bringing all coal mines under the control of the government.
- **Establishment of Coal India Limited (CIL):** The first major regulatory milestone was the establishment of **Coal India Limited (CIL)** in 1975. CIL was created to manage coal resources and production in the country after the nationalisation of coal mines.
- **Introduction of the Coal Mines (Special Provisions) Act, 2015:** This act was introduced to **facilitate the auction and allocation of coal mines** following the Supreme Court's decision to cancel certain allocations, opening the path for transparent and competitive allocation.
- **Opening up of the coal mining sector to private companies for commercial mining:** In **2020**, the Indian government allowed **private companies** to enter the coal mining sector for **commercial mining,** ending the monopoly of Coal India Limited in coal production. This was a significant step in liberalising the coal sector.

**Thus, the correct chronological order is (a) 1-3-2-4.**

**43.** *(a)* 1 and 2 only

- **Statement 1 is correct:** Under the **commercial mining policy,** the Indian government has removed **end-use restrictions** for coal mined by private companies. Earlier, coal mining was restricted to captive use for specific sectors such as power, steel, or cement industries, but now private companies can mine coal without such restrictions which allow private companies to mine coal for any purpose, including selling it in the open market this ends Coal India Limited's (CIL) monopoly.
- **Statement 2 is correct:** Private companies are allowed to sell **100% of their coal production in the open market.** This is a key feature of the commercial coal mining policy, allowing private companies to participate in coal mining without needing to tie production to a specific use or buyer.
- **Statement 3 is incorrect:** While **private players are allowed to participate in commercial coal mining, there are certain restrictions on coal exports** as per government policies, focusing mainly on meeting domestic demand.

**Therefore, the correct answer is (a) 1 and 2 only.**

## Past Learning (Answers)

| | | | | | |
|---|---|---|---|---|---|
| 1 (b) | 2 (b) | 3 (a) | 4 (c) | 5 (b) | 6 (b) |

# CHAPTER 15 Infrastructure Sector

## Assessment Round

### Topic 1 : Sector of Infrastructure

**1.** Consider the following outcomes:

1. Reduced logistics costs in India.
2. Improved multi-modal connectivity across key sectors like roads, railways and ports.
3. Enhanced India's export competitiveness by reducing infrastructure bottlenecks.
4. Promotion of infrastructure development only in urban areas.

How many of the given above is/are the possible benefits from the PM Gati Shakti Yojana?

(a) Only two (b) Only three
(c) All four (d) Only one

**2.** With reference to the 'National Infrastructure Pipeline (NIP)', consider the following statements:

1. NIP focuses on both greenfield and brownfield infrastructure projects to drive economic growth.
2. Around 80% of the total NIP investment is allocated for economic infrastructure such as transport, energy and digital infrastructure.
3. The funding for NIP projects is split evenly between the Central Government, State Governments and the private sector.

Which of the given statements are correct?

(a) 1 and 2 only (b) 1 and 3 only
(c) 2 and 3 only (d) 1, 2 and 3

**3.** The National Infrastructure Pipeline (NIP) includes various sectors to promote infrastructure development across India. In this context, which of the following sectors are part of the NIP?

1. Transportation and logistics
2. Renewable energy
3. Healthcare infrastructure
4. Financial services

Select the correct answer from the codes given below:

(a) 1 and 4 only (b) 1, 2 and 3 only
(c) 2, 3 and 4 only (d) 1, 2, 3 and 4

**4.** Which of the following best describes the purpose of the India Investment Grid (IIG)?

(a) A database exclusively for international investors seeking projects in the real estate sector in India.
(b) An online platform showcasing investment opportunities across multiple sectors and states in India to facilitate domestic, and foreign investment.
(c) A government portal for monitoring India's foreign reserves.
(d) A network of public-private partnerships for educational development.

**5.** With reference to the Sagarmala project, consider the following statements:

1. Ministry of Ports, Shipping and Waterways is the implementing authority for the Sagarmala project.
2. The Sagarmala initiative exclusively focuses on developing India's port infrastructure without involving inland waterways.
3. The project focuses on modernising only the existing ports of India.

Which of the given above statements is/are correct?

(a) 1 only (b) 2 and 3 only
(c) 1 and 3 only (d) 1, 2 and 3

**6.** Which of the following best describes the 'Landlord Port Model' in the port sector?

(a) The port authority manages both the infrastructure and cargo handling operations directly.

(b) The port authority owns the infrastructure but leases it to private operators who manage cargo handling and terminal operations.

(c) Private entities own and operate the entire port infrastructure, and services without government involvement.

(d) The port authority manages only administrative functions, while all operations are handled by multiple private companies.

**7.** With reference to the 'Bharatmala Pariyojana', consider the following statements:

1. The scheme is implemented by the Ministry of Road Transport and Highways (MoRTH).
2. It focuses on developing economic corridors and improving national highways.
3. The project primarily aims to boost connectivity across coastal areas of India.

How many of the given above statements is/are correct?

(a) Only one (b) Only two
(c) All three (d) None

**8.** Which of the following statements about the 'National Sagarmala Apex Committee (NSAC)' is/are correct?

1. It is chaired by the Union Minister of Ports, Shipping and Waterways.
2. The committee has the authority to directly allocate funds for Sagarmala projects.
3. It includes representatives from the private sector along with representatives from Central and State Governments.

Select the correct answer from the codes given below:

(a) 1 only
(b) 2 and 3 only
(c) 1 and 3 only
(d) 1, 2 and 3

**9.** With reference to the UDAN Scheme (Ude Desh Ka Aam Nagrik), consider the following statements:

1. The maximum airfare for UDAN routes is capped at 2,500 for one-hour journey.
2. The Central Government provides financial incentives in the form of Viability Gap Funding (VGF).
3. Under the UDAN scheme, 50% of the seats on UDAN flights are capped at subsidised rates for regional travellers.

How many of the above statements is/are correct?

(a) Only one
(b) Only two
(c) All three
(d) None

**10.** Which of the following best describes about the 'Regional Connectivity Fund (RCF)' under the UDAN Scheme?

(a) A fund exclusively provided by the Central Government to build new regional airports.

(b) A levy-funded mechanism that subsidises airfares for underserved and unserved routes under the UDAN Scheme.

(c) A public-private partnership fund aimed at financing private airlines to operate international routes.

(d) A one-time grant from international organisations to develop aviation infrastructure in rural areas.

**11.** With reference to the 'Harmonised List of Infrastructure', consider the following statements:

1. The list is notified by the Ministry of Finance.
2. Affordable housing is recognised as part of the Harmonised List of Infrastructure.
3. This list is used by the RBI to provide regulatory support to projects classified under infrastructure.

Which of the given statements is/are correct?

(a) 1 and 2 only (b) 2 and 3 only
(c) 1 and 3 only (d) 1, 2 and 3

**12.** Consider the following:

1. Eligibility for priority sector lending by banks.
2. Access to long-term funding at concessional rates.
3. Exemption from Goods and Services Tax (GST) on construction materials.
4. Reduced customs duties on imported equipment used for infrastructure projects.

How many of the above is/are actual benefits of receiving the infrastructure status?

(a) Only one (b) Only two
(c) Only three (d) All four

**13.** Which of the following sectors are notified under the Harmonised List of Infrastructure?

1. Renewable energy generation (solar, wind, hydroelectric)
2. Railways and metro rail systems
3. IT and software development
4. Water supply and sanitation

Select the correct answer from the codes given below:

(a) 1 and 2 only
(b) 1, 2 and 4 only
(c) 2 and 3 only
(d) 1, 3 and 4 only

**14.** Arrange the following modes of transport in India's logistics sector in decreasing order of their contribution to the total freight movement:

1. Road transport
2. Railways
3. Coastal shipping
4. Air freight

Select the correct answer from the codes given below:

(a) 1-2-3-4 (b) 2-1-3-4
(c) 1-3-2-4 (d) 2-3-1- 4

**15.** Which of the following best describes the World Bank's Logistics Performance Index (LPI)?

(a) A global ranking that evaluates the competitiveness of a country's trade logistics based on factors like infrastructure, customs and timeliness.
(b) A tool that ranks countries based on their energy efficiency and carbon footprint in the logistics sector.
(c) An index that measures the total volume of freight moved by each country in a given year.
(d) A framework used by the World Bank to assess the cost-effectiveness of shipping routes worldwide.

**16.** Which of the following best describes the primary objective of Multi-modal Logistics Parks (MMLPs) under the Bharatmala Pariyojana?

(a) To reduce logistics costs by integrating multiple modes of transport such as road, rail and waterways.
(b) To promote the development of urban infrastructure and smart cities.
(c) To enhance air cargo capacity by building new airports across India.
(d) To facilitate international trade by constructing ports along coastal areas.

**17.** India's first Multi-modal Logistics Park (MMLP) is being developed in which of the following locations?

(a) Chennai, Tamil Nadu
(b) Bengaluru, Karnataka
(c) Jogighopa, Assam
(d) Varanasi, Uttar Pradesh

**18.** With reference to India's National Logistics Policy (NLP), consider the following statements:

1. The policy aims to reduce India's logistics costs from 13-14% of GDP to a globally comparable level of 8%.
2. It focuses on creating a unified digital logistics platform to streamline the movement of goods.
3. The policy is implemented solely by the Ministry of Commerce and Industry.

How many of the above statements is/are correct?

(a) Only one
(b) Only two
(c) All three
(d) None

**19.** Which of the following are components of the 'National Logistics Policy (NLP), 2022'?

1. Comprehensive Logistics Action Plan (CLAP)
2. Unified Logistics Interface Platform (ULIP)
3. Sectoral Logistics Plans for agriculture, pharmaceuticals and e-commerce

Select the correct answer using the codes given below:

(a) 1 and 2 only
(b) 2 and 3 only
(c) 1 and 3 only
(d) 1, 2 and 3

**20.** Which of the following best describes the Unified Logistics Interface Platform (ULIP) under the National Logistics Policy (NLP)?

(a) A digital platform integrating data from various logistics stakeholders to enable real-time tracking of goods and better coordination among transport modes.
(b) A government-run e-commerce platform designed to facilitate the sale of logistics equipment.
(c) A platform designed exclusively for managing customs and import-export clearances for large ports in India.
(d) A financial assistance program for logistics companies seeking technology upgrades.

**21.** Which of the following best describes the Comprehensive Logistics Action Plan (CLAP) under the National Logistics Policy?

(a) A framework designed to integrate logistics infrastructure with agricultural supply chains.
(b) A detailed plan to improve infrastructure, human resource development and digital systems to reduce logistics costs, and enhance efficiency.
(c) A subsidy program for logistics companies to upgrade their transport fleets.
(d) A policy to promote international logistics service providers in India.

**22.** With reference to India's Dedicated Freight Corridors, consider the following statements:

1. Western Dedicated Freight Corridor (WDFC) connects the Jawaharlal Nehru Port (Mumbai) to Dadri in Uttar Pradesh.
2. Eastern Dedicated Freight Corridor (EDFC) runs between Ludhiana in Punjab and Dankuni in West Bengal.
3. DFC network is being developed by the Dedicated Freight Corridor Corporation of India (DFCCIL) under the Ministry of Road Transport and Highways.

How many of the above statements is/are correct?

(a) Only one
(b) Only two
(c) All three
(d) None

**23.** Consider the following states:

1. Maharashtra
2. Rajasthan
3. Gujarat
4. Madhya Pradesh
5. Haryana

How many of the given above states are directly traversed by the Western Dedicated Freight Corridor (WDFC)?

(a) Only two
(b) Only three
(c) Only four
(d) All five

## Topic 2 : Infrastructure Financing

**24.** Consider the following methods:

1. Infrastructure Investment Trusts (InvITs)
2. Municipal Bonds
3. Tax-Free Infrastructure Bonds
4. Corporate Social Responsibility (CSR) Funds

How many of the given above is/are key methods for financing infrastructure projects in India?

(a) Only one
(b) Only two
(c) Only three
(d) All four

**25.** With reference to Development Finance Institutions (DFIs) in India, consider the following statements:

1. DFIs provide long-term finance for sectors like infrastructure and housing which are not typically served by traditional commercial banks.
2. National Bank for Financing Infrastructure and Development (NaBFID) is a newly established DFI aimed at supporting infrastructure development in India.
3. DFIs are permitted to take deposits from the general public like traditional commercial banks.

How many of the given above statements is/are correct?

(a) Only one
(b) Only two
(c) All three
(d) None

**26.** Arrange the following Development Finance Institutions (DFIs) in India in the chronological order of their establishment:

1. Industrial Finance Corporation of India (IFCI)
2. National Bank for Agriculture and Rural Development (NABARD)
3. Small Industries Development Bank of India (SIDBI)
4. National Bank for Financing Infrastructure and Development (NaBFID)

Select the correct answer from the codes given below:

(a) 1-2-3-4 (b) 2-1-3-4
(c) 1-3-2-4 (d) 3-1-2-4

**27.** With reference to the 'National Bank for Financing Infrastructure and Development (NaBFID)', consider the following statements:

1. It was established under an act passed by the Parliament of India in 2021.
2. It has the authority to issue infrastructure bonds to raise capital for its operations.
3. NaBFID is allowed to take public deposits like commercial banks to fund infrastructure projects.

How many of the given above statements is/are correct?

(a) Only one (b) Only two
(c) All three (d) None

**28.** Consider the following entities:

1. Central Government
2. Pension Funds
3. Multilateral Development Banks
4. Indian Private Banks

How many of the given above entities is/are eligible to hold shares in NaBFID?

(a) Only two
(b) Only three
(c) All four
(d) Only one

**29.** Which of the following are key benefits of Asset Monetisation under the National Monetisation Pipeline (NMP)?

1. Unlocks value from underutilised public assets.
2. Attracts private sector investment into infrastructure sectors like roads and railways.
3. Leads to a permanent transfer of ownership from public to private entities.
4. Encourages innovation and modernization of public infrastructure.

Select the correct answer from the codes given below:

(a) 1, 2 and 4 only
(b) 1, 2 and 3 only
(c) 2 and 3 only
(d) 1, 2, 3 and 4

**30.** Consider the following sectors:

1. Highways
2. Airports
3. Power transmission
4. Sports stadiums

How many of the given above sectors is/are included in the National Monetisation Pipeline (NMP) for asset monetisation?

(a) Only one
(b) Only two
(c) Only three
(d) All four

**31.** With reference to the 'National Land Monetisation Corporation (NLMC)', consider the following statements:

1. It was created to reduce the financial burden of maintaining unused land for central Public Sector Enterprises (CPSEs).
2. It operates under the administrative control of the Ministry of Finance.
3. The proceeds from NLMC's activities can be reinvested by CPSEs for operational improvement.

How many of the above statements is/are correct?

(a) Only one (b) Only two
(c) All three (d) None

**32.** Match the following PPP models with their corresponding descriptions:

| PPP Model | Description |
|---|---|
| 1. Engineering, Procurement, and Construction (EPC) | A. The government pays the private entity in fixed milestones during the project, while the private player is responsible for design, construction and financial risk. |
| 2. Hybrid Annuity Model (HAM) | B. The government provides 40% of the project cost during construction and the remaining 60% is paid over a concession period based on performance. |
| 3. Build-Operate-Transfer (BOT) | C. Private entity finances, builds and operates the project, and transfers it back to the government after a concession period. |
| 4. Operations and Maintenance (O&M) | D. The private entity takes responsibility for maintaining the infrastructure without constructing or owning the asset. |

Select the correct answer from the codes given below:

(a) 1-B, 2-A, 3-C, 4-D
(b) 1-A, 2-B, 3-C, 4-D
(c) 1-A, 2-D, 3-B, 4-C
(d) 1-C, 2-B, 3-D, 4-A

**33.** Arrange the following PPP models in decreasing order of private sector risk:

1. Build-Operate-Transfer (BOT) (Annuity)
2. Build-Operate-Transfer (BOT) (Toll)
3. Hybrid Annuity Model (HAM)
4. Engineering, Procurement and Construction (EPC)

Select the correct answer from the codes given below:

(a) 2-1-3-4
(b) 1-2-4-3
(c) 3-2-1-4
(d) 1-4-3-2

**34.** With reference to the 'Hybrid Annuity Model (HAM)', consider the following statements:

1. Under HAM, the government provides 40% of the project cost during the construction phase and the private entity is responsible for the remaining 60%.
2. The private entity is responsible for the operation and maintenance of the project over a concession period after construction.
3. The revenue risk in HAM is fully borne by the private entity as payments are based on toll collection.

Which of the given statements are correct?

(a) 1 and 2 only
(b) 1 and 3 only
(c) 2 and 3 only
(d) 1, 2 and 3

**35.** Which of the following best describes the Swiss Challenge method in public procurement?

(a) A method where a government agency invites private players to submit proposals for a project and then allows other players to submit competing counter proposals.
(b) A bidding process where the government selects the lowest bidder without allowing other bidders to challenge the offer.
(c) A system where international firms are given preference in bidding for large infrastructure projects.
(d) A closed bidding system where only pre-qualified bidders can submit proposals.

**36.** With reference to the 'Infrastructure Investment Trusts (InvITs)', consider the following statements:

1. InvITs allow individual and institutional investors to invest in infrastructure projects, and receive a share of the income generated.
2. These are required to distribute at least 90% of their net distributable cash flow to investors.
3. The ownership of assets in InvITs remains solely with the government.

How many of the above statements is/are correct?

(a) Only one
(b) Only two
(c) All three
(d) None

**37.** Which of the following statements is/are correct about InvITs?

1. SEBI allows InvITs to raise funds from institutional investors and retail investors.
2. InvITs are required by SEBI to have at least 50% of their assets in projects that are operational.
3. InvIT units can be listed on stock exchanges and traded by retail investors.

Select the correct answer from the codes given below:

(a) 1 only
(b) 1 and 3 only
(c) 2 and 3 only
(d) 1, 2 and 3

**38.** Consider the following statements:

1. InvITs are regulated by the Securities and Exchange Board of India (SEBI).
2. InvITs can only invest in debt instruments issued by infrastructure companies.
3. InvITs allow investors to directly own shares in infrastructure projects.

Which of the given statements is/are correct?

(a) 1 only
(b) 1 and 3 only
(c) 2 and 3 only
(d) 1, 2 and 3

**39.** Consider the following sources of income:

1. Interest income from debt securities held by the InvIT.
2. Dividend income from equity holdings in infrastructure projects.
3. Capital gains from the sale of InvIT units on stock exchanges.
4. Royalties from intellectual property owned by InvITs.

How many of the given above is/are legitimate sources of income for InvIT unit holders?

(a) Only two
(b) Only three
(c) All four
(d) Only one

**40.** With reference to 'Real Estate Investment Trusts (REITs)', consider the following statements:

1. These are primarily focused on residential real estate properties.
2. REITs provide tax benefits to investors as the dividend income received is tax-exempt.
3. REIT units can be traded on stock exchanges, offering liquidity to investors.

Which of the given statements is/are correct?

(a) 1 and 3 only
(b) 2 and 3 only
(c) 1 , 2 and 3 only
(d) 3 only

**41.** With reference to the 'National Investment and Infrastructure Fund (NIIF)', consider the following statements:

1. It is 100% owned by the Government of India and does not accept any private or international investment.
2. It is aimed at promoting long-term capital into India's infrastructure sector, including energy, transportation and logistics.
3. NIIF also invests in social infrastructure projects such as education and healthcare.

How many of the above statements is/are correct?

(a) Only one
(b) Only two
(c) All three
(d) None

## Topic 4 : Conventional Energy

**42.** Which of the following best describes the objective of the 'Shakti Policy' in India's power sector?

(a) To promote the use of renewable energy in rural areas by providing subsidies for solar power installations.

(b) To ensure the transparent and efficient allocation of domestic coal to power generation companies through a competitive bidding process.

(c) To encourage the export of excess coal reserves to neighbouring countries.

(d) To facilitate the privatisation of coal mines owned by state-owned enterprises.

**43.** Under the Shakti Policy, which of the following entities are eligible to participate in the competitive bidding process for coal linkages?

(a) Only state-owned power generation companies

(b) Private sector power producers, including those with existing long-term power purchase agreements (PPAs)

(c) Renewable energy companies focused on wind and solar power

(d) Only companies involved in coal mining

**44.** With reference to the 'National Coal Index (NCI)', consider the following statements:

1. It is updated monthly to reflect the latest market prices of different grades of coal.
2. The index covers all types of coal mined in India, including both coking and non-coking coal.
3. It is used to determine the benchmark price for coal auctions conducted by the government.

Which of the given statements are correct?

(a) 1 and 2 only

(b) 2 and 3 only

(c) 1 and 3 only

(d) 1, 2 and 3

**45.** With reference to the 'City Gas Distribution (CGD)' network in India, consider the following statements:

1. CGD network includes the distribution of both Compressed Natural Gas (CNG) for vehicles and Piped Natural Gas (PNG) for domestic, commercial, and industrial consumers.
2. Petroleum and Natural Gas Regulatory Board (PNGRB) is the regulatory authority for CGD networks in India.
3. The CGD network is limited to Tier-1 cities and does not extend to smaller towns or rural areas.

How many of the above statements is/are correct?

(a) Only one

(b) Only two

(c) All three

(d) None

**46.** What is the primary objective of the 'Urja Ganga Project'?

(a) To provide Piped Natural Gas (PNG) and Compressed Natural Gas (CNG) to households and industries in India's North-Eastern region.

(b) To expand the City Gas Distribution (CGD) network to Eastern India, including cities like Varanasi and Patna, through the construction of a gas pipeline.

(c) To promote the usage of renewable energy sources like solar and wind power in urban areas.

(d) To develop India's hydroelectric potential in the Himalayan region.

**47.** Which of the following states are part of the Urja Ganga Project pipeline network?

(a) Uttar Pradesh, Bihar, Jharkhand, West Bengal, Odisha

(b) Punjab, Haryana, Gujarat, Maharashtra

(c) Tamil Nadu, Karnataka, Andhra Pradesh, Kerala

(d) Rajasthan, Madhya Pradesh, Maharashtra, Gujarat

**48.** Under the dual pricing mechanism of natural gas in India, what are the two distinct pricing methods?
(a) Cost-plus pricing for all fields and government-regulated pricing for international imports.
(b) Administered Pricing Mechanism (APM) for certain public sector fields and market-driven pricing for new fields.
(c) Government-fixed pricing for both public and private sectors.
(d) Uniform pricing across all domestic and international gas supplies.

**49.** Consider the following committees:
1. Kelkar Committee
2. Rangarajan Committee
3. Shunglu Committee
4. Kirit Parikh Committee

How many of the above committees has/have provided recommendations on natural gas pricing?
(a) Only one (b) Only two
(c) Only three (d) All four

**50.** With reference to India's Strategic Petroleum Reserves (SPR), consider the following statements:
1. These reserves are large stockpiles of crude oil maintained to protect against supply disruptions.
2. India's SPR facilities are located only on the Eastern Coast of the country.
3. Indian Strategic Petroleum Reserve Limited (ISPRL) is the agency responsible for maintaining these reserves.

Which of the above statements are correct?
(a) 1 and 2 only (b) 1 and 3 only
(c) 2 and 3 only (d) 1, 2 and 3

**51.** Which of the following statements about India's Strategic Petroleum Reserves (SPR) is/are correct?
1. India's SPRs are stored in underground rock caverns to ensure safety and security.
2. SPR program is meant to store both crude oil and refined petroleum products like gasoline and diesel.
3. India's SPR capacity is equivalent to more than 100 days of the country's crude oil requirements.

Which of the above statements is/are correct?
(a) 1 and 2 only (b) 2 and 3 only
(c) 1 only (d) 1, 2 and 3

**52.** Consider the following reforms:
1. Introduction of an Open Acreage Licensing Policy (OALP).
2. Introduction of a revenue-sharing model for oil and gas exploration.
3. Implementation of daily price revisions for petrol and diesel.

How many of the above steps has/have been implemented to further deregulate the oil and gas sector?
(a) Only one (b) Only two
(c) All three (d) None

**53.** What is the primary objective of the Open Acreage Licensing Policy (OALP) introduced by the Indian government?
(a) To promote public ownership of oil and gas companies in India.
(b) To allow companies to choose and bid for oil, and gas blocks throughout the year, without waiting for specific bidding rounds.
(c) To regulate the prices of oil and gas in the domestic market.
(d) To promote coal exploration and mining activities in India.

**54.** Which entity is responsible for managing the bidding and award of oil and gas exploration blocks under the Open Acreage Licensing Policy (OALP)?
(a) Directorate General of Hydrocarbons (DGH)
(b) Ministry of Coal
(c) Oil and Natural Gas Corporation (ONGC)
(d) Indian Petroleum Commission

# OMR SHEET

**Assessment Round**

| | | | | | | | | | | | | | | | | | | | |
|---|---|---|---|---|---|---|---|---|---|---|---|---|---|---|---|---|---|---|---|
| 1 | a | b | c | d | 31 | a | b | c | d | 61 | a | b | c | d | 91 | a | b | c | d |
| 2 | a | b | c | d | 32 | a | b | c | d | 62 | a | b | c | d | 92 | a | b | c | d |
| 3 | a | b | c | d | 33 | a | b | c | d | 63 | a | b | c | d | 93 | a | b | c | d |
| 4 | a | b | c | d | 34 | a | b | c | d | 64 | a | b | c | d | 94 | a | b | c | d |
| 5 | a | b | c | d | 35 | a | b | c | d | 65 | a | b | c | d | 95 | a | b | c | d |
| 6 | a | b | c | d | 36 | a | b | c | d | 66 | a | b | c | d | 96 | a | b | c | d |
| 7 | a | b | c | d | 37 | a | b | c | d | 67 | a | b | c | d | 97 | a | b | c | d |
| 8 | a | b | c | d | 38 | a | b | c | d | 68 | a | b | c | d | 98 | a | b | c | d |
| 9 | a | b | c | d | 39 | a | b | c | d | 69 | a | b | c | d | 99 | a | b | c | d |
| 10 | a | b | c | d | 40 | a | b | c | d | 70 | a | b | c | d | 100 | a | b | c | d |
| 11 | a | b | c | d | 41 | a | b | c | d | 71 | a | b | c | d | 101 | a | b | c | d |
| 12 | a | b | c | d | 42 | a | b | c | d | 72 | a | b | c | d | 102 | a | b | c | d |
| 13 | a | b | c | d | 43 | a | b | c | d | 73 | a | b | c | d | 103 | a | b | c | d |
| 14 | a | b | c | d | 44 | a | b | c | d | 74 | a | b | c | d | 104 | a | b | c | d |
| 15 | a | b | c | d | 45 | a | b | c | d | 75 | a | b | c | d | 105 | a | b | c | d |
| 16 | a | b | c | d | 46 | a | b | c | d | 76 | a | b | c | d | 106 | a | b | c | d |
| 17 | a | b | c | d | 47 | a | b | c | d | 77 | a | b | c | d | 107 | a | b | c | d |
| 18 | a | b | c | d | 48 | a | b | c | d | 78 | a | b | c | d | 108 | a | b | c | d |
| 19 | a | b | c | d | 49 | a | b | c | d | 79 | a | b | c | d | 109 | a | b | c | d |
| 20 | a | b | c | d | 50 | a | b | c | d | 80 | a | b | c | d | 110 | a | b | c | d |
| 21 | a | b | c | d | 51 | a | b | c | d | 81 | a | b | c | d | 111 | a | b | c | d |
| 22 | a | b | c | d | 52 | a | b | c | d | 82 | a | b | c | d | 112 | a | b | c | d |
| 23 | a | b | c | d | 53 | a | b | c | d | 83 | a | b | c | d | 113 | a | b | c | d |
| 24 | a | b | c | d | 54 | a | b | c | d | 84 | a | b | c | d | 114 | a | b | c | d |
| 25 | a | b | c | d | 55 | a | b | c | d | 85 | a | b | c | d | 115 | a | b | c | d |
| 26 | a | b | c | d | 56 | a | b | c | d | 86 | a | b | c | d | 116 | a | b | c | d |
| 27 | a | b | c | d | 57 | a | b | c | d | 87 | a | b | c | d | 117 | a | b | c | d |
| 28 | a | b | c | d | 58 | a | b | c | d | 88 | a | b | c | d | 118 | a | b | c | d |
| 29 | a | b | c | d | 59 | a | b | c | d | 89 | a | b | c | d | 119 | a | b | c | d |
| 30 | a | b | c | d | 60 | a | b | c | d | 90 | a | b | c | d | 120 | a | b | c | d |

## Calculate Your Score

| | |
|---|---|
| **Correct (✓)** | |
| **Incorrect (✓)** | |
| **Unattempted** | |
| **Total Score** | |
| **Accuracy (%)** | |

## Reasons for Incorrect Answers?

| | |
|---|---|
| 1. Lack of Knowledge/Existing Source Insufficient | |
| 2. Lack of Multiple Revision | |
| 3. Common Sense Mistakes | |

**Note :**

1. Calculate total score as correct answers carry 2 marks each 1/3rd marks will deducted for **Incorrect** Answers.
2. Calculate Accuracy (%) by dividing the number of correct answers to the total number of attempted questions.

## Past Learning

**1.** Consider the following airports: **(2024)**

1. Donyi Polo Airport
2. Kushinagar International Airport
3. Vijayawada International Airport

In the recent past, which of the above have been constructed as Greenfield projects?

(a) 1 and 2 only
(b) 2 and 3 only
(c) 2 and 3 only
(d) 1, 2 and 3

**2.** Consider the following statements: **(2023)**

**Statement I:** Interest income from the deposits in Infrastructure Investment Trusts (InvITs) distributed to their investors is exempted from tax, but the dividend is taxable.

**Statement II:** InviTs are recognised as borrowers under the 'Securitisation and Reconstruction of Financial Assets and Enforcement of Security Interest Act, 2002'.

Which one of the following is correct in respect of the above statements?

(a) Both Statement I and Statement II are correct, and Statement II is the correct explanation for Statement I.
(b) Both Statement I and Statement II are correct, and Statement II is not the correct explanation for Statement I.
(c) Statement I is correct, but Statement II is incorrect.
(d) Statement I is incorrect, Statement II is correct.

**3.** Which of the following is/are the aim/aims of 'Digital India' Plan of the Government of India? **(2018)**

1. Formation of India's own Internet companies like China did.
2. Establish a policy framework to encourage overseas multinational corporations that collect Big Data to build their large data centres within our national geographical boundaries.
3. Connect many of our villages to the Internet and bring Wi-Fi to many of our schools, public places, and major tourist centres.

Select the correct answer using the codes given below:

(a) 1 and 2 only
(b) 3 only
(c) 2 and 3 only
(d) 1, 2 and 3

**4.** With reference to 'National Investment and Infrastructure Fund', which of the following statements is/are correct? **(2017)**

1. It is an organ of NITI Aayog.
2. It has a corpus of ₹ 4, 00,000 crore at present.

Select the correct answer using the codes given below:

(a) 1 only (b) 2 only
(c) Both 1 and 2 (d) Neither 1 nor 2

**5.** Which one of the following is a purpose of 'UDAY', a scheme of the Government? **(2016)**

(a) Providing technical and financial assistance to start-up entrepreneurs in the field of renewable sources of energy
(b) Providing electricity to every household in the country by 2018
(c) Replacing the coal-based power plants with natural gas, nuclear, solar, wind and tidal power plants over a period of time.
(d) Providing for financial turnaround and revival of power distribution companies

# Detailed Solutions

## Assessment Round

**1.** *(b)* Only three

- **Statement 1 is correct: Reducing logistics costs** is a major objective of PM Gati Shakti Yojana, aimed at bringing India's logistics costs in line with global standards.
- **Statement 2 is correct:** The scheme focuses on **improving multi-modal connectivity** by integrating road, rail, aviation, and maritime infrastructure.
- **Statement 3 is correct: Enhancing export competitiveness** is also a key benefit, as better logistics and infrastructure will allow faster movement of goods, improving India's trade prospects.
- **Statement 4 is incorrect: Infrastructure development is not limited to urban areas.** PM Gati Shakti Yojana aims to cover **both urban and rural areas** across the country to enhance connectivity at all levels.

**Therefore, the correct answer is (b) Only three.**

**2.** *(a)* 1 and 2 only

The Government launched the NIP with a forward-looking approach and with a projected infrastructure investment of around **111 lakh crore during FY20-25** to provide high quality infrastructure across the country. As of 12 April 2024, out of the total capital outlay under NIP, the **transportation sector dominates with a contribution of 58%, followed by the energy sector at 24%, and the water, and sanitation sector at 12 per cent, and balance five per cent by other sectors such as social infrastructure, communication, etc**

- **Statement 1 is correct:** The NIP covers a combination of **greenfield projects** (new infrastructure) and **brownfield projects** (upgrading or expanding existing infrastructure) to foster development in multiple sectors.
- **Statement 2 is correct:** A significant portion of the NIP's budget is allocated to **economic infrastructure**, which includes sectors like **transport, energy and digital infrastructure**– around 80% of the total investment focuses on these sectors.
- **Statement 3 is incorrect:** The funding for NIP projects is not evenly split. The investment comes from **40% central government, 40% state governments and 20% private sector** participation.

**Therefore, the correct answer is (a) 1 and 2 only.**

**3.** *(b)* 1, 2 and 3 only

- **Option 1 is correct: Transportation and logistics** is one of the key sectors under the National Infrastructure Pipeline, which aims to enhance connectivity and improve supply chain efficiency through road, rail, and air infrastructure.
- **Option 2 is correct: Renewable energy** is included in the NIP, focusing on expanding India's renewable energy capacity. This aligns with India's commitment to sustainable development and lowering carbon emissions through solar, wind, and other renewable sources.
- **Option 3 is correct: Healthcare infrastructure** is also prioritised under the NIP to strengthen healthcare services across the country, ensuring accessible and high-quality medical facilities for all citizens.
- **Option 4 is incorrect: Financial services** are not included as a dedicated sector in the NIP since the initiative focuses on physical infrastructure projects rather than service-oriented financial systems.

**Therefore, the correct answer is (b) 1, 2 and 3 only.**

**4.** *(b)* An online platform showcasing investment opportunities across multiple sectors and states in India to facilitate domestic, and foreign investment.

- The **India Investment Grid (IIG)** is an online platform designed by the Government of India to enhance accessibility and transparency for potential investors.

- It provides a centralised source of investment opportunities across various sectors such as **infrastructure, manufacturing, renewable energy, healthcare and transportation.**
- The IIG helps both **domestic and foreign investors** explore viable projects with detailed project information, financial estimates, and project statuses, enabling investors to make well-informed decisions.
- Additionally, by covering opportunities across different states, IIG promotes balanced regional development and showcases India's diverse investment landscape, contributing to India's objective of creating a business-friendly environment.

**Thus, option (b) is the correct answer.**

**5.** *(a)* 1 only

- **Statement 1 is correct: Ministry of Ports, Shipping and Waterways** is the key implementing authority for the **Sagarmala project**, responsible for improving port-led development and coastal infrastructure.
- **Statement 2 is incorrect**: The **Sagarmala** project aims to improve **port-led development** and focuses on integrating **inland** waterways into the national logistics system to create a more efficient, multi-modal transport network.
  - It aims to reduce **logistics costs** and increase **trade efficiency** by improving India's maritime, and coastal infrastructure through a comprehensive approach to port modernisation, including the development of coastal economic zones (CEZs).
- **Statement 3 is incorrect**: The Sagarmala project focuses on both **modernising existing ports** and **developing new ports** to enhance India's maritime logistics capabilities.

**Thus, the correct answer is (a) 1 only.**

**6.** *(b)* The port authority owns the infrastructure but leases it to private operators who manage cargo handling and terminal operations.

- In the **Landlord Port Model**, the **port authority retains ownership of the port infrastructure** (such as docks and warehouses) but **leases it to private operators** for managing terminal operations, and cargo handling.
- This public-private collaboration allows the port to leverage private sector efficiency while maintaining public control over core infrastructure.
- **JNP** has become the first major port of the country to become a **100%** landlord port having all berths being operated on PPP model.

**Thus, option (b) is the correct answer.**

**7.** *(b)* Only two

- **Statement 1 is correct**: The **Bharatmala Pariyojana** is implemented by the **Ministry of Road Transport and Highways (MoRTH)** to develop national highways and improve road infrastructure across India.
- **Statement 2 is correct**: One of the key objectives of Bharatmala Pariyojana is to develop **economic corridors** and enhance **national highways** to ensure smoother movement of goods and services.
- **Statement 3 is incorrect**: Bharatmala Pariyojana focuses on **inland road connectivity** rather than coastal areas. Coastal infrastructure is the focus of the **Sagarmala project**.

**Thus, the correct answer is (b) Only two.**

**8.** *(a)* 1 only

- **Statement 1 is correct**: The **National Sagarmala Apex Committee (NSAC)** is chaired by the **Union Minister of Ports, Shipping and Waterways** who oversees the implementation of the Sagarmala Programme at the national level. This committee oversees the overall policy framework and implementation of the **Sagarmala project.**
- **Statement 2 is incorrect**: The NSAC does not have the authority to **directly allocate funds.** Fund allocation is typically handled by the respective ministries and government bodies overseeing specific projects.
  - The NSAC provides **policy direction, overall guidance and coordination** for the implementation of the Sagarmala Programme.
- **Statement 3 is incorrect**: The **NSAC does not** include representatives from the **private sector.** The composition of NSAC includes Minister of Shipping, Cabinet Ministers

from stakeholder Ministries and Chief Ministers or Ministers in charge of Ports of Maritime States.

| Sagarmala Body | Composition | Role |
|---|---|---|
| National Sagarmala Apex Committee | Chaired by Minister of Shipping<br>Cabinet Ministers from stakeholder Ministries<br>Chief Ministers/ Ministers in charge of Ports of Maritime States | Overall policy guidance<br>High level coordination<br>Approve National Perspective Plan<br>Review various aspects of planning<br>Review and guidance for implemention |
| State Sagarmala Committee | Chaired by Chief Minister/ Minister in Charge of Ports<br>Relevant Dep. and agencies | Coordinating and facilitating Sagarmala related projects<br>Take up matters on priority as decided in the NSAC |

**Thus, the correct answer is (a) 1 only.**

**9.** *(b)* Only two

- **Statement 1 is correct:** The fare for UDAN routes is capped at ₹ 2,500 for one-hour journey under the regional connectivity initiative to make air travel affordable for common citizens.
- **Statement 2 is correct:** The Central Government provides **Viability Gap Funding (VGF)** to make regional air operations economically feasible, ensuring that airlines can offer affordable fares while maintaining financial viability.
- **Statement 3 is incorrect:** Under the UDAN scheme, **at least 50% of the seats on UDAN flights** are capped at subsidised rates, but this is not necessarily limited to regional travellers. The seats are available to all passengers, with subsidies ensuring that a significant portion of the seats is offered at affordable rates.

**Therefore, the correct answer is (b) Only two.**

**10.** *(b)* A levy-funded mechanism that subsidises airfares for underserved and unserved routes under the UDAN Scheme.

- The **Regional Connectivity Fund** (RCF) is a key component of the UDAN Scheme. It is financed by imposing a levy on scheduled commercial flights operating on domestic routes. The fund is then used to **subsidise airfares** for underserved and unserved routes, making regional air travel affordable.
- The scheme **does not focus on international routes or one-time grants** but aims to improve **domestic air connectivity** in remote regions.
- RCS operators through (i) concessions by Central Government, State Governments and airport operators to reduce the cost of airline operations on regional routes, and (ii) financial support (viability gap funding or VGF) to meet the gap, if any, between the cost of airline operations, and expected revenues on such routes.

**Thus, option (b) is the correct answer.**

**11.** *(d)* 1, 2 and 3

- **Statement 1 is correct:** The Harmonised List of Infrastructure in India is a comprehensive classification of sectors that are recognised as infrastructure for various regulatory, policy and investment purposes. It is maintained by **the Ministry of Finance** in collaboration with various sectoral ministries and it plays a crucial role in guiding investments, and policy decisions for infrastructure development.
- **Statement 2 is correct: Affordable housing is indeed part of the Harmonised List of Infrastructure,** recognising its importance in urban development and housing policies. The inclusion of affordable housing in this list allows for benefits like tax incentives and easier financing options to boost the housing sector, and meet national housing goals.
- **Statement 3 is correct:** The **Reserve Bank of India (RBI)** uses the Harmonised List to provide specific regulatory treatment, including benefits like priority sector lending to infrastructure projects.

**Thus, the correct answer is (d) 1, 2 and 3.**

**12.** *(b)* Only two

- **Eligibility for priority sector lending** is a key benefit of receiving the infrastructure tag, allowing projects to access loans at preferential rates.
- **Access to long-term funding at concessional rates** is another benefit, as infrastructure projects often require longer gestation periods for completion, making concessional loans essential for their sustainability.
- **Exemption from Goods and Services Tax** (GST) on construction materials is **not a direct benefit** of receiving the infrastructure tag. Tax exemptions are subject to other specific laws and regulations.
- **Reduced customs duties on imported equipment** may be provided in some cases but are **not a direct benefit of infrastructure status.** These benefits depend on separate policies or government schemes.

**Thus, the correct answer is (b) Only two.**

**13.** *(b)* 1, 2 and 4 only

- **Renewable energy generation** such as **solar, wind and hydroelectric power** is included in the Harmonised List of Infrastructure, as these are critical for sustainable development, and energy security.
- **Railways and metro rail systems** are part of the list as they contribute significantly to enhancing public transport infrastructure in India.
- **IT and software development** are not included under the infrastructure category, as they fall under technology and service sectors rather than physical infrastructure development.
- **Water supply and sanitation are included under the list** to ensure improved access to clean water, and sanitation facilities, which are vital for public health, and economic development.

**Thus, the correct answer is (b) 1, 2 and 4 only.**

**14.** *(a)* 1-2-3-4

- **Road transport** carries the largest share of freight in India, accounting for **around 60%** of the total freight movement.
- **Railways** follow, contributing to approximately 30% of the freight movement, mainly handling bulk goods like coal and steel.
- **Coastal shipping** and **inland waterways** handle a small portion of freight, around 6%, but are growing due to government initiatives like **Sagarmala.**
- **Air freight** contributes the least, as it primarily handles high-value, low-volume goods.

**Thus, the correct order is (a) 1-2-3-4.**

**15.** *(a)* A global ranking that evaluates the competitiveness of a country's trade logistics based on factors like infrastructure, customs, and timeliness.

- The **World Bank Logistics Performance Index (LPI)** evaluates the **efficiency of trade logistics** in countries based on six key dimensions: customs performance, infrastructure quality, ease of arranging shipments, logistics services quality, tracking and tracing capabilities, and timeliness of deliveries. The index is widely used to assess how well countries support logistics and trade, and how they compare globally.
- **India ranks 38 out of 139 countries on World Bank's Logistics Performance Index Report 2023; India's rank has improved by sixteen places from 54 in 2014**

**Thus, option (a) is the correct answer.**

**16.** *(a)* To reduce logistics costs by integrating multiple modes of transport such as road, rail and waterways.

The **primary objective** of MMLPs is to **reduce logistics costs** by providing integrated infrastructure that combines **road, rail, and waterways** for the movement of goods. These logistics parks are being developed under the **Bharatmala Pariyojana** to streamline the movement of freight and reduce overall transport costs by optimising modal shifts.

**Thus, option (a) is the correct answer.**

**17.** *(c)* Jogighopa, Assam

India's first **Multi-modal Logistics Park (MMLP)** is being developed at **Jogighopa, Assam.** This project is aimed at improving connectivity and reducing logistics costs in the North-East region, integrating rail, road, and waterways to ensure seamless freight movement. It will also provide warehousing and other logistics infrastructure for efficient handling of goods.

**Thus, option (c) is the correct answer.**

**18.** *(b)* Only two

- **Statement 1 is correct: National Logistics Policy** (NLP) aims to bring down India's logistics costs from the current **13-14% of GDP** to around **8% by 2030**, making Indian goods more competitive globally.
- **Statement 2 is correct:** One of the key aspects of the NLP is the development of a **unified digital logistics platform,** known as **ULIP (Unified Logistics Interface Platform)** to bring various stakeholders onto a single platform for seamless operations.
- **Statement 3 is incorrect:** While the Ministry of Commerce and Industry plays a significant role, the NLP is a **multi-ministerial effort,** involving several other ministries such as the Ministry of Road Transport and Highways, Ministry of Railways, and others.

**Thus, the correct answer is (b) Only two.**

**19.** *(d)* 1, 2 and 3

- **Statement 1 is correct:** The **Comprehensive Logistics Action Plan** (CLAP) is a key component of the National Logistics Policy, aiming to reduce logistics costs and enhance efficiency. CLAP includes strategies like optimising logistics infrastructure, digital transformation and human resource development to streamline the sector.
- **Statement 2 is correct:** The **Unified Logistics Interface Platform** (ULIP) is an integral part of NLP. ULIP enables **digital integration** by connecting various logistics stakeholders, promoting transparency, and enhancing coordination, which reduces delays, and improves overall efficiency.
- **Statement 3 is correct:** The policy includes **Sectoral Logistics Plans** for specific industries such as **agriculture, pharmaceuticals and e-commerce.** These plans focus on the unique logistics needs of each sector, promoting tailored infrastructure and policy measures to meet their specific demands.

**Thus, the correct answer is (d) 1, 2 and 3.**

**20.** *(a)* A digital platform integrating data from various logistics stakeholders to enable real-time tracking of goods and better coordination among transport modes.

The **Unified Logistics Interface Platform (ULIP)** is a key initiative under the **National Logistics Policy** (NLP) aimed at creating a **single digital interface** that brings together various stakeholders in the logistics sector. It enables the **real-time tracking** of goods, improves **coordination** between different modes of transport, and streamlines **logistics processes** by integrating data from multiple sources.

**Thus, option (a) is the correct answer.**

**21.** *(b)* A detailed plan to improve infrastructure, human resource development and digital systems to reduce logistics costs, and enhance efficiency.

The **Comprehensive Logistics Action Plan** (CLAP) is an integral part of the **National Logistics Policy** (NLP), focusing on improving infrastructure, **skill development** and **digital integration** within the logistics sector. It aims to reduce India's high logistics costs and enhance the overall efficiency of freight movement across the country. This action plan lays out clear strategies to address logistical bottlenecks by improving **infrastructure** and **technological systems.**

**Thus, option (b) is the correct answer.**

**22.** *(b)* Only two

- **Statement 1 is correct:** The **Western Dedicated Freight Corridor** (WDFC) connects **Jawaharlal Nehru Port** in **Mumbai** to **Dadri** in **Uttar Pradesh,** facilitating the movement of goods between the Western Ports and Northern India.
- **Statement 2 is correct:** The **Eastern Dedicated Freight Corridor** (EDFC) spans from **Ludhiana** in **Punjab** to **Dankuni** in **West Bengal,** providing an important trade route for goods moving across Northern and Eastern India.

- **Statement 3 is incorrect:** The **Dedicated Freight Corridor Corporation of India (DFCCIL) under the Ministry of Railways** is responsible for the construction and management of the DFCs.

DFC consists of two arms:

- **Western Dedicated Freight Corridor** (WDFC): The WDFC stretches from **Jawaharlal Nehru Port (Nhava Sheva), Mumbai to Dadri in Uttar Pradesh, covering a distance of approximately 1,504 km.**
  - **Purpose:** This corridor primarily serves the industrial hubs in Western India and is designed to handle the movement of goods such as containers, cement, fertilisers, and food grains.
  - **Key States Covered:** Maharashtra, Gujarat, Rajasthan, Haryana and Uttar Pradesh.
  - **Eastern Dedicated Freight Corridor** (EDFC): The EDFC runs from Ludhiana in Punjab to Dankuni in West Bengal, covering a distance of approximately 1,839 km.
  - **Purpose:** The EDFC primarily caters to coal, iron ore, steel and other industrial products, serving the coal-producing areas of Eastern India, and the steel plants in Jharkhand, and West Bengal.
  - **Key States Covered:** Punjab, Haryana, Uttar Pradesh, Bihar, Jharkhand and West Bengal.

**Thus, the correct answer is (b) Only two.**

**23.** *(c)* Only four

The **Western Dedicated Freight Corridor** (WDFC) passes through the states of:

- **Maharashtra:** The corridor starts at the **Jawaharlal Nehru Port** in Mumbai, Maharashtra.
- **Rajasthan:** It passes through various cities in Rajasthan.
- **Gujarat:** The WDFC covers several regions in Gujarat, including **Dadra and Nagar Haveli.**
- **Haryana:** The corridor reaches its final point in **Dadri, Uttar Pradesh,** after crossing through Haryana.
- **Madhya Pradesh is not on the route of the WDFC.**

**Hence, the correct answer is (c) Only four.**

**24.** *(c)* Only three

- **Method 1 (Infrastructure Investment Trusts - InvITs) is a key method: InvITs** are specialised investment vehicles that pool funds from various investors to finance and operate income-generating infrastructure assets. They are a prominent tool for raising capital for large-scale infrastructure projects in sectors like highways, power transmission and renewable energy.
- **Method 2 (Municipal Bonds) is a key method: Municipal Bonds** are issued by urban local bodies or municipal corporations to raise funds for public infrastructure projects. These bonds help in financing city-level infrastructure like water supply, sanitation and transportation, and they have gained popularity with incentives for infrastructure development.
- **Method 3 (Tax-Free Infrastructure Bonds) is a key method: Tax-Free Infrastructure Bonds** are issued by government-backed entities to fund infrastructure projects. Investors benefit from tax-free returns, making these bonds a crucial instrument for mobilising funds for projects such as railways, highways and ports.
- **Method 4 (Corporate Social Responsibility - CSR Funds) is not a key method:** Although **CSR funds** can support community development and social projects, they are not a primary or structured method for financing large-scale infrastructure projects. CSR contributions are typically directed toward social causes rather than major infrastructure financing.

**Thus, the correct answer is (c) Only three.**

**25.** *(b)* Only two

- **Statement 1 is correct: Development Finance Institutions** (DFIs) are specialised financial institutions created to provide **long-term financing** for sectors that require large capital and extended repayment periods, such as **infrastructure, housing, and industry development.** Traditional commercial banks often do not cater to these needs due to their focus on shorter-term lending.

- **Statement 2 is correct:** The **National Bank for Financing Infrastructure and Development (NaBFID)** was established in 2021 as a **new DFI** to address the infrastructure financing gap in India. NaBFID focuses on facilitating capital for infrastructure projects, providing a structured approach to fund critical infrastructure sectors.
- **Statement 3 is incorrect:** Unlike commercial banks, **DFIs do not take deposits from the general public.** DFIs typically raise funds through government backing, bonds and institutional investors rather than public deposits, allowing them to focus on specific, high-impact sectors without competing in traditional retail banking.

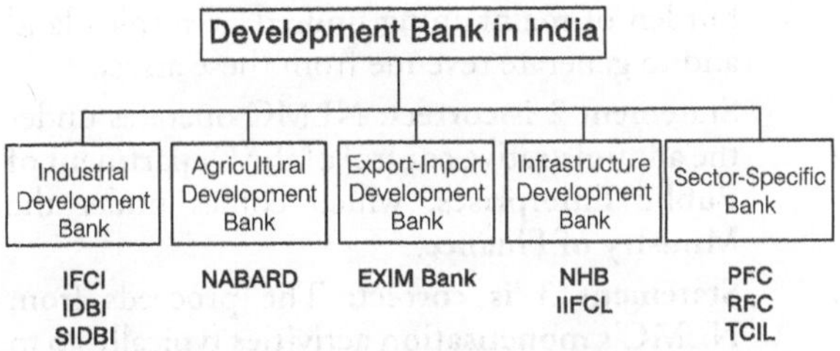


**Thus, the correct answer is (b) Only two.**

**26.** *(a)* 1-2-3-4

- **First: Industrial Finance Corporation of India (IFCI)** was established in **1948** as India's first Development Finance Institution (DFI), aimed at providing financial support to the industrial sector.
- **Second: National Bank for Agriculture and Rural Development (NABARD)** was set up in **1982** to finance, and promote agriculture, and rural development in India.
- **Third: Small Industries Development Bank of India (SIDBI)** was established in **1990** to aid the growth of micro, small, and medium enterprises (MSMEs) in India, supporting small industries, and entrepreneurship.
- **Fourth: National Bank for Financing Infrastructure and Development (NaBFID)** was established in **2021** to bridge the infrastructure financing gap, focusing on large-scale projects.

**Thus, the correct order is (a) 1-2-3-4.**

**27.** *(b)* Only two

The Government of India set up NaBFID in April 2021 as India's **fifth All India Financial Institution** in the country to support the development of long-term non-recourse infrastructure financing in India, including the development of the bonds and derivatives markets necessary for infrastructure financing. NaBFID has both developmental, and financial objectives.

**The other 4 AIFIs in India are:** National Bank for Agriculture and Rural Development, National Housing Bank (NHB), Small Industries Development Bank of India (SIDBI), Export-Import Bank of India (EXIM Bank).

- **Statement 1 is correct: NaBFID** was established in **2021** after the **NaBFID Act** was passed by the Parliament of India to address the long-term financing needs of **large infrastructure projects** in India, especially in sectors like **roads, energy** and **transport.**
- **Statement 2 is correct:** One of NaBFID's core objectives is to reduce the **financing gap** in key infrastructure sectors and provide financial support for projects that require long-term funding. **NaBFID has the authority to issue infrastructure bonds** to raise capital for long-term financing of infrastructure projects.
- **Statement 3 is incorrect:** Unlike commercial banks, **NaBFID is not allowed to take public deposits.** It raises funds through different mechanisms such as bonds and long-term loans.

**Thus, the correct answer is (b) Only two.**

**28.** *(b)* Only three

- **Central Government:** The **Government of India** is a primary shareholder in NaBFID, holding a significant stake in the institution.
- **Pension funds:** Pension funds can hold shares in NaBFID, providing long-term capital for infrastructure development.
- **Multilateral Development Banks: Multilateral Development Banks** (MDBs) can hold shares in NaBFID, as they often provide funding for infrastructure projects in India.

- **Indian Private Banks**: While **private banks** can collaborate with NaBFID in terms of co-financing infrastructure projects, they are **not eligible** to hold shares in NaBFID. NaBFID is structured to be owned by the government and large institutional investors, not traditional commercial banks.

**Thus, the correct answer is (b) Only three.**

**29.** *(a)* 1, 2 and 4 only

- **Statement 1 is correct: Asset monetisation** unlocks value from underutilised or idle public assets by leveraging them for economic benefit. It helps **unlock value** from **underutilised public assets** by transferring operational responsibilities to private entities. This allows the government to generate revenue from existing infrastructure assets without selling them outright.
- **Statement 2 is correct**: It encourages **private sector investment** in infrastructure sectors like roads, railways, airports and power transmission, bringing in fresh capital.
- **Statement 3 is incorrect**: Asset monetisation does not involve a permanent transfer of ownership, instead, assets are leased or operated under concession agreements. The private entities take over operations for a limited period through leasing or concession agreements.
- **Statement 4 is correct**: The involvement of the private sector in asset monetisation encourages **innovation** and **modernisation** of public infrastructure, as private entities bring in **technology**, **expertise**, and **efficiency** to manage, and improve these assets.

**Thus, the correct answer is (a) 1, 2 and 4 only.**

**30.** *(d)* All four

The **sectors** included are roads, ports, airports, railways, warehousing, gas and product pipeline, power generation and transmission, mining, telecom, stadium, hospitality, and housing.

The **top 5 sectors** (by estimated value) capture 83% of the aggregate pipeline value. These top 5 sectors include: Roads (27%) followed by Railways (25%), Power (15%), oil and gas pipelines (8%) and Telecom (6%).

- **Highways**: Roads and highways are a major component of the National Monetisation Pipeline (NMP).
- **Airports**: Several airports, particularly smaller and under-utilised ones, are included in the NMP for monetisation.
- **Power transmission**: The **power transmission** sector is part of the asset monetisation efforts, where assets like power grids can be monetised.
- **Sports stadiums**: Sports infrastructure, including stadiums, is also included in the NMP for potential monetisation.

**Thus, the correct answer is (d) All four.**

**31.** *(c)* All three

**Statement 1 is correct**: The **National Land Monetisation Corporation** (NLMC) was established to relieve **CPSEs** from the financial burden of maintaining unused or surplus land and to generate revenue from these assets.

**Statement 2 is correct**: NLMC operates under the administrative control of the **Department of Public Enterprises**, which comes under the **Ministry of Finance**.

**Statement 3 is correct**: The proceeds from **NLMC's monetisation activities** typically go to the **government treasury**, not directly to the CPSEs for operational improvement. However, this **proceeds** from the monetisation activities carried out by NLMC can indeed be used by CPSEs to improve their operations, repay debts, or reinvest in infrastructure and capacity-building initiatives.

**Thus, the correct answer is (c) All three.**

**32.** *(b)* 1-A, 2-B, 3-C, 4-D

- **Pair 1 is correctly matched with A**: The **Engineering, Procurement and Construction** (EPC) model involves the government providing the entire cost, and making payments at pre-set milestones.
- **Pair 2 is correctly matched with B : The Hybrid Annuity Model (HAM)** involves the government paying 40% of the project cost during construction and 60% during the concession period.
- **Pair 3 is correctly matched with C**: The **Build-Operate-Transfer (BOT) model** involves the private entity financing,

constructing and operating the asset before transferring it to the government.

- **Pair 4 is correctly matched with D**: The **Operations and Maintenance (O&M)** model involves the private entity managing the infrastructure without owning it or being involved in its construction.

**Therefore, the correct matching pairs are 1-A, 2-B, 3-C, 4-D and the correct answer is (b).**

**33.** *(a)* 2-1-3-4

- **BOT (Toll)**: The highest risk for the private sector as revenue is dependent on toll collection. The risk is higher because revenue depends on the actual traffic or usage, which can be uncertain.
- **BOT (Annuity)**: The private entity bears construction and performance risk but is paid annuities, reducing the revenue risk.
- **HAM**: The government funds 40% of the cost, and the private sector faces risk on performance but is partially shielded.
- **EPC**: The lowest risk for the private sector, as the government funds the entire project and the private entity is responsible for only construction.

**Thus, the correct order of decreasing risk is (a) 2-1-3-4.**

**34.** *(a)* 1 and 2 only

- **Statement 1 is correct**: In the **Hybrid Annuity Model (HAM)**, the government provides **40% of the project cost** during the construction phase, and the remaining 60% is provided by the private entity. This reduces the financial burden on the private sector during construction.
- **Statement 2 is correct**: The private entity is responsible for the **operation and maintenance** of the infrastructure asset during the concession period, while the government takes care of annuity payments.
- **Statement 3 is incorrect**: In HAM, **revenue risk** is borne by the **government**, not the private entity, as the payments are based on annuities and not toll collection.

**Thus, the correct answer is (a) 1 and 2 only.**

**35.** *(a)* A method where a government agency invites private players to submit proposals for a project and then allows other players to submit competing counterproposals.

The **Swiss Challenge** method is a **public procurement process** where a **private entity** submits an unsolicited proposal to the government for a project. The government then opens the proposal to **competing bids** to ensure transparency and competitive pricing. The original proposer has the right to **match the best counterproposal** to win the project.

**Thus, option (a) is the correct answer.**

**36.** *(b)* Only two

- **Statement 1 is correct: Infrastructure Investment Trusts (InvITs)** are a mechanism like a mutual fund that allows both **individual and institutional investors** to invest in **income-generating infrastructure projects**, such as roads, and power plants.
- **Statement 2 is correct**: InvITs are required by regulation to distribute at least **90% of their net distributable cash flows** to their unit holders, ensuring regular returns to investors.

  **Some of the mandatory SEBI InvITs regulations for Infrastructure Investment Trusts in India are:**

  – An InvIT must invest **at least 80%** of its total assets in completed infrastructure projects capable of generating income. The remainder of assets up to a limit of 20% held by the InvIT can be invested in under-construction infrastructure projects and various SEBI-approved Equity, Debt, and Money Market instruments.

  – InvITs must **distribute at least 90% of their income** to their unit-holders as dividends on a bi-annual basis.
- **Statement 3 is incorrect**: The **trust** created under the InvIT structure holds the assets, and the investors in the trust have an **ownership stake** in the assets through the trust. These investors may include **private sector entities, pension funds, insurance companies** and **individual investors.**

- **Government entities** may contribute assets to InvITs, but once the assets are included in the trust, they are no longer solely owned by the government. Therefore, **the ownership of assets in InvITs does not remain solely with the government. Private players can own assets through these trusts.**

**Thus, the correct answer is (b) Only two.**

***37.*** *(b)* 1 and 3 only

- **Statement 1 is correct:** SEBI regulations allow InvITs to raise funds from both **institutional investors** (such as mutual funds and insurance companies) and **retail investors** through public offerings.
- **Statement 2 is incorrect:** As per SEBI regulations, InvITs must have at least 80% (not 50%) **of their assets** in operational projects to ensure regular cash flows for investors.
- **Statement 3 is correct: InvIT units** are listed on stock exchanges and can be **traded** by retail investors, providing them with liquidity, and access to infrastructure investments.

**Thus, the correct answer is (b) 1 and 3 only.**

***38.*** *(a)* 1 only

- **Statement 1 is correct: Infrastructure Investment Trusts (InvITs)** in India are regulated by the **Securities and Exchange Board of India (SEBI)**, which oversees their registration, compliance, and investor protection norms. SEBI provides guidelines to ensure transparency and operational standards for InvITs.
- **Statement 2 is incorrect:** InvITs are not limited to investing in debt instruments. They can invest in **both equity and debt instruments** of infrastructure companies, providing flexibility in portfolio composition. This mix allows InvITs to generate income and potentially appreciate in value.
- **Statement 3 is incorrect:** InvITs do not provide investors with direct ownership in infrastructure projects. Instead, investors own **units** in the InvIT, similar to shares in a mutual fund, which represent a share in the income generated by the underlying infrastructure assets rather than direct project ownership.

**Therefore, the correct answer is (a) 1 only.**

***39.*** *(b)* Only three

InvITs (Infrastructure Investment Trusts) primarily focus on infrastructure projects such as roads, power transmission, and utilities, rather than intellectual property (IP).

- **Interest income:** InvITs can hold debt securities of infrastructure projects, generating **interest income** for unit holders.
- **Dividend income:** InvITs may hold equity in infrastructure projects, providing **dividend income** from the profits generated.
- **Capital gains:** InvIT units can be traded on stock exchanges and **capital gains** are realised when unit holders sell their units at a higher price.
- **Royalties: InvITs (Infrastructure Investment Trusts)** primarily focus on **infrastructure projects** such as roads, power transmission and utilities, rather than intellectual property (IP), and therefore do not generate royalties.

**Thus, the correct answer is (b) Only three.**

***40.*** *(d)* 3 only

- **Statement 1 is incorrect: REITs** in India primarily focus on **commercial real estate properties**, such as office buildings, retail spaces and industrial properties, rather than residential real estate. This focus is aimed at providing a stable rental income stream from commercial leases.
- **Statement 2 is incorrect:** While REITs may provide certain tax efficiencies, **dividend income from REITs is not fully tax-exempt.** In India, for example, dividends are taxed at the hands of investors based on their applicable tax slabs, though some tax advantages may apply at the trust level.
- **Statement 3 is correct: REIT units are listed and traded on stock exchanges**, making them a liquid investment option. Investors can buy and sell REIT units in the secondary market, similar to shares, allowing them to access real estate investment without the need for direct property ownership.

**Thus, the correct answer is (d) 3 only.**

**41.** *(b)* Only two

- **Statement 1 is incorrect**: The Government of India holds a **49% stake** in NIIF and contributes significant initial capital to catalyse investments, while the remaining capital comes from **private and institutional investors.**
- **Statement 2 is correct**: NIIF's primary goal is to promote **long-term capital** investment in core infrastructure sectors like **energy, transportation,** and **logistics,** which are essential for economic development.
- **Statement 3 is correct**: In addition to core infrastructure, NIIF can also invest in **social infrastructure projects,** including sectors like **education** and **healthcare,** though this is not the primary focus.

**Thus, the correct answer is (b) Only two.**

**42.** *(b)* To ensure the transparent and efficient allocation of domestic coal to power generation companies through a competitive bidding process.

- The **Shakti Policy** (Scheme for Harnessing and Allocating Koyla Transparently in India) was introduced by the Government of India in 2017 with the aims to ensure the **transparent and efficient allocation** of domestic coal to power generation companies.
- It does so through a **competitive bidding process,** providing coal linkages to companies with more efficiency and fairness. This policy is crucial in optimising coal distribution for power generation, **not related to renewable energy or coal exports.**
- Coal is a critical resource for thermal power generation in the country, and the Shakti Policy addresses the issue of coal supply shortages while promoting transparency in coal allocation.

**Thus, option (b) is the correct answer.**

**43.** *(b)* Private sector power producers, including those with existing long-term power purchase agreements (PPAs).

The **Shakti Policy** allows **private sector power producers,** particularly those with existing **long-term power purchase agreements** (PPAs), to participate in the **competitive bidding process** for coal linkages. This ensures that these companies have access to the necessary coal for generating electricity. Renewable energy companies focused on solar or wind are not the target of this policy.

**Thus, option (b) is the correct answer.**

**44.** *(d)* 1, 2 and 3

The **National Coal Index** (NCI) is an index introduced by the Government of India in June 2020 to track the prices of coal across different grades and to ensure transparency in pricing. It serves as a benchmark for determining the price of coal in India, taking into account both domestic coal production and imported coal prices.

- **Statement 1 is correct: The National Coal Index** is updated **monthly** to reflect the latest market conditions, ensuring that the index is up-to-date with current coal prices.
- **Statement 2 is correct**: The NCI covers **all types of coal** mined in India, including both **coking** (used in steel production) and **non-coking coal** (used primarily in power generation).
- **Statement 3 is correct**: The NCI serves as the benchmark for **coal auctions** conducted by the government, helping determine the pricing for coal blocks offered to private players.

**Thus, the correct answer is (d) 1, 2 and 3.**

**45.** *(b)* Only two

- **Statement 1 is correct: City Gas Distribution** (CGD) network supplies **CNG** for vehicles and **PNG** to households, commercial establishments, and industries.
  - By promoting **CNG** and **PNG** through the CGD network, India aims to reduce its dependency on **imported oil** and **LPG,** improving energy security.
- **Statement 2 is correct: Petroleum and Natural Gas Regulatory Board** (PNGRB) regulates the **CGD network** in India, ensuring proper licensing and management of these systems.
- **Statement 3 is incorrect**: The CGD network is expanding to not just **Tier-1 cities** but also to **smaller towns** and even some rural areas, as part of India's efforts to increase clean energy access.

**Thus, the correct answer is (b) Only two.**

**46.** *(b)* To expand the City Gas Distribution (CGD) network to Eastern India, including cities like Varanasi and Patna, through the construction of a gas pipeline.

The Urja Ganga Project is a major initiative launched by the Government of India in **2016** to **extend the City Gas Distribution (CGD) network**. The project aims to provide **Piped Natural Gas (PNG)** and **Compressed Natural Gas (CNG)** to households, industries, and transport in **eastern India**, with key cities such as **Varanasi, Patna, Bhubaneswar** and others benefitting from the construction of a **natural gas pipeline**. It aims to reduce reliance on traditional fuels like LPG and diesel and promote cleaner energy sources in the region.

**Thus, option (b) is the correct answer.**

**47.** *(a)* Uttar Pradesh, Bihar, Jharkhand, West Bengal and Odisha.

- The **Urja Ganga Project** involves the construction of a 2,655 km gas pipeline from Jagdishpur (Uttar Pradesh) to Haldia (West Bengal), covering major cities such as Varanasi, Patna, Ranchi and Bhubaneswar.
- This pipeline, also known as the **Jagdishpur-Haldia-Bokaro-Dhamra Natural Gas Pipeline (JHBDPL)**, is expected to play a crucial role in transporting natural gas to Eastern India.
- The **Urja Ganga Project** pipeline network passes through the Eastern states of **Uttar Pradesh, Bihar, Jharkhand, West Bengal,** and **Odisha.** This initiative is part of India's effort to expand natural gas infrastructure to underserved regions and promote clean energy.

**Thus, option (a) is the correct answer.**

**48.** *(b)* Administered Pricing Mechanism (APM) for certain public sector fields and market-driven pricing for new fields.

Under the **dual pricing mechanism** of natural gas in India, there are two distinct pricing methods:

- **Administered Pricing Mechanism (APM):** This pricing is set by the **government** for gas produced from **older fields,** primarily operated by **public sector companies** such as **ONGC** and **Oil India Ltd (OIL).** These fields were discovered before 1999 and continue to have government-regulated prices.
- **Market-Driven Pricing:** Gas produced from **new fields** (including fields auctioned under the **New Exploration Licensing Policy (NELP)** or **Hydrocarbon Exploration Licensing Policy (HELP)**) is sold at **market-determined prices.** These prices are driven by **demand and supply dynamics** and are applicable to both public and private sector entities.

**Thus, option (b) is the correct answer.**

**49.** *(c)* Only three

- **Kelkar Committee** has advocated moving to market determined pricing with rates being fixed at the highest possible level.
- The **Rangarajan Committee** played a pivotal role in recommending a **new pricing formula** for natural gas, linking domestic gas prices to international benchmarks.
- The **Shunglu Committee** primarily focused on reviewing the performance of public sector enterprises and was **not directly involved** in natural gas pricing reforms.
- The **Kirit Parikh committee** was constituted in 2022 to review the existing pricing formula for **domestically produced natural gas in India.**

**Thus, the correct answer is (c) Only three.**

**50.** *(b)* 1 and 3 only

Government of India in the interest of meeting the objective of country's energy security, decided on 7th January, 2004 to construct Strategic Petroleum Reserves (SPRs) facilities as well as a Special Purpose Vehicle (SPV) to build and operate the strategic **crude reserves.**

Today, ISPRL is a wholly owned subsidiary (WOS) of Oil Industry Development Board (OIDB), which is a Body Corporate that operates under the administrative control of the Ministry of Petroleum and Natural Gas.

- **Statement 1 is correct: Strategic Petroleum Reserves (SPR)** are stockpiles of **crude oil** that are kept to protect against **supply disruptions,** especially during geopolitical crises or natural disasters.

- **Statement 2 is incorrect:** India's SPR facilities are located on **both Eastern and Western coasts.** Key facilities are in **Visakhapatnam (Andhra Pradesh), Mangaluru (Karnataka)** and **Padur (Karnataka).**
- **Statement 3 is correct:** The **Indian Strategic Petroleum Reserve Limited (ISPRL)** is the organisation responsible for the **construction and maintenance** of these reserves.

**Thus, the correct answer is (b) 1 and 3 only.**

***51.*** *(c)* 1 only

- **Statement 1 is correct:** India's **Strategic Petroleum Reserves (SPR)** are stored in **underground rock caverns,** which provide a safe and secure environment to minimise risks such as sabotage or natural disasters.
- **Statement 2 is incorrect:** The Strategic Petroleum Reserves (SPR) store **crude oil only,** not refined products like gasoline or diesel.
- **Statement 3 is incorrect:** India's current SPR capacity covers around **9.5 days** of the country's crude oil requirements, with plans for future expansion to cover up to **22 days** of consumption (after Phase-II). Indian refiners also maintain crude oil storage (industrial stock) of 65 days making it approximately a total of 87 days after the Phase-2 of SPR.

**Thus, the correct answer is (c) 1 only.**

***52.*** *(c)* All three

- **Open Acreage Licensing Policy (OALP):** Under OALP, oil and gas exploration blocks are auctioned to private and foreign companies, allowing for greater competition and less government control, facilitating **deregulation.** It is introduced under the **Hydrocarbon Exploration and Licensing Policy (HELP)** to offer greater flexibility to oil and gas companies.
- **Revenue-sharing model:** The introduction of a revenue-sharing model for oil and gas exploration replaced the earlier production-sharing model, providing companies with more operational flexibility and encouraging private sector participation.
- **Daily price revisions:** The government introduced **daily price revisions** for **petrol and diesel** to align retail prices with global oil market fluctuations, a significant step toward deregulation.
  - The Indian government **deregulated petrol prices** in 2010, allowing prices to be determined by market conditions rather than government intervention.
  - Diesel prices were **deregulated in 2014,** allowing market forces to dictate pricing, similar to petrol, further reducing subsidies in the energy sector.

**Thus, the correct answer is (c) All three.**

***53.*** *(b)* To allow companies to choose and bid for oil and gas blocks throughout the year, without waiting for specific bidding rounds.

The **Open Acreage Licensing Policy** (OALP) was introduced to provide **greater flexibility** to oil and gas companies by allowing them to **select and bid for exploration blocks** at any time during the year, as opposed to waiting for government-announced bidding rounds. This policy aims to attract more investment into the energy sector and promote exploration activity.

**Thus, option (b) is the correct answer.**

***54.*** *(a)* The **Directorate General of Hydrocarbons (DGH)** is the key regulatory body responsible for managing the bidding, exploration, and award of oil and gas blocks under the **OALP.** It ensures that the bidding process is transparent and in line with government objectives to increase exploration and production activities in the oil and gas sector.

**Thus, option (a) is the correct answer.**

## Past Learning (Answers)

| | | | | |
|---|---|---|---|---|
| 1 (a) | 2 (d) | 3 (b) | 4 (d) | 5 (d) |